OXFORD SHAKESPEARE CONCORDANCES

OXFORD SHAKESPEARE CONCORDANCES

KING LEAR

A CONCORDANCE TO THE TEXT
OF THE FIRST FOLIO

OXFORD
AT THE CLARENDON PRESS
1971

Oxford University Press, Ely House, London W. 1

GLASGOW NEW YORK TORONTO MELBOURNE WELLINGTON
CAPE TOWN SALISBURY IBADAN NAIROBI DAR ES SALAAM LUSAKA ADDIS ABABA
BOMBAY CALCUTTA MADRAS KARACHI LAHORE DACCA
KUALA LUMPUR SINGAPORE HONG KONG TOKYO

FILMSET BY COMPUTAPRINT LIMITED
AND PRINTED IN GREAT BRITAIN
AT THE UNIVERSITY PRESS, OXFORD
BY VIVIAN RIDLER
PRINTER TO THE UNIVERSITY

GENERAL INTRODUCTION

In this series of Oxford Shakespeare Concordances, a separate volume is devoted to each of the plays. The text for each concordance is the one chosen as copy-text by Dr. Alice Walker for the Oxford Old Spelling Shakespeare now in preparation.

Each concordance takes account of every word in the text, and represents their occurrence by frequency counts, line numbers, and reference lines, or a selection of these according to the interest of the particular word. The number of words which have frequency counts only has been kept as low as possible. The introduction to each volume records the facsimile copy of the text from which the concordance was prepared, a table of Folio through line numbers and Globe edition act and scene numbers, a list of the misprints corrected in the text, and an account of the order of printing, and the proof-reading, abstracted from Professor Charlton Hinman's *The Printing and Proof-Reading of the First Folio of Shakespeare* (Oxford, 1963).

The following notes on the main features of the concordances may be helpful.[1]

A. *The Text*

The most obvious misprints have been corrected, on conservative principles, and have been listed for each play in the introduction to the corresponding concordance. Wrong-fount letters have been silently corrected.

Obvious irregularities on the part of the original compositor—for example the anomalous absence of full stops after speech prefixes—have been normalized and noted. Colons, semicolons, exclamation and interrogation marks after italicized words have been modernized to roman fount after current practice, since this aspect of

---

[1] An account of the principles and methods by which the concordances were edited appears in *Studies in Bibliography*, vol. 22, 1969.

compositorial practice would not normally be studied from a concordance. The spacing of words in the original printed texts, particularly in 'justified' lines, is extremely variable; spacing has been normalized on the basis of the compositor's practice as revealed in the particular column or page.

For ease of reference, the contractions *S.*, *L.*, *M.*, and forms such as *Mist.* and tildes, have been expanded when the compositor's own preferred practice is clear, and the expansion has been noted in the text. For M^r, the superior character has been lowered silently. Superior characters like the circumflex in *baâ* and those in ỷ, ẏ, ẙ, and ẘ, have been ignored. The reader should find little difficulty in distinguishing the original form of the pronominal contractions when they are encountered in the text. They are listed under Y and W respectively.

B. *Arrangement of entries*

The words in the text are arranged alphabetically, with numerals and & and &c listed at the end. Words starting with I and J, and U and V, will be found together under I and V respectively. The reader should note that the use of U for the medial V (and I for J) leads in some cases to an unfamiliar order of entry. For example, ADUISED is listed before ADULTERY. The reader will usually find the word he wants if he starts his inquiry at the modern spelling, for when the old spelling differs considerably from the modern spelling, a reference such as 'ENFORCE *see* inforce' will direct the reader to the entry in the concordance.

In hyphenated compounds where the hyphen is the second or third character of the heading-word (as in A-BOORD), the hyphenated form may be listed some distance from other occurrences of the same word in un-hyphenated form. In significant cases, references are given to alert the user.

Under the heading-word, the line numbers or lines of context are in the order of the text. The heading-word is followed by a frequency count of the words in short and long (that is, marked with an asterisk) lines, and the reference lines. When a word has been treated as one to have a frequency count only, or a list of the line numbers and count, any further count which follows will refer to the reference lines listed under the same heading. Where there are two counts but no reference lines (as with AN), the first count refers to the speech prefix.

C. *Special Forms*

(*a*) The following words have not been given context lines and line references but are dealt with only by the counting of their frequency:

A AM AND ARE AT BE BY HE I IN IS IT OF ON SHE THE THEY TO WAS WE WITH YOU

These forms occur so often in most texts that the reader can locate them more easily by examining the text of the play than he could by referring to an extensive listing in the concordance.

Homographs of these words (for example I = *ay*) have been listed in full and are given separate counts under the same heading-word.

(*b*) A larger number of words, consisting mainly of variant spellings, have been given line references as well as frequency counts.

These words are: ACTUS AN AR ART ATT AU BEE BEEING BEEN BEENE BEING BENE BIN BUT CAN CANST CE COULD COULDST DE DECIMA DES DID DIDD DIDDEST DIDDST DO DOE DOES DOEST DOETH DONE DOO DOOE DOOES DOOEST DOOING DOON DOONE DOOS DOOST DOOTH DOS DOST DOTH DU E EN EST ET ETC FINIS FOR FROM HA HAD HADST HAH HAS HAST HATH HAUE HEE HEEL HEELE HEL HELL HER HIM HIR HIS IE IF IL ILL ILLE INTO LA LE LES MA MAIE MAIEST MAIST MAY ME MEE MIGHT MIGHTEST MIGHTST MINE MOI MOY MY NE NO NOE NON NONA NOR NOT O OCTAUA OFF OH OR OU OUR OUT PRIMA PRIMUS QUARTA QUARTUS QUE QUINTA QUINTUS SCAENA SCENA SCOENA SECUNDA SECUNDUS SEPTIMA SEPTIMUS SEXTA SHAL SHALL SHALT SHEE SHOLD SHOLDE SHOLDST ʻSHOULD SHOULDE SHOULDST SIR SO SOE TE TERTIA TERTIUS THAT THEE THEIR THEIRE THEM THEN THER THERE THESE THEYR THIS THOSE THOU THY TIS TU VN VNE VOS VOSTRE VOUS VS WAST WEE WER WERE WERT WHAT WHEN WHER WHERE WHICH WHO WHOM WHOME WHY WIL WILL WILT WILTE WOLD WOLDE WOLDST WOULD WOULDE WOULDEST WOULDST YE YEE YF YOUE YOUR YT & &C 1 2 3 4.

Homographs of words on this list (e.g. *bee* = n.) have been listed in full, and also have separate counts.

(*c*) All speech prefixes, other than *All.*, *Both.*, and those which represent the names of actors, have been treated as count-only words. In some cases, however, where a speech prefix corresponds to a form already on the count-only list (e.g. *Is.*), a full entry has been given. In some other cases, when two counts are given for the same heading-word for no apparent reason, the count which does not correspond to the following full references or to the list of line references is that of the speech prefix form (for example AN in *The Tempest*).

(*d*) Hyphenated compounds such as *all-building-law* have been listed under the full form, and also under each main constituent after the first. In this example there are entries under ALL-BUILDING-LAW, BUILDING, and LAW. When, however, one of the constituents of the compound is a word on the count- or location-only list ((*a*) or (*b*) above), it is dealt with in whichever of these two lists applies. References such as 'AT *see also* bemock't-at-stabs' are given to assist the reader in such cases.

Simple or non-hyphenated compounds such as *o'th'King* have been listed only under the constituent parts—in this example under OTH and KING.

(*e*) 'Justified' lines where the spellings *may* have been affected by the compositor's need to fit the text to his measure are distinguished by an asterisk at the beginning of the reference line. If only location is being given, the asterisk occurs before the line reference. If only frequency counts are being given, the number *after* the asterisk records the frequency of forms occurring in 'justified' lines. Lines which do not extend to the full width of the compositor's measure have not been distinguished as 'justified' lines, even though in many cases the shorter line may have affected the spelling.

D. *Line Numbers*

The lines in each text have been numbered from the first *Actus Primus* or stage direction and thereafter in normal reading order, including all stage directions and act and scene divisions. Each typographical line has been counted as a unit when it contains matter for inclusion in the concordance. Catchwords are not included in the count. The only general exception is that turn-overs are regarded as belonging to their base-lines; where a turn-over occurs on a line by itself, it has been reckoned as part of the base-line, and the line containing only the turn-over has not been counted as a separate line. Turn-overs may readily be distinguished by vertical stroke and single bracket after the last word of the base-line; for example *brought with* | (*child,*.

When two or more lines have been joined in order to provide a fuller context, the line-endings are indicated by a vertical stroke |, and the line reference applies to that part of the line before the vertical stroke. For the true line-numbers of words in the following part of the context line, the stated line-number should be increased by one each time a vertical stroke occurs, save when the next word is a turn-over.

The numbering of the quarto texts has been fitted to that of the corresponding Folio texts; lines in the Quarto which do not occur in the Folio are prefixed by +. The line references are similarly specified. The line references of these concordances therefore provide a consistent permanent numbering of each typographical line of text, based on the First Folio.

PROGRAM CHANGES

Preparation of concordances to the first few texts, and the especial complexity of *Wiv.*, have enabled some improvements to be made to the main concordance program. For texts other than *Tmp.*, *TGV*, *MM*, and *Err.*, the concordances have been prepared with the improved program.

Speech-prefixes now have separate entries under the appropriate heading-word and follow any other entry under the same heading-word. Entries under AN in *Wiv.*, AND and TO in *TN*, and AD in *AYL* offer examples. This alteration provides a clearer record of the total number of occurrences of words which occur both as speech-prefixes and also as forms on the 'count only' or 'locations only' lists.

Another modification supplies a more precise reference to the location of words such as BEENE for which line numbers but no full lines are given. When a 'location only' word is encountered to the right of the 'end-of-line' bar (which shows that lines of text have been joined together in order to provide a sufficient context), the line number is now adjusted to supply the exact reference. In the concordances to the texts listed above, users will find that in some instances the particular occurrence of a 'location only' word which they wish to consult in the text is to be found in the line after the one specified in the concordance; this depends on whether lines have been joined in the computer-readable version of the text from which the concordance was made. It is not expected that readers will be seriously inconvenienced by this. Should a concordance to the First Folio be published, it will, of course, incorporate all improvements.

KING LEAR

THE concordance to *Lr.* was made from the Lee facsimile of the Chatsworth copy of the First Folio (Oxford, 1902). Only qq6^v and rr2 of the many variant pages recorded by Professor Charlton Hinman (*Printing and Proof-Reading of the First Folio*, Oxford, 1963, vol. 1, pp. 306–12) are in the uncorrected state in Lee. Many of the variants of the corrected pages (including some miscorrections) affect the text. This section of F was printed, according to Professor Hinman (vol. 2, p. 517), in the following order:

By Ex	Ex Ex	Ex By	By Ex	By Ex	By Ex	By By	Ex By	By By
qq3^v:4	3:4^v	2^v:5	2:5^v	1^v:6	1:6^v	rr3^v:4	3:4^v	2^v:5

	Ex		
Ex By	By Ex	By By	[Here the joint labours of B and E were interrupted
rr2:5^v	1^v:6	1:6^v	

while B alone set *Timon of Athens*.]

	By By			By B	Ex Ex	By By
	Gg3^v:4	. . . .		hhl^v:6	ss3^v:4	hh2^v:5

By By	Ex Ex	By Ex	Ex Ey	Ey Eyx	By By
hh2:5^v	ss2^v:5	ss3:4^v	ss2:5^v	ssl^v:6	1:6^v

TABLE OF LINE AND ACT/SCENE NUMBERS

Page	Col.	Comp.	F line nos.	Globe act/scene nos.
qq2	a	B	1–47	1.1.1–1.1.43
	b	E	48–94	1.1.90
qq2^v	a	E	95–160	1.1.152
	b	E	161–224	1.1.208
qq3	a	E	225–90	1.1.268
	b	E	291–352	1.2.18
qq3^v	a	B	353–418	1.2.92
	b	B	419–84	1.2.178
qq4	a	E	485–537	1.4.7
	b	E	538–602	1.4.80
qq4^v	a	E	603–68	1.4.152
	b	E	669–734	1.4.243
qq5	a	B	735–99	1.4.307
	b	B	800–63	1.4.362
qq5^v	a	E	864–922	1.5.4
	b	E	923–80	2.1.46
qq6	a	E	981–1044	2.1.106
	b	E	1045–103	2.2.33
qq6^v	a	E	1104–67	2.2.99
	b	E	1168–233	2.2.164

Page	Col.	Comp.	F line nos.	Globe act/scene nos.
rrl	a	B	1234–95	2.4.21
	b	B	1296–360	2.4.88
rrl^v	a	E	1361–425	2.4.148
	b	B	1426–91	2.4.202
rr2	a	E	1492–557	2.4.262
	b	E	1558–617	3.1.2
rr2^v	a	B	1618–78	3.1.23
	b	B	1679–744	3.2.89
rr3	a	E	1745–97	3.4.17
	b	E	1798–861	3.4.84
rr3^v	a	B	1862–926	3.4.153
	b	B	1927–86	3.5.17
rr4	a	B	1987–2046	3.6.94
	b	B	2047–106	3.7.40
rr4^v	a	B	2107–72	3.7.95
	b	B	2173–233	4.1.47
rr5	a	B	2234–94	4.2.25
	b	B	2295–354	4.4.4
rr5^v	a	B	2355–414	4.5.27
	b	B	2415–74	4.6.35
rr6	a	E	2475–540	4.6.94
	b	E	2541–606	4.6.167
rr6^v	a	B	2607–72	4.6.228
	b	B	2673–738	4.6.290
ssl	a	B	2739–95	4.7.46
	b	B	2796–853	5.1.6
ssl^v	a	E	2854–914	5.1.67
	b	E	2915–66	5.3.24
ss2	a	E	2967–3030	5.3.85
	b	E	3031–92	5.3.137
ss2^v	a	E	3093–158	5.3.195
	b	E	3159–221	5.3.261
ss3	a	B	3222–62	5.3.293
	b	B	3263–303 (Finis)	5.3.326

The following misprints, etc. were corrected in the text:

qq2^v	117	miseries		868	prai'sd
	172	*Kear.*		872	the'uent.
	173	*Lent.*		929	your
	174	swear.st	qq6	1045	yout
	205	*Bugundie,*		1075	*aad*
qq3	257	t'haue (apostrophe	qq6^v	1183	flicking
		at end of l. 256)		1228	Duke
	344	Barstadie?	rrl	1280	ahy
	351	Farhers		1331	Wirh
qq4^v	710	not		1336	the the
qq5^v	867	Your	rrl^v	1407	your

rr2	1588	an'ds	ssl^v	2871	particurlar
rr3	1787	skinso :'tis		2893	ɪhe
	1790	they		2928	*Egdar.*
	1792	free,	ss2	3037	Trmpet
	1833	though		3057	Trumper
rr4	2069	festiuate		3058	*Tumpet*
rr4^v	2176	*Exeunt,*		3090	illustirous
rr6	2505	Tyranrs	ss2^v	3104	scarely
rr6^v	2693	ice		3217	your
	2724	indinguish'd	ss3	3256	Your
	2726	rhe			*dis.*

February, 1971   T. H. H.

KING LEAR

1

ABOUT *cont*.

    *Foole. Thy Asses are gone about 'em; the reason why   908
    Hauing more man then wit about me, drew;   1318
    Do sorely ruffle, for many Miles about | There's scarce a Bush.   1604
    *breeds about her heart. Is there any cause in Nature that   2034
    With something rich about me: from that place,   2262
    *It is thy businesse that I go about: Therfore great France   2377
    And giue the Letters which thou find'st about me,   2701
    Bast. About it, and write happy, when th'hast done,   2979
ABROAD = 1*1
    there's my key: if you do stirre abroad, goe arm'd.   491
    *Cur. Nay I know not, you haue heard of the newes a- | broad, 934
ABSOLUTE = 1
    To him our absolute power, you to your rights,   3272
ABUSD = 4
    To haue her Gentleman abus'd, assaulted.   1226
    To haue his eare abus'd, wisedome bids feare.   1611
    Glou. O my Follies! then *Edgar* was abus'd,   2168
    I am mightily abus'd; I should eu'n dye with pitty   2805
ABUSE = 1
    Lear. Do not abuse me.   2836
ABUSED = 2
    The food of thy abused Fathers wrath: 2203
    Cure this great breach in his abused Nature,   2764
ACCENT = *1
    *you in a plaine accent, was a plaine Knaue, which   1187
ACCENTS = 1
    Kent. If but as will I other accents borrow,   531
ACCOMMODATE = 1
    The safer sense will ne're accommodate | His Master thus.   2528
ACCORDING = 1
    According to my bond, no more nor lesse.   99
ACCOUNT = *1
    *yeere elder then this; who, yet is no deerer in my ac- | count, 23
ACCUSE = 1
    Will quicken and accuse thee. I am your Host,   2105
ACCUSERS = *1
    *who haue the power to seale th'accusers lips. Get thee   2612
ACKNOWLEDGD = 1
    Kent. To be acknowledg'd Madam is ore-pai'd,   2750
ACKNOWLEDGE = 1*1
    *so often blush'd to acknowledge him, that now I am | braz'd too't. 13
    Then on a wretch whom Nature is asham'd | Almost t'acknowledge
    hers.   232
ACKNOWLEDGED = *1
    *be acknowledged. Doe you know this Noble Gentle- | man, *Edmond*? |
    Edm. No, my Lord.   27
ACOLD *see* cold
ACQUAINT = 1*1
    as I shall find meanes, and acquaint you withall.   432
    *acquaint my Daughter no further with any thing you   876
ACRE = 1
    Search euery Acre in the high-growne field,   2357
ACT = 3
    Which I must act, Briefenesse, and Fortune worke.   947
    Should he sit heere? This act perswades me,   1389
    Oppos'd against the act: bending his Sword   2318

ACTE = 1*1
*of my Mistris heart, and did the acte of darkenesse with   1867
Edmund, enkindle all the sparkes of Nature | To quit this horrid acte.   2162
ACTION = 1
No vnchaste action or dishonoured step   250
ACTION-TAKING = *1
*action-taking, whoreson glasse-gazing super-seruiceable   1091
ACTUS *I*.1 926 1614 2177 2844 = 5
ADDE = 1
And thereto adde such reasons of your owne,   862
ADDED = 1
And added to the gall. O *Lear*, *Lear*, *Lear*!   783
ADDER = 1
Are of the Adder. Which of them shall I take?   2904
ADDITION = 4*1
The name, and all th'addition to a King: the Sway,   144
deny'st the least sillable of thy addition.   1097
*I will peece out the comfort with what addition I | can: I will not be
long from you. *Exit*   1999
In his owne grace he doth exalt himselfe, | More then in your addition.   3008
With boote, and such addition as your Honours   3273
ADDRESSE = 1
Lear. My Lord of *Burgundie*, | We first addresse toward you, who with
this King   205
ADEW = 1
Thus *Kent*, O Princes, bids you all adew,   200
ADMIRABLE = *1
*on. An admirable euasion of Whore-master-man,   455
ADMIRATION = 1
Gon. This admiration Sir, is much o'th'fauour   746
ADO = 1
Reg. Himselfe in person there? | *Stew*. Madam with much ado: 2386
ADOPTED = 1
Vnfriended, new adopted to our hate,   222
ADORE = 1
Alb. Now Gods that we adore, | Whereof comes this?   804
ADUANCD = 1
One step I haue aduanc'd thee, if thou do'st   2971
ADUANCEMENT = 1
Deseru'd much lesse aduancement. | *Lear*. You? Did you?   1492
ADUANTAGE *see also* vantage = 1
You haue now the good aduantage of the night,   952
ADUANTAGES = *1
*which approues him an intelligent partie to the aduanta- |ges   1981
ADUERSARY = 2
Yet am I Noble as the Aduersary | I come to cope.   3075
Alb. Which is that Aduersary?   3077
ADUICE = *1
*beholding. Aduice the Duke where you are going, to a   2068
ADUISD = 1
Or whether since he is aduis'd by ought   2848
ADUISE = 3*2
Edm. Brother, I aduise you to the best, I am no honest   493
*you: what growes of it no matter, aduise your fellowes   526
Vpon his partie 'gainst the Duke of *Albany*? | Aduise your selfe.   956
Wherein we must haue vse of your aduise.   1064
Therefore I do aduise you take this note: 2416

3

ADULTERERS = *1
*and Adulterers by an inforc'd obedience of Planatary   453
ADULTERY = 2
Adultery? thou shalt not dye: dye for Adultery?   2557
ADULTRESSE = 1
Sepulchring an Adultresse. O are you free?   1410
AFARRE = 1
So should my thoughts be seuer'd from my greefes, | *Drum afarre off.*   2736
AFEARD *see* fear'd
AFFECT = 1
Who hauing beene prais'd for bluntnesse, doth affect   1171
AFFECTED = 1*1
Kent. | *I thought the King had more affected the   3
Reg. No maruaile then, though he were ill affected,   1037
AFFECTION = 1*2
That monsters it: Or your fore-voucht affection   241
*he hath writ this to feele my affection to your Honor, &   420
*with that Ceremonious affection as you were wont,   588
AFFECTIONATE = 1
Your (Wife, so I would say) affectio-|nate Seruant. Gonerill.   2722
AFFIRME = 1
Reuenge, affirme, and turne their Halcion beakes   1151
AFFLICT = 1
Gon. Neuer afflict your selfe to know more of it: 806
AFFLICTION = 3
Remember to haue heard. Mans Nature cannot carry | Th'affliction, nor
the feare.   1700
Shake patiently my great affliction off: 2475
Glou. I do remember now: henceforth Ile beare | Affliction, till it do cry
out it selfe   2520
AFOOTE *see* foote
AFORE = *1
*if your Dilligence be not speedy, I shall be there afore | you.   878
AFTER = 8*5
*after your owne wisedome. I would vnstate my | selfe, to be in a due
resolution.   429
*worse after dinner, I will not part from thee yet. Dinner   572
Foole. Why after I haue cut the egge i'th'middle and   673
You Sir, more Knaue then Foole, after your Master.   834
So the Foole followes after. *Exit*   841
Glo. Pursue him, ho: go after. By no meanes, what?   979
*great one that goes vpward, let him draw thee after: 1346
Which euen but now, demanding after you,   1719
Hot Questrists after him, met him at gate,   2076
But not without that harmefull stroke, which since | Hath pluckt him
after.   2321
Stew. I must needs after him, Madam, with my Letter.   2400
Alb. Go after her, she's desperate, gouerne her.   3120
The one the other poison'd for my sake, | And after slew herselfe.   3197
AGAINE = 16*4
Glou. He hath bin out nine yeares, and away he shall | againe. The
King is comming.   35
Cor. Nothing. | *Lear.* Nothing will come of nothing, speake againe.   95
That face of hers againe, therfore be gone,   289
*away, away, if you will measure your lubbers length a-|gaine,   620
Beweepe this cause againe, Ile plucke ye out,   821
Lear. To tak't againe perforce; Monster Ingratitude!   912

AGAINE *cont.*

Cor. Keepe peace vpon your liues, he dies that strikes | againe, what is
the matter?   1122
And in the fleshment of this dead exploit, | Drew on me here againe.   1199
*againe, I would haue none but knaues follow it, since a | Foole giues
it.   1348
Reg. And speak't againe my Lord, no more with me.   1553
*vexes. There could I haue him now, and there, and there | againe, and
there. *Storme still.*   1842
I'ld say I had eyes againe.   2205
Alb. He is not heere. | *Mes.* No my good Lord, I met him backe againe.   2338
Thy life's a Myracle. Speake yet againe.   2497
Let not my worser Spirit tempt me againe | To dye before you please.   2664
When time shall serue, let but the Herald cry, | And Ile appeare againe.
Exit.   2893
If euer I returne to you againe, | Ile bring you comfort.   2923
Edg. What in ill thoughts againe?   2932
sound of the Trumpet: he is bold in his defence. 1 Trumpet. | Her.
Againe. 2 *Trumpet.*   3063
Her. Againe. 3 *Trumpet. | Trumpet answers within.*   3065
AGAINST *see also* 'gainst = 13*8
To wage against thine enemies, nere feare to loose it, | Thy safety being
motiue.   167
*suspend your indignation against my Brother, til you can   414
*run a certaine course: where, if you violently proceed a- |gainst   416
*prediction; there's Son against Father, the King fals from   440
*byas of Nature, there's Father against Childe. We haue   441
*blessing against his will, if thou follow him, thou must   633
If I would stand against thee, would the reposall   1005
Kent. Draw you Rascall, you come with Letters a- |gainst   1108
*the King, and take Vanitie the puppets part, a- |gainst   1109
Against the Grace, and Person of my Master, | Stocking his Messenger. 1210
Displaid so sawcily against your Highnesse,   1317
Against my comming in. Thou better know'st   1461
To wage against the enmity oth'ayre,   1502
Against their Father, foole me not so much,   1575
Against the old kinde King; or something deeper,   1637
These dreadfull Summoners grace. I am a man, | More sinn'd against,
then sinning.   1712
Oppos'd against the act: bending his Sword   2318
Mes. I my good Lord: 'twas he inform'd against him   2341
All hearts against vs: *Edmund*, I thinke is gone | In pitty of his misery,
to dispatch   2396
To be oppos'd against the iarring windes?   2783
Should haue stood that night against my fire,   2785
AGASTED *see* gasted
AGD = 1
But loue, deere loue, and our ag'd Fathers Rite: 2380
AGE = 7*5
To shake all Cares and Businesse from our Age,   44
The argument of your praise, balme of your age,   236
Gon. You see how full of changes his age is, the ob- |seruation   314
Reg. 'Tis the infirmity of his age, yet he hath euer but | slenderly
knowne himselfe.   318
*rash, then must we looke from his age, to receiue not a- |lone   321
Glou. reads. This policie, and reuerence of Age, makes the   382
*it to be fit, that Sonnes at perfect age, and Fathers   406

AGE *cont*.

To be such men as may besort your Age, | Which know themselues, and
you.   760
Age is vnnecessary: on my knees I begge,   1436
As full of griefe as age, wretched in both,   1573
Life would not yeelde to age.   2192
Whose age had Charmes in it, whose Title more,   2991
AGED = *1
and fond bondage, in the oppression of aged tyranny, who swayes   385
AGU-PROOFE = *1
*me, I was euery thing: 'Tis a Lye, I am not Agu-proofe.   2551
AH *see also* a = 1
His Daughters seeke his death: Ah, that good Kent,   1943
AHANGING *see* hanging
AIAX = 1
Kent. None of these Rogues, and Cowards | But *Aiax* is there Foole.   1201
AIDANT *see* aydant
AIRE *see* ayre
AIRES *see* ayres
ALACKE = 10*3
Glo. Alacke the night comes on, and the high windes   1603
Kent. Alacke, bare-headed?   1714
Glo. Alacke, alacke *Edmund*, I like not this vnnaturall   1753
Old. Alacke sir, he is mad.   2233
Cor. Alacke, 'tis he: why he was met euen now   2351
Glou. Alacke, I haue no eyes: 2502
Glou. Alacke, alacke the day.   2623
In short, and musty straw? Alacke, alacke,   2788
(Alacke too weake the conflict to support)   3160
Seest thou this obiect *Kent*? | *Kent*. Alacke, why thus?   3194
ALARUM = 2
Alarum within. Enter with Drumme and Colours, Lear,   2918
Glo. Grace go with you Sir. *Exit*. | *Alarum and Retreat within.*   2925
ALARUMD = 1
And when he saw my best alarum'd spirits   989
ALARUMS = 1
Alb. Saue him, saue him. *Alarums. Fights.*   3107
ALAS = 2
But yet alas, stood I within his Grace,   298
Kent. Alas Sir are you here? Things that loue night,   1694
ALAY = 1
of your person, it would scarsely alay.   485
ALB = 49*3
ALBANIE = 1
Call *Burgundy*, *Cornwall*, and *Albanie*,   135
ALBANIES = 1
We make thee Lady. To thine and *Albanies* issues   71
ALBANY see also Alb. = 9*1
Duke of *Albany*, then *Cornwall*. | *Glou*. It did alwayes seeme so to vs:
But   5
*Sennet. Enter King Lear, Cornwall, Albany, Gonerill, Re-|gan,
Cordelia, and attendants.*   37
And you our no lesse louing Sonne of *Albany*,   47
Enter Albany.   768
'Twixt the Dukes of *Cornwall*, and *Albany*? | *Bast*. Not a word.   939
Vpon his partie 'gainst the Duke of *Albany*? | Aduise your selfe.   956
With mutuall cunning) 'twixt Albany, and Cornwall: 1630

ALBANY cont.
   Enter Albany.   2299
   Enter with Drum and Colours, Albany, Gonerill, Soldiers.   2864
   Flourish. Enter Albany, Gonerill, Regan, Soldiers.   2982
ALBION = *1
   *Then shal the Realme of *Albion*, come to great confusion: 1746
ALIGHT *see* a-light, light
ALIGHTS *see* lights
ALIUE = 4*1
   *Eeles, when she put 'em i'th' Paste aliue, she knapt 'em   1399
   By this had thought bin past. Aliue, or dead?   2485
   If both remaine aliue: To take the Widdow,   2906
   Her husband being aliue. Now then, wee'l vse   2909
   Alb. Produce the bodies, be they aliue or dead; | *Gonerill and Regans bodies brought out.*   3183
ALL = 77*18
   To shake all Cares and Businesse from our Age,   44
   Beyond all manner of so much I loue you.   66
   Lear. Of all these bounds euen from this Line, to this,   68
   My selfe an enemy to all other ioyes,   78
   They loue you all? Happily when I shall wed,   107
   By all the operation of the Orbes,   118
   Heere I disclaime all my Paternall care, | Propinquity and property of blood,   120
   Preheminence, and all the large effects   139
   The name, and all th'addition to a King: the Sway,   144
   Thus *Kent*, O Princes, bids you all adew,   200
   Or all of it with our displeasure piec'd,   217
   I tell you all her wealth. For you great King,   228
   Not all the Dukes of watrish *Burgundy*,   283
   Confin'd to exhibition? All this done   360
   *from my Brother, that I haue not all ore-read; and for so   372
   *treacherie, and all ruinous disorders follow vs disquietly   443
   *influence; and all that we are euill in, by a diuine thru-|sting 454
   Edg. None at all,   480
   All with me's meete, that I can fashion fit. *Exit.*   504
   That sets vs all at ods: Ile not endure it;   512
   Lear. Why my Boy? | *Fool.* If I gaue them all my liuing, I'ld keepe my Cox-|combes   636
   Weary of all, shall want some. That's a sheal'd Pescod.   711
   That all particulars of dutie know,   777
   From the fixt place: drew from my heart all loue,   782
   Turne all her Mothers paines, and benefits   800
   'Gainst Paricides did all the thunder bend,   982
   My very Character) I'ld turne it all   1009
   All Ports Ile barre, the villaine shall not scape,   1018
   I will send farre and neere, that all the kingdome   1020
   Reg. If it be true, all vengeance comes too short   1027
   Reg. Till noone? till night my Lord, and all night too.   1214
   Whose disposition all the world well knowes   1229
   Losses their remedies. All weary and o're-watch'd,   1247
   Blanket my loines, else all my haires in knots,   1261
   Resolue me with all modest haste, which way   1300
   *But for all this thou shalt haue as many Dolors for thy 1326
   *thee ther's no labouring i'th' winter. All that follow their 1341
   They haue trauail'd all the night? meere fetches,   1363
   Infirmity doth still neglect all office,   1382

ALL *cont.*

Glo. I would haue all well betwixt you. *Exit.*   1396
As cleeres her from all blame. | *Lear.* My curses on her.   1424
All the stor'd Vengeances of Heauen, fall   1444
No, rather I abiure all roofes, and chuse   1501
Lear. I gaue you all. | *Reg.* And in good time you gaue it.   1547
That all the world shall--- I will do such things,   1580
Kent. Few words, but to effect more then all yet;   1650
Cracke Natures moulds, all germaines spill at once | That makes
ingratefull Man.   1663
Lear. No, I will be the patterne of all patience, | I will say nothing.   1689
That which my Father looses: no lesse then all,   1774
Doth from my sences take all feeling else,   1793
Your old kind Father, whose franke heart gaue all,   1800
*Lear. Did'st thou giue all to thy Daughters? And art | thou come to
this?   1830
*Could'st thou saue nothing? Would'st thou giue 'em all?   1845
*Foole. Nay, he reseru'd a Blanket, else we had bin all | sham'd.   1846
*Lea. Now all the plagues that in the pendulous ayre   1848
*Foole. This cold night will turne vs all to Fooles, and | Madmen.   1858
*were like an old Letchers heart, a small spark, all the rest   1893
T'obey in all your daughters hard commands: 1927
Lear. Come, let's in all.   1956
*Kent. All the powre of his wits, haue giuen way to`his   2001
Lear. The little dogges, and all;   2020
Dogs leapt the hatch, and all are fled.   2030
With thine, and all that offer to defend him,   2053
All Cruels else subscribe: but I shall see   2137
Where is thy luster now? | *Glou.* All darke and comfortlesse?   2159
Edmund, enkindle all the sparkes of Nature | To quit this horrid acte.   2162
Thy comforts can do me no good at all, | Thee, they may hurt.   2196
Haue humbled to all strokes: that I am wretched   2250
May all the building in my fancie plucke | Vpon my hatefull life.
Another way   2332
Darnell, and all the idle weedes that grow   2355
Take all my outward worth.   2360
Cord. All blest Secrets, | All you vnpublish'd Vertues of the earth   2366
All hearts against vs: *Edmund*, I thinke is gone | In pitty of his misery,
to dispatch   2396
For all beneath the Moone would I not leape vpright.   2463
Edg. Now fare ye well, good Sir. | *Glou.* With all my heart.   2469
Edg. This is aboue all strangenesse,   2510
*Women all aboue: but to the Girdle do the Gods inhe-|rit,   2568
*beneath is all the Fiends. There's hell, there's darke-|nes,   2569
Glou. Were all thy Letters Sunnes, I could not see.   2584
*and Furr'd gownes hide all. Place sinnes with Gold, and   2608
Gent. You shall haue any thing. | *Lear.* No Seconds? All my selfe?   2637
Edg. I thanke you Sir, that's all.   2659
All my reports go with the modest truth, | Nor more, nor clipt, but so.   2751
Had not concluded all. He wakes, speake to him.   2790
What place this is: and all the skill I haue   2821
Ripenesse is all come on. | *Glo.* And that's true too. *Exeunt.*   2935
My reason all the same, and they are ready   2995
All leuied in my name, haue in my name | Tooke their discharge.   3053
Bast. I was contracted to them both, all three | Now marry in an
instant.   3179
It is a chance which do's redeeme all sorrowes | That euer I haue felt.   3228

ALL *cont.*
    Lear. A plague vpon you Murderors, Traitors all,   3233
    Haue more then merited. All Friends shall   3274
    Taste the wages of their vertue, and all Foes   3275
    And thou no breath at all? Thou'lt come no more, | Neuer, neuer,
    neuer, neuer, neuer.   3279
ALLEGEANCE = *1
    Lea. Heare me recreant, on thine allegeance heare me;   181
ALLOT = 1
    Fiue dayes we do allot thee for prouision,   187
ALLOW = 3
    Allow Obedience; if you your selues are old,   1481
    Allow not Nature, more then Nature needs: 1566
    The time will not allow the complement | Which very manners vrges.   3187
ALLOWANCE = 2
    By your allowance, which if you should, the fault   720
    Vnder th'allowance of your great aspect,   1181
ALLS = 2
    All's not offence that indiscretion findes, | And dotage termes so.   1486
    All's cheerlesse, darke, and deadly,   3258
ALL-LYCENCD = 1
    Gon. Not only Sir this, your all-lycenc'd Foole,   712
ALL-SHAKING = *1
    *Sindge my white head. And thou all-shaking Thunder,   1661
ALMES = 1
    At Fortunes almes, you haue obedience scanted,   304
ALMOST = 6
    Then on a wretch whom Nature is asham'd | Almost t'acknowledge
    hers.   232
    Peruse this Letter. Nothing almost sees miracles   1242
    Hold amity? 'Tis hard, almost impossible.   1538
    I am almost mad my selfe. I had a Sonne,   1946
    Almost too small for sight. The murmuring Surge,   2455
    For I am almost ready to dissolue, | Hearing of this.   3167
ALONE = 5*1
    And finde I am alone felicitate | In your deere Highnesse loue.   80
    *rash, then must we looke from his age, to receiue not a- | lone   321
    Lear. Let me alone. | *Kent*. Good my Lord enter heere.   1781
    Let him alone a while.   2802
    We two alone will sing like Birds i'th'Cage: 2949
    Alb. The let alone lies not in your good will. | *Bast*. Nor in thine Lord.   3023
ALONG = 1
    Glou. Take him you on. | *Kent*. Sirra, come on: go along with vs.   1962
ALOOFE = 1
    Aloofe from th'intire point, will you haue her?   263
ALOW = *2
    Edg. Pillicock sat on Pillicock hill, alow: alow, loo, loo.   1857
ALOWD = 1
    As mad as the vext Sea, singing alowd.   2352
ALREADY = *1
    *a Power already footed, we must incline to the King, I   1764
ALSO = *1
    *the generall dependants, as in the Duke himselfe also, and | your
    Daughter.   590
ALTERATION = 1
    To change the course, he's full of alteration,   2849

ALTERD = 1
Me thinkes thy voyce is alter'd, and thou speak'st   2440
ALTHOUGH = 2
Although our last and least; to whose yong loue,   89
(Although as yet the face of it is couer'd   1629
ALTITUDE = 1
Ten Masts at each, make not the altitude   2495
ALTOGETHER = 1*1
Reg. Not altogether so, | I look'd not for you yet, nor am prouided   1526
Cornw. I now perceiue, it was not altogether your   1975
ALWAIES = *1
*we haue made of it hath beene little; he alwaies   315
ALWAYES = *1
Duke of *Albany*, then *Cornwall*. | *Glou*. It did always seeme so to vs:
But   5
AM *see also* I'me = 67*16
AMBITION = 1
No blowne Ambition doth our Armes incite,   2379
AMITY = 1
Hold amity? 'Tis hard, almost impossible.   1538
AMONG = 1*2
Gon. And let his Knights haue colder lookes among   525
That such a King should play bo-peepe, | And goe the Foole among.   690
*not a nose among twenty, but can smell him that's stink-|ing;   1343
AMONGST = 1
Flew on him, and among'st them fell'd him dead,   2320
AMOROUS = 1
Long in our Court, haue made their amorous soiourne,   52
AMPLE = 1
Remaine this ample third of our faire Kingdome,   86
AN *l*.78 141 381 *384 *424 *453 *455 *659 *670 *706 *735 781 *889 899
*1088 1174 *1340 1410 *1893 *1981 *2004 2052 2188 2282 2306 2493
*2571 2816 2889 3035 3110 3180 3237 = 18*15
ANATOMIZE = *1
Lear. Then let them Anatomize *Regan*: See what   2033
ANCHORING = 1
Appeare like Mice: and yond tall Anchoring Barke,   2453
ANCIENT = 3*1
Ste. This ancient Ruffian Sir, whose life I haue spar'd | at sute of his
gray-beard.   1135
You stubborne ancient Knaue, you reuerent Bragart, | Wee'l teach you.   1204
I'th'way toward Douer, do it for ancient loue,   2230
Alb. Let's then determine with th'ancient of warre | On our proceeding.   2873
AND *see also* & = 496*134, 3*2
Lear. And you lie sirrah, wee'l haue you whipt.   694
Foole. And thou hadst beene set i'th' Stockes for that   1337
Foole. He that has and a little-tyne wit,   1729
Lear. Then there's life in't. Come, and you get it,   2644
*volke passe: and 'chud ha' bin zwaggerd out of my life,   2691
ANDS = 2
Goe tell the Duke, and's wife, Il'd speake with them: 1392
Reg. This house is little, the old man and's people, | Cannot be well
bestow'd.   1588
ANGER = 2*1
Kent. Yes Sir, but anger hath a priuiledge.   1143
To beare it tamely: touch me with Noble anger,   1576

10

ANGER *cont.*
  Corn. My Villaine? | *Seru.* Nay then come on, and take the chance of
  anger.   2152
ANGLER = *1
  Edg. Fraterretto cals me, and tells me *Nero* is an Ang-|ler   2004
ANGRIE = 1
  Cor. Why art thou angrie?   1144
ANGRING = 1
  Ang'ring it selfe, and others. Blesse thee Master.   2225
ANGUISH = 2
  Are many Simples operatiue, whose power | Will close the eye of
  Anguish.   2364
  Edg. Why then your other Senses grow imperfect | By your eyes
  anguish.   2437
ANIMALL = *1
  *man, is no more but such a poore, bare, forked A-|nimall   1887
ANNOINTED = 1
  In his Annointed flesh, sticke boarish phangs.   2130
ANON = 1
  Edg. Shall I heare from you anon? *Exit.*   497
ANOTHER = 6*1
  *my selfe, there's mine, beg another of thy | Daughters.   638
  I haue another daughter,   824
  Wee'l no more meete, no more see one another.   1514
  Reg. One side will mocke another: Th'other too.   2143
  May all the building in my fancie plucke | Vpon my hatefull life.
  Another way   2332
  Heere Friend's another purse: in it, a Iewell   2465
  To see another thus. I know not what to say: 2806
ANSWER = 11
  Shee's there, and she is yours. | *Bur.* I know no answer.   219
  You shall do well, the fault of it Ile answer.   517
  The leisure of their answer, gaue me cold lookes,   1313
  Fetch me a better answer.   1365
  Corn. Wherefore to Douer? Let him answer that.   2124
  His answer was, the worse. Of Glosters Treachery,   2273
  Which tye him to an answer: our wishes on the way   2282
  This Leter Madam, craues a speedy answer: | 'Tis from your Sister.   2328
  The Newes is not so tart. Ile read, and answer.   2334
  Your name, your quality, and why you answer | This present Summons?   3071
  By th'law of Warre, thou wast not bound to answer   3109
ANSWERD = 2
  And heere are to be answer'd. Tell me my daughters   53
  Reg. Be simple answer'd, for we know the truth.   2110
ANSWERE = 4*1
  This hideous rashnesse, answere my life, my iudgement: 161
  To answere from our home: the seuerall Messengers   1067
  Cor. Ile answere that.   1224
  Lear. Thou wert better in a Graue, then to answere   1881
  Rega. Lady I am not well, else I should answere   3016
ANSWERED = *1
  Knigh. Sir, he answered me in the roundest manner, he | would not.   583
ANSWERS = 1
  Her. Againe. 3 *Trumpet.* | *Trumpet answers within.*   3065
ANT = *1
  Foole. Wee'l set thee to schoole to an Ant, to teach   1340

11

ANTIPATHY = 1
  Kent. No contraries hold more antipathy, | Then I, and such a knaue. 1160
ANY = 9*7
  any further delay, then this very Euening. 426
  *man, if ther be any good meaning toward you: I haue told 494
  *nor so old to dote on her for any thing. I haue yeares on | my backe
  forty eight. 569
  *my peace. I had rather be any kind o'thing then a foole, 698
  Lear. Do's any heere know me? | This is not *Lear*: 738
  *acquaint my Daughter no further with any thing you 876
  Of any trust, vertue, or worth in thee 1006
  Then stands on any shoulder that I see | Before me, at this instant. 1168
  Corn. What was th'offence you gaue him? | *Ste*. I neuer gaue him any: 1190
  The Codpiece that will house, before the head has any; 1682
  of him, entreat for him, or any way sustaine him. 1757
  Edgar. Who giues any thing to poore *Tom*? Whom 1832
  *breeds about her heart. Is there any cause in Nature that 2034
  Gent. You shall haue any thing. | *Lear*. No Seconds? All my selfe? 2637
  Herald reads. | *If any man of qualitie or degree, within the lists of the*
  Ar- |*my*, 3059
  Thou worse then any name, reade thine owne euill: 3114
ANYTHING *see* thing
APACE = 1
  Vpon the Dunghill: *Regan*, I bleed apace, 2175
APISH = 1
  Their manners are so apish. 683
APOLLO = 2
  Lear. Now by *Apollo*, 172
  Kent. Now by *Apollo*, King | Thou swear'st thy Gods in vaine. 173
APOTHECARY = *1
  *of Ciuet; good Apothecary sweeten my immagination: 2572
APPARRELL *see* parrell
APPEARE = 4*3
  Kent. Fare thee well King, sith thus thou wilt appeare, 194
  Appeare like Mice: and yond tall Anchoring Barke, 2453
  *tatter'd cloathes great Vices do appeare: Robes, 2607
  When time shall serue, let but the Herald cry, | And Ile appeare againe.
  Exit. 2893
  To morrow, or at further space, t'appeare 2996
  If none appeare to proue vpon thy person, 3038
  that he is a manifold Traitor, let him appeare by the third 3062
APPEARES = 2*2
  *now in the diuision of the Kingdome, it ap-|peares 7
  hath now cast her off, appeares too grossely. 317
  *theres a great abatement of kindnesse appeares as well in 589
  Alb. Aske him his purposes, why he appeares | Vpon this Call
  o'th'Trumpet. 3068
APPERTAINES = 1
  Of what most neerely appertaines to vs both, 311
APPETITE = 1*1
  To gorge his appetite, shall to my bosome 125
  *the soyled Horse goes too't with a more riotous appe-|tite: 2566
APPLE = 1
  *for though she's as like this, as a Crabbe's like an | Apple, yet I can
  tell what I can tell. 889
APPLID = 1
  Shall be appli'd. For vs we will resigne, 3270

APPREHEND = 2
  apprehend him. Abhominable Villaine, where is he?   412
  This hurt you see, striuing to apprehend him.   1049
APPREHENSION = 1
  *seeke out where thy Father is, that hee may bee | ready for our
  apprehension.   1988
APPROACH = 2
  Approach thou Beacon to this vnder Globe,   1240
  Call by the Trumpet: he that dares approach;   3047
APPROUE = 1*1
  And your large speeches, may your deeds approue,   198
  *Kent. Good King, that must approue the common saw,   1237
APPROUES = 1*1
  Reg. I know't, my Sisters: this approues her Letter,   1470
  *which approues him an intelligent partie to the aduanta- |ges   1981
APT = 1
  And what they may incense him too, being apt,   1610
ARAIGNE = 1
  Who can araigne me for't? Exit.   3117
ARCH = 1
  My worthy Arch and Patron comes to night,   996
ARE see also y'are = 87*26
ARGUMENT = 1
  The argument of your praise, balme of your age,   236
ARGUMENTS = 1
  *I meane the whisper'd ones, for they are yet but | ear-kissing
  arguments.   935
ARIGHT = 1
  To vnderstand my purposes aright: 748
ARISE = *1
  *Kent. Come sir, arise, away, Ile teach you differences: 619
ARMD = 3
  there's my key: if you do stirre abroad, goe arm'd.   491
  Edg. Arm'd, Brother?   492
  Vntill some halfe houre past when I was arm'd,   3156
ARME = 6*2
  My vnprouided body, latch'd mine arme;   988
  *Vntimely comes this hurt. Giue me your arme. Exeunt.   2176
  Edg. Giue me thy arme; | Poore Tom shall leade thee. Exeunt.   2264
  Edg. Giue me your arme.   2507
  *the strong Lance of Iustice, hurtlesse breakes: Arme it in   2609
  Like hold on thee. Let go his arme.   2686
  Thy arme may do thee Iustice, heere is mine: 3082
  This Sword, this arme, and my best spirits are bent   3094
ARMED = 3
  Are gone with him toward Douer; where they boast | To haue well
  armed Friends.   2078
  Alb. Thou art armed Gloster, | Let the Trumpet sound: 3036
  Enter Edgar armed.   3067
ARMES = 5*1
  Glo. Weapons? Armes? what's the matter here?   1121
  Strike in their num'd and mortified Armes.   1266
  *Glou. Good friend, I prythee take him in thy armes;   2047
  Corn. Binde fast his corky armes.   2091
  No blowne Ambition doth our Armes incite,   2379
  Enter Lear with Cordelia in his armes.   3216

ARMIES = 1
Gon. Oh ho, I know the Riddle, I will goe. | *Exeunt both the Armies.* 2878
ARMY = 3*2
*him this Letter, the Army of France is landed: seeke out | the Traitor
Glouster. 2061
I told him of the Army that was Landed: 2271
Edg. But by your fauour: | How neere's the other Army? 2655
Her Army is mou'd on. *Exit.* 2661
Herald reads. | *If any man of qualitie or degree, within the lists of the
Ar-|my,* 3059
AROYNT = 2
And aroynt thee Witch, aroynt thee. 1903
ARRANT = *1
*Fortune that arrant whore, nere turns the key toth' poore. 1325
ARRAY = 1
*with mans sworne Spouse: set not thy Sweet-heart on | proud array.
Tom's a cold. 1862
ARRAYD = 1
I'th'sway of your owne will: is he array'd? 2770
ARREST = 2
Alb. Stay yet, heare reason: *Edmund*, I arrest thee 3027
On capitall Treason; and in thy arrest, 3028
ARRIUES = 1
To let him liue, Where he arriues, he moues 2395
ART *see also* thou'rt *l.*275 335 540 549 553 567 *706 *707 *708 *1076
*1093 *1098 *1101 *1130 1144 1158 1483 1515 1517 1558 1567 1708
1723 *1825 *1830 *1886 *1888 2494 2795 3036 3041 3088 3110 3124
3128 = 23*12, 3*2
If for I want that glib and oylie Art, 246
The Art of our Necessities is strange, 1725
Lear. Nature's aboue Art, in that respect. Ther's your 2533
Lear. What, art mad? A man may see how this world 2594
Who, by the Art of knowne, and feeling sorrowes, 2669
AS = 78*29
Glou. My Lord of Kent: | Remember him heereafter, as my Honourable
Friend. 30
As much as Childe ere lou'd, or Father found. 64
Reg. I am made of that selfe-mettle as my Sister, 74
I returne those duties backe as are right fit, 104
And as a stranger to my heart and me, 122
Be as well neighbour'd, pittied, and releeu'd, 126
As thou my sometime Daughter. 127
So be my graue my peace, as here I giue 133
Kent. Royall *Lear,* | Whom I haue euer honor'd as my King, 148
Lou'd as my Father, as my Master follow'd, 150
As my great Patron thought on in my praiers. 151
Kent. My life I neuer held but as pawne 166
Your faults as they are named. Loue well our Father: 296
Reg. Such vnconstant starts are we like to haue from | him, as this of
Kents banishment. 325
*Father carry authority with such disposition as he beares, 329
When my Dimensions are as well compact, 341
My minde as generous, and my shape as true 342
As honest Madams issue? Why brand they vs 343
As to th'legitimate: fine word: Legitimate. 352
*much as I haue perus'd, I finde it not fit for your ore-loo-|king. 373
The Contents, as in part I vnderstand them, | Are too blame. 377

AS *cont.*

this but as an essay, or taste of my Vertue.	381
not as it hath power, but as it is suffer'd. Come to me, that of	386
*declin'd, the Father should bee as Ward to the Son, and	407
as I shall find meanes, and acquaint you withall.	432
*Moone, and Starres, as if we were villaines on necessitie,	450
*forbearance till the speed of his rage goes slower: and as	488
Kent. If but as will I other accents borrow,	531
Lear. What art thou? | **Kent.* A very honest hearted Fellow, and as	
poore as | the King.	549
Lear. If thou be'st as poore for a subiect, as hee's for a	552
*with that Ceremonious affection as you were wont,	588
*theres a great abatement of kindnesse appeares as well in	589
*the generall dependants, as in the Duke himselfe also, and | your	
Daughter.	590
*which I haue rather blamed as mine owne iealous curio- | sitie,	598
*then as a very pretence and purpose of vnkindnesse;	599
*nay, & thou canst not smile as the wind sits, thou'lt catch	630
As you are Old, and Reuerend, should be Wise.	749
To be such men as may resort your Age, | Which know themselues, and	
you.	760
Alb. My Lord, I am guiltlesse, as I am ignorant | Of what hath moued	
you.	786
But let his disposition haue that scope | As dotage giues it.	807
As may compact it more. Get you gone,	863
*for though she's as like this, as a Crabbe's like an | Apple, yet I can	
tell what I can tell.	889
Foole. She will taste as like this as, a Crabbe do's to a	892
(As this I would, though thou didst produce	1008
Kent. That such a slaue as this should weare a Sword,	1145
Who weares no honesty: such smiling rogues as these,	1146
Smoile you my speeches, as I were a Foole?	1155
As I haue life and Honour, there shall he sit till Noone.	1213
Gent. As I learn'd, | The night before, there was no purpose in them |	
Of this remoue.	1276
*But for all this thou shalt haue as many Dolors for thy	1326
Daughters, as thou canst tell in a yeare.	1327
Foole. Cry to it Nunckle, as the Cockney did to the	1398
As cleeres her from all blame. | *Lear.* My curses on her.	1424
Our yongest borne, I could as well be brought	1506
Mans life is cheape as Beastes. Thou art a Lady;	1567
As full of griefe as age, wretched in both,	1573
(Although as yet the face of it is couer'd	1629
Who haue, as who haue not, that their great Starres	1631
(As feare not but you shall) shew her this Ring,	1644
So old, and white as this. O, ho! 'tis foule.	1679
Loue not such nights as these: The wrathfull Skies	1695
*bed, if I die for it, (as no lesse is threatned me) the King	1768
Is it not as this mouth should teare this hand	1795
In such a night as this? O *Regan, Gonerill,*	1799
From seasons such as these? O I haue tane	1813
*her. Swore as many Oathes, as I spake words, & broke	1868
*as thou art. Off, off you Lendings: Come, vn- | button heere.	1888
Glou. Vnmercifull Lady, as you are, I'me none.	2097
The Sea, with such a storme as his bare head,	2131
So long as we can say this is the worst.	2211

15

KING LEAR

AS *cont*.

As Flies to wanton Boyes, are we to th'Gods, | They kill vs for their sport. 2221
Do as I bid thee, or rather do thy pleasure: | Aboue the rest, be gone. 2236
Proper deformitie seemes not in the Fiend | So horrid as in woman. 2309
As mad as the vext Sea, singing alowd. 2352
Shew scarse so grosse as Beetles. Halfe way downe 2449
Edg. As I stood heere below, me thought his eyes 2514
*'twould not ha' bin zo long as 'tis, by a vortnight. Nay, 2692
As duteous to the vices of thy Mistris, | As badnesse would desire. 2705
For (as I am a man) I thinke this Lady | To be my childe *Cordelia*. |
Cor. And so I am: I am. 2824
Haue (as I do remember) done me wrong. 2831
Each iealous of the other, as the stung 2903
His speedy taking off. As for the mercie 2912
Men must endure | Their going hence, euen as their comming hither, 2933
and Cordelia, as prisoners, Souldiers, Captaine. 2939
As if we were Gods spies: And wee'l weare out 2957
As this instructs thee, thou dost make thy way 2972
Are as the time is; to be tender minded 2974
As I haue set it downe. *Exit Captaine*. 2981
As we shall find their merites, and our safety | May equally determine. 2987
I hold you but a subiect of this Warre, | Not as a Brother. 2999
Reg. That's as we list to grace him. 3001
Yet am I Noble as the Aduersary | I come to cope. 3075
You looke as you had something more to say. 3165
She's dead as earth: Lend me a Looking-glasse, 3221
With boote, and such addition as your Honours 3273
ASHAMD = 3
Then on a wretch whom Nature is asham'd | Almost t'acknowledge hers. 232
Life and death, I am asham'd 814
Art not asham'd to looke vpon this Beard? 1483
ASKD = 1
I ask'd his blessing, and from first to last 3158
ASKE = 7*2
Lear. Aske her forgiuenesse? 1433
*in, aske thy Daughters blessing, heere's a night pitties | neither Wisemen, nor Fooles. 1667
*him perceiued; If he aske for me, I am ill, and gone to 1767
Lear. Let me aske you one word in priuate. 1939
When thou dost aske me blessing, Ile kneele downe 2950
And aske of thee forgiuenesse: So wee'l liue, 2951
Alb. Aske him his purposes, why he appeares | Vpon this Call o'th'Trumpet. 3068
Bast. In wisedome I should aske thy name, 3097
Bast. Aske me not what I know. 3119
ASLEEPE *see also* sleepe = 1
asleepe, how now? Where's that Mungrell? 579
ASPECT = 1
Vnder th'allowance of your great aspect, 1181
ASQUINT *see* squint
ASSAULTED = 1
To haue her Gentleman abus'd, assaulted. 1226
ASSE = *2
*both parts, thou boar'st thine Asse on thy backe o're the 676
Foole. May not an Asse know, when the Cart drawes | the Horse? 735

16

ASSES = *1
    Foole. Thy Asses are gone about 'em; the reason why   908
ASSUME = 1
    Into a mad-mans rags, t'assume a semblance   3150
ASSURANCE = *1
    *assurance haue your satisfaction, and that without   425
ASSURD = 1
    I feele this pin pricke, would I were assur'd | Of my condition.   2808
ASSURE = 1
    Ile not be there. | *Cor*. Nor I, assure thee *Regan*;   1043
ASSURED = 1
    Stand in assured losse. Take vp, take vp,   2054
AT = 39*15
ATHENIAN = 1
    Lear. Come, good Athenian.   1964
ATHWART *see* thwart
ATTEMPTING = 1
    For him attempting, who was selfe-subdued,   1198
ATTEND = 3*1
    Lear. Attend the Lords of France & Burgundy, Gloster.   39
    From hence attend dispatch, our good old Friend,   1068
    Do's not attend my taking. Whiles I may scape   1256
    Commanded me to follow, and attend   1312
ATTENDANCE = *1
    Gon. Why might not you my Lord, receiue attendance   1539
ATTENDANTS = 4
    *Sennet. Enter King Lear, Cornwall, Albany, Gonerill, Re-|gan,
    Cordelia, and attendants.*   37
    Flourish. Enter Gloster with France, and Bur-|gundy, Attendants.   202
    Hornes within. Enter Lear and Attendants.   538
    Enter Cornewall, Regan, and Attendants.   1024
ATTENDED = 1
    He is attended with a desperate traine,   1609
ATWAINE *see* twaine
AUAUNT = *1
    Edg. Tom, will throw his head at them: Auaunt you   2022
AUENGE *see* venge
AUERT = 1
    T'auert your liking a more worthier way,   231
AUGHT *see* ought
AVOID = 1
    On her kind nursery. Hence and avoid my sight: 132
AUOUCH = 1
    Reg. I dare auouch it Sir, what fifty Followers?   1533
AUOUCHED = 1
    What is auouched there. If you miscarry,   2888
AURICULAR = *1
    *where you shall heare vs conferre of this, and by an Auri-|cular   424
AUSPICIOUS = 1
    Mumbling of wicked charmes, coniuring the Moone | To stand
    auspicious Mistris.   973
AUTHORITIE = 1*1
    By his authoritie I will proclaime it,   997
    *might'st behold the great image of Authoritie, a Dogg's   2602
AUTHORITY = 1*1
    *Father carry authority with such disposition as he beares,   329
    Lear. What's that? | *Kent*. Authority.   560

AWAKE = 2
Be by good Madam when we do awake him, | I doubt of his
Temperance.   2774
Gen. He's scarse awake,   2801
AWAY = 25*8
Glou. He hath bin out nine yeares, and away he shall | againe. The
King is comming.   35
The moment is thy death, away. By *Iupiter*, | This shall not be reuok'd,   192
Be it lawfull I take vp what's cast away.   278
like the image, and horror of it, pray you away.   496
Sir, the Foole hath much pined away.   603
Kent. Come sir, arise, away, Ile teach you differences: 619
*away, away, if you will measure your lubbers length a- | gaine,   620
tarry, but away, goe too, haue you wisedome, so.   621
*thou clouest thy Crownes i'th'middle, and gau'st away   675
*gau'st thy golden one away; if I speake like my selfe in   678
(Whereof I know you are fraught), and put away   732
To haue a thanklesse Childe. Away, away. *Exit*.   803
Let me still take away the harmes I feare,   851
Gon. Take you some company, and away to horse,   860
Lear. Why? | *Foole*. Why to put's head in, not to giue it away to his   903
Stew. Away, I haue nothing to do with thee.   1107
Our Sister speakes of. Come, bring away the Stocks.   1219
Corn. Come my Lord, away. *Exit*.   1227
The knaue turnes Foole that runnes away,   1356
Edg. Away, the foule Fiend followes me, through the   1827
Giue thee quicke conduct. Come, come, away. *Exeunt*   2056
Glou. Away, get thee away: good Friend be gone,   2195
Glou. Get thee away: If for my sake   2228
What are you Sir? | *Glou*. Away, and let me dye.   2488
Edgar. Away old man, giue me thy hand, away: 2928
Bast. Some Officers take them away: good guard,   2940
Lear. No, no, no, no: come let's away to prison,   2948
Bast. Take them away.   2960
Kent. O my good Master. | *Lear*. Prythee away.   3230
AWHILE *see also* while = 1*1
Kent. Now good my Lord, lye heere, and rest awhile.   2040
Alb. The Gods defend her, beare him hence awhile.   3215
AWORK *see* a-worke
AY *see* I
AYDANT = 1
Spring with my teares; be aydant, and remediate   2368
AYE = 1
Kent. I am come | To bid my King and Master aye good night.   3189
AYRE = 5*3
To wage against the enmity oth'ayre,   1502
Lea. Now all the plagues that in the pendulous ayre   1848
Glou. Heere is better then the open ayre, take it thank- | fully: 1998
Thou vnsubstantiall ayre that I embrace: 2185
Would stretch thy Spirits vp into the ayre: 2291
*The Crowes and Choughes, that wing the midway ayre   2448
Edg. Had'st thou beene ought | But Gozemore, Feathers, Ayre,   2490
Thou know'st, the first time that we smell the Ayre   2621
AYRES = 1
You taking Ayres, with Lamenesse. | *Corn*. Fye sir, fie.   1446
A-LIGHT = 1
Bid her a-light, and her troth-plight,   1902

18

A-WORKE = *1
*a prouoking merit set a-worke by a reprouable badnesse | in himselfe.   1977
BABE = 1
A Babe to honor her. If she must teeme,   795
BACKE = 8*4
I returne those duties backe as are right fit,   104
And on the sixt to turne thy hated backe   189
*nor so old to dote on her for any thing. I haue yeares on | my backe
forty eight.   569
*backe: wher's my Foole? Ho, I thinke the world's   578
*Lear. Why came not the slaue backe to me when I | call'd him?   581
*both parts, thou boar'st thine Asse on thy backe o're the   676
And not send backe my Messengers.   1275
*stockt, punish'd, and imprison'd: who hath three Suites | to his backe,
sixe shirts to his body: 1914
May proue effects. Backe *Edmond* to my Brother,   2283
Alb. He is not heere. | *Mes*. No my good Lord, I met him backe againe. 2338
*backe, thou hotly lusts to vse her in that kind, for which   2605
Backe do I tosse these Treasons to thy head,   3102
BAD = 3
Glo. I know not Madam, 'tis too bad, too bad.   1035
Bad is the Trade that must play Foole to sorrow,   2224
BADNESSE = 1*1
*a prouoking merit set a-worke by a reprouable badnesse | in himselfe. 1977
As duteous to the vices of thy Mistris, | As badnesse would desire.   2705
BAGS = *1
*But Fathers that beare bags, shall see their children kind.   1324
BALD = *1
*durt, thou hadst little wit in thy bald crowne, when thou   677
BALL = 1
Kent. Nor tript neither, you base Foot-ball plaier.   616
BALLOW = *1
*try whither your Costard, or my Ballow be the harder; | chill be plaine
with you.   2694
BALME = 1
The argument of your praise, balme of your age,   236
BANDY = 2
Lear. Do you bandy lookes with me, you Rascall?   614
To bandy hasty words, to scant my sizes,   1459
BANE = *1
*in his Pue, set Rats-bane by his Porredge, made him   1836
BANES = 1
And I her husband contradict your Banes.   3032
BANISHD = 1*3
Glo. Kent banish'd thus? and France in choller parted?   358
*Kent banish'd; his offence, honesty. 'Tis strange. *Exit*   446
*ha's banish'd two on's Daughters, and did the third a   632
He said it would be thus: poore banish'd man: 1944
BANISHMENT = 2
Freedome liues hence, and banishment is here;   195
Reg. Such vnconstant starts are we like to haue from | him, as this of
Kents banishment.   325
BANISHT = 2
Thy banisht trunke be found in our Dominions,   191
For which I raiz'd my likenesse. Now banisht *Kent*,   534
BANS = *1
*Sometimes with Lunaticke bans, sometime with Praiers   1270

BARBAROUS = 1
    Hold thee from this for euer. The barbarous *Scythian*,   123
BARBER-MONGER = 1
    *sop oth' Moonshine of you, you whoreson Cullyenly | Barber-monger,
    draw.   1105
BARE = 2*1
    *man, is no more but such a poore, bare, forked A- | nimall   1887
    The Sea, with such a storme as his bare head,   2131
    I bare it in the interest of my wife,   3030
BARE-GNAWNE = 1
    Edg. Know my name is lost | By Treasons tooth: bare-gnawne, and
    Canker-bit,   3073
BARE-HEADED = 1
    Kent. Alacke, bare-headed?   1714
BARKE = 3
    Trey, Blanch, and Sweet-heart: see, they barke at me.   2021
    Appeare like Mice: and yond tall Anchoring Barke,   2453
    dogge barke at a Beggar? | *Glou.* I Sir.   2599
BARRE = 2
    All Ports Ile barre, the villaine shall not scape,   1018
    Though their Iniunction be to barre my doores,   1928
BASE = 7*1
    Lag of a Brother? Why Bastard? Wherefore base?   340
    With Base? With basenes Bastardie? Base, Base?   344
    And my inuention thriue, *Edmond* the base | Shall to'th'Legitimate: I
    grow, I prosper: 354
    Kent. Nor tript neither, you base Foot-ball plaier.   616
    *base, proud, shallow, beggerly, three-suited-hundred   1089
    To keepe base life a foote; returne with her?   1508
BASENES = 1
    With Base? With basenes Bastardie? Base, Base?   344
BASEST = 2
    To take the basest, and most poorest shape   1258
    Lear. O reason not the need: our basest Beggers   1564
BAST = 46*21
BASTARD see also Bast. = 10
    Enter Bastard.   334
    Lag of a Brother? Why Bastard? Wherefore base?   340
    Our Fathers loue, is to the Bastard *Edmond*,   351
    Degenerate Bastard, Ile not trouble thee;   764
    Enter Bastard, and Curan, seuerally.   927
    Thou vnpossessing Bastard, dost thou thinke,   1004
    Enter Bastard, Cornewall, Regan, Gloster, Seruants.   1117
    Enter Cornewall, Regan, Gonerill, Bastard, | and Seruants.   2058
    Enter Gonerill, Bastard, and Steward.   2267
    For Glousters bastard Son was kinder to his Father,   2560
BASTARDIE = 1
    With Base? With basenes Bastardie? Base, Base?   344
BASTARDIZING = 1
    *haue bin that I am, had the maidenlest Starre in the Fir- | mament
    twinkled on my bastardizing.   460
BASTARDS = 1
    Now Gods, stand vp for Bastards.   356
BATTAILE = 3
    Edg. Before you fight the Battaile, ope this Letter: 2884
    His countenance for the Battaile, which being done,   2910
    The Battaile done, and they within our power,   2914

BATTAILES = 1
Your high-engender'd Battailes, 'gainst a head   1678
BATTELL = 1
    Edg. Do you heare ought (Sir) of a Battell toward. | *Gent*. Most sure,
and vulgar: 2652
BAUD = *1
    *would'st be a Baud in way of good seruice, and art no-|thing   1093
BAUDES = 1
And Baudes, and whores, do Churches build,   1745
BAY = *1
    *Proud of heart, to ride on a Bay trotting Horse, ouer foure   1837
BE *see also* bee, be't, shalbe = 109*34
BEACH = 1
The Fishermen, that walk'd vpon the beach   2452
BEACON = 1
Approach thou Beacon to this vnder Globe,   1240
BEADLE = *1
    *obey'd in Office. Thou, Rascall Beadle, hold thy bloody   2603
BEAKES = 1
Reuenge, affirme, and turne their Halcion beakes   1151
BEAMES = 1
That by thy comfortable Beames I may   1241
BEARD = 5*2
    Ste. This ancient Ruffian Sir, whose life I haue spar'd | at sute of his
gray-beard.   1135
Iakes with him. Spare my gray-beard, you wagtaile?   1140
Art not asham'd to looke vpon this Beard?   1483
Glou. By the kinde Gods, 'tis most ignobly done | To plucke me by the
Beard.   2100
Ser. If you did weare a beard vpon your chin,   2150
    Lear. Ha! *Gonerill* with a white beard? They flatter'd   2543
    *my Beard, ere the blacke ones were there. To say I, and   2545
BEARE = 13*1
Which, nor our nature, nor our place can beare;   185
Alb. I cannot be so partiall *Gonerill*, | To the great loue I beare you.   831
    *But Fathers that beare bags, shall see their children kind.   1324
To beare it tamely: touch me with Noble anger,   1576
The lesser is scarce felt. Thou'dst shun a Beare,   1789
Thou'dst meete the Beare i'th' mouth, when the mind's | (free,   1791
And Ile repayre the misery thou do'st beare   2261
If I could beare it longer, and not fall   2476
Glou. I do remember now: henceforth Ile beare | Affliction, till it do cry
out it selfe   2520
Edgar. Beare free and patient thoughts.   2525
Cor. Wilt please your Highnesse walke? | *Lear*. You must beare with
me: 2840
Will not beare question: either say thou'lt do't, | Or thriue by other
meanes.   2976
Alb. The Gods defend her, beare him hence awhile.   3215
Alb. Beare them from hence, our present businesse   3293
BEARER = 1
I do not bid the Thunder-bearer shoote,   1521
BEARES = *3
    *Father carry authority with such disposition as he beares,   329
    *tide by the heads, Dogges and Beares by'th'necke,   1283
    *King now beares, will be reuenged home; ther is part of   1763

BEARST = 1
Gon. Milke-Liuer'd man, | That bear'st a cheeke for blowes, a head for
wrongs,   2304
BEAST = 1*1
  Brought neere to beast; my face Ile grime with filth,   1260
  *the Worme no Silke; the Beast, no Hide; the Sheepe, no   1884
BEASTES = 1
  Mans life is cheape as Beastes. Thou art a Lady;   1567
BEASTLY = 1
  Cor. Peace sirrah, | You beastly knaue, know you no reuerence?   1141
BEATE = 2*2
  Beate at this gate that let thy Folly in,   784
  *one whom I will beate into clamours whining, if thou   1096
  *heeles, and beate thee before the King? Draw you rogue,   1103
  Or at their Chamber doore Ile beate the Drum,   1394
BEATEN = 2
  beaten for being old before thy time.   914
  Farre off methinkes I heare the beaten Drumme.   2741
BEATES = 1
  Saue what beates there, Filliall ingratitude,   1794
BEAUTY = 2
  No lesse then life, with grace, health, beauty, honor: 63
  Into her scornfull eyes: Infect her Beauty,   1449
BECAME = 1
  Their precious Stones new lost: became his guide,   3153
BECAUSE = 3
  Lear. Because they are not eight.   910
  Reg. Wherefore to Douer? | *Glou.* Because I would not see thy cruell
Nailes   2127
  Because he do's not feele, feele your powre quickly: 2254
BECOME = 1
  Do's not become a Sword, thy great imployment   2975
BECOMES = 1
  Do you but marke how this becomes the house?   1434
BED = 4*3
  *Sonne for her Cradle, ere she had a husband for her bed.   18
  Then doth within a dull stale tyred bed   347
  That you'l vouchsafe me Rayment, Bed, and Food.   1437
  *bed, if I die for it, (as no lesse is threatned me) the King   1768
  *sharpe Hauthorne blow the windes. Humh, goe to thy | bed and warme
thee.   1828
  Foole. And Ile go to bed at noone.   2043
  returne the Conqueror, then am I the Prisoner, and his bed, my   2719
BEDLAM = 1*1
  *o'Bedlam. --- O these Eclipses do portend these diui-|sions. Fa, Sol,
La, Me.   465
  Of Bedlam beggers, who with roaring voices,   1265
BEE *l.*369 *407 *427 *593 *641 *1988 *2037 = *7
BEENE *see also* bene, bin *l.*257 *315 1041 1171 1244 *1337 2300
  2490 = 6*2
BEEST *see* be'st
BEETLES = 1
  Shew scarse so grosse as Beetles. Halfe way downe   2449
BEFORE = 11*5
  *world before he was sent for: yet was his Mother fayre,   25
  Ile do't before I speake, that you make knowne   248
  Glo. Has he neuer before sounded you in this busines?   404

BEFORE *cont*.
   Lear. Go you before to *Gloster* with these Letters;   875
   beaten for being old before thy time.   914
   Yeeld, come before my Father, light hoa, here,   963
   *heeles, and beate thee before the King? Draw you rogue,   1103
   Then stands on any shoulder that I see | Before me, at this instant.   1168
   Gent. As I learn'd, | The night before, there was no purpose in them |
   Of this remoue.   1276
   The Codpiece that will house, before the head has any;   1682
   *This prophecie *Merlin* shall make, for I liue before his | (time. | *Exit*.   1749
   *his Sonne: for hee's a mad Yeoman that sees his Sonne a | Gentleman
   before him.   2011
   Pinnion him like a Theefe, bring him before vs: 2083
   Cor. 'Tis knowne before. Our preparation stands   2375
   Let not my worser Spirit tempt me againe | To dye before you please.   2664
   Edg. Before you fight the Battaile, ope this Letter: 2884
BEG = 2*1
   *my selfe, there's mine, beg another of thy | Daughters.   638
   To knee his Throne, and Squire-like pension beg,   1507
   Glou. He has some reason, else he could not beg.   2215
BEGET = 1
   Some blood drawne on me, would beget opinion   966
BEGGAR = 3
   Oldm. Madman, and beggar too.   2214
   Glou. A poore vnfortunate Beggar.   2513
   dogge barke at a Beggar? | *Glou*. I Sir.   2599
BEGGAR-MAN = 1
   Glou. Is it a Beggar-man?   2213
BEGGD = 1
   Led him, begg'd for him, sau'd him from dispaire.   3154
BEGGE = 1
   Age is vnnecessary: on my knees I begge,   1436
BEGGER = *1
   *but the composition of a Knaue, Begger, Coward,   1094
BEGGERLY = *1
   *base, proud, shallow, beggerly, three-suited-hundred   1089
BEGGERS = 2*1
   Of Bedlam beggers, who with roaring voices,   1265
   Lear. O reason not the need: our basest Beggers   1564
   *The Head, and he shall Lowse: so Beggers marry many.   1683
BEGGES = 1
   By her, that else will take the thing she begges,   757
BEGIN = 3*1
   vs, till our oldnesse cannot rellish them. I begin to finde an idle   384
   Lear. My wits begin to turne.   1722
   His wits begin t'vnsettle. | *Glou*. Canst thou blame him? *Storm still*   1941
   Edg. My teares begin to take his part so much, | They marre my
   counterfetting.   2018
BEGINS = 1*1
   Will packe, when it begins to raine,   1352
   Edg. This is the foule Flibbertigibbet; hee begins at   1895
BEGOT = 2
   Cor. Good my Lord, | You haue begot me, bred me, lou'd me.   102
   Iudicious punishment, 'twas this flesh begot | Those Pelicane Daughters.   1855
BEGUILD = 1*1
   *so much; I know Sir, I am no flatterer, he that be-|guild   1186

BEGUILD *cont.*

An vnknowne opposite: thou art not vanquish'd, | But cozend, and beguild.   3110

BEGUILE = 1

When misery could beguile the Tyrants rage, | And frustrate his proud will.   2505

BEHALFE = 1

(If you dare venture in your owne behalfe)   2288

BEHAUIOUR = *1

*behauiour, we make guilty of our disasters, the Sun, the   449

BEHIND = 1

Tript me behind: being downe, insulted, rail'd,   1195

BEHOLD = 3*2

Take vantage heauie eyes, not to behold   1248
*Behold yond simpring Dame, whose face betweene her   2563
*might'st behold the great image of Authoritie, a Dogg's   2602
Behold it is my priuiledge,   3083
Kent. If Fortune brag of two, she lou'd and hated, | One of them we behold.   3245

BEHOLDING = *1

*beholding. Aduice the Duke where you are going, to a   2068

BEING *l.*21 168 275 914 1150 1195 1217 1316 1384 1494 1555 1610 2331 2394 2411 2909 2910 = 17

BELEEUE = 3

Fall into taint, which to beleeue of her   242
comes to, he will not beleeue a Foole.   665
I can scarce speake to thee, thou'lt not beleeue   1414

BELIKE = *1

*Might not you transport her purposes by word? Belike,   2406

BELLY = *1

Lear. Rumble thy belly full: spit Fire, spowt Raine: 1669

BELOUD = 1

Bast. Yet *Edmund* was belou'd: 3196

BELOUED = 3

Reuennew, Execution of the rest, | Beloued Sonnes be yours, which to confirme,   145
him, you should enioy halfe his Reuennew for euer, and liue the | beloued of your Brother. Edgar.   388
Some other time for that. Beloued *Regan,*   1411

BELOW = 3

Thy Elements below where is this Daughter?   1330
Edg. As I stood heere below, me thought his eyes   2514
To the discent and dust below thy foote,   3092

BEMET *see* be-met

BEND = 1

'Gainst Paricides did all the thunder bend,   982

BENDING = 1*1

Glou. There is a Cliffe, whose high and bending head   2258
Oppos'd against the act: bending his Sword   2318

BENE *l.*2193 = 1

BENEATH = 1*1

For all beneath the Moone would I not leape vpright.   2463
*beneath is all the Fiends. There's hell, there's darke-|nes, 2569

BENEDICTION = 2

Thou out of Heauens benediction com'st | To the warme Sun.   1238
Cor. O looke vpon me Sir, | And hold your hand in benediction o're me,   2810

BENEFIT = 1
Is wretchednesse depriu'd that benefit | To end it selfe by death? 'Twas
yet some comfort,   2503
BENEFITS = 1
Turne all her Mothers paines, and benefits   800
BENIZON = 2
Without our Grace, our Loue, our Benizon: 290
The bountie, and the benizon of Heauen | To boot, and boot.   2673
BENT = 1*1
*Le. The bow is bent & drawne, make from the shaft.   152
This Sword, this arme, and my best spirits are bent   3094
BEREAUED = 1
In the restoring his bereaued Sense; he that helpes him,   2359
BESEECH = 6*2
To match you where I hate, therefore beseech you   230
Cor. I yet beseech your Maiesty.   245
*Bast. I beseech you Sir, pardon mee; it is a Letter   371
*Knigh. I beseech you pardon me my Lord, if I bee   593
Ste. I am none of these my Lord, | I beseech your pardon.   612
Of other your new prankes. I do beseech you   747
Glo. Let me beseech your Grace, not to do so,   1220
I do beseech your grace. | Lear. O cry you mercy, Sir: 1951
BESIDES = 2
The Duke must grant me that: besides, his picture   1019
Kent. Who's there besides foule weather?   1616
BESORT = 1
To be such men as may besort your Age, | Which know themselues, and
you.   760
BESPOKE = 1
My Lady is bespoke. | Gon. An enterlude.   3034
BEST = 14*5
And in thy best consideration checke   160
The best, the deerest, should in this trice of time   237
*Gon. The best and soundest of his time hath bin but   320
*world bitter to the best of our times: keepes our Fortunes from   383
*seene the best of our time. Machinations, hollownesse,   442
*Edm. Brother, I aduise you to the best, I am no honest   493
*Lear. If thou be'st as poore for a subiect, as hee's for a   552
*bluntly: that which ordinary men are fit for, I am qual-|lified in, and
the best of me, is Dilligence.   565
Foole. Sirrah, you were best take my Coxcombe.   627
Bast. The Duke be here to night? The better best,   943
And when he saw my best alarum'd spirits   989
Of differences, which I best thought it fit   1066
Corn. 'Tis best to giue him way, he leads himselfe.   1601
The lamentable change is from the best,   2183
Oldm. Ile bring him the best Parrell that I haue   2238
Cor. We are not the first, | Who with best meaning haue incurr'd the
worst: 2943
Reg. In my rights, | By me inuested, he compeeres the best.   3010
This Sword, this arme, and my best spirits are bent   3094
Mine eyes are not o'th'best, Ile tell you straight.   3244
BESTIRD = *1
*Kent. No Maruell, you haue so bestir'd your valour,   1127
BESTOW = 3
Kent. Kill thy Physition, and thy fee bestow   177
Lay comforts to your bosome, and bestow   1069

BESTOW *cont.*
   Come Father, Ile bestow you with a Friend. *Exeunt.*   2742
BESTOWD = 1
   Reg. This house is little, the old man and's people, | Cannot be well
   bestow'd.   1588
BET = 1
   Cor. Then be't so my good Lord: 2760
BETHINK = *1
   Bast. Bethink your selfe wherein you may haue offen-|ded   481
BETHOUGHT = 1
   I will preserue myselfe: and am bethought   1257
BETRAY = *1
   *Nor the rustling of Silkes, betray thy poore heart to wo-|man.   1875
BETTER = 21*6
   Kent. I must loue you, and sue to know you better.   33
   Kent. See better *Lear*, and let me still remaine | The true blanke of
   thine eie.   170
   Lear. Better thou had'st | Not beene borne, then not t'haue pleas'd me
   better.   256
   Thou loosest here a better where to finde.   286
   I would prefer him to a better place,   299
   *deriue from him better testimony of his intent, you shold   415
   *a figure, I am better then thou art now, I am a Foole,   707
   Striuing to better, oft we marre what's well.   870
   Bast. The Duke be here to night? The better best,   943
   I haue seene better faces in my Time,   1167
   *when a wiseman giues thee better counsell giue me mine   1347
   Fetch me a better answer.   1365
   Better then you your selfe: therefore I pray you,   1430
   Against my comming in. Thou better know'st   1461
   Mend when thou can'st, be better at thy leisure,   1523
   *better then this Rain-water out o'doore. Good Nunkle,   1666
   Lear. Thou wert better in a Graue, then to answere   1881
   Glou. What, hath your Grace no better company?   1920
   Glou. Heere is better then the open ayre, take it thank-|fully: 1998
   But better seruice haue I neuer done you, | Then now to bid you hold.   2147
   Edg. Yet better thus, and knowne to be contemn'd,   2179
   Your Sister is the better Souldier.   2388
   In better phrase, and matter then thou did'st.   2441
   Glou. Me thinkes y'are better spoken. | *Edg.* Come on Sir,   2444
   Of my huge Sorrowes? Better I were distract,   2735
   Cor. Be better suited,   2753
BETTERS = 1
   Gon. You strike my people, and your disorder'd rable, | make Seruants
   of their Betters.   766
BETWEENE *see also* 'tweene = 3*5
   Come not betweene the Dragon and his wrath,   130
   This Coronet part betweene you.   147
   Gon. There is further complement of leaue-taking be-|tweene   327
   Foole. Do'st thou know the difference my Boy, be-|tweene a bitter
   Foole, and a sweet one.   667
   Glo. Go too; say you nothing. There is diuision be-|tweene   1759
   *Loyalty, though the conflict be sore betweene that, and | my blood.   1992
   Shall passe betweene vs: ere long you are like to heare   2287
   *Behold yond simpring Dame, whose face betweene her   2563
BETWIXT *see also* 'twixt = 2*1
   To come betwixt our sentences, and our power,   184

BETWIXT *cont.*
  Glo. I would haue all well betwixt you. *Exit.*   1396
  *Postes shall be swift, and intelligent betwixt vs. Fare-|well deere
Sister, farewell my Lord of Glouster.   2070
BEWARE = *2
  *Beware my Follower. Peace Smulkin, peace thou Fiend.   1919
  *in the Lake of Darknesse: pray Innocent, and beware | the foule Fiend.   2005
BEWEEPE = 1
  Beweepe this cause againe, Ile plucke ye out,   821
BEWRAY = 1
  Glo. He did bewray his practise, and receiu'd   1048
BEYOND = 2
  Beyond what can be valewed, rich or rare,   62
  Beyond all manner of so much I loue you.   66
BE-MET = 1
  Alb. Our very louing Sister, well be-met: 2865
BIAS *see* byas
BID = 9
  Bid them farewell *Cordelia*, though vnkinde,   285
  Fra. Bid farwell to your Sisters.   292
  Now, presently: bid them come forth and heare me,   1393
  I do not bid the Thunder-bearer shoote,   1521
  Bid her a-light, and her troth-plight,   1902
  But better seruice haue I neuer done you, | Then now to bid you hold.   2147
  Do as I bid thee, or rather do thy pleasure: | Aboue the rest, be gone.   2236
  Bid me farewell, and let me heare thee going.   2468
  Kent. I am come | To bid my King and Master aye good night.   3189
BIDDING = *1
  *peace at my bidding, there I found 'em, there I smelt 'em   2549
BIDE = 1
  That bide the pelting of this pittilesse storme,   1810
BIDING = 1
  Ile leade you to some biding. | *Glou.* Heartie thankes: 2671
BIDS = 4
  Thus *Kent*, O Princes, bids you all adew,   200
  your face bids me, though you say nothing.   709
  To haue his eare abus'd, wisedome bids feare.   1611
  Bids the winde blow the Earth into the Sea,   1620
BIGGER = 1
  Me thinkes he seemes no bigger then his head.   2451
BILE *see* byle
BILLES = *1
  *Bring vp the browne Billes. O well flowne Bird: i'th'   2538
BIN *l.**12 *35 *320 *460 *916 917 929 *1132 1634 *1846 1864 1918 *2247
2484 2485 *2691 *2692 *2781 2803 3002 = 9*11
BINDE = 3
  Corn. Binde fast his corky armes.   2091
  Do me no foule play, Friends. | *Corn.* Binde him I say.   2094
  Corn. To this Chaire binde him, | Villaine, thou shalt finde.   2098
BIRD = *1
  *Bring vp the browne Billes. O well flowne Bird: i'th'   2538
BIRDS = 1
  We two alone will sing like Birds i'th'Cage: 2949
BIRTH = 1
  Let me, if not by birth, haue lands by wit,   503
BIT = 2*1
  *fed the Cuckoo so long, that it's had it head bit off by it   727

BIT *cont.*
    Mine Enemies dogge, though he had bit me,   2784
    Edg. Know my name is lost | By Treasons tooth: bare-gnawne, and
    Canker-bit,   3073
BITCH = *1
    *Pandar, and the Sonne and Heire of a Mungrill Bitch,   1095
BITE = 2
    Like Rats oft bite the holy cords a twaine,   1147
    Tooth that poysons if it bite: 2024
BITING = 1
    I haue seene the day, with my good biting Faulchion   3241
BITTER = 2*1
    world bitter to the best of our times: keepes our Fortunes from   383
    Lear. A bitter Foole.   666
    Foole. Do'st thou know the difference my Boy, be-|tweene a bitter
    Foole, and a sweet one.   667
BLACKE = 3*1
    Look'd blacke vpon me, strooke me with her Tongue   1442
    Curres, be thy mouth or blacke or white: 2023
    In Hell-blacke-night indur'd, would haue buoy'd vp   2132
    *my Beard, ere the blacke ones were there. To say I, and   2545
BLAME = 7*1
    The Contents, as in part I vnderstand them, | Are too blame.   377
    Glo. The Duke's too blame in this, | 'Twill be ill taken. *Exit.*   1235
    As cleeres her from all blame. | *Lear.* My curses on her.   1424
    Gon. 'Tis his owne blame hath put himselfe from rest,   1590
    His wits begin t'vnsettle. | *Glou.* Canst thou blame him? *Storm still*   1941
    Shall do a curt'sie to our wrath, which men | May blame, but not
    comptroll.   2086
    Leaue gentle waxe, and manners: blame vs not   2712
    To lay the blame vpon her owne dispaire, | That she for-did her selfe.   3213
BLAMED = *1
    *which I haue rather blamed as mine owne iealous curio-|sitie,   598
BLANCH = 1
    Trey, Blanch, and Sweet-heart: see, they barke at me.   2021
BLANKE = 1
    Kent. See better *Lear*, and let me still remaine | The true blanke of
    thine eie.   170
BLANKET = 1*1
    Blanket my loines, else all my haires in knots,   1261
    Foole. Nay, he reseru'd a Blanket, else we had bin all | sham'd.   1846
BLASTES = 1
    Blastes and Fogges vpon thee: 818
BLASTING = *1
    *blisse thee from Whirle-Windes, Starre-blasting, and ta-|king,   1840
BLASTS = 1
    Owes nothing to thy blasts.   2187
BLEED = 2
    Glo. But where is he? | *Bast.* Looke Sir, I bleed.   975
    Vpon the Dunghill: *Regan*, I bleed apace,   2175
BLEEDE = 1
    Blesse thy sweete eyes, they bleede.   2244
BLEEDING = 1
    Met I my Father with his bleeding Rings,   3152
BLEEDST = 1
    Hast heauy substance, bleed'st not, speak'st, art sound,   2494

BLESSE = 4*1
  Edg. Blesse thy fiue wits.   2015
  Ang'ring it selfe, and others. Blesse thee Master.   2225
  Blesse thy sweete eyes, they bleede.   2244
  *poore Tom hath bin scarr'd out of his good wits. Blesse   2247
  Burne it selfe out. If *Edgar* liue, O blesse him: 2479
BLESSING = 2*2
  *blessing against his will, if thou follow him, thou must   633
  *in, aske thy Daughters blessing, heere's a night pitties | neither
  Wisemen, nor Fooles.   1667
  When thou dost aske me blessing, Ile kneele downe   2950
  I ask'd his blessing, and from first to last   3158
BLEST = 2
  Reg. O the blest Gods! | So will you wish on me, when the rash moode
  is on.   1452
  Cord. All blest Secrets, | All you vnpublish'd Vertues of the earth   2366
BLIND = *1
  *Fathers that weare rags, do make their Children blind,   1323
BLINDE = 2*2
  *noses, are led by their eyes, but blinde men, and there's   1342
  Glou. 'Tis the times plague, | When Madmen leade the blinde: 2234
  If you do chance to heare of that blinde Traitor,   2424
  *squiny at me? No, doe thy worst blinde Cupid, Ile not   2581
BLINDING = *1
  Le. You nimble Lightnings, dart your blinding flames   1448
BLISSE = 1*2
  *Blisse thy fiue Wits, *Tom*s a cold. O do, de, do, de, do, de,   1839
  *blisse thee from Whirle-Windes, Starre-blasting, and ta- | king,   1840
  Thou art a Soule in blisse, but I am bound   2795
BLISTER = 1
  *You Fen-suck'd Fogges, drawne by the powrfull Sunne, | To fall, and
  blister.   1450
BLOCKE = 1
  To this great stage of Fooles. This a good blocke: 2625
BLOOD = 9*1
  Heere I disclaime all my Paternall care, | Propinquity and property of
  blood,   120
  Some blood drawne on me, would beget opinion   966
  Are they inform'd of this? My breath and blood: 1379
  But yet thou art my flesh, my blood, my Daughter,   1515
  In my corrupted blood. But Ile not chide thee,   1519
  Glou. Our flesh and blood, my Lord, is growne so | vilde, that it doth
  hate what gets it.   1923
  Now out-law'd from my blood: he sought my life   1947
  I smell the blood of a Brittish man. *Exeunt*   1968
  *Loyalty, though the conflict be sore betweene that, and | my blood.   1992
  I am no lesse in blood then thou art *Edmond*,   3128
BLOODED = 1
  Alb. Halfe-blooded fellow, yes.   3025
BLOODIED = 1
  Why the hot-bloodied *France*, that dowerlesse tooke   1505
BLOODY = 2*2
  *the Turke. False of heart, light of eare, bloody of hand;   1872
  *obey'd in Office. Thou, Rascall Beadle, hold thy bloody   2603
  The bloody proclamation to escape   3146
  Edg. What meanes this bloody Knife?   3173

BLOT = 1
It is no vicious blot, murther, or foulenesse,   249
BLOUDY = 1
Vnwhipt of Iustice. Hide thee, thou Bloudy hand;   1706
BLOW = 1*3
Bids the winde blow the Earth into the Sea,   1620
*Lear. Blow windes, & crack your cheeks; Rage, blow   1656
*sharpe Hauthorne blow the windes. Humh, goe to thy | bed and warme
thee.   1828
BLOWES = 2*1
*foule Fiend. Still through the Hauthorne blowes the   1878
Alb. Oh Gonerill, | You are not worth the dust which the rude winde |
Blowes in your face.   2301
Gon. Milke-Liuer'd man, | That bear'st a cheeke for blowes, a head for
wrongs,   2304
BLOWNE = 2
The Wretch that thou hast blowne vnto the worst,   2186
No blowne Ambition doth our Armes incite,   2379
BLOWS = *1
*Edg. A most poore man, made tame to Fortunes blows   2668
BLUNTLY = *1
*bluntly: that which ordinary men are fit for, I am qual- | lified in, and
the best of me, is Dilligence.   565
BLUNTNESSE = 1
Who hauing beene prais'd for bluntnesse, doth affect   1171
BLUSHD = *1
*so often blush'd to acknowledge him, that now I am | braz'd too't.   13
BOARISH = 1
In his Annointed flesh, sticke boarish phangs.   2130
BOARST = *1
*both parts, thou boar'st thine Asse on thy backe o're the   676
BOAST = 1
Are gone with him toward Douer; where they boast | To haue well
armed Friends.   2078
BOASTED = 1
That you so oft haue boasted to retaine?   2017
BOBTAILE = 1
Or Bobtaile tight, or Troudle taile,   2027
BODIE = 1
If euer thou wilt thriue, bury my bodie,   2700
BODIES = 3
The bodies delicate: the tempest in my mind,   1792
Alb. Produce the bodies, be they aliue or dead; | Gonerill and Regans
bodies brought out.   3183
BODY = 6*1
And from her derogate body, neuer spring   794
My vnprouided body, latch'd mine arme;   988
To suffer with the body; Ile forbeare,   1385
*with thy vncouer'd body, this extremitie of the Skies. Is   1882
on's body, cold: Looke, heere comes a walking fire.   1894
*stockt, punish'd, and imprison'd: who hath three Suites | to his backe,
sixe shirts to his body: 1914
To thee a Womans seruices are due, | My Foole vsurpes my body.   2296
BOG = *1
*through Sword, and Whirle-Poole, o're Bog, and Quag- | mire,   1834
BOILE see byle

30

BOLD = 4*1
Men so disorder'd, so debosh'd and bold,   751
Bold in the quarrels right, rouz'd to th'encounter,   990
You shall doe small respects, show too bold malice   1209
Stew. Wherefore, bold Pezant, | Dar'st thou support a publish'd
Traitor? Hence,   2683
sound of the Trumpet: he is bold in his defence. 1 *Trumpet.* | *Her.*
Againe. 2 *Trumpet.*   3063
BOLT = 1
And in conclusion, to oppose the bolt   1460
BOLTS = 1
Vaunt-curriors of Oake-cleauing Thunder-bolts,   1660
BOND = 3*1
According to my bond, no more nor lesse.   99
*in Pallaces, Treason; and the Bond crack'd, 'twixt   438
Spoke with how manifold, and strong a Bond   983
The Offices of Nature, bond of Childhood,   1462
BONDAGE = *1
*and fond bondage, in the oppression of aged tyranny, who swayes   385
BONES = 1
On her ingratefull top: strike her yong bones   1445
BOOKES = *1
*Plackets, thy pen from Lenders Bookes, and defye the   1877
BOONE = 1
My boone I make it, that you know me not, | Till time, and I, thinke
meet.   2758
BOOT = 2
The bountie, and the benizon of Heauen | To boot, and boot.   2673
BOOTE = 1
With boote, and such addition as your Honours   3273
BOOTES = 1
*things thou dost not. Now, now, now, now. Pull off my | Bootes:
harder, harder, so.   2614
BOOTLESSE = 1
Edg. Very bootlesse.   3265
BORE = 1
Bore the Commission of my place and person,   3004
BORNE = 6
Our eldest borne, speake first.   59
Lear. Better thou had'st | Not beene borne, then not t'haue pleas'd me
better.   256
Our yongest borne, I could as well be brought   1506
Or the hard Reine which both of them hath borne   1636
Lear. When we are borne, we cry that we are come   2624
The oldest hath borne most, we that are yong,   3300
BORROW = 1
Kent. If but as will I other accents borrow,   531
BORROWED = 1
Lear. This is a Slaue, whose easie borrowed pride   1472
BOSOME = 4
To gorge his appetite, shall to my bosome   125
Lay comforts to your bosome, and bestow   1069
To Noble *Edmund.* I know you are of her bosome. | *Stew.* I, Madam?   2413
To plucke the common bosome on his side,   2992
BOSOMES = 1
To your professed bosomes I commit him,   297

BOTH = 18*3
(Since now we will diuest vs both of Rule,   54
So farewell to you both. | *Regn.* Prescribe not vs our dutie.   300
Of what most neerely appertaines to vs both,   311
*both parts, thou boar'st thine Asse on thy backe o're the   676
*wit o'both sides, and left nothing i'th'middle; heere | comes one o'the
parings.   700
Kent. It is both he and she, | Your Son, and Daughter.   1289
Lear. Good morrow to you both.   1404
Yea, or so many? Sith that both charge and danger,   1535
As full of griefe as age, wretched in both,   1573
I will haue such reuenges on you both,   1579
Or the hard Reine which both of them hath borne   1636
And bring you where both fire, and food is ready.   1931
Both welcome, and protection. Take vp thy Master,   2051
Edg. Both style, and gate; Horseway, and foot-path: 2246
Lost he his other eye? | *Mes.* Both, both, my Lord.   2326
Gon. Oh ho, I know the Riddle, I will goe. | *Exeunt both the Armies.*   2878
Bast. To both these Sisters haue I sworne my loue: 2902
Both? One? Or neither? Neither can be enioy'd   2905
If both remaine aliue: To take the Widdow,   2906
Bast. I was contracted to them both, all three | Now marry in an
instant.   3179
BOUE = 1
Or swell the curled Waters 'boue the Maine,   1621
BOUND = 6*2
To plainnesse honour's bound,   158
My seruices are bound, wherefore should I   336
The Child was bound to'th' Father; Sir in fine,   984
Whereto our health is bound, we are not our selues,   1383
*you our Sister company: the reuenges wee are bound to   2066
*most festinate preparation: we are bound to the like. Our   2069
Thou art a Soule in blisse, but I am bound   2795
By th'law of Warre, thou wast not bound to answer   3109
BOUNDS = *1
Lear. Of all these bounds euen from this Line, to this,⸍   68
BOUNTIE = 2
That we, our largest bountie may extend   57
The bountie, and the benizon of Heauen | To boot, and boot.   2673
BOURNE = *1
Glou. But haue I falne, or no? | *Edg.* From the dread Somnet of this
Chalkie Bourne   2498
BOW = *2
Le. The bow is bent & drawne, make from the shaft.   152
*Presse-money. That fellow handles his bow, like a Crow-|keeper: 2534
BOWES = 1
Think'st thou that dutie shall haue dread to speake, | When power to
flattery bowes?   156
BOY = 11*4
Lear. Why my Boy? | *Foole.* Why? for taking ones part that's out of
fauour,   628
Lear. Why my Boy? | *Fool.* If I gaue them all my liuing, I'ld keepe my
Cox-|combes   636
Lear. Why no Boy, | Nothing can be made out of nothing.   662
Foole. Do'st thou know the difference my Boy, be-|tweene a bitter
Foole, and a sweet one.   667

BOY *cont*.
    *Foole. If a mans braines were in's heeles, wert not in | danger of
kybes? | *Lear*. I Boy.   882
    Lear. What can'st tell Boy?   891
    Gent. Ready my Lord. | *Lear*. Come Boy.   921
    (Loyall and naturall Boy) Ile worke the meanes   1022
    *Kent. With you goodman Boy, if you please, come,   1119
    Come on my boy. How dost my boy? Art cold?   1723
    *Le. True Boy: Come bring vs to this Houell. *Exit*.   1733
    In Boy, go first. You houselesse pouertie, *Exit*.   1807
    *cold winde: Sayes suum, mun, nonny, Dolphin my Boy,   1879
    Boy *Sesey*: let him trot by. *Storme still*.   1880
BOYES = 1
    As Flies to wanton Boyes, are we to th'Gods, | They kill vs for their
sport.   2221
BO-PEEPE = 1
    That such a King should play bo-peepe, | And goe the Foole among.   690
BRACH = *1
    *whipt out, when the Lady Brach may stand by'th'fire | and stinke.   642
BRACHE = 1
    Hound or Spaniell, Brache, or Hym: 2026
BRAG = 1
    Kent. If Fortune brag of two, she lou'd and hated, | One of them we
behold.   3245
BRAGART = 1
    You stubborne ancient Knaue, you reuerent Bragart, | Wee'l teach you.   1204
BRAINE = 1*1
    *hand to write this? A heart and braine to breede it in?   392
    Least my braine turne, and the deficient sight | Topple downe headlong.   2458
BRAINES = 1*1
    *Foole. If a mans braines were in's heeles, wert not in | danger of
kybes? | *Lear*. I Boy.   882
    I am cut to'th'Braines.   2636
BRAND = 2
    As honest Madams issue? Why brand they vs   343
    He that parts vs, shall bring a Brand from Heauen,   2964
BRAUE = 1
    Foole. This is a braue night to coole a Curtizan: 1734
BRAUELY = *1
    *To vse his eyes for Garden water-pots. I wil die brauely,   2640
BRAZD = 1
    *so often blush'd to acknowledge him, that now I am | braz'd too't.   13
BRAZEN-FACD = *1
    *Kent. What a brazen-fac'd Varlet art thou, to deny   1101
BREACH = 1
    Cure this great breach in his abused Nature,   2764
BREAD = 1
    Ere I taste bread, thou art in nothing lesse   3041
BREAK = *1
    *But this heart shal break into a hundred thousand flawes   1585
BREAKE = 6*1
    That thou hast sought to make vs breake our vowes,   182
    That these hot teares, which breake from me perforce   816
    *hill, least it breake thy necke with following. But the   1345
    Lear. Wilt breake my heart?   1783
    Kent. I had rather breake mine owne, | Good my Lord enter.   1784
    Kent. Breake heart, I prythee breake. | *Edg*. Looke vp my Lord.   3285

BREAKES = 1*1

Edg. I would not take this from report, | It is, and my heart breakes at
it.   2585

*the strong Lance of Iustice, hurtlesse breakes: Arme it in   2609

BREAKING = 1

Do hourely Carpe and Quarrell, breaking forth   714

BREATH = 6*2

A loue that makes breath poore, and speech vnable,   65

*Foole. Then 'tis like the breath of an vnfeed Lawyer,   659

Stew. I am scarce in breath my Lord.   1126

Are they inform'd of this? My breath and blood: 1379

Thou'dst shiuer'd like an Egge: but thou do'st breath: 2493

*Glou. You euer gentle Gods, take my breath from me,   2663

If that her breath will mist or staine the stone, | Why then she liues.   3222

And thou no breath at all? Thou'lt come no more, | Neuer, neuer,
neuer, neuer, neuer.   3279

BREATHES = 1

And that thy tongue (some say) of breeding breathes,   3099

BREATHLESSE = 1

Stew'd in his haste, halfe breathlesse, painting forth   1307

BRED = 2

Cor. Good my Lord, | You haue begot me, bred me, lou'd me.   102

Mes. A Seruant that he bred, thrill'd with remorse,   2317

BREECHES = *1

*the rod, and put'st downe thine owne breeches, then they   687

BREEDE = *1

*hand to write this? A heart and braine to breede it in?   392

BREEDING = 1*1

*Glou. His breeding Sir, hath bin at my charge. I haue   12

And that thy tongue (some say) of breeding breathes,   3099

BREEDS = *1

*breeds about her heart. Is there any cause in Nature that   2034

BREEFE = 1

Edg. By nursing them my Lord. List a breefe tale,   3144

BREEFELY = 1

Breefely thy selfe remember: the Sword is out | That must destroy thee.   2679

BREWERS = 1

When Brewers marre their Malt with water;   1737

BRIDEGROOME = *1

*Like a smugge Bridegroome. What? I will be Iouiall: 2641

BRIDGES = *1

*incht Bridges, to course his owne shadow for a Traitor.   1838

BRIEFE *see also* breefe = 1

(Be briefe in it) to'th'Castle, for my Writ   3202

BRIEFENESSE = 1

Which I must act, Briefenesse, and Fortune worke.   947

BRIMME = 1

Bring me but to the very brimme of it,   2260

BRING = 13*3

*therewithall the vnruly way-wardnesse, that infirme and | cholericke
yeares bring with them.   323

*fitly bring you to heare my Lord speake: pray ye goe,   490

Our Sister speakes of. Come, bring away the Stocks.   1219

To bring but fiue and twentie, to no more | Will I giue place or notice.   1545

*Le. True Boy: Come bring vs to this Houell. *Exit.*   1733

And bring you where both fire, and food is ready.   1931

Pinnion him like a Theefe, bring him before vs: 2083

BRING *cont.*

And bring some couering for this naked Soule, | Which Ile intreate to
leade me.   2231
Oldm. Ile bring him the best Parrell that I haue   2238
Bring me but to the very brimme of it,   2260
And bring him to our eye. What can mans wisedome   2358
*Bring vp the browne Billes. O well flowne Bird: i'th'   2538
And selfereprouing, bring his constant pleasure.   2850
If euer I returne to you againe, | Ile bring you comfort.   2923
He that parts vs, shall bring a Brand from Heauen,   2964
And more, much more, the time will bring it out.   3123
BRINGING = 1
Bringing the murderous Coward to the stake: 999
BRITTISH = 2
I smell the blood of a Brittish man. *Exeunt*   1968
Mes. Newes Madam, | The Brittish Powres are marching hitherward.   2373
BROILES = 1
For these domesticke and particular broiles, | Are not the question
heere.   2871
BROKE = *1
her. Swore as many Oathes, as I spake words, & broke   1868
BROKEN = *1
Kent. A Knaue, a Rascall, an eater of broken meates, a   1088
BROTHELL = 1
Makes it more like a Tauerne, or a Brothell,   754
BROTHELS = *1
*Keepe thy foote out of Brothels, thy hand out of   1876
BROTHER = 13*6
Lag of a Brother? Why Bastard? Wherefore base?   340
*from my Brother, that I haue not all ore-read; and for so   372
*him, you should enioy halfe his Reuennew for euer, and liue the | beloued
of your Brother.* Edgar.   388
*suspend your indignation against my Brother, til you can   414
Edg. How now Brother *Edmond*, what serious con- | templation are you
in?   467
Bast. I am thinking Brother of a prediction I read this   469
Edg. Arm'd, Brother?   492
Edm. Brother, I aduise you to the best, I am no honest   493
A Credulous Father, and a Brother Noble,   499
My Father hath set guard to take my Brother,   945
Brother, a word, discend; Brother I say,   949
Fly Brother, Torches, Torches, so farewell. | *Exit Edgar.*   964
*downe; 'twas her Brother, that in pure kindnesse to his | Horse
buttered his Hay.   1401
May proue effects. Backe *Edmond* to my Brother,   2283
And the exchange my Brother: heere, in the sands   2726
I hold you but a subiect of this Warre, | Not as a Brother.   2999
And call it selfe your Brother. | *Gon.* Not so hot: 3006
False to thy Gods, thy Brother, and thy Father,   3089
BROTHERS = 3*3
Bast. I hope for my Brothers iustification, hee wrote   380
Glou. You know the character to be your Brothers?   397
*Brothers diuide. In Cities, mutinies; in Countries, dis- | cord;   437
*Brothers euill disposition made him seeke his death: but   1976
Reg. But are my Brothers Powres set forth? | *Stew.* I Madam.   2384
Reg. But haue you neuer found my Brothers way, | To the fore-fended
place?   2858

BROUGHT = 7*2
When came you to this? Who brought it?   393
*Bast. It was not brought mee, my Lord; there's the   394
Reg. Sir, being his Knaue, I will. Stocks brought out.   1217
Brought neere to beast; my face Ile grime with filth,   1260
Our yongest borne, I could as well be brought   1506
*Lear. Ha's his Daughters brought him to this passe?   1844
Who redeemes Nature from the generall curse | Which twaine haue
brought her to.   2648
For him that brought it: wretched though I seeme,   2886
Alb. Produce the bodies, be they aliue or dead; | Gonerill and Regans
bodies brought out.   3183
BROW = 1
Let it stampe wrinkles in her brow of youth,   798
BROWES = 1
Who hast not in thy browes an eye-discerning | Thine Honor, from thy
suffering.   2306
BROWNE = *1
*Bring vp the browne Billes. O well flowne Bird: i'th'   2538
BRUISE = 1
Which for they yet glance by, and scarcely bruise,   3104
BRUTISH = *2
*Abhorred Villaine, vnnaturall, detested, brutish   410
*Villaine; worse then brutish: Go sirrah, seeke him: Ile   411
BUILD = 1
And Baudes, and whores, do Churches build,   1745
BUILDING = 1
May all the building in my fancie plucke | Vpon my hatefull life.
Another way   2332
BUOY = 1
Diminish'd to her Cocke: her Cocke, a Buoy   2454
BUOYD = 1
In Hell-blacke-night indur'd, would haue buoy'd vp   2132
BUR = 5
BURGUNDIE = 5
The Vines of France, and Milke of Burgundie,   90
Lear. My Lord of Burgundie, | We first addresse toward you, who with
this King   205
And here I take Cordelia by the hand, | Dutchesse of Burgundie.   267
Cor. Peace be with Burgundie,   272
Come Noble Burgundie. Flourish. Exeunt.   291
BURGUNDY see also Bur. = 6*2
*Lear. Attend the Lords of France & Burgundy, Gloster.   39
*May be preuented now. The Princes, France & Burgundy,   50
Call Burgundy, Cornwall, and Albanie,   135
Flourish. Enter Gloster with France, and Bur- |gundy, Attendants.   202
Cor. Heere's France and Burgundy, my Noble Lord.   204
Lear. Right Noble Burgundy, | When she was deare to vs, we did hold
her so,   213
That it intends to do: my Lord of Burgundy,   260
Not all the Dukes of watrish Burgundy,   283
BURND = 1
No Heretiques burn'd, but wenches Sutors;   1739
BURNE = 2
Do comfort, and not burne. 'Tis not in thee   1457
Burne it selfe out. If Edgar liue, O blesse him: 2479

BURNING = 1*1
  Lear. To haue a thousand with red burning spits | Come hizzing in vpon
  'em. 2013
  *there is the sulphurous pit; burning, scalding, stench, 2570
BURST = 2
  And when 'tis told, O that my heart would burst. 3145
  Twixt two extremes of passion, ioy and greefe, | Burst smilingly. 3161
BURSTS = 1
  Such sheets of Fire, such bursts of horrid Thunder, 1698
BURY = 1
  If euer thou wilt thriue, bury my bodie, 2700
BUSH = 1
  Do sorely ruffle, for many Miles about | There's scarce a Bush. 1604
BUSIE = 1
  Edg. Do you busie your selfe with that? 471
BUSINES = 1*1
  Glo. Has he neuer before sounded you in this busines? 404
  Stew. I may not Madam: | My Lady charg'd my dutie in this busines. 2403
BUSINESSE = 8*3
  To shake all Cares and Businesse from our Age, 44
  *him out: winde me into him, I pray you: frame the Bu- | sinesse 428
  Bast. I will seeke him Sir, presently: conuey the bu- | sinesse 431
  Edm. I do serue you in this businesse: 498
  My practises ride easie: I see the businesse. 502
  This weaues it selfe perforce into my businesse, 944
  Bast. If the matter of this Paper be certain, you haue | mighty
  businesse in hand. 1985
  *It is thy businesse that I go about: Therfore great France 2377
  That of thy death, and businesse, I can tell. 2731
  Your businesse of the world hath so an end, 2889
  Alb. Beare them from hence, our present businesse 3293
BUSINESSES = 1
  Your needfull counsaile to our businesses, | Which craues the instant
  vse. 1070
BUT *l.*6 *22 111 166 215 235 252 258 266 298 *318 *320 *322 330 381
  *386 *399 *402 *405 *495 531 *558 *587 *596 *600 621 713 717 807
  *901 *935 975 981 1026 *1094 *1132 1143 1153 1202 1243 *1324 *1326
  1334 *1342 *1343 *1345 *1348 1351 1354 1381 *1397 1434 1456 1491
  1515 1519 1531 1545 1550 1570 1581 *1585 1593 1600 1623 1624 1638
  1644 1650 1676 *1686 1719 1739 1788 1790 1796 1806 1852 *1887 1917
  1948 *1976 *2037 *2046 2087 2137 2147 2189 2191 2204 2260 2270 2321
  2325 2331 2380 2384 2443 2491 2493 2498 2501 2527 *2568 *2582 2655
  2752 2795 2855 2858 2893 2899 2999 3015 3098 3111 3124 3159 3164
  3267 3292 = 89*33
BUTTERED = 1
  *downe; 'twas her Brother, that in pure kindnesse to his | Horse
  buttered his Hay. 1401
BUTTERFLIES = 1
  At gilded Butterflies: and heere (poore Rogues) 2953
BUTTON = 1
  Pray you vndo this Button. Thanke you Sir, 3281
BUY = 2
  Can buy this vnpriz'd precious Maid of me. 284
  If my Cap would buy a Halter, 840
BUZ = 1
  Each buz, each fancie, each complaint, dislike, 846

BY = 57*19
BYAS = *1
   *byas of Nature, there's Father against Childe. We haue   441
BYLE = 1
   Which I must needs call mine. Thou art a Byle,   1517
BYTH = *5
   *whipt out, when the Lady Brach may stand by'th'fire | and stinke.   642
   *tide by the heads, Dogges and Beares by'th'necke,   1283
   *Monkies by'th'loynes, and Men by'th' legs: when a man   1284
   *Gon. Why not by'th'hand Sir? How haue I offended?   1485
CACKLING = 1
   I'ld driue ye cackling home to Camelot.   · 1157
CADENT = 1
   With cadent Teares fret Channels in her cheekes,   799
CAGE = 1
   We two alone will sing like Birds i'th'Cage: 2949
CAITIFFE see caytiffe
CAIUS = 1
   Where is your Seruant Caius?   3249
CALL = 16*3
   Her Fathers heart from her; call France, who stirres?   134
   Call Burgundy, Cornwall, and Albanie,   135
   And like a Sister am most loth to call   295
   *Kent. No Sir, but you haue that in your countenance, | which I would
   faine·call Master.   558
   *ho, dinner, where's my knaue? my Foole? Go you and call   573
   *Lear. What saies the Fellow there? Call the Clot-|pole   577
   *call hither my Foole; Oh you Sir, you, come you hither   606
   Which else were shame, that then necessitie | Will call discreet
   proceeding.   724
   Saddle my horses: call my Traine together.   763
   (Which I can call but now,) I haue heard strangenesse.   1026
   Corn. Why do'st thou call him Knaue?   1162
   Call not your Stocks for me, I serue the King.   1207
   Which I must needs call mine. Thou art a Byle,   1517
   Let shame come when it will, I do not call it,   1520
   But yet I call you Seruile Ministers,   1676
   I pray desire her call her wisedome to her. | So fare you well: 2422
   And call it selfe your Brother. | Gon. Not so hot: 3006
   Call by the Trumpet: he that dares approach;   3047
   Alb. Aske him his purposes, why he appeares| Vpon this Call
   o'th'Trumpet.   3068
CALLD = 4
   *Lear. Why came not the slaue backe to me when I | call'd him?   581
   I neuer gaue you Kingdome, call'd you Children;   · 1672
   *Edg. The Prince of Darkenesse is a Gentleman. Modo | he's call'd, and
   Mahu.   1921
   When I inform'd him, then he call'd me Sot,   2275
CALLS = 1
   My Master calls me, I must not say no.   3297
CALLST = 1
   Reg. Out treacherous Villaine, | Thou call'st on him, that hates thee. It
   was he   2164
CALS = 3*1
   Let pride, which she cals plainnesse, marry her: 137
   From those that she cals Seruants, or from mine?   1540
   Glo. He cals to Horse, but will I know not whether.   1600

CALS *cont.*
  Edg. Fraterretto cals me, and tells me *Nero* is an Ang-|ler   2004
CAME = 8*5
  *though this Knaue came somthing sawcily to the   24
  When came you to this? Who brought it?   393
  Lear. Why came not the slaue backe to me when I | call'd him?   581
  Corn. How now my Noble friend, since I came hither   1025
  Cor. You know not why we came to visit you?   1061
  My dutie kneeling, came there a reeking Poste,   1306
  How came my man i'th'Stockes?   1490
  Edg. Childe *Rowland* to the darke Tower came,   1966
  Which came from one that's of a newtrall heart, | And not from one
  oppos'd.   2116
  Came then into my minde, and yet my minde | Was then scarse Friends
  with him.   2218
  Diuinity. When the raine came to wet me once, and the   2547
  Thou must be patient; we came crying hither: 2620
  Gen. 'Tis hot, it smoakes, it came euen from the heart | of--- O she's .
  dead.   3174
CAMELOT = 1
  I'ld driue ye cackling home to *Camelot.*   1157
CAN *l.*11 *60 62 91 179 185 284 *414 *434 504 532 *563 *660 663 *692
  743 890 *901 1026 1028 *1343 1414 1524 *1726 2000 2196 2207 2211
  2325 2358 2654 2731 2887 2905 3117 3250 = 29*9
CANDLE = *1
  *young, so out went the Candle, and we were left dark-|ling.   728
CANKER-BIT = 1
  Edg. Know my name is lost | By Treasons tooth: bare-gnawne, and
  Canker-bit,   3073
CANNOT = 14*6
  Kent. I cannot conceiue you.   15
  Kent. I cannot wish the fault vndone, the issue of it, | being so proper.   20
  Cor. Vnhappie that I am, I cannot heaue   97
  vs, till our oldnesse cannot rellish them. I begin to finde an idle   384
  Glou. He cannot bee such a Monster. *Edmond* seeke   427
  *feare iudgement, to fight when I cannot choose, and to | eate no fish.   547
  *mistaken, for my duty cannot be silent, when I thinke | your Highnesse
  wrong'd.   594
  Alb. I cannot be so partiall *Gonerill*, | To the great loue I beare you.   831
  Alb. How farre your eies may pierce I cannot tell;   869
  that what a man cannot smell out, he may spy into.   897
  Quite from his Nature. He cannot flatter he,   1173
  Reg. I cannot thinke my Sister in the least   1420
  Reg. This house is little, the old man and's people, | Cannot be well
  bestow'd.   1588
  Remember to haue heard. Mans Nature cannot carry | Th'affliction, nor
  the feare.   1700
  Glou. Go in with me; my duty cannot suffer   1926
  Oldm. You cannot see your way.   2198
  Edg. Poore Tom's a cold. I cannot daub it further.   2241
  Cannot be heard so high. Ile looke no more,   2457
  Cannot be seene, or heard: Do but looke vp.   2501
  Lear. No, they cannot touch me for crying. I am the | King himselfe.   2530
CANST *l.*535 562 *630 891 *893 899 1327 1523 1942 = 7*2
CAP = 1*1
  If my Cap would buy a Halter,   840
  *curl'd my haire, wore Gloues in my cap; seru'd the Lust   1866

CAPABLE = 1
To make thee capable. 1023
CAPITALL = 1
On capitall Treason; and in thy arrest, 3028
CAPT = 1
CAPTAINE see also Capt. = 4
and Cordelia, as prisoners, Souldiers, Captaine. 2939
Bast. Come hither Captaine, hearke. 2969
As I haue set it downe. *Exit Captaine.* 2981
Giue it the Captaine. 3209
CAPTIUES = 1
And Fortune led you well: you haue the Captiues 2984
CARBONADO = *1
*Ile so carbonado your shanks, draw you Rascall, come | your waies. 1111
CARBUNCLE = 1
A plague sore, or imbossed Carbuncle 1518
CARE = 5*1
Halfe my loue with him, halfe my Care, and Dutie, 109
Heere I disclaime all my Paternall care, | Propinquity and property of
blood, 120
*need to care for her frowning, now thou art an O with- | out 706
Ste. Why then I care not for thee. 1082
Kent. If I had thee in *Lipsbury* Pinfold, I would make | thee care for
me. 1083
Too little care of this: Take Physicke, Pompe, 1814
CAREFULL = 1
*my old Master must be relieued. There is strange things | toward
Edmund, pray you be carefull. *Exit.* 1769
CAREFULLY = *1
*thee nothing, do it carefully: and the Noble & true-har- | ted 445
CARES = 2
To shake all Cares and Businesse from our Age, 44
Interest of Territory, Cares of State) 55
CARPE = 1
Do hourely Carpe and Quarrell, breaking forth 714
CARRIED = 1
Enter Lear in a chaire carried by Seruants 2771
CARRY = 5*1
That Lord, whose hand must take my plight, shall carry 108
*Father carry authority with such disposition as he beares, 329
May carry through it selfe to that full issue 533
Remember to haue heard. Mans Nature cannot carry | Th'affliction, nor
the feare. 1700
And hardly shall I carry out my side, 2908
Marke I say instantly, and carry it so 2980
CART = *1
Foole. May not an Asse know, when the Cart drawes | the Horse? 735
CASE = 3*1
daughters, and leaue his hornes without a case. 905
When euery Case in Law, is right; 1740
Lear. Read. | *Glou.* What with the Case of eyes? 2587
*case, your purse in a light, yet you see how this world | goes. 2591
CASEMENT = *1
*cunning of it. I found it throwne in at the Casement of | my Closset. 395
CASION = 1
Edg. Chill not let go Zir, | Without vurther 'casion. 2687

CAST = 6
    Be it lawfull I take vp what's cast away. 278
    hath now cast her off, appeares too grossely. 317
    And cast you with the waters that you loose 822
    That Ile resume the shape which thou dost thinke | I haue cast off for
    euer. *Exit* 828
    And dizie 'tis, to cast ones eyes so low, 2447
    For thee oppressed King I am cast downe, 2945
CASTLE = 1
    (Be briefe in it) to'th'Castle, for my Writ 3202
CAT = *1
    *Wooll; the Cat, no perfume. Ha? Here's three on's are 1885
CATARACTS = 1
    You Cataracts, and Hyrricano's spout, 1657
CATASTROPHE = *1
    *Pat: he comes like the Catastrophe of the old Comedie: 463
CATCH = *1
    *nay, & thou canst not smile as the wind sits, thou'lt catch 630
CAUES = 1
    And make them keepe their Caues: Since I was man, 1697
CAUGHT = 2
    A Fox, when one has caught her, 837
    Haue I caught thee? 2963
CAUSE = 8*2
    Beweepe this cause againe, Ile plucke ye out, 821
    Make it your cause: Send downe, and take my part. 1482
    No, Ile not weepe, I haue full cause of weeping. | *Storme and Tempest.* 1583
    What is the cause of Thunder? 1933
    *breeds about her heart. Is there any cause in Nature that 2034
    I pardon that mans life. What was thy cause? 2556
    *Gent. Though that the Queen on special cause is here 2660
    You haue some cause, they haue not. | *Cor.* No cause, no cause. 2832
CAUTIONS = 1
    Beene well inform'd of them, and with such cautions, 1041
CAYTIFFE = 1
    That art Incestuous. Caytiffe, to peeces shake 1708
CEASE = 4
    From whom we do exist, and cease to be, 119
    Will you require in present Dower with her, | Or cease your quest of
    Loue? 208
    That things might change, or cease. 1622
    Kent. Is this the promis'd end? | *Edg.* Or image of that horror. | *Alb.*
    Fall and cease. 3224
CEASES = 1
    And machination ceases. Fortune loues you. 2890
CENSURE = 2
    Would not scape censure, nor the redresses sleepe, 721
    Vntill their greater pleasures first be knowne | That are to censure them. 2941
CENSURED = *1
    *Bast. How my Lord, I may be censured, that Nature 1972
CENTAURES = *1
    *Downe from the waste they are Centaures, though 2567
CENTERY = 1
    In our sustaining Corne. A Centery send forth; 2356
CEREMONIOUS = *1
    *with that Ceremonious affection as you were wont, 588

CERTAIN = *1
   Bast. If the matter of this Paper be certain, you haue | mighty
businesse in hand.   1985
CERTAINE = *2
   Reg. That's most certaine, and with you: next moneth | (with vs.   313
   *run a certaine course: where, if you violently proceed a-|gainst   416
CERTAINELY = 1
   Reg. Our Sisters man is certainely miscarried. | *Bast*. 'Tis to be doubted
Madam.   2851
CHAFES = 1
   That on th'vnnumbred idle Pebble chafes   2456
CHAIRE = 2*1
   Corn. To this Chaire binde him, | Villaine, thou shalt finde.   2098
   Corn. See't shalt thou neuer. Fellowes hold y Chaire,   2139
   Enter Lear in a chaire carried by Seruants   2771
CHALKIE = *1
   Glou. But haue I falne, or no? | *Edg*. From the dread Somnet of this
Chalkie Bourne   2498
CHALLENGE = 2*1
   Where Nature doth with merit challenge. *Gonerill*,   58
   *loue. Reade thou this challenge, marke but the penning | of it.   2582
   Did challenge pitty of them. Was this a face   2782
CHAMBER = 1
   Or at their Chamber doore Ile beate the Drum,   1394
CHAMPAINS = 1
   With shadowie Forrests, and with Champains rich'd   69
CHAMPION = 1
   I can produce a Champion, that will proue   2887
CHANCD = 1
   If then they chanc'd to slacke ye,   1542
CHANCE = 2*3
   *Thy dowrelesse Daughter King, throwne to my chance,   281
   *How chance the King comes with so small a number?   1336
   Corn. My Villaine? | *Seru*. Nay then come on, and take the chance of
anger.   2152
   If you do chance to heare of that blinde Traitor,   2424
   It is a chance which do's redeeme all sorrowes | That euer I haue felt.   3228
CHANGD = 3
   *You will say they are Persian; but let them bee | chang'd.   2037
   Stew. Madam within, but neuer man so chang'd: 2270
   Edg. Y'are much deceiu'd: In nothing am I chang'd | But in my
Garments.   2442
CHANGE = 4*1
   That things might change, or cease.   1622
   The lamentable change is from the best,   2183
   I must change names at home, and giue the Distaffe   2285
   *thine eare: Change places, and handy-dandy, which is   2597
   To change the course, he's full of alteration,   2849
CHANGED = 1
   Th'vntun'd and iarring senses, O winde vp, | Of this childe-changed
Father.   2765
CHANGES = *1
   Gon. You see how full of changes his age is, the ob-|seruation   314
CHANNELS = 1
   With cadent Teares fret Channels in her cheekes,   799
CHARACTER = 2
   Glou. You know the character to be your Brothers?   397

CHARACTER *cont.*
My very Character) I'ld turne it all   1009
CHARGD = 3*1
*they tooke from me the vse of mine owne house, charg'd   1755
Was't thou not charg'd at perill.   2123
Stew. I may not Madam: | My Lady charg'd my dutie in this busines.   2403
Bast. What you haue charg'd me with, | That haue I done,   3121
CHARGE = 1*2
Glou. His breeding Sir, hath bin at my charge. I haue   12
*to lay his Goatish disposition on the charge of a Starre,   456
Yea, or so many? Sith that both charge and danger,   1535
CHARGES = 1
With his prepared Sword, he charges home   987
CHARITIE = 1*1
Inforce their charitie: poore *Turlygod* poore *Tom*,   1271
*do poore *Tom* some charitie, whom the foule Fiend   1841
CHARITY = 1*1
*maintaine talke with the Duke, that my charity be not of   1766
Edg. Let's exchange charity: 3127
CHARMES = 2
Mumbling of wicked charmes, coniuring the Moone | To stand
auspicious Mistris.   973
Whose age had Charmes in it, whose Title more,   2991
CHATTER = *1
*winde to make me chatter: when the Thunder would not   2548
CHE = *1
*come not neere th'old man: keepe out che vor'ye, or Ile   2693
CHEAPE = 1
Mans life is cheape as Beastes. Thou art a Lady;   1567
CHECKE = 1
And in thy best consideration checke   160
CHEEKE = 1
Gon. Milke-Liuer'd man, | That bear'st a cheeke for blowes, a head for
wrongs,   2304
CHEEKES = 2
With cadent Teares fret Channels in her cheekes,   799
Staine my mans cheekes. No you vnnaturall Hags,   1578
CHEEKS = *1
Lear. Blow windes, & crack your cheeks; Rage, blow   1656
CHEERLESSE = 1
All's cheerlesse, darke, and deadly,   3258
CHEESE = *1
*Mouse: peace, peace, this peece of toasted Cheese will   2536
CHIDE = 1
In my corrupted blood. But Ile not chide thee,   1519
CHIDING = *1
Gon. Did my Father strike my Gentleman for chi- | ding of his Foole? |
Ste. I Madam.   507
CHILD = 3
More hideous when thou shew'st thee in a Child, | Then the
Sea-monster.   772
The Child was bound to'th' Father; Sir in fine,   984
I will not trouble thee my Child; farewell: 1513
CHILDE = 6*1
As much as Childe ere lou'd, or Father found.   64
*byas of Nature, there's Father against Childe. We haue   441
Create her childe of Spleene, that it may liue   796

CHILDE *cont*.
To haue a thanklesse Childe. Away, away. *Exit*. 803
Edg. Childe *Rowland* to the darke Tower came, 1966
I haue seru'd you euer since I was a Childe: 2146
For (as I am a man) I thinke this Lady | To be my childe *Cordelia*. |
Cor. And so I am: I am. 2824
CHILDE-CHANGED = 1
Th'vntun'd and iarring senses, O winde vp, | Of this childe-changed
Father. 2765
CHILDHOOD = 1
The Offices of Nature, bond of Childhood, 1462
CHILDREN = 2*2
*Fathers that weare rags, do make their Children blind, 1323
*But Fathers that beare bags, shall see their children kind. 1324
I neuer gaue you Kingdome, call'd you Children; 1672
The winged Vengeance ouertake such Children. 2138
CHILD-LIKE = 1
Edmund, I heare that you haue shewne your Father | A Child-like
Office. 1045
CHILL = 2*1
Edg. Chill not let go Zir, | Without vurther 'casion. 2687
*try whither your Costard, or my Ballow be the harder; | chill be plaine
with you. 2694
**Edg*. Chill picke your teeth Zir: come, no matter vor | your foynes. 2697
CHIN = 2
These haires which thou dost rauish from my chin 2104
Ser. If you did weare a beard vpon your chin, 2150
CHOICE = 2
My Traine are men of choice, and rarest parts, 776
Gon. At your choice Sir. 1511
CHOISE = 2
*most, for qualities are so weigh'd, that curiosity in nei- | ther, can make
choise of eithers moity. 9
Most choise forsaken, and most lou'd despis'd, 276
CHOLERICKE = 1
*therewithall the vnruly way-wardnesse, that infirme and | cholericke
yeares bring with them. 323
CHOLLER = *1
Glo. Kent banish'd thus? and France in choller parted? 358
CHOOSE *see also* chuse = *1
*feare iudgement, to fight when I cannot choose, and to | eate no fish. 547
CHOUGHES = *1
*The Crowes and Choughes, that wing the midway ayre 2448
CHUD = *1
*volke passe: and 'chud ha' bin zwaggerd out of my life, 2691
CHURCHES = 1
And Baudes, and whores, do Churches build, 1745
CHUSE = 1
No, rather I abiure all roofes, and chuse 1501
CIRCLE = 1
The Wheele is come full circle, I am heere. 3136
CITIES = *1
*Brothers diuide. In Cities, mutinies; in Countries, dis- | cord; 437
CIUET = *1
*of Ciuet; good Apothecary sweeten my immagination: 2572
CLAIME = 1
This guilded Serpent: for your claime faire Sisters, 3029

CLAMOUR = 1
   Or whil'st I can vent clamour from my throate, 179
CLAMOURS = *1
   *one whom I will beate into clamours whining, if thou 1096
CLAP = 1
   Lear. What fiftie of my Followers at a clap? | Within a fortnight? 810
CLAY = 1
   To temper Clay. Ha? Let it be so. 823
CLEAUING = 1
   Vaunt-curriors of Oake-cleauing Thunder-bolts, 1660
CLEERES = 1
   As cleeres her from all blame. | *Lear*. My curses on her. 1424
CLEEREST = *1
   *Thinke that the cleerest Gods, who make them Honors 2518
CLIFFE = 1*1
   Glou. There is a Cliffe, whose high and bending head 2258
   Vpon the crowne o'th'Cliffe. What thing was that | Which parted from
   you? 2511
CLIMBE = *1
   Edg. You do climbe vp it now. Look how we labor. 2432
CLIMING = 1
   Historica passio, downe thou climing sorrow, 1329
CLIPT = 1
   All my reports go with the modest truth, | Nor more, nor clipt, but so. 2751
CLOATHES = *1
   *tatter'd cloathes great Vices do appeare: Robes, 2607
CLOATHIERS = *1
   *draw mee a Cloathiers yard. Looke, looke, a 2535
CLOSE = 2
   Ha's practis'd on mans life. Close pent-vp guilts, 1710
   Are many Simples operatiue, whose power | Will close the eye of
   Anguish. 2364
CLOSSET = 1*1
   *cunning of it. I found it throwne in at the Casement of | my Closset. 395
   *I haue lock'd the Letter in my Closset, these iniuries the 1762
CLOTPOLE = *1
   Lear. What saies the Fellow there? Call the Clot- | pole 577
CLOUEST = *1
   *thou clouest thy Crownes i'th'middle, and gau'st away 675
CLOUT = 2
   clout, i'th'clout: Hewgh. Giue the word. | *Edg*. Sweet Mariorum. 2539
COATES = 1
   Poore pelting Villages, Sheeps-Coates, and Milles, 1269
COCKE = 2*1
   *Curfew, and walkes at first Cocke: Hee giues the Web 1896
   Diminish'd to her Cocke: her Cocke, a Buoy 2454
COCKES = *1
   *Till you haue drench'd our Steeples, drown the Cockes. 1658
COCKNEY = *1
   Foole. Cry to it Nunckle, as the Cockney did to the 1398
CODPIECE = 1*1
   The Codpiece that will house, before the head has any; 1682
   Kent. Who's there? | *Foole*. Marry here's Grace, and a Codpiece, that's
   a | Wiseman, and a Foole. 1691
COLD = 8*3
   The leisure of their answer, gaue me cold lookes, 1313
   Come on my boy. How dost my boy? Art cold? 1723

COLD *cont*.

I am cold my selfe. Where is this straw, my Fellow?	1724
*Blisse thy fiue Wits, *Tom*s a cold. O do, de, do, de, do, de,	1839
Foole. This cold night will turne vs all to Fooles, and | Madmen.	1858
*with mans sworne Spouse: set not thy Sweet-heart on | proud array.	
Tom's a cold.	1862
*cold winde: Sayes suum, mun, nonny, Dolphin my Boy,	1879
on's body, cold: Looke, heere comes a walking fire.	1894
Edg. Poore Tom's a cold.	1925
Noble Philosopher, your company. | *Edg*. Tom's a cold.	1953
Edg. Poore Tom's a cold. I cannot daub it further.	2241

COLDE = *1

*colde shortly, there take my Coxcombe; why this fellow	631

COLDER = 1 *1

Gon. And let his Knights haue colder lookes among	525
Being oile to fire, snow to the colder moodes,	1150

COLDST = *1

*Gods, Gods! 'Tis strange, that from their cold'st neglect	279

COLOUR = 1

Cor. This is a Fellow of the selfe same colour,	1218

COLOURS = 5

Enter with Drum and Colours, Cordelia, Gentlemen, | and Souldiours.	2349
Enter with Drumme and Colours, Edmund, Regan. | *Gentlemen, and Souldiers*.	2845
Enter with Drum and Colours, Albany, Gonerill, Soldiers.	2864
Alarum within. Enter with Drumme and Colours, Lear,	2918
Enter in conquest with Drum and Colours, Edmund, Lear,	2938

COMBINE = 1

Gone. Combine together 'gainst the Enemie:	2870

COME = 57*17

Cor. Nothing. | *Lear*. Nothing will come of nothing, speake againe.	95
Come not betweene the Dragon and his wrath,	130
To come betwixt our sentences, and our power,	184
Come Noble *Burgundie. Flourish. Exeunt*.	291
Fra. Come my faire *Cordelia. Exit France and Cor*.	309
*such neede to hide it selfe. Let's see: come, if it bee no- | thing, I shall not neede Spectacles.	369
*not as it hath power, but as it is suffer'd. Come to me, that of	386
If you come slacke of former seruices,	516
You and your Fellowes: I'de haue it come to question;	520
So may it come, thy Master whom thou lou'st, | Shall find thee full of labours.	536
*call hither my Foole; Oh you Sir, you, come you hither	606
Kent. Come sir, arise, away, Ile teach you differences:	619
Gent. Ready my Lord. | *Lear*. Come Boy.	921
Yeeld, come before my Father, light hoa, here,	963
That if they come to soiourne at my house,	1042
Kent. Draw you Rascall, you come with Letters a- |gainst	1108
*Ile so carbonado your shanks, draw you Rascall, come | your waies.	1111
Kent. With you goodman Boy, if you please, come,	1119
Ile flesh ye, come on yong Master.	1120
Our Sister speakes of. Come, bring away the Stocks.	1219
Corn. Come my Lord, away. *Exit*.	1227
Now, presently: bid them come forth and heare me,	1393
That she would soone be heere. Is your Lady come?	1471
Dismissing halfe your traine, come then to me,	1497
Let shame come when it will, I do not call it,	1520

COME *cont.*

We could comptroll them; if you will come to me,	1543
With such a number? What, must I come to you	1551
*My *Regan* counsels well: come out oth'storme. *Exeunt*.	1613
Deny'd me to come in) returne, and force	Their scanted curtesie.	1720
Come on my boy. How dost my boy? Art cold?	1723
*And can make vilde things precious. Come, your Houel;	1726
*Le. True Boy: Come bring vs to this Houell. *Exit*.	1733
Nor Cut-purses come not to throngs;	1743
*Then shal the Realme of *Albion*, come to great confusion:	1746
*Foole. Come not in heere Nuncle, here's a spirit, helpe	me, helpe me.	1820
*Kent. What art thou that dost grumble there i'th'	straw? Come forth.	1825
*Lear. Did'st thou giue all to thy Daughters? And art	thou come to this?	1830
*as thou art. Off, off you Lendings: Come, vn-	button heere.	1888
Yet haue I ventured to come seeke you out,	1930
Lear. Come, let's in all.	1956
Glou. Take him you on.	*Kent*. Sirra, come on: go along with vs.	1962
Lear. Come, good Athenian.	1964
Lear. To haue a thousand with red burning spits	Come hizzing in vpon 'em.	2013
*Do, de, de, de: sese: Come, march to Wakes and Fayres,	2031
Glou. Come hither Friend:	Where is the King my Master?	2044
Giue thee quicke conduct. Come, come, away. *Exeunt*	2056
Corn. Come Sir.	What Letters had you late from France?	2108
Corn. My Villaine?	*Seru*. Nay then come on, and take the chance of anger.	2152
Come on't what will. *Exit*	2239
Glou. Come hither fellow.	*Edg*. And yet I must:	2242
Mes. Come with my Lady hither.	2337
And to reuenge thine eyes. Come hither Friend,	2346
Glou. When shall I come to th'top of that same hill?	2431
Glou. Me thinkes y'are better spoken.	*Edg*. Come on Sir,	2444
Lear. When we are borne, we cry that we are come	2624
Come, come, I am a King, Masters, know you that?	2642
Lear. Then there's life in't. Come, and you get it,	2644
*come not neere th'old man: keepe out che vor'ye, or Ile	2693
*Edg. Chill picke your teeth Zir: come, no matter vor	your foynes.	2697
Come Father, Ile bestow you with a Friend. *Exeunt*.	2742
Sir, this I heard, the King is come to his Daughter	2866
Giue me thy hand: Come on.	2930
Ripenesse is all come on.	*Glo*. And that's true too. *Exeunt*.	2935
Lear. No, no, no, no: come let's away to prison,	2948
Weele see 'em staru'd first: come. *Exit*.	2968
Bast. Come hither Captaine, hearke.	2969
Come hither Herald, let the Trumpet sound,	And read out this. *A Trumpet sounds*.	3057
Yet am I Noble as the Aduersary	I come to cope.	3075
The Wheele is come full circle, I am heere.	3136
Kent. I am come	To bid my King and Master aye good night.	3189
What comfort to this great decay may come,	3269
And thou no breath at all? Thou'lt come no more,	Neuer, neuer, neuer, neuer, neuer.	3279

COMEDIE = *1

*Pat: he comes like the Catastrophe of the old Comedie:	463

COMES = 14*7

Onely she comes too short, that I professe	77

COMES *cont*.

*Sonne and Father. This villaine of mine comes vnder the	439
*Pat: he comes like the Catastrophe of the old Comedie:	463
comes to, he will not beleeue a Foole.	665
*wit o'both sides, and left nothing i'th'middle; heere | comes one o'the parings.	700
Alb. Now Gods that we adore, | Whereof comes this?	804
*know, then comes from her demand out of the Letter,	877
Bast. How comes that?	933
My worthy Arch and Patron comes to night,	996
*Harke, the Dukes Trumpets, I know not wher he comes;	1017
Reg. If it be true, all vengeance comes too short	1027
*How chance the King comes with so small a number?	1336
Who comes here? O Heauens!	1479
Glo. Alacke the night comes on, and the high windes	1603
Then comes the time, who liues to see't,	1747
on's body, cold: Looke, heere comes a walking fire.	1894
*Vntimely comes this hurt. Giue me your arme. *Exeunt*.	2176
But who comes heere? My Father poorely led? | World, World, O world!	2189
Stew. Madam, here come's my Lord.	2298
But who comes heere?	2527
Edg. Here comes *Kent*.	3181

COMFORT = 4*1

Do comfort, and not burne. 'Tis not in thee	1457
*I will peece out the comfort with what addition I | can: I will not be long from you. *Exit*	1999
Is wretchednesse depriu'd that benefit | To end it selfe by death? 'Twas yet some comfort,	2503
If euer I returne to you againe, | Ile bring you comfort.	2923
What comfort to this great decay may come,	3269

COMFORTABLE = 2

Who I am sure is kinde and comfortable:	825
That by thy comfortable Beames I may	1241

COMFORTED = 1

Gent. Be comforted good Madam, the great rage	2837

COMFORTING = *1

Bast. If I finde him comforting the King, it will stuffe	1990

COMFORTLESSE = 1

Where is thy luster now? | *Glou*. All darke and comfortlesse?	2159

COMFORTS = 2

Lay comforts to your bosome, and bestow	1069
Thy comforts can do me no good at all, | Thee, they may hurt.	2196

COMMAND = 2*1

To follow in a house, where twice so many | Haue a command to tend you?	1561
A Mistresses command. Weare this; spare speech,	2289
*Which do command them. With him I sent the Queen:	2994

COMMANDED = 1

Commanded me to follow, and attend	1312

COMMANDS = 3*1

The deere Father | *Would with his Daughter speake, commands, tends, ser- |(uice,	1377
When Nature being opprest, commands the mind	1384
Should many people, vnder two commands	1537
T'obey in all your daughters hard commands:	1927

COMMEND = 3
So much commend it selfe, you shall be ours,   1056
I did commend your Highnesse Letters to them,   1304
Commend a deere thing to you. There is diuision   1628
COMMING = 8
*Glou. He hath bin out nine yeares, and away he shall | againe. The
King is comming.   35
Ste. He's comming Madam, I heare him.   518
Hee's comming hither, now i'th' night, i'th' haste,   954
Bast. I heare my Father comming, pardon me: 959
Thou might'st deserue, or they impose this vsage, | Comming from vs.   1301
Against my comming in. Thou better know'st   1461
He smil'd at it. I told him you were comming,   2272
Men must endure | Their going hence, euen as their comming hither,   2933
COMMISSION = 2
Bore the Commission of my place and person,   3004
Bast. He hath Commission from thy Wife and me, | To hang Cordelia
in the prison, and   .   3211
COMMIT = 2*1
Commit a thing so monstrous, to dismantle   238
To your professed bosomes I commit him,   297
*keepe thy words Iustice, sweare not, commit not,   1861
COMMODITIES = 1
Proue our Commodities. Oh deere Sonne Edgar,   2202
COMMON = 1*1
*Kent. Good King, that must approue the common saw,   1237
To plucke the common bosome on his side,   2992
COMPACT = 3
When my Dimensions are as well compact,   341
As may compact it more. Get you gone,   863
When he compact, and flattering his displeasure   1194
COMPANION = *1
*Reg. Was he not companion with the riotous Knights   1033
COMPANY = 3*1
Gon. Take you some company, and away to horse,   860
Glou. What, hath your Grace no better company?   1920
Noble Philosopher, your company. | Edg. Tom's a cold.   1953
*you our Sister company: the reuenges wee are bound to   2066
COMPEERES = 1
Reg. In my rights, | By me inuested, he compeeres the best.   3010
COMPLAINT = 1
Each buz, each fancie, each complaint, dislike,   846
COMPLEMENT = 1*1
*Gon. There is further complement of leaue-taking be-|tweene   327
The time will not allow the complement | Which very manners vrges.   3187
COMPOSITION = 1*1
Who in the lustie stealth of Nature, take | More composition, and fierce
qualitie,   345
*but the composition of a Knaue, Begger, Coward,   1094
COMPOUNDED = *1
*My father, compounded with my mother vnder the Dra-|gons   457
COMPTROLL = 2
We could comptroll them; if you will come to me,   1543
Shall do a curt'sie to our wrath, which men | May blame, but not
comptroll.   2086
COMPULSION = *1
*Fooles by heauenly compulsion, Knaues, Theeues, and   451

49

COMRADE = 1
To be a Comrade with the Wolfe, and Owle,   1503
COMST = 1
Thou out of Heauens benediction com'st | To the warme Sun.   1238
CONCEALES = 1
He that conceales him death.   1000
CONCEALING = 1
Riue your concealing Continents, and cry   1711
CONCEIT = 1
And yet I know not how conceit may rob   2482
CONCEIUE = 2
Kent. I cannot conceiue you.   15
Conceiue, and fare thee well.   2292
CONCEPTION = *1
Lear. Thou but remembrest me of mine owne Con-|ception,   596
CONCLUDED = 1
Had not concluded all. He wakes, speake to him.   2790
CONCLUSION = 1
And in conclusion, to oppose the bolt   1460
CONDEMND = 1
If thou canst serue where thou dost stand condemn'd,   535
CONDEMNE = 1
Though I condemne not, yet vnder pardon   866
CONDITION = 1*1
*the imperfections of long ingraffed condition, but   322
I feele this pin pricke, would I were assur'd | Of my condition.   2808
CONDITIONS = 1
Bur. Pardon me Royall Sir, | Election makes not vp in such conditions.   225
CONDUCT = 2
Giue thee quicke conduct. Come, come, away. *Exeunt*   2056
Hasten his Musters, and conduct his powres.   2284
CONFEDERACIE = *1
Corn. And what confederacie haue you with the Trai-|tors, late footed
in the Kingdome?   2111
CONFERRD = 1
Then that conferr'd on *Gonerill*. Now our Ioy,   88
CONFERRE = *1
*where you shall heare vs conferre of this, and by an Auri-|cular   424
CONFERRING = 1
Conferring them on yonger strengths, while we   45
CONFESSE = 1
Deere daughter, I confesse that I am old;   1435
CONFESSES = 1
Gen. Your Lady Sir, your Lady; and her Sister | By her is poyson'd: she
confesses it.   3177
CONFIND = 1
Confin'd to exhibition? All this done   360
CONFINE = 1
Of his confine: you should be rul'd, and led   1428
CONFINED = 1
Lookes fearfully in the confined Deepe: 2259
CONFIRMATION = 1
For confirmation that I am much more   1641
CONFIRME = 1
Reuennew, Execution of the rest, | Beloued Sonnes be yours, which to
confirme,   145

CONFLICT = 1*1
   *Loyalty, though the conflict be sore betweene that, and | my blood.   1992
   (Alacke too weake the conflict to support)   3160
CONFUSION = 1*1
   Lear. Vengeance, Plague, Death, Confusion: 1370
   *Then shal the Realme of *Albion*, come to great confusion: 1746
CONIURING = 1
   Mumbling of wicked charmes, coniuring the Moone | To stand
   auspicious Mistris.   973
CONQUEROR = *1
   returne the Conqueror, then am I the Prisoner, and his bed, my   2719
CONQUEST = 1
   Enter in conquest with Drum and Colours, Edmund, Lear,   2938
CONSIDER = 1*1
   *man no more then this? Consider him well. Thou ow'st   1883
   Good my Friends consider you are my Ghests: 2093
CONSIDERATION = 1
   And in thy best consideration checke   160
CONSORT = 1
   Bast. Yes Madam, he was of that consort.   1036
CONSPIRACY = *1
   *Hum? Conspiracy? Sleepe till I wake him, you should   390
CONSPIRANT = 1
   Conspirant 'gainst this high illustrious Prince,   3090
CONSTANT = 2
   We haue this houre a constant will to publish   48
   And selfereprouing, bring his constant pleasure.   2850
CONSTRAINES = 1
   A saucy roughnes, and constraines the garb   1172
CONSUMPTION = *1
   *consumption: Fye, fie, fie; pah, pah: Giue me an Ounce   2571
CONTAINES = 1
   What it containes. If you shall see *Cordelia*,   1643
CONTEMND = 2
   Edg. Yet better thus, and knowne to be contemn'd,   2179
   Then still contemn'd and flatter'd, to be worst: 2180
CONTEMPLATION = *1
   Edg. How now Brother *Edmond*, what serious con- | templation are you
   in?   467
CONTEMPT = 2
   To laughter, and contempt: That she may feele,   801
   That euer penury in contempt of man,   1259
CONTENDING = 1
   Gent. Contending with the fretfull Elements;   1619
CONTENT = 4
   Gon. Let your study | Be to content your Lord, who hath receiu'd you   302
   Gon. Pray you content. What *Oswald*, hoa?   833
   Must be content to thinke you old, and so,   1530
   Must make content with his Fortunes fit,   1731
CONTENTED = *1
   Foole. Prythee Nunckle be contented, 'tis a naughtie   1891
CONTENTIOUS = 1
   Lear. Thou think'st 'tis much that this contentious | (storme   1786
CONTENTS = 3
   The Contents, as in part I vnderstand them, | Are too blame.   377
   Glou. It is his. | *Bast*. It is his hand, my Lord: but I hope his heart is |
   not in the Contents.   401

CORDELIA cont.
For (as I am a man) I thinke this Lady | To be my childe *Cordelia*. |
Cor. And so I am: I am.   2824
Which he intends to *Lear* and to *Cordelia*,   2913
Cordelia, and Souldiers, ouer the Stage, and Exeunt.   2919
and Cordelia, as prisoners, Souldiers, Captaine.   2939
Lear. Vpon such sacrifices my *Cordelia*, | The Gods themselues throw
Incense.   2961
*Speake *Edmund*, where's the King? and where's *Cordelia*?   3193
Is on the life of *Lear*, and on *Cordelia*:   3203
Bast. He hath Commission from thy Wife and me, | To hang *Cordelia*
in the prison, and   3211
Enter Lear with Cordelia in his armes.   3216
Cordelia, Cordelia, stay a little. Ha: 3235
CORDS = 1
Like Rats oft bite the holy cords a twaine,   1147
CORKY = 1
Corn. Binde fast his corky armes.   2091
CORN = 31*8
CORNE = 2
Shall of a Corne cry woe, and turne his sleepe to wake.   1685
In our sustaining Corne. A Centery send forth;   2356
CORNEWALL see also Cor., Corn., Cornw. = 5
Haue you not spoken 'gainst the Duke of *Cornewall*?   953
Enter Cornewall, Regan, and Attendants.   1024
Enter Bastard, Cornewall, Regan, Gloster, Seruants.   1117
I'ld speake with the Duke of *Cornewall*, and his wife.   1372
Enter Cornewall, Regan, Gloster, Seruants.   1403
CORNW = *1
CORNWAL = *1
*Vnburthen'd crawle toward death. Our son of *Cornwal*,   46
CORNWALL = 9*1
Duke of *Albany*, then *Cornwall*. | *Glou*. It did alwayes seeme so to vs:
But   5
*Sennet. Enter King Lear, Cornwall, Albany, Gonerill, Re-|gan,
Cordelia, and attendants.*   37
Our deerest *Regan*, wife of *Cornwall*?   73
Call *Burgundy, Cornwall*, and *Albanie*,   135
That the Duke of *Cornwall*, and *Regan* his Duchesse   931
'Twixt the Dukes of *Cornwall*, and *Albany*? | *Bast*. Not a word.   939
Lear. The King would speake with *Cornwall*,   1376
With mutuall cunning) 'twixt Albany, and Cornwall: 1630
Enter Cornwall, and Edmund.   1970
Enter Cornwall, Regan, Gonerill, Bastard, | and Seruants.   2058
CORNWALS = *1
*Mes. Oh my good Lord, the Duke of *Cornwals* dead,   2313
CORONET = 1
This Coronet part betweene you.   147
CORRUPTED = 1
In my corrupted blood. But Ile not chide thee,   1519
CORRUPTER = 1
Harbour more craft, and more corrupter ends,   1177
COST = 1
The darke and vitious place where thee he got, | Cost him his eyes.   3133
COSTARD = *1
*try whither your Costard, or my Ballow be the harder; | chill be plaine
with you.   2694

COUER = 1
Alb. Euen so: couer their faces. 3199
COUERD = 1
(Although as yet the face of it is couer'd 1629
COUERING = 1
And bring some couering for this naked Soule, | Which Ile intreate to
leade me. 2231
COUERS = 1
Who couers faults, at last with shame derides: 307
COUERT = 1
That vnder couert, and conuenient seeming 1709
COULD *l*.*16 *978 *1131 *1298 1506 1543 *1842 *1851 2215 2426 2476
2505 2584 2946 = 8*6
COULDST *l*.*1845 = *1
COUNSAILE = 1*1
Lear. What seruices canst thou do? | *Kent*. I can keepe honest
counsaile, ride, run, marre a 562
Your needfull counsaile to our businesses, | Which craues the instant
vse. 1070
COUNSELL = 1*1
Gon. This man hath had good Counsell, | A hundred Knights? 842
*when a wiseman giues thee better counsell giue me mine 1347
COUNSELS = *1
*My *Regan* counsels well: come out oth'storme. *Exeunt*. 1613
COUNTENANCE = 3*1
Bast. Parted you in good termes? Found you no dis-|pleasure in him,
by word, nor countenance? 478
Kent. No Sir, but you haue that in your countenance, | which I would
faine call Master. 558
What is his fault? | *Kent*. His countenance likes me not. 1163
His countenance for the Battaile, which being done, 2910
COUNTERFETTING = 1
Edg. My teares begin to take his part so much, | They marre my
counterfetting. 2018
COUNTRIES = *1
*Brothers diuide. In Cities, mutinies; in Countries, dis-|cord; 437
COUNTRY = 2
Hee'l shape his old course, in a Country new. *Exit*. 201
The Country giues me proofe, and president 1264
COURIERS *see* curriors
COURSE = 8*5
*That troope with Maiesty. Our selfe by Monthly course, 140
Hee'l shape his old course, in a Country new. *Exit*. 201
*run a certaine course: where, if you violently proceed a-|gainst 416
*so, Ile write straight to my Sister to hold my course; pre-|pare for
dinner. *Exeunt*. 527
That you protect this course, and put it on 719
This milky gentlenesse, and course of yours 865
Of my obscured course. And shall finde time 1245
How vnremoueable and fixt he is | In his owne course. 1368
*incht Bridges, to course his owne shadow for a Traitor. 1838
*his suspition more fully. I will perseuer in my course of 1991
Glou. I am tyed to'th'Stake, | And I must stand the Course. 2125
And quit the house on purpose, that their punishment | Might haue the
freer course. 2342
To change the course, he's full of alteration, 2849

COURT = 3*1
Long in our Court, haue made their amorous soiourne, 52
That this our Court infected with their manners, 752
*Foole. O Nunkle, Court holy-water in a dry house, is 1665
Talke of Court newes, and wee'l talke with them too, 2954
COURTESIE see curtesie, curt'sie
COURTIZAN see curtizan
COWARD = 2*1
Bringing the murderous Coward to the stake: 999
*but the composition of a Knaue, Begger, Coward, 1094
He rais'd the house, with loud and coward cries, 1319
COWARDLY = *1
*you cowardly Rascall, nature disclaimes in thee: a Taylor | made thee. 1128
COWARDS = 1
Kent. None of these Rogues, and Cowards | But Aiax is there Foole. 1201
COWISH = 1
It is the Cowish terror of his spirit 2280
COW-DUNG = *1
*Cow-dung for Sallets; swallowes the old Rat, and the 1911
COXCOMBE = 2*2
Foole. Let me hire him too, here's my Coxcombe. 625
Foole. Sirrah, you were best take my Coxcombe. 627
*colde shortly, there take my Coxcombe; why this fellow 631
*needs weare my Coxcombe. How now Nunckle? would 634
COXCOMBES = 1*1
I had two Coxcombes and two Daughters. 635
Lear. Why my Boy? | *Fool. If I gaue them all my liuing, I'ld keepe my
Cox- | combes 636
COXCOMBS = *1
*o'th' coxcombs with a sticke, and cryed downe wantons, 1400
COZEND = 1
An vnknowne opposite: thou art not vanquish'd, | But cozend, and
beguild. 3110
COZENER = *1
*thou whip'st her. The Vsurer hangs the Cozener. Tho- | rough 2606
CRAB = *1
*Crab: thou canst, tell why ones nose stands i'th'middle | on's face? |
Lear. No. 893
CRABBE = *1
*Foole. She will taste as like this as, a Crabbe do's to a 892
CRABBES = *1
*for though she's as like this, as a Crabbe's like an | Apple, yet I can
tell what I can tell. 889
CRACK = 1*1
*Lear. Blow windes, & crack your cheeks; Rage, blow 1656
That Heauens vault should crack: she's gone for euer. 3219
CRACKD = 2*1
*in Pallaces, Treason; and the Bond crack'd, 'twixt 438
Glo. O Madam, my old heart is crack'd, it's crack'd. 1029
CRACKE = 1
Cracke Natures moulds, all germaines spill at once | That makes
ingratefull Man. 1663
CRADLE = *1
*Sonne for her Cradle, ere she had a husband for her bed. 18
CRAFT = 1
Harbour more craft, and more corrupter ends, 1177

CRAUE = 1
Bur. Most Royall Maiesty, | I craue no more then hath your Highnesse offer'd, 210
CRAUES = 2
Your needfull counsaile to our businesses, | Which craues the instant vse. 1070
This Leter Madam, craues a speedy answer: | 'Tis from your Sister. 2328
CRAWLE = *1
*Vnburthen'd crawle toward death. Our son of *Cornwal,* 46
CRAZD = 1
The greefe hath craz'd my wits. What a night's this? 1950
CREAKING = *1
*in madnes, Lyon in prey. Let not the creaking of shooes, 1874
CREATE = 2
Create her childe of Spleene, that it may liue 796
Witnesse the world, that I create thee heere | My Lord, and Master. 3020
CREATING = 1
Goe to th'creating a whole tribe of Fops 348
CREATURE = 1*2
Suspend thy purpose, if thou did'st intend | To make this Creature fruitfull: 790
*Mildewes the white Wheate, and hurts the poore Crea- | ture of earth. 1898
Lear. And the Creature run from the Cur: there thou 2601
CREATURES = *1
Lea. Those wicked Creatures yet do look wel fauor'd 1554
CREDULOUS = 1
A Credulous Father, and a Brother Noble, 499
CRIE = 1
Till it crie sleepe to death. 1395
CRIES = 1
He rais'd the house, with loud and coward cries, 1319
CRIME = 1
He flashes into one grosse crime, or other, 511
CRIMES = 2
That hast within thee vndivulged Crimes 1705
Alb. This shewes you are aboue | You Iustices, that these our neather crimes 2323
CROSSES = 1
And these same crosses spoile me. Who are you? 3243
CROWES = *1
*The Crowes and Choughes, that wing the midway ayre 2448
CROWKEEPER = *1
*Presse-money. That fellow handles his bow, like a Crow- | keeper: 2534
CROWND = 1
Crown'd with ranke Fenitar, and furrow weeds, 2353
CROWNE = 1*1
*durt, thou hadst little wit in thy bald crowne, when thou 677
Vpon the crowne o'th'Cliffe. What thing was that | Which parted from you? 2511
CROWNES = 2*2
Foole. Nunckle, giue me an egge, and Ile giue thee | two Crownes. 670
Lear. What two Crownes shall they be? 672
*eate vp the meate, the two Crownes of the egge: when 674
*thou clouest thy Crownes i'th'middle, and gau'st away 675
CRUELL = 2*1
Foole. Hah, ha, he weares Cruell Garters Horses are 1282

CRUELL *cont.*
  Reg. Wherefore to Douer? | *Glou.* Because I would not see thy cruell
    Nailes   2127
  Giue me some helpe. --- O cruell! O you Gods.   2142
CRUELS = 1
  All Cruels else subscribe: but I shall see   2137
CRUM = 1
  Mum, mum, he that keepes nor crust, nor crum,   710
CRUST = 1
  Mum, mum, he that keepes nor crust, nor crum,   710
CRY *see also* crie = 8*1
  Foole. Cry to it Nunckle, as the Cockney did to the   1398
  Shall of a Corne cry woe, and turne his sleepe to wake.   1685
  Riue your concealing Continents, and cry   1711
  I do beseech your grace. | *Lear.* O cry you mercy, Sir: 1951
  Glou. I do remember now: henceforth Ile beare | Affliction, till it do cry
    out it selfe   2520
  We wawle, and cry. I will preach to thee: Marke.   2622
  Lear. When we are borne, we cry that we are come   2624
  With others, whom the rigour of our State | Forc'd to cry out.   2867
  When time shall serue, let but the Herald cry, | And Ile appeare againe.
    Exit.   2893
CRYED = *1
  o'th' coxcombs with a sticke, and cryed downe wantons,   1400
CRYING = 1*1
  Lear. No, they cannot touch me for crying. I am the | King himselfe.   2530
  Thou must be patient; we came crying hither: 2620
CUCKOO = *2
  *fed the Cuckoo so long, that it's had it head bit off by it   727
  *With Hardokes, Hemlocke, Nettles, Cuckoo flowres,   2354
CUE = *1
  *my Cue is villanous Melancholly, with a sighe like *Tom*   464
CULLYENLY = *1
  *sop oth' Moonshine of you, you whoreson Cullyenly | Barber-monger,
    draw.   1105
CUNNING = 3*2
  Cor. Time shall vnfold what plighted cunning hides,   306
  *cunning of it. I found it throwne in at the Casement of | my Closset.   395
  In cunning, I must draw my Sword vpon you: 960
  With mutuall cunning) 'twixt Albany, and Cornwall: 1630
  Corn. Cunning. | *Reg.* And false.   2118
CUP = 1
  The cup of their deseruings: O see, see.   3276
CUPID = *1
  *squiny at me? No, doe thy worst blinde Cupid, Ile not   2581
CUR = *1
  Lear. And the Creature run from the Cur: there thou   2601
CUR = 3*1
CURAN *see also Cur.* = 2
  Enter Bastard, and Curan, seuerally.   927
  Bast. Saue thee *Curan.*   928
CURE = 2
  Edg. Why I do trifle thus with his dispaire, | Is done to cure it.   2471
  Cure this great breach in his abused Nature,   2764
CURFEW = *1
  *Curfew, and walkes at first Cocke: Hee giues the Web   1896

CURIOSITIE = *1
   *which I haue rather blamed as mine owne iealous curio-|sitie,   598
CURIOSITY = 1*1
   *most, for qualities are so weigh'd, that curiosity in nei-|ther, can make
   choise of eithers moity.   9
   The curiosity of Nations, to depriue me?   338
CURIOUS = *1
   *curious tale in telling it, and deliuer a plaine message   564
CURLD = *1
   *curl'd my haire, wore Gloues in my cap; seru'd the Lust   1866
CURLED = 1
   Or swell the curled Waters 'boue the Maine,   1621
CURRE = 1
   *Lear. My Ladies Father? my Lords knaue, you whor-|son dog, you
   slaue, you curre.   610
CURRES = 1
   Curres, be thy mouth or blacke or white: 2023
CURRIORS = 1
   Vaunt-curriors of Oake-cleauing Thunder-bolts,   1660
CURSE = 4
   Dow'rd with our curse, and stranger'd with our oath, | Take her or,
   leaue her.   223
   Th'vntented woundings of a Fathers curse   819
   Lear. No Regan, thou shalt neuer haue my curse: 1454
   Who redeemes Nature from the generall curse | Which twaine haue
   brought her to.   2648
CURSES = 1
   As cleeres her from all blame. | Lear. My curses on her.   1424
CURST = 1
   And found him pight to doe it, with curst speech   1002
CURTAINES = *1
   *Lear. Make no noise, make no noise, draw the Cur-|taines: 2041
CURTESIE = 3
   Effects of Curtesie, dues of Gratitude: 1463
   Deny'd me to come in) returne, and force | Their scanted curtesie.   1720
   Bast. This Curtesie forbid thee, shall the Duke   1771
CURTIZAN = 1
   Foole. This is a braue night to coole a Curtizan: 1734
CURTSIE = 1
   Shall do a curt'sie to our wrath, which men | May blame, but not
   comptroll.   2086
CUSTOME = 1
   Stand in the plague of custome, and permit   337
CUT = 3*2
   *Foole. Why after I haue cut the egge i'th'middle and   673
   Shall not be a Maid long, vnlesse things be cut shorter. | Exeunt.   924
   To grudge my pleasures, to cut off my Traine,   1458
   I am cut to'th'Braines.   2636
   *opportunities to cut him off: if your will want not, time and   2717
CUTS = 1
   Preferment fals on him, that cuts him off.   2425
CUTTER = *1
   *Kent. A Taylor Sir, a Stone-cutter, or a Painter, could   1131
CUT-PURSES = 1
   Nor Cut-purses come not to throngs;   1743

DAIES = 1
*I will looke further intoo't: but where's my Foole? I | haue not seene
him this two daies.   600
DALLY = 1
If thou should'st dally halfe an houre, his life   2052
DAME = 1*1
*Behold yond simpring Dame, whose face betweene her   2563
Alb. Shut your mouth Dame,   3112
DAMNED = 1
To thy suggestion, plot, and damned practise: 1010
DANDY = *1
*thine eare: Change places, and handy-dandy, which is   2597
DANGER = 4
to no other pretence of danger. | *Glou*. Thinke you so?   421
Foole. If a mans braines were in's heeles, wert not in | danger of
kybes? | *Lear*. I Boy.   882
Yea, or so many? Sith that both charge and danger,   1535
(For now I spie a danger) I entreate you   1544
DANGEROUS = 1*1
*receiued a Letter this night, 'tis dangerous to be spoken,   1761
Reg. Our troopes set forth to morrow, stay with vs: | The wayes are
dangerous.   2401
DARE = 3*1
*his obedience. I dare pawne downe my life for him, that   419
Reg. I dare auouch it Sir, what fifty Followers?   1533
Kent. Sir, I do know you, | And dare vpon the warrant of my note   1626
(If you dare venture in your owne behalfe)   2288
DARES = 2
That dares not vndertake: Hee'l not feele wrongs   2281
Call by the Trumpet: he that dares approach;   3047
DARK = *1
Bast. Here stood he in the dark, his sharpe Sword out,   972
DARKE = 5*1
Reg. Thus out of season, thredding darke ey'd night,   1062
Gallow the very wanderers of the darke   1696
Edg. Childe *Rowland* to the darke Tower came,   1966
Where is thy luster now? | *Glou*. All darke and comfortlesse?   2159
The darke and vitious place where thee he got, | Cost him his eyes.   3133
All's cheerlesse, darke, and deadly,   3258
DARKENES = *1
*beneath is all the Fiends. There's hell, there's darke-|nes,   2569
DARKENESSE = *2
*of my Mistris heart, and did the acte of darkenesse with   1867
Edg. The Prince of Darkenesse is a Gentleman. *Modo* | he's call'd, and
Mahu.   1921
DARKER = *1
Lear. Meane time we shal expresse our darker purpose.   41
DARKLING = *1
*young, so out went the Candle, and we were left dark-|ling.   728
DARKNESSE = 1*1
Lear. Darknesse, and Diuels.   762
*in the Lake of Darknesse: pray Innocent, and beware | the foule Fiend. 2005
DARNELL = 1
Darnell, and all the idle weedes that grow   2355
DARST = 1
Stew. Wherefore, bold Pezant, | Dar'st thou support a publish'd
Traitor? Hence,   2683

DART = *1
*Le. You nimble Lightnings, dart your blinding flames   1448
DAUB = 1
Edg. Poore Tom's a cold. I cannot daub it further.   2241
DAUBE = *1
*villaine into morter, and daube the wall of a   1139
DAUGHTER = 20*7
Be this perpetuall. What sayes our second Daughter?   72
As thou my sometime Daughter.   127
Thy yongest Daughter do's not loue thee least,   162
Hath riuald for our Daughter; what in the least   207
*Thy dowrelesse Daughter King, throwne to my chance,   281
Haue no such Daughter, nor shall euer see   288
*my Foole hither. You you Sirrah, where's my Daughter?   574
*the generall dependants, as in the Duke himselfe also, and | your
Daughter.   590
*and tell my Daughter, I would speake with her. Goe you   605
*Lear. How now Daughter? what makes that Frontlet   703
Lear. Are you our Daughter?   730
Yet haue I left a daughter.   765
I haue another daughter,   824
And such a Daughter, | Should sure to the Slaughter,   838
*acquaint my Daughter no further with any thing you   876
*Fool. Shalt see thy other Daughter will vse thee kind- | ly,   888
Kent. It is both he and she, | Your Son, and Daughter.   1289
Your Sonne and Daughter found this trespasse worth   1320
Thy Elements below where is this Daughter?   1330
The deere Father | *Would with his Daughter speake, commands, tends,
ser- | (uice,   1377
Deere daughter, I confesse that I am old;   1435
Lear. I prythee Daughter do not make me mad,   1512
But yet thou art my flesh, my blood, my Daughter,   1515
Your most deere Daughter--- | Lear. No rescue? What, a Prisoner? I am
euen   2632
Past speaking of in a King. Thou hast a Daughter   2647
Sir, this I heard, the King is come to his Daughter   2866
King Lear hath lost, he and his Daughter tane,   2929
DAUGHTERS = 20*7
Our daughters seuerall Dowers, that future strife   49
Great Riuals in our yongest daughters loue,   51
And heere are to be answer'd. Tell me my daughters   53
With my two Daughters Dowres, digest the third,   136
*Knigh. He saies my Lord, your Daughters is not well.   580
*ha's banish'd two on's Daughters, and did the third a   632
I had two Coxcombes and two Daughters.   635
*my selfe, there's mine, beg another of thy | Daughters.   638
*thy Daughters thy Mothers, for when thou gau'st them   686
*Foole. I maruell what kin thou and thy daughters are,   695
daughters, and leaue his hornes without a case.   905
Daughters, as thou canst tell in a yeare.   1327
If it be you that stirres these Daughters hearts   1574
*in, aske thy Daughters blessing, heere's a night pitties | neither
Wisemen, nor Fooles.   1667
Nor Raine, Winde, Thunder, Fire are my Daughters;   1670
That will with two pernicious Daughters ioyne   1677
*Lear. Did'st thou giue all to thy Daughters? And art | thou come to
this?   1830

DAUGHTERS *cont*.
*Lear. Ha's his Daughters brought him to this passe?	1844
Hang fated o're mens faults, light on thy Daughters.	1849
Kent. He hath no Daughters Sir.	1850
To such a lownesse, but his vnkind Daughters.	1852
Iudicious punishment, 'twas this flesh begot | Those Pelicane Daughters.	1855
T'obey in all your daughters hard commands:	1927
His Daughters seeke his death: Ah, that good Kent,	1943
Then my Daughters got 'tweene the lawfull sheets.	2561
Shall we not see these Daughters, and these Sisters?	2947
Your eldest Daughters haue fore-done themselues,	3259

DAWNING = *1
*Stew. Good dawning to thee Friend, art of this house? | *Kent*. I.	1076

DAY = 7*1
Vpon our kingdome: if on the tenth day following,	190
other day, what should follow these Eclipses.	470
Gon. By day and night, he wrongs me, euery howre	510
Though the Raine it raineth euery day.	1732
Glou. Alacke, alacke the day.	2623
Where am I? Faire day light?	2804
*Alb. Sir, you haue shew'd to day your valiant straine	2983
I haue seene the day, with my good biting Faulchion	3241

DAYES *see also* daies = 2*1
Fiue dayes we do allot thee for prouision,	187
*thou knowest me? Is it two dayes since I tript vp thy	1102
Who were the opposites of this dayes strife:	2985

DAYLIGHT *see* day
DE = *6
*Blisse thy fiue Wits, *Tom*s a cold. O do, de, do, de, do, de,	1839
*Do, de, de, de: sese: Come, march to Wakes and Fayres,	2031

DEAD = 15*1
And in the fleshment of this dead exploit, | Drew on me here againe.	1199
*Mes. Oh my good Lord, the Duke of *Cornwal*s dead,	2313
Flew on him, and among'st them fell'd him dead,	2320
My Lord is dead: *Edmond*, and I haue talk'd,	2417
By this had thought bin past. Aliue, or dead?	2485
Glou. What, is he dead?	2707
May be my Friends: hee's dead; I am onely sorry	2710
*Gen. 'Tis hot, it smoakes, it came euen from the heart | of--- O she's dead.	3174
Alb. Who dead? Speake man.	3176
Alb. Produce the bodies, be they aliue or dead; | *Gonerill and Regans bodies brought out*.	3183
I know when one is dead, and when one liues,	3220
She's dead as earth: Lend me a Looking-glasse,	3221
He'le strike and quickly too, he's dead and rotten.	3251
And desperately are dead | *Lear*. I so I thinke.	3260
Mess. Edmund is dead my Lord. | *Alb*. That's but a trifle heere:	3266
Shall neuer see so much, nor liue so long. | *Exeunt with a dead March*. | FINIS.	3301

DEADLY = 1
All's cheerlesse, darke, and deadly,	3258

DEALE = 3
And put vpon him such a deale of Man,	1196
Makes thee the happier: Heauens deale so still:	2251
And to deale plainely, | I feare I am not in my perfect mind.	2817

DEALING = *1
*dealing; when I desired their leaue that I might pity him,   1754
DEARE *see also* deere = 3
Lear. O Vassall! Miscreant. | *Alb. Cor.* Deare Sir forbeare.   175
Lear. Right Noble *Burgundy*, | When she was deare to vs, we did hold
her so,   213
But Mice, and Rats, and such small Deare,   1917
DEATH = 16*3
*Vnburthen'd crawle toward death. Our son of *Cornwal*,   46
The moment is thy death, away. By *Iupiter*, | This shall not be reuok'd,   192
Life and death, I am asham'd   814
He that conceales him death.   1000
If they not thought the profits of my death   1012
'Tis they haue put him on the old mans death,   1038
Lear. Vengeance, Plague, Death, Confusion: 1370
For the sound man. Death on my state: wherefore   1388
Till it crie sleepe to death.   1395
Lear. Death Traitor, nothing could haue subdu'd | (Nature   1851
His Daughters seeke his death: Ah, that good Kent,   1943
*Brothers euill disposition made him seeke his death: but   1976
I haue ore-heard a plot of death vpon him: 2048
Bast. Yours in the rankes of death. *Exit*.   2293
Is wretchednesse depriu'd that benefit | To end it selfe by death? 'Twas
yet some comfort,   2503
Vpon the English party. Oh vntimely death, death.   2703
That of thy death, and businesse, I can tell.   2731
That we the paine of death would hourely dye,   3148
DEATHSMAN = 1
He had no other Deathsman. Let vs see: 2711
DEATH-PRACTISD = 1
Of the death-practis'd Duke: for him 'tis well,   2730
DEBATE = 1
Stands on me to defend, not to debate. *Exit*.   2916
DEBOSHD = 1
Men so disorder'd, so debosh'd and bold,   751
DEBT = 1
No Squire in debt, nor no poore Knight;   1741
DECAY = 2
Kent. That from your first of difference and decay, | Haue follow'd your
sad steps.   3254
What comfort to this great decay may come,   3269
DECEIUD = 1
Edg. Y'are much deceiu'd: In nothing am I chang'd | But in my
Garments.   2442
DECLIND = *1
*declin'd, the Father should bee as Ward to the Son, and   407
DECLINE = 1
Decline your head. This kisse, if it durst speake   2290
DEEDE = 1
I finde she names my very deede of loue: 76
DEEDS = 1
And your large speeches, may your deeds approue,   198
DEEPE = 2
Nature's of such deepe trust, we shall much need: | You we first seize
on.   1057
Lookes fearfully in the confined Deepe: 2259

DEEPER = 1
    Against the old kinde King; or something deeper,   1637
DEERE = 19
    And finde I am alone felicitate | In your deere Highnesse loue.   80
    The Gods to their deere shelter take thee Maid,   196
    And thy deere Iudgement out. Go, go, my people.   785
    Lear. It may be so, my Lord. | Heare Nature, heare deere Goddesse,
    heare: 788
    Glo. My deere Lord, | You know the fiery quality of the Duke,   1366
    The deere Father | *Would with his Daughter speake, commands, tends,
    ser- |(uice,   1377
    Deere daughter, I confesse that I am old;   1435
    Commend a deere thing to you. There is diuision   1628
    Corn. I will lay trust vpon thee: and thou shalt finde | a deere Father
    in my loue. *Exeunt*.   1994
    *Postes shall be swift, and intelligent betwixt vs. Fare- |well deere
    Sister, farewell my Lord of Glouster.   2070
    Proue our Commodities. Oh deere Sonne *Edgar*,   2202
    Gon. My most deere Gloster.   2294
    In expectation of them. O deere Father,   2376
    But loue, deere loue, and our ag'd Fathers Rite: 2380
    Your most deere Daughter--- | *Lear*. No rescue? What, a Prisoner? I am
    euen   2632
    I prythee put them off. | *Kent*. Pardon deere Madam,   2755
    Cor. O my deere Father, restauratian hang   2776
    Kent. Kind and deere Princesse.   2780
    Reg. I neuer shall endure her, deere my Lord | Be not familiar with her.   2861
DEERELY = *2
    *deerely, Dice deerely; and in Woman, out-Paramour'd   1871
DEERER = 2*1
    *yeere elder then this; who, yet is no deerer in my ac- |count,   23
    Deerer then eye-sight, space, and libertie,   61
    No Father his Sonne deerer: true to tell thee,   1949
DEEREST = 2
    Our deerest *Regan*, wife of *Cornwall*?   73
    The best, the deerest, should in this trice of time   237
DEFECTS = 1
    Our meanes secure vs, and our meere defects   2201
DEFENCE = *1
    sound of the Trumpet: he is bold in his defence. 1 *Trumpet*. | *Her*.
    Againe. 2 *Trumpet*.   3063
DEFEND = 5
    Draw, seeme to defend your selfe, | Now quit you well.   961
    Your lop'd, and window'd raggednesse defend you   1812
    With thine, and all that offer to defend him,   2053
    Stands on me to defend, not to debate. *Exit*.   2916
    Alb. The Gods defend her, beare him hence awhile.   3215
DEFICIENT = 1
    Least my braine turne, and the deficient sight | Topple downe headlong.   2458
DEFORMITIE = 1
    Proper deformitie seemes not in the Fiend | So horrid as in woman.   2309
DEFUSE = 1
    That can my speech defuse, my good intent   532
DEFYE = *1
    *Plackets, thy pen from Lenders Bookes, and defye the   1877
DEGENERATE = 1
    Degenerate Bastard, Ile not trouble thee;   764

DEGREE = 1*1
Must be of such vnnaturall degree,   240
*Herald reads. | *If any man of qualitie or degree, within the lists of the*
Ar- |my,   3059
DEIECTED = 1
The lowest, and most deiected thing of Fortune,   2181
DELAY = 2
any further delay, then this very Euening.   426
What safe, and nicely I might well delay,   3100
DELICATE = 2
The bodies delicate: the tempest in my mind,   1792
It were a delicate stratagem to shoo | A Troope of Horse with Felt: Ile
put't in proofe,   2626
DELIUER = *2
*curious tale in telling it, and deliuer a plaine message   564
Gaole, from the loathed warmth whereof, deliuer me, and sup- |ply the
place for your Labour.   2720
DELIUERD = 1
Deliuer'd Letters spight of intermission,   1309
DELIUERED = *1
Kent. I will not sleepe my Lord, till I haue deliuered | your Letter.
Exit.   880
DEMAND = *1
*know, then comes from her demand out of the Letter,   877
DEMANDED = 1
Methinkes our pleasure might haue bin demanded   3002
DEMANDING = 1
Which euen but now, demanding after you,   1719
DENIE = 1
Make thy words faith'd? No, what should I denie,   1007
DENY = 2*1
Glo. O strange and fastned Villaine, | Would he deny his Letter, said he? 1015
Kent. What a brazen-fac'd Varlet art thou, to deny   1101
Lear. Deny to speake with me?   1361
DENYD = 1
Deny'd me to come in) returne, and force | Their scanted curtesie.   1720
DENYST = 1
deny'st the least sillable of thy addition.   1097
DEPART = 1*1
Lea. 'Tis strange that they should so depart from home,   1274
Corn. I will haue my reuenge, ere I depart his house.   1971
DEPARTURE = *1
Fool. She that's a Maid now, & laughs at my departure,   923
DEPEND = 1
And the remainders that shall still depend,   759
DEPENDANTS = 1*1
*the generall dependants, as in the Duke himselfe also, and | your
Daughter.   590
Who, with some other of the Lords, dependants,   2077
DEPOSITARIES = 1
Lear. Made you my Guardians, my Depositaries,   1549
DEPRAUD = 1
With how deprau'd a quality. Oh *Regan.*   1415
DEPRIUD = 2
That hath depriu'd me of your Grace and fauour,   251
Is wretchednesse depriu'd that benefit | To end it selfe by death? 'Twas
yet some comfort,   2503

DEPRIUE = 1
   The curiosity of Nations, to depriue me?   338
DERIDES = 1
   Who couers faults, at last with shame derides: 307
DERIUE = *1
   *deriue from him better testimony of his intent, you shold   415
DEROGATE = 1
   And from her derogate body, neuer spring   794
DESCENT *see* discent
DESCRY = 2
   His nighted life: Moreouer to descry | The strength o'th'Enemy.   2398
   Gent. Neere, and on speedy foot: the maine descry | Stands on the
   hourely thought.   2657
DESERT = 1
   You lesse know how to value her desert, | Then she to scant her dutie.   1417
DESERUD = 2
   question, thoud'st well deseru'd it. | *Kent*. Why Foole?   1338
   Deseru'd much lesse aduancement. | *Lear*. You? Did you?   1492
DESERUE = 2
   That he which finds him shall deserue our thankes,   998
   Thou might'st deserue, or they impose this vsage, | Comming from vs.   1301
DESERUING = 2
   Edm. Sir, I shall study deseruing.   34
   This seemes a faire deseruing, and must draw me   1773
DESERUINGS = 1
   The cup of their deseruings: O see, see.   3276
DESIRD = 1
   For instant remedy. Be then desir'd   756
DESIRE = 3
   I pray desire her call her wisedome to her. | So fare you well: 2422
   As duteous to the vices of thy Mistris, | As badnesse would desire.   2705
   You see is kill'd in him: desire him to go in,   2838
DESIRED = *1
   *dealing; when I desired their leaue that I might pity him,   1754
DESIRES = 1
   In the Goodmans desires: seeke, seeke for him,   2369
DESPAIRE *see* dispaire
DESPERATE = 2
   He is attended with a desperate traine,   1609
   Alb. Go after her, she's desperate, gouerne her.   3120
DESPERATELY = 1
   And desperately are dead | *Lear*. I so I thinke.   3260
DESPIGHT = 1
   Despight of mine owne Nature. Quickly send,   3201
DESPISD *see also* dispis'd = 1
   Most choise forsaken, and most lou'd despis'd,   276
DESPISE = 1
   Despise thy victor-Sword, and fire new Fortune,   3087
DESTROY = 1
   Breefely thy selfe remember: the Sword is out | That must destroy thee.   2679
DETAINE = 1
   Bast. I shall offend, either to detaine, or giue it: 376
DETECTOR = 1
   *of France. O Heauens! that this Treason were not; | or not I the
   detector.   1982
DETERMINE = 2
   Alb. Let's then determine with th'ancient of warre | On our proceeding.   2873

DETERMINE *cont.*
As we shall find their merites, and our safety | May equally determine. 2987
DETESTED = 2*1
*Abhorred Villaine, vnnaturall, detested, brutish 410
Lear. Detested Kite, thou lyest. 775
Perswade me rather to be slaue and sumpter | To this detested groome. 1509
DEUILL *see* diuell
DEUILLS *see* diuels
DEUISE = 1
Let her who would be rid of him, deuise 2911
DEUOURE = 1
The good yeares shall deuoure them, flesh and fell, 2966
DIALECT = *1
Kent. To go out of my dialect, which you discom- |mend 1185
DICE = *1
*deerely, Dice deerely; and in Woman, out-Paramour'd 1871
DID *see also* for-did *l.**6 214 *507 *632 688 898 982 *1030 1048 1304
*1398 1493 *1867 2150 2336 2782 2799 2823 3137 3140 3214 3239
3240 = 17*6
DIDST = 5*1
How vgly did'st thou in *Cordelia* shew? 780
Suspend thy purpose, if thou did'st intend | To make this Creature
fruitfull: 790
(As this I would, though thou didst produce 1008
Thou did'st not know on't. 1478
Lear. Did'st thou giue all to thy Daughters? And art | thou come to
this? 1830
In better phrase, and matter then thou did'st. 2441
DIE *see also* dye = 1*2
*bed, if I die for it, (as no lesse is threatned me) the King 1768
*To vse his eyes for Garden water-pots. I wil die brauely, 2640
Rather then die at once) taught me to shift 3149
DIES = 1*1
Cor. Keepe peace vpon your liues, he dies that strikes | againe, what is
the matter? 1122
Looke there, looke there. *He dies*. 3283
DIEST *see* dy'st
DIETED = 1
Let the superfluous, and Lust-dieted man, 2252
DIFFERENCE = 3*1
Foole. Do'st thou know the difference my Boy, be- |tweene a bitter
Foole, and a sweet one. 667
Cor. What is your difference, speake? 1125
Oh, the difference of man, and man, 2295
Kent. That from your first of difference and decay, | Haue follow'd your
sad steps. 3254
DIFFERENCES = 1*1
Kent. Come sir, arise, away, Ile teach you differences: 619
Of differences, which I best thought it fit 1066
DIFUSE *see* defuse
DIGEST = 1
With my two Daughters Dowres, digest the third, 136
DILLIGENCE = 1*1
*bluntly: that which ordinary men are fit for, I am qual- |lified in, and
the best of me, is Dilligence. 565
*if your Dilligence be not speedy, I shall be there afore | you. 878

DILLIGENT = 1
By dilligent discouerie, but your hast | Is now vrg'd on you.   2899
DIMENSIONS = 1
When my Dimensions are as well compact,   341
DIMINISHD = 1
Diminish'd to her Cocke: her Cocke, a Buoy   2454
DINNER = 1 *4
*so, Ile write straight to my Sister to hold my course; pre- | pare for
dinner. *Exeunt*.   527
Lear. Let me not stay a iot for dinner, go get it rea- | dy: 539
*worse after dinner, I will not part from thee yet. Dinner   572
*ho, dinner, where's my knaue? my Foole? Go you and call   573
DIRT *see* durt
DISASTERS = 1 *1
To shield thee from disasters of the world,   188
*behauiour, we make guilty of our disasters, the Sun, the   449
DISCARDED = 1
Is it the fashion, that discarded Fathers,   1853
DISCEND = 1
Brother, a word, discend; Brother I say,   949
DISCENT = 1
To the discent and dust below thy foote,   3092
DISCERNES = 1
By some discretion, that discernes your state   1429
DISCERNING = 1
Who hast not in thy browes an eye-discerning | Thine Honor, from thy
suffering.   2306
DISCERNINGS = 1
Either his Notion weakens, his Discernings   741
DISCHARGE = 1
All leuied in my name, haue in my name | Tooke their discharge.   3053
DISCLAIME = 1
Heere I disclaime all my Paternall care, | Propinquity and property of
blood,   120
DISCLAIMES = *1
*you cowardly Rascall, nature disclaimes in thee: a Taylor | made thee. 1128
DISCOMMEND = *1
Kent. To go out of my dialect, which you discom- | mend   1185
DISCORD = *1
*Brothers diuide. In Cities, mutinies; in Countries, dis- | cord;   437
DISCOUER = 1
I threaten'd to discouer him; he replied,   1003
DISCOUERIE = 1
By dilligent discouerie, but your hast | Is now vrg'd on you.   2899
DISCREET = 1
Which else were shame, that then necessitie | Will call discreet
proceeding.   724
DISCRETION = 1
By some discretion, that discernes your state   1429
DISDAIND = 1
That very Dogges disdain'd: and in this habit   3151
DISDAINE = 1
By rule of Knight-hood, I disdaine and spurne: 3101
DISEASE = 2
Vpon the foule disease, reuoke thy guift,   178
Or rather a disease that's in my flesh,   1516

DISHONOURED = 1
No vnchaste action or dishonoured step   250
DISLIKE = 2
Each buz, each fancie, each complaint, dislike,   846
What most he should dislike, seemes pleasant to him; | What like, offensiue.   2277
DISMANTLE = 1
Commit a thing so monstrous, to dismantle   238
DISMISSD = 1
Lear. Returne to her? and fifty men dismiss'd?   1500
DISMISSING = 1
Dismissing halfe your traine, come then to me,   1497
DISNATURD = 1
And be a thwart disnatur'd torment to her.   797
DISORDERD = 1*1
Men so disorder'd, so debosh'd and bold,   751
Gon. You strike my people, and your disorder'd rable, | make Seruants of their Betters.   766
DISORDERS = 1*1
*treacherie, and all ruinous disorders follow vs disquietly   443
Corn. I set him there, Sir: but his owne Disorders   1491
DISPAIRE = 3
Edg. Why I do trifle thus with his dispaire, | Is done to cure it.   2471
Led him, begg'd for him, sau'd him from dispaire.   3154
To lay the blame vpon her owne dispaire, | That she for-did her selfe.   3213
DISPATCH = 3*1
Glou. No? what needed then that terrible dispatch of   367
And found; dispatch, the Noble Duke my Master,   995
From hence attend dispatch, our good old Friend,   1068
All hearts against vs: *Edmund,* I thinke is gone | In pitty of his misery, to dispatch   2396
DISPISD = 1
A poore, infirme, weake, and dispis'd old man: 1675
DISPLAID = 1
Displaid so sawcily against your Highnesse,   1317
DISPLEASURE = 3*4
Or all of it with our displeasure piec'd,   217
Bast. Parted you in good termes? Found you no dis- |pleasure in him, by word, nor countenance?   478
*some little time hath qualified the heat of his displeasure,   483
*for my part I will not be, though I should win your | displeasure to entreat me too't.   1188
When he compact, and flattering his displeasure   1194
*me on paine of perpetuall displeasure, neither to speake   1756
Corn. Leaue him to my displeasure. *Edmond,* keepe   2065
DISPOSE = 1
Dispose of them, of me, the walls is thine: 3019
DISPOSITION = 2*3
*Father carry authority with such disposition as he beares,   329
*to lay his Goatish disposition on the charge of a Starre,   456
But let his disposition haue that scope | As dotage giues it.   807
Whose disposition all the world well knowes   1229
*Brothers euill disposition made him seeke his death: but   1976
DISPOSITIONS = 1
These dispositions, which of late transport you | From what you rightly are.   733

DISQUANTITY = 1
A little to disquantity your Traine,   758
DISQUIETLY = *1
*treacherie, and all ruinous disorders follow vs disquietly   443
DISSOLUE = 2
Least his vngouern'd rage, dissolue the life | That wants the meanes to
leade it.   2370
For I am almost ready to dissolue, | Hearing of this.   3167
DISSWADED = 1
Bast. When I disswaded him from his intent,   1001
DISTAFFE = 1
I must change names at home, and giue the Distaffe   2285
DISTASTE = 1
If he distaste it, let him to my Sister,   521
DISTINGUISH = 1
Euery one heares that, which can distinguish sound.   2654
DISTRACT = 1
Of my huge Sorrowes? Better I were distract,   2735
DISTRIBUTION = 1
So distribution should vndoo excesse,   2255
DITCH-DOGGE = *1
*ditch-Dogge; drinkes the green Mantle of the standing   1912
DIUELL = 1
Alb. See thy selfe diuell: 2308
DIUELS = 1
Lear. Darknesse, and Diuels.   762
DIUEST = 1
(Since now we will diuest vs both of Rule,   54
DIUIDE = *1
*Brothers diuide. In Cities, mutinies; in Countries, dis- | cord;   437
DIUIDED = 1
Giue me the Map there. Know, that we haue diuided   42
DIUINE = *1
*influence; and all that we are euill in, by a diuine thru- | sting   454
DIUINITY = *1
*Diuinity. When the raine came to wet me once, and the   2547
DIUISION = 1*2
*now in the diuision of the Kingdome, it ap- | peares   7
Commend a deere thing to you. There is diuision   1628
Glo. Go too; say you nothing. There is diuision be- | tweene   1759
DIUISIONS = *1
*o'Bedlam. --- O these Eclipses do portend these diui- | sions. Fa, Sol,
La, Me.   465
DIUORCE = 1
I would diuorce me from thy Mother Tombe,   1409
DIZIE = 1
And dizie 'tis, to cast ones eyes so low,   2447
DO *see also* doe, doo't, do't *l.*19 119 155 187 260 *332 *413 *445 *465 471
491 498 517 *544 562 614 646 714 723 747 750 830 941 968 1107 1220
*1231 1299 *1323 1431 1434 1457 1480 1512 1520 1521 *1554 1580 1604
1626 1640 1646 1742 1745 *1841 1951 *2036 2086 2094 2107 2151 2196
2230 2236 2416 2420 2424 2427 *2432 2435 2471 2474 2501 2520 2521
*2552 2555 *2568 *2607 2652 2774 2791 2794 2797 2798 2813 2823 2830
2831 2836 2856 2986 *2994 3013 3082 3102 3116 3126 3164 3200 3282 =
77*15, *4
*Blisse thy fiue Wits, *Tom*s a cold. O do, de, do, de, do, de,   1839
*Do, de, de, de: sese: Come, march to Wakes and Fayres,   2031

DOE *l*.*27 138 1002 1209 *1870 *2581 = 3*3
DOES *see also* do's *l*.1531 2792 = 2
DOG = 3*2
  *Lear. My Ladies Father? my Lords knaue, you whor-|son dog, you
slaue, you curre.   610
  *Foole. Truth's a dog must to kennell, hee must bee   641
  Kent. Why Madam, if I were your Fathers dog, | You should not vse
me so.   1215
  *Hog in sloth, Foxe in stealth, Wolfe in greedinesse, Dog   1873
  Why should a Dog, a Horse, a Rat haue life,   3278
DOGGE = 3*2
  *ditch-Dogge; drinkes the green Mantle of the standing   1912
  Reg. How now, you dogge?   2149
  *me like a Dogge, and told mee I had the white hayres in   2544
  dogge barke at a Beggar? | *Glou*. I Sir.   2599
  Mine Enemies dogge, though he had bit me,   2784
DOGGES = 3*1
  Knowing naught (like dogges) but following: 1153
  *tide by the heads, Dogges and Beares by'th'necke,   1283
  Lear. The little dogges, and all;   2020
  That very Dogges disdain'd: and in this habit   3151
DOGGS = *1
  *might'st behold the great image of Authoritie, a Dogg's   2602
DOGS = 1
  Dogs leapt the hatch, and all are fled.   2030
DOING = 2
  Whose nature is so farre from doing harmes,   500
  Be fear'd of doing harme, make your owne purpose,   1053
DOLORS = *1
  *But for all this thou shalt haue as many Dolors for thy   1326
DOLPHIN = *1
  *cold winde: Sayes suum, mun, nonny, Dolphin my Boy,   1879
DOMESTICKE = 1
  For these domesticke and particular broiles, | Are not the question
heere.   2871
DOMINIONS = 1
  Thy banisht trunke be found in our Dominions,   191
DONE *see also* fore-done *l*.360 486 718 2100 2147 2472 *2718 2831 2910
  2914 2979 3122 3259 = 12*1
DOORE = 1*1
  Or at their Chamber doore Ile beate the Drum,   1394
  *better then this Rain-water out o'doore. Good Nunkle,   1666
DOORES = 2*1
  Must be their Schoole-Masters: shut vp your doores,   1608
  *Cor. Shut vp your doores my Lord, 'tis a wil'd night,   1612
  Though their Iniunction be to barre my doores,   1928
DOOT = *1
  *doo't. There's my Gauntlet, Ile proue it on a Gyant.   2537
DORE = 1
  Leaue thy drinke and thy whore, | And keepe in a dore,   654
DOS *l*.162 738 *740 *892 *1165 1256 2254 2410 2559 *2564 *2610 2761
  2975 3228 = 9*6
DOST *l*.180 535 *542 557 626 *667 828 1004 1028 1085 1087 1162 *1374
  1723 *1825 2104 2256 2261 2493 2579 *2580 *2604 *2614 2950 2971
  2972 = 19*7
DOT = 4*1
  Ile do't before I speake, that you make knowne   248

DOT *cont.*
  Lear. They durst not do't: 1297
  *They could not, would not do't: 'tis worse then murther,   1298
  Will not beare question: either say thou'lt do't, | Or thriue by other
  meanes.   2976
  Capt. Ile do't my Lord.   2978
DOTAGE = 3
  But let his disposition haue that scope | As dotage giues it.   807
  He may enguard his dotage with their powres,   847
  All's not offence that indiscretion findes, | And dotage termes so.   1486
DOTE = *1
  *nor so old to dote on her for any thing. I haue yeares on | my backe
  forty eight.   569
DOTH *l.*56 58 347 755 1055 1171 1382 1557 1775 1793 1924 2379
  3008 = 13
DOUBLE = 1
  Thy fifty yet doth double fiue and twenty,   1557
DOUBT = 1
  Be by good Madam when we do awake him, | I doubt of his
  Temperance.   2774
DOUBTED = 1
  Reg. Our Sisters man is certainely miscarried. | *Bast*. 'Tis to be doubted
  Madam.   2851
DOUBTFULL = 1
  Yet I am doubtfull: For I am mainely ignorant   2820
DOUER = 9*1
  *And driue toward Douer friend, where thou shalt meete   2050
  Are gone with him toward Douer; where they boast | To haue well
  armed Friends.   2078
  Corn. Where hast thou sent the King? | *Glou*. To Douer.   2120
  Reg. Wherefore to Douer?   2122
  Corn. Wherefore to Douer? Let him answer that.   2124
  Reg. Wherefore to Douer? | *Glou*. Because I would not see thy cruell
  Nailes   2127
  Reg. Go thrust him out at gates, and let him smell | His way to Douer.
  Exit with Glouster.   2170
  I'th'way toward Douer, do it for ancient loue,   2230
  Glou. Know'st thou the way to Douer?   2245
  And each man haue enough. Dost thou know Douer? | *Edg*. I Master.   2256
DOWER = 1
  Will you require in present Dower with her, | Or cease your quest of
  Loue?   208
DOWERLESSE = 1
  Why the hot-bloodied *France*, that dowerlesse tooke   1505
DOWERS = 1
  Our daughters seuerall Dowers, that future strife   49
DOWNE = 11*7
  *his obedience. I dare pawne downe my life for him, that   419
  *the rod, and put'st downe thine owne breeches, then they   687
  Tript me behind: being downe, insulted, rail'd,   1195
  Historica passio, downe thou climing sorrow,   1329
  *let go thy hold when a great wheele runs downe a   1344
  Lear. Oh my heart! My rising heart! But downe.   1397
  *o'th' coxcombs with a sticke, and cryed downe wantons,   1400
  *downe; 'twas her Brother, that in pure kindnesse to his | Horse
  buttered his Hay.   1401
  Make it your cause: Send downe, and take my part.   1482

DOWNE *cont.*
  Glou. I haue a Letter guessingly set downe 2115
  Shew scarse so grosse as Beetles. Halfe way downe 2449
  Least my braine turne, and the deficient sight | Topple downe headlong. 2458
  (So many fathome downe precipitating) 2492
  *Downe from the waste they are Centaures, though 2567
  Edg. Sit you downe Father: rest you. 2708
  For thee oppressed King I am cast downe, 2945
  When thou dost aske me blessing, Ile kneele downe 2950
  As I haue set it downe. *Exit Captaine.* 2981
DOWRD = 1
  Dow'rd with our curse, and stranger'd with our oath, | Take her or, leaue her. 223
DOWRE = 1
  Lear. Let it be so, thy truth then be thy dowre: 115
DOWRELESSE = *1
  *Thy dowrelesse Daughter King, throwne to my chance, 281
DOWRES = 1
  With my two Daughters Dowres, digest the third, 136
DOWRIE = 1
  She is herselfe a Dowrie. 264
DRAGON = 1
  Come not betweene the Dragon and his wrath, 130
DRAGONS = *1
  *My father compounded with my mother vnder the Dra-|gons 457
DRAW = 7*7
  Striue to be interest. What can you say, to draw 91
  In cunning, I must draw my Sword vpon you: 960
  Draw, seeme to defend your selfe, | Now quit you well. 961
  *heeles, and beate thee before the King? Draw you rogue, 1103
  *sop oth' Moonshine of you, you whoreson Cullyenly | Barber-monger, draw. 1105
  Kent. Draw you Rascall, you come with Letters a-|gainst 1108
  *the Royaltie of her Father: draw you Rogue, or 1110
  *Ile so carbonado your shanks, draw you Rascall, come | your waies. 1111
  *great one that goes vpward, let him draw thee after: 1346
  This seemes a faire deseruing, and must draw me 1773
  Lear. Make no noise, make no noise, draw the Cur-|taines: 2041
  *draw mee a Cloathiers yard. Looke, looke, a 2535
  Bast. The Enemy's in view, draw vp your powers, 2897
  Bast. Himselfe, what saist thou to him? | *Edg*. Draw thy Sword, 3079
DRAWES = *1
  Foole. May not an Asse know, when the Cart drawes | the Horse? 735
DRAWNE = 1*2
  Le. The bow is bent & drawne, make from the shaft. 152
  Some blood drawne on me, would beget opinion 966
  *You Fen-suck'd Fogges, drawne by the powrfull Sunne, | To fall, and blister. 1450
DREAD = 1*1
  Think'st thou that dutie shall haue dread to speake, | When power to flattery bowes? 156
  Glou. But haue I falne, or no? | *Edg*. From the dread Somnet of this Chalkie Bourne 2498
DREADFULL = 3
  Lear. Let the great Goddes | That keepe this dreadfull pudder o're our heads, 1702

DREADFULL *cont.*

These dreadfull Summoners grace. I am a man, | More sinn'd against,
then sinning. 1712

Hangs one that gathers Sampire: dreadfull Trade: 2450

DREAME = *1

*At point a hundred Knights: yes, that on euerie dreame, 845

DRENCHD = *1

*Till you haue drench'd our Steeples, drown the Cockes. 1658

DREW = 3

From the fixt place: drew from my heart all loue, 782

And in the fleshment of this dead exploit, | Drew on me here againe. 1199

Hauing more man then wit about me, drew; 1318

DRIE = 1

Drie vp in her the Organs of increase, 793

DRINKE = 2

Leaue thy drinke and thy whore, | And keepe in a dore, 654

If you haue poyson for me, I will drinke it: 2829

DRINKES = *1

*ditch-Dogge; drinkes the green Mantle of the standing 1912

DRIUE = 1 *1

I'ld driue ye cackling home to *Camelot*. 1157

*And driue toward Douer friend, where thou shalt meete 2050

DROPS = 1

And let not womens weapons, water drops, 1577

DROWN = *1

*Till you haue drench'd our Steeples, drown the Cockes. 1658

DRUM = 6

Or at their Chamber doore Ile beate the Drum, 1394

Enter with Drum and Colours, Cordelia, Gentlemen, | and Souldiours. 2349

So should my thoughts be seuer'd from my greefes, | *Drum afarre off.* 2736

Enter with Drum and Colours, Albany, Gonerill, Soldiers. 2864

Enter in conquest with Drum and Colours, Edmund, Lear, 2938

Reg. Let the Drum strike, and proue my title thine. 3026

DRUMME = 3

Farre off methinkes I heare the beaten Drumme. 2741

*Enter with Drumme and Colours, Edmund, Regan. | Gentlemen, and
Souldiers.* 2845

Alarum within. Enter with Drumme and Colours, Lear, 2918

DRUNKARDS = 1 *1

*Treachers by Sphericall predominance. Drunkards, Ly- | ars, 452

Of my more fierce endeauour. I haue seene drunkards 967

DRY *see also* drie = 1 *1

Foole. O Nunkle, Court holy-water in a dry house, is 1665

And Market Townes: poore Tom thy horne is dry, 2032

DUCHESSE *see also* dutchesse = 1

That the Duke of *Cornwall*, and *Regan* his Duchesse 931

DUCKING = 1

Then twenty silly-ducking obseruants, 1178

DUE = 4

Make with you by due turne, onely we shall retaine 143

*after your owne wisedome. I would vnstate my | selfe, to be in a due
resolution. 429

May haue due note of him, and of my land, 1021

To thee a Womans seruices are due, | My Foole vsurpes my body. 2296

DUES = 1

Effects of Curtesie, dues of Gratitude: 1463

DUKE = 17*4
Duke of *Albany*, then *Cornwall*. | **Glou*. It did alwayes seeme so to vs:
But   5
*the generall dependants, as in the Duke himselfe also, and | your
Daughter.   590
That the Duke of *Cornwall*, and *Regan* his Duchesse   931
Bast. The Duke be here to night? The better best,   943
Haue you not spoken 'gainst the Duke of *Cornewall*?   953
Vpon his partie 'gainst the Duke of *Albany*? | Aduise your selfe.   956
And found; dispatch, the Noble Duke my Master,   995
The Duke must grant me that: besides, his picture   1019
Glo. My deere Lord, | You know the fiery quality of the Duke,   1366
I'ld speake with the Duke of *Cornewall*, and his wife.   1372
Fiery? The fiery Duke, tell the hot Duke that---   1380
That this remotion of the Duke and her   1390
Goe tell the Duke, and's wife, Il'd speake with them: 1392
*maintaine talke with the Duke, that my charity be not of   1766
Bast. This Curtesie forbid thee, shall the Duke   1771
*beholding. Aduice the Duke where you are going, to a   2068
*Mes. Oh my good Lord, the Duke of *Cornwal*s dead,   2313
Of the death-practis'd Duke: for him 'tis well,   2730
Bast. Know of the Duke if his last purpose hold,   2847
Bast. Feare not, she and the Duke her husband.   2863
DUKES = 4*4
*not which of the Dukes hee valewes   8
Not all the Dukes of watrish *Burgundy*,   283
'Twixt the Dukes of *Cornwall*, and *Albany*? | *Bast*. Not a word.   939
*Harke, the Dukes Trumpets, I know not wher he comes;   1017
*Glo. I am sorry for there friend, 'tis the Dukes pleasure,   1228
Glo. The Duke's too blame in this, | 'Twill be ill taken. *Exit*.   1235
Either in snuffes, and packings of the Dukes,   1635
*the Dukes, and a worsse matter then that: I haue   1760
DULL = 2
Then doth within a dull stale tyred bed   347
Lear. This is a dull sight, are you not *Kent*? | *Kent*. The same: your
Seruant *Kent*,   3247
DULLARD = 1
And thou must make a dullard of the world,   1011
DUNG = *1
*Cow-dung for Sallets; swallowes the old Rat, and the   1911
DUNGHILL = 2
Vpon the Dunghill: *Regan*, I bleed apace,   2175
Stew. Out Dunghill.   2696
DURING = 1
During the life of this old Maiesty   3271
DURST = 3*1
Which we durst neuer yet; and with strain'd pride,   183
*Bast. If the matter were good my Lord, I durst swear   398
Lear. They durst not do't: 1297
Decline your head. This kisse, if it durst speake   2290
DURT = *1
*durt, thou hadst little wit in thy bald crowne, when thou   677
DUST = 2
Alb. Oh *Gonerill*, | You are not worth the dust which the rude winde |
Blowes in your face.   2301
To the discent and dust below thy foote,   3092

DUTCHESSE = 2
And here I take *Cordelia* by the hand, | Dutchesse of *Burgundie*.   267
Corn. Go with me to the Dutchesse.   1984
DUTEOUS = 1
As duteous to the vices of thy Mistris, | As badnesse would desire.   2705
DUTIE = 7
Halfe my loue with him, halfe my Care, and Dutie,   109
Think'st thou that dutie shall haue dread to speake, | When power to
flattery bowes?   156
So farewell to you both. | *Regn*. Prescribe not vs our dutie.   300
That all particulars of dutie know,   777
My dutie kneeling, came there a reeking Poste,   1306
You lesse know how to value her desert, | Then she to scant her dutie.   1417
Stew. I may not Madam: | My Lady charg'd my dutie in this busines.   2403
DUTIES = 2
I returne those duties backe as are right fit,   104
That stretch their duties nicely.   1179
DUTY = 2*1
*mistaken, for my duty cannot be silent, when I thinke | your Highnesse
wrong'd.   594
Bast. It was my duty Sir.   1047
Glou. Go in with me; my duty cannot suffer   1926
DWELS = 1
Dwels in the sickly grace of her he followes.   1473
DYE = 8
What are you Sir? | *Glou*. Away, and let me dye.   2488
Enough, enough, and dye. That thing you speake of,   2522
Adultery? thou shalt not dye: dye for Adultery?   2557
Let not my worser Spirit tempt me againe | To dye before you please.   2664
Cor. Sir, do you know me? | *Lear*. You are a spirit I know, where did
you dye?   2798
I am mightily abus'd; I should eu'n dye with pitty   2805
That we the paine of death would hourely dye,   3148
DYST = 1
Stew. Let go Slaue, or thou dy'st.   2689
EACH = 6
Each buz, each fancie, each complaint, dislike,   846
And each man haue enough. Dost thou know Douer? | *Edg*. I Master.   2256
Ten Masts at each, make not the altitude   2495
Each iealous of the other, as the stung   2903
EARE = 2*2
For your fit welcome, giue eare Sir to my Sister,   1528
To haue his eare abus'd, wisedome bids feare.   1611
*the Turke. False of heart, light of eare, bloody of hand;   1872
*thine eare: Change places, and handy-dandy, which is   2597
EARES = *1
*goes, with no eyes. Looke with thine eares: See how   2595
EARLE = 2*3
Kent. With the Earle Sir, here within.   1331
Corn. True or false, it hath made thee Earle of Glou- | cester: 1987
To *Edmund* Earle of Glouster: seeke him out   2702
*will maintaine vpon Edmund, supposed Earle of Gloster,   3061
Edg. What's he that speakes for *Edmund* Earle of Glo- | (ster?   3078
EARNEST = 1
Lear. Now my friendly knaue I thanke thee, there's | earnest of thy
seruice.   622

EARNESTLY = *1
  *Glou. Why so earnestly seeke you to put vp y Letter?   363
EARTH = 5
  The terrors of the earth? you thinke Ile weepe,   1582
  Bids the winde blow the Earth into the Sea,   1620
  *Mildewes the white Wheate, and hurts the poore Crea-|ture of earth.   1898
  Cord. All blest Secrets, | All you vnpublish'd Vertues of the earth   2366
  She's dead as earth: Lend me a Looking-glasse,   3221
EAR-KISSING = 1
  *I meane the whisper'd ones, for they are yet but | ear-kissing
  arguments.   935
EASE = 1
  Lear. Prythee go in thy selfe, seeke thine owne ease,   1804
EASIE = 2
  My practises ride easie: I see the businesse.   502
  Lear. This is a Slaue, whose easie borrowed pride   1472
EATE = 1*1
  *feare iudgement, to fight when I cannot choose, and to | eate no fish.   547
  *eate vp the meate, the two Crownes of the egge: when   674
EATER = *1
  *Kent. A Knaue, a Rascall, an eater of broken meates, a   1088
EATES = *1
  *Edg. Poore Tom, that eates the swimming Frog, the   1908
EATS = *1
  *in the furie of his heart, when the foule Fiend rages, eats   1910
EBBE = 1
  In a wall'd prison, packs and sects of great ones, | That ebbe and flow
  by th'Moone.   2958
ECLIPSES = 1*2
  *Glou. These late Eclipses in the Sun and Moone por-|tend   433
  *o'Bedlam. --- O these Eclipses do portend these diui-|sions. Fa, Sol,
  La, Me.   465
  other day, what should follow these Eclipses.   470
EDG = 69*19
EDGAR see also Edg. = 20*1
  Legitimate Edgar, I must haue your land,   350
  *him, you should enioy halfe his Reuennew for euer, and liue the | beloued
  of your Brother. Edgar.   388
  *enioy halfe his Reuennew: my Sonne Edgar, had hee a   391
  Enter Edgar.   462
  Enter Edgar.   948
  Fly Brother, Torches, Torches, so farewell. | Exit Edgar.   964
  He whom my Father nam'd, your Edgar?   1031
  Enter Edgar.   1251
  That's something yet: Edgar I nothing am. Exit.   1272
  Enter Edgar, and Foole.   1818
  Enter Lear, Edgar, and Foole.   2003
  Glou. O my Follies! then Edgar was abus'd,   2168
  Enter Edgar.   2178
  Proue our Commodities. Oh deere Sonne Edgar,   2202
  Enter Gloucester, and Edgar.   2430
  Burne it selfe out. If Edgar liue, O blesse him: 2479
  Enter Edgar.   2880
  Enter Edgar, and Gloster.   2920
  Enter Edgar.   2927
  Enter Edgar armed.   3067
  My name is Edgar and thy Fathers Sonne,   3130

EDGAR = 2*2
EDM = 4*2
EDMOND = 8*4
  Enter Kent, Gloucester, and Edmond.   2
  *be acknowledged. Doe you know this Noble Gentle- | man, *Edmond*? |
  Edm. No, my Lord.   27
  Our Fathers loue, is to the Bastard *Edmond*,   351
  And my inuention thriue, *Edmond* the base | Shall to'th'Legitimate: I
  grow, I prosper: 354
  Vpon the gad? *Edmond*, how now? What newes?   361
  Glou. He cannot bee such a Monster. *Edmond* seeke   427
  *to our Graues. Find out this Villain, *Edmond*, it shall lose   444
  Edg. How now Brother *Edmond*, what serious con- | templation are you
  in?   467
  Corn. Leaue him to my displeasure. *Edmond*, keepe   2065
  May proue effects. Backe *Edmond* to my Brother,   2283
  My Lord is dead: *Edmond*, and I haue talk'd,   2417
  I am no lesse in blood then thou art *Edmond*,   3128
EDMUND see also Edm. = 19*6
  Glo. Now *Edmund*, where's the villaine?   971
  Glo. Where is the villaine, *Edmund*?   977
  Edmund, I heare that you haue shewne your Father | A Child-like
  Office.   1045
  How in my strength you please: for you *Edmund*,   1054
  Enter Gloster, and Edmund.   1752
  Glo. Alacke, alacke *Edmund*, I like not this vnnaturall   1753
  *my old Master must be relieued. There is strange things | toward
  Edmund, pray you be carefull. *Exit*.   1769
  Enter Cornwall, and Edmund.   1970
  Corn. Edmund farewell: go seek the Traitor Gloster,   2082
  Where's my Sonne *Edmund*?   2161
  Edmund, enkindle all the sparkes of Nature | To quit this horrid acte.   2162
  Reg. Lord *Edmund* spake not with your Lord at home? | *Stew*. No
  Madam.   2389
  All hearts against vs: *Edmund*, I thinke is gone | In pitty of his misery,
  to dispatch   2396
  Reg. Why should she write to *Edmund*?   2405
  To Noble *Edmund*. I know you are of her bosome. | *Stew*. I, Madam?   2413
  To *Edmund* Earle of Glouster: seeke him out   2702
  Enter with Drumme and Colours, Edmund, Regan. | Gentlemen, and
  Souldiers.   2845
  Enter Edmund.   2896
  Enter in conquest with Drum and Colours, Edmund, Lear,   2938
  Alb. Stay yet, heare reason: *Edmund*, I arrest thee   3027
  will maintaine vpon Edmund, supposed Earle of Gloster,   3061
  Edg. What's he that speakes for *Edmund* Earle of Glo- |(ster?   3078
  *Speake *Edmund*, where's the King? and where's *Cordelia*?   3193
  Bast. Yet *Edmund* was belou'd: 3196
  Mess. Edmund is dead my Lord. | *Alb*. That's but a trifle heere: 3266
EELES = *1
  *Eeles, when she put 'em i'th' Paste aliue, she knapt 'em   1399
EEUEN = 1
  Glou. Me thinkes the ground is euen. | *Edg*. Horrible steepe.   2433
EFFECT = 1
  Kent. Few words, but to effect more then all yet;   1650
EFFECTS = 4*2
  Preheminence, and all the large effects   139

EFFECTS *cont.*
That good effects may spring from words of loue: 199
*by the sequent effects. Loue cooles, friendship falls off, 436
Bast. I promise you, the effects he writes of, succeede | vnhappily. 472
Effects of Curtesie, dues of Gratitude: 1463
May proue effects. Backe *Edmond* to my Brother, 2283
EGGE = 1*3
Foole. Nunckle, giue me an egge, and Ile giue thee | two Crownes. 670
Foole. Why after I haue cut the egge i'th'middle and 673
*eate vp the meate, the two Crownes of the egge: when 674
Thou'dst shiuer'd like an Egge: but thou do'st breath: 2493
EIE = 1
Kent. See better *Lear*, and let me still remaine | The true blanke of
thine eie. 170
EIES = 3*2
Cor. The Iewels of our Father, with wash'd eies 293
*Do's *Lear* walke thus? Speake thus? Where are his eies? 740
Alb. How farre your eies may pierce I cannot tell; 869
Lear. Oh ho, are you there with me? No eies in your 2589
And turne our imprest Launces in our eies 2993
EIGHT = 2
*nor so old to dote on her for any thing. I haue yeares on | my backe
forty eight. 569
Lear. Because they are not eight. 910
EITHER = 4*1
Bast. I shall offend, either to detaine, or giue it: 376
Either his Notion weakens, his Discernings 741
Foole. Why to keepe ones eyes of either side 's nose, 896
Either in snuffes, and packings of the Dukes, 1635
Will not beare question: either say thou'lt do't, | Or thriue by other
meanes. 2976
EITHERS = 1
*most, for qualities are so weigh'd, that curiosity in nei- | ther, can make
choise of eithers moity. 9
ELDER = *1
*yeere elder then this; who, yet is no deerer in my ac- | count, 23
ELDEST = 2
Our eldest borne, speake first. 59
Your eldest Daughters haue fore-done themselues, 3259
ELECTION = 1
Bur. Pardon me Royall Sir, | Election makes not vp in such conditions. 225
ELEMENTS = 3
Thy Elements below where is this Daughter? 1330
Gent. Contending with the fretfull Elements; 1619
I taxe not you, you Elements with vnkindnesse. 1671
ELIADS = 1
She gaue strange Eliads, and most speaking lookes 2412
ELSE = 10*1
Which else were shame, that then necessitie | Will call discreet
proceeding. 724
By her, that else will take the thing she begges, 757
Bast. I shall serue you Sir truely, how euer else. 1059
Blanket my loines, else all my haires in knots, 1261
Doth from my sences take all feeling else, 1793
Foole. Nay, he reseru'd a Blanket, else we had bin all | sham'd. 1846
All Cruels else subscribe: but I shall see 2137
Glou. He has some reason, else he could not beg. 2215

ELSE *cont.*
My selfe could else out-frowne false Fortunes frowne.   2946
Rega. Lady I am not well, else I should answere   3016
Lear. You are welcome hither. | *Kent.* Nor no man else: 3256
EM = 2*7
Foole. Thy Asses are gone about 'em; the reason why   908
*Eeles, when she put 'em i'th' Paste aliue, she knapt 'em   1399
*Could'st thou saue nothing? Would'st thou giue 'em all?   1845
Lear. To haue a thousand with red burning spits | Come hizzing in vpon
'em.   2013
*peace at my bidding, there I found 'em, there I smelt 'em   2549
*none, I say none, Ile able 'em; take that of me my Friend,   2611
Weele see 'em staru'd first: come. *Exit.*   2968
EMBOSSED *see* imbossed
EMBRACE = 2
Thou vnsubstantiall ayre that I embrace: 2185
A Royall Noblenesse: I must embrace thee,   3138
EMINENCE = 1
Maugre thy strength, place, youth, and eminence,   3086
EMPLOYMENT *see* imployment
EMPTY = 1
Nor are those empty hearted, whose low sounds | Reuerbe no
hollownesse.   163
ENCOUNTER = 1
Bold in the quarrels right, rouz'd to th'encounter,   990
END = 4
'Tis on such ground, and to such wholesome end,   1423
Is wretchednesse depriu'd that benefit | To end it selfe by death? 'Twas
yet some comfort,   2503
Your businesse of the world hath so an end,   2889
Kent. Is this the promis'd end? | *Edg.* Or image of that horror. | *Alb.*
Fall and cease.   3224
ENDEAUOUR = 1
Of my more fierce endeauour. I haue seene drunkards   967
ENDOWD = 1
Thy halfe o'th'Kingdome hast thou not forgot, | Wherein I thee
endow'd.   1464
ENDS = 1
Harbour more craft, and more corrupter ends,   1177
ENDURD *see also* indur'd = 2
In ranke, and (not to be endur'd) riots Sir.   715
Kent. The wonder is, he hath endur'd so long, | He but vsurpt his life. 3291
ENDURE = 5
That sets vs all at ods: Ile not endure it;   512
The tirrany of the open night's too rough | For Nature to endure.
Storme still   1779
To shut me out? Poure on, I will endure: 1798
Reg. I neuer shall endure her, deere my Lord | Be not familiar with her. 2861
Men must endure | Their going hence, euen as their comming hither,   2933
ENEMIE = 1
Gone. Combine together 'gainst the Enemie: 2870
ENEMIES = 4
To wage against thine enemies, nere feare to loose it, | Thy safety being
motiue.   167
Finde out their enemies now. Tremble thou Wretch,   1704
To know our enemies mindes, we rip their hearts,   2713
Mine Enemies dogge, though he had bit me,   2784

ENEMY = 2
My selfe an enemy to all other ioyes, 78
His nighted life: Moreouer to descry | The strength o'th'Enemy. 2398
ENEMYS = 1
Bast. The Enemy's in view, draw vp your powers, 2897
ENFLAMD = 1
My Loue should kindle to enflam'd respect. 280
ENFORCD *see* inforc'd
ENFORCE *see* inforce
ENGENDERD = 1
Your high-engender'd Battailes, 'gainst a head 1678
ENGINE = 1
Which like an Engine, wrencht my frame of Nature 781
ENGLISH = 1
Vpon the English party. Oh vntimely death, death. 2703
ENGRAFFED *see* ingraffed
ENGUARD = 1
He may enguard his dotage with their powres, 847
ENIOY = 1*2
him, you should enioy halfe his Reuennew for euer, and liue the | beloued
of your Brother. Edgar. 388
enioy halfe his Reuennew: my Sonne Edgar, had hee a 391
Gon. Meane you to enioy him? 3022
ENIOYD = 1
Both? One? Or neither? Neither can be enioy'd 2905
ENKINDLE = 1
Edmund, enkindle all the sparkes of Nature | To quit this horrid acte. 2162
ENMITY = 1
To wage against the enmity oth'ayre, 1502
ENORMOUS = 1
From this enormous State, seeking to giue 1246
ENOUGH = 6*1
King, thou art poore enough. What wouldst thou? | *Kent.* Seruice. 553
And each man haue enough. Dost thou know Douer? | *Edg.* I Master. 2256
Enough, enough, and dye. That thing you speake of, 2522
Do'st thou know me? | *Lear.* I remember thine eyes well enough: dost
thou 2579
I know thee well enough, thy name is Glouster: 2619
Glou. Now let thy friendly hand | Put strength enough too't. 2681
ENRAGD = 1
To his great Master, who, threat-enrag'd 2319
ENRAGED = 1
Hornes wealk'd, and waued like the enraged Sea: 2516
ENTER = 75*2
Enter Kent, Gloucester, and Edmond. 2
Sennet. Enter King Lear, Cornwall, Albany, Gonerill, Re- | gan,
Cordelia, and attendants. 37
Flourish. Enter Gloster with France, and Bur- | gundy, Attendants. 202
Enter Bastard. 334
Enter Gloucester. 357
Enter Edgar. 462
Enter Gonerill, and Steward. 506
Enter Kent. 530
Hornes within. Enter Lear and Attendants. 538
Enter Steward. 575
Sir, who am I Sir? | *Enter Steward.* | *Ste.* My Ladies Father. 607
Enter Foole. 624

ENTER *cont.*

Enter *Edgar, and Gloster.* 2920

Enter *Edgar.* 2927

Enter *in conquest with Drum and Colours, Edmund, Lear,* 2938

Flourish. Enter *Albany, Gonerill, Regan, Soldiers.* 2982

Enter *a Herald.* 3050

Enter *Edgar armed.* 3067

Enter *a Gentleman.* 3169

Enter *Kent.* 3182

Enter *Lear with Cordelia in his armes.* 3216

Enter *a Messenger.* 3264

ENTERLUDE = 1

My Lady is bespoke. | *Gon.* An enterlude. 3034

ENTERTAIND = *1

*but to my iudgement your Highnesse is not entertain'd 587

ENTERTAINE = *1

*make these hard-hearts. You sir, I entertaine for one of 2035

ENTERTAINEMENT = 1

Which shall be needfull for your entertainement. 1499

ENTIRE *see* intire

ENTREAT = 3

*for my part I will not be, though I should win your | displeasure to

entreat me too't. 1188

Will not be rub'd nor stopt, Ile entreat for thee. 1230

of him, entreat for him, or any way sustaine him. 1757

ENTREATE *see also* intreate = 2

(For now I spie a danger) I entreate you 1544

Gon. My Lord, entreate him by no meanes to stay. 1602

ENTREATY = *1

*him: and at my entreaty forbeare his presence, vntill 482

EPICURISME = 1

Shewes like a riotous Inne; Epicurisme and Lust 753

EPILEPTICKE = 1

A plague vpon your Epilepticke visage, 1154

EQUALLY = 1

As we shall find their merites, and our safety | May equally determine. 2987

ERE = 11 *4

*Sonne for her Cradle, ere she had a husband for her bed. 18

As much as Childe ere lou'd, or Father found. 64

Foole. I haue vsed it Nunckle, ere since thou mad'st 685

Ere I was risen from the place, that shewed 1305

Or ere Ile weepe; O Foole, I shall go mad. *Exeunt.* 1586

Ile speake a Prophesie ere I go: 1735

Poore naked wretches, where so ere you are 1809

Corn. I will haue my reuenge, ere I depart his house. 1971

I am worse then ere I was. 2208

Shall passe betweene vs: ere long you are like to heare 2287

*my Beard, ere the blacke ones were there. To say I, and 2545

Edg. If ere your Grace had speech with man so poore, | Heare me one

word. 2881

Ere they shall make vs weepe? 2967

Ere you had spoke so farre. He led our Powers, 3003

Ere I taste bread, thou art in nothing lesse 3041

ESCAPD = 1

Escap'd the hunt. No Port is free, no place 1254

ESCAPE *see also* scape = 1

The bloody proclamation to escape 3146

ESPERANCE = 1
Stands still in esperance, liues not in feare: 2182
ESSAY = 1
this but as an essay, or taste of my Vertue.   381
EUASION = *1
*on. An admirable euasion of Whore-master-man,   455
EUEN *see also* eeuen, eu'n = 8*2
*Lear. Of all these bounds euen from this Line, to this,   68
That she whom euen but now, was your obiect,   235
But euen for want of that, for which I am richer,   252
Which euen but now, demanding after you,   1719
Cor. Alacke, 'tis he: why he was met euen now   2351
Your most deere Daughter--- | Lear. No rescue? What, a Prisoner? I am
euen   2632
Glo. No further Sir, a man may rot euen heere.   2931
Men must endure | Their going hence, euen as their comming hither,   2933
*Gen. 'Tis hot, it smoakes, it came euen from the heart | of--- O she's
dead.   3174
Alb. Euen so: couer their faces.   3199
EUENING = 2
any further delay, then this very Euening.   426
I haue this present euening from my Sister   1040
EUENT = 1
Gon. Nay then--- | Alb. Well, well, th'euent. *Exeunt*   871
EUER *see also* ere = 16*3
Lear. To thee, and thine hereditarie euer,   85
Hold thee from this for euer. The barbarous *Scythian*,   123
Kent. Royall *Lear*, | Whom I haue euer honor'd as my King,   148
Haue no such Daughter, nor shall euer see   288
*Reg. 'Tis the infirmity of his age, yet he hath euer but | slenderly
knowne himselfe.   318
*him, you should enioy halfe his Reuennew for euer, and liue the | beloued
of your Brother. Edgar.   388
That Ile resume the shape which thou dost thinke | I haue cast off for
euer. *Exit*   828
Bast. I shall serue you Sir truely, how euer else.   1059
That euer penury in contempt of man,   1259
I haue seru'd you euer since I was a Childe: 2146
*Glou. You euer gentle Gods, take my breath from me,   2663
If euer thou wilt thriue, bury my bodie,   2700
If euer I returne to you againe, | Ile bring you comfort.   2923
Where they shall rest for euer. Trumpets speake.   3106
Let sorrow split my heart, if euer I | Did hate thee, or thy Father.   3139
That Heauens vault should crack: she's gone for euer.   3219
It is a chance which do's redeeme all sorrowes | That euer I haue felt.   3228
I might haue sau'd her, now she's gone for euer: 3234
What is't thou saist? Her voice was euer soft,   3236
EUERIE = 1*1
Pierce euerie sense about thee. Old fond eyes,   820
*At point a hundred Knights: yes, that on euerie dreame,   845
EUERY = 10*2
Gon. By day and night, he wrongs me, euery howre   510
On euery trifle. When he returnes from hunting,   514
Which are t'intrince, t'vnloose: smooth euery passion   1148
With euery gall, and varry of their Masters,   1152
Though the Raine it raineth euery day.   1732
When euery Case in Law, is right;   1740

EUERY *cont.*
Search euery Acre in the high-growne field,	2357
*no, to euery thing that I said: I, and no too, was no good	2546
*me, I was euery thing: 'Tis a Lye, I am not Agu-proofe.	2551
Is't not the King? | *Lear.* I, euery inch a King.	2553
Euery one heares that, which can distinguish sound.	2654
My life will be too short, | And euery measure faile me.	2748

EUERYONE *see* euery
EUERYTHING *see* euery
EUILL = 2*2
Ile tell thee thou dost euill.	180
*influence; and all that we are euill in, by a diuine thru-|sting	454
*Brothers euill disposition made him seeke his death: but	1976
Thou worse then any name, reade thine owne euill:	3114

EUN = 1
I am mightily abus'd; I should eu'n dye with pitty	2805

EXACT = 1
And in the most exact regard, support	778

EXALT = 1
In his owne grace he doth exalt himselfe, | More then in your addition.	3008

EXASPERATES = 1
Exasperates, makes mad her Sister *Gonerill*,	2907

EXCELLENT = 1*1
Bast. This is the excellent foppery of the world, that	447
Gentle, and low, an excellent thing in woman.	3237

EXCESSE = 1
So distribution should vndoo excesse,	2255

EXCHANGE = 3
And the exchange my Brother: heere, in the sands	2726
Bast. There's my exchange, what in the world hes	3045
Edg. Let's exchange charity:	3127

EXECUTING = 1
You Sulph'rous and Thought-executing Fires,	1659

EXECUTION = 1
Reuennew, Execution of the rest, | Beloued Sonnes be yours, which to confirme,	145

EXEUNT = 20*3
Come Noble *Burgundie. Flourish. Exeunt.*	291
Gon. We must do something, and i'th' heate. *Exeunt.*	332
*so, Ile write straight to my Sister to hold my course; pre-|pare for dinner. *Exeunt.*	527
Gon. Nay then---| *Alb.* Well, well, th'euent. *Exeunt*	871
Shall not be a Maid long, vnlesse things be cut shorter. | *Exeunt.*	924
Glo. I serue you Madam, | Your Graces are right welcome. *Exeunt. Flourish.*	1072
Or ere Ile weepe; O Foole, I shall go mad. *Exeunt.*	1586
*My *Regan* counsels well: come out oth'storme. *Exeunt.*	1613
That way, Ile this: He that first lights on him, | Holla the other. *Exeunt.*	1652
I smell the blood of a Brittish man. *Exeunt*	1968
Corn. I will lay trust vpon thee: and thou shalt finde | a deere Father in my loue. *Exeunt.*	1994
Giue thee quicke conduct. Come, come, away. *Exeunt*	2056
*Vntimely comes this hurt. Giue me your arme. *Exeunt.*	2176
Edg. Giue me thy arme; | Poore Tom shall leade thee. *Exeunt.*	2264
Tell me what more thou know'st. *Exeunt.*	2347
Soone may I heare, and see him. *Exeunt.*	2381
Reg. Fare thee well. *Exeunt*	2428

EXEUNT *cont.*

Come Father, Ile bestow you with a Friend. *Exeunt.*	2742
Pray you now forget, and forgiue,	I am old and foolish. *Exeunt*	2842
Gon. Oh ho, I know the Riddle, I will goe.	*Exeunt both the Armies.*	2878
Cordelia, and Souldiers, ouer the Stage, and Exeunt.	2919
Ripenesse is all come on.	*Glo.* And that's true too. *Exeunt.*	2935
Shall neuer see so much, nor liue so long.	*Exeunt with a dead March.*	
FINIS.	3301

EXHIBITION = 1

Confin'd to exhibition? All this done	360

EXIST = 1

From whom we do exist, and cease to be,	119

EXIT = 35*2

Glou. I shall, my Lord. *Exit.*	40
Hee'l shape his old course, in a Country new. *Exit.*	201
Fra. Come my faire *Cordelia. Exit France and Cor.*	309
*Kent banish'd; his offence, honesty. 'Tis strange. *Exit*	446
Edg. Shall I heare from you anon? *Exit.*	497
All with me's meete, that I can fashion fit. *Exit.*	504
Ste. So please you--- *Exit.*	576
To haue a thanklesse Childe. Away, away. *Exit.*	803
That Ile resume the shape which thou dost thinke	I haue cast off for	
euer. *Exit*	828
So the Foole followes after. *Exit*	841
Kent. I will not sleepe my Lord, till I haue deliuered	your Letter.	
Exit.	880
Fare you well Sir. *Exit.*	942
Fly Brother, Torches, Torches, so farewell.	*Exit Edgar.*	964
Corn. Come my Lord, away. *Exit.*	1227
Glo. The Duke's too blame in this,	'Twill be ill taken. *Exit.*	1235
That's something yet: *Edgar* I nothing am. *Exit.*	1272
Lear. Follow me not, stay here. *Exit.*	1332
Glo. I would haue all well betwixt you. *Exit.*	1396
Le. True Boy: Come bring vs to this Houell. *Exit.*	1733
*This prophecie *Merlin* shall make, for I liue before his	(time.	*Exit.*	1749
*my old Master must be relieued. There is strange things	toward	
Edmund, pray you be carefull. *Exit.*	1769
The yonger rises, when the old doth fall. *Exit.*	1775
In Boy, go first. You houselesse pouertie, *Exit.*	1807
*I will peece out the comfort with what addition I	can: I will not be	
long from you. *Exit*	1999
Gon. Farewell sweet Lord, and Sister. *Exit*	2081
Reg. Go thrust him out at gates, and let him smell	His way to Douer.	
Exit with Glouster.	2170
Come on't what will. *Exit*	2239
Bast. Yours in the rankes of death. *Exit.*	2293
You shall get it by running: Sa, sa, sa, sa. *Exit.*	2645
Her Army is mou'd on. *Exit.*	2661
When time shall serue, let but the Herald cry,	And Ile appeare againe.	
Exit.	2893
Alb. We will greet the time. *Exit.*	2901
Stands on me to defend, not to debate. *Exit.*	2916
Glo. Grace go with you Sir. *Exit.*	*Alarum and Retreat within.*	2925
Weele see 'em staru'd first: come. *Exit.*	2968
As I haue set it downe. *Exit Captaine.*	2981
Who can araigne me for't? *Exit.*	3117

EXPECTATION = 1
In expectation of them. O deere Father,   2376
EXPENCE = 1
To haue th'expence and wast of his Reuenues: 1039
EXPIRATION = 1
If till the expiration of your Moneth   1495
EXPLOIT = 1
And in the fleshment of this dead exploit, | Drew on me here againe.   1199
EXPOSE = 1
Expose thy selfe to feele what wretches feele,   1815
EXPRESSE = *1
*Lear. Meane time we shal expresse our darker purpose.   41
EXTEND = 1
That we, our largest bountie may extend   57
EXTREME = 1
You are now within a foote of th'extreme Verge: 2462
EXTREMES = 1
Twixt two extremes of passion, ioy and greefe, | Burst smilingly.   3161
EXTREMEST = 1
And from th'extremest vpward of thy head,   3091
EXTREMITIE = *1
*with thy vncouer'd body, this extremitie of the Skies. Is   1882
EYD = *1
*Reg. Thus out of season, thredding darke ey'd night,   1062
EYE see also eie = 6*2
A still soliciting eye, and such a tongue,   253
*and the Pin, squints the eye, and makes the Hare-lippe;   1897
*Ser. Oh I am slaine: my Lord, you haue one eye left   2156
Slaine by his Seruant, going to put out | The other eye of Glouster.   2314
Lost he his other eye? | Mes. Both, both, my Lord.   2326
And bring him to our eye. What can mans wisedome   2358
Are many Simples operatiue, whose power | Will close the eye of
Anguish.   2364
Gon. Hola, hola, | That eye that told you so, look'd but a squint.   3014
EYELESSE = 2
Turne out that eyelesse Villaine: throw this Slaue   2174
That eyelesse head of thine, was first fram'd flesh   2677
EYES see also eies = 23*8
Pierce euerie sense about thee. Old fond eyes,   820
*Foole. Why to keepe ones eyes of either side 's nose,   896
Take vantage heauie eyes, not to behold   1248
*noses, are led by their eyes, but blinde men, and there's   1342
Into her scornfull eyes: Infect her Beauty,   1449
Thee o're to harshnesse: Her eyes are fierce, but thine   1456
Gon. Plucke out his eyes.   2064
Plucke out his poore old eyes: nor thy fierce Sister,   2129
Vpon these eyes of thine, Ile set my foote.   2140
Glou. I haue no way, and therefore want no eyes: 2199
I'ld say I had eyes againe.   2205
Blesse thy sweete eyes, they bleede.   2244
Alb. Glousters eyes.   2316
Alb. Where was his Sonne, | When they did take his eyes?   2335
And to reuenge thine eyes. Come hither Friend,   2346
It was great ignorance, Glousters eyes being out   2394
Edg. Why then your other Senses grow imperfect | By your eyes
anguish.   2437
And dizie 'tis, to cast ones eyes so low,   2447

EYES *cont.*
  Glou. Alacke, I haue no eyes: 2502
  Edg. As I stood heere below, me thought his eyes   2514
  Do'st thou know me? | *Lear.* I remember thine eyes well enough: dost thou   2579
  Lear. Read. | *Glou.* What with the Case of eyes?   2587
  *head, nor no mony in your purse? Your eyes are in a hea-|uy   2590
  *goes, with no eyes. Looke with thine eares: See how   2595
  *glasse-eyes, and like a scuruy Politician, seeme to see the   2613
  Lear. If thou wilt weepe my Fortunes, take my eyes.   2618
  *To vse his eyes for Garden water-pots. I wil die brauely,   2640
  And fire vs hence, like Foxes: wipe thine eyes,   2965
  The darke and vitious place where thee he got, | Cost him his eyes.   3133
  Had I your tongues and eyes, Il'd vse them so,   3218
  Mine eyes are not o'th'best, Ile tell you straight.   3244
EYE-DISCERNING = 1
  Who hast not in thy browes an eye-discerning | Thine Honor, from thy suffering.   2306
EYE-SIGHT = 1
  Deerer then eye-sight, space, and libertie,   61
FA = 1
  *o'Bedlam. --- O these Eclipses do portend these diui-|sions. Fa, Sol, La, Me.   465
FACD = *1
  Kent. What a brazen-fac'd Varlet art thou, to deny   1101
FACE = 8*2
  That face of hers againe, therfore be gone,   289
  your face bids me, though you say nothing.   709
  *Crab: thou canst, tell why ones nose stands i'th'middle | on's face? | *Lear.* No.   893
  Brought neere to beast; my face Ile grime with filth,   1260
  And with presented nakednesse out-face   1262
  (Although as yet the face of it is couer'd   1629
  *them in the sweet face of Heauen. One, that slept in the   1869
  Alb. Oh *Gonerill,* | You are not worth the dust which the rude winde | Blowes in your face.   2301
  *Behold yond simpring Dame, whose face betweene her   2563
  Did challenge pitty of them. Was this a face   2782
FACES = 2
  I haue seene better faces in my Time,   1167
  Alb. Euen so: couer their faces.   3199
FAILE = 2
  Would faile her Obligation. If Sir perchance   1421
  My life will be too short, | And euery measure faile me.   2748
FAINE = 3*1
  *it were his: but in respect of that, I would faine thinke it | were not.   399
  Kent. No Sir, but you haue that in your countenance, | which I would faine call Master.   558
  thy Foole to lie, I would faine learne to lie.   693
  And was't thou faine (poore Father)   2786
FAINT = *1
  *I haue perceiued a most faint neglect of late,   597
FAINTLY = *1
  *you what I haue seene, and heard: But faintly. Nothing   495
FAINTS = 1
  Edg. He faints, my Lord, my Lord.   3284

FAIRE *see also* fayre = 8*1
  Remaine this ample third of our faire Kingdome,   86
  Is Queene of vs, of ours, and our faire *France*:   282
  Fra. Come my faire *Cordelia. Exit France and Cor.*   309
  Lear. Your name, faire Gentlewoman?   745
  *For there was neuer yet faire woman, but shee made | mouthes in a glasse.   1686
  This seemes a faire deseruing, and must draw me   1773
  Where am I? Faire day light?   2804
  This guilded Serpent: for your claime faire Sisters,   3029
  But since thy out-side lookes so faire and Warlike,   3098
FAIRES *see* fayres
FAIREST = 1
  Fra. Fairest *Cordelia*, that art most rich being poore,   275
FAIRIES *see* fayries
FAITH = 4
  Must be a faith that reason without miracle | Should neuer plant in me.   243
  Kent. Sir, in good faith, in sincere verity,   1180
  Reg. Faith he is poasted hence on serious matter: 2393
  Yes faith: I pray weepe not,   2828
FAITHD = 1
  Make thy words faith'd? No, what should I denie,   1007
FALL = 8
  Kent. Let it fall rather, though the forke inuade   153
  Fall into taint, which to beleeue of her   242
  All the stor'd Vengeances of Heauen, fall   1444
  *You Fen-suck'd Fogges, drawne by the powrfull Sunne, | To fall, and blister.   1450
  You owe me no subscription. Then let fall   1673
  The yonger rises, when the old doth fall. *Exit.*   1775
  If I could beare it longer, and not fall   2476
  Kent. Is this the promis'd end? | *Edg.* Or image of that horror. | *Alb.* Fall and cease.   3224
FALLEN = 2
  But now her price is fallen: Sir, there she stands,   215
  And am fallen out with my more headier will,   1386
FALLS = 1*1
  When Maiesty falls to folly, reserue thy state,   159
  *by the sequent effects. Loue cooles, friendship falls off,   436
FALNE = 1
  Glou. But haue I falne, or no? | *Edg.* From the dread Somnet of this Chalkie Bourne   2498
FALS = 1*1
  *prediction; there's Son against Father, the King fals from   440
  Preferment fals on him, that cuts him off.   2425
FALSE = 3*2
  *the Turke. False of heart, light of eare, bloody of hand;   1872
  Corn. True or false, it hath made thee Earle of Glou-|cester: 1987
  Corn. Cunning. | *Reg.* And false.   2118
  My selfe could else out-frowne false Fortunes frowne.   2946
  False to thy Gods, thy Brother, and thy Father,   3089
FAMILIAR = 1
  Reg. I neuer shall endure her, deere my Lord | Be not familiar with her.   2861
FANCIE = 2
  Each buz, each fancie, each complaint, dislike,   846
  May all the building in my fancie plucke | Vpon my hatefull life. Another way   2332

```
FANGS see phangs
FARE = 6*1
  *Kent. Fare thee well King, sith thus thou wilt appeare,      194
  Fare you well Sir. Exit.                                      942
  Conceiue, and fare thee well.                                2292
  I pray desire her call her wisedome to her. | So fare you well: 2422
  Reg. Fare thee well. Exeunt                                  2428
  Edg. Now fare ye well, good Sir. | Glou. With all my heart.  2469
  Now Fellow, fare thee well. | Edg. Gone Sir, farewell:       2480
FARES = 2
  Kent. How fares your Grace? | Lear. What's he?               1904
  Cor. How does my Royall Lord? | How fares your Maiesty?      2792
FARETHEE = *1
  *Alb. Why farethee well, I will o're-looke thy paper.        2895
FAREWELL = 8*2
  Bid them farewell Cordelia, though vnkinde,                  285
  So farewell to you both. | Regn. Prescribe not vs our dutie. 300
  Fly Brother, Torches, Torches, so farewell. | Exit Edgar.    964
  I will not trouble thee my Child; farewell:                  1513
  *Postes shall be swift, and intelligent betwixt vs. Fare-|well deere
  Sister, farewell my Lord of Glouster.                        2070
  Gon. Farewell sweet Lord, and Sister. Exit                   2081
  *Corn. Edmund farewell: go seek the Traitor Gloster,        2082
  Bid me farewell, and let me heare thee going.                2468
  Now Fellow, fare thee well. | Edg. Gone Sir, farewell:       2480
FARMERS = *1
  *the Iustice, which is the theefe: Thou hast seene a Far-|mers 2598
FARMES = 1
  And with this horrible obiect, from low Farmes,              1268
FARRE = 10
  Whose nature is so farre from doing harmes,                  500
  Alb. Well, you may feare too farre.                          849
  Gon. Safer then trust too farre;                             850
  Alb. How farre your eies may pierce I cannot tell;           869
  Glost. Let him fly farre:                                    993
  I will send farre and neere, that all the kingdome           1020
  Looke vp a height, the shrill-gorg'd Larke so farre          2500
  Farre off methinkes I heare the beaten Drumme.               2741
  Cor. Still, still, farre wide.                               2800
  Ere you had spoke so farre. He led our Powers,               3003
FARWELL = 1
  Fra. Bid farwell to your Sisters.                            292
FASHION = 2*1
  All with me's meete, that I can fashion fit. Exit.           504
  Is it the fashion, that discarded Fathers,                   1853
  *my hundred; only, I do not like the fashion of your gar-|ments. 2036
FAST = 2
  In three our Kingdome: and 'tis our fast intent,             43
  Corn. Binde fast his corky armes.                            2091
FASTNED = 1
  Glo. O strange and fastned Villaine, | Would he deny his Letter, said he? 1015
FATED = 1
  Hang fated o're mens faults, light on thy Daughters.         1849
FATHER = 43*14
  As much as Childe ere lou'd, or Father found.                64
  Lou'd as my Father, as my Master follow'd,                   150
  Bur. I am sorry then you haue so lost a Father,              270
```

FATHER *cont.*

Cor. The Iewels of our Father, with wash'd eies	293
Your faults as they are named. Loue well our Father:	296
I thinke our Father will hence to night.	312
*Father carry authority with such disposition as he beares,	329
this I may speake more. If our Father would sleepe till I wak'd	387
*declin'd, the Father should bee as Ward to the Son, and	407
*Sonne and Father. This villaine of mine comes ynder the	439
*prediction; there's Son against Father, the King fals from	440
*byas of Nature, there's Father against Childe. We haue	441
*My father compounded with my mother vnder the Dra- | gons	457
When saw you my Father last? | *Edg*. The night gone by.	474
A Credulous Father, and a Brother Noble,	499
Gon. Did my Father strike my Gentleman for chi- | ding of his Foole? |	
Ste. I Madam.	507
Sir, who am I Sir? | *Enter Steward*. | *Ste*. My Ladies Father.	607
Lear. My Ladies Father? my Lords knaue, you whor- | son dog, you	
slaue, you curre.	610
Lear. I will forget my Nature, so kind a Father? Be | my Horsses	
ready?	906
Cur. And you Sir, I haue bin | With your Father, and giuen him notice	929
My Father hath set guard to take my Brother,	945
My Father watches: O Sir, fly this place,	950
Bast. I heare my Father comming, pardon me:	959
Yeeld, come before my Father, light hoa, here,	963
Do more then this in sport; Father, Father,	968
The Child was bound to'th' Father; Sir in fine,	984
He whom my Father nam'd, your *Edgar*?	1031
That tended vpon my Father?	1034
Edmund, I heare that you haue shewne your Father | A Child-like	
Office.	1045
Our Father he hath writ, so hath our Sister,	1065
*the Royaltie of her Father: draw you Rogue, or	1110
The deere Father | *Would with his Daughter speake, commands, tends,	
ser- | (uice,	1377
Reg. I pray you Father being weake, seeme so.	1494
Against their Father, foole me not so much,	1575
That which my Father looses: no lesse then all,	1774
Your old kind Father, whose franke heart gaue all,	1800
No Father his Sonne deerer: true to tell thee,	1949
*seeke out where thy Father is, that hee may bee | ready for our	
apprehension.	1988
Corn. I will lay trust vpon thee: and thou shalt finde | a deere Father	
in my loue. *Exeunt*.	1994
*take vppon your Traitorous Father, are not fit for your	2067
But who comes heere? My Father poorely led? | World, World, O	
world!	2189
In expectation of them. O deere Father,	2376
It was some Fiend: Therefore thou happy Father,	2517
For Glousters bastard Son was kinder to his Father,	2560
Edg. Well pray you Father.	2666
Edg. Sit you downe Father: rest you.	2708
Come Father, Ile bestow you with a Friend. *Exeunt*.	2742
Th'vntun'd and iarring senses, O winde vp, | Of this childe-changed	
Father.	2765
Cor. O my deere Father, restauratian hang	2776
Cor. Had you not bin their Father, these white flakes	2781

FATHER *cont.*
And was't thou faine (poore Father)	2786
Edg. Heere Father, take the shadow of this Tree	2921
False to thy Gods, thy Brother, and thy Father,	3089
Let sorrow split my heart, if euer I | Did hate thee, or thy Father.	3139
How haue you knowne the miseries of your Father?	3143
Met I my Father with his bleeding Rings,	3152

FATHERS = 9*4
Her Fathers heart from her; call *France*, who stirres?	134
Our Fathers loue, is to the Bastard *Edmond*,	351
*it to be fit, that Sonnes at perfect age, and Fathers	406
Th'vntented woundings of a Fathers curse	819
Reg. What, did my Fathers Godsonne seeke your life?	1030
Kent. Why Madam, if I were your Fathers dog, | You should not vse me so.	1215
*Fathers that weare rags, do make their Children blind,	1323
*But Fathers that beare bags, shall see their children kind.	1324
Is it the fashion, that discarded Fathers,	1853
And your Fathers Tenant, these fourescore yeares.	2194
The food of thy abused Fathers wrath:	2203
But loue, deere loue, and our ag'd Fathers Rite:	2380
My name is *Edgar* and thy Fathers Sonne,	3130

FATHOM = *2
Edg. Fathom, and halfe, Fathom and halfe; poore *Tom*.	1819

FATHOME = 1
(So many fathome downe precipitating)	2492

FAULCHION = 1
I haue seene the day, with my good biting Faulchion	3241

FAULT = 6*1
Do you smell a fault?	19
Kent. I cannot wish the fault vndone, the issue of it, | being so proper.	20
You shall do well, the fault of it Ile answer.	517
By your allowance, which if you should, the fault	720
The worships of their name. O most small fault,	779
What is his fault? | *Kent.* His countenance likes me not.	1163
Neuer (O fault) reueal'd my selfe vnto him,	3155

FAULTS = 3
Your faults as they are named. Loue well our Father:	296
Who couers faults, at last with shame derides:	307
Hang fated o're mens faults, light on thy Daughters.	1849

FAUORD = *1
Lea. Those wicked Creatures yet do look wel fauor'd	1554

FAUOUR = 4*1
So many folds of fauour: sure her offence	239
That hath depriu'd me of your Grace and fauour,	251
Lear. Why my Boy? | *Foole.* Why? for taking ones part that's out of fauour,	628
Gon. This admiration Sir, is much o'th'fauour	746
Edg. But by your fauour: | How neere's the other Army?	2655

FAUOURS = 1
With Robbers hands, my hospitable fauours	2106

FAYRE = *1
*world before he was sent for: yet was his Mother fayre,	25

FAYRES = *1
*Do, de, de, de: sese: Come, march to Wakes and Fayres,	2031

FAYRIES = 1
Well worth a poore mans taking. Fayries, and Gods	2466

FEARD = 1
Be fear'd of doing harme, make your owne purpose,   1053
FEARE = 11*2
   To wage against thine enemies, nere feare to loose it, | Thy safety being
motiue.   167
*Edm. That's my feare, I pray you haue a continent   487
*feare iudgement, to fight when I cannot choose, and to | eate no fish.   547
Alb. Well, you may feare too farre.   849
Let me still take away the harmes I feare,   851
Not feare still to be taken. I know his heart,   852
Informe her full of my particular feare,   861
To haue his eare abus'd, wisedome bids feare.   1611
(As feare not but you shall) shew her this Ring,   1644
Remember to haue heard. Mans Nature cannot carry | Th'affliction, nor
the feare.   1700
Stands still in esperance, liues not in feare: 2182
And to deale plainely, | I feare I am not in my perfect mind.   2817
Bast. Feare not, she and the Duke her husband.   2863
FEAREFULL = 2
To haue found a safe redresse, but now grow fearefull   717
Heere's the place: stand still: how fearefull   2446
FEARES = *1
*thus giues way to Loyaltie, something feares mee to | thinke of.   1973
FEARFULLY = 1
Lookes fearfully in the confined Deepe: 2259
FEATHER = 1
Lear. This feather stirs, she liues: if it be so,   3227
FEATHERS = 1
Edg. Had'st thou beene ought | But Gozemore, Feathers, Ayre,   2490
FED = *1
*fed the Cuckoo so long, that it's had it head bit off by it   727
FEE = 1
Kent. Kill thy Physition, and thy fee bestow   177
FEELE = 9*1
*he hath writ this to feele my affection to your Honor, &   420
To laughter, and contempt: That she may feele,   801
Expose thy selfe to feele what wretches feele,   1815
Because he do's not feele, feele your powre quickly: 2254
That dares not vndertake: Hee'l not feele wrongs   2281
Vp, so: How is't? Feele you your Legges? You stand. | Glou. Too well,
too well.   2508
I feele this pin pricke, would I were assur'd | Of my condition.   2808
Speake what we feele, not what we ought to say: 3299
FEELING = 3
Doth from my sences take all feeling else,   1793
Who, by the Art of knowne, and feeling sorrowes,   2669
How stiffe is my vilde sense | That I stand vp, and haue ingenious
feeling   2733
FEELINGLY = 1
Glou. I see it feelingly.   2593
FEET = 1
That going shalbe vs'd with feet.   1748
FELICITATE = 1
And finde I am alone felicitate | In your deere Highnesse loue.   80
FELL = 4
To his vnnaturall purpose, in fell motion   986
Glost. How fell you out, say that?   1159

FELL *cont*.
    Which thou hast perpendicularly fell,   2496
    The good yeares shall deuoure them, flesh and fell,   2966
FELLD = 1
    Flew on him, and among'st them fell'd him dead,   2320
FELLOW = 19*8
    Lear. What art thou? | *Kent*. A very honest hearted Fellow, and as
    poore as | the King.   549
    Lear. Do'st thou know me fellow?   557
    Lear. What saies the Fellow there? Call the Clot-|pole   577
    Lear. I thanke thee fellow. | Thou seru'st me, and Ile loue thee.   617
    *colde shortly, there take my Coxcombe; why this fellow   631
    Foole. Thou wast a pretty fellow when thou hadst no   705
    Kent. Fellow I know thee.   1086
    Stew. Why, what a monstrous Fellow art thou, thus   1098
    Cor. Thou art a strange fellow, a Taylor make a man?   1130
    Corn. What art thou mad old Fellow?   1158
    Corn. This is some Fellow,   1170
    Cor. This is a Fellow of the selfe same colour,   1218
    Being the very fellow which of late   1316
    And she will tell you who that Fellow is   1645
    I am cold my selfe. Where is this straw, my Fellow?   1724
    Glou. In fellow there, into th'Houel; keep thee warm.   1955
    Let him take the Fellow.   1961
    Oldm. Fellow, where goest?   2212
    I'th'last nights storme, I such a fellow saw;   2216
    Glou. Is that the naked Fellow? | *Oldm*. I, my Lord.   2226
    Glou. Sirrah, naked fellow.   2240
    Glou. Come hither fellow. | *Edg*. And yet I must: 2242
    Now Fellow, fare thee well. | *Edg*. Gone Sir, farewell: 2480
    *Presse-money. That fellow handles his bow, like a Crow-|keeper: 2534
    Alb. Halfe-blooded fellow, yes.   3025
    Lear. Did I not fellow?   3240
    Lear. He's a good fellow, I can tell you that,   3250
FELLOWES = 1*3
    Glou. Sir, this yong Fellowes mother could; where-|vpon   16
    You and your Fellowes: I'de haue it come to question;   520
    *you: what growes of it no matter, aduise your fellowes   526
    Corn. See't shalt thou neuer. Fellowes hold y Chaire,   2139
FELT = 3
    The lesser is scarce felt. Thou'dst shun a Beare,   1789
    It were a delicate stratagem to shoo | A Troope of Horse with Felt: Ile
    put't in proofe,   2626
    It is a chance which do's redeeme all sorrowes | That euer I haue felt.   3228
FENDED = 1
    Reg. But haue you neuer found my Brothers way, | To the fore-fended
    place?   2858
FENITAR = 1
    Crown'd with ranke Fenitar, and furrow weeds,   2353
FEN-SUCKD = *1
    *You Fen-suck'd Fogges, drawne by the powrfull Sunne, | To fall, and
    blister.   1450
FESTINATE = *1
    *most festinate preparation: we are bound to the like. Our   2069
FETCH = 3
    Corn. Fetch forth the Stocks?   1203
    Corn. Fetch forth the Stocks;   1212

FETCH *cont.*
   Fetch me a better answer.   1365
FETCHES = 1
   They haue trauail'd all the night? meere fetches,   1363
FEW = 1
   Kent. Few words, but to effect more then all yet;   1650
FIE *see also* fye = 2*2
   You taking Ayres, with Lamenesse. | *Corn.* Fye sir, fie.   1446
   His word was still, fie, foh, and fumme,   1967
   *consumption: Fye, fie, fie; pah, pah: Giue me an Ounce   2571
FIELD = 2*1
   When Vsurers tell their Gold i'th'Field,   1744
   *night to swimme in. Now a little fire in a wilde Field,   1892
   Search euery Acre in the high-growne field,   2357
FIEND = 7*8
   Ingratitude! thou Marble-hearted Fiend,   771
   Edg. Away, the foule Fiend followes me, through the   1827
   *the foule fiend hath led through Fire, and through Flame,   1833
   *do poore *Tom* some charitie, whom the foule Fiend   1841
   Edgar. Take heed o'th'foule Fiend, obey thy Pa-|rents,   1860
   *foule Fiend. Still through the Hauthorne blowes the   1878
   *in the furie of his heart, when the foule Fiend rages, eats   1910
   *Beware my Follower. Peace Smulkin, peace thou Fiend.   1919
   What is your study? | *Edg.* How to preuent the Fiend, and to kill
   Vermine.   1937
   *in the Lake of Darknesse: pray Innocent, and beware | the foule Fiend.   2005
   thee good mans sonne, from the foule Fiend.   2248
   Proper deformitie seemes not in the Fiend | So horrid as in woman.   2309
   It was some Fiend: Therefore thou happy Father,   2517
   The Fiend, the Fiend, he led me to that place.   2524
FIENDS = *1
   *beneath is all the Fiends. There's hell, there's darke-|nes,   2569
FIERCE = 4
   Who in the lustie stealth of Nature, take | More composition, and fierce
   qualitie,   345
   Of my more fierce endeauour. I haue seene drunkards   967
   Thee o're to harshnesse: Her eyes are fierce, but thine   1456
   Plucke out his poore old eyes: nor thy fierce Sister,   2129
FIERY = 4
   Glo. My deere Lord, | You know the fiery quality of the Duke,   1366
   Fiery? What quality? Why *Gloster, Gloster,*   1371
.   Fiery? The fiery Duke, tell the hot Duke that---   1380
FIFTIE = 1
   Lear. What fiftie of my Followers at a clap? | Within a fortnight?   810
FIFTY = 3
   Lear. Returne to her? and fifty men dismiss'd?   1500
   Reg. I dare auouch it Sir, what fifty Followers?   1533
   Thy fifty yet doth double fiue and twenty,   1557
FIGHT = 1*1
   *feare iudgement, to fight when I cannot choose, and to | eate no fish.   547
   Edg. Before you fight the Battaile, ope this Letter: 2884
FIGHTS = 1
   Alb. Saue him, saue him. *Alarums. Fights.*   3107
FIGURE = *1
   *a figure, I am better then thou art now, I am a Foole,   707
FILLIALL = 1
   Saue what beates there, Filliall ingratitude,   1794

FILTH = 1
Brought neere to beast; my face Ile grime with filth,   1260
FILTHY = 1*1
*pound, filthy woosted-stocking knaue, a Lilly-liuered,   1090
Reg. Hard, hard: O filthy Traitor.   2096
FIND = 3*1
as I shall find meanes, and acquaint you withall.   432
*to our Graues. Find out this Villain, *Edmond*, it shall lose   444
So may it come, thy Master whom thou lou'st, | Shall find thee full of
labours.   536
As we shall find their merites, and our safety | May equally determine.   2987
FINDE = 8*4
I finde she names my very deede of loue: 76
And finde I am alone felicitate | In your deere Highnesse loue.   80
Thou loosest here a better where to finde.   286
*much as I haue perus'd, I finde it not fit for your ore-loo-|king.   373
*vs, *till our oldnesse cannot rellish them. I begin to finde an idle*   384
Shee'l flea thy Woluish visage. Thou shalt finde,   827
Of my obscured course. And shall finde time   1245
Finde out their enemies now. Tremble thou Wretch,   1704
Bast. If I finde him comforting the King, it will stuffe   1990
Corn. I will lay trust vpon thee: and thou shalt finde | a deere Father
in my loue. *Exeunt.*   1994
Corn. To this Chaire binde him, | Villaine, thou shalt finde.   2098
If you do finde him, pray you giue him this;   2420
FINDES = 2
this, let him be whipt that first findes it so.   679
All's not offence that indiscretion findes, | And dotage termes so.   1486
FINDS = 1*1
*reason it thus, and thus, yet Nature finds it selfe scourg'd   435
That he which finds him shall deserue our thankes,   998
FINDST = 1
And giue the Letters which thou find'st about me,   2701
FINE = 2
As to th'legitimate: fine word: Legitimate.   352
The Child was bound to'th' Father; Sir in fine,   984
FINICALL = *1
*finicall Rogue, one Trunke-inheriting slaue, one that   1092
FINIS *l*.3303 = 1
FIRE = 10*4
*whipt out, when the Lady Brach may stand by'th'fire | and stinke.   642
Being oile to fire, snow to the colder moodes,   1150
Whose influence like the wreath of radient fire | On flickring *Phoebus*
front.   1182
Lear. Rumble thy belly full: spit Fire, spowt Raine: 1669
Nor Raine, Winde, Thunder, Fire are my Daughters;   1670
Such sheets of Fire, such bursts of horrid Thunder,   1698
*the foule fiend hath led through Fire, and through Flame,   1833
*night to swimme in. Now a little fire in a wilde Field,   1892
on's body, cold: Looke, heere comes a walking fire.   1894
And bring you where both fire, and food is ready.   1931
Should haue stood that night against my fire,   2785
Vpon a wheele of fire, that mine owne teares | Do scal'd, like molten
Lead.   2796
And fire vs hence, like Foxes: wipe thine eyes,   2965
Despise thy victor-Sword, and fire new Fortune,   3087

FIRES = 2
You Sulph'rous and Thought-executing Fires,   1659
And quench'd the Stelled fires: 2133
FIRMAMENT = *1
*haue bin that I am, had the maidenlest Starre in the Fir-|mament
twinkled on my bastardizing.   460
FIRME = 1
Lear. Nothing, I haue sworne, I am firme.   269
FIRMELY = 1
On him, on you, who not, I will maintaine | My truth and honor
firmely.   3048
FIRST = 15*1
Our eldest borne, speake first.   59
Lear. My Lord of *Burgundie*, | We first addresse toward you, who with
this King   205
this, let him be whipt that first findes it so.   679
Nature's of such deepe trust, we shall much need: | You we first seize
on.   1057
That way, Ile this: He that first lights on him, | Holla the other. *Exeunt.* 1652
In Boy, go first. You houselesse pouertie, *Exit.*   1807
*Curfew, and walkes at first Cocke: Hee giues the Web 1896
Lear. First let me talke with this Philosopher,   1932
Glou. O let me kisse that hand. | *Lear*. Let me wipe it first, 2574
Thou know'st, the first time that we smell the Ayre 2621
That eyelesse head of thine, was first fram'd flesh 2677
Vntill their greater pleasures first be knowne | That are to censure them. 2941
Cor. We are not the first, | Who with best meaning haue incurr'd the
worst: 2943
Weele see 'em staru'd first: come. *Exit.*   2968
I ask'd his blessing, and from first to last   3158
Kent. That from your first of difference and decay, | Haue follow'd your
sad steps.   3254
FISH = 1
*feare iudgement, to fight when I cannot choose, and to | eate no fish. 547
FISHERMEN = 1
The Fishermen, that walk'd vpon the beach   2452
FIT = 7*4
I returne those duties backe as are right fit,   104
*much as I haue perus'd, I finde it not fit for your ore-loo-|king. 373
*it to be fit, that Sonnes at perfect age, and Fathers 406
All with me's meete, that I can fashion fit. *Exit.*   504
*bluntly: that which ordinary men are fit for, I am qual-|lified in, and
the best of me, is Dilligence.   565
Of differences, which I best thought it fit   1066
To take the indispos'd and sickly fit,   1387
For your fit welcome, giue eare Sir to my Sister, 1528
Must make content with his Fortunes fit,   1731
*take vppon your Traitorous Father, are not fit for your 2067
Bast. Sir, I thought it fit, | To send the old and miserable King to some
retention,   2989
FITCHEW = *1
*the head to heare of pleasures name. The Fitchew, nor 2565
FITLY = 1*1
And nothing more may fitly like your Grace,   218
*fitly bring you to heare my Lord speake: pray ye goe, 490
FITTEST = 1
Gen. Madam do you, 'tis fittest.   2791

FIUE = 8*1
Fiue dayes we do allot thee for prouision,   187
To bring but fiue and twentie, to no more | Will I giue place or notice.   1545
With fiue and twenty? *Regan*, said you so?   1552
Thy fifty yet doth double fiue and twenty,   1557
Gon. Heare me my Lord; | What need you fiue and twenty? Ten? Or
fiue?   1559
*Blisse thy fiue Wits, *Tom*s a cold. O do, de, do, de, do, de,   1839
Edg. Blesse thy fiue wits.   2015
Some fiue or six and thirty of his Knights   2075
FIXT = 3
From the fixt place: drew from my heart all loue,   782
How vnremoueable and fixt he is | In his owne course.   1368
But where the greater malady is fixt,   1788
FLAKES = *1
Cor. Had you not bin their Father, these white flakes   2781
FLAME = *1
*the foule fiend hath led through Fire, and through Flame,   1833
FLAMES = *1
Le. You nimble Lightnings, dart your blinding flames   1448
FLASHES = 1
He flashes into one grosse crime, or other,   511
FLAT = 1
Strike flat the thicke Rotundity o'th'world,   1662
FLATTER = 1
Quite from his Nature. He cannot flatter he,   1173
FLATTERD = 1*1
Then still contemn'd and flatter'd, to be worst: 2180
Lear. Ha! *Gonerill* with a white beard? They flatter'd   2543
FLATTERER = *1
*so much; I know Sir, I am no flatterer, he that be-|guild   1186
FLATTERING = 1
When he compact, and flattering his displeasure   1194
FLATTERY = 1
Think'st thou that dutie shall haue dread to speake, | When power to
flattery bowes?   156
FLAWD = 1
Told him our pilgrimage. But his flaw'd heart   3159
FLAWES = *1
*But this heart shal break into a hundred thousand flawes   1585
FLEA = 1
Shee'l flea thy Woluish visage. Thou shalt finde,   827
FLED = 2*1
Bast. Fled this way Sir, when by no meanes he could.   978
Or whether gasted by the noyse I made, | Full sodainely he fled.   991
Dogs leapt the hatch, and all are fled.   2030
FLESH = 8*1
Ile flesh ye, come on yong Master.   1120
But yet thou art my flesh, my blood, my Daughter,   1515
Or rather a disease that's in my flesh,   1516
Should haue thus little mercy on their flesh: 1854
Iudicious punishment, 'twas this flesh begot | Those Pelicane Daughters.   1855
Glou. Our flesh and blood, my Lord, is growne so | vilde, that it doth
hate what gets it.   1923
In his Annointed flesh, sticke boarish phangs.   2130
That eyelesse head of thine, was first fram'd flesh   2677
The good yeares shall deuoure them, flesh and fell,   2966

FLESHMENT = 1
And in the fleshment of this dead exploit, | Drew on me here againe.   1199
FLEW = 1
Flew on him, and among'st them fell'd him dead,   2320
FLIBBERTIGIBBET = *1
*Edg. This is the foule Flibbertigibbet; hee begins at   1895
FLICKRING = 1
Whose influence like the wreath of radient fire | On flickring *Phoebus*
front.   1182
FLIE = 1
And let the wiseman flie: 1355
FLIES = 1
As Flies to wanton Boyes, are we to th'Gods, | They kill vs for their
sport.   2221
FLIGHT = 1
But if thy flight lay toward the roaring sea,   1790
FLOURISH = 4
Flourish. Enter Gloster with France, and Bur-|gundy, Attendants.   202
Come Noble *Burgundie. Flourish. Exeunt.*   291
Glo. I serue you Madam, | Your Graces are right welcome. *Exeunt.
Flourish.*   1072
Flourish. Enter Albany, Gonerill, Regan, Soldiers.   2982
FLOW = 1
In a wall'd prison, packs and sects of great ones, | That ebbe and flow
by th'Moone.   2958
FLOWING = 1
From a full flowing stomack. Generall,   3017
FLOWNE = *1
*Bring vp the browne Billes. O well flowne Bird: i'th'   2538
FLOWRES = *1
*With Hardokes, Hemlocke, Nettles, Cuckoo flowres,   2354
FLY *see also* flie = 4*1
My Father watches: O Sir, fly this place,   950
Fly Brother, Torches, Torches, so farewell. | *Exit Edgar*.   964
Glost. Let him fly farre: 993
Foole. Winters not gon yet, if the wil'd Geese fly that | (way,   1322
No, the Wren goes too't, and the small gilded Fly   2558
FLYING = 1
The images of reuolt and flying off.   1364
FOES = 1
Taste the wages of their vertue, and all Foes   3275
FOGGES = 1*1
Blastes and Fogges vpon thee: 818
*You Fen-suck'd Fogges, drawne by the powrfull Sunne, | To fall, and
blister.   1450
FOH = 1
His word was still, fie, foh, and fumme,   1967
FOINES *see* foynes
FOLD = 1
He met the Night-Mare, and her nine-fold;   1901
FOLDS = 1
So many folds of fauour: sure her offence   239
FOLKE *see* volke
FOLLIES = 1
Glou. O my Follies! then *Edgar* was abus'd,   2168
FOLLOW = 8*5
*treacherie, and all ruinous disorders follow vs disquietly   443

FOLLOW *cont.*

other day, what should follow these Eclipses.	470
Lear. Follow me, thou shalt serue me, if I like thee no	571
*blessing against his will, if thou follow him, thou must	633
Commanded me to follow, and attend	1312
Lear. Follow me not, stay here. *Exit*.	1332
*thee ther's no labouring i'th' winter. All that follow their	1341

*againe, I would haue none but knaues follow it, since a | Foole giues
it. 1348

To follow in a house, where twice so many | Haue a command to tend
you? 1561

And follow me, that will to some prouision	2055
Corn. I haue receiu'd a hurt: Follow me Lady;	2173

Stew. Would I could meet Madam, I should shew | What party I do
follow. 2426

Take thou this note, go follow them to prison,	2970

FOLLOWD = 3

Lou'd as my Father, as my Master follow'd,	150
That follow'd me so neere, (O our liues sweetnesse,	3147

Kent. That from your first of difference and decay, | Haue follow'd your
sad steps. 3254

FOLLOWED = 2

But kept a reseruation to be followed	1550
Corn. Followed the old man forth, he is return'd.	1597

FOLLOWER = 1*1

Reg. For his particular, Ile receiue him gladly,	But not one follower.	1592
*Beware my Follower. Peace Smulkin, peace thou Fiend.	1919

FOLLOWERS = 2

Lear. What fiftie of my Followers at a clap?	Within a fortnight?	810
Reg. I dare auouch it Sir, what fifty Followers?	1533

FOLLOWES = 3*2

*that it followes, I am rough and Leacherous. I should	459
So the Foole followes after. *Exit*	841
And followes but for forme;	1351
Dwels in the sickly grace of her he followes.	1473
Edg. Away, the foule Fiend followes me, through the	1827

FOLLOWING = 2*1

Vpon our kingdome: if on the tenth day following,	190
Knowing naught (like dogges) but following:	1153
*hill, least it breake thy necke with following. But the	1345

FOLLOWRES = 1

She haue restrained the Riots of your Followres,	1422

FOLLY = 3

When Maiesty falls to folly, reserue thy state,	159
Beate at this gate that let thy Folly in,	784
And must needs taste his folly.	1591

FOND = 2*1

and fond bondage, in the oppression of aged tyranny, who swayes	385
Pierce euerie sense about thee. Old fond eyes,	820
I am a very foolish fond old man,	2814

FOOD = 5

That you'l vouchsafe me Rayment, Bed, and Food.	1437
For lifting food too't? But I will punish home;	1796
Haue bin Toms food, for seuen long yeare:	1918
And bring you where both fire, and food is ready.	1931
The food of thy abused Fathers wrath:	2203

FOOL = *3
FOOLE see also Fool. = 37*10

Gon. Did my Father strike my Gentleman for chi- | ding of his Foole? |	
Ste. I Madam.	507
*ho, dinner, where's my knaue? my Foole? Go you and call	573
*my Foole hither. You you Sirrah, where's my Daughter?	574
*backe: wher's my Foole? Ho, I thinke the world's	578
*I will looke further intoo't: but where's my Foole? I | haue not seene	
him this two daies.	600
Sir, the Foole hath much pined away.	603
*call hither my Foole; Oh you Sir, you, come you hither	606
Enter Foole.	624
Kent. This is nothing Foole.	658
comes to, he will not beleeue a Foole.	665
Lear. A bitter Foole.	666
Foole. Do'st thou know the difference my Boy, be- | tweene a bitter	
Foole, and a sweet one.	667
That such a King should play bo-peepe, | And goe the Foole among.	690
thy Foole to lie, I would faine learne to lie.	693
*my peace. I had rather be any kind o'thing then a foole,	698
*a figure, I am better then thou art now, I am a Foole,	707
Gon. Not only Sir this, your all-lycenc'd Foole,	712
You Sir, more Knaue then Foole, after your Master.	834
Tarry, take the Foole with thee:	836
So the Foole followes after. *Exit*	841
Enter Lear, Kent, Gentleman, and Foole.	874
Foole. Yes indeed, thou would'st make a good Foole.	911
Foole. If thou wert my Foole Nunckle, Il'd haue thee	913
Smoile you my speeches, as I were a Foole?	1155
Kent. None of these Rogues, and Cowards | But *Aiax* is there Foole.	1201
Enter Lear, Foole, and Gentleman.	1273
question, thoud'st well deseru'd it. | *Kent.* Why Foole?	1338
*againe, I would haue none but knaues follow it, since a | Foole giues	
it.	1348
But I will tarry, the Foole will stay,	1354
The knaue turnes Foole that runnes away,	1356
The Foole no knaue perdie.	1357
Kent. Where learn'd you this Foole? | *Foole.* Not i'th' Stocks Foole.	1359
Against their Father, foole me not so much,	1575
Or ere Ile weepe; O Foole, I shall go mad. *Exeunt.*	1586
Gent. None but the Foole, who labours to out-iest | His heart-strooke	
iniuries.	1624
Storme still. Enter Lear, and Foole.	1655
Kent. Who's there? | *Foole.* Marry here's Grace, and a Codpiece, that's	
a | Wiseman, and a Foole.	1691
Poore Foole, and Knaue, I haue one part in my heart | That's sorry yet	
for thee.	1727
Enter Lear, Kent, and Foole.	1777
Enter Edgar, and Foole.	1818
Enter Lear, Edgar, and Foole.	2003
Bad is the Trade that must play Foole to sorrow,	2224
To thee a Womans seruices are due, | My Foole vsurpes my body.	2296
Gon. Oh vaine Foole.	2311
The Naturall Foole of Fortune. Vse me well,	2634
Lear. And my poore Foole is hang'd: no, no, no life?	3277

FOOLE = 11*37

FOOLES = 3*2
*Fooles by heauenly compulsion, Knaues, Theeues, and 451
Fooles had nere lesse grace in a yeere, 680
*in, aske thy Daughters blessing, heere's a night pitties | neither
Wisemen, nor Fooles. 1667
*Foole. This cold night will turne vs all to Fooles, and | Madmen. 1858
To this great stage of Fooles. This a good blocke: 2625
FOOLISH = 3
That he suspects none: on whose foolish honestie 501
I am a very foolish fond old man, 2814
Pray you now forget, and forgiue, | I am old and foolish. *Exeunt* 2842
FOOT = 1
Gent. Neere, and on speedy foot: the maine descry | Stands on the
hourely thought. 2657
FOOTE = 4*1
To keepe base life a foote; returne with her? 1508
*Keepe thy foote out of Brothels, thy hand out of 1876
Vpon these eyes of thine, Ile set my foote. 2140
You are now within a foote of th'extreme Verge: 2462
To the discent and dust below thy foote, 3092
FOOTED = 2*1
*a Power already footed, we must incline to the King, I 1764
Swithold footed thrice the old, 1900
Corn. And what confederacie haue you with the Trai-|tors, late footed
in the Kingdome? 2111
FOOT-BALL = 1
Kent. Nor tript neither, you base Foot-ball plaier. 616
FOOT-PATH = *1
Edg. Both style, and gate; Horseway, and foot-path: 2246
FOPPERY = *1
Bast. This is the excellent foppery of the world, that 447
FOPPISH = 1
For wisemen are growne foppish, 681
FOPS = 1
Goe to th'creating a whole tribe of Fops 348
FOR *see also* for't, vor *l.**9 *18 *25 116 123 187 207 *227 228 246 252 287
339 356 *372 *373 *380 *388 *419 *507 529 534 *539 *552 *565 *568
*569 *594 *629 681 *686 688 689 *696 *697 *706 *726 756 829 867 868
*889 914 *935 1054 1060 1082 1084 1087 *1104 1171 *1188 1198 1207
*1228 1230 *1326 *1337 1350 1351 1388 1411 1499 1527 1528 1529 1544
1570 1592 1604 1641 *1686 1728 *1749 1757 *1767 *1768 1780 1796
*1838 *1911 1918 1989 *2011 2029 *2035 *2067 2080 2110 2222 2228
2230 2231 2305 2345 2369 2418 2419 2455 2463 2523 *2530 2557 2560
2562 2573 *2605 *2640 2722 2730 2820 2824 2829 2830 2871 2886 2910
2912 2915 2922 2945 3029 3052 *3078 3104 3106 3154 3167 3197 3200
3202 3210 3219 3234 3270 = 95*46
FORBEARANCE = *1
*forbearance till the speed of his rage goes slower: and as 488
FORBEARE = 2*1
Lear. O Vassall! Miscreant. | *Alb. Cor.* Deare Sir forbeare. 175
*him: and at my entreaty forbeare his presence, vntill 482
To suffer with the body; Ile forbeare, 1385
FORBID = 2
Bast. This Curtesie forbid thee, shall the Duke 1771
Alb. Stay till I haue read the Letter. | *Edg.* I was forbid it: 2891
FORCD = 1
With others, whom the rigour of our State | Forc'd to cry out. 2867

FORCE = 1
Deny'd me to come in) returne, and force | Their scanted curtesie.   1720
FORCES = 1
Heere is the guesse of their true strength and Forces,   2898
FOREUER *see* euer
FORE-DONE = 1
Your eldest Daughters haue fore-done themselues,   3259
FORE-FENDED = 1
Reg. But haue you neuer found my Brothers way, | To the fore-fended
place?   2858
FORE-VOUCHT = 1
That monsters it: Or your fore-voucht affection   241
FORGET = 1*1
Lear. I will forget my Nature, so kind a Father? Be | my Horsses
ready?   906
Pray you now forget, and forgiue, | I am old and foolish. *Exeunt*   2842
FORGIUE = 3
Kinde Gods, forgiue me that, and prosper him.   2169
Pray you now forget, and forgiue, | I am old and foolish. *Exeunt*   2842
That hast this Fortune on me? If thou'rt Noble, | I do forgiue thee.   3125
FORGIUENESSE = 2
Lear. Aske her forgiuenesse?   1433
And aske of thee forgiuenesse: So wee'l liue,   2951
FORGOT = 2
Thy halfe o'th'Kingdome hast thou not forgot, | Wherein I thee
endow'd.   1464
Is he not here? | *Alb.* Great thing of vs forgot,   3191
FORKE = 1
Kent. Let it fall rather, though the forke inuade   153
FORKED = *1
*man, is no more but such a poore, bare, forked A- | nimall   1887
FORKES = *1
*Forkes presages Snow; that minces Vertue, & do's shake   2564
FORLORNE = 1
To houell thee with Swine and Rogues forlorne,   2787
FORME = 2
And followes but for forme;   1351
Without the forme of Iustice: yet our power   2085
FORMER = 1
If you come slacke of former seruices,   516
FORRESTS = 1
With shadowie Forrests, and with Champains rich'd   69
FORSAKEN = 1
Most choise forsaken, and most lou'd despis'd,   276
FORSOOTH = *1
*thou art nothing. Yes forsooth I will hold my tongue, so   708
FORT = 1*1
*you gaue me nothing for't, can you make no vse of no- | thing Nuncle?   660
Who can araigne me for't? *Exit.*   3117
FORTH = 11
Do hourely Carpe and Quarrell, breaking forth   714
Corn. Fetch forth the Stocks?   1203
Corn. Fetch forth the Stocks;   1212
Stew'd in his haste, halfe breathlesse, painting forth   1307
Is practise only. Giue me my Seruant forth;   1391
Now, presently: bid them come forth and heare me,   1393
Corn. Followed the old man forth, he is return'd.   1597

FORTH *cont*.
    Kent. What art thou that dost grumble there i'th' | straw? Come forth.   1825
In our sustaining Corne. A Centery send forth;   2356
    Reg. But are my Brothers Powres set forth? | *Stew*. I Madam.   2384
    Reg. Our troopes set forth to morrow, stay with vs: | The wayes are
    dangerous.   2401
FORTNIGHT *see also* vortnight = 1
    Lear. What fiftie of my Followers at a clap? | Within a fortnight?   810
FORTUNATELY = 1
    Who hath most fortunately beene inform'd   1244
FORTUNE = 11*3
    *when we are sicke in fortune, often the surfets of our own   448
Which I must act, Briefenesse, and Fortune worke.   947
A good mans fortune may grow out at heeles: 1233
This shamefull lodging. Fortune goodnight,   1249
*Fortune that arrant whore, nere turns the key toth' poore.   1325
Bast. How malicious is my fortune, that I must re- | pent   1979
The lowest, and most deiected thing of Fortune,   2181
The Naturall Foole of Fortune. Vse me well,   2634
Least that th'infection of his fortune take   2685
And machination ceases. Fortune loues you.   2890
And Fortune led you well: you haue the Captiues   2984
Despise thy victor-Sword, and fire new Fortune,   3087
That hast this Fortune on me? If thou'rt Noble, | I do forgiue thee.   3125
    Kent. If Fortune brag of two, she lou'd and hated, | One of them we
    behold.   3245
FORTUNES = 7*3
    ‣Least you may marre your Fortunes.   101
Since that respect and Fortunes are his loue,   273
At Fortunes almes, you haue obedience scanted,   304
world bitter to the best of our times: keepes our Fortunes from   383
Must make content with his Fortunes fit,   1731
Lear. If thou wilt weepe my Fortunes, take my eyes.   2618
Edg. A most poore man, made tame to Fortunes blows   2668
To raise my fortunes. Thou old, vnhappy Traitor,   2678
My selfe could else out-frowne false Fortunes frowne.   2946
To Noble Fortunes: know thou this, that men   2973
FORTY = 1
    *nor so old to dote on her for any thing. I haue yeares on | my backe
    forty eight.   569
FOR-DID = 1
    To lay the blame vpon her owne dispaire, | That she for-did her selfe.   3213
FOSTER = 1
    Our foster Nurse of Nature, is repose,   2362
FOULE = 6*7
    Vpon the foule disease, reuoke thy guift,   178
    Kent. Who's there besides foule weather?   1616
So old, and white as this. O, ho! 'tis foule.   1679
Edg. Away, the foule Fiend followes me, through the   1827
*the foule fiend hath led through Fire, and through Flame,   1833
*do poore *Tom* some charitie, whom the foule Fiend   1841
Edgar. Take heed o'th'foule Fiend, obey thy Pa- | rents,   1860
*foule Fiend. Still through the Hauthorne blowes the   1878
Edg. This is the foule Flibbertigibbet; hee begins at   1895
*in the furie of his heart, when the foule Fiend rages, eats   1910
*in the Lake of Darknesse: pray Innocent, and beware | the foule Fiend.   2005
Do me no foule play, Friends. | *Corn*. Binde him I say.   2094

FOULE *cont*.
thee good mans sonne, from the foule Fiend. 2248
FOULENESSE = 1
It is no vicious blot, murther, or foulenesse, 249
FOUND = 7*4
As much as Childe ere lou'd, or Father found. 64
Thy banisht trunke be found in our Dominions, 191
*cunning of it. I found it throwne in at the Casement of | my Closset. 395
*Bast. Parted you in good termes? Found you no dis-|pleasure in him,
by word, nor countenance? 478
To haue found a safe redresse, but now grow fearefull 717
And found; dispatch, the Noble Duke my Master, 995
And found him pight to doe it, with curst speech 1002
Your Sonne and Daughter found this trespasse worth 1320
*That when we haue found the King, in which your pain 1651
*peace at my bidding, there I found 'em, there I smelt 'em 2549
Reg. But haue you neuer found my Brothers way, | To the fore-fended
place? 2858
FOURE = *1
*Proud of heart, to ride on a Bay trotting Horse, ouer foure 1837
FOURESCORE = 2
And your Fathers Tenant, these fourescore yeares. 2194
Fourescore and vpward, | Not an houre more, nor lesse: 2815
FOURTEENE = 1
For that I am some twelue, or fourteene Moonshines 339
FOX = 2
A Fox, when one has caught her, 837
Who's there? the Traitor? | *Reg*. Ingratefull Fox, 'tis he. 2089
FOXE = *1
*Hog in sloth, Foxe in stealth, Wolfe in greedinesse, Dog 1873
FOXES = 1
And fire vs hence, like Foxes: wipe thine eyes, 2965
FOYNES = 1
*Edg. Chill picke your teeth Zir: come, no matter vor | your foynes. 2697
FRA = 5
FRAMD = 1
That eyelesse head of thine, was first fram'd flesh 2677
FRAME = 1*1
*him out: winde me into him, I pray you: frame the Bu-|sinesse 428
Which like an Engine, wrencht my frame of Nature 781
FRANCE see also Fra. = 11*8
*Lear. Attend the Lords of France & Burgundy, Gloster. 39
*May be preuented now. The Princes, *France* & *Burgundy*, 50
The Vines of France, and Milke of Burgundie, 90
Her Fathers heart from her; call *France*, who stirres? 134
Flourish. Enter Gloster with France, and Bur-|gundy, Attendants. 202
*Cor. Heere's *France* and *Burgundy*, my Noble Lord. 204
Is Queene of vs, of ours, and our faire *France*: 282
Lear. Thou hast her *France*, let her be thine, for we 287
Fra. Come my faire *Cordelia. Exit France and Cor*. 309
France and him, pray you let vs sit together, if our 328
Glo. Kent banish'd thus? and France in choller parted? 358
Knight. Since my young Ladies going into *France* 602
Why the hot-bloodied *France*, that dowerlesse tooke 1505
Which are to France the Spies and Speculations 1633
*of France. O Heauens! that this Treason were not; | or not I the
detector. 1982

FRANCE cont.

*him this Letter, the Army of France is landed: seeke out | the Traitor	
Glouster.	2061
Corn. Come Sir. | What Letters had you late from France?	2108
*It is thy businesse that I go about: Therfore great France	2377
Lear. Am I in France? | *Kent.* In your owne kingdome Sir.	2834

FRANKE = 1

Your old kind Father, whose franke heart gaue all,	1800

FRATERRETTO = *1

Edg. Fraterretto cals me, and tells me *Nero* is an Ang-|ler	2004

FRAUGHT = 1

(Whereof I know you are fraught), and put away	732

FREE = 4

Escap'd the hunt. No Port is free, no place	1254
Sepulchring an Adulteresse. O are you free?	1410
Thou'dst meete the Beare i'th' mouth, when the mind's | (free,	1791
Edgar. Beare free and patient thoughts.	2525

FREEDOME = 1

Freedome liues hence, and banishment is here;	195

FREER = 1

And quit the house on purpose, that their punishment | Might haue the	
freer course.	2342

FRESH = 1

Gent. I Madam: in the heauinesse of sleepe, | We put fresh garments on	
him.	2772

FRET = 1

With cadent Teares fret Channels in her cheekes,	799

FRETFULL = 1

Gent. Contending with the fretfull Elements;	1619

FRIEND = 10*6

Glou. My Lord of Kent: | Remember him heereafter, as my Honourable	
Friend.	30
Corn. How now my Noble friend, since I came hither	1025
From hence attend dispatch, our good old Friend,	1068
Stew. Good dawning to thee Friend, art of this house? | *Kent.* I.	1076
Glo. I am sorry for thee friend, 'tis the Dukes pleasure,	1228
Thou sayest the King growes mad, Ile tell thee Friend	1945
But lately: very late: I lou'd him (Friend)	1948
Glou. Come hither Friend: | Where is the King my Master?	2044
Glou. Good friend, I prythee take him in thy armes;	2047
*And driue toward Douer friend, where thou shalt meete	2050
Glou. Away, get thee away: good Friend be gone,	2195
And to reuenge thine eyes. Come hither Friend,	2346
Hoa, you Sir: Friend, heare you Sir, speake:	2486
*none, I say none, Ile able 'em; take that of me my Friend,	2611
Come Father, Ile bestow you with a Friend. *Exeunt.*	2742
Edg. 'Tis Noble *Kent* your Friend.	3232

FRIENDLY = 1*1

Lear. Now my friendly knaue I thanke thee, there's | earnest of thy	
seruice.	622
Glou. Now let thy friendly hand | Put strength enough too't.	2681

FRIENDS = 9

Are gone with him toward Douer; where they boast | To haue well	
armed Friends.	2078
Good my Friends consider you are my Ghests:	2093
Do me no foule play, Friends. | *Corn.* Binde him I say.	2094

FRIENDS *cont*.
    Came then into my minde, and yet my minde | Was then scarse Friends
    with him.   2218
    Heere Friend's another purse: in it, a Iewell   2465
    May be my Friends: hee's dead; I am onely sorry   2710
    You Lords and Noble Friends, know our intent,   3268
    Haue more then merited. All Friends shall   3274
    Is generall woe: Friends of my soule, you twaine,   3294
FRIENDSHIP = 1*1
    *by the sequent effects. Loue cooles, friendship falls off,   436
    Some friendship will it lend you 'gainst the Tempest: 1716
FROG = *1
    Edg. Poore Tom, that eates the swimming Frog, the   1908
FROM *l*.44 *68 119 123 134 *152 179 188 199 229 263 *279 *321 *325
    *372 *383 *415 *440 *489 497 500 514 *572 734 782 794 816 *877 1001
    1040 1067 1068 *1124 1173 1243 1246 1268 *1274 1302 1305 1308 1409
    1424 1474 1498 1540 *1590 *1755 1793 1813 *1840 *1877 *1913 1947
    2000 2104 2109 2116 2117 2183 2248 2262 2307 2329 2421 *2499 2512
    *2567 2585 *2601 2648 *2663 *2720 2736 2964 3017 3091 3154 3158
    *3174 3211 3254 3293 = 60*25
FRONT = 1
    Whose influence like the wreath of radient fire | On flickring *Phoebus*
    front.   1182
FRONTLET = *1
    Lear. How now Daughter? what makes that Frontlet   703
FROWNE = 3
    on? You are too much of late i'th'frowne.   704
    My selfe could else out-frowne false Fortunes frowne.   2946
FROWNING = *1
    *need to care for her frowning, now thou art an O with-|out   706
FRUITFULL = 1
    Suspend thy purpose, if thou did'st intend | To make this Creature
    fruitfull: 790
FRUITFULLY = *1
    place will be fruitfully offer'd. There is nothing done. If hee   2718
FRUSTRATE = 1
    When misery could beguile the Tyrants rage, | And frustrate his proud
    will.   2505
FULL = 11*3
    Gon. You see how full of changes his age is, the ob-|seruation   314
    May carry through it selfe to that full issue   533
    So may it come, thy Master whom thou lou'st, | Shall find thee full of
    labours.   536
    Le. When were you wont to be so full of Songs sirrah?   684
    Informe her full of my particular feare,   861
    Or whether gasted by the noyse I made, | Full sodainely he fled.   991
    As full of griefe as age, wretched in both,   1573
    No, Ile not weepe, I haue full cause of weeping. | *Storme and Tempest*.   1583
    Lear. Rumble thy belly full: spit Fire, spowt Raine: 1669
    I stumbled when I saw. Full oft 'tis seene,   2200
    Were two full Moones: he had a thousand Noses,   2515
    To change the course, he's full of alteration,   2849
    From a full flowing stomack. Generall,   3017
    The Wheele is come full circle, I am heere.   3136
FULLY = *1
    *his suspition more fully. I will perseuer in my course of   1991

FUMITAR *see* fenitar
FUMME = 1
  His word was still, fie, foh, and fumme,   1967
FURIE = *1
  *in the furie of his heart, when the foule Fiend rages, eats   1910
FURNISHINGS = 1
  Whereof (perchance) these are but furnishings.   1638
FURRD = *1
  *and Furr'd gownes hide all. Place sinnes with Gold, and   2608
FURROW = 1
  Crown'd with ranke Fenitar, and furrow weeds,   2353
FURTHER *see also* vurther = 9*3
  Gon. There is further complement of leaue-taking be-|tweene   327
  Reg. We shall further thinke of it.   331
  any further delay, then this very Euening.   426
  *I will looke further intoo't: but where's my Foole? I | haue not seene
  him this two daies.   600
  *acquaint my Daughter no further with any thing you   876
  Gent. I will talke further with you. | *Kent*. No, do not: 1639
  Edg. Poore Tom's a cold. I cannot daub it further.   2241
  Gon. Then shall you go no further.   2279
  Prosper it with thee. Go thou further off,   2467
  Trouble him no more till further setling.   2839
  Glo. No further Sir, a man may rot euen heere.   2931
  To morrow, or at further space, t'appeare   2996
FUTURE = 1
  Our daughters seuerall Dowers, that future strife   49
FYE = 2*1
  You taking Ayres, with Lamenesse. | *Corn*. Fye sir, fie.   1446
  That yet you do not know. Fye on this Storme,   1646
  *consumption: Fye, fie, fie; pah, pah: Giue me an Ounce   2571
GAD = 1
  Vpon the gad? *Edmond*, how now? What newes?   361
GAINE = 1
  That Sir, which serues and seekes for gaine,   1350
GAINST = 8
  Haue you not spoken 'gainst the Duke of *Cornewall*?   953
  Vpon his partie 'gainst the Duke of *Albany*? | Aduise your selfe. 956
  'Gainst Paricides did all the thunder bend,   982
  Speake 'gainst so great a number? How in one house   1536
  Your high-engender'd Battailes, 'gainst a head   1678
  Some friendship will it lend you 'gainst the Tempest: 1716
  Gone. Combine together 'gainst the Enemie: 2870
  Conspirant 'gainst this high illustrious Prince,   3090
GAIT *see* gate
GALL = 3
  Lear. A pestilent gall to me.   644
  And added to the gall. O *Lear, Lear, Lear*!   783
  With euery gall, and varry of their Masters,   1152
GALLOW = 1
  Gallow the very wanderers of the darke   1696
GAOLE = *1
  Gaole, from the loathed warmth whereof, deliuer me, and sup-|ply the
  place for your Labour.   2720
GAP = *1
  *gap in your owne Honor, and shake in peeces, the heart of 418

GARB = 1
A saucy roughnes, and constraines the garb   1172
GARDEN = *1
*To vse his eyes for Garden water-pots. I wil die brauely,   2640
GARMENTS = 3*1
*my hundred; only, I do not like the fashion of your gar-|ments.   2036
Edg. Y'are much deceiu'd: In nothing am I chang'd | But in my
Garments.   2442
Gent. I Madam: in the heauinesse of sleepe, | We put fresh garments on
him.   2772
Remembers not these garments: nor I know not   2822
GARTERS = *1
Foole. Hah, ha, he weares Cruell Garters Horses are   1282
GASTED = 1
Or whether gasted by the noyse I made, | Full sodainely he fled.   991
GATE = 4*2
Beate at this gate that let thy Folly in,   784
Hot Questrists after him, met him at gate,   2076
If Wolues had at thy Gate howl'd that sterne time,   2135
Edg. Both style, and gate; Horseway, and foot-path: 2246
Edg. Good Gentleman goe your gate, and let poore   2690
Alb. Me thought thy very gate did prophesie   3137
GATES = 1
Reg. Go thrust him out at gates, and let him smell | His way to Douer.
Exit with Glouster.   2170
GATHER = 1
Then for your Ladies: You may gather more: 2419
GATHERS = 1
Hangs one that gathers Sampire: dreadfull Trade: 2450
GAUE = 8*2
Lear. Why my Boy? | *Fool.* If I gaue them all my liuing, I'ld keepe my
Cox-|combes   636
*you gaue me nothing for't, can you make no vse of no-|thing Nuncle?   660
Corn. What was th'offence you gaue him? | *Ste.* I neuer gaue him any: 1190
The leisure of their answer, gaue me cold lookes,   1313
Lear. I gaue you all. | *Reg.* And in good time you gaue it.   1547
I neuer gaue you Kingdome, call'd you Children;   1672
Your old kind Father, whose franke heart gaue all,   1800
She gaue strange Eliads, and most speaking lookes   2412
GAUNTLET = *1
*doo't. There's my Gauntlet, Ile proue it on a Gyant.   2537
GAUST = *3
*thou clouest thy Crownes i'th'middle, and gau'st away   675
*gau'st thy golden one away; if I speake like my selfe in   678
*thy Daughters thy Mothers, for when thou gau'st them   686
GAZING = *1
*action-taking, whoreson glasse-gazing super-seruiceable   1091
GEESE = *1
Foole. Winters not gon yet, if the wil'd Geese fly that | (way,   1322
GELLY = 1
Corn. Lest it see more, preuent it; Out vilde gelly: 2158
GEN = 6*1
GENERALL = 3*1
*the generall dependants, as in the Duke himselfe also, and | your
Daughter.   590
Who redeemes Nature from the generall curse | Which twaine haue
brought her to.   2648

GENERALL *cont*.
  From a full flowing stomack. Generall,   3017
  Is generall woe: Friends of my soule, you twaine,   3294
GENERATION = 1
  Or he that makes his generation messes   124
GENEROUS = 1
  My minde as generous, and my shape as true   342
GENT = 19*1
GENTLE = 3*1
  Edg. Haile gentle Sir.   2650
  Glou. You euer gentle Gods, take my breath from me,   2663
  Leaue gentle waxe, and manners: blame vs not   2712
  Gentle, and low, an excellent thing in woman.   3237
GENTLEMAN *see also Gen*., *Gent*. = 9*5
  *be acknowledged. Doe you know this Noble Gentle- | man, *Edmond*? |
  Edm. No, my Lord.   27
  Gon. Did my Father strike my Gentleman for chi- | ding of his Foole? |
  Ste. I Madam.   507
  Enter Lear, Kent, Gentleman, and Foole.   874
  To haue her Gentleman abus'd, assaulted.   1226
  Enter Lear, Foole, and Gentleman.   1273
  Storme still. Enter Kent, and a Gentleman, seuerally.   1615
  Edg. The Prince of Darkenesse is a Gentleman. *Modo* | he's call'd, and
  Mahu.   1921
  Foole. Prythee Nunkle tell me, whether a madman be | a Gentleman,
  or a Yeoman,   2007
  Foole. No, he's a Yeoman, that ha's a Gentleman to   2010
  *his Sonne: for hee's a mad Yeoman that sees his Sonne a | Gentleman
  before him.   2011
  Enter a Gentleman.   2630
  Edg. Good Gentleman goe your gate, and let poore   2690
  Enter Cordelia, Kent, and Gentleman.   2744
  Enter a Gentleman.   3169
GENTLEMEN = 2
  Enter with Drum and Colours, Cordelia, Gentlemen, | *and Souldiours*.   2349
  Enter with Drumme and Colours, Edmund, Regan. | *Gentlemen, and
  Souldiers*.   2845
GENTLENESSE = 1
  This milky gentlenesse, and course of yours   865
GENTLEWOMAN = 1
  Lear. Your name, faire Gentlewoman?   745
GERMAINES = 1
  Cracke Natures moulds, all germaines spill at once | That makes
  ingratefull Man.   1663
GET = 7*2
  Lear. Let me not stay a iot for dinner, go get it rea- | dy: 539
  As may compact it more. Get you gone,   863
  Nay get thee in; Ile pray, and then Ile sleepe.   1808
  Corn. Get horses for your Mistris.   2080
  Glou. Away, get thee away: good Friend be gone,   2195
  Glou. Get thee away: If for my sake   2228
  *who haue the power to seale th'accusers lips. Get thee   2612
  Lear. Then there's life in't. Come, and you get it,   2644
  You shall get it by running: Sa, sa, sa, sa. *Exit*.   2645
GETS = 1
  Glou. Our flesh and blood, my Lord, is growne so | vilde, that it doth
  hate what gets it.   1923

GHESTS = 1
   Good my Friends consider you are my Ghests: 2093
GHOST = *1
   *Kent. Vex not his ghost, O let him passe, he hates him,   3287
GIANT see gyant
GIFT see guift
GILDED see also guilded = 2
   No, the Wren goes too't, and the small gilded Fly   2558
   At gilded Butterflies: and heere (poore Rogues)   2953
GIRDLE = *1
   *Women all aboue: but to the Girdle do the Gods inhe-|rit,   2568
GIUE = 32*9
   Giue me the Map there. Know, that we haue diuided   42
   So be my graue my peace, as here I giue   133
   Bur. Royall King, | Giue but that portion which your selfe propos'd,   265
   Glou. Giue me the Letter, Sir.   375
   Bast. I shall offend, either to detaine, or giue it: 376
   *Foole. Nunckle, giue me an egge, and Ile giue thee | two Crownes.   670
   Lear. Why? | *Foole. Why to put's head in, not to giue it away to his   903
   *my Lord, if you will giue me leaue, I will tread this vn-|boulted   1138
   Giue you good morrow.   1234
   From this enormous State, seeking to giue   1246
   *when a wiseman giues thee better counsell giue me mine   1347
   Is practise only. Giue me my Seruant forth;   1391
   Thy tender-hefted Nature shall not giue   1455
   For your fit welcome, giue eare Sir to my Sister,   1528
   To bring but fiue and twentie, to no more | Will I giue place or notice.   1545
   You Heauens, giue me that patience, patience I need,   1571
   Corn. 'Tis best to giue him way, he leads himselfe.   1601
   Gent. Giue me your hand, | Haue you no more to say?   1648
   This tempest will not giue me leaue to ponder   1805
   Kent. Giue my thy hand, who's there?   1822
   *Lear. Did'st thou giue all to thy Daughters? And art | thou come to
this?   1830
   *Could'st thou saue nothing? Would'st thou giue 'em all?   1845
   Giue thee quicke conduct. Come, come, away. Exeunt   2056
   Giue me some helpe. --- O cruell! O you Gods.   2142
   Reg. Giue me thy Sword. A pezant stand vp thus? | Killes him.   2154
   *Vntimely comes this hurt. Giue me your arme. Exeunt.   2176
   Edg. Giue me thy arme; | Poore Tom shall leade thee. Exeunt.   2264
   I must change names at home, and giue the Distaffe   2285
   If you do finde him, pray you giue him this;   2420
   Edg. Giue me your hand: 2461
   Edg. Giue me your arme.   2507
   clout, i'th'clout: Hewgh. Giue the word. | Edg. Sweet Mariorum.   2539
   *consumption: Fye, fie, fie; pah, pah: Giue me an Ounce   2571
   Am pregnant to good pitty. Giue me your hand,   2670
   And giue the Letters which thou find'st about me,   2701
   Edg. Giue me your hand: 2740
   Edgar. Away old man, giue me thy hand, away: 2928
   Giue me thy hand: Come on.   2930
   This Sword of mine shall giue them instant way,   3105
   Giue it the Captaine.   3209
GIUEN = 2*1
   Cur. And you Sir, I haue bin | With your Father, and giuen him notice   929
   Intelligence is giuen where you are hid;   951
   *Kent. All the powre of his wits, haue giuen way to his   2001

GIUES = 3*4
    But let his disposition haue that scope | As dotage giues it.   807
    The Country giues me proofe, and president   1264
    *when a wiseman giues thee better counsell giue me mine   1347
    *againe, I would haue none but knaues follow it, since a | Foole giues
    it.   1348
    *Edgar. Who giues any thing to poore Tom? Whom   1832
    *Curfew, and walkes at first Cocke: Hee giues the Web   1896
    *thus giues way to Loyaltie, something feares mee to | thinke of.   1973
GLAD = 3
    That I am glad I haue not, though not to haue it,   254
    Reg. I am glad to see your Highnesse.   1406
    I haue to thinke so, if thou should'st not be glad,   1408
GLADLY = 1
    Reg. For his particular, Ile receiue him gladly, | But not one follower.   1592
GLANCE = 1
    Which for they yet glance by, and scarcely bruise,   3104
GLASSE = 2
    *For there was neuer yet faire woman, but shee made | mouthes in a
    glasse.   1686
    She's dead as earth: Lend me a Looking-glasse,   3221
GLASSE-EYES = *1
    *glasse-eyes, and like a scuruy Politician, seeme to see the   2613
GLASSE-GAZING = *1
    *action-taking, whoreson glasse-gazing super-seruiceable   1091
GLIB = 1
    If for I want that glib and oylie Art,   246
GLO = 24*6
GLOBE = 1
    Approach thou Beacon to this vnder Globe,   1240
GLOST = 2
GLOSTER = 16*5
    *Lear. Attend the Lords of France & Burgundy, Gloster.   39
    Flourish. Enter Gloster with France, and Bur-|gundy, Attendants.   202
    *Lear. Go you before to Gloster with these Letters;   875
    Enter Gloster, and Seruants with Torches.   970
    Occasions Noble Gloster of some prize,   1063
    Enter Bastard, Cornewall, Regan, Gloster, Seruants.   1117
    Enter Lear, and Gloster.   1358
    Fiery? What quality? Why Gloster, Gloster,   1371
    Enter Cornewall, Regan, Gloster, Seruants.   1403
    Gon. So am I purpos'd, | Where is my Lord of Gloster?   1594
    Enter Gloster.   1596
    Enter Gloster, and Edmund.   1752
    Enter Gloster.   2039
    *Corn. Edmund farewell: go seek the Traitor Gloster,   2082
    Gon. My most deere Gloster.   2294
    Enter Edgar, and Gloster.   2920
    Alb. Thou art armed Gloster, | Let the Trumpet sound: 3036
    *will maintaine vpon Edmund, supposed Earle of Gloster,   3061
    *Edg. What's he that speakes for Edmund Earle of Glo-|(ster?   3078
    Gon. This is practise Gloster,   3108
GLOSTERS = 1
    His answer was, the worse. Of Glosters Treachery,   2273
GLOU = 64*19
GLOUCESTER see also Glo., Glost., Glou. = 6*1
    Enter Kent, Gloucester, and Edmond.   2

GLOUCESTER cont.

Enter Gloucester.	357
Enter Gloucester, with a Torch.	1890
*Corn. True or false, it hath made thee Earle of Glou-|cester:	1987
Enter Kent, and Gloucester.	1997
Enter Gloucester, and Seruants.	2088
Enter Gloucester, and Edgar.	2430

GLOUES = *1

*curl'd my haire, wore Gloues in my cap; seru'd the Lust	1866

GLOUSTER = 10*1

*him this Letter, the Army of France is landed: seeke out | the Traitor Glouster.	2061
*Postes shall be swift, and intelligent betwixt vs. Fare-|well deere Sister, farewell my Lord of Glouster.	2070
*Stew. My Lord of Glouster hath conuey'd him hence	2074
Reg. Go thrust him out at gates, and let him smell | His way to Douer.	
Exit with Glouster.	2170
Enter Glouster, and an Oldman.	2188
Slaine by his Seruant, going to put out | The other eye of Glouster.	2314
So speedily can venge. But (O poore Glouster)	2325
But being widdow, and my Glouster with her,	2331
Alb. Glouster, I liue | To thanke thee for the loue thou shew'dst the King,	2344
I know thee well enough, thy name is Glouster:	2619
To Edmund Earle of Glouster: seeke him out	2702

GLOUSTERS = 3

Alb. Glousters eyes.	2316
It was great ignorance, Glousters eyes being out	2394
For Glousters bastard Son was kinder to his Father,	2560

GNAWNE = 1

Edg. Know my name is lost | By Treasons tooth: bare-gnawne, and Canker-bit,	3073

GO see also goe = 32*11

*Villaine; worse then brutish: Go sirrah, seeke him: Ile	411
*Lear. Let me not stay a iot for dinner, go get it rea-|dy:	539
*ho, dinner, where's my knaue? my Foole? Go you and call	573
And thy deere Iudgement out. Go, go, my people.	785
*Lear. Go you before to Gloster with these Letters;	875
*Foole. Then I prythee be merry, thy wit shall not go | slip-shod. | Lear. Ha, ha, ha.	885
Glo. Pursue him, ho: go after. By no meanes, what?	979
*Kent. To go out of my dialect, which you discom-|mend	1185
*let go thy hold when a great wheele runs downe a	1344
Stands in some ranke of praise, Ile go with thee,	1556
If onely to go warme were gorgeous,	1568
Or ere Ile weepe; O Foole, I shall go mad. Exeunt.	1586
I will go seeke the King.	1647
Ile speake a Prophesie ere I go:	1735
*Glo. Go too; say you nothing. There is diuision be-|tweene	1759
Lear. Prythee go in thy selfe, seeke thine owne ease,	1804
In Boy, go first. You houselesse pouertie, Exit.	1807
Glou. Go in with me; my duty cannot suffer	1926
Kent. Good my Lord take his offer, | Go into th'house.	1934
Kent. Importune him once more to go my Lord,	1940
Glou. Take him you on. | Kent. Sirra, come on: go along with vs.	1962
Corn. Go with me to the Dutchesse.	1984
so, so, wee'l go to Supper i'th'morning.	2042

GO *cont.*
Foole. And Ile go to bed at noone. 2043
*Corn. Edmund farewell: go seek the Traitor Gloster, 2082
Reg. Go thrust him out at gates, and let him smell | His way to Douer.
Exit with Glouster. 2170
Gon. Then shall you go no further. 2279
*It is thy businesse that I go about: Therfore great France 2377
Glou. Let go my hand: 2464
Prosper it with thee. Go thou further off, 2467
*out. Go too, they are not men o'their words; they told 2550
Like hold on thee. Let go his arme. 2686
Edg. Chill not let go Zir, | Without vurther 'casion. 2687
Stew. Let go Slaue, or thou dy'st. 2689
All my reports go with the modest truth, | Nor more, nor clipt, but so. 2751
You see is kill'd in him: desire him to go in, 2838
Reg. Sister you'le go with vs? | *Gon.* No. 2875
Reg. 'Tis most conuenient, pray go with vs. 2877
Glo. Grace go with you Sir. *Exit.* | *Alarum and Retreat within.* 2925
Take thou this note, go follow them to prison, 2970
Alb. Go after her, she's desperate, gouerne her. 3120
Kent. I haue a iourney Sir, shortly to go, 3296
GOATISH = *1
*to lay his Goatish disposition on the charge of a Starre, 456
GODDES = 1
Lear. Let the great Goddes | That keepe this dreadfull pudder o're our
heads, 1702
GODDESSE = 2
Bast. Thou Nature art my Goddesse, to thy Law 335
Lear. It may be so, my Lord. | Heare Nature, heare deere Goddesse,
heare: 788
GODS = 21*5
Kent. Now by *Apollo*, King | Thou swear'st thy Gods in vaine. 173
The Gods to their deere shelter take thee Maid. 196
*Gods, Gods! 'Tis strange, that from their cold'st neglect 279
Now Gods, stand vp for Bastards. 356
Alb. Now Gods that we adore, | Whereof comes this? 804
But that I told him the reuenging Gods, 981
Reg. O the blest Gods! | So will you wish on me, when the rash moode
is on. 1452
You see me heere (you Gods) a poore old man, 1572
impatience: the Gods reward your kindnesse. 2002
Glou. By the kinde Gods, 'tis most ignobly done | To plucke me by the
Beard. 2100
Giue me some helpe. --- O cruell! O you Gods. 2142
Kinde Gods, forgiue me that, and prosper him. 2169
Edg. O Gods! Who is't can say I am at the worst? 2207
As Flies to wanton Boyes, are we to th'Gods, | They kill vs for their
sport. 2221
Well worth a poore mans taking. Fayries, and Gods 2466
Glou. O you mighty Gods! | This world I do renounce, and in your
sights 2473
*Thinke that the cleerest Gods, who make them Honors 2518
*Women all aboue: but to the Girdle do the Gods inhe-|rit, 2568
Glou. You euer gentle Gods, take my breath from me, 2663
Cor. O you kind Gods! 2763
As if we were Gods spies: And wee'l weare out 2957

GODS *cont*.

Lear. Vpon such sacrifices my *Cordelia*, | The Gods themselues throw Incense.	2961
False to thy Gods, thy Brother, and thy Father,	3089
The Gods are iust, and of our pleasant vices | Make instruments to plague vs:	3131
Alb. The Gods defend her, beare him hence awhile.	3215

GODSONNE = *1

Reg. What, did my Fathers Godsonne seeke your life?	1030

GOE = 7*6

Goe to th'creating a whole tribe of Fops	348
*fitly bring you to heare my Lord speake: pray ye goe,	490
there's my key: if you do stirre abroad, goe arm'd.	491
Lear. No more of that, I haue noted it well, goe you	604
*and tell my Daughter, I would speake with her. Goe you	605
tarry, but away, goe too, haue you wisedome, so.	621
That such a King should play bo-peepe, | And goe the Foole among.	690
Goe tell the Duke, and's wife, Il'd speake with them:	1392
*will looke him, and priuily relieue him; goe you and	1765
On things would hurt me more, but Ile goe in,	1806
*sharpe Hauthorne blow the windes. Humh, goe to thy | bed and warme thee.	1828
Edg. Good Gentleman goe your gate, and let poore	2690
Gon. Oh ho, I know the Riddle, I will goe. | *Exeunt both the Armies*.	2878

GOES = 3*4

Lear. But goes thy heart with this? | *Cor*. I my good Lord.	111
*forbearance till the speed of his rage goes slower: and as	488
*great one that goes vpward, let him draw thee after:	1346
No, the Wren goes too't, and the small gilded Fly	2558
*the soyled Horse goes too't with a more riotous appe-|tite:	2566
*case, your purse in a light, yet you see how this world | goes.	2591
*goes, with no eyes. Looke with thine eares: See how	2595

GOEST = 2

Ride more then thou goest,	651
Oldm. Fellow, where goest?	2212

GOING = 5*2

Knight. Since my young Ladies going into *France*	602
Corn. Whether is he going?	1599
That going shalbe vs'd with feet.	1748
*beholding. Aduice the Duke where you are going, to a	2068
Slaine by his Seruant, going to put out | The other eye of Glouster.	2314
Bid me farewell, and let me heare thee going.	2468
Men must endure | Their going hence, euen as their comming hither,	2933

GOLD = 1*1

When Vsurers tell their Gold i'th'Field,	1744
*and Furr'd gownes hide all. Place sinnes with Gold, and	2608

GOLDEN = *1

*gau'st thy golden one away; if I speake like my selfe in	678

GON = 1*2

Foole. Winters not gon yet, if the wil'd Geese fly that | (way,	1322
Kent. Here Sir, but trouble him not, his wits are gon.	2046
Edg. He is gon indeed.	3290

GON = 34*13

GONE *see also* begone = 11*2

That face of hers againe, therfore be gone,	289
And the King gone to night? Prescrib'd his powre,	359
When saw you my Father last? | *Edg*. The night gone by.	474

GONE *cont*.

As may compact it more. Get you gone,   863
Foole. Thy Asses are gone about 'em; the reason why   908
*him perceiued; If he aske for me, I am ill, and gone to   1767
Are gone with him toward Douer; where they boast | To haue well
armed Friends.   2078
Glou. Away, get thee away: good Friend be gone,   2195
Do as I bid thee, or rather do thy pleasure: | Aboue the rest, be gone.   2236
All hearts against vs: *Edmund*, I thinke is gone | In pitty of his misery,
to dispatch   2396
Now Fellow, fare thee well. | *Edg*. Gone Sir, farewell: 2480
That Heauens vault should crack: she's gone for euer.   3219
I might haue sau'd her, now she's gone for euer: 3234
GONE = 1
GONERILL *see also Gon., Gone*. = 16*2
*Sennet. Enter King Lear, Cornwall, Albany, Gonerill, Re-|gan,
Cordelia, and attendants.*   37
Where Nature doth with merit challenge. *Gonerill*,   58
Then that conferr'd on *Gonerill*. Now our Ioy,   88
Enter Gonerill, and Steward.   506
Enter Gonerill.   702
Alb. I cannot be so partiall *Gonerill*, | To the great loue I beare you. 831
From *Gonerill* his Mistris, salutations;   1308
Enter Gonerill.   1476
In such a night as this? O *Regan, Gonerill*,   1799
Enter Cornwall, Regan, Gonerill, Bastard, | and Seruants.   2058
Enter Gonerill, Bastard, and Steward.   2267
Alb. Oh *Gonerill*, | You are not worth the dust which the rude winde |
Blowes in your face.   2301
Lear. Ha! *Gonerill* with a white beard? They flatter'd   2543
Your (Wife, so I would say) affectio-|nate Seruant. Gonerill.   2722
Enter with Drum and Colours, Albany, Gonerill, Soldiers.   2864
Exasperates, makes mad her Sister *Gonerill*,   2907
Flourish. Enter Albany, Gonerill, Regan, Soldiers;   2982
Alb. Produce the bodies, be they aliue or dead; | *Gonerill and Regans
bodies brought out.*   3183
GOOD = 53*23
*there was good sport at his making, and the horson must   26
Cor. Good my Lord, | You haue begot me, bred me, lou'd me.   102
Lear. But goes thy heart with this? | *Cor*. I my good Lord.   111
Kent. Good my Liege. | *Lear*. Peace *Kent*,   128
Our potencie made good, take thy reward.   186
That good effects may spring from words of loue: 199
Bast. If the matter were good my Lord, I durst swear   398
*no good to vs: though the wisedome of Nature can   434
Bast. Parted you in good termes? Found you no dis-|pleasure in him,
by word, nor countenance?   478
*man, if ther be any good meaning toward you: I haue told   494
That can my speech defuse, my good intent   532
Gon. I would you would make vse of your good wise-|(dome   731
Gon. This man hath had good Counsell, | A hundred Knights?   842
Foole. Yes indeed, thou would'st make a good Foole.   911
You haue now the good aduantage of the night,   952
Cor. Is he pursued? | *Glo*. I my good Lord.   1050
From hence attend dispatch, our good old Friend,   1068
Stew. Good dawning to thee Friend, art of this house? | *Kent*. I.   1076
*would'st be a Baud in way of good seruice, and art no-|thing   1093

GOOD *cont.*

Kent. Sir, in good faith, in sincere verity,	1180
A good mans fortune may grow out at heeles:	1233
Giue you good morrow.	1234
*Kent. Good King, that must approue the common saw,	1237
Glo. Well my good Lord, I haue inform'd them so.	1373
*Lear. Inform'd them? Do'st thou vnderstand me man. | *Glo.* I my good Lord.	1374
Lear. Good morrow to you both.	1404
*Reg. Good Sir, no more: these are vnsightly trickes:	1438
Reg. Good Sir, to'th'purpose. *Tucket within.*	1466
*Lear. Who stockt my Seruant? *Regan,* I haue good hope	1477
Lear. I gaue you all. | *Reg.* And in good time you gaue it.	1547
**better then this Rain-water out o'doore. Good Nunkle,	1666
*Foole. He that has a house to put's head in, has a good | Head-peece:	1680
*Kent. Here is the place my Lord, good my Lord enter,	1778
Lear. Let me alone. | *Kent.* Good my Lord enter heere.	1781
Kent. I had rather breake mine owne, | Good my Lord enter.	1784
Kent. Good my Lord enter here.	1803
Kent. Good my Lord take his offer, | Go into th'house.	1934
His Daughters seeke his death: Ah, that good Kent,	1943
Kent. Good my Lord, sooth him:	1960
Lear. Come, good Athenian.	1964
*Kent. Now good my Lord, lye heere, and rest awhile.	2040
*Glou. Good friend, I prythee take him in thy armes;	2047
Good my Friends consider you are my Ghests:	2093
Thou should'st haue said, good Porter turne the Key:	2136
Who is too good to pitty thee.	2167
Oldm. O my good Lord, I haue bene your Tenant,	2193
Glou. Away, get thee away: good Friend be gone,	2195
Thy comforts can do me no good at all, | Thee, they may hurt.	2196
**poore Tom hath bin scarr'd out of his good wits. Blesse	2247
thee good mans sonne, from the foule Fiend.	2248
*Mes. Oh my good Lord, the Duke of *Cornwals* dead,	2313
Alb. He is not heere. | *Mes.* No my good Lord, I met him backe againe.	2338
*Mes. I my good Lord: 'twas he inform'd against him	2341
Edg. Now fare ye well, good Sir. | *Glou.* With all my heart.	2469
**no, to euery thing that I said: I, and no too, was no good	2546
**of Ciuet; good Apothecary sweeten my immagination:	2572
To this great stage of Fooles. This a good blocke:	2625
Glou. Now good sir, what are you?	2667
Am pregnant to good pitty. Giue me your hand,	2670
*Edg. Good Gentleman goe your gate, and let poore	2690
Cor. O thou good *Kent,* | How shall I liue and worke | To match thy goodnesse?	2745
Cor. Then be't so my good Lord:	2760
Be by good Madam when we do awake him, | I doubt of his Temperance.	2774
Gent. Be comforted good Madam, the great rage	2837
For your good hoast: pray that the right may thriue:	2922
Bast. Some Officers take them away: good guard,	2940
The good yeares shall deuoure them, flesh and fell,	2966
Alb. The let alone lies not in your good will. | *Bast.* Nor in thine Lord.	3023
Not sure, though hoping of this good successe,	3157
And shall perchance do good, but speake you on,	3164
Kent. I am come | To bid my King and Master aye good night.	3189
Bast. I pant for life: some good I meane to do	3200

GOOD *cont.*
Kent. O my good Master. | *Lear.* Prythee away.	3230
I haue seene the day, with my good biting Faulchion	3241
Lear. He's a good fellow, I can tell you that,	3250
Kent. No my good Lord, I am the very man. | *Lear.* Ile see that straight.	3252

GOODMAN = *1
*Kent. With you goodman Boy, if you please, come,	1119

GOODMANS = 1
In the Goodmans desires: seeke, seeke for him,	2369

GOODNESSE = 2
Cor. O thou good *Kent,* | How shall I liue and worke | To match thy goodnesse?	2745
You know the goodnesse I intend vpon you:	2854

GOODNIGHT *see also* good = 1
This shamefull lodging. Fortune goodnight,	1249

GOOSE = 1
Goose, if I had you vpon *Sarum* Plaine,	1156

GORD = 1
Rule in this Realme, and the gor'd state sustaine.	3295

GORGD = 1
Looke vp a height, the shrill-gorg'd Larke so farre	2500

GORGE = 1
To gorge his appetite, shall to my bosome	125

GORGEOUS = 2
If onely to go warme were gorgeous,	1568
Why Nature needs not what thou gorgeous wear'st,	1569

GOT = 4
Got 'tweene a sleepe, and wake? Well then,	349
That worthied him, got praises of the King,	1197
Then my Daughters got 'tweene the lawfull sheets.	2561
The darke and vitious place where thee he got, | Cost him his eyes.	3133

GOUERND = 1
Cor. Be gouern'd by your knowledge, and proceede	2769

GOUERNE = 1
Alb. Go after her, she's desperate, gouerne her.	3120

GOWNES = *1
**and Furr'd gownes hide all. Place sinnes with Gold, and	2608

GOZEMORE = 1
Edg. Had'st thou beene ought | But Gozemore, Feathers, Ayre,	2490

GRACD = 1
Then a grac'd Pallace. The shame it selfe doth speake	755

GRACE = 19*2
No lesse then life, with grace, health, beauty, honor:	63
And nothing more may fitly like your Grace,	218
That hath depriu'd me of your Grace and fauour,	251
Without our Grace, our Loue, our Benizon:	290
But yet alas, stood I within his Grace,	298
Fooles had nere lesse grace in a yeere,	680
Glo. For him I thanke your Grace.	1060
Against the Grace, and Person of my Master, | Stocking his Messenger.	1210
Glo. Let me beseech your Grace, not to do so,	1220
Corn. Haile to your Grace. *Kent here set at liberty.*	1405
Dwels in the sickly grace of her he followes.	1473
Corn. What meanes your Grace?	1475
Kent. Who's there? | **Foole.* Marry here's Grace, and a Codpiece, that's a | Wiseman, and a Foole.	1691

GRACE *cont.*

These dreadfull Summoners grace. I am a man, | More sinn'd against,
then sinning. 1712
Kent. How fares your Grace? | *Lear.* What's he? 1904
Glou. What, hath your Grace no better company? 1920
I do beseech your grace. | *Lear.* O cry you mercy, Sir: 1951
*Edg. If ere your Grace had speech with man so poore, | Heare me one
word. 2881
Glo. Grace go with you Sir. *Exit.* | *Alarum and Retreat within.* 2925
Reg. That's as we list to grace him. 3001
In his owne grace he doth exalt himselfe, | More then in your addition. 3008
GRACES = 2
Glo. I serue you Madam, | Your Graces are right welcome. *Exeunt.*
Flourish. 1072
Glou. What meanes your Graces? 2092
GRACIOUS = 1
Gracious my Lord, hard by heere is a Houell, 1715
GRANT = 1
The Duke must grant me that: besides, his picture 1019
GRATITUDE ≠ 1
Effects of Curtesie, dues of Gratitude: 1463
GRAUE = 2*1
So be my graue my peace, as here I giue 133
*Lear. Thou wert better in a Graue, then to answere 1881
Lear. You do me wrong to take me out o'th'graue, 2794
GRAUES = *1
*to our Graues. Find out this Villain, *Edmond*, it shall lose 444
GRAY-BEARD = 2
*Ste. This ancient Ruffian Sir, whose life I haue spar'd | at sute of his
gray-beard. 1135
Iakes with him. Spare my gray-beard, you wagtaile? 1140
GREAT = 20*8
Great Riuals in our yongest daughters loue, 51
As my great Patron thought on in my praiers. 151
I tell you all her wealth. For you great King, 228
*him, mistaking his purpose, it would make a great 417
*theres a great abatement of kindnesse appeares as well in 589
Alb. I cannot be so partiall *Gonerill*, | To the great loue I beare you. 831
Vnder th'allowance of your great aspect, 1181
*let go thy hold when a great wheele runs downe a 1344
*great one that goes vpward, let him draw thee after: 1346
Speake 'gainst so great a number? How in one house 1536
Who haue, as who haue not, that their great Starres 1631
Lear. Let the great Goddes | That keepe this dreadfull pudder o're our
heads, 1702
*Then shal the Realme of *Albion*, come to great confusion: 1746
To his great Master, who, threat-enrag'd 2319
*It is thy businesse that I go about: Therfore great France 2377
It was great ignorance, Glousters eyes being out 2394
Shake patiently my great affliction off: 2475
To quarrell with your great opposelesse willes, 2477
Glou. O ruin'd peece of Nature, this great world | Shall so weare out to
naught. 2577
*might'st behold the great image of Authoritie, a Dogg's 2602
*tatter'd cloathes great Vices do appeare: Robes, 2607
To this great stage of Fooles. This a good blocke: 2625
Cure this great breach in his abused Nature, 2764

GREAT *cont.*

Gent. Be comforted good Madam, the great rage | 2837
In a wall'd prison, packs and sects of great ones, | That ebbe and flow
by th'Moone. | 2958
Do's not become a Sword, thy great imployment | 2975
Is he not here? | *Alb.* Great thing of vs forgot, | 3191
What comfort to this great decay may come, | 3269
GREATER = 2
But where the greater malady is fixt, | 1788
Vntill their greater pleasures first be knowne | That are to censure them. | 2941
GREEDINESSE = *1
*Hog in sloth, Foxe in stealth, Wolfe in greedinesse, Dog | 1873
GREEFE = 2
The greefe hath craz'd my wits. What a night's this? | 1950
Twixt two extremes of passion, ioy and greefe, | Burst smilingly. | 3161
GREEFES = 1
So should my thoughts be seuer'd from my greefes, | *Drum afarre off.* | 2736
GREEN = *1
*ditch-Dogge; drinkes the green Mantle of the standing | 1912
GREET = 1
Alb. We will greet the time. *Exit.* | 2901
GREW = 1*1
*she grew round womb'd, and had indeede (Sir) a | 17
Cor. Speake yet, how grew your quarrell? | 1134
GREY-HOUND = 1
Mastiffe, Grey-hound, Mongrill, Grim, | 2025
GRIEFE *see also* greefe = 1
As full of griefe as age, wretched in both, | 1573
GRIEFES *see* greefes
GRIM = 1
Mastiffe, Grey-hound, Mongrill, Grim, | 2025
GRIME = 1
Brought neere to beast; my face Ile grime with filth, | 1260
GROANES = 1
Such groanes of roaring Winde, and Raine, I neuer | 1699
GROOME = 1
Perswade me rather to be slaue and sumpter | To this detested groome. | 1509
GROSSE = 2
He flashes into one grosse crime, or other, · | 511
Shew scarse so grosse as Beetles. Halfe way downe | 2449
GROSSELY = 1
hath now cast her off, appeares too grossely. | 317
GROUND = 2
'Tis on such ground, and to such wholesome end, | 1423
Glou. Me thinkes the ground is eeuen. | *Edg.* Horrible steepe. | 2433
GROW = 6
And my inuention thriue, *Edmond* the base | Shall to'th'Legitimate: I
grow, I prosper: | 354
His Knights grow riotous, and himselfe vpbraides vs | 513
To haue found a safe redresse, but now grow fearefull | 717
A good mans fortune may grow out at heeles: | 1233
Darnell, and all the idle weedes that grow | 2355
Edg. Why then your other Senses grow imperfect | By your eyes
anguish. | 2437
GROWES = 2*1
*you: what growes of it no matter, aduise your fellowes | 526
Thou sayest the King growes mad, Ile tell thee Friend | 1945

GROWES *cont.*
Regan. My sicknesse growes vpon me. 3055
GROWNE = 2*1
    For wisemen are growne foppish, 681
    *Glou. Our flesh and blood, my Lord, is growne so | vilde, that it doth
    hate what gets it. 1923
    Search euery Acre in the high-growne field, 2357
GRUDGE = 1
    To grudge my pleasures, to cut off my Traine, 1458
GRUMBLE = *1
    *Kent. What art thou that dost grumble there i'th' | straw? Come forth. 1825
GUARD = 3
    My Father hath set guard to take my Brother, 945
    That guard, and most vnusall vigilance 1255
    Bast. Some Officers take them away: good guard, 2940
GUARDIANS = 1
    Lear. Made you my Guardians, my Depositaries, 1549
GUESSE = 1
    Heere is the guesse of their true strength and Forces, 2898
GUESSINGLY = 1
    Glou. I haue a Letter guessingly set downe 2115
GUESTS *see* ghests
GUIDE = 1
    Their precious Stones new lost: became his guide, 3153
GUIFT = 1
    Vpon the foule disease, reuoke thy guift, 178
GUILDED = 1
    This guilded Serpent: for your claime faire Sisters, 3029
GUILTLESSE = 1
    Alb. My Lord, I am guiltlesse, as I am ignorant | Of what hath moued
    you. 786
GUILTS = 1
    Ha's practis'd on mans life. Close pent-vp guilts, 1710
GUILTY = *1
    *behauiour, we make guilty of our disasters, the Sun, the 449
GYANT = *1
    *doo't. There's my Gauntlet, Ile proue it on a Gyant. 2537
HA *l.*592 742 823 887 1280 *1282 *1885 *2543 3235 = 8*3, *2
    *volke passe: and 'chud ha' bin zwaggerd out of my life, 2691
    *'twould not ha' bin zo long as 'tis, by a vortnight. Nay, 2692
HABIT = 1
    That very Dogges disdain'd: and in this habit 3151
HAD *l.*4 *17 *18 *391 *460 635 680 *698 716 *727 842 *1083 *1132 1156
    1315 1784 *1846 1946 2109 2135 2205 2276 2409 2484 2485 2515 *2544
    2711 *2781 2784 2790 *2881 2991 3003 3165 3218 = 23*13
HADST *see also* thou'dst *l.*256 *677 *705 *916 *1337 2490 = 2*4
HAGS = 1
    Staine my mans cheekes. No you vnnaturall Hags, 1578
HAH *l.**1282 = *1
HAILE = 3
    Kent. Haile to thee Noble Master. 1279
    Corn. Haile to your Grace. *Kent here set at liberty.* 1405
    Edg. Haile gentle Sir. 2650
HAIRE = *1
    *curl'd my haire, wore Gloues in my cap; seru'd the Lust 1866
HAIRES = 2
    Blanket my loines, else all my haires in knots, 1261

HAIRES *cont.*
   These haires which thou dost rauish from my chin   2104
HALCION = 1
   Reuenge, affirme, and turne their Halcion beakes   1151
HALFE = 9*4
   Halfe my loue with him, halfe my Care, and Dutie,   109
   *him, you should enioy halfe his Reuennew for euer, and liue the | beloued
   of your Brother*. Edgar.   388
   *enioy halfe his Reuennew: my Sonne *Edgar*, had hee a   391
   Stew'd in his haste, halfe breathlesse, painting forth   1307
   She hath abated me of halfe my Traine;   1441
   Thy halfe o'th'Kingdome hast thou not forgot, | Wherein I thee
   endow'd.   1464
   Dismissing halfe your traine, come then to me,   1497
   Edg. Fathom, and halfe, Fathom and halfe; poore *Tom*.   1819
   If thou should'st dally halfe an houre, his life   2052
   Shew scarse so grosse as Beetles. Halfe way downe   2449
   Vntill some halfe houre past when I was arm'd,   3156
HALFE-BLOODED = 1
   Alb. Halfe-blooded fellow, yes.   3025
HALTER = 1
   If my Cap would buy a Halter,   840
HALTERS = *1
   *that hath laid Kniues vnder his Pillow, and Halters   1835
HAND = 20*6
   That Lord, whose hand must take my plight, shall carry   108
   And here I take *Cordelia* by the hand, | Dutchesse of *Burgundie*. 267
   *hand to write this? A heart and braine to breede it in?   392
   Glou. It is his. | *Bast*. It is his hand, my Lord: but I hope his heart is |
   not in the Contents.   401
   O *Regan*, will you take her by the hand?   1484
   Gon. Why not by'th'hand Sir? How haue I offended?   1485
   Gent. Giue me your hand, | Haue you no more to say?   1648
   Vnwhipt of Iustice. Hide thee, thou Bloudy hand;   1706
   Is it not as this mouth should teare this hand   1795
   Kent. Giue my thy hand, who's there?   1822
   *the Turke. False of heart, light of eare, bloody of hand;   1872
   *Keepe thy foote out of Brothels, thy hand out of   1876
   Bast. If the matter of this Paper be certain, you haue | mighty
   businesse in hand.   1985
   Corn. If you see vengeance. | *Seru*. Hold your hand, my Lord: 2144
   And more conuenient is he for my hand   2418
   Edg. Giue me your hand: 2461
   Glou. Let go my hand: 2464
   Glou. O let me kisse that hand. | *Lear*. Let me wipe it first, 2574
   *hand: why dost thou lash that Whore? Strip thy owne   2604
   Gent. Oh heere he is: lay hand vpon him, Sir.   2631
   Am pregnant to good pitty. Giue me your hand,   2670
   Glou. Now let thy friendly hand | Put strength enough too't. 2681
   Edg. Giue me your hand: 2740
   Cor. O looke vpon me Sir, | And hold your hand in benediction o're
   me,   2810
   Edgar. Away old man, giue me thy hand, away: 2928
   Giue me thy hand: Come on.   2930
HANDLES = *1
   *Presse-money. That fellow handles his bow, like a Crow-|keeper: 2534

HANDS = 4
With Robbers hands, my hospitable fauours 2106
Reg. To whose hands | You haue sent the Lunaticke King: Speake. 2113
Into my Husbands hands. This trustie Seruant 2286
I will not sweare these are my hands: let's see, 2807
HANDY-DANDY = *1
*thine eare: Change places, and handy-dandy, which is 2597
HANG = 4
Hang fated o're mens faults, light on thy Daughters. 1849
Reg. Hang him instantly. 2063
Cor. O my deere Father, restauratian hang 2776
Bast. He hath Commission from thy Wife and me, | To hang *Cordelia*
in the prison, and 3211
HANGD = *1
Lear. And my poore Foole is hang'd: no, no, no life? 3277
HANGING = 1
I kill'd the Slaue that was a hanging thee. | *Gent.* 'Tis true (my Lords)
he did. 3238
HANGS = 1 *1
Hangs one that gathers Sampire: dreadfull Trade: 2450
*thou whip'st her. The Vsurer hangs the Cozener. Tho- | rough 2606
HAPPIE = 1
Stew. A proclaim'd prize: most happie 2676
HAPPIER = 1
Makes thee the happier: Heauens deale so still: 2251
HAPPILY = 1
They loue you all? Happily when I shall wed, 107
HAPPY = 3
And by the happy hollow of a Tree, 1253
It was some Fiend: Therefore thou happy Father, 2517
Bast. About it, and write happy, when th'hast done, 2979
HARBOUR = 1
Harbour more craft, and more corrupter ends, 1177
HARD = 7 *1
Kent. Pray do not Sir, I haue watch'd and trauail'd hard, 1231
Hold amity? 'Tis hard, almost impossible. 1538
Or the hard Reine which both of them hath borne 1636
Gracious my Lord, hard by heere is a Houell, 1715
Repose you there, while I to this hard house, 1717
T'obey in all your daughters hard commands: 1927
Reg. Hard, hard: O filthy Traitor. 2096
HARDER = 3 *1
(More harder then the stones whereof 'tis rais'd, 1718
*things thou dost not. Now, now, now, now. Pull off my | Bootes:
harder, harder, so. 2614
*try whither your Costard, or my Ballow be the harder; | chill be plaine
with you. 2694
HARDLY = 1
And hardly shall I carry out my side, 2908
HARDOKES = *1
*With Hardokes, Hemlocke, Nettles, Cuckoo flowres, 2354
HARD-HEARTS = *1
*make these hard-hearts. You sir, I entertaine for one of 2035
HARE-LIPPE = *1
*and the Pin, squints the eye, and makes the Hare-lippe; 1897
HARKE *see also* hearke = *1
*Harke, the Dukes Trumpets, I know not wher he comes; 1017

HARME = 1
　Be fear'd of doing harme, make your owne purpose,　　　　　1053
HARMEFULL = 2
　Then prais'd for harmefull mildnesse.　　　　　　　　　　868
　But not without that harmefull stroke, which since | Hath pluckt him
　after.　　　　　　　　　　　　　　　　　　　　　　　2321
HARMES = 3
　Whose nature is so farre from doing harmes,　　　　　　　500
　Let me still take away the harmes I feare,　　　　　　　　851
　Repaire those violent harmes, that my two Sisters | Haue in thy
　Reuerence made.　　　　　　　　　　　　　　　　　　2778
HARSHNESSE = 1
　Thee o're to harshnesse: Her eyes are fierce, but thine　　1456
HART = *1
　*The man y makes his Toe, what he his Hart shold make,　　1684
HARTED = 1
　*thee nothing, do it carefully: and the Noble & true-har-|ted　445
HAS see also it's l.*404 *632 837 *901 *1680 1682 1710 1729 *1844 *2010
　2215 3206 = 6*7
HAST see also th'hast l.182 197 287 *699 815 1464 1705 1864 2120 2186
　2306 2494 2496 *2598 2647 *2699 3125 = 14*3, 2
　By dilligent discouerie, but your hast | Is now vrg'd on you.　2899
　Edg. Hast thee for thy life.　　　　　　　　　　　　　3210
HASTE see also hast = 3
　Hee's comming hither, now i'th' night, i'th' haste,　　　　954
　Resolue me with all modest haste, which way　　　　　　1300
　Stew'd in his haste, halfe breathlesse, painting forth　　　1307
HASTEN = 2
　And hasten your returne; no, no, my Lord,　　　　　　　864
　Hasten his Musters, and conduct his powres.　　　　　　2284
HASTY = 1
　To bandy hasty words, to scant my sizes,　　　　　　　　1459
HATCH = 1
　Dogs leapt the hatch, and all are fled.　　　　　　　　　2030
HATE = 5
　Vnfriended, new adopted to our hate,　　　　　　　　　222
　To match you where I hate, therefore beseech you　　　　230
　*Glou. Our flesh and blood, my Lord, is growne so | vilde, that it doth
　hate what gets it.　　　　　　　　　　　　　　　　　1923
　But that thy strange mutations make vs hate thee,　　　　2191
　Let sorrow split my heart, if euer I | Did hate thee, or thy Father.　3139
HATED = 3
　And on the sixt to turne thy hated backe　　　　　　　　189
　With the hell-hated Lye, ore-whelme thy heart,　　　　　3103
　Kent. If Fortune brag of two, she lou'd and hated, | One of them we
　behold.　　　　　　　　　　　　　　　　　　　　　3245
HATEFULL = 1
　May all the building in my fancie plucke | Vpon my hatefull life.
　Another way　　　　　　　　　　　　　　　　　　　2332
HATES = 1*1
　Reg. Out treacherous Villaine, | Thou call'st on him, that hates thee. It
　was he　　　　　　　　　　　　　　　　　　　　　2164
　*Kent. Vex not his ghost, O let him passe, he hates him,　3287
HATH l.*12 *35 207 211 251 255 303 *315 317 *318 *320 *368 *386 *420
　*483 486 603 787 842 853 945 1065 1143 1244 1287 1412 1441 *1590
　1634 1636 *1833 *1835 1850 *1914 1920 1950 *1987 *2074 *2247 2322
　2378 2768 2889 2929 3163 3211 3291 3300 = 33*16

HAUE *see also* ha', t'haue *l.**12 *22 42 48 52 103 106 149 156 254 263 269
270 288 304 305 310 *315 *325 350 *372 *373 *405 *425 *441 *460 *481
*487 *494 *495 503 520 523 *525 *558 *569 *597 *598 601 *604 621 648
656 *673 *685 694 *696 717 718 765 803 807 824 829 853 855 858 *880
*913 *916 929 *934 938 946 952 953 955 967 1021 1026 1032 1038 1039
1040 1045 1064 1107 *1127 *1132 *1135 1167 1213 1223 1226 *1231
*1326 *1348 1363 1373 1396 1408 1416 1422 1432 1454 *1477 *1485
1562 1579 1583 1611 1631 1649 *1651 *1658 1700 1727 *1760 *1762
1813 *1842 *1851 1854 1918 1930 1971 *1985 *2001 2013 2017 2048
2079 *2111 2114 2115 2132 2136 2146 2147 *2156 2173 2193 2199 2220
2238 2250 2256 2300 2343 2417 2498 2502 2519 *2612 2628 2635 2637
2649 *2716 2734 2779 2785 2803 2821 2829 2831 2832 2858 2885 2891
2902 2944 2963 2971 2981 *2983 2984 3002 3042 3053 3121 3122 3142
3143 3229 3234 3241 3242 3255 3259 3274 3278 3296 = 139*49
HAUING = 2

Who hauing beene prais'd for bluntnesse, doth affect	1171
Hauing more man then wit about me, drew;	1318

HAUTHORNE = *2

*sharpe Hauthorne blow the windes. Humh, goe to thy | bed and warme thee.	1828
*foule Fiend. Still through the Hauthorne blowes the	1878

HAY = 1

*downe; 'twas her Brother, that in pure kindnesse to his | Horse buttered his Hay.	1401

HAYRES = *1

*me like a Dogge, and told mee I had the white hayres in	2544

HE *see also* hee, hee'l, hee's, he'le, he'sheart *see also* hart = 117*35
HEAD = 10*9

*fed the Cuckoo so long, that it's had it head bit off by it	727
Lear. Why? | **Foole.* Why to put's head in, not to giue it away to his	903
*Sindge my white head. And thou all-shaking Thunder,	1661
Your high-engender'd Battailes, 'gainst a head	1678
**Foole.* He that has a house to put's head in, has a good | Head-peece:	1680
The Codpiece that will house, before the head has any;	1682
*The Head, and he shall Lowse: so Beggers marry many.	1683
**Edg.* Tom, will throw his head at them: Auaunt you	2022
For with throwing thus my head;	2029
The Sea, with such a storme as his bare head,	2131
**Glou.* There is a Cliffe, whose high and bending head	2258
Decline your head. This kisse, if it durst speake	2290
Gon. Milke-Liuer'd man, | That bear'st a cheeke for blowes, a head for wrongs,	2304
Me thinkes he seemes no bigger then his head.	2451
*the head to heare of pleasures name. The Fitchew, nor	2565
*head, nor no mony in your purse? Your eyes are in a hea-|uy	2590
That eyelesse head of thine, was first fram'd flesh	2677
And from th'extremest vpward of thy head,	3091
Backe do I tosse these Treasons to thy head,	3102

HEADED = 1

Kent. Alacke, bare-headed?	1714

HEADIER = 1

And am fallen out with my more headier will,	1386

HEADLONG = 1

Least my braine turne, and the deficient sight | Topple downe headlong.	2458

HEADS = 2*1

*tide by the heads, Dogges and Beares by'th'necke,	1283

HEADS *cont.*

Lear. Let the great Goddes | That keepe this dreadfull pudder o're our
heads,   1702
How shall your House-lesse heads, and vnfed sides,   1811
HEAD-PEECE = 1
Foole. He that has a house to put's head in, has a good | Head-peece: 1680
HEALTH = 2
No lesse then life, with grace, health, beauty, honor: 63
Whereto our health is bound, we are not our selues,   1383
HEARD = 9*3
Bast. Neuer my Lord. But I haue heard him oft main- | taine   405
*you what I haue seene, and heard: But faintly. Nothing   495
Cur. Nay I know not, you haue heard of the newes a- | broad,   934
Cur. Haue you heard of no likely Warres toward,   938
(Which I can call but now,) I haue heard strangenesse.   1026
Edg. I heard my selfe proclaim'd,   1252
Remember to haue heard. Mans Nature cannot carry | Th'affliction, nor
the feare.   1700
I haue ore-heard a plot of death vpon him: 2048
I haue heard more since: 2220
Cannot be heard so high. Ile looke no more,   2457
Cannot be seene, or heard: Do but looke vp.   2501
Sir, this I heard, the King is come to his Daughter   2866
HEARE = 20*5
Lea. Heare me recreant, on thine allegeance heare me;   181
*where you shall heare vs conferre of this, and by an Auri- | cular   424
*fitly bring you to heare my Lord speake: pray ye goe,   490
Edg. Shall I heare from you anon? *Exit.*   497
Ste. He's comming Madam, I heare him.   518
Lear. It may be so, my Lord. | Heare Nature, heare deere Goddesse,
heare: 788
When she shall heare this of thee, with her nailes   826
Bast. I heare my Father comming, pardon me: 959
Edmund, I heare that you haue shewne your Father | A Child-like
Office.   1045
Now, presently: bid them come forth and heare me,   1393
Gon. Heare me my Lord; | What need you fiue and twenty? Ten? Or
fiue?   1559
Shall passe betweene vs: ere long you are like to heare   2287
Soone may I heare, and see him. *Exeunt.*   2381
If you do chance to heare of that blinde Traitor,   2424
Hearke, do you heare the Sea? | *Glou.* No truly.   2435
Bid me farewell, and let me heare thee going.   2468
Hoa, you Sir: Friend, heare you Sir, speake: 2486
*the head to heare of pleasures name. The Fitchew, nor   2565
Edg. Do you heare ought (Sir) of a Battell toward. | *Gent.* Most sure,
and vulgar: 2652
Farre off methinkes I heare the beaten Drumme.   2741
Edg. If ere your Grace had speech with man so poore, | Heare me one
word.   2881
Alb. Stay yet, heare reason: *Edmund*, I arrest thee   3027
HEARES = 2
And when your Mistris heares thus much from you,   2421
Euery one heares that, which can distinguish sound.   2654
HEARING = 1
For I am almost ready to dissolue, | Hearing of this.   3167

HEARKE = 2*1
| | |
Hearke, do you heare the Sea? | *Glou*. No truly. | 2435
*yond Iustice railes vpon yond simple theefe. Hearke in | 2596
Bast. Come hither Captaine, hearke. | 2969

HEART = 27*17

And prize me at her worth. In my true heart, — 75
My heart into my mouth: I loue your Maiesty — 98
Lear. But goes thy heart with this? | *Cor*. I my good Lord. — 111
And as a stranger to my heart and me, — 122
Her Fathers heart from her; call *France*, who stirres? — 134
The region of my heart, be *Kent* vnmannerly, — 154
*hand to write this? A heart and braine to breede it in? — 392
Glou. It is his. | *Bast. It is his hand, my Lord: but I hope his heart is | not in the Contents. — 401
*gap in your owne Honor, and shake in peeces, the heart of — 418
From the fixt place: drew from my heart all loue, — 782
Not feare still to be taken. I know his heart, — 852
Glo. O Madam, my old heart is crack'd, it's crack'd. — 1029
*Lear. Oh how this Mother swels vp toward my heart! — 1328
*Lear. Oh me my heart! My rising heart! But downe. — 1397
Most Serpent-like, vpon the very Heart. — 1443
*But this heart shal break into a hundred thousand flawes — 1585
Poore Foole, and Knaue, I haue one part in my heart | That's sorry yet for thee. — 1727
Lear. Wilt breake my heart? — 1783
Your old kind Father, whose franke heart gaue all, — 1800
*Proud of heart, to ride on a Bay trotting Horse, ouer foure — 1837
*with mans sworne Spouse: set not thy Sweet-heart on | proud array. *Tom*'s a cold. — 1862
Lear. What hast thou bin? | *Edg. A Seruingman? Proud in heart, and minde; that — 1864
*of my Mistris heart, and did the acte of darkenesse with — 1867
*the Turke. False of heart, light of eare, bloody of hand; — 1872
*Nor the rustling of Silkes, betray thy poore heart to wo-|man. — 1875
*were like an old Letchers heart, a small spark, all the rest — 1893
*in the furie of his heart, when the foule Fiend rages, eats — 1910
Trey, Blanch, and Sweet-heart: see, they barke at me. — 2021
*breeds about her heart. Is there any cause in Nature that — 2034
Which came from one that's of a newtrall heart, | And not from one oppos'd. — 2116
Yet poore old heart, he holpe the Heauens to raine. — 2134
Edg. Now fare ye well, good Sir. | *Glou*. With all my heart. — 2469
Edg. I would not take this from report, | It is, and my heart breakes at it. — 2585
There is my pledge: Ile make it on thy heart — 3040
That if my speech offend a Noble heart, — 3081
Thy valor, and thy heart, thou art a Traitor: — 3088
To proue vpon thy heart, where to I speake, | Thou lyest. — 3095
With the hell-hated Lye, ore-whelme thy heart, — 3103
Let sorrow split my heart, if euer I | Did hate thee, or thy Father. — 3139
And when 'tis told, O that my heart would burst. — 3145
Told him our pilgrimage. But his flaw'd heart — 3159
*Gen. 'Tis hot, it smoakes, it came euen from the heart | of--- O she's dead. — 3174
Kent. Breake heart, I prythee breake. | *Edg*. Looke vp my Lord. — 3285

HEARTED *see also* harted = 2*1
  Nor are those empty hearted, whose low sounds | Reuerbe no
hollownesse.   163
  Lear. What art thou? | *Kent*. A very honest hearted Fellow, and as
poore as | the King.   549
  Ingratitude! thou Marble-hearted Fiend,   771
HEARTIE = 1
  Ile leade you to some biding. | *Glou*. Heartie thankes: 2671
HEARTS = 3*1
  If it be you that stirres these Daughters hearts   1574
  *make these hard-hearts. You sir, I entertaine for one of   2035
  All hearts against vs: *Edmund*, I thinke is gone | In pitty of his misery,
to dispatch   2396
  To know our enemies mindes, we rip their hearts,   2713
HEART-STROOKE = 1
  Gent. None but the Foole, who labours to out-iest | His heart-strooke
iniuries.   1624
HEAT = *1
  *some little time hath qualified the heat of his displeasure,   483
HEATE = *1
  Gon. We must do something, and i'th' heate. *Exeunt*.   332
HEAUE = 1
  Cor. Vnhappie that I am, I cannot heaue   97
HEAUEN = 3*2
  Lear. O let me not be mad, not mad sweet Heauen: 918
  All the stor'd Vengeances of Heauen, fall   1444
  *them in the sweet face of Heauen. One, that slept in the   1869
  The bountie, and the benizon of Heauen | To boot, and boot.   2673
  He that parts vs, shall bring a Brand from Heauen,   2964
HEAUENLY = *1
  *Fooles by heauenly compulsion, Knaues, Theeues, and   451
HEAUENS = 8*1
  Thou out of Heauens benediction com'st | To the warme Sun.   1238
  Who comes here? O Heauens!   1479
  You Heauens, giue me that patience, patience I need,   1571
  And shew the Heauens more iust.   1817
  *of France. O Heauens! that this Treason were not; | or not I the
detector.   1982
  Yet poore old heart, he holpe the Heauens to raine.   2134
  Makes thee the happier: Heauens deale so still: 2251
  This iudgement of the Heauens that makes vs tremble.   3185
  That Heauens vault should crack: she's gone for euer.   3219
HEAUIE = 1
  Take vantage heauie eyes, not to behold   1248
HEAUINESSE = 1
  Gent. I Madam: in the heauinesse of sleepe, | We put fresh garments on
him.   2772
HEAUNS = *1
  Glou. Here take this purse, y whom the heau'ns plagues   2249
HEAUY = 1*1
  Hast heauy substance, bleed'st not, speak'st, art sound,   2494
  *head, nor no mony in your purse? Your eyes are in a hea-|uy   2590
HECCAT = 1
  The misteries of *Heccat* and the night: 117
HEDGE-SPARROW = *1
  Foole. For you know Nunckle, the Hedge-Sparrow   726

HEE *l.**8 *380 *391 *641 *1895 *1896 *1980 *1988 *2718 = *9
HEED = 1*1
    Lear. Take heed Sirrah, the whip.   640
    *Edgar. Take heed o'th'foule Fiend, obey thy Pa- | rents,   1860
HEEL *l.*201 2281 = 2
HEELES = 1*2
    *Foole. If a mans braines were in's heeles, wert not in | danger of
kybes? | *Lear*. I Boy.   882
    *heeles, and beate thee before the King? Draw you rogue,   1103
A good mans fortune may grow out at heeles: 1233
HEERE = 34*4
And heere are to be answer'd. Tell me my daughters   53
Heere I disclaime all my Paternall care, | Propinquity and property of
blood,   120
    *wit o'both sides, and left nothing i'th'middle; heere | comes one o'the
parings.   700
    Lear. Do's any heere know me? | This is not *Lear*:   738
Heere do you keepe a hundred Knights and Squires,   750
    Lear. What's he, | That hath so much thy place mistooke | To set thee
heere?   1286
And meeting heere the other Messenger,   1314
The shame which heere it suffers.   1321
Should he sit heere? This act perswades me,   1389
Sharpe-tooth'd vnkindnesse, like a vulture heere,   1413
That she would soone be heere. Is your Lady come?   1471
You see me heere (you Gods) a poore old man,   1572
Your horrible pleasure. Heere I stand your Slaue,   1674
Gracious my Lord, hard by heere is a Houell,   1715
    Lear. Let me alone. | *Kent*. Good my Lord enter heere.   1781
    *Foole. Come not in heere Nuncle, here's a spirit, helpe | me, helpe me.   1820
    *as thou art. Off, off you Lendings: Come, vn- | button heere.   1888
on's body, cold: Looke, heere comes a walking fire.   1894
    *Glou. Heere is better then the open ayre, take it thank- | fully: 1998
    *Kent. Now good my Lord, lye heere, and rest awhile.   2040
But who comes heere? My Father poorely led? | World, World, O
world!   2189
    Alb. He is not heere. | *Mes*. No my good Lord, I met him backe againe.   2338
I am sure of that: and at her late being heere,   2411
Heere Friend's another purse: in it, a Iewell   2465
    Edg. As I stood heere below, me thought his eyes   2514
But who comes heere?   2527
    Gent. Oh heere he is: lay hand vpon him, Sir.   2631
And the exchange my Brother: heere, in the sands   2726
For these domesticke and particular broiles, | Are not the question
heere.   2871
Heere is the guesse of their true strength and Forces,   2898
    Edg. Heere Father, take the shadow of this Tree   2921
    Glo. No further Sir, a man may rot euen heere.   2931
At gilded Butterflies: and heere (poore Rogues)   2953
Witnesse the world, that I create thee heere | My Lord, and Master.   3020
Then I haue heere proclaim'd thee.   3042
Thy arme may do thee Iustice, heere is mine: 3082
The Wheele is come full circle, I am heere.   3136
    Mess. *Edmund* is dead my Lord. | *Alb*. That's but a trifle heere: 3266
HEEREAFTER = 1
    Glou. My Lord of Kent: | Remember him heereafter, as my Honourable
Friend.   30

HEERES = 2*1
   Cor. Heere's *France* and *Burgundy*, my Noble Lord.   204
   *in, aske thy Daughters blessing, heere's a night pitties | neither
Wisemen, nor Fooles.   1667
   Heere's the place: stand still: how fearefull   2446
HEES = 3*2
   Lear. If thou be'st as poore for a subiect, as hee's for a   552
   Hee's comming hither, now i'th' night, i'th' haste,   954
   And they will take it so, if not, hee's plaine.   1175
   *his Sonne: for hee's a mad Yeoman that sees his Sonne a | Gentleman
before him.   2011
   May be my Friends: hee's dead; I am onely sorry   2710
HEFTED = 1
   Thy tender-hefted Nature shall not giue   1455
HEIGHT = 1
   Looke vp a height, the shrill-gorg'd Larke so farre   2500
HEIGH-HO = 1
   With heigh-ho, the Winde and the Raine,   1730
HEINOUS *see* heynous
HEIRE = *1
   *Pandar, and the Sonne and Heire of a Mungrill Bitch,   1095
HELD = 1
   Kent. My life I neuer held but as pawne   166
HELE = 1
   He'le strike and quickly too, he's dead and rotten.   3251
HELL = *1
   *beneath is all the Fiends. There's hell, there's darke- |nes,   2569
HELL-BLACKE-NIGHT = 1
   In Hell-blacke-night indur'd, would haue buoy'd vp   2132
HELL-HATED = 1
   With the hell-hated Lye, ore-whelme thy heart,   3103
HELPE = 10*1
   Stop, stop, no helpe?   969
   Ste. Helpe, ho, murther, helpe.   1113
   Stew. Helpe hoa, murther, murther.   1116
   Foole. Come not in heere Nuncle, here's a spirit, helpe | me, helpe me.   1820
   Giue me some helpe. --- O cruell! O you Gods.   2142
   Gen. Helpe, helpe: O helpe.   3170
   Edg. What kinde of helpe? | *Alb*. Speake man.   3171
HELPES = 1
   In the restoring his bereaued Sense; he that helpes him,   2359
HEMLOCKE = *1
   *With Hardokes, Hemlocke, Nettles, Cuckoo flowres,   2354
HENCE = 11*1
   On her kind nursery. Hence and avoid my sight: 132
   Freedome liues hence, and banishment is here;   195
   I thinke our Father will hence to night.   312
   From hence attend dispatch, our good old Friend,   1068
   Stew. My Lord of Glouster hath conuey'd him hence   2074
   Thou wilt ore-take vs hence a mile or twaine   2229
   Reg. Faith he is poasted hence on serious matter: 2393
   Stew. Wherefore, bold Pezant, | Dar'st thou support a publish'd
Traitor? Hence,   2683
   Men must endure | Their going hence, euen as their comming hither,   2933
   And fire vs hence, like Foxes: wipe thine eyes,   2965
   Alb. The Gods defend her, beare him hence awhile.   3215
   Alb. Beare them from hence, our present businesse   3293

HENCEFORTH = 1
Glou. I do remember now: henceforth Ile beare | Affliction, till it do cry
out it selfe 2520
HER *l.**18 75 131 132 134 137 208 214 215 224 *227 228 239 242 263 287
317 *569 *605 *706 757 792 793 794 795 796 797 798 799 800 826 837
861 *877 898 *1110 1226 1390 *1401 1417 1418 1421 1424 1425 1432
1433 1442 1445 1449 1456 1470 1473 1484 1500 1504 1508 1558 1644
*1868 1901 1902 *2034 2331 *2406 2410 2411 2413 2422 2454 *2563
*2605 *2606 2649 2661 2725 2861 2862 2863 2907 2909 2911 3032 3056
3120 3177 3178 3213 3214 3215 3222 3234 3236 3282 = 90*15
HER = 3
HERALD see also Her. = 5
When time shall serue, let but the Herald cry, | And Ile appeare againe.
Exit. 2893
Enter a Herald. 3050
Alb. A Herald, ho. 3051
Come hither Herald, let the Trumpet sound, | And read out this. *A
Trumpet sounds.* 3057
Herald reads. | **If any man of qualitie or degree, within the lists of the
Ar-|my,* 3059
HERE *see also* heere = 19*5
So be my graue my peace, as here I giue 133
Freedome liues hence, and banishment is here; 195
And here I take *Cordelia* by the hand, | Dutchesse of *Burgundie.* 267
Thee and thy vertues here I seize vpon, 277
Thou loosest here a better where to finde. 286
Will be here with him this night. 932
Bast. The Duke be here to night? The better best, 943
Yeeld, come before my Father, light hoa, here, 963
*Bast. Here stood he in the dark, his sharpe Sword out, 972
Glo. Weapons? Armes? what's the matter here? 1121
And in the fleshment of this dead exploit, | Drew on me here againe. 1199
Kent. With the Earle Sir, here within. 1331
Lear. Follow me not, stay here. *Exit.* 1332
Corn. Haile to your Grace. *Kent here set at liberty.* 1405
Who comes here? O Heauens! 1479
Kent. Alas Sir are you here? Things that loue night, 1694
*Kent. Here is the place my Lord, good my Lord enter, 1778
Kent. Good my Lord enter here. 1803
*Kent. Here Sir, but trouble him not, his wits are gon. 2046
*Glou. Here take this purse, y whom the heau'ns plagues 2249
Stew. Madam, here come's my Lord. 2298
*Gent. Though that the Queen on special cause is here 2660
Edg. Here comes *Kent.* 3181
Is he not here? | *Alb.* Great thing of vs forgot, 3191
HEREDITARIE = 1
Lear. To thee, and thine hereditarie euer, 85
HERES = 1*3
Foole. Let me hire him too, here's my Coxcombe. 625
Kent. Who's there? | **Foole.* Marry here's Grace, and a Codpiece, that's
a | Wiseman, and a Foole. 1691
*Foole. Come not in heere Nuncle, here's a spirit, helpe | me, helpe me. 1820
*Wooll; the Cat, no perfume. Ha? Here's three on's are 1885
HERETIQUES = 1
No Heretiques burn'd, but wenches Sutors; 1739

HERS = 2*1
  Then on a wretch whom Nature is asham'd | Almost t'acknowledge
  hers.   232
  That face of hers againe, therfore be gone,   289
  *Cor. No more perchance do's mine, nor his, nor hers.   1165
HERSELFE see also selfe = 2
  She is herselfe a Dowrie.   264
  The one the other poison'd for my sake, | And after slew herselfe. 3197
HES = 7*1
  Ste. He's comming Madam, I heare him.   518
  *Edg. The Prince of Darkenesse is a Gentleman. Modo | he's call'd, and
  Mahu.   1921
  *Foole. No, he's a Yeoman, that ha's a Gentleman to   2010
  Gen. He's scarse awake,   2801
  To change the course, he's full of alteration,   2849
  Bast. There's my exchange, what in the world hes   3045
  Lear. He's a good fellow, I can tell you that,   3250
  He'le strike and quickly too, he's dead and rotten.   3251
HEWGH = 1
  clout, i'th'clout: Hewgh. Giue the word. | Edg. Sweet Mariorum. 2539
HEYNOUS = 1
  Thy heynous, manifest, and many Treasons,   3039
HID = 3
  Intelligence is giuen where you are hid;   951
  Glo. O Lady, Lady, shame would haue it hid.   1032
  Alb. Where haue you hid your selfe?   3142
HIDE = 1*3
  *such neede to hide it selfe. Let's see: come, if it bee no-|thing, I shall
  not neede Spectacles.   369
  Vnwhipt of Iustice. Hide thee, thou Bloudy hand;   1706
  *the Worme no Silke; the Beast, no Hide; the Sheepe, no 1884
  *and Furr'd gownes hide all. Place sinnes with Gold, and 2608
HIDEOUS = 2
  This hideous rashnesse, answere my life, my iudgement: 161
  More hideous when thou shew'st thee in a Child, | Then the
  Sea-monster.   772
HIDES = *1
  *Cor. Time shall vnfold what plighted cunning hides,   306
HIGH = 4*2
  Glo. The King is in high rage.   1598
  *Glo. Alacke the night comes on, and the high windes 1603
  Thron'd and set high; Seruants, who seeme no lesse, 1632
  *Glou. There is a Cliffe, whose high and bending head 2258
  Cannot be heard so high. Ile looke no more,   2457
  Conspirant 'gainst this high illustrious Prince,   3090
HIGHNESSE = 7*1
  And finde I am alone felicitate | In your deere Highnesse loue. 80
  Bur. Most Royall Maiesty, | I craue no more then hath your Highnesse
  offer'd,   210
  *but to my iudgement your Highnesse is not entertain'd 587
  *mistaken, for my duty cannot be silent, when I thinke | your Highnesse
  wrong'd.   594
  I did commend your Highnesse Letters to them,   1304
  Displaid so sawcily against your Highnesse,   1317
  Reg. I am glad to see your Highnesse.   1406
  Cor. Wilt please your Highnesse walke? | Lear. You must beare with
  me: 2840

HIGH-ENGENDERD = 1
Your high-engender'd Battailes, 'gainst a head   1678
HIGH-GROWNE = 1
Search euery Acre in the high-growne field,   2357
HIGH-IUDGING = 1
Nor tell tales of thee to high-iudging *Ioue*,   1522
HILL = 1*2
*hill, least it breake thy necke with following. But the   1345
*Edg. Pillicock sat on Pillicock hill, alow: alow, loo, loo.   1857
Glou. When shall I come to th'top of that same hill?   2431
HIM *l*.*13 31 109 297 299 326 *328 *388 *390 *405 *411 412 *415 *417
*419 *428 *431 476 480 *482 *484 515 518 521 *545 *546 582 601 625
*633 *664 679 844 854 930 932 955 979 981 993 998 1000 1001 1002
1003 1021 1038 1049 1060 *1132 1140 1162 1190 1191 1196 1197 1198
1223 *1343 *1346 1491 1592 1601 1602 1610 1623 1652 *1754 1757
*1765 *1767 *1836 *1842 *1844 1880 *1883 1940 1942 1948 1958 1960
1961 1962 *1976 *1981 *1990 2012 2028 *2046 *2047 2048 2049 2053
*2061 2063 *2065 *2074 2076 2078 2083 2095 2098 2124 2155 2157 2165
2169 2170 2219 2238 2271 2272 2275 2277 2282 2320 2322 2339 *2341
2358 2359 2363 2369 2381 2391 2395 *2400 2420 2425 2479 2631 2702
*2717 2730 2773 2774 2790 2802 2838 2839 2886 2911 *2994 3001 3022
3048 *3062 3068 3079 3107 3134 3154 3155 3159 3215 3242 3263 3272
*3287 3289 = 131*45
HIMSELFE = 8*2
*Reg. 'Tis the infirmity of his age, yet he hath euer but | slenderly
knowne himselfe.   318
His Knights grow riotous, and himselfe vpbraides vs   513
*the generall dependants, as in the Duke himselfe also, and | your
Daughter.   590
*Gon. 'Tis his owne blame hath put himselfe from rest,   1590
Corn. 'Tis best to giue him way, he leads himselfe.   1601
*a prouoking merit set a-worke by a reprouable badnesse | in himselfe.   1977
Reg. Himselfe in person there? | *Stew*. Madam with much ado: 2386
*Lear. No, they cannot touch me for crying. I am the | King himselfe.   2530
In his owne grace he doth exalt himselfe, | More then in your addition.   3008
Bast. Himselfe, what saist thou to him? | *Edg*. Draw thy Sword,   3079
HIRE = 1
Foole. Let me hire him too, here's my Coxcombe.   625
HIS *see also* and's, in's, on's, put's, 's *l*.*12 *25 *26 124 125 130 201 273
274 298 *314 *318 *320 *321 330 359 *388 *391 *399 401 *402 408 *409
*415 *417 *419 *446 *456 *482 *483 *488 509 513 *525 *633 *664 *740
741 807 847 852 854 899 *904 905 931 956 *972 986 987 997 1001 1016
1019 1039 1048 1136 1163 1164 *1165 1173 1192 1193 1194 1211 1217
1221 1222 1307 1308 1369 1372 *1378 *1401 1402 1428 1491 1507 *1590
1591 1592 1611 1625 *1684 1685 1731 *1749 *1823 *1835 *1836 *1838
*1844 1852 *1910 1915 1934 1941 1943 1949 1967 1971 *1976 *1991
*2001 *2011 2018 *2022 *2046 2052 2064 2075 2084 2091 2129 2130
2131 2171 *2247 2273 2274 2280 2284 2314 2318 2319 2326 2335 2336
2359 2370 2397 2398 2451 2471 2506 2514 2529 *2534 2560 *2640 2685
2686 *2719 2764 2775 2847 2850 2866 2910 2912 2915 2929 2992 3008
*3063 3068 3134 3152 3153 3158 3159 3216 *3287 3292 = 118*55
HISSING *see* hizzing
HISTORICA = 1
Historica passio, downe thou climing sorrow,   1329
HISTORY = 1
Which often leaues the history vnspoke   259

HITHER = 10*4
*my Foole hither. You you Sirrah, where's my Daughter?	574
*call hither my Foole; Oh you Sir, you, come you hither	606
Hee's comming hither, now i'th' night, i'th' haste,	954
*Corn. How now my Noble friend, since I came hither	1025
Glou. Come hither Friend: | Where is the King my Master?	2044
Glou. Come hither fellow. | Edg. And yet I must:	2242
Mes. Come with my Lady hither.	2337
And to reuenge thine eyes. Come hither Friend,	2346
Thou must be patient; we came crying hither:	2620
Men must endure | Their going hence, euen as their comming hither,	2933
Bast. Come hither Captaine, hearke.	2969
Come hither Herald, let the Trumpet sound, | And read out this. A Trumpet sounds.	3057
Lear. You are welcome hither. | Kent. Nor no man else:	3256

HITHERWARD = 1
Mes. Newes Madam, | The Brittish Powres are marching hitherward.	2373

HIZZING = 1
Lear. To haue a thousand with red burning spits | Come hizzing in vpon 'em.	2013

HO = 6*3
*ho, dinner, where's my knaue? my Foole? Go you and call	573
*backe: wher's my Foole? Ho, I thinke the world's	578
Glo. Pursue him, ho: go after. By no meanes, what?	979
Ste. Helpe, ho, murther, helpe.	1113
So old, and white as this. O, ho! 'tis foule.	1679
With heigh-ho, the Winde and the Raine,	1730
*Lear. Oh ho, are you there with me? No eies in your	2589
Gon. Oh ho, I know the Riddle, I will goe. | Exeunt both the Armies.	2878
Alb. A Herald, ho.	3051

HOA = 4
Gon. Pray you content. What Oswald, hoa?	833
Yeeld, come before my Father, light hoa, here,	963
Stew. Helpe hoa, murther, murther.	1116
Hoa, you Sir: Friend, heare you Sir, speake:	2486

HOAST = 1
For your good hoast: pray that the right may thriue:	2922

HOG = *1
*Hog in sloth, Foxe in stealth, Wolfe in greedinesse, Dog	1873

HOLA = 2
Gon. Hola, hola, | That eye that told you so, look'd but a squint.	3014

HOLD = 16*5
Hold thee from this for euer. The barbarous Scythian,	123
Lear. Right Noble Burgundy, | When she was deare to vs, we did hold her so,	213
*so, Ile write straight to my Sister to hold my course; pre-|pare for dinner. Exeunt.	527
*thou art nothing. Yes forsooth I will hold my tongue, so	708
And hold our liues in mercy. Oswald, I say.	848
Kent. No contraries hold more antipathy, | Then I, and such a knaue.	1160
*let go thy hold when a great wheele runs downe a	1344
Will you yet hold?	1489
Hold amity? 'Tis hard, almost impossible.	1538
And let this Tyrannous night take hold vpon you,	1929
*Corn. See't shalt thou neuer. Fellowes hold y Chaire,	2139
Corn. If you see vengeance. | Seru. Hold your hand, my Lord:	2144
But better seruice haue I neuer done you, | Then now to bid you hold.	2147

HOLD *cont*.

*obey'd in Office. Thou, Rascall Beadle, hold thy bloody	2603
Like hold on thee. Let go his arme.	2686
Cor. O looke vpon me Sir, | And hold your hand in benediction o're me,	2810
Bast. Know of the Duke if his last purpose hold,	2847
Where you shall hold your Session.	2997
I hold you but a subiect of this Warre, | Not as a Brother.	2999
Or with this paper shall I stop it: hold Sir,	3113
Alb. If there be more, more wofull, hold it in,	3166

HOLDING = *1

*whipt for lying, and sometimes I am whipt for holding	697

HOLLA = 1

That way, Ile this: He that first lights on him, | Holla the other. *Exeunt.*	1652

HOLLOW = 1

And by the happy hollow of a Tree,	1253

HOLLOWNESSE = 1*1

Nor are those empty hearted, whose low sounds | Reuerbe no hollownesse.	163
*seene the best of our time. Machinations, hollownesse,	442

HOLPE = 1

Yet poore old heart, he holpe the Heauens to raine.	2134

HOLY = 1

Like Rats oft bite the holy cords a twaine,	1147

HOLY-WATER = *1

Foole. O Nunkle, Court holy-water in a dry house, is	1665

HOME = 7*3

With his prepared Sword, he charges home	987
To answere from our home: the seuerall Messengers	1067
I'ld driue ye cackling home to *Camelot*.	1157
Lea. 'Tis strange that they should so depart from home,	1274
Kent. My Lord, when at their home	1303
I am now from home, and out of that prouision	1498
*King now beares, will be reuenged home; ther is part of	1763
For lifting food too't? But I will punish home;	1796
I must change names at home, and giue the Distaffe	2285
Reg. Lord *Edmund* spake not with your Lord at home? | *Stew.* No Madam.	2389

HONEST = 2*4

As honest Madams issue? Why brand they vs	343
Edm. Brother, I aduise you to the best, I am no honest	493
*honest, to conuerse with him that is wise and saies little, to	546
Lear. What art thou? | *Kent.* A very honest hearted Fellow, and as poore as | the King.	549
Lear. What seruices canst thou do? | *Kent.* I can keepe honest counsaile, ride, run, marre a	562
An honest mind and plaine, he must speake truth,	1174

HONESTIE = 1

That he suspects none: on whose foolish honestie	501

HONESTY = 1*1

*Kent banish'd; his offence, honesty. 'Tis strange. *Exit*	446
Who weares no honesty: such smiling rogues as these,	1146

HONOR = 4*3

No lesse then life, with grace, health, beauty, honor:	63
*gap in your owne Honor, and shake in peeces, the heart of	418
*he hath writ this to feele my affection to your Honor, z	420
Bast. If your Honor iudge it meete, I will place you	423

HONOR *cont*.
A Babe to honor her. If she must teeme,   795
Who hast not in thy browes an eye-discerning | Thine Honor, from thy
suffering.   2306
On him, on you, who not, I will maintaine | My truth and honor
firmely.   3048
HONORD = 1
Kent. Royall *Lear*, | Whom I haue euer honor'd as my King,   148
HONORS = *1
*Thinke that the cleerest Gods, who make them Honors   2518
HONOUR = 3
Obey you, Loue you, and most Honour you.   105
As I haue life and Honour, there shall he sit till Noone.   1213
Bast. No by mine honour, Madam.   2860
HONOURABLE = 1
Glou. My Lord of Kent: | Remember him heereafter, as my Honourable
Friend.   30
HONOURD = 1
Do you not loue my Sister? | *Bast*. In honour'd Loue.   2856
HONOURS = 3
To plainnesse honour's bound,   158
The priuiledge of mine Honours,   3084
With boote, and such addition as your Honours   3273
HOOD = 1
By rule of Knight-hood, I disdaine and spurne: 3101
HOPE = 1*3
Bast. I hope for my Brothers iustification, hee wrote   380
Glou. It is his. | *Bast*. It is his hand, my Lord: but I hope his heart is |
not in the Contents.   401
Reg. I pray you Sir, take patience, I haue hope   1416
Lear. Who stockt my Seruant? *Regan*, I haue good hope   1477
HOPING = 1
Not sure, though hoping of this good successe,   3157
HORNE = 1
And Market Townes: poore Tom thy horne is dry,   2032
HORNES = 3
Hornes within. Enter Lear and Attendants.   538
daughters, and leaue his hornes without a case.   905
Hornes wealk'd, and waued like the enraged Sea: 2516
HORRIBLE = 3
And with this horrible obiect, from low Farmes,   1268
Your horrible pleasure. Heere I stand your Slaue,   1674
Glou. Me thinkes the ground is eeuen. | *Edg*. Horrible steepe. 2433
HORRID = 3
Such sheets of Fire, such bursts of horrid Thunder,   1698
Edmund, enkindle all the sparkes of Nature | To quit this horrid acte. 2162
Proper deformitie seemes not in the Fiend | So horrid as in woman. 2309
HORROR = 2
like the image, and horror of it, pray you away.   496
Kent. Is this the promis'd end? | *Edg*. Or image of that horror. | *Alb*.
Fall and cease.   3224
HORSE = 8*2
Foole. May not an Asse know, when the Cart drawes | the Horse? 735
Gon. Take you some company, and away to horse,   860
They summon'd vp their meiney, straight tooke Horse,   1311
*downe; 'twas her Brother, that in pure kindnesse to his | Horse
buttered his Hay.   1401

HORSE *cont.*

Glo. He cals to Horse, but will I know not whether.	1600
*Proud of heart, to ride on a Bay trotting Horse, ouer foure	1837
Horse to ride, and weapon to weare:	1916
*the soyled Horse goes too't with a more riotous appe- | tite:	2566
It were a delicate stratagem to shoo | A Troope of Horse with Felt: Ile put't in proofe,	2626
Why should a Dog, a Horse, a Rat haue life,	3278

HORSES = 5*1

Saddle my horses: call my Traine together.	763
Is it your will, speake Sir? Prepare my Horses.	770
*keepe me in temper, I would not be mad. How now are | the Horses ready?	919
Stew. Where may we set our horses? | *Kent*. I'th'myre.	1078
Foole. Hah, ha, he weares Cruell Garters Horses are	1282
Corn. Get horses for your Mistris.	2080

HORSEWAY = *1

Edg. Both style, and gate; Horseway, and foot-path:	2246

HORSON = *1

*there was good sport at his making, and the horson must	26

HORSSES = 1

Lear. I will forget my Nature, so kind a Father? Be | my Horsses ready?	906

HOSPITABLE = 1

With Robbers hands, my hospitable fauours	2106

HOST = 1

Will quicken and accuse thee. I am your Host,	2105

HOT = 4*1

That these hot teares, which breake from me perforce	816
Fiery? The fiery Duke, tell the hot Duke that---	1380
Hot Questrists after him, met him at gate,	2076
And call it selfe your Brother. | *Gon*. Not so hot:	3006
Gen. 'Tis hot, it smoakes, it came euen from the heart | of--- O she's dead.	3174

HOTLY = *1

*backe, thou hotly lusts to vse her in that kind, for which	2605

HOT-BLOODIED = 1

Why the hot-bloodied *France*, that dowerlesse tooke	1505

HOUEL = *2

*And can make vilde things precious. Come, your Houel;	1726
Glou. In fellow there, into th'Houel; keep thee warm.	1955

HOUELL = 2*1

Gracious my Lord, hard by heere is a Houell,	1715
Le. True Boy: Come bring vs to this Houell. *Exit*.	1733
To houell thee with Swine and Rogues forlorne,	2787

HOUND = 2

Mastiffe, Grey-hound, Mongrill, Grim,	2025
Hound or Spaniell, Brache, or Hym:	2026

HOURE *see also* howre = 4

We haue this houre a constant will to publish	48
If thou should'st dally halfe an houre, his life	2052
Fourescore and vpward, | Not an houre more, nor lesse:	2815
Vntill some halfe houre past when I was arm'd,	3156

HOURELY = 3

Do hourely Carpe and Quarrell, breaking forth	714
Gent. Neere, and on speedy foot: the maine descry | Stands on the hourely thought.	2657

HOURELY *cont.*
That we the paine of death would hourely dye,   3148
HOURES = 2
Bast. Spake you with him? | *Edg.* I, two houres together.   476
These weedes are memories of those worser houres: 2754
HOUSE = 12*4
Foole. Nor I neither; but I can tell why a Snaile ha's | a house.   901
That if they come to soiourne at my house,   1042
Stew. Good dawning to thee Friend, art of this house? | *Kent.* I.   1076
He rais'd the house, with loud and coward cries,   1319
Do you but marke how this becomes the house?   1434
Speake 'gainst so great a number? How in one house   1536
To follow in a house, where twice so many | Haue a command to tend
you?   1561
Reg. This house is little, the old man and's people, | Cannot be well
bestow'd.   1588
Foole. O Nunkle, Court holy-water in a dry house, is   1665
Foole. He that has a house to put's head in, has a good | Head-peece: 1680
The Codpiece that will house, before the head has any;   1682
Repose you there, while I to this hard house;   1717
*they tooke from me the vse of mine owne house, charg'd   1755
Kent. Good my Lord take his offer, | Go into th'house.   1934
Corn. I will haue my reuenge, ere I depart his house.   1971
And quit the house on purpose, that their punishment | Might haue the
freer course.   2342
HOUSELESSE = 1
In Boy, go first. You houselesse pouertie, *Exit.*   1807
HOUSE-LESSE = 1
How shall your House-lesse heads, and vnfed sides,   1811
HOW = 48*18
Lear. How, how *Cordelia*? Mend your speech a little,   100
Gon. You see how full of changes his age is, the ob- | seruation   314
Vpon the gad? *Edmond*, how now? What newes?   361
Edg. How now Brother *Edmond*, what serious con- | templation are you
in?   467
how now, what art thou? | *Kent.* A man Sir.   540
Lear. How old art thou? | *Kent.* Not so young Sir to loue a woman for
singing,   567
asleepe, how now? Where's that Mungrell?   579
Lear. How now my pretty knaue, how dost thou?   626
*needs weare my Coxcombe. How now Nunckle? would   634
And know not how their wits to weare,   682
Lear. How now Daughter? what makes that Frontlet   703
How vgly did'st thou in *Cordelia* shew?   780
How sharper then a Serpents tooth it is,   802
How now *Oswald*?   857
Alb. How farre your eies may pierce I cannot tell;   869
Foole. Can'st tell how an Oyster makes his shell? | *Lear.* No.   899
*keepe me in temper, I would not be mad. How now are | the Horses
ready?   919
Bast. How comes that?   933
Spoke with how manifold, and strong a Bond   983
Seeing how lothly opposite I stood   985
Corn. How now my Noble friend, since I came hither   1025
Which can pursue th'offender; how dost my Lord?   1028
How in my strength you please: for you *Edmund*,   1054
Bast. I shall serue you Sir truely, how euer else.   1059

HOW *cont.*

Bast. How now, what's the matter? Part.	1118
Cor. Speake yet, how grew your quarrell?	1134
Glost. How fell you out, say that?	1159
Lear. Oh how this Mother swels vp toward my heart!	1328
*How chance the King comes with so small a number?	1336
How vnremoueable and fixt he is | In his owne course.	1368
With how deprau'd a quality. Oh *Regan.*	1415
You lesse know how to value her desert, | Then she to scant her dutie.	1417
Lear. Say? How is that?	1419
Do you but marke how this becomes the house?	1434
Gon. Why not by'th'hand Sir? How haue I offended?	1485
How came my man i'th'Stockes?	1490
Speake 'gainst so great a number? How in one house	1536
Come on my boy. How dost my boy? Art cold?	1723
How shall your House-lesse heads, and vnfed sides,	1811
Kent. How fares your Grace? | *Lear.* What's he?	1904
What is your study? | *Edg.* How to preuent the Fiend, and to kill Vermine.	1937
Bast. How my Lord, I may be censured, that Nature	1972
Bast. How malicious is my fortune, that I must re-|pent	1979
How now? Where's the King?	2073
Reg. How now, you dogge?	2149
How is't my Lord? How looke you?	2172
Oldm. How now? who's there?	2206
Edg. How should this be?	2223
Edg. You do climbe vp it now. Look how we labor.	2432
Heere's the place: stand still: how fearefull	2446
And yet I know not how conceit may rob	2482
Vp, so: How is't? Feele you your Legges? You stand. | *Glou.* Too well, too well.	2508
When I do stare, see how the Subiect quakes.	2555
*case, your purse in a light, yet you see how this world | goes.	2591
Lear. What, art mad? A man may see how this world	2594
*goes, with no eyes. Looke with thine eares: See how	2595
Edg. But by your fauour: | How neere's the other Army?	2655
How stiffe is my vilde sense | That I stand vp, and haue ingenious feeling	2733
Cor. O thou good *Kent,* | How shall I liue and worke | To match thy goodnesse?	2745
How do's the King? | *Gent.* Madam sleepes still.	2761
Cor. How does my Royall Lord? | How fares your Maiesty?	2792
How haue you knowne the miseries of your Father?	3143

HOWEUER *see* how

HOWLD = 1

If Wolues had at thy Gate howl'd that sterne time,	2135

HOWLE = *3

Lear. Howle, howle, howle: O you are men of stones,	3217

HOWRE = 1

Gon. By day and night, he wrongs me, euery howre	510

HOWS = 1

Lear. How's that?	915

HUGE = 1

Of my huge Sorrowes? Better I were distract,	2735

HUM = *1

*Hum? Conspiracy? Sleepe till I wake him, you should	390

HUMBLED = 1
Haue humbled to all strokes: that I am wretched   2250
HUMH = *1
    *sharpe Hauthorne blow the windes. Humh, goe to thy | bed and warme
    thee.   1828
HUNDRED = 5*4
    With reseruation of an hundred Knights,   141
    Heere do you keepe a hundred Knights and Squires,   750
    Gon. This man hath had good Counsell, | A hundred Knights?   842
    *At point a hundred Knights: yes, that on euerie dreame,   845
    If she sustaine him, and his hundred Knights   854
    *base, proud, shallow, beggerly, three-suited-hundred   1089
    I can be patient, I can stay with *Regan*, | I and my hundred Knights. 1524
    *But this heart shal break into a hundred thousand flawes   1585
    *my hundred; only, I do not like the fashion of your gar- | ments.   2036
HUNT = 1
    Escap'd the hunt. No Port is free, no place   1254
HUNTING = 1
    On euery trifle. When he returnes from hunting,   514
HURRICANOES *see* hyrricano's
HURT = 4*1
    This hurt you see, striuing to apprehend him.   1049
    On things would hurt me more, but Ile goe in,   1806
    Corn. I haue receiu'd a hurt: Follow me Lady;   2173
    *Vntimely comes this hurt. Giue me your arme. *Exeunt*.   2176
    Thy comforts can do me no good at all, | Thee, they may hurt.   2196
HURTLESSE = *1
    *the strong Lance of Iustice, hurtlesse breakes: Arme it in   2609
HURTS = *1
    *Mildewes the white Wheate, and hurts the poore Crea- | ture of earth. 1898
HUSBAND = 5*4
    *Sonne for her Cradle, ere she had a husband for her bed.   18
    That you must loose a husband.   271
    Corn. Poste speedily to my Lord your husband, shew   2060
    Gon. Welcome my Lord. I meruell our mild husband   2268
    Stew. Madam, I had rather--- | *Reg*. I know your Lady do's not loue her
    Husband,   2409
    Bast. Feare not, she and the Duke her husband.   2863
    Her husband being aliue. Now then, wee'l vse   2909
    Alb. That were the most, if he should husband you.   3012
    And I her husband contradict your Banes.   3032
HUSBANDS = 3
    Why haue my Sisters Husbands, if they say   106
    Into my Husbands hands. This trustie Seruant   2286
    A plot vpon her vertuous Husbands life,   2725
HUSH = 1
    Glou. No words, no words, hush.   1965
HYM = 1
    Hound or Spaniell, Brache, or Hym: 2026
HYRRICANOS = 1
    You Cataracts, and Hyrricano's spout,   1657
I *see also* che, chill, 'chud = 445*141, 16*3
    Lear. But goes thy heart with this? | *Cor*. I my good Lord.   111
    Bast. Spake you with him? | *Edg*. I, two houres together.   476
    Gon. Did my Father strike my Gentleman for chi- | ding of his Foole? |
    Ste. I Madam.   507
    What haue you writ that Letter to my Sister? | *Stew*. I Madam.   858

I *cont.*

Foole. If a mans braines were in's heeles, wert not in | danger of kybes? | *Lear*. I Boy. 882

Cor. Is he pursued? | *Glo*. I my good Lord. 1050

Stew. Good dawning to thee Friend, art of this house? | *Kent*. I. 1076

Kent. By *Iuno*, I sweare I. 1296

Lear. Inform'd them? Do'st thou vnderstand me man. | *Glo*. I my good Lord. 1374

Glou. Is that the naked Fellow? | *Oldm*. I, my Lord. 2226

And each man haue enough. Dost thou know Douer? | *Edg*. I Master. 2256

Mes. I my good Lord: 'twas he inform'd against him 2341

Reg. But are my Brothers Powres set forth? | *Stew*. I Madam. 2384

*my Beard, ere the blacke ones were there. To say I, and 2545

*no, to euery thing that I said: I, and no too, was no good 2546

Is't not the King? | *Lear*. I, euery inch a King. 2553

dogge barke at a Beggar? | *Glou*. I Sir. 2599

Gent. I Madam: in the heauinesse of sleepe, | We put fresh garments on him. 2772

And desperately are dead | *Lear*. I so I thinke. 3260

IAKES = 1

Iakes with him. Spare my gray-beard, you wagtaile? 1140

IARRING = 2

Th'vntun'd and iarring senses, O winde vp, | Of this childe-changed Father. 2765

To be oppos'd against the iarring windes? 2783

IDE = 1

You and your Fellowes: I'de haue it come to question; 520

IDLE = 2*1

vs, till our oldnesse cannot rellish them. I begin to finde an idle 384

Darnell, and all the idle weedes that grow 2355

That on th'vnnumbred idle Pebble chafes 2456

IEALOUS = 1*1

*which I haue rather blamed as mine owne iealous curio-|sitie, 598

Each iealous of the other, as the stung 2903

IELLY *see* gelly

IEST = 1

Gent. None but the Foole, who labours to out-iest | His heart-strooke iniuries. 1624

IESTERS = 1

Reg. Iesters do oft proue Prophets. 3013

IEWELL = 1

Heere Friend's another purse: in it, a Iewell 2465

IEWELS = 1

Cor. The Iewels of our Father, with wash'd eies 293

IF *l.*106 190 216 246 *328 353 *369 *387 *398 *413 *416 *423 *450 491 *494 503 516 521 531 535 *552 *571 *593 *620 *633 *637 *678 720 790 795 840 854 *878 *882 *913 1005 1012 1027 1042 1052 1080 *1083 *1096 *1119 *1138 1156 1175 1215 *1322 1408 1421 1480 1481 1495 1542 1543 1568 1574 1643 *1767 *1768 1790 *1985 *1990 2024 2052 2135 2144 2150 2228 2288 2290 2420 2424 2476 2479 *2618 2700 *2717 *2718 2829 2847 *2881 2885 2888 2906 2923 2957 2971 *3012 3033 3038 3044 *3060 3081 3116 3125 3129 3139 3166 3222 3227 3245 = 70*34

IGNOBLY = 1

Glou. By the kinde Gods, 'tis most ignobly done | To plucke me by the Beard. 2100

IGNORANCE = 1

It was great ignorance, Glousters eyes being out 2394

IGNORANT = 2
  Alb. My Lord, I am guiltlesse, as I am ignorant | Of what hath moued
  you.   786
  Yet I am doubtfull: For I am mainely ignorant   2820
ILD = 7*2
  Lear. Why my Boy? | *Fool*. If I gaue them all my liuing, I'ld keepe my
  Cox- | combes   636
  Foole. If thou wert my Foole Nunckle, Il'd haue thee   913
  My very Character) I'ld turne it all   1009
  I'ld driue ye cackling home to *Camelot*.   1157
  I'ld speake with the Duke of *Cornewall*, and his wife.   1372
  Goe tell the Duke, and's wife, Il'd speake with them: 1392
  I'ld shake it on this quarrell. What do you meane?   2151
  I'ld say I had eyes againe.   2205
  Had I your tongues and eyes, Il'd vse them so,   3218
ILE *l*.180 248 *411 512 517 *527 615 618 *619 645 *670 764 813 821 828
  1018 1022 1043 *1104 *1111 1120 1224 1230 1232 1260 1385 1394 1519
  1556 1582 1583 1586 1592 1652 1735 1806 1808 *1936 1945 2043 2140
  2232 2238 2261 2334 2407 2457 2520 *2537 *2581 *2611 2627 2671
  *2693 2727 2742 2883 2894 2924 2950 2978 3040 3044 3244
  3253 = 55*11
ILL = 4*2
  Reg. No maruaile then, though he were ill affected,   1037
  *not haue made him so ill, though they had bin but two | yeares
  oth'trade.   1132
  The King his Master, needs must take it ill   1221
  Glo. The Duke's too blame in this, | 'Twill be ill taken. *Exit*.   1235
  *him perceiued; If he aske for me, I am ill, and gone to   1767
  Edg. What in ill thoughts againe?   2932
ILLUSTRIOUS = 1
  Conspirant 'gainst this high illustrious Prince,   3090
IMAGE = 2*1
  like the image, and horror of it, pray you away.   496
  *might'st behold the great image of Authoritie, a Dogg's   2602
  Kent. Is this the promis'd end? | *Edg*. Or image of that horror. | *Alb*.
  Fall and cease.   3224
IMAGES = 1
  The images of reuolt and flying off.   1364
IMAGINATIONS = 1
  And woes, by wrong imaginations loose   2738
IMBOSSED = 1
  A plague sore, or imbossed Carbuncle   1518
IME = 1
  Glou. Vnmercifull Lady, as you are, I'me none.   2097
IMMAGINATION = *1
  *of Ciuet; good Apothecary sweeten my immagination: 2572
IMMEDIACIE = 1
  The which immediacie may well stand vp,   3005
IMPATIENCE = 1
  impatience: the Gods reward your kindnesse.   2002
IMPERFECT = 1
  Edg. Why then your other Senses grow imperfect | By your eyes
  anguish.   2437
IMPERFECTIONS = *1
  *the imperfections of long ingraffed condition, but   322
IMPERTINENCY = 1
  Edg. O matter, and impertinency mixt, | Reason in Madnesse.   2616

IMPLOYMENT = 2
  On whose imployment I was sent to you,   1208
  Do's not become a Sword, thy great imployment   2975
IMPORT = 1
  Reg. What might import my Sisters Letter to him? | *Stew.* I know not,
  Lady.   2391
IMPORTUND = 1
  My mourning, and importun'd teares hath pittied: 2378
IMPORTUNE = 1
  Kent. Importune him once more to go my Lord,   1940
IMPOSE = 1
  Thou might'st deserue, or they impose this vsage, | Comming from vs.   1301
IMPOSSIBILITIES = 1
  Of mens Impossibilities, haue preserued thee.   2519
IMPOSSIBLE = 1
  Hold amity? 'Tis hard, almost impossible.   1538
IMPREST = 1
  And turne our imprest Launces in our eies   2993
IMPRISOND = *1
  *stockt, punish'd, and imprison'd: who hath three Suites | to his backe,
  six shirts to his body: 1914
IN *see also* a, in's, in't, i'th' = 185*76
INCENSE = 2
  And what they may incense him too, being apt,   1610
  Lear. Vpon such sacrifices my *Cordelia*, | The Gods themselues throw
  Incense.   2961
INCESTUOUS = 1
  That art Incestuous. Caytiffe, to peeces shake   1708
INCH = 1
  Is't not the King? | *Lear.* I, euery inch a King.   2553
INCHT = *1
  *incht Bridges, to course his owne shadow for a Traitor.   1838
INCITE = 1
  No blowne Ambition doth our Armes incite,   2379
INCLINE = *1
  *a Power already footed, we must incline to the King, I   1764
INCREASE = 1
  Drie vp in her the Organs of increase,   793
INCURRD = 1
  Cor. We are not the first, | Who with best meaning haue incurr'd the
  worst: 2943
INDEED = 3*1
  Foole. Yes indeed, thou would'st make a good Foole.   911
  Glou. So may it be indeed.   2439
  Thus might he passe indeed: yet he reuiues.   2487
  Edg. He is gon indeed.   3290
INDEEDE = *1
  *she grew round womb'd, and had indeede (Sir) a   17
INDIGNATION = *1
  *suspend your indignation against my Brother, til you can   414
INDISCRETION = 1
  All's not offence that indiscretion findes, | And dotage termes so.   1486
INDISPOSD = 1
  To take the indispos'd and sickly fit,   1387
INDISTINGUISHD = 1
  Oh indistinguish'd space of Womans will,   2724

INDURD = 1
In Hell-blacke-night indur'd, would haue buoy'd vp   2132
INFECT = 1
Into her scornfull eyes: Infect her Beauty,   1449
INFECTED = 1
That this our Court infected with their manners,   752
INFECTION = 1
Least that th'infection of his fortune take   2685
INFIRME = 1*1
*therewithall the vnruly way-wardnesse, that infirme and | cholericke
yeares bring with them.   323
A poore, infirme, weake, and dispis'd old man: 1675
INFIRMITIES = 1
Lear. Will you with those infirmities she owes,   221
INFIRMITY = 1*1
Reg. 'Tis the infirmity of his age, yet he hath euer but | slenderly
knowne himselfe.   318
Infirmity doth still neglect all office,   1382
INFLAMD *see* enflam'd
INFLUENCE = 1*1
*influence; and all that we are euill in, by a diuine thru-|sting   454
Whose influence like the wreath of radient fire | On flickring *Phoebus*
front.   1182
INFORCD = *1
*and Adulterers by an inforc'd obedience of Planatary   453
INFORCE = 1
Inforce their charitie: poore *Turlygod* poore *Tom*,   1271
INFORMD = 5*2
Beene well inform'd of them, and with such cautions,   1041
Who hath most fortunately beene inform'd   1244
Glo. Well my good Lord, I haue inform'd them so.   1373
Lear. Inform'd them? Do'st thou vnderstand me man. | *Glo*. I my good
Lord.   1374
Are they inform'd of this? My breath and blood: 1379
When I inform'd him, then he call'd me Sot,   2275
Mes. I my good Lord: 'twas he inform'd against him   2341
INFORME = 1
Informe her full of my particular feare,   861
INGENIOUS = 1
How stiffe is my vilde sense | That I stand vp, and haue ingenious
feeling   2733
INGRAFFED = *1
*the imperfections of long ingraffed condition, but   322
INGRATEFULL = 3
On her ingratefull top: strike her yong bones   1445
Cracke Natures moulds, all germaines spill at once | That makes
ingratefull Man.   1663
Who's there? the Traitor? | *Reg*. Ingratefull Fox, 'tis he.   2089
INGRATITUDE = 2*1
Ingratitude! thou Marble-hearted Fiend,   771
Lear. To tak't againe perforce; Monster Ingratitude!   912
Saue what beates there, Filliall ingratitude,   1794
INHERIT = *1
*Women all aboue: but to the Girdle do the Gods inhe-|rit,   2568
INHERITING = *1
*finicall Rogue, one Trunke-inheriting slaue, one that   1092

INIUNCTION = 1
Though their Iniunction be to barre my doores,   1928
INIURIES = 2*1
Reg. O Sir, to wilfull men, | The iniuries that they themselues procure,   1606
Gent. None but the Foole, who labours to out-iest | His heart-strooke
iniuries.   1624
*I haue lock'd the Letter in my Closset, these iniuries the   1762
INNE = 1
Shewes like a riotous Inne; Epicurisme and Lust   753
INNOCENT = *1
*in the Lake of Darknesse: pray Innocent, and beware | the foule Fiend.   2005
INS = *1
Foole. If a mans braines were in's heeles, wert not in | danger of
kybes? | *Lear*. I Boy.   882
INSOLENT = 1
But other of your insolent retinue   713
INSTANT = 6*1
*which at this instant so rageth in him, that with the mis- | chiefe   484
For instant remedy. Be then desir'd   756
Whose vertue and obedience doth this instant   1055
Your needfull counsaile to our businesses, | Which craues the instant
vse.   1070
Then stands on any shoulder that I see | Before me, at this instant.   1168
This Sword of mine shall giue them instant way,   3105
Bast. I was contracted to them both, all three | Now marry in an
instant.   3179
INSTANTLY = 3
Instantly know, and of that Letter too;   1772
Reg. Hang him instantly.   2063
Marke I say instantly, and carry it so   2980
INSTRUCTS = 1
As this instructs thee, thou dost make thy way   2972
INSTRUMENTS = 1
The Gods are iust, and of our pleasant vices | Make instruments to
plague vs: 3131
INSULTED = 1
Tript me behind: being downe, insulted, rail'd,   1195
INT = 2
There is a Litter ready, lay him in't,   2049
Lear. Then there's life in't. Come, and you get it,   2644
INTELLIGENCE = 1
Intelligence is giuen where you are hid;   951
INTELLIGENT = 1*2
Intelligent of our State. What hath bin seene,   1634
*which approues him an intelligent partie to the aduanta- | ges   1981
*Postes shall be swift, and intelligent betwixt vs. Fare- | well deere
Sister, farewell my Lord of Glouster.   2070
INTEND = 3
To speake and purpose not, since what I will intend,   247
Suspend thy purpose, if thou did'st intend | To make this Creature
fruitfull: 790
You know the goodnesse I intend vpon you: 2854
INTENDS = 2
That it intends to do: my Lord of *Burgundy*,   260
Which he intends to *Lear* and to *Cordelia*,   2913
INTENT = 5*1
In three our Kingdome: and 'tis our fast intent,   43

144

INTENT *cont.*

   *deriue from him better testimony of his intent, you shold   415
   That can my speech defuse, my good intent   532
   Bast. When I disswaded him from his intent,   1001
   Yet to be knowne shortens my made intent,   2757
   You Lords and Noble Friends, know our intent,   3268

INTEREST = 3

   Interest of Territory, Cares of State)   55
   Striue to be interest. What can you say, to draw   91
   I bare it in the interest of my wife,   3030

INTERLUDE *see* enterlude

INTERMISSION = 1

   Deliuer'd Letters spight of intermission,   1309

INTIRE = 1

   Aloofe from th'intire point, will you haue her?   263

INTO *l.*98 242 *368 *428 511 *602 792 897 944 *1096 *1139 1449 *1585
   1620 1935 *1955 2218 2286 2291 3150 = 13*7

INTOOT = *1

   *I will looke further intoo't: but where's my Foole? I | haue not seene
   him this two daies.   600

INTREATE = 1

   And bring some couering for this naked Soule, | Which Ile intreate to
   leade me.   2231

INTRINCE = 1

   Which are t'intrince, t'vnloose: smooth euery passion   1148

INUADE = 1

   Kent. Let it fall rather, though the forke inuade   153

INUADES = 1

   Inuades vs to the skin so: 'tis to thee,   1787

INUENTION = 1

   And my inuention thriue, *Edmond* the base | Shall to'th'Legitimate: I
   grow, I prosper: 354

INUEST = 1

   I doe inuest you ioyntly with my power,   138

INUESTED = 1

   Reg. In my rights, | By me inuested, he compeeres the best.   3010

IOINE *see* ioyne

IOINTLY *see* ioyntly

IOT = *1

   **Lear.* Let me not stay a iot for dinner, go get it rea- | dy: 539

IOUE = 1

   Nor tell tales of thee to high-iudging *Ioue*,   1522

IOUIALL = *1

   *Like a smugge Bridegroome. What? I will be Iouiall: 2641

IOURNEY = 1

   Kent. I haue a iourney Sir, shortly to go,   3296

IOY = 3

   Then that conferr'd on *Gonerill.* Now our Ioy,   88
   For sodaine ioy did weepe, | And I for sorrow sung,   688
   Twixt two extremes of passion, ioy and greefe, | Burst smilingly.   3161

IOYES = 1

   My selfe an enemy to all other ioyes,   78

IOYNE = 1

   That will with two pernicious Daughters ioyne   1677

IOYNTLY = 1

   I doe inuest you ioyntly with my power,   138

IS *see also* all's, and's, bodies, *Cornwal*s, crabbe's, dogg's, duke's, enemy's, friend's, heere's, hee's, here's, he's, honour's, how's, it's, life's, loue's, me's, mind's, name's, nature's, neere's, night's, shee's, she's, sisters, that's, there's, ther's, 'tis, *Tom*'s, trumpet's, truth's, what's, where's, wher's, who's, winters = 151*48

ISSUE = 2*1

Kent. I cannot wish the fault vndone, the issue of it, | being so proper.	20
As honest Madams issue? Why brand they vs	343
May carry through it selfe to that full issue	533

ISSUES = 1

We make thee Lady. To thine and *Albanies* issues	71

IST = 6

Kent. Who's there? What is't you seeke?	1906
How is't my Lord? How looke you?	2172
Edg. O Gods! Who is't can say I am at the worst?	2207
Vp, so: How is't? Feele you your Legges? You stand. | *Glou.* Too well, too well.	2508
Is't not the King? | *Lear.* I, euery inch a King.	2553
What is't thou saist? Her voice was euer soft,	3236

IT *see also* be't, doo't, do't, for't, in't, intoo't, is't, know't, on't, put't, see't, speak't, 't, tak't, 'tis, too't, wert, wilt = 135*52, *2

*fed the Cuckoo so long, that it's had it head bit off by it	727

ITH = 15*10

Gon. We must do something, and i'th' heate. *Exeunt.*	332
Foole. Why after I haue cut the egge i'th'middle and	673
*thou clouest thy Crownes i'th'middle, and gau'st away	675
*wit o'both sides, and left nothing i'th'middle; heere | comes one o'the parings.	700
on? You are too much of late i'th'frowne.	704
*Crab: thou canst, tell why ones nose stands i'th'middle | on's face? | *Lear.* No.	893
Hee's comming hither, now i'th' night, i'th' haste,	954
Stew. Where may we set our horses? | *Kent.* I'th'myre.	1078
Foole. And thou hadst beene set i'th' Stockes for that	1337
*thee ther's no labouring i'th' winter. All that follow their	1341
Kent. Where learn'd you this Foole? | *Foole.* Not i'th' Stocks Foole.	1359
*Eeles, when she put 'em i'th' Paste aliue, she knapt 'em	1399
Lear. Who put my man i'th'Stockes?	1467
How came my man i'th'Stockes?	1490
When Vsurers tell their Gold i'th'Field,	1744
Thou'dst meete the Beare i'th' mouth, when the mind's | (free,	1791
Kent. What art thou that dost grumble there i'th' | straw? Come forth.	1825
so, so, wee'l go to Supper i'th'morning.	2042
I'th'last nights storme, I such a fellow saw;	2216
I'th'way toward Douer, do it for ancient loue,	2230
*Bring vp the browne Billes. O well flowne Bird: i'th'	2538
clout, i'th'clout: Hewgh. Giue the word. | *Edg.* Sweet Mariorum.	2539
I'th'sway of your owne will: is he array'd?	2770
We two alone will sing like Birds i'th'Cage:	2949

ITS *see also* it = 1*1

*fed the Cuckoo so long, that it's had it head bit off by it	727
Glo. O Madam, my old heart is crack'd, it's crack'd.	1029

ITSELFE *see* selfe

IUDGE = *1

Bast. If your Honor iudge it meete, I will place you	423

IUDGEMENT = 3*3

This hideous rashnesse, answere my life, my iudgement:	161

IUDGEMENT *cont.*
*lou'd our Sister most, and with what poore iudgement he	316
*feare iudgement, to fight when I cannot choose, and to | eate no fish.	547
*but to my iudgement your Highnesse is not entertain'd	587
And thy deere Iudgement out. Go, go, my people.	785
This iudgement of the Heauens that makes vs tremble.	3185

IUDGING = 1
Nor tell tales of thee to high-iudging *Ioue,*	1522

IUDICIOUS = 1
Iudicious punishment, 'twas this flesh begot | Those Pelicane Daughters.	1855

IUGGE = 1
Whoop Iugge I loue thee.	737

IUNO = 1
Kent. By *Iuno,* I sweare I.	1296

IUPITER = 2
The moment is thy death, away. By *Iupiter,* | This shall not be reuok'd,	192
Lear. By *Iupiter* I sweare no.	1295

IUST = 2*1
And shew the Heauens more iust.	1817
*to be iust? This is the Letter which hee spoake of;	1980
The Gods are iust, and of our pleasant vices | Make instruments to plague vs:	3131

IUSTICE = 3*4
Vnwhipt of Iustice. Hide thee, thou Bloudy hand;	1706
*keepe thy words Iustice, sweare not, commit not,	1861
Without the forme of Iustice: yet our power	2085
*yond Iustice railes vpon yond simple theefe. Hearke in	2596
*the Iustice, which is the theefe: Thou hast seene a Far-|mers	2598
*the strong Lance of Iustice, hurtlesse breakes: Arme it in	2609
Thy arme may do thee Iustice, heere is mine:	3082

IUSTICES = 1
Alb. This shewes you are aboue | You Iustices, that these our neather crimes	2323

IUSTIFICATION = *1
Bast. I hope for my Brothers iustification, hee wrote	380

IUSTLY = 1
That iustly think'st, and hast most rightly said:	197

KEEP = *1
Glou. In fellow there, into th'Houel; keep thee warm.	1955

KEEPE = 7*10
Lear. What seruices canst thou do? | *Kent.* I can keepe honest counsaile, ride, run, marre a	562
Lear. Why my Boy? | *Fool.* If I gaue them all my liuing, I'ld keepe my Cox-|combes	636
Leaue thy drinke and thy whore, | And keepe in a dore,	654
*Pry'thy Nuncle keepe a Schoolemaster that can teach	692
Heere do you keepe a hundred Knights and Squires,	750
'Tis politike, and safe to let him keepe	844
Foole. Why to keepe ones eyes of either side 's nose,	896
*keepe me in temper, I would not be mad. How now are | the Horses ready?	919
Cor. Keepe peace vpon your liues, he dies that strikes | againe, what is the matter?	1122
To keepe base life a foote; returne with her?	1508
And make them keepe their Caues: Since I was man,	1697
Lear. Let the great Goddes | That keepe this dreadfull pudder o're our heads,	1702

KEEPE *cont.*

*keepe thy words Iustice, sweare not, commit not,	1861
*Keepe thy foote out of Brothels, thy hand out of	1876
I will keepe still with my Philosopher.	1959
*Corn. Leaue him to my displeasure. *Edmond*, keepe	2065
*come not neere th'old man: keepe out che vor'ye, or Ile	2693

KEEPES = 2*1

*world bitter to the best of our times: keepes our Fortunes from	383
Mum, mum, he that keepes nor crust, nor crum,	710
Which scarcely keepes thee warme, but for true need:	1570

KENNELL = *1

*Foole. Truth's a dog must to kennell, hee must bee	641

KENT = 24*2

Enter Kent, Gloucester, and Edmond.	2
Glou. My Lord of Kent: | Remember him heereafter, as my Honourable Friend.	30
Kent. Good my Liege. | Lear. Peace Kent,	128
The region of my heart, be *Kent* vnmannerly,	154
Lear. Kent, on thy life no more.	165
Thus Kent, O Princes, bids you all adew,	200
*Glo. Kent banish'd thus? and France in choller parted?	358
*Kent banish'd; his offence, honesty. 'Tis strange. Exit	446
Enter Kent.	530
For which I raiz'd my likenesse. Now banisht Kent,	534
Enter Lear, Kent, Gentleman, and Foole.	874
Enter Kent, and Steward seuerally.	1075
Corn. Haile to your Grace. Kent here set at liberty.	1405
Storme still. Enter Kent, and a Gentleman, seuerally.	1615
Enter Kent.	1688
Enter Lear, Kent, and Foole.	1777
His Daughters seeke his death: Ah, that good Kent,	1943
Enter Kent, and Gloucester.	1997
Enter Cordelia, Kent, and Gentleman.	2744
Cor. O thou good Kent, | How shall I liue and worke | To match thy goodnesse?	2745
Edg. Here comes Kent.	3181
Enter Kent.	3182
Seest thou this obiect Kent? | Kent. Alacke, why thus?	3194
Edg. 'Tis Noble Kent your Friend.	3232
Lear. This is a dull sight, are you not Kent? | Kent. The same: your Seruant Kent,	3247

KENT = 79*28

KENTS = 1

*Reg. Such vnconstant starts are we like to haue from | him, as this of Kents banishment.	325

KEPT = 1

But kept a reseruation to be followed	1550

KEY = 2*1

there's my key: if you do stirre abroad, goe arm'd.	491
*Fortune that arrant whore, nere turns the key toth' poore.	1325
Thou should'st haue said, good Porter turne the Key:	2136

KIBES *see* kybes

KILL = 8*1

Kent. Kill thy Physition, and thy fee bestow	177
What is your study? | *Edg. How to preuent the Fiend, and to kill Vermine.	1937

KILL *cont*.
As Flies to wanton Boyes, are we to th'Gods, | They kill vs for their
sport.   2221
Then kill, kill, kill, kill, kill, kill.   2629
KILLD = 2
You see is kill'd in him: desire him to go in,   2838
I kill'd the Slaue that was a hanging thee. | *Gent*. 'Tis true (my Lords)
he did.   3238
KILLES = 1
Reg. Giue me thy Sword. A pezant stand vp thus? | *Killes him*.   2154
KIN = *1
Foole. I maruell what kin thou and thy daughters are,   695
KIND = 5*4
On her kind nursery. Hence and avoid my sight: 132
*my peace. I had rather be any kind o'thing then a foole,   698
Lear. I will forget my Nature, so kind a Father? Be | my Horsses
ready?   906
These kind of Knaues I know, which in this plainnesse   1176
*But Fathers that beare bags, shall see their children kind.   1324
Your old kind Father, whose franke heart gaue all,   1800
*backe, thou hotly lusts to vse her in that kind, for which   2605
Cor. O you kind Gods!   2763
Kent. Kind and deere Princesse.   2780
KINDE = 5
Who I am sure is kinde and comfortable: 825
Against the old kinde King; or something deeper,   1637
Glou. By the kinde Gods, 'tis most ignobly done | To plucke me by the
Beard.   2100
Kinde Gods, forgiue me that, and prosper him.   2169
Edg. What kinde of helpe? | *Alb*. Speake man.   3171
KINDER = 1
For Glousters bastard Son was kinder to his Father,   2560
KINDLE = 1
My Loue should kindle to enflam'd respect.   280
KINDLY = *1
Fool. Shalt see thy other Daughter will vse thee kind-|ly,   888
KINDNESSE = 1*2
*theres a great abatement of kindnesse appeares as well in   589
*downe; 'twas her Brother, that in pure kindnesse to his | Horse
buttered his Hay.   1401
impatience: the Gods reward your kindnesse.   2002
KING = 42*16
Kent. | *I thought the King had more affected the   3
Glou. He hath bin out nine yeares, and away he shall | againe. The
King is comming.   35
Sennet. *Enter King Lear, Cornwall, Albany, Gonerill, Re-|gan,
Cordelia, and attendants*.   37
The name, and all th'addition to a King: the Sway,   144
Kent. Royall *Lear*, | Whom I haue euer honor'd as my King,   148
Kent. Now by *Apollo*, King | Thou swear'st thy Gods in vaine.   173
Kent. Fare thee well King, sith thus thou wilt appeare,   194
Lear. My Lord of *Burgundie*, | We first addresse toward you, who with
this King   205
I tell you all her wealth. For you great King,   228
Bur. Royall King, | Giue but that portion which your selfe propos'd,   265
*Thy dowrelesse Daughter King, throwne to my chance,   281
And the King gone to night? Prescrib'd his powre,   359

KING *cont*.

*prediction; there's Son against Father, the King fals from	440
Lear. What art thou? | *Kent*. A very honest hearted Fellow, and as	
poore as | the King.	549
King, thou art poore enough. What wouldst thou? | *Kent*. Seruice.	553
That such a King should play bo-peepe, | And goe the Foole among.	690
*heeles, and beate thee before the King? Draw you rogue,	1103
*the King, and take Vanitie the puppets part, a- | gainst	1109
Reg. The Messengers from our Sister, and the King?	1124
It pleas'd the King his Master very late	1192
That worthied him, got praises of the King,	1197
Call not your Stocks for me, I serue the King.	1207
The King his Master, needs must take it ill	1221
Kent. Good King, that must approue the common saw,	1237
*How chance the King comes with so small a number?	1336
Lear. The King would speake with *Cornwall*,	1376
Glo. The King is in high rage.	1598
Kent. I know you: Where's the King?	1618
Against the old kinde King; or something deeper,	1637
I will go seeke the King.	1647
*That when we haue found the King, in which your pain	1651
*King now beares, will be reuenged home; ther is part of	1763
*a Power already footed, we must incline to the King, I	1764
*bed, if I die for it, (as no lesse is threatned me) the King	1768
Thou sayest the King growes mad, Ile tell thee Friend	1945
Bast. If I finde him comforting the King, it will stuffe	1990
Lear. A King, a King.	2009
Glou. Come hither Friend: | Where is the King my Master?	2044
How now? Where's the King?	2073
Reg. To whose hands | You haue sent the Lunaticke King: Speake.	2113
Corn. Where hast thou sent the King? | *Glou*. To Douer.	2120
Alb. Glouster, I liue | To thanke thee for the loue thou shew'dst the	
King,	2344
Lear. No, they cannot touch me for crying. I am the | King himselfe.	2530
Is't not the King? | *Lear*. I, euery inch a King.	2553
Come, come, I am a King, Masters, know you that?	2642
Past speaking of in a King. Thou hast a Daughter	2647
Glou. The King is mad:	2732
How do's the King? | *Gent*. Madam sleepes still.	2761
Gent. So please your Maiesty, | That we may wake the King, he hath	
slept long?	2767
Sir, this I heard, the King is come to his Daughter	2866
King *Lear* hath lost, he and his Daughter tane,	2929
For thee oppressed King I am cast downe,	2945
Bast. Sir, I thought it fit, | To send the old and miserable King to some	
retention,	2989
Kent. I am come | To bid my King and Master aye good night.	3189
*Speake *Edmund*, where's the King? and where's *Cordelia*?	3193
THE TRAGEDIE OF | KING LEAR.	3304

KINGDOME = 8*1

*now in the diuision of the Kingdome, it ap- | peares	7
In three our Kingdome: and 'tis our fast intent,	43
Remaine this ample third of our faire Kingdome,	86
Vpon our kingdome: if on the tenth day following,	190
I will send farre and neere, that all the kingdome	1020
Thy halfe o'th'Kingdome hast thou not forgot, | Wherein I thee	
endow'd.	1464

KINGDOME *cont.*
I neuer gaue you Kingdome, call'd you Children;   1672
Corn. And what confederacie haue you with the Trai- | tors, late footed
in the Kingdome?   2111
Lear. Am I in France? | *Kent.* In your owne kingdome Sir.   2834

KISSE = 3
Decline your head. This kisse, if it durst speake   2290
Glou. O let me kisse that hand. | *Lear.* Let me wipe it first,   2574
Thy medicine on my lippes, and let this kisse   2777

KISSING = 1
*I meane the whisper'd ones, for they are yet but | ear-kissing
arguments.   935

KITE = 1
Lear. Detested Kite, thou lyest.   775

KNAPT = *1
*Eeles, when she put 'em i'th' Paste aliue, she knapt 'em   1399

KNAUE = 10*8
*though this Knaue came somthing sawcily to the   24
*ho, dinner, where's my knaue? my Foole? Go you and call   573
Lear. My Ladies Father? my Lords knaue, you whor- | son dog, you
slaue, you curre.   610
Lear. Now my friendly knaue I thanke thee, there's | earnest of thy
seruice.   622
Lear. How now my pretty knaue, how dost thou?   626
You Sir, more Knaue then Foole, after your Master.   834
Kent. A Knaue, a Rascall, an eater of broken meates, a   1088
*pound, filthy woosted-stocking knaue, a Lilly-liuered,   1090
*but the composition of a Knaue, Begger, Coward,   1094
Cor. Peace sirrah, | You beastly knaue, know you no reuerence?   1141
Kent. No contraries hold more antipathy, | Then I, and such a knaue.   1160
Corn. Why do'st thou call him Knaue?   1162
*you in a plaine accent, was a plaine Knaue, which   1187
You stubborne ancient Knaue, you reuerent Bragart, | Wee'l teach you.   1204
Reg. Sir, being his Knaue, I will. *Stocks brought out.*   1217
The knaue turnes Foole that runnes away,   1356
The Foole no knaue perdie.   1357
Poore Foole, and Knaue, I haue one part in my heart | That's sorry yet
for thee.   1727

KNAUES = 1*2
*Fooles by heauenly compulsion, Knaues, Theeues, and   451
These kind of Knaues I know, which in this plainnesse   1176
*againe, I would haue none but knaues follow it, since a | Foole giues
it.   1348

KNEE = 1
To knee his Throne, and Squire-like pension beg,   1507

KNEELE = 2
You must not kneele. | *Lear.* Pray do not mocke me: 2812
When thou dost aske me blessing, Ile kneele downe   2950

KNEELING = 1
My dutie kneeling, came there a reeking Poste,   1306

KNEES = 1
Age is vnnecessary: on my knees I begge,   1436

KNIFE = 1
Edg. What meanes this bloody Knife?   3173

KNIGH = *3
KNIGHT *see also Knigh.* = 1
No Squire in debt, nor no poore Knight;   1741

KNIGHT = *2
KNIGHTS = 7*3

With reseruation of an hundred Knights,	141
His Knights grow riotous, and himselfe vpbraides vs	513
*Gon. And let his Knights haue colder lookes among	525
Heere do you keepe a hundred Knights and Squires,	750
Gon. This man hath had good Counsell, | A hundred Knights?	842
*At point a hundred Knights: yes, that on euerie dreame,	845
If she sustaine him, and his hundred Knights	854
*Reg. Was he not companion with the riotous Knights	1033
I can be patient, I can stay with *Regan*, | I and my hundred Knights.	1524
Some fiue or six and thirty of his Knights	2075

KNIGHT-HOOD = 1

By rule of Knight-hood, I disdaine and spurne:	3101

KNIUES = *1

*that hath laid Kniues vnder his Pillow, and Halters	1835

KNOTS = 1

Blanket my loines, else all my haires in knots,	1261

KNOW = 63*10

*be acknowledged. Doe you know this Noble Gentle-|man, *Edmond*? | *Edm*. No, my Lord.	27
Kent. I must loue you, and sue to know you better.	33
Giue me the Map there. Know, that we haue diuided	42
Shee's there, and she is yours. | *Bur*. I know no answer.	219
Cordelia leaues you, I know you what you are,	294
Bast. I know no newes, my Lord.	364
Glou. You know the character to be your Brothers?	397
Bast. I do not well know my L.(ord) If it shall please you to	413
Whose mind and mine I know in that are one,	522
Lear. Do'st thou know me fellow?	557
Lear. He would not? | *Knight*. My Lord, I know not what the matter is,	585
Foole. Do'st thou know the difference my Boy, be-|tweene a bitter Foole, and a sweet one.	667
And know not how their wits to weare,	682
Foole. For you know Nunckle, the Hedge-Sparrow	726
(Whereof I know you are fraught), and put away	732
Foole. May not an Asse know, when the Cart drawes | the Horse?	735
Lear. Do's any heere know me? | This is not *Lear*:	738
To be such men as may besort your Age, | Which know themselues, and you.	760
That all particulars of dutie know,	777
Gon. Neuer afflict your selfe to know more of it:	806
Not feare still to be taken. I know his heart,	852
*know, then comes from her demand out of the Letter,	877
Cur. Nay I know not, you haue heard of the newes a-|broad,	934
*Harke, the Dukes Trumpets, I know not wher he comes;	1017
Glo. I know not Madam, 'tis too bad, too bad.	1035
Cor. You know not why we came to visit you?	1061
Ste. Why do'st thou vse me thus? I know thee not.	1085
Kent. Fellow I know thee.	1086
Ste. What do'st thou know me for?	1087
Cor. Peace sirrah, | You beastly knaue, know you no reuerence?	1141
These kind of Knaues I know, which in this plainnesse	1176
*so much; I know Sir, I am no flatterer, he that be-|guild	1186
But miserie. I know 'tis from *Cordelia*,	1243
Glo. My deere Lord, | You know the fiery quality of the Duke,	1366

KNOW *cont.*

Lear. Regan, I thinke you are. I know what reason	1407
You lesse know how to value her desert,	Then she to scant her dutie.	1417
Thou did'st not know on't.	1478
What they are yet, I know not, but they shalbe	1581
Glo. He cals to Horse, but will I know not whether.	1600
Kent. I know you: Where's the King?	1618
Kent. Sir, I do know you,	And dare vpon the warrant of my note	1626
That yet you do not know. Fye on this Storme,	1646
Instantly know, and of that Letter too;	1772
Reg. Be simple answer'd, for we know the truth.	2110
And each man haue enough. Dost thou know Douer?	*Edg.* I Master.	2256
Reg. What might import my Sisters Letter to him?	*Stew.* I know not, Lady.	2391
Some things, I know not what. Ile loue thee much	2407
Stew. Madam, I had rather---	*Reg.* I know your Lady do's not loue her Husband,	2409
To Noble *Edmund.* I know you are of her bosome.	*Stew.* I, Madam?	2413
And yet I know not how conceit may rob	2482
Lear. Passe.	*Glou.* I know that voice.	2541
Do'st thou know me?	**Lear.* I remember thine eyes well enough: dost thou	2579
I know thee well enough, thy name is Glouster:	2619
Come, come, I am a King, Masters, know you that?	2642
Edg. I know thee well. A seruiceable Villaine,	2704
To know our enemies mindes, we rip their hearts,	2713
My boone I make it, that you know me not,	Till time, and I, thinke meet.	2758
Cor. Sir, do you know me?	*Lear.* You are a spirit I know, where did you dye?	2798
To see another thus. I know not what to say:	2806
Me thinkes I should know you, and know this man,	2819
Remembers not these garments: nor I know not	2822
I know you do not loue me, for your Sisters	2830
Bast. Know of the Duke if his last purpose hold,	2847
You know the goodnesse I intend vpon you:	2854
Gon. Oh ho, I know the Riddle, I will goe.	*Exeunt both the Armies.*	2878
To Noble Fortunes: know thou this, that men	2973
Edg. Know my name is lost	By Treasons tooth: bare-gnawne, and Canker-bit,	3073
No tearing Lady, I perceiue you know it.	3115
Bast. Aske me not what I know.	3119
I know when one is dead, and when one liues,	3220
You Lords and Noble Friends, know our intent,	3268

KNOWES = 5

*to raile on one, that is neither knowne of thee, nor	knowes thee?	1099
Whose disposition all the world well knowes	1229
But she knowes what she doe's.	1531
Alb. Knowes he the wickednesse?	2340
Alb. He knowes not what he saies, and vaine is it	That we present vs to him.	3262

KNOWEST = 1*1

Speake lesse then thou knowest,	649
*thou knowest me? Is it two dayes since I tript vp thy	1102

KNOWING = 1

Knowing naught (like dogges) but following:	1153

KNOWLEDGE = 2
The knowledge of themselues.   2739
Cor. Be gouern'd by your knowledge, and proceede   2769
KNOWNE = 9*1
Ile do't before I speake, that you make knowne   248
Reg. 'Tis the infirmity of his age, yet he hath euer but | slenderly
knowne himselfe.   318
I had thought by making this well knowne vnto you,   716
*to raile on one, that is neither knowne of thee, nor | knowes thee?   1099
Edg. Yet better thus, and knowne to be contemn'd,   2179
Cor. 'Tis knowne before. Our preparation stands   2375
Who, by the Art of knowne, and feeling sorrowes,   2669
Yet to be knowne shortens my made intent,   2757
Vntill their greater pleasures first be knowne | That are to censure them.   2941
How haue you knowne the miseries of your Father?   3143
KNOWST = 5
Against my comming in. Thou better know'st   1461
Glou. Know'st thou the way to Douer?   2245
Tell me what more thou know'st. *Exeunt.*   2347
Thou know'st, the first time that we smell the Ayre   2621
Alb. Most monstrous! O, know'st thou this paper?   3118
KNOWT = 3
Reg. I know't, my Sisters: this approues her Letter,   1470
Reg. I speake in vnderstanding: Y'are: I know't,   2415
Edg. Worthy Prince I know't.   3141
KYBES = 1
Foole. If a mans braines were in's heeles, wert not in | danger of
kybes? | *Lear.* I Boy.   882
LA = 1
*o'Bedlam. --- O these Eclipses do portend these diui-|sions. Fa, Sol,
La, Me.   465
LABOR = *1
Edg. You do climbe vp it now. Look how we labor.   2432
LABOUR = 1
*Gaole, from the loathed warmth whereof, deliuer me, and sup-|ply the
place for your Labour.*   2720
LABOURING = *1
*thee ther's no labouring i'th' winter. All that follow their   1341
LABOURS = 2
So may it come, thy Master whom thou lou'st, | Shall find thee full of
labours.   536
Gent. None but the Foole, who labours to out-iest | His heart-strooke
iniuries.   1624
LACKE = 1
Too't Luxury pell-mell, for I lacke Souldiers.   2562
LACKES = 1
The which he lackes: that to prouoke in him   2363
LAD = 1
Lear. No Lad, teach me.   669
LADIE = 1
Reg. So white, and such a Traitor? | *Glou.* Naughty Ladie,   2102
LADIES = 2*2
Knight. Since my young Ladies going into *France*   602
Sir, who am I Sir? | *Enter Steward.* | *Ste.* My Ladies Father.   607
Lear. My Ladies Father? my Lords knaue, you whor-|son dog, you
slaue, you curre.   610
Then for your Ladies: You may gather more: 2419

LADY = 18*1
We make thee Lady. To thine and *Albanies* issues 71
What say you to the Lady? Loue's not loue 261
*whipt out, when the Lady Brach may stand by'th'fire | and stinke. 642
Glo. O Lady, Lady, shame would haue it hid. 1032
That she would soone be heere. Is your Lady come? 1471
Mans life is cheape as Beastes. Thou art a Lady; 1567
Glou. Vnmercifull Lady, as you are, I'me none. 2097
Corn. I haue receiu'd a hurt: Follow me Lady; 2173
Mes. Come with my Lady hither. 2337
Reg. What might import my Sisters Letter to him? | *Stew*. I know not,
Lady. 2391
Stew. I may not Madam: | My Lady charg'd my dutie in this busines. 2403
Stew. Madam, I had rather--- | *Reg*. I know your Lady do's not loue her
Husband, 2409
For (as I am a man) I thinke this Lady | To be my childe *Cordelia*. |
Cor. And so I am: I am. 2824
Rega. Lady I am not well, else I should answere 3016
My Lady is bespoke. | *Gon*. An enterlude. 3034
No tearing Lady, I perceiue you know it. 3115
Gen. Your Lady Sir, your Lady; and her Sister | By her is poyson'd: she
confesses it. 3177
LAG = 1
Lag of a Brother? Why Bastard? Wherefore base? 340
LAID = *1
*that hath laid Kniues vnder his Pillow, and Halters 1835
LAKE = *1
*in the Lake of Darknesse: pray Innocent, and beware | the foule Fiend. 2005
LAMENESSE = 1
You taking Ayres, with Lamenesse. | *Corn*. Fye sir, fie. 1446
LAMENTABLE = 1
The lamentable change is from the best, 2183
LANCE = *1
*the strong Lance of Iustice, hurtlesse breakes: Arme it in 2609
LANCES *see* launces
LAND = 3*1
Legitimate *Edgar*, I must haue your land, 350
*Foole. Prythee tell him, so much the rent of his land 664
Not in this Land shall he remaine vncaught 994
May haue due note of him, and of my land, 1021
LANDED = 1*1
*him this Letter, the Army of France is landed: seeke out | the Traitor
Glouster. 2061
I told him of the Army that was Landed: 2271
LANDS = 1
Let me, if not by birth, haue lands by wit, 503
LARGE = 2
Preheminence, and all the large effects 139
And your large speeches, may your deeds approue, 198
LARGEST = 1
That we, our largest bountie may extend 57
LARKE = 1
Looke vp a height, the shrill-gorg'd Larke so farre 2500
LASH = *1
*hand: why dost thou lash that Whore? Strip thy owne 2604
LAST = 8
Although our last and least; to whose yong loue, 89

LAST *cont.*

Who couers faults, at last with shame derides:	307
this last surrender of his will but offend vs.	330
When saw you my Father last? | *Edg.* The night gone by.	474
I'th'last nights storme, I such a fellow saw;	2216
Where I did lodge last night. Do not laugh at me,	2823
Bast. Know of the Duke if his last purpose hold,	2847
I ask'd his blessing, and from first to last	3158

LATCHD = 1

My vnprouided body, latch'd mine arme;	988

LATE = 10*2

Glou. These late Eclipses in the Sun and Moone por-|tend	433
*I haue perceiued a most faint neglect of late,	597
on? You are too much of late i'th'frowne.	704
By what your selfe too late haue spoke and done,	718
These dispositions, which of late transport you | From what you rightly are.	733
Lear. Woe, that too late repents:	769
It pleas'd the King his Master very late	1192
Being the very fellow which of late	1316
But lately: very late: I lou'd him (Friend)	1948
Corn. Come Sir. | What Letters had you late from France?	2108
Corn. And what confederacie haue you with the Trai-|tors, late footed in the Kingdome?	2111
I am sure of that: and at her late being heere,	2411

LATELY = 1

But lately: very late: I lou'd him (Friend)	1948

LAUGH = 2

Where I did lodge last night. Do not laugh at me,	2823
And pray, and sing, and tell old tales, and laugh	2952

LAUGHS = *1

Fool. She that's a Maid now, & laughs at my departure,	923

LAUGHTER = 2

To laughter, and contempt: That she may feele,	801
The worst returnes to laughter. Welcome then,	2184

LAUNCES = 1

And turne our imprest Launces in our eies	2993

LAW = 3*1

Glou. But I haue a Sonne, Sir, by order of Law, some	22
Bast. Thou Nature art my Goddesse, to thy Law	335
When euery Case in Law, is right;	1740
By th'law of Warre, thou wast not bound to answer	3109

LAWD = 1

Now out-law'd from my blood: he sought my life	1947

LAWES = 2

And when I haue stolne vpon these Son in Lawes,	2628
Gon. Say if I do, the Lawes are mine not thine,	3116

LAWFULL = 3

Be it lawfull I take vp what's cast away.	278
Then my Daughters got 'tweene the lawfull sheets.	2561
Their Papers is more lawfull. | *Reads the Letter.*	2714

LAWYER = *1

Foole. Then 'tis like the breath of an vnfeed Lawyer,	659

LAY = 5*2

*to lay his Goatish disposition on the charge of a Starre,	456
Lay comforts to your bosome, and bestow	1069
But if thy flight lay toward the roaring sea,	1790

LAY *cont.*
Corn. I will lay trust vpon thee: and thou shalt finde | a deere Father
in my loue. *Exeunt.*   1994
There is a Litter ready, lay him in't,   2049
Gent. Oh heere he is: lay hand vpon him, Sir.   2631
To lay the blame vpon her owne dispaire, | That she for-did her selfe.   3213
LE = *5
LEA = *4
LEACHEROUS = *1
*that it followes, I am rough and Leacherous. I should   459
LEAD = 1
Vpon a wheele of fire, that mine owne teares | Do scal'd, like molten
Lead.   2796
LEADE = 5
And bring some couering for this naked Soule, | Which Ile intreate to
leade me.   2231
Glou. 'Tis the times plague, | When Madmen leade the blinde: 2234
Edg. Giue me thy arme; | Poore Tom shall leade thee. *Exeunt.*   2264
Least his vngouern'd rage, dissolue the life | That wants the meanes to
leade it.   2370
Ile leade you to some biding. | *Glou.* Heartie thankes: 2671
LEADING = 1
I shall no leading neede.   2263
LEADS = 1
Corn. 'Tis best to giue him way, he leads himselfe.   1601
LEAPE = 1
For all beneath the Moone would I not leape vpright.   2463
LEAPT = 1
Dogs leapt the hatch, and all are fled.   2030
LEAR see also Le., Lea. = 26*1
*Sennet. Enter King Lear, Cornwall, Albany, Gonerill, Re-|gan,
Cordelia, and attendants.*   37
Kent. Royall *Lear,* | Whom I haue euer honor'd as my King,   148
When *Lear* is mad, what wouldest thou do old man?   155
Kent. See better *Lear,* and let me still remaine | The true blanke of
thine eie.   170
Hornes within. Enter Lear and Attendants.   538
Lear. Do's any heere know me? | This is not *Lear*:   738
And added to the gall. O *Lear, Lear, Lear!*   783
Enter Lear.   809
Foole. Nunkle *Lear,* Nunkle *Lear,*   835
Enter Lear, Kent, Gentleman, and Foole.   874
Enter Lear, Foole, and Gentleman.   1273
Enter Lear, and Gloster: 1358
Storme still. Enter Lear, and Foole.   1655
Enter Lear, Kent, and Foole.   1777
Enter Lear, Edgar, and Foole.   2003
Enter Lear.   2526
Enter Lear in a chaire carried by Seruants   2771
Which he intends to *Lear* and to *Cordelia,*   2913
Alarum within. Enter with Drumme and Colours, Lear,   2918
King *Lear* hath lost, he and his Daughter tane,   2929
Enter in conquest with Drum and Colours, Edmund, Lear,   2938
Is on the life of *Lear,* and on *Cordelia*:   3203
Enter Lear with Cordelia in his armes.   3216
THE TRAGEDIE OF | KING LEAR.   3304

LEAR = 129*43
LEARND *see also* lerned = 2
  Gent. As I learn'd, | The night before, there was no purpose in them |
  Of this remoue. ... 1276
  Kent. Where learn'd you this Foole? | *Foole.* Not i'th' Stocks Foole. ... 1359
LEARNE = 3
  Learne more then thou trowest, ... 652
  thy Foole to lie, I would faine learne to lie. ... 693
  Kent. Sir, I am too old to learne: ... 1206
LEARS = 1
  Who is it that can tell me who I am? | *Foole. Lears* shadow. ... 743
LEAST = 9*1
  Although our last and least; to whose yong loue, ... 89
  Least you may marre your Fortunes. ... 101
  Thy yongest Daughter do's not loue thee least, ... 162
  Hath riuald for our Daughter; what in the least ... 207
  deny'st the least sillable of thy addition. ... 1097
  *hill, least it breake thy necke with following. But the ... 1345
  Reg. I cannot thinke my Sister in the least ... 1420
  Least his vngouern'd rage, dissolue the life | That wants the meanes to
  leade it. ... 2370
  Least my braine turne, and the deficient sight | Topple downe headlong. ... 2458
  Least that th'infection of his fortune take ... 2685
LEAUE = 6*4
  Dow'rd with our curse, and stranger'd with our oath, | Take her or,
  leaue her. ... 223
  Le. Then leaue her sir, for by the powre that made me, ... 227
  Leaue thy drinke and thy whore, | And keepe in a dore, ... 654
  daughters, and leaue his hornes without a case. ... 905
  *my Lord, if you will giue me leaue, I will tread this vn- | boulted ... 1138
  And leaue thee in the storme, ... 1353
  *dealing; when I desired their leaue that I might pity him, ... 1754
  This tempest will not giue me leaue to ponder ... 1805
  Corn. Leaue him to my displeasure. *Edmond,* keepe ... 2065
  Leaue gentle waxe, and manners: blame vs not ... 2712
LEAUES = 2
  Which often leaues the history vnspoke ... 259
  Cordelia leaues you, I know you what you are, ... 294
LEAUE-TAKING = *1
  Gon. There is further complement of leaue-taking be- | tweene ... 327
LECHER *see* letcher
LECHERS *see* letchers
LED = 6*2
  *noses, are led by their eyes, but blinde men, and there's ... 1342
  Of his confine: you should be rul'd, and led ... 1428
  *the foule fiend hath led through Fire, and through Flame, ... 1833
  But who comes heere? My Father poorely led? | World, World, O
  world! ... 2189
  The Fiend, the Fiend, he led me to that place. ... 2524
  And Fortune led you well: you haue the Captiues ... 2984
  Ere you had spoke so farre. He led our Powers, ... 3003
  Led him, begg'd for him, sau'd him from dispaire. ... 3154
LEFT = 1*3
  *wit o'both sides, and left nothing i'th'middle; heere | comes one o'the
  parings. ... 700
  *young, so out went the Candle, and we were left dark- | ling. ... 728
  Yet haue I left a daughter. ... 765

LEFT *cont*.
   *Ser. Oh I am slaine: my Lord, you haue one eye left   2156
LEGGES = 1
   Vp, so: How is't? Feele you your Legges? You stand. | *Glou*. Too well,
   too well.   2508
LEGITIMATE = 4
   Legitimate *Edgar*, I must haue your land,   350
   As to th'legitimate: fine word: Legitimate.   352
   And my inuention thriue, *Edmond* the base | Shall to'th'Legitimate: I
   grow, I prosper: 354
LEGITTIMATE = 1
   Well, my Legittimate, if this Letter speed,   353
LEGS = *2
   *Monkies by'th'loynes, and Men by'th' legs: when a man   1284
   *ouerlustie at legs, then he weares wodden nether-stocks.   1285
LEISURE = 2
   The leisure of their answer, gaue me cold lookes,   1313
   Mend when thou can'st, be better at thy leisure,   1523
LEND = 3
   Lend lesse then thou owest,   650
   Some friendship will it lend you 'gainst the Tempest: 1716
   She's dead as earth: Lend me a Looking-glasse,   3221
LENDERS = *1
   *Plackets, thy pen from Lenders Bookes, and defye the   1877
LENDINGS = *1
   *as thou art. Off, off you Lendings: Come, vn- | button heere.   1888
LENGTH = *1
   *away, away, if you will measure your lubbers length a- | gaine,   620
LERNED = *1
   *Lear. Ile talke a word with this same lerned Theban: 1936
LESSE = 17*2
   And you our no lesse louing Sonne of *Albany*,   47
   No lesse then life, with grace, health, beauty, honor: 63
   No lesse in space, validitie, and pleasure   87
   According to my bond, no more nor lesse.   99
   Nor will you tender lesse?   212
   *Kent. I do professe to be no lesse then I seeme; to serue   544
   Speake lesse then thou knowest,   649
   Lend lesse then thou owest,   650
   Set lesse then thou throwest;   653
   Fooles had nere lesse grace in a yeere,   680
   You lesse know how to value her desert, | Then she to scant her dutie.   1417
   Deseru'd much lesse aduancement. | *Lear*. You? Did you?   1492
   Thron'd and set high; Seruants, who seeme no lesse,   1632
   *bed, if I die for it, (as no lesse is threatned me) the King   1768
   That which my Father looses: no lesse then all,   1774
   How shall your House-lesse heads, and vnfed sides,   1811
   Fourescore and vpward, | Not an houre more, nor lesse: 2815
   Ere I taste bread, thou art in nothing lesse   3041
   I am no lesse in blood then thou art *Edmond*,   3128
LESSER = 1
   The lesser is scarce felt. Thou'dst shun a Beare,   1789
LEST *see also* least = 1
   Corn. Lest it see more, preuent it; Out vilde gelly: 2158
LET = 59*13
   Lear. Let it be so, thy truth then be thy dowre: 115
   Let pride, which she cals plainnesse, marry her: 137

LET *cont*.

Kent. Let it fall rather, though the forke inuade	153
Kent. See better *Lear*, and let me still remaine | The true blanke of thine eie.	170
Lear. Thou hast her *France*, let her be thine, for we	287
Gon. Let your study | Be to content your Lord, who hath receiu'd you	302
*France and him, pray you let vs sit together, if our	328
Let me, if not by birth, haue lands by wit,	503
If he distaste it, let him to my Sister,	521
*Gon. And let his Knights haue colder lookes among	525
*Lear. Let me not stay a iot for dinner, go get it rea- | dy:	539
Foole. Let me hire him too, here's my Coxcombe.	625
this, let him be whipt that first findes it so.	679
Beate at this gate that let thy Folly in,	784
Let it stampe wrinkles in her brow of youth,	798
But let his disposition haue that scope | As dotage giues it.	807
To temper Clay. Ha? Let it be so.	823
'Tis politike, and safe to let him keepe	844
Let me still take away the harmes I feare,	851
*Lear. O let me not be mad, not mad sweet Heauen:	918
Glost. Let him fly farre:	993
Glo. Let me beseech your Grace, not to do so,	1220
**let go thy hold when a great wheele runs downe a	1344
**great one that goes vpward, let him draw thee after:	1346
And let the wiseman flie:	1355
Let shame come when it will, I do not call it,	1520
And let not womens weapons, water drops,	1577
Corn. Let vs withdraw, 'twill be a Storme.	1587
You owe me no subscription. Then let fall	1673
Lear. Let the great Goddes | That keepe this dreadfull pudder o're our heads,	1702
Lear. Let me alone. | *Kent*. Good my Lord enter heere.	1781
O that way madnesse lies, let me shun that: | No more of that.	1801
**in madnes, Lyon in prey. Let not the creaking of shooes,	1874
Boy *Sesey*: let him trot by. *Storme still*.	1880
And let this Tyrannous night take hold vpon you,	1929
Lear. First let me talke with this Philosopher,	1932
Lear. Let me aske you one word in priuate.	1939
Let him take the Fellow.	1961
*Lear. Then let them Anatomize *Regan*: See what	2033
**You will say they are Persian; but let them bee | chang'd.	2037
Corn. Wherefore to Douer? Let him answer that.	2124
Reg. Go thrust him out at gates, and let him smell | His way to Douer. *Exit with Glouster*.	2170
Let the superfluous, and Lust-dieted man,	2252
To let him liue. Where he arriues, he moues	2395
Let me vnseale the Letter.	2408
Glou. Let go my hand:	2464
Bid me farewell, and let me heare thee going.	2468
What are you Sir? | *Glou*. Away, and let me dye.	2488
Do's letcher in my sight. Let Copulation thriue:	2559
Glou. O let me kisse that hand. | *Lear*. Let me wipe it first,	2574
You shall haue ransome. Let me haue Surgeons,	2635
Let not my worser Spirit tempt me againe | To dye before you please.	2664
Glou. Now let thy friendly hand | Put strength enough too't.	2681
Like hold on thee. Let go his arme.	2686
Edg. Chill not let go Zir, | Without vurther 'casion.	2687

LET *cont.*
Stew. Let go Slaue, or thou dy'st.	2689
Edg. Good Gentleman goe your gate, and let poore	2690
He had no other Deathsman. Let vs see:	2711
Let our reciprocall vowes be remembred. You haue manie	2716
Thy medicine on my lippes, and let this kisse	2777
Let him alone a while.	2802
If you haue victory, let the Trumpet sound	2885
When time shall serue, let but the Herald cry, | And Ile appeare againe.	
Exit.	2893
Let her who would be rid of him, deuise	2911
Alb. The let alone lies not in your good will. | *Bast.* Nor in thine Lord.	3023
Reg. Let the Drum strike, and proue my title thine.	3026
Alb. Thou art armed *Gloster*, | Let the Trumpet sound:	3036
Come hither Herald, let the Trumpet sound, | And read out this. *A*	
Trumpet sounds.	3057
that he is a manifold Traitor, let him appeare by the third	3062
Let sorrow split my heart, if euer I | Did hate thee, or thy Father.	3139
Kent. Vex not his ghost, O let him passe, he hates him,	3287

LETCHER = 1
Do's letcher in my sight. Let Copulation thriue:	2559

LETCHERS = 1*1
*were like an old Letchers heart, a small spark, all the rest	1893
Of murtherous Letchers: and in the mature time,	2728

LETER = 1
This Leter Madam, craues a speedy answer: | 'Tis from your Sister.	2328

LETHARGIED = 1
Are Lethargied. Ha! Waking? 'Tis not so?	742

LETS = 8*1
*such neede to hide it selfe. Let's see: come, if it bee no-|thing, I shall	
not neede Spectacles.	369
Glou. Let's see, let's see.	379
Lear. Come, let's in all.	1956
Let's see these Pockets; the Letters that he speakes of	2709
I will not sweare these are my hands: let's see,	2807
Alb. Let's then determine with th'ancient of warre | On our proceeding.	2873
Lear. No, no, no, no: come let's away to prison,	2948
Edg. Let's exchange charity:	3127

LETTER *see also* leter = 14*10
Well, my Legittimate, if this Letter speed,	353
Glou. Why so earnestly seeke you to put vp y Letter?	363
Bast. I beseech you Sir, pardon mee; it is a Letter	371
Glou. Giue me the Letter, Sir.	375
Glou. O Villain, villain: his very opinion in the Let-|ter.	409
What haue you writ that Letter to my Sister? | *Stew.* I Madam.	858
*know, then comes from her demand out of the Letter,	877
Kent. I will not sleepe my Lord, till I haue deliuered | your Letter.	
Exit.	880
Glo. O strange and fastned Villaine, | Would he deny his Letter, said he?	1015
Kent. Thou whoreson Zed, thou vnnecessary letter:	1137
Peruse this Letter. Nothing almost sees miracles	1242
Reg. I know't, my Sisters: this approues her Letter,	1470
*receiued a Letter this night, 'tis dangerous to be spoken,	1761
*I haue lock'd the Letter in my Closset, these iniuries the	1762
Instantly know, and of that Letter too;	1772
*to be iust? This is the Letter which hee spoake of;	1980

LETTER *cont*.

*him this Letter, the Army of France is landed: seeke out | the Traitor
Glouster.   2061
Glou. I haue a Letter guessingly set downe   2115
Reg. What might import my Sisters Letter to him? | *Stew*. I know not,
Lady.   2391
*Stew. I must needs after him, Madam, with my Letter.   2400
Let me vnseale the Letter.   2408
Their Papers is more lawfull. | *Reads the Letter*.   2714
Edg. Before you fight the Battaile, ope this Letter: 2884
Alb. Stay till I haue read the Letter. | *Edg*. I was forbid it: 2891
LETTERS = 6*2
*Lear. Go you before to *Gloster* with these Letters;   875
*Kent. Draw you Rascall, you come with Letters a- | gainst   1108
I did commend your Highnesse Letters to them,   1304
Deliuer'd Letters spight of intermission,   1309
Corn. Come Sir. | What Letters had you late from France?   2108
Glou. Were all thy Letters Sunnes, I could not see.   2584
And giue the Letters which thou find'st about me,   2701
Let's see these Pockets; the Letters that he speakes of   2709
LEUIED = 1
All leuied in my name, haue in my name | Tooke their discharge.   3053
LIARS *see* lyars
LIBERTIE = 1
Deerer then eye-sight, space, and libertie,   61
LIBERTY = 1
Corn. Haile to your Grace. *Kent here set at liberty*.   1405
LICENCD *see* lycenc'd
LIE *see also* lye = 3
thy Foole to lie, I would faine learne to lie.   693
Lear. And you lie sirrah, wee'l haue you whipt.   694
LIEGE = 1
Kent. Good my Liege. | *Lear*. Peace *Kent*,   128
LIES = 3
O that way madnesse lies, let me shun that: | No more of that.   1801
Alb. The let alone lies not in your good will. | *Bast*. Nor in thine Lord.   3023
That names me Traitor, villain-like he lies,   3046
LIEST *see* lyest
LIFE = 29*5
No lesse then life, with grace, health, beauty, honor: 63
This hideous rashnesse, answere my life, my iudgement: 161
Lear. *Kent*, on thy life no more.   165
Kent. My life I neuer held but as pawne   166
*his obedience. I dare pawne downe my life for him, that   419
Life and death, I am asham'd   814
*Reg. What, did my Fathers Godsonne seeke your life?   1030
*Ste. This ancient Ruffian Sir, whose life I haue spar'd | at sute of his
gray-beard.   1135
As I haue life and Honour, there shall he sit till Noone.   1213
To keepe base life a foote; returne with her?   1508
Mans life is cheape as Beastes. Thou art a Lady;   1567
Ha's practis'd on mans life. Close pent-vp guilts,   1710
Now out-law'd from my blood: he sought my life   1947
If thou should'st dally halfe an houre, his life   2052
Though well we may not passe vpon his life   2084
Life would not yeelde to age.   2192

LIFE *cont.*

May all the building in my fancie plucke | Vpon my hatefull life.
Another way   2332
Least his vngouern'd rage, dissolue the life | That wants the meanes to
leade it.   2370
His nighted life: Moreouer to descry | The strength o'th'Enemy.   2398
The Treasury of life, when life it selfe   2483
I pardon that mans life. What was thy cause?   2556
Lear. Then there's life in't. Come, and you get it,   2644
*volke passe: and 'chud ha' bin zwaggerd out of my life,   2691
A plot vpon her vertuous Husbands life,   2725
My life will be too short, | And euery measure faile me.   2748
'Tis wonder that thy life and wits, at once   2789
Bast. I pant for life: some good I meane to do   3200
Is on the life of *Lear*, and on *Cordelia*:   3203
Edg. Hast thee for thy life.   3210
During the life of this old Maiesty   3271
Lear. And my poore Foole is hang'd: no, no, no life?   3277
Why should a Dog, a Horse, a Rat haue life,   3278
Kent. The wonder is, he hath endur'd so long, | He but vsurpt his life. 3291

LIFES = 1

Thy life's a Myracle. Speake yet againe.   2497

LIFTING = 1

For lifting food too't? But I will punish home;   1796

LIGHT = 4*2

Yeeld, come before my Father, light hoa, here,   963
Hang fated o're mens faults, light on thy Daughters.   1849
*the Turke. False of heart, light of eare, bloody of hand;   1872
Bid her a-light, and her troth-plight,   1902
*case, your purse in a light, yet you see how this world | goes.   2591
Where am I? Faire day light?   2804

LIGHTNINGS = *1

Le. You nimble Lightnings, dart your blinding flames   1448

LIGHTS = 1

That way, Ile this: He that first lights on him, | Holla the other. *Exeunt.* 1652

LIKE = 27*17

Sure I shall neuer marry like my Sisters.   110
And nothing more may fitly like your Grace,   218
And like a Sister am most loth to call   295
Reg. Such vnconstant starts are we like to haue from | him, as this of
Kents banishment.   325
*Pat: he comes like the Catastrophe of the old Comedie: 463
*my Cue is villanous Melancholly, with a sighe like *Tom*   464
like the image, and horror of it, pray you away.   496
Lear. Follow me, thou shalt serue me, if I like thee no   571
Foole. Then 'tis like the breath of an vnfeed Lawyer,   659
*gau'st thy golden one away; if I speake like my selfe in   678
Shewes like a riotous Inne; Epicurisme and Lust   753
Makes it more like a Tauerne, or a Brothell,   754
Which like an Engine, wrencht my frame of Nature   781
*for though she's as like this, as a Crabbe's like an | Apple, yet I can
tell what I can tell.   889
Foole. She will taste as like this as, a Crabbe do's to a   892
Edmund, I heare that you haue shewne your Father | A Child-like
Office.   1045
Like Rats oft bite the holy cords a twaine,   1147
Knowing naught (like dogges) but following: 1153

LIKE *cont.*

Whose influence like the wreath of radient fire | On flickring *Phoebus*
front.   1182
Sharpe-tooth'd vnkindnesse, like a vulture heere,   1413
Most Serpent-like, vpon the very Heart.   1443
To knee his Throne, and Squire-like pension beg,   1507
Gen. One minded like the weather, most vnquietly.   1617
Glo. Alacke, alacke *Edmund*, I like not this vnnaturall   1753
*were like an old Letchers heart, a small spark, all the rest   1893
*my hundred; only, I do not like the fashion of your gar-|ments.   2036
*most festinate preparation: we are bound to the like. Our   2069
Pinnion him like a Theefe, bring him before vs: 2083
What most he should dislike, seemes pleasant to him; | What like,
offensiue.   2277
Shall passe betweene vs: ere long you are like to heare   2287
Gon. One way I like this well.   2330
Appeare like Mice: and yond tall Anchoring Barke,   2453
Thou'dst shiuer'd like an Egge: but thou do'st breath: 2493
Hornes wealk'd, and waued like the enraged Sea: 2516
*Presse-money. That fellow handles his bow, like a Crow-|keeper: 2534
*me like a Dogge, and told mee I had the white hayres in   2544
*glasse-eyes, and like a scuruy Politician, seeme to see the   2613
*Like a smugge Bridegroome. What? I will be Iouiall: 2641
Like hold on thee. Let go his arme.   2686
Vpon a wheele of fire, that mine owne teares | Do scal'd, like molten
Lead.   2796
We two alone will sing like Birds i'th'Cage: 2949
And fire vs hence, like Foxes: wipe thine eyes,   2965
That names me Traitor, villain-like he lies,   3046
LIKELY = 1

Cur. Haue you heard of no likely Warres toward,   938
LIKENESSE = 1

For which I raiz'd my likenesse. Now banisht *Kent*,   534
LIKES = 1

What is his fault? | *Kent.* His countenance likes me not.   1163
LIKING = 2

T'auert your liking a more worthier way,   231
Hath lost me in your liking.   255
LILLY-LIUERED = *1

*pound, filthy woosted-stocking knaue, a Lilly-liuered,   1090
LINE = *1

Lear. Of all these bounds euen from this Line, to this,   68
LION *see* lyon
LIPPE = *1

*and the Pin, squints the eye, and makes the Hare-lippe;   1897
LIPPES = 1

Thy medicine on my lippes, and let this kisse   2777
LIPS = 1 *1

*who haue the power to seale th'accusers lips. Get thee   2612
Do you see this? Looke on her? Looke her lips,   3282
LIPSBURY = *1

*Kent. If I had thee in *Lipsbury* Pinfold, I would make | thee care for
me.   1083
LIST = 2

Reg. That's as we list to grace him.   3001
Edg. By nursing them my Lord. List a breefe tale,   3144

LISTS = *1
Herald reads. | *If any man of qualitie or degree, within the lists of the*
Ar-|my, — 3059
LITTER = 1
There is a Litter ready, lay him in't, — 2049
LITTLE = 8*6
Lear. How, how *Cordelia*? Mend your speech a little, — 100
If ought within that little seeming substance, — 216
Gon. Sister, it is not little I haue to say, — 310
*we haue made of it hath beene little; he alwaies — 315
*some little time hath qualified the heat of his displeasure, — 483
*honest, to conuerse with him that is wise and saies little, to — 546
*durt, thou hadst little wit in thy bald crowne, when thou — 677
A little to disquantity your Traine, — 758
Reg. This house is little, the old man and's people, | Cannot be well
bestow'd. — 1588
Too little care of this: Take Physicke, Pompe, — 1814
Should haue thus little mercy on their flesh: — 1854
*night to swimme in. Now a little fire in a wilde Field, — 1892
Lear. The little dogges, and all; — 2020
Cordelia, Cordelia, stay a little. Ha: — 3235
LITTLE-TYNE = 1
Foole. He that has and a little-tyne wit, — 1729
LIUE = 10*2
*him, you should enioy halfe his Reuennew for euer, and liue the | beloued
of your Brother.* Edgar. — 388
Create her childe of Spleene, that it may liue — 796
When Slanders do not liue in Tongues; — 1742
*This prophecie *Merlin* shall make, for I liue before his | (time. | *Exit.* — 1749
Glou. He that will thinke to liue, till he be old, — 2141
Might I but liue to see thee in my touch, — 2204
Alb. Glouster, I liue | To thanke thee for the loue thou shew'dst the
King, — 2344
To let him liue. Where he arriues, he moues — 2395
Burne it selfe out. If *Edgar* liue, O blesse him: — 2479
Cor. O thou good *Kent,* | How shall I liue and worke | To match thy
goodnesse? — 2745
And aske of thee forgiuenesse: So wee'l liue, — 2951
Shall neuer see so much, nor liue so long. | *Exeunt with a dead March.* |
FINIS. — 3301
LIUERD = 1
Gon. Milke-Liuer'd man, | That bear'st a cheeke for blowes, a head for
wrongs, — 2304
LIUERED = *1
*pound, filthy woosted-stocking knaue, a Lilly-liuered, — 1090
LIUES = 8*1
Freedome liues hence, and banishment is here; — 195
And hold our liues in mercy. *Oswald,* I say. — 848
Cor. Keepe peace vpon your liues, he dies that strikes | againe, what is
the matter? — 1122
Then comes the time, who liues to see't, — 1747
Stands still in esperance, liues not in feare: — 2182
That follow'd me so neere, (O our liues sweetnesse, — 3147
I know when one is dead, and when one liues, — 3220
If that her breath will mist or staine the stone, | Why then she liues. — 3222
Lear. This feather stirs, she liues: if it be so, — 3227

LIUING = *1
  Lear. Why my Boy? | *Fool.* If I gaue them all my liuing, I'ld keepe my
  Cox-|combes 636
LOATH *see* loth
LOATHED = 1*1
  My snuffe, and loathed part of Nature should 2478
  Gaole, from the loathed warmth whereof, deliuer me, and sup-|ply the
  place for your Labour. 2720
LOATHLY *see* lothly
LOCKD = *1
  *I haue lock'd the Letter in my Closset, these iniuries the 1762
LODGE = 1
  Where I did lodge last night. Do not laugh at me, 2823
LODGING = 1*1
  *I say, retire with me to my lodging, from whence I will 489
  This shamefull lodging. Fortune goodnight, 1249
LOINES *see also* loynes = 1
  Blanket my loines, else all my haires in knots, 1261
LONG = 9*3
  Long in our Court, haue made their amorous soiourne, 52
  *the imperfections of long ingraffed condition, but 322
  *fed the Cuckoo so long, that it's had it head bit off by it 727
  Shall not be a Maid long, vnlesse things be cut shorter. | *Exeunt.* 924
  Haue bin Toms food, for seuen long yeare: 1918
  *I will peece out the comfort with what addition I | can: I will not be
  long from you. *Exit* 1999
  So long as we can say this is the worst. 2211
  Shall passe betweene vs: ere long you are like to heare 2287
  *'twould not ha' bin zo long as 'tis, by a vortnight. Nay, 2692
  Gent. So please your Maiesty, | That we may wake the King, he hath
  slept long? 2767
  Kent. The wonder is, he hath endur'd so long, | He but vsurpt his life. 3291
  Shall neuer see so much, nor liue so long. | *Exeunt with a dead March.* |
  FINIS. 3301
LONGER = 2
  If I could beare it longer, and not fall 2476
  That would vpon the wracke of this tough world | Stretch him out
  longer. 3288
LOO = *2
  Edg. Pillicock sat on Pillicock hill, alow: alow, loo, loo. 1857
LOOK = *2
  Lea. Those wicked Creatures yet do look wel fauor'd 1554
  Edg. You do climbe vp it now. Look how we labor. 2432
LOOKD = 3
  Look'd blacke vpon me, strooke me with her Tongue 1442
  Reg. Not altogether so, | I look'd not for you yet, nor am prouided 1526
  Gon. Hola, hola, | That eye that told you so, look'd but a squint. 3014
LOOKE = 14*7
  *rash, then must we looke from his age, to receiue not a-|lone 321
  *I will looke further intoo't: but where's my Foole? I | haue not seene
  him this two daies. 600
  Glo. But where is he? | *Bast.* Looke Sir, I bleed. 975
  Art not asham'd to looke vpon this Beard? 1483
  *will looke him, and priuily relieue him; goe you and 1765
  on's body, cold: Looke, heere comes a walking fire. 1894
  How is't my Lord? How looke you? 2172
  Cannot be heard so high. Ile looke no more, 2457

LOOKE *cont*.
  Looke vp a height, the shrill-gorg'd Larke so farre   2500
  Cannot be seene, or heard: Do but looke vp.   2501
  *draw mee a Cloathiers yard. Looke, looke, a   2535
  *goes, with no eyes. Looke with thine eares: See how   2595
  Cor. O looke vpon me Sir, | And hold your hand in benediction o're
  me,   .   2810
  Alb. Why farethee well, I will o're-looke thy paper.   2895
  You looke as you had something more to say.   3165
  Do you see this? Looke on her? Looke her lips,   3282
  Looke there, looke there. *He dies*.   3283
  Kent. Breake heart, I prythee breake. | *Edg*. Looke vp my Lord.   3285
LOOKES = 5*1
  Gon. And let his Knights haue colder lookes among   525
  Lear. Do you bandy lookes with me, you Rascall?   614
  The leisure of their answer, gaue me cold lookes,   1313
  Lookes fearfully in the confined Deepe: 2259
  She gaue strange Eliads, and most speaking lookes   2412
  But since thy out-side lookes so faire and Warlike,   3098
LOOKING = 1
  *much as I haue perus'd, I finde it not fit for your ore-loo- | king.   373
LOOKING-GLASSE = 1
  She's dead as earth: Lend me a Looking-glasse,   3221
LOOSE = 4
  To wage against thine enemies, nere feare to loose it, | Thy safety being
  motiue.   167
  That you must loose a husband.   271
  And cast you with the waters that you loose   822
  And woes, by wrong imaginations loose   2738
LOOSES = 2
  That which my Father looses: no lesse then all,   1774
  Who looses, and who wins; who's in, who's out;   2955
LOOSEST = 1
  Thou loosest here a better where to finde.   286
LOPD = 1
  Your lop'd, and window'd raggednesse defend you   1812
LORD = 67*28
  Kent. Is not this your Son, my Lord?   11
  *be acknowledged. Doe you know this Noble Gentle- | man, *Edmond*? |
  Edm. No, my Lord.   27
  Glou. My Lord of Kent: | Remember him heereafter, as my Honourable
  Friend.   30
  Glou. I shall, my Lord. *Exit*.   40
  Cor. Nothing my Lord. | *Lear*. Nothing?   93
  Cor. Good my Lord, | You haue begot me, bred me, lou'd me.   102
  That Lord, whose hand must take my plight, shall carry   108
  Lear. But goes thy heart with this? | *Cor*. I my good Lord.   111
  Lear. So young, and so vntender? | *Cor*. So young my Lord, and true.   113
  Cor. Heere's *France* and *Burgundy*, my Noble Lord.   204
  Lear. My Lord of *Burgundie*, | We first addresse toward you, who with
  this King   205
  That it intends to do: my Lord of *Burgundy*,   260
  Gon. Let your study | Be to content your Lord, who hath receiu'd you   302
  Bast. I know no newes, my Lord.   364
  Glou. What Paper were you reading? | *Bast*. Nothing my Lord.   365
  Bast. It was not brought mee, my Lord; there's the   394
  Bast. If the matter were good my Lord, I durst swear   398

LORD *cont*.

Glou. It is his. | **Bast*. It is his hand, my Lord: but I hope his heart is | not in the Contents.	401
*Bast. Neuer my Lord. But I haue heard him oft main-|taine	405
*Bast. I do not well know my L.(ord) If it shall please you to	413
**fitly bring you to heare my Lord speake: pray ye goe,	490
*Knigh. He saies my Lord, your Daughters is not well.	580
Lear. He would not? | **Knight*. My Lord, I know not what the matter is,	585
*Knigh. I beseech you pardon me my Lord, if I bee	593
Ste. I am none of these my Lord, | I beseech your pardon.	612
Ste. Ile not be strucken my Lord.	615
Alb. My Lord, I am guiltlesse, as I am ignorant | Of what hath moued you.	786
Lear. It may be so, my Lord. | Heare Nature, heare deere Goddesse, heare:	788
And hasten your returne; no, no, my Lord,	864
*Kent. I will not sleepe my Lord, till I haue deliuered | your Letter. *Exit*.	880
Gent. Ready my Lord. | *Lear*. Come Boy.	921
Which can pursue th'offender; how dost my Lord?	1028
Cor. Is he pursued? | *Glo*. I my good Lord.	1050
Stew. I am scarce in breath my Lord.	1126
*my Lord, if you will giue me leaue, I will tread this vn-|boulted	1138
*Reg. Till noone? till night my Lord, and all night too.	1214
Corn. Come my Lord, away. *Exit*.	1227
Lear. Ha? Mak'st thou this shame thy pastime? | *Kent*. No my Lord.	1280
Kent. My Lord, when at their home	1303
Glo. My deere Lord, | You know the fiery quality of the Duke,	1366
Glo. Well my good Lord, I haue inform'd them so.	1373
*Lear. Inform'd them? Do'st thou vnderstand me man. | *Glo*. I my good Lord.	1374
*Gon. Why might not you my Lord, receiue attendance	1539
Reg. Why not my Lord?	1541
*Reg. And speak't againe my Lord, no more with me.	1553
Gon. Heare me my Lord; | What need you fiue and twenty? Ten? Or fiue?	1559
Gon. So am I purpos'd, | Where is my Lord of *Gloster*?	1594
Gon. My Lord, entreate him by no meanes to stay.	1602
*Cor. Shut vp your doores my Lord, 'tis a wil'd night,	1612
Gracious my Lord, hard by heere is a Houell,	1715
*Kent. Here is the place my Lord, good my Lord enter,	1778
Lear. Let me alone. | *Kent*. Good my Lord enter heere.	1781
Kent. I had rather breake mine owne, | Good my Lord enter.	1784
Kent. Good my Lord enter here.	1803
*Glou. Our flesh and blood, my Lord, is growne so | vilde, that it doth hate what gets it.	1923
Kent. Good my Lord take his offer, | Go into th'house.	1934
Kent. Importune him once more to go my Lord,	1940
Kent. This way, my Lord. | *Lear*. With him;	1957
Kent. Good my Lord, sooth him:	1960
*Bast. How my Lord, I may be censured, that Nature	1972
*Kent. Now good my Lord, lye heere, and rest awhile.	2040
*Corn. Poste speedily to my Lord your husband, shew	2060
**Postes shall be swift, and intelligent betwixt vs. Fare-|well deere Sister, farewell my Lord of Glouster.	2070
*Stew. My Lord of Glouster hath conuey'd him hence	2074

LORD *cont.*

Gon. Farewell sweet Lord, and Sister. *Exit*	2081
Corn. If you see vengeance. | *Seru.* Hold your hand, my Lord:	2144
*Ser. Oh I am slaine: my Lord, you haue one eye left	2156
How is't my Lord? How looke you?	2172
Oldm. O my good Lord, I haue bene your Tenant,	2193
Glou. Is that the naked Fellow? | *Oldm.* I, my Lord.	2226
*Gon. Welcome my Lord. I meruell our mild husband	2268
Stew. Madam, here come's my Lord.	2298
*Mes. Oh my good Lord, the Duke of *Cornwal*s dead,	2313
Lost he his other eye? | *Mes.* Both, both, my Lord.	2326
Alb. He is not heere. | *Mes.* No my good Lord, I met him backe againe.	2338
*Mes. I my good Lord: 'twas he inform'd against him	2341
*Reg. Lord *Edmund* spake not with your Lord at home? | *Stew.* No Madam.	2389
My Lord is dead: *Edmond*, and I haue talk'd,	2417
Cor. Then be't so my good Lord:	2760
Cor. How does my Royall Lord? | How fares your Maiesty?	2792
Reg. Now sweet Lord,	2853
Reg. I neuer shall endure her, deere my Lord | Be not familiar with her.	2861
Capt. Ile do't my Lord.	2978
Witnesse the world, that I create thee heere | My Lord, and Master.	3020
Alb. The let alone lies not in your good will. | *Bast.* Nor in thine Lord.	3023
'Tis she is sub-contracted to this Lord,	3031
Edg. By nursing them my Lord. List a breefe tale,	3144
Edg. To who my Lord? Who ha's the Office?	3206
Kent. No my good Lord, I am the very man. | *Lear.* Ile see that straight.	3252
Mess. Edmund is dead my Lord. | *Alb.* That's but a trifle heere:	3266
Edg. He faints, my Lord, my Lord.	3284
Kent. Breake heart, I prythee breake. | *Edg.* Looke vp my Lord.	3285

LORDS = 4*2

*Lear. Attend the Lords of France & Burgundy, Gloster.	39
*Lear. My Ladies Father? my Lords knaue, you whor-|son dog, you slaue, you curre.	610
That in the natures of their Lords rebell,	1149
Who, with some other of the Lords, dependants,	2077
I kill'd the Slaue that was a hanging thee. | *Gent.* 'Tis true (my Lords) he did.	3238
You Lords and Noble Friends, know our intent,	3268

LORDSHIP = 2*1

Edm. My seruices to your Lordship.	32
Bast. So please your Lordship, none.	362
*Bast. Perswade me to the murther of your Lordship,	980

LOSE *see also* loose = *1

**to our Graues. Find out this Villain, *Edmond*, it shall lose	444

LOSES *see* looses

LOSEST *see* loosest

LOSSE = 1

Stand in assured losse. Take vp, take vp,	2054

LOSSES = 1

Losses their remedies. All weary and o're-watch'd,	1247

LOST = 6

Hath lost me in your liking.	255
Bur. I am sorry then you haue so lost a Father,	270
Lost he his other eye? | *Mes.* Both, both, my Lord.	2326
King *Lear* hath lost, he and his Daughter tane,	2929

LOST *cont*.

Edg. Know my name is lost | By Treasons tooth: bare-gnawne, and
Canker-bit, 3073
Their precious Stones new lost: became his guide, 3153
LOTH = 1
And like a Sister am most loth to call 295
LOTHLY = 1
Seeing how lothly opposite I stood 985
LOUD = 8*2
As much as Childe ere lou'd, or Father found. 64
Cor. Good my Lord, | You haue begot me, bred me, lou'd me. 102
I lou'd her most, and thought to set my rest 131
Lou'd as my Father, as my Master follow'd, 150
Most choise forsaken, and most lou'd despis'd, 276
*lou'd our Sister most, and with what poore iudgement he 316
He rais'd the house, with loud and coward cries, 1319
*contriuing of Lust, and wak'd to doe it. Wine lou'd I 1870
But lately: very late: I lou'd him (Friend) 1948
Kent. If Fortune brag of two, she lou'd and hated, | One of them we
behold. 3245
LOUE = 42*6
Kent. I must loue you, and sue to know you better. 33
Great Riuals in our yongest daughters loue, 51
Which of you shall we say doth loue vs most, 56
Gon. Sir, I loue you more then word can weild y matter, 60
A loue that makes breath poore, and speech vnable, 65
Beyond all manner of so much I loue you. 66
Cor. What shall *Cordelia* speake? Loue, and be silent. 67
I finde she names my very deede of loue: 76
And finde I am alone felicitate | In your deere Highnesse loue. 80
Although our last and least; to whose yong loue, 89
My heart into my mouth: I loue your Maiesty 98
Obey you, Loue you, and most Honour you. 105
They loue you all? Happily when I shall wed, 107
Halfe my loue with him, halfe my Care, and Dutie, 109
Thy yongest Daughter do's not loue thee least, 162
That good effects may spring from words of loue: 199
Will you require in present Dower with her, | Or cease your quest of
Loue? 208
I would not from your loue make such a stray, 229
What say you to the Lady? Loue's not loue 261
Since that respect and Fortunes are his loue, 273
My Loue should kindle to enflam'd respect. 280
Without our Grace, our Loue, our Benizon: 290
Your faults as they are named. Loue well our Father: 296
Our Fathers loue, is to the Bastard *Edmond*, 351
*by the sequent effects. Loue cooles, friendship falls off, 436
*him truely that will put me in trust, to loue him that is 545
Lear. How old art thou? | *Kent*. Not so young Sir to loue a woman for
singing, 567
Lear. I thanke thee fellow. | Thou seru'st me, and Ile loue thee. 617
Whoop Iugge I loue thee. 737
From the fixt place: drew from my heart all loue, 782
Alb. I cannot be so partiall *Gonerill*, | To the great loue I beare you. 831
Stew. Prythee, if thou lou'st me, tell me. | *Kent*. I loue thee not. 1080
If you do loue old men; if your sweet sway 1480
And thou art twice her Loue. 1558

LOUE *cont.*
Kent. Alas Sir are you here? Things that loue night,   1694
Loue not such nights as these: The wrathfull Skies   1695
*Corn. I will lay trust vpon thee: and thou shalt finde | a deere Father
in my loue. *Exeunt.*   1994
I'th'way toward Douer, do it for ancient loue,   2230
Alb. Glouster, I liue | To thanke thee for the loue thou shew'dst the
King,   2344
But loue, deere loue, and our ag'd Fathers Rite: 2380
Some things, I know not what. Ile loue thee much   2407
Stew. Madam, I had rather--- | *Reg.* I know your Lady do's not loue her
Husband,   2409
*loue. Reade thou this challenge, marke but the penning | of it.   2582
I know you do not loue me, for your Sisters   2830
Do you not loue my Sister? | *Bast.* In honour'd Loue.   2856
Bast. To both these Sisters haue I sworne my loue: 2902
LOUES = 4
Cor. Then poore *Cordelia,* | And yet not so, since I am sure my loue's   82
What say you to the Lady? Loue's not loue   261
And machination ceases. Fortune loues you.   2890
If you will marry, make your loues to me,   3033
LOUING = 2
And you our no lesse louing Sonne of *Albany,*   47
Alb. Our very louing Sister, well be-met: 2865
LOUST = 2
So may it come, thy Master whom thou lou'st, | Shall find thee full of
labours.   536
Stew. Prythee, if thou lou'st me, tell me. | *Kent.* I loue thee not.   1080
LOW = 4
Nor are those empty hearted, whose low sounds | Reuerbe no
hollownesse.   163
And with this horrible obiect, from low Farmes,   1268
And dizie 'tis, to cast ones eyes so low,   2447
Gentle, and low, an excellent thing in woman.   3237
LOWEST = 1
The lowest, and most deiected thing of Fortune,   2181
LOWNESSE = 1
To such a lownesse, but his vnkind Daughters.   1852
LOWSE = *1
*The Head, and he shall Lowse: so Beggers marry many.   1683
LOYALL = 2
(Loyall and naturall Boy) Ile worke the meanes   1022
And of the loyall Seruice of his Sonne   2274
LOYALTIE = *1
*thus giues way to Loyaltie, something feares mee to | thinke of.   1973
LOYALTY = *1
*Loyalty, though the conflict be sore betweene that, and | my blood.   1992
LOYNES = *1
*Monkies by'th'loynes, and Men by'th' legs: when a man   1284
LUBBERS = *1
*away, away, if you will measure your lubbers length a- | gaine,   620
LUNATICKE = 1*1
*Sometimes with Lunaticke bans, sometime with Praiers   1270
Reg. To whose hands | You haue sent the Lunaticke King: Speake.   2113
LUST = 1*2
Shewes like a riotous Inne; Epicurisme and Lust   753
*curl'd my haire, wore Gloues in my cap; seru'd the Lust   1866

LUST *cont.*
*contriuing of Lust, and wak'd to doe it. Wine lou'd I   1870
LUSTER = 1
Where is thy luster now? | *Glou.* All darke and comfortlesse?   2159
LUSTIE = 1
Who in the lustie stealth of Nature, take | More composition, and fierce
qualitie,   345
LUSTS = *1
*backe, thou hotly lusts to vse her in that kind, for which   2605
LUST-DIETED = 1
Let the superfluous, and Lust-dieted man,   2252
LUXURY = 1
Too't Luxury pell-mell, for I lacke Souldiers.   2562
LYARS = *1
*Treachers by Sphericall predominance. Drunkards, Ly- | ars,   452
LYCENCD = 1
Gon. Not only Sir this, your all-lycenc'd Foole,   712
LYE = 1*2
Kent. Now good my Lord, lye heere, and rest awhile.   2040
*me, I was euery thing: 'Tis a Lye, I am not Agu-proofe.   2551
With the hell-hated Lye, ore-whelme thy heart,   3103
LYEST = 2
Lear. Detested Kite, thou lyest.   775
To proue vpon thy heart, where to I speake, | Thou lyest.   3095
LYING = *1
*whipt for lying, and sometimes I am whipt for holding   697
LYM *see* hym
LYON = *1
*in madnes, Lyon in prey. Let not the creaking of shooes,   1874
MACHINATION = 1
And machination ceases. Fortune loues you.   2890
MACHINATIONS = *1
*seene the best of our time. Machinations, hollownesse,   442
MAD = 11*5
When *Lear* is mad, what wouldest thou do old man?   155
Lear. O let me not be mad, not mad sweet Heauen: 918
*keepe me in temper, I would not be mad. How now are | the Horses
ready?   919
Corn. What art thou mad old Fellow?   1158
Lear. I prythee Daughter do not make me mad,   1512
Or ere Ile weepe; O Foole, I shall go mad. *Exeunt.*   1586
Thou sayest the King growes mad, Ile tell thee Friend   1945
I am almost mad my selfe. I had a Sonne,   1946
*his Sonne: for hee's a mad Yeoman that sees his Sonne a | Gentleman
before him.   2011
Old. 'Tis poore mad Tom.   2209
Old. Alacke sir, he is mad.   2233
As mad as the vext Sea, singing alowd.   2352
Lear. What, art mad? A man may see how this world   2594
Glou. The King is mad: 2732
Exasperates, makes mad her Sister *Gonerill,*   2907
MADAM = 30*1
Gon. Did my Father strike my Gentleman for chi- | ding of his Foole? |
Ste. I Madam.   507
Ste. He's comming Madam, I heare him.   518
Remember what I haue said. | *Ste.* Well Madam.   523
What haue you writ that Letter to my Sister? | *Stew.* I Madam.   858

MADAM *cont*.

Glo. O Madam, my old heart is crack'd, it's crack'd.	1029
Glo. I know not Madam, 'tis too bad, too bad.	1035
Bast. Yes Madam, he was of that consort.	1036
Glo. I serue you Madam, | Your Graces are right welcome. *Exeunt.*	
Flourish.	1072
Kent. Why Madam, if I were your Fathers dog, | You should not vse	
me so.	1215
Stew. Madam within, but neuer man so chang'd:	2270
Stew. Madam, here come's my Lord.	2298
This Leter Madam, craues a speedy answer: | 'Tis from your Sister.	2328
Gent. There is meanes Madam:	2361
Mes. Newes Madam, | The Brittish Powres are marching hitherward.	2373
Reg. But are my Brothers Powres set forth? | *Stew.* I Madam.	2384
Reg. Himselfe in person there? | *Stew.* Madam with much ado:	2386
*Reg. Lord *Edmund* spake not with your Lord at home? | *Stew.* No	
Madam.	2389
*Stew. I must needs after him, Madam, with my Letter.	2400
Stew. I may not Madam: | My Lady charg'd my dutie in this busines.	2403
Stew. Madam, I had rather--- | *Reg.* I know your Lady do's not loue her	
Husband,	2409
To Noble *Edmund.* I know you are of her bosome. | *Stew.* I, Madam?	2413
Stew. Would I could meet Madam, I should shew | What party I do	
follow.	2426
Kent. To be acknowledg'd Madam is ore-pai'd,	2750
I prythee put them off. | *Kent.* Pardon deere Madam,	2755
How do's the King? | *Gent.* Madam sleepes still.	2761
Gent. I Madam: in the heauinesse of sleepe, | We put fresh garments on	
him.	2772
Be by good Madam when we do awake him, | I doubt of his	
Temperance.	2774
Gen. Madam do you, 'tis fittest.	2791
Gent. Be comforted good Madam, the great rage	2837
Reg. Our Sisters man is certainely miscarried. | *Bast.* 'Tis to be doubted	
Madam.	2851
Bast. No by mine honour, Madam.	2860

MADAMS = 1

As honest Madams issue? Why brand they vs	343

MADE = 13*8

Long in our Court, haue made their amorous soiourne,	52
Reg. I am made of that selfe-mettle as my Sister,	74
Our potencie made good, take thy reward.	186
*Le. Then leaue her sir, for by the powre that made me,	227
*we haue made of it hath beene little; he alwaies	315
Lear. Why no Boy, | Nothing can be made out of nothing.	662
Or whether gasted by the noyse I made, | Full sodainely he fled.	991
*you cowardly Rascall, nature disclaimes in thee: a Taylor | made thee.	1128
*not haue made him so ill, though they had bin but two | yeares	
oth'trade.	1132
Gen. Made you no more offence, | But what you speake of? | *Kent.*	
None:	1333
Lear. Made you my Guardians, my Depositaries,	1549
*For there was neuer yet faire woman, but shee made | mouthes in a	
glasse.	1686
*in his Pue, set Rats-bane by his Porredge, made him	1836
*Brothers euill disposition made him seeke his death: but	1976
Corn. True or false, it hath made thee Earle of Glou- |cester:	1987

MADE *cont.*

That made the ouerture of thy Treasons to vs:	2166
Which made me thinke a Man, a Worme. My Sonne	2217
Edg. A most poore man, made tame to Fortunes blows	2668
Yet to be knowne shortens my made intent,	2757
Repaire those violent harmes, that my two Sisters | Haue in thy Reuerence made.	2778
I would haue made him skip: I am old now,	3242

MADMAN = 1*1

Foole. Prythee Nunkle tell me, whether a madman be | a Gentleman, or a Yeoman.	2007
Oldm. Madman, and beggar too.	2214

MADMEN = 2

Foole. This cold night will turne vs all to Fooles, and | Madmen.	1858
Glou. 'Tis the times plague, | When Madmen leade the blinde:	2234

MADNES = *1

*in madnes, Lyon in prey. Let not the creaking of shooes,	1874

MADNESSE = 2

O that way madnesse lies, let me shun that: | No more of that.	1801
Edg. O matter, and impertinency mixt, | Reason in Madnesse.	2616

MADST = *1

Foole. I haue vsed it Nunckle, ere since thou mad'st	685

MAD-MANS = 1

Into a mad-mans rags, t'assume a semblance	3150

MAHU = 1

Edg. The Prince of Darkenesse is a Gentleman. *Modo* | he's call'd, and *Mahu.*	1921

MAID = 3*1

The Gods to their deere shelter take thee Maid,	196
Can buy this vnpriz'd precious Maid of me.	284
Fool. She that's a Maid now, & laughs at my departure,	923
Shall not be a Maid long, vnlesse things be cut shorter. | *Exeunt.*	924

MAIDENLEST = *1

*haue bin that I am, had the maidenlest Starre in the Fir-|mament twinkled on my bastardizing.	460

MAIESTY = 7*1

My heart into my mouth: I loue your Maiesty	98
*That troope with Maiesty. Our selfe by Monthly course,	140
When Maiesty falls to folly, reserue thy state,	159
Bur. Most Royall Maiesty, | I craue no more then hath your Highnesse offer'd,	210
Cor. I yet beseech your Maiesty.	245
Gent. So please your Maiesty, | That we may wake the King, he hath slept long?	2767
Cor. How does my Royall Lord? | How fares your Maiesty?	2792
During the life of this old Maiesty	3271

MAINE = 2

Or swell the curled Waters 'boue the Maine,	1621
Gent. Neere, and on speedy foot: the maine descry | Stands on the hourely thought.	2657

MAINELY = 1

Yet I am doubtfull: For I am mainely ignorant	2820

MAINTAINE = 1*3

Bast. Neuer my Lord. But I haue heard him oft main-|taine	405
*maintaine talke with the Duke, that my charity be not of	1766
On him, on you, who not, I will maintaine | My truth and honor firmely.	3048

MAINTAINE *cont.*
*will maintaine vpon Edmund, supposed Earle of Gloster,   3061
MAIOR = *1
*taile, and my Natiuity was vnder *Vrsa Maior*, so   458
MAIST *l.*1816 = 1
MAKE = 29*18
*most, for qualities are so weigh'd, that curiosity in nei- |ther, can make
choise of eithers moity.   9
We make thee Lady. To thine and *Albanies* issues   71
Make with you by due turne, onely we shall retaine   143
*Le. The bow is bent & drawne, make from the shaft.   152
That thou hast sought to make vs breake our vowes,   182
I would not from your loue make such a stray,   229
Ile do't before I speake, that you make knowne   248
*him, mistaking his purpose, it would make a great   417
*behauiour, we make guilty of our disasters, the Sun, the   449
*you gaue me nothing for't, can you make no vse of no- |thing Nuncle?   660
*Gon. I would you would make vse of your good wise- |(dome   731
*Gon. You strike my people, and your disorder'd rable, | make Seruants
of their Betters.   766
Suspend thy purpose, if thou did'st intend | To make this Creature
fruitfull: 790
Should make thee worth them.   817
*Foole. Yes indeed, thou would'st make a good Foole.   911
Make thy words faith'd? No, what should I denie,   1007
And thou must make a dullard of the world,   1011
To make thee seeke it. *Tucket within.*   1014
To make thee capable.   1023
Be fear'd of doing harme, make your owne purpose,   1053
*Kent. If I had thee in *Lipsbury* Pinfold, I would make | thee care for
me.   1083
*for though it be night, yet the Moone shines, Ile make a   1104
*Cor. Thou art a strange fellow, a Taylor make a man?   1130
*Fathers that weare rags, do make their Children blind,   1323
That to our Sister, you do make returne,   1431
Make it your cause: Send downe, and take my part.   1482
Lear. I prythee Daughter do not make me mad,   1512
*The man y makes his Toe, what he his Hart shold make,   1684
And make them keepe their Caues: Since I was man,   1697
*And can make vilde things precious. Come, your Houel;   1726
Must make content with his Fortunes fit,   1731
*This prophecie *Merlin* shall make, for I liue before his | (time. | *Exit.* 1749
Tom will make him weepe and waile,   2028
*make these hard-hearts. You sir, I entertaine for one of   2035
*Lear. Make no noise, make no noise, draw the Cur- |taines: 2041
But that thy strange mutations make vs hate thee,   2191
Ten Masts at each, make not the altitude   2495
*Thinke that the cleerest Gods, who make them Honors   2518
*winde to make me chatter: when the Thunder would not   2548
Why, this would make a man, a man of Salt   2639
My boone I make it, that you know me not, | Till time, and I, thinke
meet.   2758
Ere they shall make vs weepe?   2967
As this instructs thee, thou dost make thy way   2972
If you will marry, make your loues to me,   3033
There is my pledge: Ile make it on thy heart   3040

MAKE *cont.*
The Gods are iust, and of our pleasant vices | Make instruments to
plague vs: 3131
MAKES = 9*4
A loue that makes breath poore, and speech vnable,   65
Or he that makes his generation messes   124
Bur. Pardon me Royall Sir, | Election makes not vp in such conditions. 225
Glou. reads. This policie, and reuerence of Age, makes the   382
*Lear. How now Daughter? what makes that Frontlet   703
Makes it more like a Tauerne, or a Brothell,   754
Foole. Can'st tell how an Oyster makes his shell? | *Lear.* No.   899
Cracke Natures moulds, all germaines spill at once | That makes
ingratefull Man.   1663
*The man y makes his Toe, what he his Hart shold make,   1684
*and the Pin, squints the eye, and makes the Hare-lippe;   1897
Makes thee the happier: Heauens deale so still: 2251
Exasperates, makes mad her Sister *Gonerill*,   2907
This iudgement of the Heauens that makes vs tremble.   3185
MAKING = 1*1
*there was good sport at his making, and the horson must   26
I had thought by making this well knowne vnto you,   716
MAKST = 1
Lear. Ha? Mak'st thou this shame thy pastime? | *Kent.* No my Lord.   1280
MALADY = 1
But where the greater malady is fixt,   1788
MALICE = 1
You shall doe small respects, show too bold malice   1209
MALICIOUS = *1
*Bast. How malicious is my fortune, that I must re-|pent   1979
MALT = 1
When Brewers marre their Malt with water;   1737
MAN = 40*13
When *Lear* is mad, what wouldest thou do old man?   155
*on. An admirable euasion of Whore-master-man,   455
*man, if there be any good meaning toward you: I haue told   494
how now, what art thou? | *Kent.* A man Sir.   540
Gon. This man hath had good Counsell, | A hundred Knights?   842
that what a man cannot smell out, he may spy into.   897
*Cor. Thou art a strange fellow, a Taylor make a man?   1130
And put vpon him such a deale of Man,   1196
That euer penury in contempt of man,   1259
*Monkies by'th'loynes, and Men by'th' legs: when a man   1284
Hauing more man then wit about me, drew;   1318
*Lear. Inform'd them? Do'st thou vnderstand me man. | *Glo.* I my good
Lord.   1374
For the sound man. Death on my state: wherefore   1388
Lear. Who put my man i'th'Stockes?   1467
How came my man i'th'Stockes?   1490
You see me heere (you Gods) a poore old man,   1572
Reg. This house is little, the old man and's people, | Cannot be well
bestow'd.   1588
Corn. Followed the old man forth, he is return'd.   1597
Cracke Natures moulds, all germaines spill at once | That makes
ingratefull Man.   1663
A poore, infirme, weake, and dispis'd old man: 1675
*The man y makes his Toe, what he his Hart shold make,   1684
And make them keepe their Caues: Since I was man,   1697

MAN *cont.*

These dreadfull Summoners grace. I am a man, | More sinn'd against,
then sinning. 1712
*man no more then this? Consider him well. Thou ow'st 1883
*man, is no more but such a poore, bare, forked A-|nimall 1887
He said it would be thus: poore banish'd man: 1944
I smell the blood of a Brittish man. *Exeunt* 1968
Glou. Is it a Beggar-man? 2213
Which made me thinke a Man, a Worme. My Sonne 2217
Let the superfluous, and Lust-dieted man, 2252
And each man haue enough. Dost thou know Douer? | *Edg.* I Master. 2256
Stew. Madam within, but neuer man so chang'd: 2270
Oh, the difference of man, and man, 2295
Gon. Milke-Liuer'd man, | That bear'st a cheeke for blowes, a head for
wrongs, 2304
I tooke it for a man: often 'twould say 2523
Lear. What, art mad? A man may see how this world 2594
Why, this would make a man, a man of Salt 2639
Edg. A most poore man, made tame to Fortunes blows 2668
*come not neere th'old man: keepe out che vor'ye, or Ile 2693
I am a very foolish fond old man, 2814
Me thinkes I should know you, and know this man, 2819
For (as I am a man) I thinke this Lady | To be my childe *Cordelia.* |
Cor. And so I am: I am. 2824
Reg. Our Sisters man is certainely miscarried. | *Bast.* 'Tis to be doubted
Madam. 2851
Edg. If ere your Grace had speech with man so poore, | Heare me one
word. 2881
Edgar. Away old man, giue me thy hand, away: 2928
Glo. No further Sir, a man may rot euen heere. 2931
Herald reads. | *If any man of qualitie or degree, within the lists of the
Ar-|my,* 3059
Edg. What kinde of helpe? | *Alb.* Speake man. 3171
Alb. Who dead? Speake man. 3176
Kent. No my good Lord, I am the very man.| *Lear.* Ile see that
straight. 3252
Lear. You are welcome hither. | *Kent.* Nor no man else: 3256
MANAGE = 1
the Sonne manage his Reuennew. 408
MANHOOD = 1
That thou hast power to shake my manhood thus, 815
MANIE = *1
*Let our reciprocall vowes be remembred. You haue manie 2716
MANIFEST = 1
Thy heynous, manifest, and many Treasons, 3039
MANIFOLD = 1*1
Spoke with how manifold, and strong a Bond 983
*that he is a manifold Traitor, let him appeare by the third 3062
MANNER = 1*1
Beyond all manner of so much I loue you. 66
*Knigh. Sir, he answered me in the roundest manner, he | would not. 583
MANNERS = 4
Their manners are so apish. 683
That this our Court infected with their manners, 752
Leaue gentle waxe, and manners: blame vs not 2712
The time will not allow the complement | Which very manners vrges. 3187

MANS = 11*2
*_Foole_. If a mans braines were in's heeles, wert not in | danger of
kybes? | _Lear_. I Boy.   882
'Tis they haue put him on the old mans death,   1038
A good mans fortune may grow out at heeles: 1233
Mans life is cheape as Beastes. Thou art a Lady;   1567
Staine my mans cheekes. No you vnnaturall Hags,   1578
Remember to haue heard. Mans Nature cannot carry | Th'affliction, nor
the feare.   1700
Ha's practis'd on mans life. Close pent-vp guilts,   1710
*with mans sworne Spouse: set not thy Sweet-heart on | proud array.
Tom's a cold.   1862
thee good mans sonne, from the foule Fiend.   2248
And bring him to our eye. What can mans wisedome   2358
Well worth a poore mans taking. Fayries, and Gods   2466
I pardon that mans life. What was thy cause?   2556
Into a mad-mans rags, t'assume a semblance   3150
MANTLE = *1
*ditch-Dogge; drinkes the green Mantle of the standing   1912
MANY = 8*3
So many folds of fauour: sure her offence   239
*But for all this thou shalt haue as many Dolors for thy   1326
Yea, or so many? Sith that both charge and danger,   1535
Should many people, vnder two commands   1537
To follow in a house, where twice so many | Haue a command to tend
you?   1561
Do sorely ruffle, for many Miles about | There's scarce a Bush.   1604
*The Head, and he shall Lowse: so Beggers marry many.   1683
*her. Swore as many Oathes, as I spake words, & broke   1868
Are many Simples operatiue, whose power | Will close the eye of
Anguish.   2364
(So many fathome downe precipitating)   2492
Thy heynous, manifest, and many Treasons,   3039
MAP = 1
Giue me the Map there. Know, that we haue diuided   42
MARBLE-HEARTED = 1
Ingratitude! thou Marble-hearted Fiend,   771
MARCH = 1*1
*Do, de, de, de: sese: Come, march to Wakes and Fayres,   2031
Shall neuer see so much, nor liue so long. | _Exeunt with a dead March_. |
FINIS.   3301
MARCHING = 1
Mes. Newes Madam, | The Brittish Powres are marching hitherward.   2373
MARE = 1
He met the Night-Mare, and her nine-fold;   1901
MARIORUM = 1
clout, i'th'clout: Hewgh. Giue the word. | _Edg_. Sweet Mariorum.   2539
MARKE = 5*1
Foole. Marke it Nuncle; | Haue more then thou showest,   647
Gon. Do you marke that?   830
Do you but marke how this becomes the house?   1434
*loue. Reade thou this challenge, marke but the penning | of it.   2582
We wawle, and cry. I will preach to thee: Marke.   2622
Marke I say instantly, and carry it so   2980
MARKET = 1
And Market Townes: poore Tom thy horne is dry,   2032

MARRE = 4*1
Least you may marre your Fortunes.   101
Lear. What seruices canst thou do? | *Kent*. I can keepe honest
counsaile, ride, run, marre a   562
Striuing to better, oft we marre what's well.   870
When Brewers marre their Malt with water;   1737
Edg. My teares begin to take his part so much, | They marre my
counterfetting.   2018
MARRY = 4*2
Sure I shall neuer marry like my Sisters.   110
Let pride, which she cals plainnesse, marry her: 137
*The Head, and he shall Lowse: so Beggers marry many.   1683
Kent. Who's there? | *Foole*. Marry here's Grace, and a Codpiece, that's
a | Wiseman, and a Foole.   1691
If you will marry, make your loues to me,   3033
Bast. I was contracted to them both, all three | Now marry in an
instant.   3179
MARUAILE = 1
Reg. No maruaile then, though he were ill affected,   1037
MARUELL *see also* meruell = *2
Foole. I maruell what kin thou and thy daughters are,   695
Kent. No Maruell, you haue so bestir'd your valour,   1127
MASTER = 21*2
Lou'd as my Father, as my Master follow'd,   150
*on. An admirable euasion of Whore-master-man,   455
So may it come, thy Master whom thou lou'st, | Shall find thee full of
labours.   536
Kent. No Sir, but you haue that in your countenance, | which I would
faine call Master.   558
You Sir, more Knaue then Foole, after your Master.   834
And found; dispatch, the Noble Duke my Master,   995
Ile flesh ye, come on yong Master.   1120
It pleas'd the King his Master very late   1192
Against the Grace, and Person of my Master, | Stocking his Messenger.   1210
The King his Master, needs must take it ill   1221
Kent. Haile to thee Noble Master.   1279
*my old Master must be relieued. There is strange things | toward
Edmund, pray you be carefull. *Exit*.   1769
Glou. Come hither Friend: | Where is the King my Master?   2044
Both welcome, and protection. Take vp thy Master,   2051
Ang'ring it selfe, and others. Blesse thee Master.   2225
And each man haue enough. Dost thou know Douer? | *Edg*. I Master.   2256
Not met vs on the way. Now, where's your Master?   2269
To his great Master, who, threat-enrag'd   2319
The safer sense will ne're accommodate | His Master thus.   2528
Witnesse the world, that I create thee heere | My Lord, and Master.   3020
Kent. I am come | To bid my King and Master aye good night.   3189
Kent. O my good Master. | *Lear*. Prethee away.   3230
My Master calls me, I must not say no.   3297
MASTERS = 3
With euery gall, and varry of their Masters,   1152
Must be their Schoole-Masters: shut vp your doores,   1608
Come, come, I am a King, Masters, know you that?   2642
MASTIFFE = 1
Mastiffe, Grey-hound, Mongrill, Grim,   2025
MASTS = 1
Ten Masts at each, make not the altitude   2495

MATCH = 2

To match you where I hate, therefore beseech you   230
Cor. O thou good *Kent,* | How shall I liue and worke | To match thy
goodnesse?   2745
MATTER = 8*7

*Gon. Sir, I loue you more then word can weild y matter,   60
*Bast. If the matter were good my Lord, I durst swear   398
*you: what growes of it no matter, aduise your fellowes   526
Lear. He would not? | *Knight. My Lord, I know not what the matter
is,   585
Alb. What's the matter, Sir? | *Lear.* Ile tell thee: 812
Bast. How now, what's the matter? Part.   1118
Glo. Weapons? Armes? what's the matter here?   1121
*Cor. Keepe peace vpon your liues, he dies that strikes | againe, what is
the matter?   1122
When Priests are more in word, then matter;   1736
*the Dukes, and a worsse matter then that: I haue   1760
*Bast. If the matter of this Paper be certain, you haue | mighty
businesse in hand.   1985
Reg. Faith he is poasted hence on serious matter: 2393
In better phrase, and matter then thou did'st.   2441
Edg. O matter, and impertinency mixt, | Reason in Madnesse.   2616
*Edg. Chill picke your teeth Zir: come, no matter vor | your foynes.   2697
MATURE = 1

Of murtherous Letchers: and in the mature time,   2728
MAUGRE = 1

Maugre thy strength, place, youth, and eminence,   3086
MAY *l.**50 57 101 198 199 218 308 *387 *481 533 536 *642 *735 760 788
796 801 847 849 863 869 897 941 1021 1078 1225 1233 1241 1256 1381
1610 *1972 *1988 2084 2087 2197 2210 2283 2332 2381 2403 2419 2439
2482 *2594 2710 2768 2922 2931 2988 3005 3082 3269 = 45*8
ME *see also* mee *l.*42 53 75 103 122 170 *181 225 *227 244 251 255 257
284 338 375 *386 *428 486 *489 503 510 *539 *545 557 567 *571 *581
*583 *593 *596 614 618 625 644 *660 669 *670 *696 709 738 743 816
851 *918 *919 959 966 *980 1019 1080 1084 1085 1087 *1102 *1138
1164 1169 1189 1193 1195 1200 1207 1216 1220 1264 1300 1312 1313
1318 1332 *1347 1361 1365 *1374 1389 1391 1393 *1397 1409 1437 1441
1442 1453 1497 1509 1512 1543 *1553 1559 1571 1572 1575 1576 1648
1673 1720 *1755 *1756 *1767 *1768 1773 1781 1798 1801 1805 1806
1821 *1827 1926 1932 1939 1984 *2004 *2007 2021 2055 2094 2101 2142
2154 2169 2173 *2176 2196 2217 2232 2260 2262 2264 2275 2276 2347
2408 2433 2440 2444 2451 2460 2461 2468 2489 2507 2514 2524 *2530
*2544 *2547 *2548 *2551 *2571 2574 2575 2579 *2581 *2589 *2611 2634
2635 *2663 2664 2670 *2699 2701 *2720 2740 2749 2758 2784 2794 2798
2810 2811 2813 2819 2823 2829 2830 2831 2836 2841 2855 2882 2916
2928 2930 2950 3011 3019 3033 3046 3055 3117 3119 3121 3125 3129
3137 3147 3149 3163 3211 3221 3243 3297 = 168*48, 1
*o'Bedlam. --- O these Eclipses do portend these diui- | sions. Fa, Sol,
La, Me.   465
MEADES = 1

With plenteous Riuers, and wide-skirted Meades   70
MEANE = 3*2

*Lear. Meane time we shal expresse our darker purpose.   41
*I meane the whisper'd ones, for they are yet but | ear-kissing
arguments.   935
I'ld shake it on this quarrell. What do you meane?   2151
Gon. Meane you to enioy him?   3022

MEANE *cont.*

   Bast. I pant for life: some good I meane to do   3200
MEANES = 11*1

    as I shall find meanes, and acquaint you withall.   432
    Bast. Fled this way Sir, when by no meanes he could.   978
    Glo. Pursue him, ho: go after. By no meanes, what?   979
    (Loyall and naturall Boy) Ile worke the meanes   1022
    Corn. What meanes your Grace?   1475
    Gon. My Lord, entreate him by no meanes to stay.   1602
    Glou. What meanes your Graces?   2092
    Our meanes secure vs, and our meere defects   2201
    Gent. There is meanes Madam: 2361
    Least his vngouern'd rage, dissolue the life | That wants the meanes to
    leade it.   2370
    Will not beare question: either say thou'lt do't, | Or thriue by other
    meanes.   2976
    Edg. What meanes this bloody Knife?   3173
MEANEST = 1

   Gent. A sight most pittifull in the meanest wretch,   2646
MEANETIME *see* meane
MEANING = 1*1

    *man, if ther be any good meaning toward you: I haue told   494
    Cor. We are not the first, | Who with best meaning haue incurr'd the
    worst: 2943
MEANST = 1

   Corn. What mean'st by this?   1184
MEASURE = 1*1

    *away, away, if you will measure your lubbers length a-|gaine, 620
    My life will be too short, | And euery measure faile me.   2748
MEATE = *1

    *eate vp the meate, the two Crownes of the egge: when   674
MEATES = *1

    Kent. A Knaue, a Rascall, an eater of broken meates, a   1088
MEDICINE = 2

    Thy medicine on my lippes, and let this kisse   2777
    Reg. Sicke, O sicke. | *Gon.* If not, Ile nere trust medicine. 3043
MEE *l.**371 *394 *1973 *2535 *2544 = *5
MEERE = 2

    They haue trauail'd all the night? meere fetches,   1363
    Our meanes secure vs, and our meere defects   2201
MEET = 2

   Stew. Would I could meet Madam, I should shew | What party I do
    follow.   2426
    My boone I make it, that you know me not, | Till time, and I, thinke
    meet.   2758
MEETE = 3*2

    Bast. If your Honor iudge it meete, I will place you   423
    All with me's meete, that I can fashion fit. *Exit.*   504
    Wee'l no more meete, no more see one another.   1514
    Thou'dst meete the Beare i'th' mouth, when the mind's | (free, 1791
    *And driue toward Douer friend, where thou shalt meete   2050
MEETING = 1

    And meeting heere the other Messenger,   1314
MEINEY = 1

    They summon'd vp their meiney, straight tooke Horse,   1311
MELANCHOLLY = *1

    *my Cue is villanous Melancholly, with a sighe like *Tom* 464

MELL = 1
Too't Luxury pell-mell, for I lacke Souldiers.   2562
MEMORIES = 1
These weedes are memories of those worser houres: 2754
MEN = 9*5
*bluntly: that which ordinary men are fit for, I am qual-|lified in, and
the best of me, is Dilligence.   565
Men so disorder'd, so debosh'd and bold,   751
To be such men as may besort your Age, | Which know themselues, and
you.   760
My Traine are men of choice, and rarest parts,   776
*Monkies by'th'loynes, and Men by'th' legs: when a man   1284
*noses, are led by their eyes, but blinde men, and there's   1342
If you do loue old men; if your sweet sway   1480
Lear. Returne to her? and fifty men dismiss'd?   1500
Reg. O Sir, to wilfull men, | The iniuries that they themselues procure,   1606
Shall do a curt'sie to our wrath, which men | May blame, but not
comptroll.   2086
*out. Go too, they are not men o'their words; they told   2550
Men must endure | Their going hence, euen as their comming hither,   2933
To Noble Fortunes: know thou this, that men   2973
*Lear. Howle, howle, howle: O you are men of stones,   3217
MEND = 1*1
*Lear. How, how Cordelia? Mend your speech a little,   100
Mend when thou can'st, be better at thy leisure,   1523
MENS = 2
Hang fated o're mens faults, light on thy Daughters.   1849
Of mens Impossibilities, haue preserued thee.   2519
MERCIE = 1
His speedy taking off. As for the mercie   2912
MERCY = 3
And hold our liues in mercy. Oswald, I say.   848
Should haue thus little mercy on their flesh: 1854
I do beseech your grace. | Lear. O cry you mercy, Sir: 1951
MERIT = 1*1
Where Nature doth with merit challenge. Gonerill,   58
*a prouoking merit set a-worke by a reprouable badnesse | in himselfe.   1977
MERITED = 1
Haue more then merited. All Friends shall   3274
MERITES = 1
As we shall find their merites, and our safety | May equally determine.   2987
MERLIN = *1
*This prophecie Merlin shall make, for I liue before his | (time. | Exit.   1749
MERRY = *1
*Foole. Then I prythee be merry, thy wit shall not go | slip-shod. | Lear.
Ha, ha, ha.   885
MERUELL = *1
*Gon. Welcome my Lord. I meruell our mild husband   2268
MES = 1
All with me's meete, that I can fashion fit. Exit.   504
MES = 5*2
MESS = 1
MESSAGE = *1
*curious tale in telling it, and deliuer a plaine message   564
MESSENGER see also Mes., Mess. = 6
Against the Grace, and Person of my Master, | Stocking his Messenger.   1210

MESSENGER cont.
That he so slightly valued in his Messenger, | Should haue him thus
restrained.   1222
And meeting heere the other Messenger,   1314
Enter a Messenger.   2312
Enter Messenger.   2372
Enter a Messenger.   3264
MESSENGERS = 2*1
To answere from our home: the seuerall Messengers   1067
Reg. The Messengers from our Sister, and the King?   1124
And not send backe my Messengers.   1275
MESSES = 1
Or he that makes his generation messes   124
MET = 7
He met the Night-Mare, and her nine-fold;   1901
Hot Questrists after him, met him at gate,   2076
Not met vs on the way. Now, where's your Master?   2269
Alb. He is not heere. | *Mes.* No my good Lord, I met him backe againe. 2338
Cor. Alacke, 'tis he: why he was met euen now   2351
Alb. Our very louing Sister, well be-met: 2865
Met I my Father with his bleeding Rings,   3152
METHINKES *see also* thinkes = 2
Farre off methinkes I heare the beaten Drumme.   2741
Methinkes our pleasure might haue bin demanded   3002
METHOUGHT *see* thought
METTLE = 1
Reg. I am made of that selfe-mettle as my Sister,   74
MICE = 2
But Mice, and Rats, and such small Deare,   1917
Appeare like Mice: and yond tall Anchoring Barke,   2453
MIDDLE = *4
Foole. Why after I haue cut the egge i'th'middle and   673
*thou clouest thy Crownes i'th'middle, and gau'st away   675
*wit o'both sides, and left nothing i'th'middle; heere | comes one o'the
parings.   700
*Crab: thou canst, tell why ones nose stands i'th'middle | on's face? |
Lear. No.   893
MIDWAY = *1
*The Crowes and Choughes, that wing the midway ayre   2448
MIGHT *l.**1539 1622 *1754 2204 2343 2391 *2406 2487 3002 3100
3234 = 8*3
MIGHTILY = 1
I am mightily abus'd; I should eu'n dye with pitty   2805
MIGHTST *l.*1301 *2602 = 1*1
MIGHTY = 3
Mighty in their working do you that offence,   723
Bast. If the matter of this Paper be certain, you haue | mighty
businesse in hand.   1985
Glou. O you mighty Gods! | This world I do renounce, and in your
sights   2473
MILD = *1
Gon. Welcome my Lord. I meruell our mild husband   2268
MILDEWES = *1
*Mildewes the white Wheate, and hurts the poore Crea-|ture of earth.   1898
MILDNESSE = 1
Then prais'd for harmefull mildnesse.   868

MILE = 1
Thou wilt ore-take vs hence a mile or twaine   2229
MILES = 1
Do sorely ruffle, for many Miles about | There's scarce a Bush.   1604
MILKE = 1
The Vines of France, and Milke of Burgundie,   90
MILKE-LIUERD = 1
Gon. Milke-Liuer'd man, | That bear'st a cheeke for blowes, a head for
wrongs,   2304
MILKY = 1
This milky gentlenesse, and course of yours   865
MILLES = 1
Poore pelting Villages, Sheeps-Coates, and Milles,   1269
MINCES = *1
*Forkes presages Snow; that minces Vertue, & do's shake   2564
MIND = 5
Whose mind and mine I know in that are one,   522
An honest mind and plaine, he must speake truth,   1174
When Nature being opprest, commands the mind   1384
The bodies delicate: the tempest in my mind,   1792
And to deale plainely, | I feare I am not in my perfect mind.   2817
MINDE = 3*1
My minde as generous, and my shape as true   342
Lear. What hast thou bin? | *Edg.* A Seruingman? Proud in heart, and
minde; that   1864
Came then into my minde, and yet my minde | Was then scarse Friends
with him.   2218
MINDED = 2
Gen. One minded like the weather, most vnquietly.   1617
Are as the time is; to be tender minded   2974
MINDES = 1
To know our enemies mindes, we rip their hearts,   2713
MINDS = 1
Thou'dst meete the Beare i'th' mouth, when the mind's | (free,   1791
MINE *l.*439 522 *596 *598 *638 988 *1165 1315 *1347 1517 1540 *1755
1784 2784 2796 2860 3082 3084 3105 3116 3201 3244 = 15*7
MINGLE = 1
For those that mingle reason with your passion,   1529
MINGLED = 1
When it is mingled with regards, that stands   262
MINISTERS = 1
But yet I call you Seruile Ministers,   1676
MIRACLE *see also* myracle = 1
Must be a faith that reason without miracle | Should neuer plant in me.   243
MIRACLES = 1
Peruse this Letter. Nothing almost sees miracles   1242
MIRE *see also* myre
MISCARRIED = 1
Reg. Our Sisters man is certainely miscarried. | *Bast.* 'Tis to be doubted
Madam.   2851
MISCARRY = 1
What is auouched there. If you miscarry,   2888
MISCHEFE = 1
To see some mischefe on him. Oh.   2157
MISCHIEFE = *1
*which at this instant so rageth in him, that with the mis-|chiefe   484

MISCONSTRUCTION = 1
To strike at me vpon his misconstruction, 1193
MISCREANT = 1
Lear. O Vassall! Miscreant. | *Alb. Cor.* Deare Sir forbeare. 175
MISERABLE = 1
Bast. Sir, I thought it fit, | To send the old and miserable King to some
retention, 2989
MISERIE = 1
But miserie. I know 'tis from *Cordelia*, 1243
MISERIES = 1
How haue you knowne the miseries of your Father? 3143
MISERY = 3
And Ile repayre the misery thou do'st beare 2261
All hearts against vs: *Edmund*, I thinke is gone | In pitty of his misery,
to dispatch 2396
When misery could beguile the Tyrants rage, | And frustrate his proud
will. 2505
MIST = 1
If that her breath will mist or staine the stone, | Why then she liues. 3222
MISTAKEN = *1
*mistaken, for my duty cannot be silent, when I thinke | your Highnesse
wrong'd. 594
MISTAKING = *1
*him, mistaking his purpose, it would make a great 417
MISTERIES = 1
The misteries of *Heccat* and the night: 117
MISTOOKE = 1
Lear. What's he, | That hath so much thy place mistooke | To set thee
heere? 1286
MISTRESSES = 1
A Mistresses command. Weare this; spare speech, 2289
MISTRIS = 5*1
Mumbling of wicked charmes, coniuring the Moone | To stand
auspicious Mistris. 973
From *Gonerill* his Mistris, salutations; 1308
*of my Mistris heart, and did the acte of darkenesse with 1867
Corn. Get horses for your Mistris. 2080
And when your Mistris heares thus much from you, 2421
As duteous to the vices of thy Mistris, | As badnesse would desire. 2705
MIXT = 1
Edg. O matter, and impertinency mixt, | Reason in Madnesse. 2616
MO = *1
*the seuen Starres are no mo then seuen, is a pretty reason. 909
MOCKE = 2
Reg. One side will mocke another: Th'other too. 2143
You must not kneele. | *Lear.* Pray do not mocke me: 2812
MODEST = 2
Resolue me with all modest haste, which way 1300
All my reports go with the modest truth, | Nor more, nor clipt, but so. 2751
MODO = *1
Edg. The Prince of Darkenesse is a Gentleman. *Modo* | he's call'd, and
Mahu. 1921
MOITY = 1
*most, for qualities are so weigh'd, that curiosity in nei- | ther, can make
choise of eithers moity. 9

MOLTEN = 1
Vpon a wheele of fire, that mine owne teares | Do scal'd, like molten
Lead.   2796
MOMENT = 1
The moment is thy death, away. By *Iupiter*, | This shall not be reuok'd,   192
MONETH = 1*1
Reg. That's most certaine, and with you: next moneth | (with vs.   313
If till the expiration of your Moneth   1495
MONEY *see also* mony = 1*1
*Presse-money. That fellow handles his bow, like a Crow-|keeper: 2534
There's money for thee.   2573
MONGER = 1
*sop oth' Moonshine of you, you whoreson Cullyenly | Barber-monger,
draw.   1105
MONGRILL *see also* mungrell, mungrill = 1
Mastiffe, Grey-hound, Mongrill, Grim,   2025
MONKIES = *1
*Monkies by'th'loynes, and Men by'th' legs: when a man   1284
MONSTER = 1*2
Glou. He cannot bee such a Monster. *Edmond* seeke   427
More hideous when thou shew'st thee in a Child, | Then the
Sea-monster.   772
Lear. To tak't againe perforce; Monster Ingratitude!   912
MONSTERS = 1
That monsters it: Or your fore-voucht affection   241
MONSTROUS = 2*1
Commit a thing so monstrous, to dismantle   238
Stew. Why, what a monstrous Fellow art thou, thus   1098
Alb. Most monstrous! O, know'st thou this paper?   3118
MONTH *see* moneth
MONTHLY = *1
*That troope with Maiesty. Our selfe by Monthly course,   140
MONY = *1
*head, nor no mony in your purse? Your eyes are in a hea-|uy   2590
MOODE = 1
Reg. O the blest Gods! | So will you wish on me, when the rash moode
is on.   1452
MOODES = 1
Being oile to fire, snow to the colder moodes,   1150
MOONE = 3*3
Glou. These late Eclipses in the Sun and Moone por-|tend   433
*Moone, and Starres, as if we were villaines on necessitie,   450
Mumbling of wicked charmes, coniuring the Moone | To stand
auspicious Mistris.   973
*for though it be night, yet the Moone shines, Ile make a   1104
For all beneath the Moone would I not leape vpright.   2463
In a wall'd prison, packs and sects of great ones, | That ebbe and flow
by th'Moone.   2958
MOONES = 1
Were two full Moones: he had a thousand Noses,   2515
MOONSHINE = *1
*sop oth' Moonshine of you, you whoreson Cullyenly | Barber-monger,
draw.   1105
MOONSHINES = 1
For that I am some twelue, or fourteene Moonshines   339
MORE *see also* mo = 67*11
Kent. | *I thought the King had more affected the   3

MORE *cont.*
   Gon. Sir, I loue you more then word can weild y matter,   60
More ponderous then my tongue.   84
A third, more opilent then your Sisters? speake.   92
According to my bond, no more nor lesse.   99
Lear. Kent, on thy life no more.   165
Bur. Most Royall Maiesty, | I craue no more then hath your Highnesse
offer'd,   210
And nothing more may fitly like your Grace,   218
T'auert your liking a more worthier way,   231
Who in the lustie stealth of Nature, take | More composition, and fierce
qualitie,   345
this I may speake more. If our Father would sleepe till I wak'd   387
Lear. No more of that, I haue noted it well, goe you   604
Foole. Marke it Nuncle; | Haue more then thou showest,   647
Ride more then thou goest,   651
Learne more then thou trowest,   652
And thou shalt haue more, | Then two tens to a score.   656
Makes it more like a Tauerne, or a Brothell,   754
More hideous when thou shew'st thee in a Child, | Then the
Sea-monster.   772
Gon. Neuer afflict your selfe to know more of it: 806
You Sir, more Knaue then Foole, after your Master.   834
As may compact it more. Get you gone,   863
You are much more at task for want of wisedome,   867
Of my more fierce endeauour. I haue seene drunkards   967
Do more then this in sport; Father, Father,   968
Cor. If he be taken, he shall neuer more   1052
Kent. No contraries hold more antipathy, | Then I, and such a knaue.   1160
Cor. No more perchance do's mine, nor his, nor hers.   1165
Harbour more craft, and more corrupter ends,   1177
Reg. My Sister may recieue it much more worsse,   1225
Smile once more, turne thy wheele.   1250
Hauing more man then wit about me, drew;   1318
Gen. Made you no more offence, | But what you speake of? | *Kent.*
None: 1333
And am fallen out with my more headier will,   1386
Reg. Good Sir, no more: these are vnsightly trickes: 1438
Wee'l no more meete, no more see one another.   1514
Is it not well? What should you need of more?   1534
To bring but fiue and twentie, to no more | Will I giue place or notice.   1545
Reg. And speak't againe my Lord, no more with me.   1553
When others are much wicked, not being the worst   1555
Allow not Nature, more then Nature needs: 1566
For confirmation that I am much more   1641
Gent. Giue me your hand, | Haue you no more to say?   1648
Kent. Few words, but to effect more then all yet;   1650
These dreadfull Summoners grace. I am a man, | More sinn'd against,
then sinning.   1712
(More harder then the stones whereof 'tis rais'd,   1718
When Priests are more in word, then matter;   1736
No, I will weepe no more; in such a night,   1797
O that way madnesse lies, let me shun that: | No more of that.   1801
On things would hurt me more, but Ile goe in,   1806
And shew the Heauens more iust.   1817
*man no more then this? Consider him well. Thou ow'st   1883
*man, is no more but such a poore, bare, forked A-|nimall   1887

MORE *cont*.

Kent. Importune him once more to go my Lord,	1940
*his suspition more fully. I will perseuer in my course of	1991
Corn. Lest it see more, preuent it; Out vilde gelly:	2158
I haue heard more since:	2220
Tell me what more thou know'st. *Exeunt*.	2347
And more conuenient is he for my hand	2418
Then for your Ladies: You may gather more:	2419
Cannot be heard so high. Ile looke no more,	2457
*the soyled Horse goes too't with a more riotous appe-|tite:	2566
Their Papers is more lawfull. | *Reads the Letter*.	2714
All my reports go with the modest truth, | Nor more, nor clipt, but so.	2751
Fourescore and vpward, | Not an houre more, nor lesse:	2815
Trouble him no more till further setling.	2839
Whose age had Charmes in it, whose Title more,	2991
In his owne grace he doth exalt himselfe, | More then in your addition.	3008
And more, much more, the time will bring it out.	3123
If more, the more th'hast wrong'd me.	3129
You looke as you had something more to say.	3165
Alb. If there be more, more wofull, hold it in,	3166
Haue more then merited. All Friends shall	3274
And thou no breath at all? Thou'lt come no more, | Neuer, neuer, neuer, neuer, neuer.	3279

MOREOUER = 1

His nighted life: Moreouer to descry | The strength o'th'Enemy.	2398

MORNING = 1

so, so, wee'l go to Supper i'th'morning.	2042

MORROW = 4

Giue you good morrow.	1234
Lear. Good morrow to you both.	1404
Reg. Our troopes set forth to morrow, stay with vs: | The wayes are dangerous.	2401
To morrow, or at further space, t'appeare	2996

MORTALITY = 1

It smelles of Mortality.	2576

MORTER = *1

*villaine into morter, and daube the wall of a	1139

MORTIFIED = 1

Strike in their num'd and mortified Armes.	1266

MOST = 33*7

*most, for qualities are so weigh'd, that curiosity in nei-|ther, can make choise of eithers moity.	9
Which of you shall we say doth loue vs most,	56
Which the most precious square of sense professes,	79
Obey you, Loue you, and most Honour you.	105
I lou'd her most, and thought to set my rest	131
That iustly think'st, and hast most rightly said:	197
Bur. Most Royall Maiesty, | I craue no more then hath your Highnesse offer'd,	210
Fra. This is most strange,	234
Fra. Fairest *Cordelia*, that art most rich being poore,	275
Most choise forsaken, and most lou'd despis'd,	276
And like a Sister am most loth to call	295
Of what most neerely appertaines to vs both,	311
Reg. That's most certaine, and with you: next moneth | (with vs.	313
*lou'd our Sister most, and with what poore iudgement he	316
*I haue perceiued a most faint neglect of late,	597

MOST *cont*.

And in the most exact regard, support	778
The worships of their name. O most small fault,	779
Who hath most fortunately beene inform'd	1244
That guard, and most vnusall vigilance	1255
To take the basest, and most poorest shape	1258
Most Serpent-like, vpon the very Heart.	1443
Gen. One minded like the weather, most vnquietly.	1617
Bast. Most sauage and vnnaturall.	1758
*most festinate preparation: we are bound to the like. Our	2069
Glou. By the kinde Gods, 'tis most ignobly done | To plucke me by the Beard.	2100
The lowest, and most deiected thing of Fortune,	2181
What most he should dislike, seemes pleasant to him; | What like, offensiue.	2277
Gon. My most deere Gloster.	2294
She gaue strange Eliads, and most speaking lookes	2412
Your most deere Daughter--- | *Lear*. No rescue? What, a Prisoner? I am euen	2632
Gent. A sight most pittifull in the meanest wretch,	2646
Edg. Do you heare ought (Sir) of a Battell toward. | *Gent*. Most sure, and vulgar:	2652
Edg. A most poore man, made tame to Fortunes blows	2668
Stew. A proclaim'd prize: most happie	2676
Reg. 'Tis most conuenient, pray go with vs.	2877
Alb. That were the most, if he should husband you.	3012
A most Toad-spotted Traitor. Say thou no,	3093
Alb. Most monstrous! O, know'st thou this paper?	3118
The oldest hath borne most, we that are yong,	3300

MOTHER = 1*4

Glou. Sir, this yong Fellowes mother could; where- | vpon	16
*world before he was sent for: yet was his Mother fayre,	25
*My father compounded with my mother vnder the Dra- | gons	457
Lear. Oh how this Mother swels vp toward my heart!	1328
I would diuorce me from thy Mother Tombe,	1409

MOTHERS = 1*1

*thy Daughters thy Mothers, for when thou gau'st them	686
Turne all her Mothers paines, and benefits	800

MOTION = 1

To his vnnaturall purpose, in fell motion	986

MOTIUE = 1

To wage against thine enemies, nere feare to loose it, | Thy safety being motiue.	167

MOUD = 2

Her Army is mou'd on. *Exit*.	2661
Bast. This speech of yours hath mou'd me,	3163

MOUED = 1

Alb. My Lord, I am guiltlesse, as I am ignorant | Of what hath moued you.	786

MOUES = 1

To let him liue. Where he arriues, he moues	2395

MOULDS = 1

Cracke Natures moulds, all germaines spill at once | That makes ingratefull Man.	1663

MOURNING = 1

My mourning, and importun'd teares hath pittied:	2378

MOUSE = *1
*Mouse: peace, peace, this peece of toasted Cheese will 2536
MOUTH = 5
My heart into my mouth: I loue your Maiesty 98
Thou'dst meete the Beare i'th' mouth, when the mind's | (free, 1791
Is it not as this mouth should teare this hand 1795
Curres, be thy mouth or blacke or white: 2023
Alb. Shut your mouth Dame, 3112
MOUTHES = 1
*For there was neuer yet faire woman, but shee made | mouthes in a
glasse. 1686
MUCH = 21*3
As much as Childe ere lou'd, or Father found. 64
Beyond all manner of so much I loue you. 66
*much as I haue perus'd, I finde it not fit for your ore-loo-|king. 373
Sir, the Foole hath much pined away. 603
Foole. Prythee tell him, so much the rent of his land 664
on? You are too much of late i'th'frowne. 704
Gon. This admiration Sir, is much o'th'fauour 746
You are much more at task for want of wisedome, 867
So much commend it selfe, you shall be ours, 1056
Nature's of such deepe trust, we shall much need: | You we first seize
on. 1057
*so much; I know Sir, I am no flatterer, he that be-|guild 1186
Reg. My Sister may recieue it much more worsse, 1225
Lear. What's he, | That hath so much thy place mistooke | To set thee
heere? 1286
Deseru'd much lesse aduancement. | *Lear.* You? Did you? 1492
Against their Father, foole me not so much, 1575
For confirmation that I am much more 1641
Lear. Thou think'st 'tis much that this contentious | (storme 1786
Edg. My teares begin to take his part so much, | They marre my
counterfetting. 2018
Reg. Himselfe in person there? | *Stew.* Madam with much ado: 2386
Some things, I know not what. Ile loue thee much 2407
And when your Mistris heares thus much from you, 2421
Edg. Y'are much deceiu'd: In nothing am I chang'd | But in my
Garments. 2442
And more, much more, the time will bring it out. 3123
Shall neuer see so much, nor liue so long. | *Exeunt with a dead March.* |
FINIS. 3301
MUM = 2
Mum, mum, he that keepes nor crust, nor crum, 710
MUMBLING = 1
Mumbling of wicked charmes, coniuring the Moone | To stand
auspicious Mistris. 973
MUN = *1
*cold winde: Sayes suum, mun, nonny, Dolphin my Boy, 1879
MUNGRELL = 1
asleepe, how now? Where's that Mungrell? 579
MUNGRILL = *1
*Pandar, and the Sonne and Heire of a Mungrill Bitch, 1095
MURDERORS = 1
Lear. A plague vpon you Murderors, Traitors all, 3233
MURDEROUS = 1
Bringing the murderous Coward to the stake: 999

MURMURING = 1
Almost too small for sight. The murmuring Surge,	2455

MURTHER = 4*2
It is no vicious blot, murther, or foulenesse,	249
*Bast. Perswade me to the murther of your Lordship,	980
Ste. Helpe, ho, murther, helpe.	1113
Stew. Helpe hoa, murther, murther.	1116
*They could not, would not do't: 'tis worse then murther,	1298

MURTHEROUS = 1
Of murtherous Letchers: and in the mature time,	2728

MUST = 33*11
*there was good sport at his making, and the horson must	26
Kent. I must loue you, and sue to know you better.	33
That Lord, whose hand must take my plight, shall carry	108
Must be of such vnnaturall degree,	240
Must be a faith that reason without miracle | Should neuer plant in me.	243
That you must loose a husband.	271
*rash, then must we looke from his age, to receiue not a- |lone	321
*Gon. We must do something, and i'th' heate. Exeunt.	332
Legitimate Edgar, I must haue your land,	350
*blessing against his will, if thou follow him, thou must	633
*Foole. Truth's a dog must to kennell, hee must bee	641
A Babe to honor her. If she must teeme,	795
Which I must act, Briefenesse, and Fortune worke.	947
In cunning, I must draw my Sword vpon you:	960
And thou must make a dullard of the world,	1011
The Duke must grant me that: besides, his picture	1019
Wherein we must haue vse of your aduise.	1064
An honest mind and plaine, he must speake truth,	1174
The King his Master, needs must take it ill	1221
*Kent. Good King, that must approue the common saw,	1237
Which I must needs call mine. Thou art a Byle,	1517
Must be content to thinke you old, and so,	1530
With such a number? What, must I come to you	1551
And must needs taste his folly.	1591
Must be their Schoole-Masters: shut vp your doores,	1608
Must make content with his Fortunes fit,	1731
*a Power already footed, we must incline to the King, I	1764
*my old Master must be relieued. There is strange things | toward	
Edmund, pray you be carefull. Exit.	1769
This seemes a faire deseruing, and must draw me	1773
*Bast. How malicious is my fortune, that I must re-|pent	1979
Glou. I am tyed to'th'Stake, | And I must stand the Course.	2125
Bad is the Trade that must play Foole to sorrow,	2224
Glou. Come hither fellow. | Edg. And yet I must:	2242
I must change names at home, and giue the Distaffe	2285
*Stew. I must needs after him, Madam, with my Letter.	2400
Thou must be patient; we came crying hither:	2620
Breefely thy selfe remember: the Sword is out | That must destroy thee.	2679
You must not kneele. | Lear. Pray do not mocke me:	2812
Cor. Wilt please your Highnesse walke? | Lear. You must beare with me:	2840
Men must endure | Their going hence, euen as their comming hither,	2933
A Royall Noblenesse: I must embrace thee,	3138
My Master calls me, I must not say no.	3297
Edg. The waight of this sad time we must obey,	3298

MUSTERS = 1
   Hasten his Musters, and conduct his powres.   2284
MUSTY = 1
   In short, and musty straw? Alacke, alacke,   2788
MUTATIONS = 1
   But that thy strange mutations make vs hate thee,   2191
MUTINIES = *1
   *Brothers diuide. In Cities, mutinies; in Countries, dis-|cord;   437
MUTUALL = 1
   With mutuall cunning) 'twixt Albany, and Cornwall: 1630
MY *l*.11 *12 *23 30 31 32 40 53 74 75 76 78 83 84 93 98 99 102 106 108
109 110 112 114 120 122 125 127 128 131 132 133 136 138 149 150 151
154 161 166 169 179 204 205 260 280 *281 309 335 336 341 342 353 354
364 366 *372 *380 381 *391 *394 396 *398 *402 *405 *413 *414 *419
*420 *429 *457 *458 462 *464 474 *482 *487 *489 *490 491 502 *507
521 *527 532 534 570 *573 *574 *578 *580 *586 *587 *593 *594 *600
*602 *605 *606 609 *610 612 615 *622 625 626 627 628 *631 *634 636
*637 *638 *667 *678 *698 *708 748 763 *766 770 776 781 782 785 786
788 810 815 840 853 858 861 864 *876 *880 *906 907 *913 921 *923 944
945 950 959 960 963 967 988 989 995 996 1009 1012 1021 *1025 1028
1029 *1030 1031 1034 1040 1042 1047 1051 1054 1126 *1138 1140 1155
1166 1167 *1185 *1188 1210 *1214 1225 1227 1245 1252 1256 1260 1261
1275 1281 1303 1306 *1328 1366 1373 1375 1379 1386 1388 1391 *1397
1420 1425 1436 1439 1441 1454 1458 1459 1461 1467 1470 1474 *1477
1482 1490 1496 1513 1515 1516 1519 1525 1528 *1539 1541 1549 *1553
1559 1578 1595 1602 *1612 *1613 1627 1642 *1661 1670 1715 1722 1723
1724 1727 *1762 *1766 *1769 1774 *1778 1782 1783 1785 1792 1793
1803 1822 *1866 *1867 *1879 *1919 *1923 1926 1928 1934 1940 1946
1947 1950 1957 1959 1960 1971 *1972 *1979 *1991 1993 1995 2018 2019
2029 *2036 *2040 2045 *2060 *2065 2072 *2074 2093 2104 2106 2140
2145 2152 *2156 2161 2168 2172 2189 2193 2204 2217 2218 2227 2228
*2268 2283 2286 2294 2297 2298 *2313 2327 2331 2332 2333 2337 2339
*2341 2360 2368 2378 2384 2391 *2400 2404 2417 2418 2443 2458 2464
2470 2475 2478 *2537 *2545 *2549 2559 2561 *2572 2586 *2611 *2614
*2618 2638 *2663 2664 2678 *2691 *2694 *2699 2700 2710 *2719 2726
2733 2735 2736 2748 2751 2757 2758 2760 2776 2777 2778 2785 2792
2807 2809 2818 2825 2856 2858 2861 2902 2908 2915 2946 2961 2978
2995 3004 3010 3018 3021 3026 3030 3034 3040 3045 3049 3053 3055
3056 3073 3081 3083 3085 3094 3130 3139 3144 3145 3152 3155 3190
3197 3202 3206 3208 3230 3239 3241 3252 3266 *3277 3284 3286 3294
3297 = 339*112
MYRACLE = 1
   Thy life's a Myracle. Speake yet againe.   2497
MYRE = 1
   Stew. Where may we set our horses? | *Kent.* I'th'myre.   1078
MYSELFE *see also* selfe = 1
   I will preserue myselfe: and am bethought   1257
MYSTERY = 1
   And take vpon's the mystery of things,   2956
NAILES *see also* nayles = 2
   When she shall heare this of thee, with her nailes   826
   Reg. Wherefore to Douer? | *Glou.* Because I would not see thy cruell   2127
   Nailes
NAKED = 4
   Poore naked wretches, where so ere you are   1809
   Glou. Is that the naked Fellow? | *Oldm.* I, my Lord.   2226

NAKED *cont.*

And bring some couering for this naked Soule, | Which Ile intreate to
leade me. 2231
Glou. Sirrah, naked fellow. 2240
NAKEDNESSE = 1

And with presented nakednesse out-face 1262
NAMD = 1

He whom my Father nam'd, your *Edgar*? 1031
NAME = 11*1

The name, and all th'addition to a King: the Sway, 144
Lear. Your name, faire Gentlewoman? 745
The worships of their name. O most small fault, 779
*the head to heare of pleasures name. The Fitchew, nor 2565
I know thee well enough, thy name is Glouster: 2619
All leuied in my name, haue in my name | Tooke their discharge. 3053
Your name, your quality, and why you answer | This present Summons? 3071
Edg. Know my name is lost | By Treasons tooth: bare-gnawne, and
Canker-bit, 3073
Bast. In wisedome I should aske thy name, 3097
Thou worse then any name, reade thine owne euill: 3114
My name is *Edgar* and thy Fathers Sonne, 3130
NAMED = 1

Your faults as they are named. Loue well our Father: 296
NAMES = 4*1

I finde she names my very deede of loue: 76
Foole. A spirite, a spirite, he sayes his name's poore | *Tom.* 1823
Glou. What are you there? Your Names? 1907
I must change names at home, and giue the Distaffe 2285
That names me Traitor, villain-like he lies, 3046
NATIONS = 1

The curiosity of Nations, to depriue me? 338
NATIUITY = *1

*taile, and my Natiuity was vnder *Vrsa Maior*, so 458
NATURALL = 2

(Loyall and naturall Boy) Ile worke the meanes 1022
The Naturall Foole of Fortune. Vse me well, 2634
NATURE = 27*7

Where Nature doth with merit challenge. *Gonerill*, 58
Which, nor our nature, nor our place can beare; 185
Then on a wretch whom Nature is asham'd | Almost t'acknowledge
hers. 232
Fra. Is it but this? A tardinesse in nature, 258
Bast. Thou Nature art my Goddesse, to thy Law 335
Who in the lustie stealth of Nature, take | More composition, and fierce
qualitie, 345
*no good to vs: though the wisedome of Nature can 434
*reason it thus, and thus, yet Nature finds it selfe scourg'd 435
*byas of Nature, there's Father against Childe. We haue 441
Whose nature is so farre from doing harmes, 500
Which like an Engine, wrencht my frame of Nature 781
Lear. It may be so, my Lord. | Heare Nature, heare deere Goddesse,
heare: 788
Lear. I will forget my Nature, so kind a Father? Be | my Horsses
ready? 906
*you cowardly Rascall, nature disclaimes in thee: a Taylor | made thee. 1128
Quite from his Nature. He cannot flatter he, 1173
When Nature being opprest, commands the mind 1384

NATURE *cont.*
Nature in you stands on the very Verge 1427
Thy tender-hefted Nature shall not giue 1455
The Offices of Nature, bond of Childhood, 1462
Allow not Nature, more then Nature needs: 1566
Why Nature needs not what thou gorgeous wear'st, 1569
Remember to haue heard. Mans Nature cannot carry | Th'affliction, nor
the feare. 1700
The tirrany of the open night's too rough | For Nature to endure.
Storme still 1779
Lear. Death Traitor, nothing could haue subdu'd | (Nature 1851
Bast. How my Lord, I may be censured, that Nature 1972
*breeds about her heart. Is there any cause in Nature that 2034
Edmund, enkindle all the sparkes of Nature | To quit this horrid acte. 2162
Our foster Nurse of Nature, is repose, 2362
My snuffe, and loathed part of Nature should 2478
Glou. O ruin'd peece of Nature, this great world | Shall so weare out to
naught. 2577
Who redeemes Nature from the generall curse | Which twaine haue
brought her to. 2648
Cure this great breach in his abused Nature, 2764
Despight of mine owne Nature. Quickly send, 3201
NATURES = 3*1
Nature's of such deepe trust, we shall much need: | You we first seize
on. 1057
That in the natures of their Lords rebell, 1149
Cracke Natures moulds, all germaines spill at once | That makes
ingratefull Man. 1663
Lear. Nature's aboue Art, in that respect. Ther's your 2533
NAUGHT = 3
Knowing naught (like dogges) but following: 1153
Thy Sisters naught: oh *Regan,* she hath tied 1412
Glou. O ruin'd peece of Nature, this great world | Shall so weare out to
naught. 2577
NAUGHTIE = *1
Foole. Prythee Nunckle be contented, 'tis a naughtie 1891
NAUGHTY = 1
Reg. So white, and such a Traitor? | *Glou.* Naughty Ladie, 2102
NAY = 3*5
*nay, & thou canst not smile as the wind sits, thou'lt catch 630
Gon. Nay then--- | *Alb.* Well, well, th'euent. *Exeunt* 871
Cur. Nay I know not, you haue heard of the newes a-|broad, 934
Nay get thee in; Ile pray, and then Ile sleepe. 1808
Foole. Nay, he reseru'd a Blanket, else we had bin all | sham'd. 1846
Corn. My Villaine? | *Seru.* Nay then come on, and take the chance of
anger. 2152
*'twould not ha' bin zo long as 'tis, by a vortnight. Nay, 2692
Nay, send in time. | *Alb.* Run, run, O run. 3204
NAYLES = 1
Pins, Wodden-prickes, Nayles, Sprigs of Rosemarie: 1267
NEAT = *1
Kent. Strike you slaue: stand rogue, stand you neat | slaue, strike. 1114
NEATHER = 1
Alb. This shewes you are aboue | You Iustices, that these our neather
crimes 2323
NECESSITIE = 1*1
*Moone, and Starres, as if we were villaines on necessitie, 450

NECESSITIE *cont*.
 Which else were shame, that then necessitie | Will call discreet
 proceeding.   724
NECESSITIES = 2
 Necessities sharpe pinch. Returne with her? 1504
 The Art of our Necessities is strange, 1725
NECKE = *2
 *tide by the heads, Dogges and Beares by'th'necke, 1283
 *hill, least it breake thy necke with following. But the 1345
NEED = 7*1
 *need to care for her frowning, now thou art an O with-|out 706
 Nature's of such deepe trust, we shall much need: | You we first seize
 on. 1057
 Is it not well? What should you need of more? 1534
 Gon. Heare me my Lord; | What need you fiue and twenty? Ten? Or
 fiue? 1559
 Reg. What need one? 1563
 Lear. O reason not the need: our basest Beggers 1564
 Which scarcely keepes thee warme, but for true need: 1570
 You Heauens, giue me that patience, patience I need, 1571
NEEDE = 2*1
 *such neede to hide it selfe. Let's see: come, if it bee no-|thing, I shall
 not neede Spectacles. 369
 I shall no leading neede. 2263
NEEDED = *1
 Glou. No? what needed then that terrible dispatch of 367
NEEDFULL = 2
 Your needfull counsaile to our businesses, | Which craues the instant
 vse. 1070
 Which shall be needfull for your entertainement. 1499
NEEDS = 5*2
 *needs weare my Coxcombe. How now Nunckle? would 634
 The King his Master, needs must take it ill 1221
 Which I must needs call mine. Thou art a Byle, 1517
 Allow not Nature, more then Nature needs: 1566
 Why Nature needs not what thou gorgeous wear'st, 1569
 And must needs taste his folly. 1591
 Stew. I must needs after him, Madam, with my Letter. 2400
NEERE = 4*1
 I will send farre and neere, that all the kingdome 1020
 Brought neere to beast; my face Ile grime with filth, 1260
 Gent. Neere, and on speedy foot: the maine descry | Stands on the
 hourely thought. 2657
 *come not neere th'old man: keepe out che vor'ye, or Ile 2693
 That follow'd me so neere, (O our liues sweetnesse, 3147
NEERELY = 1
 Of what most neerely appertaines to vs both, 311
NEERES = 1
 Edg. But by your fauour: | How neere's the other Army? 2655
NEGLECT = 1*2
 *Gods, Gods! 'Tis strange, that from their cold'st neglect 279
 *I haue perceiued a most faint neglect of late, 597
 Infirmity doth still neglect all office, 1382
NEGLIGENCE = 1
 Gon. Put on what weary negligence you please, 519
NEIGHBOURD = 1
 Be as well neighbour'd, pittied, and releeu'd, 126

NEITHER = 4*4
    *most, for qualities are so weigh'd, that curiosity in nei-|ther, can make
    choise of eithers moity.   9
    Kent. Nor tript neither, you base Foot-ball plaier.   616
    *Foole. Nor I neither; but I can tell why a Snaile ha's | a house.   901
    *to raile on one, that is neither knowne of thee, nor | knowes thee?   1099
    *in, aske thy Daughters blessing, heere's a night pitties | neither
    Wisemen, nor Fooles.   1667
    *me on paine of perpetuall displeasure, neither to speake   1756
    Both? One? Or neither? Neither can be enioy'd   2905
NERE = 4*1
    To wage against thine enemies, nere feare to loose it, | Thy safety being
    motiue.   167
    Fooles had nere lesse grace in a yeere,   680
    *Fortune that arrant whore, nere turns the key toth' poore.   1325
    The safer sense will ne're accommodate | His Master thus.   2528
    Reg. Sicke, O sicke. | *Gon*. If not, Ile nere trust medicine.   3043
NERO = *1
    **Edg. Fraterretto* cals me, and tells me *Nero* is an Ang-|ler   2004
NETHER-STOCKS = *1
    *ouerlustie at legs, then he weares wodden nether-stocks.   1285
NETTLES = *1
    *With Hardokes, Hemlocke, Nettles, Cuckoo flowres,   2354
NEUER *see also* nere = 24*4
    Sure I shall neuer marry like my Sisters.   110
    Kent. My life I neuer held but as pawne   166
    Which we durst neuer yet; and with strain'd pride,   183
    Must be a faith that reason without miracle | Should neuer plant in me.   243
    *Glo. Has he neuer before sounded you in this busines?   404
    *Bast. Neuer my Lord. But I haue heard him oft main-|taine   405
    And from her derogate body, neuer spring   794
    Gon. Neuer afflict your selfe to know more of it: 806
    Cor. If he be taken, he shall neuer more   1052
    Corn. What was th'offence you gaue him? | *Ste*. I neuer gaue him any: 1190
    Returne you to my Sister. | *Lear*. Neuer *Regan*:   1439
    Lear. No *Regan*, thou shalt neuer haue my curse: 1454
    I neuer gaue you Kingdome, call'd you Children;   1672
    *For there was neuer yet faire woman, but shee made | mouthes in a
    glasse.   1686
    Such groanes of roaring Winde, and Raine, I neuer   1699
    *Corn. See't shalt thou neuer. Fellowes hold y Chaire,   2139
    But better seruice haue I neuer done you, | Then now to bid you hold.   2147
    Stew. Madam within, but neuer man so chang'd: 2270
    Reg. But haue you neuer found my Brothers way, | To the fore-fended
    place?   2858
    Reg. I neuer shall endure her, deere my Lord | Be not familiar with her.   2861
    Shall neuer see his pardon: for my state,   2915
    Neuer (O fault) reueal'd my selfe vnto him,   3155
    And thou no breath at all? Thou'lt come no more, | Neuer, neuer,
    neuer, neuer, neuer.   3279
    Shall neuer see so much, nor liue so long. | *Exeunt with a dead March*. |
    FINIS.   3301
NEUT = *1
    *Toad, the Tod-pole, the wall-Neut, and the water: that   1909
NEW = 5
    Hee'l shape his old course, in a Country new. *Exit*.   201
    Vnfriended, new adopted to our hate,   222

NEW *cont.*

Of other your new prankes. I do beseech you	747
Despise thy victor-Sword, and fire new Fortune,	3087
Their precious Stones new lost: became his guide,	3153

NEWES = 5*1

Vpon the gad? *Edmond*, how now? What newes?	361
Bast. I know no newes, my Lord.	364
Cur. Nay I know not, you haue heard of the newes a- | broad,	934
The Newes is not so tart. Ile read, and answer.	2334
Mes. Newes Madam, | The Brittish Powres are marching hitherward.	2373
Talke of Court newes, and wee'l talke with them too,	2954

NEWTRALL = 1

Which came from one that's of a newtrall heart, | And not from one oppos'd.	2116

NEXT = *1

Reg. That's most certaine, and with you: next moneth | (with vs.	313

NICELY = 2

That stretch their duties nicely.	1179
What safe, and nicely I might well delay,	3100

NIGHT = 21*10

The misteries of *Heccat* and the night:	117
I thinke our Father will hence to night.	312
And the King gone to night? Prescrib'd his powre,	359
When saw you my Father last? | *Edg.* The night gone by.	474
Gon. By day and night, he wrongs me, euery howre	510
Will be here with him this night.	932
Bast. The Duke be here to night? The better best,	943
You haue now the good aduantage of the night,	952
Hee's comming hither, now i'th' night, i'th' haste,	954
My worthy Arch and Patron comes to night,	996
Reg. Thus out of season, thredding darke ey'd night,	1062
*for though it be night, yet the Moone shines, Ile make a	1104
Reg. Till noone? till night my Lord, and all night too.	1214
Gent. As I learn'd, | The night before, there was no purpose in them | Of this remoue.	1276
They haue trauail'd all the night? meere fetches,	1363
Glo. Alacke the night comes on, and the high windes	1603
Cor. Shut vp your doores my Lord, 'tis a wil'd night,	1612
*in, aske thy Daughters blessing, heere's a night pitties | neither Wisemen, nor Fooles.	1667
Kent. Alas Sir are you here? Things that loue night,	1694
Foole. This is a braue night to coole a Curtizan:	1734
*receiued a Letter this night, 'tis dangerous to be spoken,	1761
No, I will weepe no more; in such a night,	1797
In such a night as this? O *Regan, Gonerill*,	1799
Foole. This cold night will turne vs all to Fooles, and | Madmen.	1858
*night to swimme in. Now a little fire in a wilde Field,	1892
And let this Tyrannous night take hold vpon you,	1929
In Hell-blacke-night indur'd, would haue buoy'd vp	2132
Should haue stood that night against my fire,	2785
Where I did lodge last night. Do not laugh at me,	2823
Kent. I am come | To bid my King and Master aye good night.	3189

NIGHTED = 1

His nighted life: Moreouer to descry | The strength o'th'Enemy.	2398

NIGHTS = 4

Loue not such nights as these: The wrathfull Skies	1695

NIGHTS *cont*.
The tirrany of the open night's too rough | For Nature to endure.
Storme still 1779
The greefe hath craz'd my wits. What a night's this? 1950
I'th'last nights storme, I such a fellow saw; 2216
NIGHT-MARE = 1
He met the Night-Mare, and her nine-fold; 1901
NIMBLE = *1
Le. You nimble Lightnings, dart your blinding flames 1448
NINE = *1
Glou. He hath bin out nine yeares, and away he shall | againe. The
King is comming. 35
NINE-FOLD = 1
He met the Night-Mare, and her nine-fold; 1901
NO *l*.*23 30 47 63 87 99 164 165 211 220 249 250 288 364 *367 421 *434
*478 *493 *526 *544 548 *558 *571 *604 *660 662 669 *705 864 *876
895 900 *909 938 969 *978 979 1007 1037 *1127 1142 1146 1160 *1165
*1186 1254 1277 1281 1291 1293 1295 1333 *1341 1357 1381 *1438 1454
1501 1514 1545 *1553 1578 1583 1602 1632 1640 1649 1673 1689 1739
1741 *1768 1774 1797 1802 1850 *1883 *1884 *1885 *1887 1920 1949
1965 *2010 *2041 2094 2196 2199 2263 2279 2339 2379 2390 2436 2451
2457 2498 2502 *2530 *2546 2558 *2581 *2589 *2590 *2595 2633 2638
*2697 2711 2833 2839 2860 2876 2931 2948 3093 3115 3128 3252 3257
*3277 3279 3297 = 100*43
NOBLE = 16*3
*be acknowledged. Doe you know this Noble Gentle- | man, *Edmond?* |
Edm. No, my Lord. 27
Cor. Heere's *France* and *Burgundy*, my Noble Lord. 204
Lear. Right Noble *Burgundy*, | When she was deare to vs, we did hold
her so, 213
Come Noble *Burgundie. Flourish. Exeunt*. 291
*thee nothing, do it carefully: and the Noble & true-har- | ted 445
A Credulous Father, and a Brother Noble, 499
And found; dispatch, the Noble Duke my Master, 995
Corn. How now my Noble friend, since I came hither 1025
Occasions Noble *Gloster* of some prize, 1063
Kent. Haile to thee Noble Master. 1279
To beare it tamely: touch me with Noble anger, 1576
Noble Philosopher, your company. | *Edg*. Tom's a cold. 1953
To Noble *Edmund*. I know you are of her bosome. | *Stew*. I, Madam? 2413
To Noble Fortunes: know thou this, that men 2973
Yet am I Noble as the Aduersary | I come to cope. 3075
That if my speech offend a Noble heart, 3081
That hast this Fortune on me? If thou'rt Noble, | I do forgiue thee. 3125
Edg. 'Tis Noble *Kent* your Friend. 3232
You Lords and Noble Friends, know our intent, 3268
NOBLENESSE = 1
A Royall Noblenesse: I must embrace thee, 3138
NOBLES = 1
When Nobles are their Taylors Tutors, 1738
NOISE *see also* noyse = *2
Lear. Make no noise, make no noise, draw the Cur- | taines: 2041
NONE = 9*4
Bast. So please your Lordship, none. 362
Edg. None at all, 480
That he suspects none: on whose foolish honestie 501
Ste. I am none of these my Lord, | I beseech your pardon. 612

NONE *cont.*
Kent. None of these Rogues, and Cowards | But *Aiax* is there Foole.   1201
Gen. Made you no more offence, | But what you speake of? | *Kent.*
None: 1333
*againe, I would haue none but knaues follow it, since a | Foole giues
it.   1348
Gent. None but the Foole, who labours to out-iest | His heart-strooke
iniuries.   1624
Glou. Vnmercifull Lady, as you are, I'me none.   2097
*ragges, a Pigmies straw do's pierce it. None do's offend,   2610
*none, I say none, Ile able 'em; take that of me my Friend,   2611
If none appeare to proue vpon thy person,   3038
NONNY = *1
*cold winde: Sayes suum, mun, nonny, Dolphin my Boy,   1879
NOONE = 2*1
As I haue life and Honour, there shall he sit till Noone.   1213
Reg. Till noone? till night my Lord, and all night too.   1214
Foole. And Ile go to bed at noone.   2043
NOR *l.*99 163 185 212 288 480 *569 616 710 721 *901 1044 *1099 *1165
1230 1522 1527 1668 1670 1701 1741 1743 *1875 2129 *2565 *2590 2752
2816 2822 3024 3257 3301 = 28*8
NOSE = *3
*Crab: thou canst, tell why ones nose stands i'th'middle | on's face? |
Lear. No.   893
Foole. Why to keepe ones eyes of either side 's nose,   896
*not a nose among twenty, but can smell him that's stink-|ing;   1343
NOSES = 1*1
*noses, are led by their eyes, but blinde men, and there's   1342
Were two full Moones: he had a thousand Noses,   2515
NOT *l.*8 11 83 130 162 193 226 229 247 254 257 261 274 283 301 310
*321 *368 371 *372 *373 *386 *394 400 403 *413 503 512 515 *539 *568
*572 *580 *581 584 585 *586 *587 601 615 *630 665 682 *699 712 715
721 *735 739 742 764 852 866 *878 *880 *882 *885 *904 910 *916 *918
*919 924 *934 937 940 953 958 994 1012 *1017 1018 *1033 1035 1043
1061 1081 1082 1085 *1132 1164 1175 *1188 1207 1216 1220 1230 *1231
1248 1256 1275 1297 *1298 *1322 1332 *1343 1360 1381 1383 1408 1414
1455 1457 1464 1478 1483 *1485 1486 1512 1513 1519 1520 1521 1526
1527 1534 *1539 1541 1555 1564 1566 1569 1575 1577 1581 1583 1593
1600 1631 1640 1644 1646 1671 1695 1742 1743 *1753 *1766 1795 1805
*1820 *1861 *1862 *1874 *1975 *1982 1983 2000 *2036 *2046 *2067
2084 2087 2107 2117 2123 2128 2182 2192 2210 2215 2253 2254 2269
2281 2302 2306 2309 2321 2334 2338 *2389 2392 2403 *2406 2407 2410
2463 2476 2482 2494 2495 *2548 *2550 *2551 2553 2557 *2581 2584
2585 *2614 2664 2687 *2692 *2693 2712 *2717 2758 *2781 2790 2806
2807 2812 2813 2816 2818 2822 2823 2828 2830 2832 2836 2856 2862
2863 2872 2916 2943 2947 2975 2976 3000 3007 3016 3023 3044 3048
3056 3109 3110 3116 3119 3157 3186 3187 3191 3240 3244 3247 3262
*3287 3297 3299 = 189*63
NOTE = 4
May haue due note of him, and of my land,   1021
Kent. Sir, I do know you, | And dare vpon the warrant of my note   1626
Therefore I do aduise you take this note: 2416
Take thou this note, go follow them to prison,   2970
NOTED = *1
Lear. No more of that, I haue noted it well, goe you   604
NOTHING = 20*13
Cor. Nothing my Lord. | *Lear.* Nothing?   93

NOTHING *cont.*

Cor. Nothing. | *Lear.* Nothing will come of nothing, speake againe.	95
And nothing more may fitly like your Grace,	218
Lear. Nothing, I haue sworne, I am firme.	269
Glou. What Paper were you reading? | *Bast.* Nothing my Lord.	365
*it into your Pocket? The quality of nothing, hath not	368
*such neede to hide it selfe. Let's see: come, if it bee no- | thing, I shall	
not neede Spectacles.	369
*thee nothing, do it carefully: and the Noble & true-har- | ted	445
*you what I haue seene, and heard: But faintly. Nothing	495
Kent. This is nothing Foole.	658
*you gaue me nothing for't, can you make no vse of no- | thing Nuncle?	660
Lear. Why no Boy, | Nothing can be made out of nothing.	662
*wit o'both sides, and left nothing i'th'middle; heere | comes one o'the	
parings.	700
*thou art nothing. Yes forsooth I will hold my tongue, so	708
your face bids me, though you say nothing.	709
And *Regan* with him, haue you nothing said	955
*would'st be a Baud in way of good seruice, and art no- | thing	1093
Stew. Away, I haue nothing to do with thee.	1107
Peruse this Letter. Nothing almost sees miracles	1242
That's something yet: *Edgar* I nothing am. *Exit.*	1272
Lear. No, I will be the patterne of all patience, | I will say nothing.	1689
Glo. Go too; say you nothing. There is diuision be- | tweene	1759
*Could'st thou saue nothing? Would'st thou giue 'em all?	1845
Lear. Death Traitor, nothing could haue subdu'd | (Nature	1851
Owes nothing to thy blasts.	2187
Edg. Y'are much deceiu'd: In nothing am I chang'd | But in my	
Garments.	2442
place will be fruitfully offer'd. There is nothing done. If hee	2718
Ere I taste bread, thou art in nothing lesse	3041

NOTICE = 2

Cur. And you Sir, I haue bin | With your Father, and giuen him notice	929
To bring but fiue and twentie, to no more | Will I giue place or notice.	1545

NOTION = 1

Either his Notion weakens, his Discernings	741

NOW = 49*23

*now in the diuision of the Kingdome, it ap- | peares	7
*so often blush'd to acknowledge him, that now I am | braz'd too't.	13
*May be preuented now. The Princes, *France* & *Burgundy*,	50
(Since now we will diuest vs both of Rule,	54
Then that conferr'd on *Gonerill*. Now our Ioy,	88
Lear. Now by *Apollo*,	172
Kent. Now by *Apollo*, King | Thou swear'st thy Gods in vaine.	173
But now her price is fallen: Sir, there she stands,	215
That she whom euen but now, was your obiect,	235
hath now cast her off, appeares too grossely.	317
Now Gods, stand vp for Bastards.	356
Vpon the gad? *Edmond*, how now? What newes?	361
Edg. How now Brother *Edmond*, what serious con- | templation are you	
in?	467
For which I raiz'd my likenesse. Now banisht *Kent*,	534
how now, what art thou? | *Kent.* A man Sir.	540
asleepe, how now? Where's that Mungrell?	579
Lear. Now my friendly knaue I thanke thee, there's | earnest of thy	
seruice.	622
Lear. How now my pretty knaue, how dost thou?	626

NOW *cont*.

*needs weare my Coxcombe. How now Nunckle? would	634
*Lear. How now Daughter? what makes that Frontlet	703
*need to care for her frowning, now thou art an O with- |out	706
*a figure, I am better then thou art now, I am a Foole,	707
To haue found a safe redresse, but now grow fearefull	717
Alb. Now Gods that we adore, | Whereof comes this?	804
How now Oswald?	857
*keepe me in temper, I would not be mad. How now are | the Horses ready?	919
*Fool. She that's a Maid now, & laughs at my departure,	923
You haue now the good aduantage of the night,	952
Hee's comming hither, now i'th' night, i'th' haste,	954
Draw, seeme to defend your selfe, | Now quit you well.	961
Glo. Now Edmund, where's the villaine?	971
*Corn. How now my Noble friend, since I came hither	1025
(Which I can call but now,) I haue heard strangenesse.	1026
Bast. How now, what's the matter? Part.	1118
Now, presently: bid them come forth and heare me,	1393
I am now from home, and out of that prouision	1498
(For now I spie a danger) I entreate you	1544
Finde out their enemies now. Tremble thou Wretch,	1704
Which euen but now, demanding after you,	1719
*King now beares, will be reuenged home; ther is part of	1763
*vexes. There could I haue him now, and there, and there | againe, and there. *Storme still*.	1842
*Lea. Now all the plagues that in the pendulous ayre	1848
*night to swimme in. Now a little fire in a wilde Field,	1892
Now out-law'd from my blood: he sought my life	1947
*Cornw. I now perceiue, it was not altogether your	1975
Kent. O pitty: Sir, where is the patience now	2016
*Kent. Now good my Lord, lye heere, and rest awhile.	2040
How now? Where's the King?	2073
But better seruice haue I neuer done you, | Then now to bid you hold.	2147
Reg. How now, you dogge?	2149
Where is thy luster now? | Glou. All darke and comfortlesse?	2159
Oldm. How now? who's there?	2206
Not met vs on the way. Now, where's your Master?	2269
Cor. Alacke, 'tis he: why he was met euen now	2351
*Edg. You do climbe vp it now. Look how we labor.	2432
You are now within a foote of th'extreme Verge:	2462
Edg. Now fare ye well, good Sir. | Glou. With all my heart.	2469
Now Fellow, fare thee well. | Edg. Gone Sir, farewell:	2480
Glou. I do remember now: henceforth Ile beare | Affliction, till it do cry out it selfe	2520
*things thou dost not. Now, now, now, now. Pull off my | Bootes: harder, harder, so.	2614
Glou. Now good sir, what are you?	2667
Glou. Now let thy friendly hand | Put strength enough too't.	2681
Pray you now forget, and forgiue, | I am old and foolish. *Exeunt*	2842
Reg. Now sweet Lord,	2853
By dilligent discouerie, but your hast | Is now vrg'd on you.	2899
Her husband being aliue. Now then, wee'l vse	2909
Bast. I was contracted to them both, all three | Now marry in an instant.	3179
I might haue sau'd her, now she's gone for euer:	3234
I would haue made him skip: I am old now,	3242

NOYSE = 1
Or whether gasted by the noyse I made, | Full sodainely he fled.　991
NUMBER = 2*1
*How chance the King comes with so small a number?　1336
Speake 'gainst so great a number? How in one house　1536
With such a number? What, must I come to you　1551
NUMD = 1
Strike in their num'd and mortified Armes.　1266
NUNCKLE = *9
*needs weare my Coxcombe. How now Nunckle? would　634
*Foole. Nunckle, giue me an egge, and Ile giue thee | two Crownes.　670
*Foole. I haue vsed it Nunckle, ere since thou mad'st　685
*Pry'thy Nunckle keepe a Schoolemaster that can teach　692
*and yet I would not be thee Nunckle, thou hast pared thy　699
*Foole. For you know Nunckle, the Hedge-Sparrow　726
*Foole. If thou wert my Foole Nunckle, Il'd haue thee　913
*Foole. Cry to it Nunckle, as the Cockney did to the　1398
*Foole. Prythee Nunckle be contented, 'tis a naughtie　1891
NUNCLE = 2*1
Foole. Marke it Nuncle; | Haue more then thou showest,　647
*you gaue me nothing for't, can you make no vse of no- | thing Nuncle?　660
*Foole. Come not in heere Nuncle, here's a spirit, helpe | me, helpe me.　1820
NUNKLE = 2*3
Foole. Nunkle Lear, Nunkle Lear,　835
*Foole. O Nunkle, Court holy-water in a dry house, is　1665
*better then this Rain-water out o'doore. Good Nunkle,　1666
*Foole. Prythee Nunkle tell me, whether a madman be | a Gentleman,
or a Yeoman.　2007
NURSE = 1
Our foster Nurse of Nature, is repose,　2362
NURSERY = 1
On her kind nursery. Hence and avoid my sight:　132
NURSING = 1
Edg. By nursing them my Lord. List a breefe tale,　3144
O l.175 200 *409 *465 779 783 *918 950 1015 1029 1032 1410 1426 1452
1479 1484 1488 1564 1586 1606 *1665 1679 1799 1801 1813 *1839 1952
*1982 2016 2096 2142 2168 2190 2193 2207 2325 2376 2473 2479 2532
*2538 2574 2577 2616 2745 2763 2765 2776 2810 3043 3118 3145 3147
3155 3170 3175 3186 3205 *3217 3230 3276 *3287 = 54*9, *5
*o'Bedlam. --- O these Eclipses do portend these diui- | sions. Fa, Sol,
La, Me.　465
*my peace. I had rather be any kind o'thing then a foole,　698
*wit o'both sides, and left nothing i'th'middle; heere | comes one o'the
parings.　700
*need to care for her frowning, now thou art an O with- | out　706
*better then this Rain-water out o'doore. Good Nunkle,　1666
OAKE-CLEAUING = 1
Vaunt-curriors of Oake-cleauing Thunder-bolts,　1660
OATH = 2
Dow'rd with our curse, and stranger'd with our oath, | Take her or,
leaue her.　223
My oath, and my profession. I protest,　3085
OATHES = *1
*her. Swore as many Oathes, as I spake words, & broke　1868
OBEDIENCE = 3*2
At Fortunes almes, you haue obedience scanted,　304
*his obedience. I dare pawne downe my life for him, that　419

OBEDIENCE *cont.*
*and Adulterers by an inforc'd obedience of Planatary	453
Whose vertue and obedience doth this instant	1055
Allow Obedience; if you your selues are old,	1481

OBEY = 4*1
Obey you, Loue you, and most Honour you.	105
Edgar. Take heed o'th'foule Fiend, obey thy Pa-|rents,	1860
T'obey in all your daughters hard commands:	1927
Gent. You are a Royall one, and we obey you.	2643
Edg. The waight of this sad time we must obey,	3298

OBEYD = *1
*obey'd in Office. Thou, Rascall Beadle, hold thy bloody	2603

OBIECT = 3
That she whom euen but now, was your obiect,	235
And with this horrible obiect, from low Farmes,	1268
Seest thou this obiect *Kent*? | *Kent.* Alacke, why thus?	3194

OBLIGATION = 1
Would faile her Obligation. If Sir perchance	1421

OBSCURED = 1
Of my obscured course. And shall finde time	1245

OBSERUANTS = 1
Then twenty silly-ducking obseruants,	1178

OBSERUATION = *1
Gon. You see how full of changes his age is, the ob-|seruation	314

OCCASION *see* 'casion
OCCASIONS = 1
Occasions Noble *Gloster* of some prize,	1063

OCCUPATION = 1
Kent. Sir, 'tis my occupation to be plaine,	1166

ODS = 1
That sets vs all at ods: Ile not endure it;	512

OEILLADES *see* eliads
OF *see also* o', o'the, o'their = 307*119
OFF *l.*317 *436 *727 829 1364 1458 *1888 2425 2467 2475 *2614 *2717
2737 2741 2755 2912 = 11*6
OFFENCE = 5*1
So many folds of fauour: sure her offence	239
*Kent banish'd; his offence, honesty. 'Tis strange. *Exit*	446
Mighty in their working do you that offence,	723
Corn. What was th'offence you gaue him? | *Ste.* I neuer gaue him any:	1190
Gen. Made you no more offence, | But what you speake of? | *Kent.* None:	1333
All's not offence that indiscretion findes, | And dotage termes so.	1486

OFFEND = 3*1
this last surrender of his will but offend vs.	330
Bast. I shall offend, either to detaine, or giue it:	376
*ragges, a Pigmies straw do's pierce it. None do's offend,	2610
That if my speech offend a Noble heart,	3081

OFFENDED = *2
Bast. Bethink your selfe wherein you may haue offen-|ded	481
Gon. Why not by'th'hand Sir? How haue I offended?	1485

OFFENDER = 1
Which can pursue th'offender; how dost my Lord?	1028

OFFENSIUE = 1
What most he should dislike, seemes pleasant to him; | What like, offensiue.	2277

OFFER = 2
   Kent. Good my Lord take his offer, | Go into th'house.   1934
   With thine, and all that offer to defend him,   2053
OFFERD = 1*1
   Bur. Most Royall Maiesty, | I craue no more then hath your Highnesse
   offer'd,   210
   place will be fruitfully offer'd. There is nothing done. If hee   2718
OFFICE = 3*1
   Edmund, I heare that you haue shewne your Father | A Child-like
   Office.   1045
   Infirmity doth still neglect all office,   1382
   *obey'd in Office. Thou, Rascall Beadle, hold thy bloody   2603
   Edg. To who my Lord? Who ha's the Office?   3206
OFFICERS = 1
   Bast. Some Officers take them away: good guard,   2940
OFFICES = 1
   The Offices of Nature, bond of Childhood,   1462
OFT = 5*1
   Bast. Neuer my Lord. But I haue heard him oft main-|taine   405
   Striuing to better, oft we marre what's well.   870
   Like Rats oft bite the holy cords a twaine,   1147
   That you so oft haue boasted to retaine?   2017
   I stumbled when I saw. Full oft 'tis seene,   2200
   Reg. Iesters do oft proue Prophets.   3013
OFTEN = 2*2
   *so often blush'd to acknowledge him, that now I am | braz'd too't.   13
   Which often leaues the history vnspoke   259
   *when we are sicke in fortune, often the surfets of our own   448
   I tooke it for a man: often 'twould say   2523
OH *see also* O *l*.*606 *1328 *1397 1412 1415 *2156 2157 2202 2295 2301
   2311 *2313 *2589 2631 2703 2724 2878 = 11*6
OILE = 1
   Being oile to fire, snow to the colder moodes,   1150
OILIE *see* oylie
OLD = 36*7
   When *Lear* is mad, what wouldest thou do old man?   155
   Hee'l shape his old course, in a Country new. *Exit*.   201
   *Pat: he comes like the Catastrophe of the old Comedie: 463
   Lear. How old art thou? | *Kent*. Not so young Sir to loue a woman for
   singing,   567
   *nor so old to dote on her for any thing. I haue yeares on | my backe
   forty eight.   569
   As you are Old, and Reuerend, should be Wise.   749
   Pierce euerie sense about thee. Old fond eyes,   820
   beaten for being old before thy time.   914
   Foole. Thou shouldst not haue bin old, till thou hadst | bin wise.   916
   Glo. O Madam, my old heart is crack'd, it's crack'd.   1029
   'Tis they haue put him on the old mans death,   1038
   From hence attend dispatch, our good old Friend,   1068
   Corn. What art thou mad old Fellow?   1158
   Kent. Sir, I am too old to learne: 1206
   Reg. O Sir, you are old,   1426
   Deere daughter, I confesse that I am old;   1435
   If you do loue old men; if your sweet sway   1480
   Allow Obedience; if you your selues are old,   1481
   Must be content to thinke you old, and so,   1530
   You see me heere (you Gods) a poore old man,   1572

OLD *cont.*

Reg. This house is little, the old man and's people, | Cannot be well
bestow'd.   1588

Corn. Followed the old man forth, he is return'd.   1597

Against the old kinde King; or something deeper,   1637

A poore, infirme, weake, and dispis'd old man: 1675

So old, and white as this. O, ho! 'tis foule.   1679

*my old Master must be relieued. There is strange things | toward

Edmund, pray you be carefull. *Exit.*   1769

The yonger rises, when the old doth fall. *Exit.*   1775

Your old kind Father, whose franke heart gaue all,   1800

*were like an old Letchers heart, a small spark, all the rest   1893

Swithold footed thrice the old,   1900

*Cow-dung for Sallets; swallowes the old Rat, and the   1911

Plucke out his poore old eyes: nor thy fierce Sister,   2129

Yet poore old heart, he holpe the Heauens to raine.   2134

Glou. He that will thinke to liue, till he be old,   2141

To raise my fortunes. Thou old, vnhappy Traitor,   2678

*come not neere th'old man: keepe out che vor'ye, or Ile   2693

I am a very foolish fond old man,   2814

Pray you now forget, and forgiue, | I am old and foolish. *Exeunt*   2842

Edgar. Away old man, giue me thy hand, away: 2928

And pray, and sing, and tell old tales, and laugh   2952

Bast. Sir, I thought it fit, | To send the old and miserable King to some
retention,   2989

I would haue made him skip: I am old now,   3242

During the life of this old Maiesty   3271

OLD = 2

OLDEST = 1

The oldest hath borne most, we that are yong,   3300

OLDM = 7

OLDMAN see also Old., Oldm. = 1

Enter Glouster, and an Oldman.   2188

OLDNESSE = *1

*vs, till our oldnesse cannot rellish them. I begin to finde an idle   384

ON *see also* a, on't = 75*17

ONCE = 5*1

Smile once more, turne thy wheele.   1250

Cracke Natures moulds, all germaines spill at once | That makes
ingratefull Man.   1663

Kent. Importune him once more to go my Lord,   1940

*Diuinity. When the raine came to wet me once, and the   2547

'Tis wonder that thy life and wits, at once   2789

Rather then die at once) taught me to shift   3149

ONE *see also* 1. = 27*9

He flashes into one grosse crime, or other,   511

Whose mind and mine I know in that are one,   522

Foole. Do'st thou know the difference my Boy, be-|tweene a bitter
Foole, and a sweet one.   667

*gau'st thy golden one away; if I speake like my selfe in   678

*wit o'both sides, and left nothing i'th'middle; heere | comes one o'the
parings.   700

A Fox, when one has caught her,   837

And I haue one thing of a queazie question   946

*finicall Rogue, one Trunke-inheriting slaue, one that   1092

*one whom I will beate into clamours whining, if thou   1096

*to raile on one, that is neither knowne of thee, nor ⊦ knowes thee?   1099

ONE *cont.*
*great one that goes vpward, let him draw thee after:	1346
Wee'l no more meete, no more see one another.	1514
Speake 'gainst so great a number? How in one house	1536
Reg. What need one?	1563
Reg. For his particular, Ile receiue him gladly, | But not one follower.	1592
Gen. One minded like the weather, most vnquietly.	1617
Poore Foole, and Knaue, I haue one part in my heart | That's sorry yet for thee.	1727
*them in the sweet face of Heauen. One, that slept in the	1869
Lear. Let me aske you one word in priuate.	1939
*make these hard-hearts. You sir, I entertaine for one of	2035
Which came from one that's of a newtrall heart, | And not from one oppos'd.	2116
Reg. One side will mocke another: Th'other too.	2143
Ser. Oh I am slaine: my Lord, you haue one eye left	2156
Gon. One way I like this well.	2330
Hangs one that gathers Sampire: dreadfull Trade:	2450
Gent. You are a Royall one, and we obey you.	2643
Euery one heares that, which can distinguish sound.	2654
Edg. If ere your Grace had speech with man so poore, | Heare me one word.	2881
Both? One? Or neither? Neither can be enioy'd	2905
One step I haue aduanc'd thee, if thou do'st	2971
The one the other poison'd for my sake, | And after slew herselfe.	3197
I know when one is dead, and when one liues,	3220
Kent. If Fortune brag of two, she lou'd and hated, | One of them we behold.	3245

ONELY = 4
Only she comes too short, that I professe	77
Make with you by due turne, onely we shall retaine	143
If onely to go warme were gorgeous,	1568
May be my Friends: hee's dead; I am onely sorry	2710

ONES = 2*5
Lear. Why my Boy? | *Foole.* Why? for taking ones part that's out of fauour,	628
*Crab: thou canst, tell why ones nose stands i'th'middle | on's face? | *Lear.* No.	893
Foole. Why to keepe ones eyes of either side 's nose,	896
*I meane the whisper'd ones, for they are yet but | ear-kissing arguments.	935
And dizie 'tis, to cast ones eyes so low,	2447
*my Beard, ere the blacke ones were there. To say I, and	2545
In a wall'd prison, packs and sects of great ones, | That ebbe and flow by th'Moone.	2958

ONLY = 2*1
Gon. Not only Sir this, your all-lycenc'd Foole,	712
Is practise only. Giue me my Seruant forth;	1391
*my hundred; only, I do not like the fashion of your gar- |ments.	2036

ONS = 2*2
*ha's banish'd two on's Daughters, and did the third a	632
*Crab: thou canst, tell why ones nose stands i'th'middle | on's face? | *Lear.* No.	893
*Wooll; the Cat, no perfume. Ha? Here's three on's are	1885
on's body, cold: Looke, heere comes a walking fire.	1894

ONT = 3
Edg. I am sure on't, not a word.	958

ONT *cont*.
    Thou did'st not know on't.   1478
    Come on't what will. *Exit*   2239
OPE = 1
    Edg. Before you fight the Battaile, ope this Letter: 2884
OPEN = 2*1
    Then my out-wall; open this Purse, and take   1642
    The tirrany of the open night's too rough | For Nature to endure.
    Storme still   1779
    Glou. Heere is better then the open ayre, take it thank- | fully: 1998
OPERATION = 1
    By all the operation of the Orbes,   118
OPERATIUE = 1
    Are many Simples operatiue, whose power | Will close the eye of
    Anguish.   2364
OPILENT = 1
    A third, more opilent then your Sisters? speake.   92
OPINION = 1*1
    Glou. O Villain, villain: his very opinion in the Let- | ter.   409
    Some blood drawne on me, would beget opinion   966
OPPORTUNITIES = *1
    opportunities to cut him off: if your will want not, time and   2717
OPPOSD = 3
    Which came from one that's of a newtrall heart, | And not from one
    oppos'd.   2116
    Oppos'd against the act: bending his Sword   2318
    To be oppos'd against the iarring windes?   2783
OPPOSE = 1
    And in conclusion, to oppose the bolt   1460
OPPOSELESSE = 1
    To quarrell with your great opposelesse willes,   2477
OPPOSITE = 2
    Seeing how lothly opposite I stood   985
    An vnknowne opposite: thou art not vanquish'd, | But cozend, and
    beguild.   3110
OPPOSITES = 1
    Who were the opposites of this dayes strife: 2985
OPPRESSED = 1
    For thee oppressed King I am cast downe,   2945
OPPRESSION = *1
    and fond bondage, in the oppression of aged tyranny, who swayes   385
OPPREST = 1
    When Nature being opprest, commands the mind   1384
OR *l*.62 64 124 179 209 217 224 241 249 250 339 376 381 511 754 991 1006
    *1110 *1131 1301 1394 1516 1518 1535 1540 1546 1560 1586 1621 1622
    1636 1637 1757 1983 *1987 2008 2023 2026 2027 2075 2229 2236 2485
    2498 2501 2689 *2693 *2694 2848 2905 2977 2996 *3060 3113 3140 3183
    3222 3225 = 55*6
ORBES = 1
    By all the operation of the Orbes,   118
ORDER = *1
    Glou. But I haue a Sonne, Sir, by order of Law, some   22
ORDINANCE = 1
    That slaues your ordinance, that will not see   2253
ORDINARY = *1
    *bluntly: that which ordinary men are fit for, I am qual- | lified in, and
    the best of me, is Dilligence.*   565

ORE = 4*2
*both parts, thou boar'st thine Asse on thy backe o're the — 676
Thee o're to harshnesse: Her eyes are fierce, but thine — 1456
Lear. Let the great Goddes | That keepe this dreadfull pudder o're our heads, — 1702
*through Sword, and Whirle-Poole, o're Bog, and Quag- | mire, — 1834
Hang fated o're mens faults, light on thy Daughters. — 1849
Cor. O looke vpon me Sir, | And hold your hand in benediction o're me, — 2810
ORE-HEARD = 1
I haue ore-heard a plot of death vpon him: — 2048
ORE-LOOKE = *1
*Alb. Why farethee well, I will o're-looke thy paper. — 2895
ORE-LOOKING = 1
*much as I haue perus'd, I finde it not fit for your ore-loo- | king. — 373
ORE-PAID = 1
Kent. To be acknowledg'd Madam is ore-pai'd, — 2750
ORE-READ = *1
*from my Brother, that I haue not all ore-read; and for so — 372
ORE-TAKE = 1
Thou wilt ore-take vs hence a mile or twaine — 2229
ORE-WATCHD = 1
Losses their remedies. All weary and o're-watch'd, — 1247
ORE-WHELME = 1
With the hell-hated Lye, ore-whelme thy heart, — 3103
ORGANS = 1
Drie vp in her the Organs of increase, — 793
OSWALD = 3
Gon. Pray you content. What Oswald, hoa? — 833
And hold our liues in mercy. Oswald, I say. — 848
How now Oswald? — 857
OTH = 10*4
Gon. This admiration Sir, is much o'th'fauour — 746
*sop oth' Moonshine of you, you whoreson Cullyenly | Barber-monger, draw. — 1105
*not haue made him so ill, though they had bin but two | yeares oth'trade. — 1132
*o'th' coxcombs with a sticke, and cryed downe wantons, — 1400
Thy halfe o'th'Kingdome hast thou not forgot, | Wherein I thee endow'd. — 1464
To wage against the enmity oth'ayre, — 1502
*My Regan counsels well: come out oth'storme. Exeunt. — 1613
Strike flat the thicke Rotundity o'th'world, — 1662
*Edgar. Take heed o'th'foule Fiend, obey thy Pa- | rents, — 1860
His nighted life: Moreouer to descry | The strength o'th'Enemy. — 2398
Vpon the crowne o'th'Cliffe. What thing was that | Which parted from you? — 2511
Lear. You do me wrong to take me out o'th'graue, — 2794
Alb. Aske him his purposes, why he appeares | Vpon this Call o'th'Trumpet. — 3068
Mine eyes are not o'th'best, Ile tell you straight. — 3244
OTHE = 1
*wit o'both sides, and left nothing i'th'middle; heere | comes one o'the parings. — 700
OTHEIR = *1
*out. Go too, they are not men o'their words; they told — 2550

OTHER = 20*1
My selfe an enemy to all other ioyes,	78
to no other pretence of danger. | *Glou*. Thinke you so?	421
other day, what should follow these Eclipses.	470
He flashes into one grosse crime, or other,	511
Kent. If but as will I other accents borrow,	531
But other of your insolent retinue	713
Of other your new prankes. I do beseech you	747
Fool. Shalt see thy other Daughter will vse thee kind-|ly,	888
And meeting heere the other Messenger,	1314
Some other time for that. Beloued *Regan*,	1411
That way, Ile this: He that first lights on him, | Holla the other. *Exeunt*.	1652
Who, with some other of the Lords, dependants,	2077
Reg. One side will mocke another: Th'other too.	2143
Slaine by his Seruant, going to put out | The other eye of Glouster.	2314
Lost he his other eye? | *Mes*. Both, both, my Lord.	2326
Edg. Why then your other Senses grow imperfect | By your eyes anguish.	2437
Edg. But by your fauour: | How neere's the other Army?	2655
He had no other Deathsman. Let vs see:	2711
Each iealous of the other, as the stung	2903
Will not beare question: either say thou'lt do't, | Or thriue by other meanes.	2976
The one the other poison'd for my sake, | And after slew herselfe.	3197

OTHERS = 3
When others are more wicked, not being the worst	1555
Ang'ring it selfe, and others. Blesse thee Master.	2225
With others, whom the rigour of our State | Forc'd to cry out.	2867

OUER *see* ore = 1*1
*Proud of heart, to ride on a Bay trotting Horse, ouer foure	1837
Cordelia, and Souldiers, ouer the Stage, and Exeunt.	2919

OUERLUSTIE = *1
*ouerlustie at legs, then he weares wodden nether-stocks.	1285

OUERTAKE = 2
The winged Vengeance ouertake such Children.	2138
Alb. Ile ouertake you, speake.	2883

OUERTURE = 1
That made the ouerture of thy Treasons to vs:	2166

OUGHT = 5
If ought within that little seeming substance,	216
Edg. Had'st thou beene ought | But Gozemore, Feathers, Ayre,	2490
Edg. Do you heare ought (Sir) of a Battell toward. | *Gent*. Most sure, and vulgar:	2652
Or whether since he is aduis'd by ought	2848
Speake what we feele, not what we ought to say:	3299

OUNCE = *1
*consumption: Fye, fie, fie; pah, pah: Giue me an Ounce	2571

OUR *l*.*41 43 44 *46 47 49 51 52 57 59 72 73 86 88 89 *140 142 182 184
185 186 190 191 207 217 222 223 282 290 293 296 301 312 *316 *328
351 *383 *384 *387 *442 *444 *448 *449 730 752 848 998 1065 1067
1068 1070 1078 *1124 1219 1383 1431 1506 1564 1634 *1658 1703 1725
*1923 1989 *2066 *2069 2085 2086 2201 2202 *2268 2282 2324 2356
2358 2362 2375 2379 2380 2401 2713 *2716 2851 2865 2867 2874 2914
2987 2993 3002 3003 3131 3147 3159 3268 3272 3293 = 88*20

OURS = 2
Is Queene of vs, of ours, and our faire *France*:	282
So much commend it selfe, you shall be ours,	1056

OURSELFE *see* selfe
OURSELUES *see* selues
OUT *l.**35 169 *428 *444 *629 *642 663 *728 785 821 *877 897 *972
  *1062 1159 *1185 1217 1232 1233 1238 1386 1474 1498 *1613 *1666
  1704 1798 *1876 1930 *1988 *1999 *2061 2064 2129 2158 2164 2170
  2174 *2247 2276 2314 2394 2479 2521 *2550 2578 2679 *2691 *2693
  2696 2702 2794 2868 2908 2955 2957 3058 3123 3184 3289 = 40*21
OUTRAGE = 1
  To do vpon respect such violent outrage: 1299
OUTWARD = 1
  Take all my outward worth. 2360
OUT-FACE = 1
  And with presented nakednesse out-face 1262
OUT-FROWNE = 1
  My selfe could else out-frowne false Fortunes frowne. 2946
OUT-IEST = 1
  Gent. None but the Foole, who labours to out-iest | His heart-strooke
  iniuries. 1624
OUT-LAWD = 1
  Now out-law'd from my blood: he sought my life 1947
OUT-PARAMOURD = *1
  *deerely, Dice deerely; and in Woman, out-Paramour'd 1871
OUT-SIDE = 1
  But since thy out-side lookes so faire and Warlike, 3098
OUT-WALL = 1
  Then my out-wall; open this Purse, and take 1642
OWE = 1
  You owe me no subscription. Then let fall 1673
OWES = 2
  Lear. Will you with those infirmities she owes, 221
  Owes nothing to thy blasts. 2187
OWEST = 1
  Lend lesse then thou owest, 650
OWLE = 1
  To be a Comrade with the Wolfe, and Owle, 1503
OWN = *1
  *when we are sicke in fortune, often the surfets of our own 448
OWNE = 14*9
  *gap in your owne Honor, and shake in peeces, the heart of 418
  *after your owne wisedome. I would vnstate my | selfe, to be in a due
  resolution. 429
  Lear. Thou but remembrest me of mine owne Con-|ception, 596
  *which I haue rather blamed as mine owne iealous curio-|sitie, 598
  *the rod, and put'st downe thine owne breeches, then they 687
  And thereto adde such reasons of your owne, 862
  Be fear'd of doing harme, make your owne purpose, 1053
  How vnremoueable and fixt he is | In his owne course. 1368
  Corn. I set him there, Sir: but his owne Disorders 1491
  Gon. 'Tis his owne blame hath put himselfe from rest, 1590
  *they tooke from me the vse of mine owne house, charg'd 1755
  Kent. I had rather breake mine owne, | Good my Lord enter. 1784
  Lear. Prythee go in thy selfe, seeke thine owne ease, 1804
  *incht Bridges, to course his owne shadow for a Traitor. 1838
  (If you dare venture in your owne behalfe) 2288
  *hand: why dost thou lash that Whore? Strip thy owne 2604
  I'th'sway of your owne will: is he array'd? 2770

OWNE *cont.*
Vpon a wheele of fire, that mine owne teares | Do scal'd, like molten
Lead.   2796
Lear. Am I in France? | *Kent.* In your owne kingdome Sir.   2834
In his owne grace he doth exalt himselfe, | More then in your addition.   3008
Thou worse then any name, reade thine owne euill: 3114
Despight of mine owne Nature. Quickly send,   3201
To lay the blame vpon her owne dispaire, | That she for-did her selfe.   3213
OWST = *1
*man no more then this? Consider him well. Thou ow'st   1883
OYLIE = 1
If for I want that glib and oylie Art,   246
OYSTER = 1
Foole. Can'st tell how an Oyster makes his shell? | *Lear.* No.   899
PACKE = 1
Will packe, when it begins to raine,   1352
PACKINGS = 1
Either in snuffes, and packings of the Dukes,   1635
PACKS = 1
In a wall'd prison, packs and sects of great ones, | That ebbe and flow
by th'Moone.   2958
PAH = *2
*consumption: Fye, fie, fie; pah, pah: Giue me an Ounce   2571
PAID = 1
Kent. To be acknowledg'd Madam is ore-pai'd,   2750
PAIN = *1
*That when we haue found the King, in which your pain   1651
PAINE = 1*1
*me on paine of perpetuall displeasure, neither to speake   1756
That we the paine of death would hourely dye,   3148
PAINES = 1
Turne all her Mothers paines, and benefits   800
PAINTER = *1
Kent. A Taylor Sir, a Stone-cutter, or a Painter, could   1131
PAINTING = 1
Stew'd in his haste, halfe breathlesse, painting forth   1307
PALLACE = 1
Then a grac'd Pallace. The shame it selfe doth speake   755
PALLACES = *1
*in Pallaces, Treason; and the Bond crack'd, 'twixt   438
PANDAR = *1
*Pandar, and the Sonne and Heire of a Mungrill Bitch,   1095
PANT = 1
Bast. I pant for life: some good I meane to do   3200
PAPER = 4*2
Glou. What Paper were you reading? | *Bast.* Nothing my Lord.   365
Bast. If the matter of this Paper be certain, you haue | mighty
businesse in hand.   1985
With this vngracious paper strike the sight   2729
Alb. Why farethee well, I will o're-looke thy paper.   2895
Or with this paper shall I stop it: hold Sir,   3113
Alb. Most monstrous! O, know'st thou this paper?   3118
PAPERS = 1
Their Papers is more lawfull. | *Reads the Letter.*   2714
PARAMOURD = *1
*deerely, Dice deerely; and in Woman, out-Paramour'd   1871

PARDON = 7*2
  Bur. Pardon me Royall Sir, | Election makes not vp in such conditions.   225
  Bast. I beseech you Sir, pardon mee; it is a Letter   371
  Knigh. I beseech you pardon me my Lord, if I bee   593
  Ste. I am none of these my Lord, | I beseech your pardon.   612
  Though I condemne not, yet vnder pardon   866
  Bast. I heare my Father comming, pardon me: 959
  I pardon that mans life. What was thy cause?   2556
  I prythee put them off. | *Kent.* Pardon deere Madam,   2755
  Shall neuer see his pardon: for my state,   2915
PARED = *1
  *and yet I would not be thee Nunckle, thou hast pared thy   699
PARENTS = *1
  Edgar. Take heed o'th'foule Fiend, obey thy Pa-|rents,   1860
PARICIDES = 1
  'Gainst Paricides did all the thunder bend,   ·982
PARINGS = 1
  *wit o'both sides, and left nothing i'th'middle; heere | comes one o'the
  parings.   700
PARRELL = 1
  Oldm. Ile bring him the best Parrell that I haue   2238
PART = 7*5
  This Coronet part betweene you.   147
  The Contents, as in part I vnderstand them, | Are too blame.   377
  *worse after dinner, I will not part from thee yet. Dinner   572
  Lear. Why my Boy? | *Foole.* Why? for taking ones part that's out of
  fauour,   628
  *the King, and take Vanitie the puppets part, a-|gainst   1109
  Bast. How now, what's the matter? Part.   1118
  *for my part I will not be, though I should win your | displeasure to
  entreat me too't.   1188
  Make it your cause: Send downe, and take my part.   1482
  Poore Foole, and Knaue, I haue one part in my heart | That's sorry yet
  for thee.   1727
  *King now beares, will be reuenged home; ther is part of   1763
  Edg. My teares begin to take his part so much, | They marre my
  counterfetting.   2018
  My snuffe, and loathed part of Nature should   2478
PARTED = 1*2
  Glo. Kent banish'd thus? and France in choller parted?   358
  Bast. Parted you in good termes? Found you no dis-|pleasure in him,
  by word, nor countenance?   478
  Vpon the crowne o'th'Cliffe. What thing was that | Which parted from
  you?   2511
PARTIALL = 1
  Alb. I cannot be so partiall *Gonerill*, | To the great loue I beare you.   831
PARTICULAR = 3
  Informe her full of my particular feare,   861
  Reg. For his particular, Ile receiue him gladly, | But not one follower.   1592
  For these domesticke and particular broiles, | Are not the question
  heere.   2871
PARTICULARS = 1
  That all particulars of dutie know,   777
PARTIE = 1*1
  Vpon his partie 'gainst the Duke of *Albany*? | Aduise your selfe.   956
  *which approues him an intelligent partie to the aduanta-|ges   1981

PARTS = 2*1
*both parts, thou boar'st thine Asse on thy backe o're the   676
My Traine are men of choice, and rarest parts,   776
He that parts vs, shall bring a Brand from Heauen,   2964
PARTY = 2
Stew. Would I could meet Madam, I should shew | What party I do
follow.   2426
Vpon the English party. Oh vntimely death, death.   2703
PASSE = 4*3
Lear. Ha's his Daughters brought him to this passe?   1844
Though well we may not passe vpon his life   2084
Shall passe betweene vs: ere long you are like to heare   2287
Thus might he passe indeed: yet he reuiues.   2487
Lear. Passe. | *Glou*. I know that voice.   2541
*volke passe: and 'chud ha' bin zwaggerd out of my life,   2691
Kent. Vex not his ghost, O let him passe, he hates him,   3287
PASSIO = 1
Historica passio, downe thou climing sorrow,   1329
PASSION = 3
Which are t'intrince, t'vnloose: smooth euery passion   1148
For those that mingle reason with your passion,   1529
Twixt two extremes of passion, ioy and greefe, | Burst smilingly. 3161
PAST = 4
By this had thought bin past. Aliue, or dead?   2485
Past speaking of in a King. Thou hast a Daughter   2647
'Tis past, and so am I: But what art thou   3124
Vntill some halfe houre past when I was arm'd,   3156
PASTE = *1
*Eeles, when she put 'em i'th' Paste aliue, she knapt 'em   1399
PASTIME = 1
Lear. Ha? Mak'st thou this shame thy pastime? | *Kent*. No my Lord. 1280
PAT = *1
*Pat: he comes like the Catastrophe of the old Comedie: 463
PATERNALL = 1
Heere I disclaime all my Paternall care, | Propinquity and property of
blood,   120
PATH = *1
Edg. Both style, and gate; Horseway, and foot-path: 2246
PATIENCE = 6
Reg. I pray you Sir, take patience, I haue hope   1416
You Heauens, giue me that patience, patience I need,   1571
Lear. No, I will be the patterne of all patience, | I will say nothing. 1689
Kent. O pitty: Sir, where is the patience now   2016
Alb. Sir, by your patience,   2998
PATIENT = 4
Alb. Pray Sir be patient.   774
I can be patient, I can stay with *Regan*, | I and my hundred Knights. 1524
Edgar. Beare free and patient thoughts.   2525
Thou must be patient; we came crying hither: 2620
PATIENTLY = 1
Shake patiently my great affliction off: 2475
PATRIMONY = 1
Take thou my Souldiers, prisoners, patrimony,   3018
PATRON = 2
As my great Patron thought on in my praiers.   151
My worthy Arch and Patron comes to night,   996

PATTERNE = 1
Lear. No, I will be the patterne of all patience, | I will say nothing. 1689
PAWNE = 1*1
   Kent. My life I neuer held but as pawne 166
   *his obedience. I dare pawne downe my life for him, that 419
PEACE = 4*7
   Kent. Good my Liege. | *Lear*. Peace *Kent*, 128
   So be my graue my peace, as here I giue 133
   Cor. Peace be with *Burgundie*, 272
   *my peace. I had rather be any kind o'thing then a foole, 698
   **Cor*. Keepe peace vpon your liues, he dies that strikes | againe, what is
   the matter? 1122
   Cor. Peace sirrah, | You beastly knaue, know you no reuerence? 1141
   *Beware my Follower. Peace Smulkin, peace thou Fiend. 1919
   *Mouse: peace, peace, this peece of toasted Cheese will 2536
   *peace at my bidding, there I found 'em, there I smelt 'em 2549
PEASANT *see* pezant
PEBBLE = 1
   That on th'vnnumbred idle Pebble chafes 2456
PEECE = 2*2
   **Foole*. He that has a house to put's head in, has a good | Head-peece: 1680
   *I will peece out the comfort with what addition I | can: I will not be
   long from you. *Exit* 1999
   *Mouse: peace, peace, this peece of toasted Cheese will 2536
   Glou. O ruin'd peece of Nature, this great world | Shall so weare out to
   naught. 2577
PEECES = 1*1
   *gap in your owne Honor, and shake in peeces, the heart of 418
   That art Incestuous. Caytiffe, to peeces shake 1708
PEEPE = 1
   That such a King should play bo-peepe, | And goe the Foole among. 690
PELICANE = 1
   Iudicious punishment, 'twas this flesh begot | Those Pelicane Daughters. 1855
PELL-MELL = 1
   Too't Luxury pell-mell, for I lacke Souldiers. 2562
PELTING = 2
   Poore pelting Villages, Sheeps-Coates, and Milles, 1269
   That bide the pelting of this pittilesse storme, 1810
PEN = *1
   *Plackets, thy pen from Lenders Bookes, and defye the 1877
PENDULOUS = *1
   Lea. Now all the plagues that in the pendulous ayre 1848
PENNING = *1
   *loue. Reade thou this challenge, marke but the penning | of it. 2582
PENSION = 1
   To knee his Throne, and Squire-like pension beg, 1507
PENT-VP = 1
   Ha's practis'd on mans life. Close pent-vp guilts, 1710
PENURY = 1
   That euer penury in contempt of man, 1259
PEOPLE = 3*1
   **Gon*. You strike my people, and your disorder'd rable, | make Seruants
   of their Betters. 766
   And thy deere Iudgement out. Go, go, my people. 785
   Should many people, vnder two commands 1537
   Reg. This house is little, the old man and's people, | Cannot be well
   bestow'd. 1588

PERCEIUD = 1
  Whose welcome I perceiu'd had poison'd mine,   1315
PERCEIUE = 1*1
  Cornw. I now perceiue, it was not altogether your   1975
  No tearing Lady, I perceiue you know it.   3115
PERCEIUED = *2
  *I haue perceiued a most faint neglect of late,   597
  *him perceiued; If he aske for me, I am ill, and gone to   1767
PERCHANCE = 3*1
  Cor. No more perchance do's mine, nor his, nor hers.   1165
  Would faile her Obligation. If Sir perchance   1421
  Whereof (perchance) these are but furnishings.   1638
  And shall perchance do good, but speake you on,   3164
PERDIE = 1
  The Foole no knaue perdie.   1357
PERFECT = 1*1
  *it to be fit, that Sonnes at perfect age, and Fathers   406
  And to deale plainely, | I feare I am not in my perfect mind.   2817
PERFORCE = 2*1
  That these hot teares, which breake from me perforce   816
  Lear. To tak't againe perforce; Monster Ingratitude!   912
  This weaues it selfe perforce into my businesse,   944
PERFUME = *1
  *Wooll; the Cat, no perfume. Ha? Here's three on's are   1885
PERILL = 1
  Was't thou not charg'd at perill.   2123
PERIURD = 1
  Thou Periur'd, and thou Simular of Vertue   1707
PERMIT = 1
  Stand in the plague of custome, and permit   337
PERNICIOUS = 1
  That will with two pernicious Daughters ioyne   1677
PERPENDICULARLY = 1
  Which thou hast perpendicularly fell,   2496
PERPETUALL = 1*1
  Be this perpetuall. What sayes our second Daughter?   72
  *me on paine of perpetuall displeasure, neither to speake   1756
PERSECUTIONS = 1
  The Windes, and persecutions of the skie;   1263
PERSEUER = *1
  *his suspition more fully. I will perseuer in my course of   1991
PERSIAN = *1
  *You will say they are Persian; but let them bee | chang'd.   2037
PERSON = 5
  of your person, it would scarsely alay.   485
  Against the Grace, and Person of my Master, | Stocking his Messenger.   1210
  Reg. Himselfe in person there? | *Stew*. Madam with much ado: 2386
  Bore the Commission of my place and person,   3004
  If none appeare to proue vpon thy person,   3038
PERSWADE = 1*1
  Bast. Perswade me to the murther of your Lordship,   980
  Perswade me rather to be slaue and sumpter | To this detested groome.   1509
PERSWADES = 1
  Should he sit heere? This act perswades me,   1389
PERUSD = *1
  *much as I haue perus'd, I finde it not fit for your ore-loo-|king.   373

PERUSE = 1
Peruse this Letter. Nothing almost sees miracles 1242
PESCOD = 1
Weary of all, shall want some. That's a sheal'd Pescod. 711
PESTILENT = 1
Lear. A pestilent gall to me. 644
PEW *see* pue
PEZANT = 2
Reg. Giue me thy Sword. A pezant stand vp thus? | *Killes him.* 2154
Stew. Wherefore, bold Pezant, | Dar'st thou support a publish'd
Traitor? Hence, 2683
PHANGS = 1
In his Annointed flesh, sticke boarish phangs. 2130
PHILOSOPHER = 3
Lear. First let me talke with this Philosopher, 1932
Noble Philosopher, your company. | *Edg.* Tom's a cold. 1953
I will keepe still with my Philosopher. 1959
PHOEBUS = 1
Whose influence like the wreath of radient fire | On flickring *Phoebus*
front. 1182
PHRASE = 1
In better phrase, and matter then thou did'st. 2441
PHYSICKE = 1
Too little care of this: Take Physicke, Pompe, 1814
PHYSITION = 1
Kent. Kill thy Physition, and thy fee bestow 177
PICKE = *1
Edg. Chill picke your teeth Zir: come, no matter vor | your foynes. 2697
PICTURE = 1
The Duke must grant me that: besides, his picture 1019
PIECD = 1
Or all of it with our displeasure piec'd, 217
PIECE *see* peece
PIECES *see* peeces
PIERCE = 2*1
Pierce euerie sense about thee. Old fond eyes, 820
Alb. How farre your eies may pierce I cannot tell; 869
*ragges, a Pigmies straw do's pierce it. None do's offend, 2610
PIERCING = 1
Edg. O thou side-piercing sight! 2532
PIGHT = 1
And found him pight to doe it, with curst speech 1002
PIGMIES = *1
*ragges, a Pigmies straw do's pierce it. None do's offend, 2610
PILGRIMAGE = 1
Told him our pilgrimage. But his flaw'd heart 3159
PILLICOCK = *2
Edg. Pillicock sat on Pillicock hill, alow: alow, loo, loo. 1857
PILLOW = *1
*that hath laid Kniues vnder his Pillow, and Halters 1835
PIN = 1*1
*and the Pin, squints the eye, and makes the Hare-lippe; 1897
I feele this pin pricke, would I were assur'd | Of my condition. 2808
PINCH = 1
Necessities sharpe pinch. Returne with her? 1504
PINED = 1
Sir, the Foole hath much pined away. 603

PINFOLD = *1
  Kent. If I had thee in *Lipsbury* Pinfold, I would make | thee care for
  me.   1083
PINNION = 1
  Pinnion him like a Theefe, bring him before vs: 2083
PINS = 1
  Pins, Wodden-prickes, Nayles, Sprigs of Rosemarie: 1267
PIT = *1
  *there is the sulphurous pit; burning, scalding, stench,   2570
PITTIED = 2
  Be as well neighbour'd, pittied, and releeu'd,   126
  My mourning, and importun'd teares hath pittied: 2378
PITTIES = *1
  *in, aske thy Daughters blessing, heere's a night pitties | neither
  Wisemen, nor Fooles.   1667
PITTIFULL = 1
  Gent. A sight most pittifull in the meanest wretch,   2646
PITTILESSE = 1
  That bide the pelting of this pittilesse storme,   1810
PITTY = 7
  Kent. O pitty: Sir, where is the patience now   2016
  Who is too good to pitty thee.   2167
  All hearts against vs: *Edmund*, I thinke is gone | In pitty of his misery,
  to dispatch   2396
  Am pregnant to good pitty. Giue me your hand,   2670
  Did challenge pitty of them. Was this a face   2782
  I am mightily abus'd; I should eu'n dye with pitty   2805
  Touches vs not with pitty: O, is this he?   3186
PITY = *1
  *dealing; when I desired their leaue that I might pity him,   1754
PLACE = 17*4
  Which, nor our nature, nor our place can beare;   185
  I would prefer him to a better place,   299
  Bast. If your Honor iudge it meete, I will place you   423
  From the fixt place: drew from my heart all loue,   782
  My Father watches: O Sir, fly this place,   950
  Escap'd the hunt. No Port is free, no place   1254
  Lear. What's he, | That hath so much thy place mistooke | To set thee
  heere?   1286
  Ere I was risen from the place, that shewed   1305
  To bring but fiue and twentie, to no more | Will I giue place or notice.   1545
  Kent. Here is the place my Lord, good my Lord enter,   1778
  With something rich about me: from that place,   2262
  Heere's the place: stand still: how fearefull   2446
  The Fiend, the Fiend, he led me to that place.   2524
  *and Furr'd gownes hide all. Place sinnes with Gold, and   2608
  place will be fruitfully offer'd. There is nothing done. If hee   2718
  *Gaole, from the loathed warmth whereof, deliuer me, and sup-|ply the
  place for your Labour.*   2720
  What place this is: and all the skill I haue   2821
  Reg. But haue you neuer found my Brothers way, | To the fore-fended
  place?   2858
  Bore the Commission of my place and person,   3004
  Maugre thy strength, place, youth, and eminence,   3086
  The darke and vitious place where thee he got, | Cost him his eyes.   3133
PLACES = *1
  *thine eare: Change places, and handy-dandy, which is   2597

PLACKETS = *1
*Plackets, thy pen from Lenders Bookes, and defye the 1877
PLAGUE = 7
Stand in the plague of custome, and permit 337
A plague vpon your Epilepticke visage, 1154
Lear. Vengeance, Plague, Death, Confusion: 1370
A plague sore, or imbossed Carbuncle 1518
Glou. 'Tis the times plague, | When Madmen leade the blinde: 2234
The Gods are iust, and of our pleasant vices | Make instruments to
plague vs: 3131
Lear. A plague vpon you Murderors, Traitors all, 3233
PLAGUES = *2
Lea. Now all the plagues that in the pendulous ayre 1848
Glou. Here take this purse, y whom the heau'ns plagues 2249
PLAIER = 1
Kent. Nor tript neither, you base Foot-ball plaier. 616
PLAINE = 5*3
*curious tale in telling it, and deliuer a plaine message 564
Goose, if I had you vpon *Sarum* Plaine, 1156
Kent. Sir, 'tis my occupation to be plaine, 1166
An honest mind and plaine, he must speake truth, 1174
And they will take it so, if not, hee's plaine. 1175
*you in a plaine accent, was a plaine Knaue, which 1187
*try whither your Costard, or my Ballow be the harder; | chill be plaine
with you. 2694
PLAINELY = 1
And to deale plainely, | I feare I am not in my perfect mind. 2817
PLAINNESSE = 3
Let pride, which she cals plainnesse, marry her: 137
To plainnesse honour's bound, ·158
These kind of Knaues I know, which in this plainnesse 1176
PLANATARY = *1
*and Adulterers by an inforc'd obedience of Planatary 453
PLANT = 1
Must be a faith that reason without miracle | Should neuer plant in me. 243
PLAY = 3
That such a King should play bo-peepe, | And goe the Foole among. 690
Do me no foule play, Friends. | *Corn.* Binde him I say. 2094
Bad is the Trade that must play Foole to sorrow, 2224
PLAYER *see* plaier
PLEASANT = 2
What most he should dislike, seemes pleasant to him; | What like,
offensiue. 2277
The Gods are iust, and of our pleasant vices | Make instruments to
plague vs: 3131
PLEASD = 2
Lear. Better thou had'st | Not beene borne, then not t'haue pleas'd me
better. 256
It pleas'd the King his Master very late 1192
PLEASE = 7*2
Bast. So please your Lordship, none. 362
Bast. I do not well know my L.(ord) If it shall please you to 413
Gon. Put on what weary negligence you please, 519
Ste. So please you--- *Exit.* 576
How in my strength you please: for you *Edmund,* 1054
Kent. With you goodman Boy, if you please, come, 1119
Let not my worser Spirit tempt me againe | To dye before you please. 2664

PLEASE *cont.*

Gent. So please your Maiesty, | That we may wake the King, he hath
slept long? 2767
Cor. Wilt please your Highnesse walke? | *Lear.* You must beare with
me: 2840
PLEASURE = 5*1
No lesse in space, validitie, and pleasure 87
Glo. I am sorry for thee friend, 'tis the Dukes pleasure, 1228
Your horrible pleasure. Heere I stand your Slaue, 1674
Do as I bid thee, or rather do thy pleasure: | Aboue the rest, be gone. 2236
And selfereprouing, bring his constant pleasure. 2850
Methinkes our pleasure might haue bin demanded 3002
PLEASURES = 2*1
To grudge my pleasures, to cut off my Traine, 1458
*the head to heare of pleasures name. The Fitchew, nor 2565
Vntill their greater pleasures first be knowne | That are to censure them. 2941
PLEDGE = 1
There is my pledge: Ile make it on thy heart 3040
PLENTEOUS = 1
With plenteous Riuers, and wide-skirted Meades 70
PLIGHT = 2
That Lord, whose hand must take my plight, shall carry 108
Bid her a-light, and her troth-plight, 1902
PLIGHTED = *1
Cor. Time shall vnfold what plighted cunning hides, 306
PLOT = 3
To thy suggestion, plot, and damned practise: 1010
I haue ore-heard a plot of death vpon him: 2048
A plot vpon her vertuous Husbands life, 2725
PLUCKE = 6
Beweepe this cause againe, Ile plucke ye out, 821
Gon. Plucke out his eyes. 2064
Glou. By the kinde Gods, 'tis most ignobly done | To plucke me by the
Beard. 2100
Plucke out his poore old eyes: nor thy fierce Sister, 2129
May all the building in my fancie plucke | Vpon my hatefull life.
Another way 2332
To plucke the common bosome on his side, 2992
PLUCKT = 1
But not without that harmefull stroke, which since | Hath pluckt him
after. 2321
POASTED = 1
Reg. Faith he is poasted hence on serious matter: 2393
POCKET = *1
*it into your Pocket? The quality of nothing, hath not 368
POCKETS = 1
Let's see these Pockets; the Letters that he speakes of 2709
POINT = 1*1
Aloofe from th'intire point, will you haue her? 263
*At point a hundred Knights: yes, that on euerie dreame, 845
POISON *see* poyson
POISOND *see also* poyson'd = 2
Whose welcome I perceiu'd had poyson'd mine, 1315
The one the other poyson'd for my sake, | And after slew herselfe. 3197
POISONS *see* poysons
POLE = *1
*Toad, the Tod-pole, the wall-Neut, and the water: that 1909

POLICIE = *1
   *Glou. reads. This policie, and reuerence of Age, makes the   382
POLITICIAN = *1
   *glasse-eyes, and like a scuruy Politician, seeme to see the   2613
POLITIKE = 1
   'Tis politike, and safe to let him keepe   844
POMPE = 1
   Too little care of this: Take Physicke, Pompe,   1814
PONDER = 1
   This tempest will not giue me leaue to ponder   1805
PONDEROUS = 1
   More ponderous then my tongue.   84
POOLE = *2
   *through Sword, and Whirle-Poole, o're Bog, and Quag- | mire,   1834
   *Poole: who is whipt from Tything to Tything, and   1913
POORE = 25*17
   A loue that makes breath poore, and speech vnable,   65
   Cor. Then poore Cordelia, | And yet not so, since I am sure my loue's   82
   Fra. Fairest Cordelia, that art most rich being poore,   275
   *lou'd our Sister most, and with what poore iudgement he   316
   Lear. What art thou? | *Kent. A very honest hearted Fellow, and as
   poore as | the King.   549
   *Lear. If thou be'st as poore for a subiect, as hee's for a   552
   King, thou art poore enough. What wouldst thou? | Kent. Seruice.   553
   Poore pelting Villages, Sheeps-Coates, and Milles,   1269
   Inforce their charitie: poore Turlygod poore Tom,   1271
   *Fortune that arrant whore, nere turns the key toth' poore.   1325
   You see me heere (you Gods) a poore old man,   1572
   A poore, infirme, weake, and dispis'd old man: 1675
   Poore Foole, and Knaue, I haue one part in my heart | That's sorry yet
   for thee.   1727
   No Squire in debt, nor no poore Knight;   1741
   Poore naked wretches, where so ere you are   1809
   *Edg. Fathom, and halfe, Fathom and halfe; poore Tom.   1819
   *Foole. A spirite, a spirite, he sayes his name's poore | Tom.   1823
   *Edgar. Who giues any thing to poore Tom? Whom   1832
   *do poore Tom some charitie, whom the foule Fiend   1841
   *Nor the rustling of Silkes, betray thy poore heart to wo- | man.   1875
   *man, is no more but such a poore, bare, forked A- | nimall   1887
   *Mildewes the white Wheate, and hurts the poore Crea- | ture of earth.   1898
   *Edg. Poore Tom, that eates the swimming Frog, the   1908
   Edg. Poore Tom's a cold.   1925
   He said it would be thus: poore banish'd man: 1944
   And Market Townes: poore Tom thy horne is dry,   2032
   Plucke out his poore old eyes: nor thy fierce Sister,   2129
   Yet poore old heart, he holpe the Heauens to raine.   2134
   Old. 'Tis poore mad Tom.   2209
   Edg. Poore Tom's a cold. I cannot daub it further.   2241
   *poore Tom hath bin scarr'd out of his good wits. Blesse   2247
   Edg. Giue me thy arme; | Poore Tom shall leade thee. Exeunt.   2264
   So speedily can venge. But (O poore Glouster)   2325
   Well worth a poore mans taking. Fayries, and Gods   2466
   Glou. A poore vnfortunate Beggar.   2513
   *Edg. A most poore man, made tame to Fortunes blows   2668
   *Edg. Good Gentleman goe your gate, and let poore   2690
   And was't thou faine (poore Father)   2786

POORE *cont.*

Edg. If ere your Grace had speech with man so poore, | Heare me one
word.   2881
At gilded Butterflies: and heere (poore Rogues)   2953
Lear. And my poore Foole is hang'd: no, no, no life?   3277
POORELY = 1
But who comes heere? My Father poorely led? | World, World, O
world!   2189
POOREST = 2
To take the basest, and most poorest shape   1258
Are in the poorest thing superfluous.   1565
PORREDGE = *1
*in his Pue, set Rats-bane by his Porredge, made him   1836
PORT = 1
Escap'd the hunt. No Port is free, no place   1254
PORTEND = *2
Glou. These late Eclipses in the Sun and Moone por- | tend   433
*o'Bedlam. --- O these Eclipses do portend these diui- | sions. Fa, Sol,
La, Me.   465
PORTER = 1
Thou should'st haue said, good Porter turne the Key: 2136
PORTION = 1
Bur. Royall King, | Giue but that portion which your selfe propos'd,   265
PORTS = 1
All Ports Ile barre, the villaine shall not scape,   1018
POSTE = 2*1
My dutie kneeling, came there a reeking Poste,   1306
Corn. Poste speedily to my Lord your husband, shew   2060
Thee Ile rake vp, the poste vnsanctified   2727
POSTES = *1
*Postes shall be swift, and intelligent betwixt vs. Fare- | well deere
Sister, farewell my Lord of Glouster.   2070
POTENCIE = 1
Our potencie made good, take thy reward.   186
POTENTIALL = 1
Were very pregnant and potentiall spirits   1013
POTS = *1
*To vse his eyes for Garden water-pots. I wil die brauely,   2640
POUERTIE = 1
In Boy, go first. You houselesse pouertie, *Exit.*   1807
POUND = *1
*pound, filthy woosted-stocking knaue, a Lilly-liuered,   1090
POURE = 1
To shut me out? Poure on, I will endure: 1798
POWER = 8*3
I doe inuest you ioyntly with my power,   138
Think'st thou that dutie shall haue dread to speake, | When power to
flattery bowes?   156
To come betwixt our sentences, and our power,   184
not as it hath power, but as it is suffer'd. Come to me, that of   386
That thou hast power to shake my manhood thus,   815
*a Power already footed, we must incline to the King, I   1764
Without the forme of Iustice: yet our power   2085
Are many Simples operatiue, whose power | Will close the eye of
Anguish.   2364
*who haue the power to seale th'accusers lips. Get thee   2612
The Battaile done, and they within our power,   2914

POWER *cont*.

To him our absolute power, you to your rights,   3272
POWERS = 2
  Bast. The Enemy's in view, draw vp your powers,   2897
  Ere you had spoke so farre. He led our Powers,   3003
POWRE = 2*2
  Le. Then leaue her sir, for by the powre that made me,   227
  And the King gone to night? Prescrib'd his powre,   359
  Kent. All the powre of his wits, haue giuen way to his   2001
  Because he do's not feele, feele your powre quickly: 2254
POWRES = 4
  He may enguard his dotage with their powres,   847
  Hasten his Musters, and conduct his powres.   2284
  Mes. Newes Madam, | The Brittish Powres are marching hitherward.   2373
  Reg. But are my Brothers Powres set forth? | *Stew*. I Madam.   2384
POWRFULL = *1
  *You Fen-suck'd Fogges, drawne by the powrfull Sunne, | To fall, and
blister.   1450
POYSON = 1
  If you haue poyson for me, I will drinke it: 2829
POYSOND = 1
  Gen. Your Lady Sir, your Lady; and her Sister | By her is poyson'd: she
confesses it.   3177
POYSONS = 1
  Tooth that poysons if it bite: 2024
PRACTISD = 2
  Ha's practis'd on mans life. Close pent-vp guilts,   1710
  Of the death-practis'd Duke: for him 'tis well,   2730
PRACTISE = 4
  To thy suggestion, plot, and damned practise: 1010
  Glo. He did bewray his practise, and receiu'd   1048
  Is practise only. Giue me my Seruant forth;   1391
  Gon. This is practise *Gloster*,   3108
PRACTISES = 1
  My practises ride easie: I see the businesse.   502
PRAIERS = 1*1
  As my great Patron thought on in my praiers.   151
  *Sometimes with Lunaticke bans, sometime with Praiers   1270
PRAISD = 2
  Then prais'd for harmefull mildnesse.   868
  Who hauing beene prais'd for bluntnesse, doth affect   1171
PRAISE = 2
  The argument of your praise, balme of your age,   236
  Stands in some ranke of praise, Ile go with thee,   1556
PRAISES = 1
  That worthied him, got praises of the King,   1197
PRANKES = 1
  Of other your new prankes. I do beseech you   747
PRAY = 19*6
  France and him, pray you let vs sit together, if our   328
  *him out: winde me into him, I pray you: frame the Bu-|sinesse   428
  Edm. That's my feare, I pray you haue a continent   487
  *fitly bring you to heare my Lord speake: pray ye goe,   490
  like the image, and horror of it, pray you away.   496
  Alb. Pray Sir be patient.   774
  Gon. Pray you content. What *Oswald*, hoa?   833
  Bast. Not I: pray you what are they?   937

PRAY *cont.*
 Kent. Pray do not Sir, I haue watch'd and trauail'd hard, 1231
Reg. I pray you Sir, take patience, I haue hope 1416
Better then you your selfe: therefore I pray you, 1430
Reg. I pray you Father being weake, seeme so. 1494
*my old Master must be relieued. There is strange things | toward
Edmund, pray you be carefull. *Exit.* 1769
Nay get thee in; Ile pray, and then Ile sleepe. 1808
*in the Lake of Darknesse: pray Innocent, and beware | the foule Fiend. 2005
If you do finde him, pray you giue him this; 2420
I pray desire him call her wisedome to her. | So fare you well: 2422
Edg. Well pray you Father. 2666
You must not kneele. | *Lear.* Pray do not mocke me: 2812
Yes faith: I pray weepe not, 2828
Pray you now forget, and forgiue, | I am old and foolish. *Exeunt* 2842
Reg. 'Tis most conuenient, pray go with vs. 2877
For your good hoast: pray that the right may thriue: 2922
And pray, and sing, and tell old tales, and laugh 2952
Pray you vndo this Button. Thanke you Sir, 3281
PRAYERS *see* praiers
PREACH = 1
 We wawle, and cry. I will preach to thee: Marke. 2622
PRECIOUS = 3*1
 Which the most precious square of sense professes, 79
Can buy this vnpriz'd precious Maid of me. 284
*And can make vilde things precious. Come, your Houel; 1726
Their precious Stones new lost: became his guide, 3153
PRECIPITATING = 1
 (So many fathome downe precipitating) 2492
PREDICTION = *2
 *prediction; there's Son against Father, the King fals from 440
Bast. I am thinking Brother of a prediction I read this 469
PREDOMINANCE = *1
 *Treachers by Sphericall predominance. Drunkards, Ly- |ars, 452
PREFER = 1
 I would prefer him to a better place, 299
PREFERMENT = 1
 Preferment fals on him, that cuts him off. 2425
PREGNANT = 2
 Were very pregnant and potentiall spirits 1013
Am pregnant to good pitty. Giue me your hand, 2670
PREHEMINENCE = 1
 Preheminence, and all the large effects 139
PREPARATION = 1*1
 *most festinate preparation: we are bound to the like. Our 2069
Cor. 'Tis knowne before. Our preparation stands 2375
PREPARE = 1*1
 *so, Ile write straight to my Sister to hold my course; pre- |pare for
dinner. *Exeunt.* 527
Is it your will, speake Sir? Prepare my Horses. 770
PREPARED = 1
 With his prepared Sword, he charges home 987
PRESAGES = *1
 *Forkes presages Snow; that minces Vertue, & do's shake 2564
PRESCRIBD = 1
 And the King gone to night? Prescrib'd his powre, 359

PRESCRIBE = 1
So farewell to you both. | *Regn.* Prescribe not vs our dutie. 300
PRESENCE = *1
*him: and at my entreaty forbeare his presence, vntill 482
PRESENT = 5
Will you require in present Dower with her, | Or cease your quest of
Loue? 208
I haue this present euening from my Sister 1040
Your name, your quality, and why you answer | This present Summons? 3071
Alb. He knowes not what he saies, and vaine is it | That we present vs
to him. 3262
Alb. Beare them from hence, our present businesse 3293
PRESENTED = 1
And with presented nakednesse out-face 1262
PRESENTLY = 2*1
**Bast.* I will seeke him Sir, presently: conuey the bu-|sinesse 431
Which presently they read; on those contents 1310
Now, presently: bid them come forth and heare me, 1393
PRESERUE = 1
I will preserue myselfe: and am bethought 1257
PRESERUED = 1
Of mens Impossibilities, haue preserued thee. 2519
PRESIDENT = 1
The Country giues me proofe, and president 1264
PRESSE-MONEY = *1
*Presse-money. That fellow handles his bow, like a Crow-|keeper: 2534
PRETENCE = 1*1
to no other pretence of danger. | *Glou.* Thinke you so? 421
*then as a very pretence and purpose of vnkindnesse; 599
PRETTY = 1*2
Lear. How now my pretty knaue, how dost thou? 626
**Foole.* Thou wast a pretty fellow when thou hadst no 705
*the seuen Starres are no mo then seuen, is a pretty reason. 909
PREUENT = 1*1
What is your study? | *Edg.* How to preuent the Fiend, and to kill
Vermine. 1937
Corn. Lest it see more, preuent it; Out vilde gelly: 2158
PREUENTED = *1
*May be preuented now. The Princes, *France* & *Burgundy*, 50
PREY = *1
*in madnes, Lyon in prey. Let not the creaking of shooes, 1874
PRICE = 1
But now her price is fallen: Sir, there she stands, 215
PRICKE = 1
I feele this pin pricke, would I were assur'd | Of my condition. 2808
PRICKES = 1
Pins, Wodden-prickes, Nayles, Sprigs of Rosemarie: 1267
PRIDE = 3
Let pride, which she cals plainnesse, marry her: 137
Which we durst neuer yet; and with strain'd pride, 183
Lear. This is a Slaue, whose easie borrowed pride 1472
PRIESTS = 1
When Priests are more in word, then matter; 1736
PRIMA *l.*1 926 1614 2177 2844 = 5
PRIMUS *l.*1 = 1

PRINCE = 2*1
    *Edg. The Prince of Darkenesse is a Gentleman. *Modo* | he's call'd, and
    Mahu.   1921
    Conspirant 'gainst this high illustrious Prince,   3090
    Edg. Worthy Prince I know't.   3141
PRINCES = 1*1
    *May be preuented now. The Princes, *France* & *Burgundy*,   50
    Thus *Kent*, O Princes, bids you all adew,   200
PRINCESSE = 1
    Kent. Kind and deere Princesse.   2780
PRISON = 4
    Lear. No, no, no, no: come let's away to prison,   2948
    In a wall'd prison, packs and sects of great ones, | That ebbe and flow
    by th'Moone.   2958
    Take thou this note, go follow them to prison,   2970
    Bast. He hath Commission from thy Wife and me, | To hang *Cordelia*
    in the prison, and   3211
PRISONER = 1*1
    Your most deere Daughter--- | *Lear*. No rescue? What, a Prisoner? I am
    euen   2632
    returne the Conqueror, then am I the Prisoner, and his bed, my   2719
PRISONERS = 2
    and Cordelia, as prisoners, Souldiers, Captaine.   2939
    Take thou my Souldiers, prisoners, patrimony,   3018
PRITHEE *see* prythee, prythy
PRIUATE = 1
    Lear. Let me aske you one word in priuate.   1939
PRIUILEDGE = 3
    Kent. Yes Sir, but anger hath a priuiledge.   1143
    Behold it is my priuiledge,   3083
    The priuiledge of mine Honours,   3084
PRIUILY = *1
    *will looke him, and priuily relieue him; goe you and   1765
PRIZE = 3
    And prize me at her worth. In my true heart,   75
    Occasions Noble *Gloster* of some prize,   1063
    Stew. A proclaim'd prize: most happie   2676
PROCEED = *1
    *run a certaine course: where, if you violently proceed a- | gainst   416
PROCEEDE = 1
    Cor. Be gouern'd by your knowledge, and proceede   2769
PROCEEDING = 2
    Which else were shame, that then necessitie | Will call discreet
    proceeding.   ·724
    Alb. Let's then determine with th'ancient of warre | On our proceeding. 2873
PROCLAIMD = 3
    Edg. I heard my selfe proclaim'd,   1252
    Stew. A proclaim'd prize: most happie   2676
    Then I haue heere proclaim'd thee.   .   3042
PROCLAIME = 1
    By his authoritie I will proclaime it,   997
PROCLAMATION = 1
    The bloody proclamation to escape   3146
PROCURE = 1
    Reg. O Sir, to wilfull men, | The iniuries that they themselues procure, 1606
PRODUCE = 3
    (As this I would, though thou didst produce   1008

PRODUCE *cont.*

I can produce a Champion, that will proue 2887

Alb. Produce the bodies, be they aliue or dead; | *Gonerill and Regans*
bodies brought out. 3183

PROFESSE = 1*2

Onely she comes too short, that I professe 77

*Lear. What dost thou professe? What would'st thou | with vs? 542

*Kent. I do professe to be no lesse then I seeme; to serue 544

PROFESSED = 1

To your professed bosomes I commit him, 297

PROFESSES = 1

Which the most precious square of sense professes, 79

PROFESSION = 1

My oath, and my profession. I protest, 3085

PROFITS = 1

If they not thought the profits of my death 1012

PROMISD = 1

Kent. Is this the promis'd end? | *Edg.* Or image of that horror. | *Alb.*
Fall and cease. 3224

PROMISE = *1

*Bast. I promise you, the effects he writes of, succeede | vnhappily. 472

PROOFE = 2*1

The Country giues me proofe, and president 1264

*me, I was euery thing: 'Tis a Lye, I am not Agu-proofe. 2551

It were a delicate stratagem to shoo | A Troope of Horse with Felt: Ile
put't in proofe, 2626

PROPER = 2

*Kent. I cannot wish the fault vndone, the issue of it, | being so proper. 20

Proper deformitie seemes not in the Fiend | So horrid as in woman. 2309

PROPERTY = 1

Heere I disclaime all my Paternall care, | Propinquity and property of
blood, 120

PROPHECIE = *1

**This prophecie *Merlin* shall make, for I liue before his | (time. | *Exit.* 1749

PROPHESIE = 2

Ile speake a Prophesie ere I go: 1735

Alb. Me thought thy very gate did prophesie 3137

PROPHETS = 1

Reg. Iesters do oft proue Prophets. 3013

PROPINQUITY = 1

Heere I disclaime all my Paternall care, | Propinquity and property of
blood, 120

PROPOSD = 1

Bur. Royall King, | Giue but that portion which your selfe propos'd, 265

PROSPER = 4

Well may you prosper. 308

And my inuention thriue, *Edmond* the base | Shall to'th'Legitimate: I
grow, I prosper: 354

Kinde Gods, forgiue me that, and prosper him. 2169

Prosper it with thee. Go thou further off, 2467

PROTECT = 1

That you protect this course, and put it on 719

PROTECTION = 1

Both welcome, and protection. Take vp thy Master, 2051

PROTEST = 1

My oath, and my profession. I protest, 3085

PROUD = 2*3
*base, proud, shallow, beggerly, three-suited-hundred   1089
*Proud of heart, to ride on a Bay trotting Horse, ouer foure   1837
*with mans sworne Spouse: set not thy Sweet-heart on | proud array. *Tom*'s a cold.   1862
Lear. What hast thou bin? | *Edg.* A Seruingman? Proud in heart, and minde; that   1864
When misery could beguile the Tyrants rage, | And frustrate his proud will.   2505
PROUE = 7*1
Proue our Commodities. Oh deere Sonne *Edgar*,   2202
May proue effects. Backe *Edmond* to my Brother,   2283
*doo't. There's my Gauntlet, Ile proue it on a Gyant.   2537
I can produce a Champion, that will proue   2887
Reg. Iesters do oft proue Prophets.   3013
Reg. Let the Drum strike, and proue my title thine.   3026
If none appeare to proue vpon thy person,   3038
To proue vpon thy heart, where to I speake, | Thou lyest.   3095
PROUIDED = 1
Reg. Not altogether so, | I look'd not for you yet, nor am prouided   1526
PROUISION = 3
Fiue dayes we do allot thee for prouision,   187
I am now from home, and out of that prouision   1498
And follow me, that will to some prouision   2055
PROUOKE = 1
The which he lackes: that to prouoke in him   2363
PROUOKING = *1
*a prouoking merit set a-worke by a reprouable badnesse | in himselfe.   1977
PRYTHEE = 6*5
Foole. Prythee tell him, so much the rent of his land   664
Foole. Then I prythee be merry, thy wit shall not go | slip-shod. | *Lear.* Ha, ha, ha.   885
Stew. Prythee, if thou lou'st me, tell me. | *Kent.* I loue thee not.   1080
Lear. I prythee Daughter do not make me mad,   1512
Lear. Prythee go in thy selfe, seeke thine owne ease,   1804
Foole. Prythee Nunckle be contented, 'tis a naughtie   1891
Foole. Prythee Nunckle tell me, whether a madman be | a Gentleman, or a Yeoman.   2007
Glou. Good friend, I prythee take him in thy armes;   2047
I prythee put them off. | *Kent.* Pardon deere Madam,   2755
Kent. O my good Master. | *Lear.* Prythee away.   3230
Kent. Breake heart, I prythee breake. | *Edg.* Looke vp my Lord.   3285
PRYTHY = *1
*Pry'thy Nunckle keepe a Schoolemaster that can teach   692
PUBLISH = 1
We haue this houre a constant will to publish   48
PUBLISHD = 1
Stew. Wherefore, bold Pezant, | Dar'st thou support a publish'd Traitor? Hence,   2683
PUDDER = 1
Lear. Let the great Goddes | That keepe this dreadfull pudder o're our heads,   1702
PUE = *1
*in his Pue, set Rats-bane by his Porredge, made him   1836
PULL = *1
*things thou dost not. Now, now, now, now. Pull off my | Bootes: harder, harder, so.   2614

PUNISH = 1

For lifting food too't? But I will punish home; 1796

PUNISHD = *1

*stockt, punish'd, and imprison'd: who hath three Suites | to his backe,
sixe shirts to his body: 1914

PUNISHMENT = 2

Iudicious punishment, 'twas this flesh begot | Those Pelicane Daughters. 1855
And quit the house on purpose, that their punishment | Might haue the
freer course. 2342

PUPPETS = *1

*the King, and take Vanitie the puppets part, a-|gainst 1109

PURE = *1

*downe; 'twas her Brother, that in pure kindnesse to his | Horse
buttered his Hay. 1401

PURPOSD = 1

Gon. So am I purpos'd, | Where is my Lord of *Gloster?* 1594

PURPOSE = 8*3

Lear. Meane time we shal expresse our darker purpose. 41
To speake and purpose not, since what I will intend, 247
*him, mistaking his purpose, it would make a great 417
*then as a very pretence and purpose of vnkindnesse; 599
Suspend thy purpose, if thou did'st intend | To make this Creature
fruitfull: 790
To his vnnaturall purpose, in fell motion 986
Be fear'd of doing harme, make your owne purpose, 1053
Gent. As I learn'd, | The night before, there was no purpose in them |
Of this remoue. 1276
Reg. Good Sir, to'th'purpose. *Tucket within.* 1466
And quit the house on purpose, that their punishment | Might haue the
freer course. 2342
Bast. Know of the Duke if his last purpose hold, 2847

PURPOSES = 2*1

To vnderstand my purposes aright: 748
*Might not you transport her purposes by word? Belike, 2406
Alb. Aske him his purposes, why he appeares | Vpon this Call
o'th'Trumpet. 3068

PURSE = 2*4

Then my out-wall; open this Purse, and take 1642
Glou. Here take this purse, y whom the heau'ns plagues 2249
Heere Friend's another purse: in it, a Iewell 2465
*head, nor no mony in your purse? Your eyes are in a hea-|uy 2590
*case, your purse in a light, yet you see how this world | goes. 2591
Stew. Slaue thou hast slaine me: Villain, take my purse; 2699

PURSES = 1

Nor Cut-purses come not to throngs; 1743

PURSUE = 2

Glo. Pursue him, ho: go after. By no meanes, what? 979
Which can pursue th'offender; how dost my Lord? 1028

PURSUED = 1

Cor. Is he pursued? | *Glo.* I my good Lord. 1050

PUT = 10*4

Glou. Why so earnestly seeke you to put vp y Letter? 363
Gon. Put on what weary negligence you please, 519
*him truely that will put me in trust, to loue him that is 545
That you protect this course, and put it on 719
(Whereof I know you are fraught), and put away 732
'Tis they haue put him on the old mans death, 1038

PUT *cont.*
  And put vpon him such a deale of Man,   1196
  *Eeles, when she put 'em i'th' Paste aliue, she knapt 'em   1399
  Lear. Who put my man i'th'Stockes?   1467
  Gon. 'Tis his owne blame hath put himselfe from rest,   1590
  Slaine by his Seruant, going to put out | The other eye of Glouster.   2314
  Glou. Now let thy friendly hand | Put strength enough too't.   2681
  I prythee put them off. | *Kent.* Pardon deere Madam,   2755
  Gent. I Madam: in the heauinesse of sleepe, | We put fresh garments on
  him.   2772
PUTS = *2
  Lear. Why? | *Foole.* Why to put's head in, not to giue it away to his   903
  Foole. He that has a house to put's head in, has a good | Head-peece: 1680
PUTST = *1
  *the rod, and put'st downe thine owne breeches, then they   687
PUTT = 1
  It were a delicate stratagem to shoo | A Troope of Horse with Felt: Ile
  put't in proofe,   2626
QUAGMIRE = *1
  *through Sword, and Whirle-Poole, o're Bog, and Quag-|mire,   1834
QUAKES = 1
  When I do stare, see how the Subiect quakes.   2555
QUALIFIED = *1
  *some little time hath qualified the heat of his displeasure,   483
QUALITIE = 1*1
  Who in the lustie stealth of Nature, take | More composition, and fierce
  qualitie,   345
  Herald reads. | *If any man of qualitie or degree, within the lists of the
  Ar-|my,*   3059
QUALITIES = *1
  *most, for qualities are so weigh'd, that curiosity in nei-|ther, can make
  choise of eithers moity.   9
QUALITY = 4*1
  *it into your Pocket? The quality of nothing, hath not   368
  Glo. My deere Lord, | You know the fiery quality of the Duke,   1366
  Fiery? What quality? Why *Gloster, Gloster,*   1371
  With how deprau'd a quality. Oh *Regan.*   1415
  Your name, your quality, and why you answer | This present Summons?   3071
QUALLIFIED = *1
  *bluntly: that which ordinary men are fit for, I am qual-|lified in, and
  the best of me, is Dilligence.   565
QUARRELL = 4
  Do hourely Carpe and Quarrell, breaking forth   714
  Cor. Speake yet, how grew your quarrell?   1134
  I'ld shake it on this quarrell. What do you meane?   2151
  To quarrell with your great opposelesse willes,   2477
QUARRELS = 1
  Bold in the quarrels right, rouz'd to th'encounter,   990
QUARTA *l.*529 1776 2382 = 3
QUARTUS *l.*2177 = 1
QUEAZIE = 1
  And I haue one thing of a queazie question   946
QUEEN = *2
  Gent. Though that the Queen on special cause is here   2660
  *Which do command them. With him I sent the Queen: 2994
QUEENE = 1
  Is Queene of vs, of ours, and our faire *France*:   282

QUENCHD = 1
And quench'd the Stelled fires: 2133
QUEST = 1
Will you require in present Dower with her, | Or cease your quest of
Loue? 208
QUESTION = 5
You and your Fellowes: I'de haue it come to question; 520
And I haue one thing of a queazie question 946
question, thoud'st well deseru'd it. | *Kent*. Why Foole? 1338
For these domesticke and particular broiles, | Are not the question
heere. 2871
Will not beare question: either say thou'lt do't, | Or thriue by other
meanes. 2976
QUESTRISTS = 1
Hot Questrists after him, met him at gate, 2076
QUICKE = 1
Giue thee quicke conduct. Come, come, away. *Exeunt* 2056
QUICKEN = 1
Will quicken and accuse thee. I am your Host, 2105
QUICKLY = 3
Because he do's not feele, feele your powre quickly: 2254
Despight of mine owne Nature. Quickly send, 3201
He'le strike and quickly too, he's dead and rotten. 3251
QUINTA *l*.873 1969 2429 = 3
QUINTUS *l*.2844 = 1
QUIT = 3
Draw, seeme to defend your selfe, | Now quit you well. 961
Edmund, enkindle all the sparkes of Nature | To quit this horrid acte. 2162
And quit the house on purpose, that their punishment | Might haue the
freer course. 2342
QUITE = 1
Quite from his Nature. He cannot flatter he, 1173
RABLE = *1
Gon. You strike my people, and your disorder'd rable, | make Seruants
of their Betters. 766
RACKE *see* wracke
RADIENCE = 1
For by the sacred radience of the Sunne, 116
RADIENT = 1
Whose influence like the wreath of radient fire | On flickring *Phoebus*
front. 1182
RAGE = 4*2
*forbearance till the speed of his rage goes slower: and as 488
Glo. The King is in high rage. 1598
Lear. Blow windes, & crack your cheeks; Rage, blow 1656
Least his vngouern'd rage, dissolue the life | That wants the meanes to
leade it. 2370
When misery could beguile the Tyrants rage, | And frustrate his proud
will. 2505
Gent. Be comforted good Madam, the great rage 2837
RAGES = *1
*in the furie of his heart, when the foule Fiend rages, eats 1910
RAGETH = *1
*which at this instant so rageth in him, that with the mis-|chiefe 484
RAGGEDNESSE = 1
Your lop'd, and window'd raggednesse defend you 1812

RAGGES = *1
  *ragges, a Pigmies straw do's pierce it. None do's offend,   2610
RAGS = 1*1
  *Fathers that weare rags, do make their Children blind,   1323
  Into a mad-mans rags, t'assume a semblance   3150
RAILD = 1
  Tript me behind: being downe, insulted, rail'd,   1195
RAILE = *1
  *to raile on one, that is neither knowne of thee, nor | knowes thee?   1099
RAILES = *1
  *yond Iustice railes vpon yond simple theefe. Hearke in   2596
RAIMENT see rayment
RAINE = 6*2
  Will packe, when it begins to raine,   1352
  *Lear. Rumble thy belly full: spit Fire, spowt Raine: 1669
  Nor Raine, Winde, Thunder, Fire are my Daughters;   1670
  Such groanes of roaring Winde, and Raine, I neuer   1699
  With heigh-ho, the Winde and the Raine,   1730
  Though the Raine it raineth euery day.   1732
  Yet poore old heart, he holpe the Heauens to raine.   2134
  *Diuinity. When the raine came to wet me once, and the   2547
RAINETH = 1
  Though the Raine it raineth euery day.   1732
RAIN-WATER = *1
  *better then this Rain-water out o'doore. Good Nunkle,   1666
RAISD = 2
  He rais'd the house, with loud and coward cries,   1319
  (More harder then the stones whereof 'tis rais'd,   1718
RAISE = 1
  To raise my fortunes. Thou old, vnhappy Traitor,   2678
RAIZD = 1
  For which I raiz'd my likenesse. Now banisht Kent,   534
RAKE = 1
  Thee Ile rake vp, the poste vnsanctified   2727
RANKE = 3
  In ranke, and (not to be endur'd) riots Sir.   715
  Stands in some ranke of praise, Ile go with thee,   1556
  Crown'd with ranke Fenitar, and furrow weeds,   2353
RANKES = 1
  Bast. Yours in the rankes of death. Exit.   2293
RANSOME = 1
  You shall haue ransome. Let me haue Surgeons,   2635
RARE = 1
  Beyond what can be valewed, rich or rare,   62
RAREST = 1
  My Traine are men of choice, and rarest parts,   776
RASCALL = 1*5
  Lear. Do you bandy lookes with me, you Rascall?   614
  *Kent. A Knaue, a Rascall, an eater of broken meates, a   1088
  *Kent. Draw you Rascall, you come with Letters a- |gainst   1108
  *Ile so carbonado your shanks, draw you Rascall, come | your waies.   1111
  *you cowardly Rascall, nature disclaimes in thee: a Taylor | made thee.   1128
  *obey'd in Office. Thou, Rascall Beadle, hold thy bloody   2603
RASH = 1*1
  *rash, then must we looke from his age, to receiue not a- |lone   321
  Reg. O the blest Gods! | So will you wish on me, when the rash moode   1452
  is on.

RASHNESSE = 1
This hideous rashnesse, answere my life, my iudgement: 161
RAT = 1*1
*Cow-dung for Sallets; swallowes the old Rat, and the   1911
Why should a Dog, a Horse, a Rat haue life,   3278
RATHER = 8*2
Kent. Let it fall rather, though the forke inuade   153
*which I haue rather blamed as mine owne iealous curio- |sitie,   598
*my peace. I had rather be any kind o'thing then a foole,   698
No, rather I abiure all roofes, and chuse   1501
Perswade me rather to be slaue and sumpter | To this detested groome.   1509
Or rather a disease that's in my flesh,   1516
Kent. I had rather breake mine owne, | Good my Lord enter.   1784
Do as I bid thee, or rather do thy pleasure: | Aboue the rest, be gone.   2236
Stew. Madam, I had rather--- | *Reg*. I know your Lady do's not loue her
Husband,   2409
Rather then die at once) taught me to shift   3149
RATS = 2
Like Rats oft bite the holy cords a twaine,   1147
But Mice, and Rats, and such small Deare,   1917
RATS-BANE = *1
*in his Pue, set Rats-bane by his Porredge, made him   1836
RAUISH = 1
These haires which thou dost rauish from my chin   2104
RAYMENT = 1
That you'l vouchsafe me Rayment, Bed, and Food.   1437
READ = 5*2
*from my Brother, that I haue not all ore-read; and for so   372
Bast. I am thinking Brother of a prediction I read this   469
Which presently they read; on those contents   1310
The Newes is not so tart. Ile read, and answer.   2334
Lear. Read. | *Glou*. What with the Case of eyes?   2587
Alb. Stay till I haue read the Letter. | *Edg*. I was forbid it: 2891
Come hither Herald, let the Trumpet sound, | And read out this. *A
Trumpet sounds*.   3057
READE = 1*1
*loue. Reade thou this challenge, marke but the penning | of it.   2582
Thou worse then any name, reade thine owne euill: 3114
READING = 1
Glou. What Paper were you reading? | *Bast*. Nothing my Lord.   365
READS = 2*1
Glou. *reads*. *This policie, and reuerence of Age, makes the*   382
Their Papers is more lawfull. | *Reads the Letter*.   2714
Herald reads. | *If any man of qualitie or degree, within the lists of the
Ar- |my*,   3059
READY = 8*1
Lear. Let me not stay a iot for dinner, go get it rea- |dy: 539
Lear. I will forget my Nature, so kind a Father? Be | my Horsses
ready?   906
*keepe me in temper, I would not be mad. How now are | the Horses
ready?   919
Gent. Ready my Lord. | *Lear*. Come Boy.   921
And bring you where both fire, and food is ready.   1931
*seeke out where thy Father is, that hee may bee | ready for our
apprehension.   1988
There is a Litter ready, lay him in't,   2049
My reason all the same, and they are ready   2995

READY *cont*.
    For I am almost ready to dissolue, | Hearing of this.   3167
REALME = 1*1
    *Then shal the Realme of *Albion*, come to great confusion: 1746
    Rule in this Realme, and the gor'd state sustaine.   3295
REASON = 8*3
    Must be a faith that reason without miracle | Should neuer plant in me.   243
    *reason it thus, and thus, yet Nature finds it selfe scourg'd   435
    Foole. Thy Asses are gone about 'em; the reason why   908
    *the seuen Starres are no mo then seuen, is a pretty reason.   909
    Lear. *Regan*, I thinke you are. I know what reason   1407
    For those that mingle reason with your passion,   1529
    Lear. O reason not the need: our basest Beggers   1564
    Glou. He has some reason, else he could not beg.   2215
    Edg. O matter, and impertinency mixt, | Reason in Madnesse.   2616
    My reason all the same, and they are ready   2995
    Alb. Stay yet, heare reason: *Edmund*, I arrest thee   3027
REASOND = 1
    Regan. Why is this reasond?   2869
REASONS = 1
    And thereto adde such reasons of your owne,   862
REBELL = 1
    That in the natures of their Lords rebell,   1149
RECEIUD = 3
    Gon. Let your study | Be to content your Lord, who hath receiu'd you   302
    Glo. He did bewray his practise, and receiu'd   1048
    Corn. I haue receiu'd a hurt: Follow me Lady;   2173
RECEIUE = 1*2
    *rash, then must we looke from his age, to receiue not a- | lone   321
    Gon. Why might not you my Lord, receiue attendance   1539
    Reg. For his particular, Ile receiue him gladly, | But not one follower.   1592
RECEIUED = *1
    *receiued a Letter this night, 'tis dangerous to be spoken,   1761
RECIEUE = 1
    Reg. My Sister may recieue it much more worsse,   1225
RECIPROCALL = *1
    Let our reciprocall vowes be remembred. You haue manie   2716
RECREANT = *1
    Lea. Heare me recreant, on thine allegeance heare me;   181
RED = 1
    Lear. To haue a thousand with red burning spits | Come hizzing in vpon
    'em.   2013
REDEEME = 1
    It is a chance which do's redeeme all sorrowes | That euer I haue felt.   3228
REDEEMES = 1
    Who redeemes Nature from the generall curse | Which twaine haue
    brought her to.   2648
REDRESSE = 1
    To haue found a safe redresse, but now grow fearefull   717
REDRESSES = 1
    Would not scape censure, nor the redresses sleepe,   721
REEKING = 1
    My dutie kneeling, came there a reeking Poste,   1306
REG = 56*11
REGA = 1

REGAN see also Reg., Rega., Regn. = 22*4

REGAN = 2

REGANS = 1

REGARD = 1

REGARDS = 1

REGION = 1 *

REGN = 1

REINE = 1

RELEEUD = 1

RELIEUE = *1

RELIEUED = *1

RELLISH = *1

REMAINDERS = 1

REMAINE = 4

REMAINE *cont.*

Not in this Land shall he remaine vncaught   994
If both remaine aliue: To take the Widdow,   2906
REMEDIATE = 1

Spring with my teares; be aydant, and remediate   2368
REMEDIES = 1

Losses their remedies. All weary and o're-watch'd,   1247
REMEDY = 1

For instant remedy. Be then desir'd   756
REMEMBER = 6*2

Glou. My Lord of Kent: | Remember him heereafter, as my Honourable
Friend.   30
Remember what I haue said. | *Ste.* Well Madam.   523
Remember to haue heard. Mans Nature cannot carry | Th'affliction, nor
the feare.   1700
Glou. I do remember now: henceforth Ile beare | Affliction, till it do cry
out it selfe   2520
Glou. The tricke of that voyce, I do well remember: 2552
Do'st thou know me? | *Lear.* I remember thine eyes well enough: dost
thou   2579
Breefely thy selfe remember: the Sword is out | That must destroy thee.   2679
Haue (as I do remember) done me wrong.   2831
REMEMBERS = 1

Remembers not these garments: nor I know not   2822
REMEMBRED = *1

Let our reciprocall vowes be remembred. You haue manie   2716
REMEMBREST = *1

Lear. Thou but remembrest me of mine owne Con-|ception,   596
REMORSE = 1

Mes. A Seruant that he bred, thrill'd with remorse,   2317
REMOTION = 1

That this remotion of the Duke and her   1390
REMOUE = 1

Gent. As I learn'd, | The night before, there was no purpose in them |
Of this remoue.   1276
RENOUNCE = 1

Glou. O you mighty Gods! | This world I do renounce, and in your
sights   2473
RENT = *1

Foole. Prythee tell him, so much the rent of his land   664
REPAIRE = 1

Repaire those violent harmes, that my two Sisters | Haue in thy
Reuerence made.   2778
REPAYRE = 1

And Ile repayre the misery thou do'st beare   2261
REPENT = *1

Bast. How malicious is my fortune, that I must re-|pent   1979
REPENTS = 1

Lear. Woe, that too late repents: 769
REPLIED = 1

I threaten'd to discouer him; he replied,   1003
REPORT = 1

Edg. I would not take this from report, | It is, and my heart breakes at
it.   2585
REPORTS = 1

All my reports go with the modest truth, | Nor more, nor clipt, but so.   2751

REPOSALL = 1
  If I would stand against thee, would the reposall   1005
REPOSE = 2
  Repose you there, while I to this hard house,   1717
  Our foster Nurse of Nature, is repose,   2362
REPREEUE = 1
  Send thy token of repreeue.   3207
REPROUABLE = *1
  *a prouoking merit set a-worke by a reprouable badnesse | in himselfe.   1977
REPROUING see selfereprouing
REQUIRE = 2
  Will you require in present Dower with her, | Or cease your quest of
  Loue?   208
  I do require them of you so to vse them,   2986
RESCUE = 1
  Your most deere Daughter--- | Lear. No rescue? What, a Prisoner? I am
  euen   2632
RESERUATION = 2
  With reseruation of an hundred Knights,   141
  But kept a reseruation to be followed   1550
RESERUD = *1
  *Foole. Nay, he reseru'd a Blanket, else we had bin all | sham'd.   1846
RESERUE = 1
  When Maiesty falls to folly, reserue thy state,   159
RESIGNE = 1
  Shall be appli'd. For vs we will resigne,   3270
RESOLUE = 1
  Resolue me with all modest haste, which way   1300
RESOLUTION = 1
  *after your owne wisedome. I would vnstate my | selfe, to be in a due
  resolution.   429
RESPECT = 3*2
  Since that respect and Fortunes are his loue,   273
  My Loue should kindle to enflam'd respect.   280
  *it were his: but in respect of that, I would faine thinke it | were not.   399
  To do vpon respect such violent outrage: 1299
  *Lear. Nature's aboue Art, in that respect. Ther's your   2533
RESPECTS = 1
  You shall doe small respects, show too bold malice   1209
REST = 6*3
  I lou'd her most, and thought to set my rest   131
  Reuennew, Execution of the rest, | Beloued Sonnes be yours, which to
  confirme,   145
  Some time I shall sleepe out, the rest Ile whistle: 1232
  *Gon. 'Tis his owne blame hath put himselfe from rest,   1590
  *were like an old Letchers heart, a small spark, all the rest   1893
  *Kent. Now good my Lord, lye heere, and rest awhile.   2040
  Do as I bid thee, or rather do thy pleasure: | Aboue the rest, be gone.   2236
  Edg. Sit you downe Father: rest you.   2708
  Where they shall rest for euer. Trumpets speake.   3106
RESTAURATIAN = 1
  Cor. O my deere Father, restauratian hang   2776
RESTORING = 1
  In the restoring his bereaued Sense; he that helpes him,   2359
RESTRAINED = 2
  That he so slightly valued in his Messenger, | Should haue him thus
  restrained.   1222

RESTRAINED *cont.*
She haue restrained the Riots of your Followres,   1422
RESUME = 1
That Ile resume the shape which thou dost thinke | I haue cast off for
euer. *Exit*   828
RETAINE = 2
Make with you by due turne, onely we shall retaine   143
That you so oft haue boasted to retaine?   2017
RETENTION = 1
Bast. Sir, I thought it fit, | To send the old and miserable King to some
retention,   2989
RETINUE = 1
But other of your insolent retinue   713
RETIRE = *1
*I say, retire with me to my lodging, from whence I will   489
RETREAT = 1
Glo. Grace go with you Sir. *Exit.* | *Alarum and Retreat within.*   2925
RETURND = 1
Corn. Followed the old man forth, he is return'd.   1597
RETURNE = 10*1
I returne those duties backe as are right fit,   104
And hasten your returne; no, no, my Lord,   864
That to our Sister, you do make returne,   1431
Returne you to my Sister. | *Lear.* Neuer *Regan*:   1439
You will returne and soiourne with my Sister,   1496
Lear. Returne to her? and fifty men dismiss'd?   1500
Necessities sharpe pinch. Returne with her?   1504
To keepe base life a foote; returne with her?   1508
Deny'd me to come in) returne, and force | Their scanted curtesie.   1720
returne the Conqueror, then am I the Prisoner, and his bed, my   2719
If euer I returne to you againe, | Ile bring you comfort.   2923
RETURNES = 2
On euery trifle. When he returnes from hunting,   514
The worst returnes to laughter. Welcome then,   2184
REUEALD = 1
Neuer (O fault) reueal'd my selfe vnto him,   3155
REUENGE = 3
Reuenge, affirme, and turne their Halcion beakes   1151
Corn. I will haue my reuenge, ere I depart his house.   1971
And to reuenge thine eyes. Come hither Friend,   2346
REUENGED = *1
*King now beares, will be reuenged home; ther is part of   1763
REUENGES = 1*1
I will haue such reuenges on you both,   1579
*you our Sister company: the reuenges wee are bound to   2066
REUENGING = 1
But that I told him the reuenging Gods,   981
REUENNEW = 2*2
Reuennew, Execution of the rest, | Beloued Sonnes be yours, which to
confirme,   145
him, you should enioy halfe his Reuennew for euer, and liue the | beloued
of your Brother. Edgar.   388
*enioy halfe his Reuennew: my Sonne *Edgar*, had hee a   391
the Sonne manage his Reuennew.   408
REUENUES = 1
To haue th'expence and wast of his Reuenues: 1039

REUERBE = 1
  Nor are those empty hearted, whose low sounds | Reuerbe no
  hollownesse.   163
REUERENCE = 2*1
  *Glou. reads. This policie, and reuerence of Age, makes the   382
  Cor. Peace sirrah, | You beastly knaue, know you no reuerence?   1141
  Repaire those violent harmes, that my two Sisters | Haue in thy
  Reuerence made.   2778
REUEREND = 1
  As you are Old, and Reuerend, should be Wise.   749
REUERENT = 1
  You stubborne ancient Knaue, you reuerent Bragart, | Wee'l teach you.   1204
REUIUES = 1
  Thus might he passe indeed: yet he reuiues.   2487
REUOKD = 1
  The moment is thy death, away. By Iupiter, | This shall not be reuok'd,   192
REUOKE = 1
  Vpon the foule disease, reuoke thy guift,   178
REUOLT = 1
  The images of reuolt and flying off.   1364
REWARD = 2
  Our potencie made good, take thy reward.   186
  impatience: the Gods reward your kindnesse.   2002
RICH = 3
  Beyond what can be valewed, rich or rare,   62
  Fra. Fairest Cordelia, that art most rich being poore,   275
  With something rich about me: from that place,   2262
RICHD = 1
  With shadowie Forrests, and with Champains rich'd   69
RICHER = 1
  But euen for want of that, for which I am richer,   252
RID = 1
  Let her who would be rid of him, deuise   2911
RIDDLE = 1
  Gon. Oh ho, I know the Riddle, I will goe. | Exeunt both the Armies.   2878
RIDE = 3*2
  My practises ride easie: I see the businesse.   502
  Lear. What seruices canst thou do? | *Kent. I can keepe honest
  counsaile, ride, run, marre a   562
  Ride more then thou goest,   651
  *Proud of heart, to ride on a Bay trotting Horse, ouer foure   1837
  Horse to ride, and weapon to weare: 1916
RIGHT see also rite = 7
  I returne those duties backe as are right fit,   104
  Lear. Right Noble Burgundy, | When she was deare to vs, we did hold
  her so,   213
  Bold in the quarrels right, rouz'd to th'encounter,   990
  Glo. I serue you Madam, | Your Graces are right welcome. Exeunt.
  Flourish.   1072
  When euery Case in Law, is right;   1740
  For your good hoast: pray that the right may thriue: 2922
  Bast. Th'hast spoken right, 'tis true,   3135
RIGHTLY = 2
  That iustly think'st, and hast most rightly said: 197
  These dispositions, which of late transport you | From what you rightly
  are.   733

RIGHTS = 2
Reg. In my rights, | By me inuested, he compeeres the best.   3010
To him our absolute power, you to your rights,   3272
RIGOUR = 1
With others, whom the rigour of our State | Forc'd to cry out.   2867
RING = 1
(As feare not but you shall) shew her this Ring,   1644
RINGS = 1
Met I my Father with his bleeding Rings,   3152
RIOTOUS = 2*2
His Knights grow riotous, and himselfe vpbraides vs   513
Shewes like a riotous Inne; Epicurisme and Lust   753
Reg. Was he not companion with the riotous Knights   1033
*the soyled Horse goes too't with a more riotous appe- | tite: 2566
RIOTS = 2
In ranke, and (not to be endur'd) riots Sir.   715
She haue restrained the Riots of your Followres,   1422
RIP = 1
To know our enemies mindes, we rip their hearts,   2713
RIPENESSE = 1
Ripenesse is all come on. | *Glo.* And that's true too. *Exeunt.*   2935
RISEN = 1
Ere I was risen from the place, that shewed   1305
RISES = 1
The yonger rises, when the old doth fall. *Exit.*   1775
RISING = *1
Lear. Oh me my heart! My rising heart! But downe.   1397
RITE = 1
But loue, deere loue, and our ag'd Fathers Rite: 2380
RIUALD = 1
Hath riuald for our Daughter; what in the least   207
RIUALS = 1
Great Riuals in our yongest daughters loue,   51
RIUE = 1
Riue your concealing Continents, and cry   1711
RIUERS = 1
With plenteous Riuers, and wide-skirted Meades   70
ROARING = 3
Of Bedlam beggers, who with roaring voices,   1265
Such groanes of roaring Winde, and Raine, I neuer   1699
But if thy flight lay toward the roaring sea,   1790
ROB = 1
And yet I know not how conceit may rob   2482
ROBBERS = 1
With Robbers hands, my hospitable fauours   2106
ROBES = *1
*tatter'd cloathes great Vices do appeare: Robes,   2607
ROD = *1
*the rod, and put'st downe thine owne breeches, then they   687
ROGUE = *4
*finicall Rogue, one Trunke-inheriting slaue, one that   1092
*heeles, and beate thee before the King? Draw you rogue,   1103
*the Royaltie of her Father: draw you Rogue, or   1110
*Kent. Strike you slaue: stand rogue, stand you neat | slaue, strike. 1114
ROGUES = 4
Who weares no honesty: such smiling rogues as these,   1146
Kent. None of these Rogues, and Cowards | But *Aiax* is there Foole. 1201

ROGUES *cont.*
  To houell thee with Swine and Rogues forlorne,   2787
  At gilded Butterflies: and heere (poore Rogues)   2953
ROOFES = 1
  No, rather I abiure all roofes, and chuse   1501
ROSEMARIE = 1
  Pins, Wodden-prickes, Nayles, Sprigs of Rosemarie: 1267
ROT = 1
  Glo. No further Sir, a man may rot euen heere.   2931
ROTTEN = 1
  He'le strike and quickly too, he's dead and rotten.   3251
ROTUNDITY = 1
  Strike flat the thicke Rotundity o'th'world,   1662
ROUGH = 1*1
  *that it followes, I am rough and Leacherous. I should   459
  The tirrany of the open night's too rough | For Nature to endure.
  Storme still   1779
ROUGHNES = 1
  A saucy roughnes, and constraines the garb   1172
ROUND = *1
  *she grew round womb'd, and had indeede (Sir) a   17
ROUNDEST = *1
  Knigh. Sir, he answered me in the roundest manner, he | would not.   583
ROUZD = 1
  Bold in the quarrels right, rouz'd to th'encounter,   990
ROWLAND = 1
  Edg. Childe *Rowland* to the darke Tower came,   1966
ROYALL = 7
  Kent. Royall *Lear*, | Whom I haue euer honor'd as my King,   148
  Bur. Most Royall Maiesty, | I craue no more then hath your Highnesse
  offer'd,   210
  Bur. Pardon me Royall Sir, | Election makes not vp in such conditions. 225
  Bur. Royall King, | Giue but that portion which your selfe propos'd, 265
  Gent. You are a Royall one, and we obey you.   2643
  Cor. How does my Royall Lord? | How fares your Maiesty?   2792
  A Royall Noblenesse: I must embrace thee,   3138
ROYALTIE = *1
  *the Royaltie of her Father: draw you Rogue, or   1110
RUBD = 1
  Will not be rub'd nor stopt, Ile entreat for thee.   1230
RUDE = 1
  Alb. Oh *Gonerill*, | You are not worth the dust which the rude winde |
  Blowes in your face.   2301
RUFFIAN = *1
  Ste. This ancient Ruffian Sir, whose life I haue spar'd | at sute of his
  gray-beard.   1135
RUFFLE = 2
  Do sorely ruffle, for many Miles about | There's scarce a Bush.   1604
  You should not ruffle thus. What will you do?   2107
RUIND = 1
  Glou. O ruin'd peece of Nature, this great world | Shall so weare out to
  naught.   2577
RUINOUS = *1
  *treacherie, and all ruinous disorders follow vs disquietly   443
RULD = 1
  Of his confine: you should be rul'd, and led   1428

RULE = 3

(Since now we will diuest vs both of Rule,   54
By rule of Knight-hood, I disdaine and spurne: 3101
Rule in this Realme, and the gor'd state sustaine.   3295

RUMBLE = *1

*Lear. Rumble thy belly full: spit Fire, spowt Raine: 1669

RUN = 3*3

*run a certaine course: where, if you violently proceed a-|gainst   416
Lear. What seruices canst thou do? | *Kent. I can keepe honest
counsaile, ride, run, marre a   562
*Lear. And the Creature run from the Cur: there thou   2601
Nay, send in time. | Alb. Run, run, O run.   3204

RUNNES = 1

The knaue turnes Foole that runnes away,   1356

RUNNING = 1

You shall get it by running: Sa, sa, sa, sa. Exit.   2645

RUNS = *1

*let go thy hold when a great wheele runs downe a   1344

RUSTLING = *1

*Nor the rustling of Silkes, betray thy poore heart to wo-|man.   1875

S = *1

*Foole. Why to keepe ones eyes of either side 's nose,   896

SA = 4

You shall get it by running: Sa, sa, sa, sa. Exit.   2645

SACRED = 1

For by the sacred radience of the Sunne,   116

SACRIFICES = 1

Lear. Vpon such sacrifices my Cordelia, | The Gods themselues throw
Incense.   2961

SAD = 2

Kent. That from your first of difference and decay, | Haue follow'd your
sad steps.   3254
Edg. The waight of this sad time we must obey,   3298

SADDLE = 1

Saddle my horses: call my Traine together.   763

SAFE = 3

To haue found a safe redresse, but now grow fearefull   717
'Tis politike, and safe to let him keepe   · 844
What safe, and nicely I might well delay,   3100

SAFER = 2

Gon. Safer then trust too farre;   850
The safer sense will ne're accommodate | His Master thus.   2528

SAFETY = 2

To wage against thine enemies, nere feare to loose it, | Thy safety being
motiue.   167
As we shall find their merites, and our safety | May equally determine.   2987

SAID = 7*1

That iustly think'st, and hast most rightly said: 197
Remember what I haue said. | Ste. Well Madam.   523
And Regan with him, haue you nothing said   955
Glo. O strange and fastned Villaine, | Would he deny his Letter, said he?   1015
With fiue and twenty? Regan, said you so?   1552
He said it would be thus: poore banish'd man: 1944
Thou should'st haue said, good Porter turne the Key: 2136
*no, to euery thing that I said: I, and no too, was no good   2546

SAIES = 1*3

*honest, to conuerse with him that is wise and saies little, to   546

SAIES *cont.*
  Lear. What saies the Fellow there? Call the Clot-|pole   577
  Knigh. He saies my Lord, your Daughters is not well.   580
  Alb. He knowes not what he saies, and vaine is it | That we present vs
    to him.   3262
SAIST = 3
  Lear. Ha? Saist thou so?   592
  Bast. Himselfe, what saist thou to him? | *Edg.* Draw thy Sword,   3079
  What is't thou saist? Her voice was euer soft,   3236
SAKE = 2
  Glou. Get thee away: If for my sake   2228
  The one the other poison'd for my sake, | And after slew herselfe.   3197
SALLETS = *1
  *Cow-dung for Sallets; swallowes the old Rat, and the   1911
SALT = 1
  Why, this would make a man, a man of Salt   2639
SALUTATIONS = 1
  From *Gonerill* his Mistris, salutations;   1308
SAME = 5*1
  Cor. This is a Fellow of the selfe same colour,   1218
  Lear. Ile talke a word with this same lerned Theban: 1936
  Glou. When shall I come to th'top of that same hill?   2431
  My reason all the same, and they are ready   2995
  And these same crosses spoile me. Who are you?   3243
  Lear. This is a dull sight, are you not *Kent*? | *Kent.* The same: your
    Seruant *Kent,*   3247
SAMPIRE = 1
  Hangs one that gathers Sampire: dreadfull Trade: 2450
SANDS = 1
  And the exchange my Brother: heere, in the sands   2726
SARUM = 1
  Goose, if I had you vpon *Sarum* Plaine,   1156
SAT = *1
  Edg. Pillicock sat on Pillicock hill, alow: alow, loo, loo.   .1857
SATISFACTION = *1
  *assurance haue your satisfaction, and that without   425
SAUAGE = 1
  Bast. Most sauage and vnnaturall.   1758
SAUCY = 1
  A saucy roughnes, and constraines the garb   1172
SAUD = 2
  Led him, begg'd for him, sau'd him from dispaire.   3154
  I might haue sau'd her, now she's gone for euer: 3234
SAUE = 4*1
  Bast. Saue thee *Curan.*   928
  Saue what beates there, Filliall ingratitude,   1794
  *Could'st thou saue nothing? Would'st thou giue 'em all?   1845
  Alb. Saue him, saue him. *Alarums. Fights.*   3107
SAW = 4*1
  When saw you my Father last? | *Edg.* The night gone by.   474
  And when he saw my best alarum'd spirits   989
  Kent. Good King, that must approue the common saw,   1237
  I stumbled when I saw. Full oft 'tis seene,   2200
  I'th'last nights storme, I such a fellow saw;   2216
SAWCILY = 1*1
  *though this Knaue came somthing sawcily to the   24
  Displaid so sawcily against your Highnesse,   1317

SAY = 31*5

Which of you shall we say doth loue vs most,	56
Striue to be interest. What can you say, to draw	91
Why haue my Sisters Husbands, if they say	106
What say you to the Lady? Loue's not loue	261
Gon. Sister, it is not little I haue to say,	310
*I say, retire with me to my lodging, from whence I will	489
I will not speake with him, say I am sicke,	515
your face bids me, though you say nothing.	709
And hold our liues in mercy. *Oswald,* I say.	848
Brother, a word, discend; Brother I say,	949
Glost. How fell you out, say that?	1159
Lear. No.	*Kent.* Yes.	*Lear.* No I say.	*Kent.* I say yea.	1291
Lear. Say? How is that?	1419
Say you haue wrong'd her.	1432
Gent. Giue me your hand,	Haue you no more to say?	1648
Lear. No, I will be the patterne of all patience,	I will say nothing.	1689
Glo. Go too; say you nothing. There is diuision be-|tweene	1759
*You will say they are Persian; but let them bee	chang'd.	2037
Do me no foule play, Friends.	*Corn.* Binde him I say.	2094
I'ld say I had eyes againe.	2205
Edg. O Gods! Who is't can say I am at the worst?	2207
So long as we can say this is the worst.	2211
I tooke it for a man: often 'twould say	2523
*my Beard, ere the blacke ones were there. To say I, and	2545
*none, I say none, Ile able 'em; take that of me my Friend,	2611
Your (Wife, so I would say) affectio-|nate Seruant. Gonerill.	2722
To see another thus. I know not what to say:	2806
Will not beare question: either say thou'lt do't,	Or thriue by other	
meanes.	2976
Marke I say instantly, and carry it so	2980
A most Toad-spotted Traitor. Say thou no,	3093
And that thy tongue (some say) of breeding breathes,	3099
Gon. Say if I do, the Lawes are mine not thine,	3116
You looke as you had something more to say.	3165
My Master calls me, I must not say no.	3297
Speake what we feele, not what we ought to say:	3299

SAYES *see also* saies = 1*2

Be this perpetuall. What sayes our second Daughter?	72
Foole. A spirite, a spirite, he sayes his name's poore	*Tom.*	1823
*cold winde: Sayes suum, mun, nonny, Dolphin my Boy,	1879

SAYEST *see also* sai'st = 1

| Thou sayest the King growes mad, Ile tell thee Friend | 1945 |

SCAENA *l.*1751 2743 = 2

SCALD = 1

| Vpon a wheele of fire, that mine owne teares | Do scal'd, like molten | |
| Lead. | 2796 |

SCALDING = *1

| *there is the sulphurous pit; burning, scalding, stench, | 2570 |

SCANT = 2

| You lesse know how to value her desert, | Then she to scant her dutie. | 1417 |
| To bandy hasty words, to scant my sizes, | 1459 |

SCANTED = 2

| At Fortunes almes, you haue obedience scanted, | 304 |
| Deny'd me to come in) returne, and force | Their scanted curtesie. | 1720 |

SCAPE = 3

| Would not scape censure, nor the redresses sleepe, | 721 |

243

SCAPE *cont.*
All Ports Ile barre, the villaine shall not scape,　1018
Do's not attend my taking. Whiles I may scape　1256
SCARCE = 4
Stew. I am scarce in breath my Lord.　1126
I can scarce speake to thee, thou'lt not beleeue　1414
Do sorely ruffle, for many Miles about | There's scarce a Bush.　1604
The lesser is scarce felt. Thou'dst shun a Beare,　1789
SCARCELY = 2
Which scarcely keepes thee warme, but for true need:　1570
Which for they yet glance by, and scarcely bruise,　3104
SCARRD = *1
*poore Tom hath bin scarr'd out of his good wits. Blesse　2247
SCARSE = 3
Came then into my minde, and yet my minde | Was then scarse Friends
with him.　2218
Shew scarse so grosse as Beetles. Halfe way downe　2449
Gen. He's scarse awake,　2801
SCARSELY = 1
of your person, it would scarsely alay.　485
SCENA *see also* scaena, scoena *l.*333 505 529 873 926 1074 1614 1654
1776 1969 1996 2057 2177 2266 2348 2382 2429 2844 2917 2937 = 20
SCHOOLE = *1
Foole. Wee'l set thee to schoole to an Ant, to teach　1340
SCHOOLEMASTER = *1
*Pry'thy Nunckle keepe a Schoolemaster that can teach　692
SCHOOLE-MASTERS = 1
Must be their Schoole-Masters: shut vp your doores,　1608
SCOENA *l.*1 = 1
SCOPE = 1
But let his disposition haue that scope | As dotage giues it.　807
SCORE = 1
And thou shalt haue more, | Then two tens to a score.　656
SCORNFULL = 1
Into her scornfull eyes: Infect her Beauty,　1449
SCOURGD = *1
*reason it thus, and thus, yet Nature finds it selfe scourg'd　435
SCURUY = *1
*glasse-eyes, and like a scuruy Politician, seeme to see the　2613
SCYTHIAN = 1
Hold thee from this for euer. The barbarous *Scythian*,　123
SEA = 6
Bids the winde blow the Earth into the Sea,　1620
But if thy flight lay toward the roaring sea,　1790
The Sea, with such a storme as his bare head,　2131
As mad as the vext Sea, singing alowd.　2352
Hearke, do you heare the Sea? | *Glou.* No truly.　2435
Hornes wealk'd, and waued like the enraged Sea:　2516
SEALE = *1
*who haue the power to seale th'accusers lips. Get thee　2612
SEARCH = 1
Search euery Acre in the high-growne field,　2357
SEASON = *1
Reg. Thus out of season, thredding darke ey'd night,　1062
SEASONS = 1
From seasons such as these? O I haue tane　1813

SEA-MONSTER = 1
More hideous when thou shew'st thee in a Child, | Then the
Sea-monster.   772
SECOND = 1
Be this perpetuall. What sayes our second Daughter?   72
SECONDS = 1
Gent. You shall haue any thing. | *Lear.* No Seconds? All my selfe?   2637
SECRETS = 1
Cord. All blest Secrets, | All you vnpublish'd Vertues of the earth   2366
SECTS = 1
In a wall'd prison, packs and sects of great ones, | That ebbe and flow
by th'Moone.   2958
SECUNDA *l*.333 1074 1654 2266 2917 = 5
SECUNDUS *l*.926 = 1
SECURE = 1
Our meanes secure vs, and our meere defects   2201
SEE = 38*9
Kent. See better *Lear*, and let me still remaine | The true blanke of
thine eie.   170
Haue no such Daughter, nor shall euer see   288
Gon. You see how full of changes his age is, the ob- | seruation   314
*such neede to hide it selfe. Let's see: come, if it bee no- | thing, I shall
not neede Spectacles.   369
Glou. Let's see, let's see.   379
My practises ride easie: I see the businesse.   502
Fool. Shalt see thy other Daughter will vse thee kind- | ly,   888
This hurt you see, striuing to apprehend him.   1049
Then stands on any shoulder that I see | Before me, at this instant. 1168
*But Fathers that beare bags, shall see their children kind.   1324
Reg. I am glad to see your Highnesse.   1406
Wee'l no more meete, no more see one another.   1514
You see me heere (you Gods) a poore old man,   1572
What it containes. If you shall see *Cordelia*,   1643
Trey, Blanch, and Sweet-heart: see, they barke at me.   2021
Lear. Then let them Anatomize *Regan*: See what   2033
Reg. Wherefore to Douer? | *Glou.* Because I would not see thy cruell
Nailes   2127
All Cruels else subscribe: but I shall see   2137
Corn. If you see vengeance. | *Seru.* Hold your hand, my Lord: 2144
To see some mischefe on him. Oh.   2157
Corn. Lest it see more, preuent it; Out vilde gelly: 2158
Oldm. You cannot see your way.   2198
Might I but liue to see thee in my touch,   2204
That slaues your ordinance, that will not see   2253
Alb. See thy selfe diuell: 2308
Soone may I heare, and see him. *Exeunt*.   2381
When I do stare, see how the Subiect quakes.   2555
Glou. Were all thy Letters Sunnes, I could not see.   2584
*case, your purse in a light, yet you see how this world | goes.   2591
Glou. I see it feelingly.   2593
Lear. What, art mad? A man may see how this world   2594
*goes, with no eyes. Looke with thine eares: See how   2595
*glasse-eyes, and like a scuruy Politician, seeme to see the   2613
Let's see these Pockets; the Letters that he speakes of   2709
He had no other Deathsman. Let vs see: 2711·
To see another thus. I know not what to say: 2806
I will not sweare these are my hands: let's see,   2807

SEE *cont.*

You see is kill'd in him: desire him to go in,	2838
Shall neuer see his pardon: for my state,	2915
Shall we not see these Daughters, and these Sisters?	2947
Weele see 'em staru'd first: come. *Exit.*	2968
Kent. No my good Lord, I am the very man. | *Lear.* Ile see that straight.	3252
The cup of their deseruings: O see, see.	3276
Do you see this? Looke on her? Looke her lips,	3282
Shall neuer see so much, nor liue so long. | *Exeunt with a dead March.* | FINIS.	3301

SEEING = 1

Seeing how lothly opposite I stood	985

SEEK = *1

Corn. Edmund farewell: go seek the Traitor Gloster,	2082

SEEKE = 9*8

Glou. Why so earnestly seeke you to put vp y Letter?	363
*Villaine; worse then brutish: Go sirrah, seeke him: Ile	411
Glou. He cannot bee such a Monster. *Edmond* seeke	427
Bast. I will seeke him Sir, presently: conuey the bu-|sinesse	431
To make thee seeke it. *Tucket within.*	1014
Reg. What, did my Fathers Godsonne seeke your life?	1030
I will go seeke the King.	1647
Lear. Prythee go in thy selfe, seeke thine owne ease,	1804
Kent. Who's there? What is't you seeke?	1906
Yet haue I ventured to come seeke you out,	1930
His Daughters seeke his death: Ah, that good Kent,	1943
*Brothers euill disposition made him seeke his death: but	1976
*seeke out where thy Father is, that hee may bee | ready for our apprehension.	1988
*him this Letter, the Army of France is landed: seeke out | the Traitor Glouster.	2061
In the Goodmans desires: seeke, seeke for him,	2369
To *Edmund* Earle of Glouster: seeke him out	2702

SEEKES = 1

That Sir, which serues and seekes for gaine,	1350

SEEKING = 1

From this enormous State, seeking to giue	1246

SEEME = 4*3

Duke of *Albany*, then *Cornwall.* | *Glou.* It did alwayes seeme so to vs: But	5
Kent. I do professe to be no lesse then I seeme; to serue	544
Draw, seeme to defend your selfe, | Now quit you well.	961
Reg. I pray you Father being weake, seeme so.	1494
Thron'd and set high; Seruants, who seeme no lesse,	1632
*glasse-eyes, and like a scuruy Politician, seeme to see the	2613
For him that brought it: wretched though I seeme,	2886

SEEMES = 4

This seemes a faire deseruing, and must draw me	1773
What most he should dislike, seemes pleasant to him; | What like, offensiue.	2277
Proper deformitie seemes not in the Fiend | So horrid as in woman.	2309
Me thinkes he seemes no bigger then his head.	2451

SEEMING = 2

If ought within that little seeming substance,	216
That vnder couert, and conuenient seeming	1709

SEENE = 7*3
*seene the best of our time. Machinations, hollownesse,   442
*you what I haue seene, and heard: But faintly. Nothing   495
*I will looke further intoo't: but where's my Foole? I | haue not seene
him this two daies.   600
Of my more fierce endeauour. I haue seene drunkards   967
I haue seene better faces in my Time,   1167
Intelligent of our State. What hath bin seene,   1634
I stumbled when I saw. Full oft 'tis seene,   2200
Cannot be seene, or heard: Do but looke vp.   2501
*the Iustice, which is the theefe: Thou hast seene a Far-|mers   2598
I haue seene the day, with my good biting Faulchion   3241
SEES = 1*1
Peruse this Letter. Nothing almost sees miracles   1242
*his Sonne: for hee's a mad Yeoman that sees his Sonne a | Gentleman
before him.   2011
SEEST = 1
Seest thou this obiect *Kent*? | *Kent*. Alacke, why thus?   3194
SEET = 1*1
Then comes the time, who liues to see't,   1747
Corn. See't shalt thou neuer. Fellowes hold y Chaire,   2139
SEIZE = 2
Thee and thy vertues here I seize vpon,   277
Nature's of such deepe trust, we shall much need: | You we first seize
on.   1057
SELFE = 32*7
My selfe an enemy to all other ioyes,   78
*That troope with Maiesty. Our selfe by Monthly course,   140
Bur. Royall King, | Giue but that portion which your selfe propos'd,   265
*such neede to hide it selfe. Let's see: come, if it bee no-|thing, I shall
not neede Spectacles.   369
*after your owne wisedome. I would vnstate my | selfe, to be in a due
resolution.   429
*reason it thus, and thus, yet Nature finds it selfe scourg'd   435
Edg. Do you busie your selfe with that?   471
Bast. Bethink your selfe wherein you may haue offen-|ded   481
May carry through it selfe to that full issue   533
*my selfe, there's mine, beg another of thy | Daughters.   638
*gau'st thy golden one away; if I speake like my selfe in   678
By what your selfe too late haue spoke and done,   718
Then a grac'd Pallace. The shame it selfe doth speake   755
Gon. Neuer afflict your selfe to know more of it: 806
This weaues it selfe perforce into my businesse,   944
Vpon his partie 'gainst the Duke of *Albany*? | Aduise your selfe.   956
Draw, seeme to defend your selfe, | Now quit you well.   961
So much commend it selfe, you shall be ours,   1056
Cor. This is a Fellow of the selfe same colour,   1218
Edg. I heard my selfe proclaim'd,   1252
Better then you your selfe: therefore I pray you,   1430
I am cold my selfe. Where is this straw, my | Fellow?   1724
Lear. Prythee go in thy selfe, seeke thine owne ease,   1804
Expose thy selfe to feele what wretches feele,   1815
*sophisticated. Thou art the thing it selfe; vnaccommo-|dated   1886
I am almost mad my selfe. I had a Sonne,   1946
Ang'ring it selfe, and others. Blesse thee Master.   2225
Alb. See thy selfe diuell: 2308
Burne it selfe out. If *Edgar* liue, O blesse him: 2479

SELFE *cont*.
The Treasury of life, when life it selfe	2483
Is wretchednesse depriu'd that benefit | To end it selfe by death? 'Twas yet some comfort,	2503
Glou. I do remember now: henceforth Ile beare | Affliction, till it do cry out it selfe	2520
Gent. You shall haue any thing. | *Lear*. No Seconds? All my selfe?	2637
Breefely thy selfe remember: the Sword is out | That must destroy thee.	2679
My selfe could else out-frowne false Fortunes frowne.	2946
And call it selfe your Brother. | *Gon*. Not so hot:	3006
Alb. Where haue you hid your selfe?	3142
Neuer (O fault) reueal'd my selfe vnto him,	3155
To lay the blame vpon her owne dispaire, | That she for-did her selfe.	3213

SELFEREPROUING = 1
And selfereprouing, bring his constant pleasure.	2850

SELFE-METTLE = 1
Reg. I am made of that selfe-mettle as my Sister,	74

SELFE-SAME *see* selfe

SELFE-SUBDUED = 1
For him attempting, who was selfe-subdued,	1198

SELUES = 2
Whereto our health is bound, we are not our selues,	1383
Allow Obedience; if you your selues are old,	1481

SEMBLANCE = 1
Into a mad-mans rags, t'assume a semblance	3150

SENCES = 1
Doth from my sences take all feeling else,	1793

SEND = 8
I will send farre and neere, that all the kingdome	1020
And not send backe my Messengers.	1275
Make it your cause: Send downe, and take my part.	1482
In our sustaining Corne. A Centery send forth;	2356
Bast. Sir, I thought it fit, | To send the old and miserable King to some retention,	2989
Despight of mine owne Nature. Quickly send,	3201
Nay, send in time. | *Alb*. Run, run, O run.	3204
Send thy token of repreeue.	3207

SENNET = *1
*Sennet. Enter King Lear, Cornwall, Albany, Gonerill, Re-|gan, Cordelia, and attendants.	37

SENSE = 5
Which the most precious square of sense professes,	79
Pierce euerie sense about thee. Old fond eyes,	820
In the restoring his bereaued Sense; he that helpes him,	2359
The safer sense will ne're accommodate | His Master thus.	2528
How stiffe is my vilde sense | That I stand vp, and haue ingenious feeling	2733

SENSES = 2
Edg. Why then your other Senses grow imperfect | By your eyes anguish.	2437
Th'vntun'd and iarring senses, O winde vp, | Of this childe-changed Father.	2765

SENT = 3*2
**world before he was sent for: yet was his Mother fayre,	25
On whose imployment I was sent to you,	1208
Reg. To whose hands | You haue sent the Lunaticke King: Speake.	2113
Corn. Where hast thou sent the King? | *Glou*. To Douer.	2120

248

SENT *cont.*

  *Which do command them. With him I sent the Queen: 2994
SENTENCES = 1

  To come betwixt our sentences, and our power,   184
SENTRY *see* centery
SEPTIMA *l.*2057 2743 = 2
SEPULCHRING = 1

  Sepulchring an Adultresse. O are you free?   1410
SEQUENT = *1

  *by the sequent effects. Loue cooles, friendship falls off,   436
SER = 1*1
SERIOUS = 1*1

  Edg. How now Brother *Edmond,* what serious con- | templation are you
in?   467
  Reg. Faith he is poasted hence on serious matter: 2393
SERPENT = 1

  This guilded Serpent: for your claime faire Sisters,   3029
SERPENTS = 1

  How sharper then a Serpents tooth it is,   802
SERPENT-LIKE = 1

  Most Serpent-like, vpon the very Heart.   1443
SERU = 1*1
SERUANT *see also Ser., Seru.* = 7*1

  Is practise only. Giue me my Seruant forth;   1391
  Lear. Who stockt my Seruant? *Regan,* I haue good hope   1477
  Into my Husbands hands. This trustie Seruant   2286
  Slaine by his Seruant, going to put out | The other eye of Glouster.   2314
  Mes. A Seruant that he bred, thrill'd with remorse,   2317
  Your (*Wife, so I would say*) affectio- |*nate Seruant.* Gonerill.   2722
  Lear. This is a dull sight, are you not *Kent?* | *Kent.* The same: your
Seruant *Kent,*   3247
  Where is your Seruant *Caius?*   3249
SERUANTS = 9

  Gon. You strike my people, and your disorder'd rable, | make Seruants
of their Betters.   766
  Enter Gloster, and Seruants with Torches.   970
  Enter Bastard, Cornewall, Regan, Gloster, Seruants.   1117
  Enter Cornewall, Regan, Gloster, Seruants.   1403
  From those that she cals Seruants, or from mine?   1540
  Thron'd and set high; Seruants, who seeme no lesse,   1632
  Enter Cornwall, Regan, Gonerill, Bastard, | *and Seruants.*   2058
  Enter Gloucester, and Seruants.   2088
  Enter Lear in a chaire carried by Seruants   2771
SERUD = 1*1

  *curl'd my haire, wore Gloues in my cap; seru'd the Lust   1866
  I haue seru'd you euer since I was a Childe: 2146
SERUE = 7*2

  Edm. I do serue you in this businesse: 498
  If thou canst serue where thou dost stand condemn'd,   535
  Kent. I do professe to be no lesse then I seeme; to serue   544
  Lear. Who wouldst thou serue? | *Kent.* You.   555
  Lear. Follow me, thou shalt serue me, if I like thee no   571
  Bast. I shall serue you Sir truely, how euer else.   1059
  Glo. I serue you Madam, | Your Graces are right welcome. *Exeunt.*
Flourish.   1072
  Call not your Stocks for me, I serue the King.   1207

SERUE *cont.*
When time shall serue, let but the Herald cry, | And Ile appeare againe.
Exit.   2893
SERUES = 1
That Sir, which serues and seekes for gaine,   1350
SERUICE = 4*2
King, thou art poore enough. What wouldst thou? | *Kent.* Seruice.   553
Lear. Now my friendly knaue I thanke thee, there's | earnest of thy
seruice.   622
*would'st be a Baud in way of good seruice, and art no-|thing   1093
The deere Father | *Would with his Daughter speake, commands, tends,
ser-|(uice,   1377
But better seruice haue I neuer done you, | Then now to bid you hold.   2147
And of the loyall Seruice of his Sonne   2274
SERUICEABLE = 1*1
*action-taking, whoreson glasse-gazing super-seruiceable   1091
Edg. I know thee well. A seruiceable Villaine,   2704
SERUICES = 5
Edm. My seruices to your Lordship.   32
My seruices are bound, wherefore should I   336
If you come slacke of former seruices,   516
Lear. What seruices canst thou do? | *Kent.* I can keepe honest
counsaile, ride, run, marre a   562
To thee a Womans seruices are due, | My Foole vsurpes my body.   2296
SERUILE = 1
But yet I call you Seruile Ministers,   1676
SERUINGMAN = *1
Lear. What hast thou bin? | *Edg.* A Seruingman? Proud in heart, and
minde; that   1864
SERUST = 1
Lear. I thanke thee fellow. | Thou seru'st me, and Ile loue thee.   617
SESE = *1
*Do, de, de, de: sese: Come, march to Wakes and Fayres,   2031
SESEY = 1
Boy *Sesey*: let him trot by. *Storme still.*   1880
SESSA *see* sese, sesey
SESSION = 1
Where you shall hold your Session.   2997
SET = 14*5
I lou'd her most, and thought to set my rest   131
Set lesse then thou throwest;   653
My Father hath set guard to take my Brother,   945
Stew. Where may we set our horses? | *Kent.* I'th'myre.   1078
Lear. What's he, | That hath so much thy place mistooke | To set thee
heere?   1286
Foole. And thou hadst beene set i'th' Stockes for that   1337
Foole. Wee'l set thee to schoole to an Ant, to teach   1340
Corn. Haile to your Grace. *Kent here set at liberty.*   1405
Corn. I set him there, Sir: but his owne Disorders   1491
Thron'd and set high; Seruants, who seeme no lesse,   1632
*in his Pue, set Rats-bane by his Porredge, made him   1836
*with mans sworne Spouse: set not thy Sweet-heart on | proud array.
Tom's a cold.   1862
*a prouoking merit set a-worke by a reprouable badnesse | in himselfe.   1977
Glou. I haue a Letter guessingly set downe   2115
Vpon these eyes of thine, Ile set my foote.   2140
Reg. But are my Brothers Powres set forth? | *Stew.* I Madam.   2384

SET *cont.*

Reg. Our troopes set forth to morrow, stay with vs: | The wayes are
dangerous. 2401
Glou. Set me where you stand. 2460
As I haue set it downe. *Exit Captaine.* 2981
SETLING = 1
Trouble him no more till further setling. 2839
SETS = 1
That sets vs all at ods: Ile not endure it; 512
SEUEN = 1*2
*the seuen Starres are no mo then seuen, is a pretty reason. 909
Haue bin Toms food, for seuen long yeare: 1918
SEUERALL = 2
Our daughters seuerall Dowers, that future strife 49
To answere from our home: the seuerall Messengers 1067
SEUERALLY = 3
Enter Bastard, and Curan, seuerally. 927
Enter Kent, and Steward seuerally. 1075
Storme still. Enter Kent, and a Gentleman, seuerally. 1615
SEUERD = 1
So should my thoughts be seuer'd from my greefes, | *Drum afarre off.* 2736
SEXTA *l.*1996 = 1
SHADOW = 2*1
Who is it that can tell me who I am? | *Foole. Lears* shadow. 743
*incht Bridges, to course his owne shadow for a Traitor. 1838
Edg. Heere Father, take the shadow of this Tree 2921
SHADOWIE = 1
With shadowie Forrests, and with Champains rich'd 69
SHAFT = *1
Le. The bow is bent & drawne, make from the shaft. 152
SHAKE = 6*2
To shake all Cares and Businesse from our Age, 44
*gap in your owne Honor, and shake in peeces, the heart of 418
That thou hast power to shake my manhood thus, 815
That art Incestuous. Caytiffe, to peeces shake 1708
That thou maist shake the superflux to them, 1816
I'ld shake it on this quarrell. What do you meane? 2151
Shake patiently my great affliction off: 2475
*Forkes presages Snow; that minces Vertue, & do's shake 2564
SHAKING = *1
*Sindge my white head. And thou all-shaking Thunder, 1661
SHAL *l.**41 *1585 *1746 = *3
SHALBE = 2
What they are yet, I know not, but they shalbe 1581
That going shalbe vs'd with feet. 1748
SHALL *l.*34 *35 40 56 *67 107 108 110 125 142 143 156 193 274 288 *306
331 355 371 376 *413 *424 432 *444 497 517 537 672 711 759 826 *878
*885 924 994 998 1018 1052 1056 1057 1059 1209 1213 1232 1245 *1324
1455 1499 1580 1586 1643 1644 *1683 1685 *1749 1771 1811 *2070 2086
2137 2263 2265 2279 2287 2431 2578 2635 2637 2645 2746 2861 2893
2904 2908 2915 2947 2964 2966 2967 2987 2997 3105 3106 3113 3164
3270 3274 3301 = 76*12
SHALLOW = *1
*base, proud, shallow, beggerly, three-suited-hundred 1089
SHALT *l.**571 656 827 *888 *1326 1454 *1994 *2050 2099 *2139
2557 = 5*6

SHAMD = 1
  Foole. Nay, he reseru'd a Blanket, else we had bin all | sham'd.   1846
SHAME = 7
  Who couers faults, at last with shame derides: 307
  Which else were shame, that then necessitie | Will call discreet
  proceeding.   724
  Then a grac'd Pallace. The shame it selfe doth speake   755
  Glo. O Lady, Lady, shame would haue it hid.   1032
  Lear. Ha? Mak'st thou this shame thy pastime? | *Kent*. No my Lord.   1280
  The shame which heere it suffers.   1321
  Let shame come when it will, I do not call it,   1520
SHAMEFULL = 1
  This shamefull lodging. Fortune goodnight,   1249
SHANKS = *1
  *Ile so carbonado your shanks, draw you Rascall, come | your waies.   1111
SHAPE = 4
  Hee'l shape his old course, in a Country new. *Exit*.   201
  My minde as generous, and my shape as true   342
  That Ile resume the shape which thou dost thinke | I haue cast off for
  euer. *Exit*   828
  To take the basest, and most poorest shape   1258
SHARPE = 1*2
  Bast. Here stood he in the dark, his sharpe Sword out,   972
  Necessities sharpe pinch. Returne with her?   1504
  *sharpe Hauthorne blow the windes. Humh, goe to thy | bed and warme
  thee.   1828
SHARPER = 1
  How sharper then a Serpents tooth it is,   802
SHARPE-TOOTHD = 1
  Sharpe-tooth'd vnkindnesse, like a vulture heere,   1413
SHE *see also* shee, shee'l, shee's, she's = 34*6
SHEALD = 1
  Weary of all, shall want some. That's a sheal'd Pescod.   711
SHEE *l*.*1686 = *1
SHEEL = 1
  Shee'l flea thy Woluish visage. Thou shalt finde,   827
SHEEPE = *1
  *the Worme no Silke; the Beast, no Hide; the Sheepe, no   1884
SHEEPS-COATES = 1
  Poore pelting Villages, Sheeps-Coates, and Milles,   1269
SHEES = 1
  Shee's there, and she is yours. | *Bur*. I know no answer.   219
SHEETS = 2
  Such sheets of Fire, such bursts of horrid Thunder,   1698
  Then my Daughters got 'tweene the lawfull sheets.   2561
SHELL = 1
  Foole. Can'st tell how an Oyster makes his shell? | *Lear*. No.   899
SHELTER = 1
  The Gods to their deere shelter take thee Maid,   196
SHES = 5*1
  *for though she's as like this, as a Crabbe's like an | Apple, yet I can
  tell what I can tell.   889
  Alb. Go after her, she's desperate, gouerne her.   3120
  Gen. 'Tis hot, it smoakes, it came euen from the heart | of--- O she's
  dead.   3174
  That Heauens vault should crack: she's gone for euer.   3219
  She's dead as earth: Lend me a Looking-glasse,   3221

SHES *cont*.
I might haue sau'd her, now she's gone for euer: 3234
SHEW = 5*1
    How vgly did'st thou in *Cordelia* shew?   780
    (As feare not but you shall) shew her this Ring,   1644
    And shew the Heauens more iust.   1817
    Corn. Poste speedily to my Lord your husband, shew   2060
    Stew. Would I could meet Madam, I should shew | What party I do
    follow.   2426
    Shew scarse so grosse as Beetles. Halfe way downe   2449
SHEWD = 1*1
    When I haue shew'd th'vnfitnesse.   855
    Alb. Sir, you haue shew'd to day your valiant straine   2983
SHEWDST = 1
    Alb. Glouster, I liue | To thanke thee for the loue thou shew'dst the
    King,   2344
SHEWED = 1
    Ere I was risen from the place, that shewed   1305
SHEWES = 2
    Shewes like a riotous Inne; Epicurisme and Lust   753
    Alb. This shewes you are aboue | You Iustices, that these our neather
    crimes   2323
SHEWNE = 1
    Edmund, I heare that you haue shewne your Father | A Child-like
    Office.   1045
SHEWST = 1
    More hideous when thou shew'st thee in a Child, | Then the
    Sea-monster.   772
SHIELD = 1
    To shield thee from disasters of the world,   188
SHIFT = 1
    Rather then die at once) taught me to shift   3149
SHINES = *1
    *for though it be night, yet the Moone shines, Ile make a   1104
SHIRTS = 1
    *stockt, punish'd, and imprison'd: who hath three Suites | to his backe,
    sixe shirts to his body: 1914
SHIUERD = 1
    Thou'dst shiuer'd like an Egge: but thou do'st breath: 2493
SHOD = 1
    Foole. Then I prythee be merry, thy wit shall not go | slip-shod. | *Lear*.
    Ha, ha, ha.   885
SHOLD *l*.*415 *1684 = *2
SHOO = 1
    It were a delicate stratagem to shoo | A Troope of Horse with Felt: Ile
    put't in proofe,   2626
SHOOES = *1
    *in madnes, Lyon in prey. Let not the creaking of shooes,   1874
SHOOTE = 1
    I do not bid the Thunder-bearer shoote,   1521
SHORT = 4
    Onely she comes too short, that I professe   77
    Reg. If it be true, all vengeance comes too short   1027
    My life will be too short, | And euery measure faile me.   2748
    In short, and musty straw? Alacke, alacke,   2788
SHORTENS = 1
    Yet to be knowne shortens my made intent,   2757

SHORTER = 1
  Shall not be a Maid long, vnlesse things be cut shorter. | *Exeunt.*   924
SHORTLY = 1*1
  *colde shortly, there take my Coxcombe; why this fellow   631
  Kent. I haue a iourney Sir, shortly to go,   3296
SHOULD *see also* shold *l.*237 244 280 336 *388 *390 *407 *459 470 690
  720 749 817 839 1007 *1145 *1188 1216 1223 *1274 1389 1428 1534
  1537 1795 1854 2107 2223 2255 2277 2405 2426 2478 2736 2785 2805
  2819 *3012 3016 3097 3219 3278 = 34*8
SHOULDER = 1
  Then stands on any shoulder that I see | Before me, at this instant.   1168
SHOULDST *l.*916 1408 2052 2136 = 3*1
SHOW *see also* shew = 1
  You shall doe small respects, show too bold malice   1209
SHOWD *see* shew'd
SHOWDST *see* shew'dst
SHOWED *see* shewed
SHOWES *see* shewes
SHOWEST = 1
  Foole. Marke it Nuncle; | Haue more then thou showest,   647
SHOWNE *see* shewne
SHOWST *see* shew'st
SHRILL-GORGD = 1
  Looke vp a height, the shrill-gorg'd Larke so farre   2500
SHUN = 2
  The lesser is scarce felt. Thou'dst shun a Beare,   1789
  O that way madnesse lies, let me shun that: | No more of that.   1801
SHUT = 3*1
  Must be their Schoole-Masters: shut vp your doores,   1608
  Cor. Shut vp your doores my Lord, 'tis a wil'd night,   1612
  To shut me out? Poure on, I will endure: 1798
  Alb. Shut your mouth Dame,   3112
SICKE = 4*1
  *when we are sicke in fortune, often the surfets of our own   448
  I will not speake with him, say I am sicke,   515
  They are sicke, they are weary,   1362
  Reg. Sicke, O sicke. | *Gon.* If not, Ile nere trust medicine.   3043
SICKLY = 2
  To take the indispos'd and sickly fit,   1387
  Dwels in the sickly grace of her he followes.   1473
SICKNESSE = 1
  Regan. My sicknesse growes vpon me.   3055
SIDE = 5*1
  Foole. Why to keepe ones eyes of either side 's nose,   896
  Reg. One side will mocke another: Th'other too.   2143
  And told me I had turn'd the wrong side out: 2276
  And hardly shall I carry out my side,   2908
  To plucke the common bosome on his side,   2992
  But since thy out-side lookes so faire and Warlike,   3098
SIDES = 2*1
  *wit o'both sides, and left nothing i'th'middle; heere | comes one o'the
  parings.   700
  Lear. O sides, you are too tough!   1488
  How shall your House-lesse heads, and vnfed sides,   1811
SIDE-PIERCING = 1
  Edg. O thou side-piercing sight!   2532

SIGHE = *1

*my Cue is villanous Melancholly, with a sighe like *Tom*   464
SIGHT = 11

Deerer then eye-sight, space, and libertie,   61
On her kind nursery. Hence and auoid my sight: 132
Lear. Out of my sight.   169
Out Varlet, from my sight.   1474
Almost too small for sight. The murmuring Surge,   2455
Least my braine turne, and the deficient sight | Topple downe headlong.   2458
Edg. O thou side-piercing sight!   2532
Do's letcher in my sight. Let Copulation thriue: 2559
Gent. A sight most pittifull in the meanest wretch,   2646
With this vngracious paper strike the sight   2729
Lear. This is a dull sight, are you not *Kent?* | *Kent.* The same: your
Seruant *Kent,*   3247
SIGHTS = 1

Glou. O you mighty Gods! | This world I do renounce, and in your
sights   2473
SILENT = *2

Cor. What shall *Cordelia* speake? Loue, and be silent.   67
*mistaken, for my duty cannot be silent, when I thinke | your Highnesse
wrong'd.   594
SILKE = *1

*the Worme no Silke; the Beast, no Hide; the Sheepe, no   1884
SILKES = *1

*Nor the rustling of Silkes, betray thy poore heart to wo- | man.   1875
SILLABLE = 1

deny'st the least sillable of thy addition.   1097
SILLY-DUCKING = 1

Then twenty silly-ducking obseruants,   1178
SIMPLE = 1*1

Reg. Be simple answer'd, for we know the truth.   2110
*yond Iustice railes vpon yond simple theefe. Hearke in   2596
SIMPLES = 1

Are many Simples operatiue, whose power | Will close the eye of
Anguish.   2364
SIMPRING = *1

*Behold yond simpring Dame, whose face betweene her   2563
SIMULAR = 1

Thou Periur'd, and thou Simular of Vertue   1707
SINCE = 10*5

(Since now we will diuest vs both of Rule,   54
Cor. Then poore *Cordelia,* | And yet not so, since I am sure my loue's   82
To speake and purpose not, since what I will intend,   247
Since that respect and Fortunes are his loue,   273
Knight. Since my young Ladies going into *France*   602
Foole. I haue vsed it Nunckle, ere since thou mad'st   685
Corn. How now my Noble friend, since I came hither   1025
*thou knowest me? Is it two dayes since I tript vp thy   1102
*againe, I would haue none but knaues follow it, since a | Foole giues
it.   1348
And make them keepe their Caues: Since I was man,   1697
I haue seru'd you euer since I was a Childe: 2146
I haue heard more since: 2220
But not without that harmefull stroke, which since | Hath pluckt him
after.   2321
Or whether since he is aduis'd by ought   2848

SINCE *cont.*
But since thy out-side lookes so faire and Warlike, 3098
SINCERE = 1 1180
Kent. Sir, in good faith, in sincere verity,
SINDGE = *1 1661
*Sindge my white head. And thou all-shaking Thunder,
SING = 2
We two alone will sing like Birds i'th'Cage: 2949
And pray, and sing, and tell old tales, and laugh 2952
SINGING = 1*1
Lear. How old art thou? | *Kent.* Not so young Sir to loue a woman for
singing, 567
As mad as the vext Sea, singing alowd. 2352
SINGLE = 1
Trust to thy single vertue, for thy Souldiers 3052
SINND = 1
These dreadfull Summoners grace. I am a man, | More sinn'd against,
then sinning. 1712
SINNES = *1
*and Furr'd gownes hide all. Place sinnes with Gold, and 2608
SINNING = 1
These dreadfull Summoners grace. I am a man, | More sinn'd against,
then sinning. 1712
SIR *see also* zir *l.*12 *16 *17 *22 34 *60 176 215 225 *227 *371 375 *431
541 *558 *568 *583 603 *606 607 *619 712 715 746 770 774 812 834 929
942 950 976 *978 984 1047 1059 *1131 *1135 1143 1166 1180 *1186
1206 1217 *1231 1331 1416 1421 1426 *1438 1447 1466 *1485 1491 1511
1528 1533 1606 1626 1694 1850 1952 2016 *2035 *2046 2108 2233 2445
2469 2481 2486 2488 2600 2631 2650 2651 2652 2659 2662 2667 2798
2810 2835 2866 2925 2931 *2983 2989 2998 3113 3177 3281 3296 =
72*23, 1
That Sir, which serues and seekes for gaine, 1350
SIRHA = 1
Foole. Sirha, Ile teach thee a speech. | *Lear.* Do. 645
SIRRA = 1
Glou. Take him you on. | *Kent.* Sirra, come on: go along with vs. 1962
SIRRAH = 5*3
*Villaine; worse then brutish: Go sirrah, seeke him: Ile 411
*my Foole hither. You you Sirrah, where's my Daughter? 574
Foole. Sirrah, you were best take my Coxcombe. 627
Lear. Take heed Sirrah, the whip. 640
Le. When were you wont to be so full of Songs sirrah? 684
Lear. And you lie sirrah, wee'l haue you whipt. 694
Cor. Peace sirrah, | You beastly knaue, know you no reuerence? 1141
Glou. Sirrah, naked fellow. 2240
SISTER = 25*4
Reg. I am made of that selfe-mettle as my Sister, 74
And like a Sister am most loth to call 295
Gon. Sister, it is not little I haue to say, 310
*lou'd our Sister most, and with what poore iudgement he 316
If he distaste it, let him to my Sister, 521
*so, Ile write straight to my Sister to hold my course; pre-|pare for
dinner. *Exeunt.* 527
What he hath vtter'd I haue writ my Sister: 853
What haue you writ that Letter to my Sister? | *Stew.* I Madam. 858
I haue this present euening from my Sister 1040
Our Father he hath writ, so hath our Sister, 1065

SISTER *cont.*

Reg. The Messengers from our Sister, and the King? 1124
Our Sister speakes of. Come, bring away the Stocks. 1219
Reg. My Sister may recieue it much more worsse, 1225
Reg. I cannot thinke my Sister in the least 1420
That to our Sister, you do make returne, 1431
Returne you to my Sister. | *Lear.* Neuer *Regan*: 1439
You will returne and soiourne with my Sister, 1496
For your fit welcome, giue eare Sir to my Sister, 1528
*you our Sister company: the reuenges wee are bound to 2066
*Postes shall be swift, and intelligent betwixt vs. Fare-|well deere
Sister, farewell my Lord of Glouster. 2070
Gon. Farewell sweet Lord, and Sister. *Exit* 2081
Plucke out his poore old eyes: nor thy fierce Sister, 2129
This Leter Madam, craues a speedy answer: | 'Tis from your Sister. 2328
Your Sister is the better Souldier. 2388
Do you not loue my Sister? | *Bast.* In honour'd Loue. 2856
Alb. Our very louing Sister, well be-met: 2865
Reg. Sister you'le go with vs? | *Gon.* No. 2875
Exasperates, makes mad her Sister *Gonerill*, 2907
Gen. Your Lady Sir, your Lady; and her Sister | By her is poyson'd: she
confesses it. 3177
SISTERS = 13

A third, more opilent then your Sisters? speake. 92
Why haue my Sisters Husbands, if they say 106
Sure I shall neuer marry like my Sisters. 110
Fra. Bid farwell to your Sisters. 292
Thy Sisters naught: oh *Regan*, she hath tied 1412
Reg. I know't, my Sisters: this approues her Letter, 1470
Reg. What might import my Sisters Letter to him? | *Stew.* I know not,
Lady. 2391
Repaire those violent harmes, that my two Sisters | Haue in thy
Reuerence made. 2778
I know you do not loue me, for your Sisters 2830
Reg. Our Sisters man is certainely miscarried. | *Bast.* 'Tis to be doubted
Madam. 2851
Bast. To both these Sisters haue I sworne my loue: 2902
Shall we not see these Daughters, and these Sisters? 2947
This guilded Serpent: for your claime faire Sisters, 3029
SIT = 3*1

*France and him, pray you let vs sit together, if our 328
As I haue life and Honour, there shall he sit till Noone. 1213
Should he sit heere? This act perswades me, 1389
Edg. Sit you downe Father: rest you. 2708
SITH = 1*1

**Kent.* Fare thee well King, sith thus thou wilt appeare, 194
Yea, or so many? Sith that both charge and danger, 1535
SITS = *1

*nay, & thou canst not smile as the wind sits, thou'lt catch 630
SIX = 1

Some fiue or six and thirty of his Knights 2075
SIXE = 1

*stockt, punish'd, and imprison'd: who hath three Suites | to his backe,
sixe shirts to his body: 1914
SIXT = 1

And on the sixt to turne thy hated backe 189

SIZES = 1
　　To bandy hasty words, to scant my sizes,　　　　　　　　　　　1459
SKIE = 1
　　The Windes, and persecutions of the skie;　　　　　　　　　　1263
SKIES = 1*1
　　Loue not such nights as these: The wrathfull Skies　　　　　　1695
　　*with thy vncouer'd body, this extremitie of the Skies. Is　　　1882
SKILL = 1
　　What place this is: and all the skill I haue　　　　　　　　　2821
SKIN = 1
　　Inuades vs to the skin so: 'tis to thee,　　　　　　　　　　1787
SKIP = 1
　　I would haue made him skip: I am old now,　　　　　　　　　3242
SKIRTED = 1
　　With plenteous Riuers, and wide-skirted Meades　　　　　　　70
SLACKE = 2
　　If you come slacke of former seruices,　　　　　　　　　　　516
　　If then they chanc'd to slacke ye,　　　　　　　　　　　　1542
SLAINE = 1*2
　　*Ser. Oh I am slaine: my Lord, you haue one eye left　　　　　2156
　　Slaine by his Seruant, going to put out | The other eye of Glouster.　2314
　　*Stew. Slaue thou hast slaine me: Villain, take my purse;　　　2699
SLANDERS = 1
　　When Slanders do not liue in Tongues;　　　　　　　　　　1742
SLAUE = 8*5
　　*Lear. Why came not the slaue backe to me when I | call'd him?　581
　　*Lear. My Ladies Father? my Lords knaue, you whor-|son dog, you
　　slaue, you curre.　　　　　　　　　　　　　　　　　　610
　　*finicall Rogue, one Trunke-inheriting slaue, one that　　　　1092
　　*Kent. Strike you slaue: stand rogue, stand you neat | slaue, strike.　1114
　　*Kent. That such a slaue as this should weare a Sword,　　　　1145
　　Lear. This is a Slaue, whose easie borrowed pride　　　　　　1472
　　Perswade me rather to be slaue and sumpter | To this detested groome.　1509
　　Your horrible pleasure. Heere I stand your Slaue,　　　　　　1674
　　Turne out that eyelesse Villaine: throw this Slaue　　　　　　2174
　　Stew. Let go Slaue, or thou dy'st.　　　　　　　　　　　2689
　　*Stew. Slaue thou hast slaine me: Villain, take my purse;　　　2699
　　I kill'd the Slaue that was a hanging thee. | Gent. 'Tis true (my Lords)
　　he did.　　　　　　　　　　　　　　　　　　　　3238
SLAUES = 1
　　That slaues your ordinance, that will not see　　　　　　　　2253
SLAUGHTER = 1
　　And such a Daughter, | Should sure to the Slaughter,　　　　　838
SLEEPE = 7*3
　　Got 'tweene a sleepe, and wake? Well then,　　　　　　　　349
　　*this I may speake more. If our Father would sleepe till I wak'd　387
　　*Hum? Conspiracy? Sleepe till I wake him, you should　　　　390
　　Would not scape censure, nor the redresses sleepe,　　　　　721
　　*Kent. I will not sleepe my Lord, till I haue deliuered | your Letter.
　　Exit.　　　　　　　　　　　　　　　　　　　　880
　　Some time I shall sleepe out, the rest Ile whistle:　　　　　1232
　　Till it crie sleepe to death.　　　　　　　　　　　　　1395
　　Shall of a Corne cry woe, and turne his sleepe to wake.　　　1685
　　Nay get thee in; Ile pray, and then Ile sleepe.　　　　　　1808
　　Gent. I Madam: in the heauinesse of sleepe, | We put fresh garments on
　　him.　　　　　　　　　　　　　　　　　　　　2772

SLEEPES = 1
　How do's the King? | *Gent.* Madam sleepes still.　　　　2761
SLENDERLY = 1
　Reg. 'Tis the infirmity of his age, yet he hath euer but | slenderly
　knowne himselfe.　　　　318
SLEPT = 1*1
　*them in the sweet face of Heauen. One, that slept in the　　1869
　Gent. So please your Maiesty, | That we may wake the King, he hath
　slept long?　　　　2767
SLEW = 1
　The one the other poison'd for my sake, | And after slew herselfe.　3197
SLIGHTLY = 1
　That he so slightly valued in his Messenger, | Should haue him thus
　restrained.　　　　1222
SLIP-SHOD = 1
　Foole. Then I prythee be merry, thy wit shall not go | slip-shod. | *Lear.*
　Ha, ha, ha.　　　　885
SLOTH = *1
　*Hog in sloth, Foxe in stealth, Wolfe in greedinesse, Dog　　1873
SLOWER = *1
　*forbearance till the speed of his rage goes slower: and as　　488
SMALL = 5*2
　The worships of their name. O most small fault,　　　779
　You shall doe small respects, show too bold malice　　　1209
　*How chance the King comes with so small a number?　　　1336
　*were like an old Letchers heart, a small spark, all the rest　　1893
　But Mice, and Rats, and such small Deare,　　　1917
　Almost too small for sight. The murmuring Surge,　　　2455
　No, the Wren goes too't, and the small gilded Fly　　　2558
SMELL = 5*1
　Do you smell a fault?　　　　19
　that what a man cannot smell out, he may spy into.　　　897
　*not a nose among twenty, but can smell him that's stink-|ing;　1343
　I smell the blood of a Brittish man. *Exeunt*　　　1968
　Reg. Go thrust him out at gates, and let him smell | His way to Douer.
　Exit with Glouster.　　　　2170
　Thou know'st, the first time that we smell the Ayre　　　2621
SMELLES = 1
　It smelles of Mortality.　　　　2576
SMELT = *1
　*peace at my bidding, there I found 'em, there I smelt 'em　　2549
SMILD = 1
　He smil'd at it. I told him you were comming,　　　2272
SMILE = 1*1
　*nay, & thou canst not smile as the wind sits, thou'lt catch　630
　Smile once more, turne thy wheele.　　　　1250
SMILING = 1
　Who weares no honesty: such smiling rogues as these,　　1146
SMILINGLY = 1
　Twixt two extremes of passion, ioy and greefe, | Burst smilingly.　3161
SMOAKES = *1
　Gen. 'Tis hot, it smoakes, it came euen from the heart | of--- O she's
　dead.　　　　3174
SMOILE = 1
　Smoile you my speeches, as I were a Foole?　　　1155
SMOOTH = 1
　Which are t'intrince, t'vnloose: smooth euery passion　　1148

SMUGGE = *1
  *Like a smugge Bridegroome. What? I will be Iouiall: 2641
SMULKIN = *1
  *Beware my Follower. Peace Smulkin, peace thou Fiend.   1919
SNAILE = *1
  *Foole. Nor I neither; but I can tell why a Snaile ha's | a house.   901
SNOW = 1*1
  Being oile to fire, snow to the colder moodes,   1150
  *Forkes presages Snow; that minces Vertue, & do's shake   2564
SNUFFE = 1
  My snuffe, and loathed part of Nature should   2478
SNUFFES = 1
  Either in snuffes, and packings of the Dukes,   1635
SO see also zo l.*6 *9 *13 21 66 83 113 114 115 133 214 238 239 270 300
  362 *363 *372 422 *458 *484 500 *527 536 *568 *569 576 592 621 *664
  679 683 *684 *708 *727 *728 742 751 788 823 831 841 *906 964 1056
  1065 *1111 *1127 *1132 1175 *1186 1216 1220 1222 *1274 1287 1317
  *1336 1373 1408 1453 1487 1494 1526 1530 1535 1536 1552 1561 1575
  1594 1679 *1683 1787 1809 *1923 2017 2018 2042 2102 2211 2251 2255
  2270 2310 2325 2334 2423 2439 2447 2449 2457 2492 2500 2508 2578
  2615 2722 2736 2752 2760 2767 2826 *2881 2889 2951 2980 2986 3003
  3007 3015 3098 3124 3147 3199 3218 3227 3261 3291 3301 = 99*25
SODAINE = 1
  For sodaine ioy did weepe, | And I for sorrow sung,   688
SODAINELY = 1
  Or whether gasted by the noyse I made, | Full sodainely he fled.   991
SOFT = 1
  What is't thou saist? Her voice was euer soft,   3236
SOILED see soyled
SOIOURNE = 3
  Long in our Court, haue made their amorous soiourne,   52
  That if they come to soiourne at my house,   1042
  You will returne and soiourne with my Sister,   1496
SOL = 1
  *o'Bedlam. --- O these Eclipses do portend these diui-|sions. Fa, Sol,
  La, Me.   465
SOLDIERS see also souldiers, souldiours = 2
  Enter with Drum and Colours, Albany, Gonerill, Soldiers.   2864
  Flourish. Enter Albany, Gonerill, Regan, Soldiers.   2982
SOLICITING = 1
  A still soliciting eye, and such a tongue,   253
SOME = 29*3
  *Glou. But I haue a Sonne, Sir, by order of Law, some   22
  For that I am some twelue, or fourteene Moonshines   339
  *some little time hath qualified the heat of his displeasure,   483
  Edg. Some Villaine hath done me wrong.   486
  Weary of all, shall want some. That's a sheal'd Pescod.   711
  Gon. Take you some company, and away to horse,   860
  Some blood drawne on me, would beget opinion   966
  Occasions Noble Gloster of some prize,   1063
  Corn. This is some Fellow,   1170
  Some time I shall sleepe out, the rest Ile whistle: 1232
  Some other time for that. Beloued Regan,   1411
  By some discretion, that discernes your state   1429
  Stands in some ranke of praise, Ile go with thee,   1556
  Some friendship will it lend you 'gainst the Tempest: 1716
  *do poore Tom some charitie, whom the foule Fiend   1841

KING LEAR

SOME *cont.*

And follow me, that will to some prouision   2055
Some fiue or six and thirty of his Knights   2075
Who, with some other of the Lords, dependants,   2077
Giue me some helpe. --- O cruell! O you Gods.   2142
To see some mischefe on him. Oh.   2157
Glou. He has some reason, else he could not beg.   2215
And bring some couering for this naked Soule, | Which Ile intreate to
leade me.   2231
Some things, I know not what. Ile loue thee much   2407
Is wretchednesse depriu'd that benefit | To end it selfe by death? 'Twas
yet some comfort,   2503
It was some Fiend: Therefore thou happy Father,   2517
Ile leade you to some biding. | *Glou.* Heartie thankes: 2671
You haue some cause, they haue not. | *Cor.* No cause, no cause. 2832
Bast. Some Officers take them away: good guard,   2940
Bast. Sir, I thought it fit, | To send the old and miserable King to some
retention,   2989
And that thy tongue (some say) of breeding breathes,   3099
Vntill some halfe houre past when I was arm'd,   3156
Bast. I pant for life: some good I meane to do   .   3200
SOMETHING = 4*2
  *Gon. We must do something, and i'th' heate. *Exeunt.*   332
  That's something yet: *Edgar* I nothing am. *Exit.*   1272
  Against the old kinde King; or something deeper,   1637
  *thus giues way to Loyaltie, something feares mee to | thinke of. 1973
  With something rich about me: from that place,   2262
  You looke as you had something more to say.   3165
SOMETIME = 1*1
  As thou my sometime Daughter.   127
  *Sometimes with Lunaticke bans, sometime with Praiers   1270
SOMETIMES = *2
  *whipt for lying, and sometimes I am whipt for holding   697
  *Sometimes with Lunaticke bans, sometime with Praiers   1270
SOMNET = *1
  Glou. But haue I falne, or no? | *Edg.* From the dread Somnet of this
  Chalkie Bourne   2498
SOMTHING = *1
  *though this Knaue came somthing sawcily to the   24
SON = 4*3
  Kent. Is not this your Son, my Lord?   11
  *Vnburthen'd crawle toward death. Our son of *Cornwal*,   46
  *declin'd, the Father should bee as Ward to the Son, and   407
  *prediction; there's Son against Father, the King fals from 440
  Kent. It is both he and she, | Your Son, and Daughter.   1289
  For Gloursters bastard Son was kinder to his Father,   2560
  And when I haue stolne vpon these Son in Lawes,   2628
SONGS = *1
  Le. When were you wont to be so full of Songs sirrah?   684
SONNE = 12*7
  *Sonne for her Cradle, ere she had a husband for her bed.   18
  Glou. But I haue a Sonne, Sir, by order of Law, some   22
  And you our no lesse louing Sonne of *Albany*,   47
  *enioy halfe his Reuennew: my Sonne *Edgar*, had hee a   391
  the Sonne manage his Reuennew.   408
  *Sonne and Father. This villaine of mine comes vnder the   439
  *Pandar, and the Sonne and Heire of a Mungrill Bitch,   1095

261

SONNE *cont*.

Your Sonne and Daughter found this trespasse worth	1320
I am almost mad my selfe. I had a Sonne,	1946
No Father his Sonne deerer: true to tell thee,	1949
*his Sonne: for hee's a mad Yeoman that sees his Sonne a | Gentleman	
before him.	2011
Where's my Sonne *Edmund*?	2161
Proue our Commodities. Oh deere Sonne *Edgar*,	2202
Which made me thinke a Man, a Worme. My Sonne	2217
thee good mans sonne, from the foule Fiend.	2248
And of the loyall Seruice of his Sonne	2274
Alb. Where was his Sonne, | When they did take his eyes?	2335
My name is *Edgar* and thy Fathers Sonne,	3130

SONNES = 1*1

Reuennew, Execution of the rest, | Beloued Sonnes be yours, which to	
confirme,	145
*it to be fit, that Sonnes at perfect age, and Fathers	406

SOONE = 2

That she would soone be heere. Is your Lady come?	1471
Soone may I heare, and see him. *Exeunt*.	2381

SOOTH = 1

Kent. Good my Lord, sooth him:	1960

SOP = *1

*sop oth' Moonshine of you, you whoreson Cullyenly | Barber-monger,	
draw.	1105

SOPHISTICATED = *1

*sophisticated. Thou art the thing it selfe; vnaccommo- |dated	1886

SORE = 1*1

A plague sore, or imbossed Carbuncle	1518
*Loyalty, though the conflict be sore betweene that, and | my blood.	1992

SORELY = 1

Do sorely ruffle, for many Miles about | There's scarce a Bush.	1604

SORROW = 4

For sodaine ioy did weepe, | And I for sorrow sung,	688
Historica passio, downe thou climing sorrow,	1329
Bad is the Trade that must play Foole to sorrow,	2224
Let sorrow split my heart, if euer I | Did hate thee, or thy Father.	3139

SORROWES = 3

Who, by the Art of knowne, and feeling sorrowes,	2669
Of my huge Sorrowes? Better I were distract,	2735
It is a chance which do's redeeme all sorrowes | That euer I haue felt.	3228

SORRY = 3*1

Bur. I am sorry then you haue so lost a Father,	270
Glo. I am sorry for thee friend, 'tis the Dukes pleasure,	1228
Poore Foole, and Knaue, I haue one part in my heart | That's sorry yet	
for thee.	1727
May be my Friends: hee's dead; I am onely sorry	2710

SOT = 1

When I inform'd him, then he call'd me Sot,	2275

SOUGHT = 2

That thou hast sought to make vs breake our vowes,	182
Now out-law'd from my blood: he sought my life	1947

SOULDIER = 1

Your Sister is the better Souldier.	2388

SOULDIERS = 6

Too't Luxury pell-mell, for I lacke Souldiers.	2562

SOULDIERS *cont.*

  Enter with Drumme and Colours, Edmund, Regan. | Gentlemen, and
  Souldiers. 2845
  Cordelia, and Souldiers, ouer the Stage, and Exeunt. 2919
  and Cordelia, as prisoners, Souldiers, Captaine. 2939
  Take thou my Souldiers, prisoners, patrimony, 3018
  Trust to thy single vertue, for thy Souldiers 3052
SOULDIOURS = 1
  Enter with Drum and Colours, Cordelia, Gentlemen, | and Souldiours. 2349
SOULE = 3
  And bring some couering for this naked Soule, | Which Ile intreate to
  leade me. 2231
  Thou art a Soule in blisse, but I am bound 2795
  Is generall woe: Friends of my soule, you twaine, 3294
SOUND = 6*1
  For the sound man. Death on my state: wherefore 1388
  Hast heauy substance, bleed'st not, speak'st, art sound, 2494
  Euery one heares that, which can distinguish sound. 2654
  If you haue victory, let the Trumpet sound 2885
  Alb. Thou art armed *Gloster,* | Let the Trumpet sound: 3036
  Come hither Herald, let the Trumpet sound, | And read out this. *A*
  Trumpet sounds. 3057
  *sound of the Trumpet: he is bold in his defence. 1 *Trumpet. | Her.*
  Againe. 2 *Trumpet.* 3063
SOUNDED = *1
  *Glo. Has he neuer before sounded you in this busines? 404
SOUNDEST = *1
  *Gon. The best and soundest of his time hath bin but 320
SOUNDS = 2
  Nor are those empty hearted, whose low sounds | Reuerbe no
  hollownesse. 163
  Come hither Herald, let the Trumpet sound, | And read out this. *A*
  Trumpet sounds. 3057
SOYLED = *1
  *the soyled Horse goes too't with a more riotous appe-|tite: 2566
SPACE = 4
  Deerer then eye-sight, space, and libertie, 61
  No lesse in space, validitie, and pleasure 87
  Oh indistinguish'd space of Womans will, 2724
  To morrow, or at further space, t'appeare 2996
SPAKE = 1*2
  Bast. Spake you with him? | *Edg.* I, two houres together. 476
  *her. Swore as many Oathes, as I spake words, & broke 1868
  *Reg. Lord *Edmund* spake not with your Lord at home? | *Stew.* No
  Madam. 2389
SPANIELL = 1
  Hound or Spaniell, Brache, or Hym: 2026
SPARD = *1
  *Ste. This ancient Ruffian Sir, whose life I haue spar'd | at sute of his
  gray-beard. 1135
SPARE = 2
  Iakes with him. Spare my gray-beard, you wagtaile? 1140
  A Mistresses command. Weare this; spare speech, 2289
SPARK = *1
  *were like an old Letchers heart, a small spark, all the rest 1893
SPARKES = 1
  Edmund, enkindle all the sparkes of Nature | To quit this horrid acte. 2162

SPARROW = *1
  Foole. For you know Nunckle, the Hedge-Sparrow   726
SPEAKE = 36*9
  Our eldest borne, speake first.   59
  Cor. What shall *Cordelia* speake? Loue, and be silent.   67
  A third, more opilent then your Sisters? speake.   92
  Cor. Nothing. | *Lear*. Nothing will come of nothing, speake againe.   95
  Think'st thou that dutie shall haue dread to speake, | When power to
flattery bowes?   156
  To speake and purpose not, since what I will intend,   247
  Ile do't before I speake, that you make knowne   248
  *this I may speake more. If our Father would sleepe till I wak'd   387
  *fitly bring you to heare my Lord speake: pray ye goe,   490
  I will not speake with him, say I am sicke,   515
  *and tell my Daughter, I would speake with her. Goe you   605
  Speake lesse then thou knowest,   649
  *gau'st thy golden one away; if I speake like my selfe in   678
  *Do's *Lear* walke thus? Speake thus? Where are his eies?   740
  Then a grac'd Pallace. The shame it selfe doth speake   755
  Is it your will, speake Sir? Prepare my Horses.   770
  Cor. What is your difference, speake?   1125
  Cor. Speake yet, how grew your quarrell?   1134
  An honest mind and plaine, he must speake truth,   1174
  Gen. Made you no more offence, | But what you speake of? | *Kent*.
None: 1333
  Lear. Deny to speake with me?   1361
  I'ld speake with the Duke of *Cornewall*, and his wife.   1372
  Lear. The King would speake with *Cornwall*,   1376
  The deere Father | *Would with his Daughter speake, commands, tends,
ser-|(uice.   1377
  Goe tell the Duke, and's wife, Il'd speake with them: 1392
  I can scarce speake to thee, thou'lt not beleeue   1414
  Speake 'gainst so great a number? How in one house   1536
  Ile speake a Prophesie ere I go: 1735
  *me on paine of perpetuall displeasure, neither to speake   1756
  Reg. To whose hands | You haue sent the Lunaticke King: Speake.   2113
  Decline your head. This kisse, if it durst speake   2290
  Reg. I speake in vnderstanding: Y'are: I know't,   2415
  Hoa, you Sir: Friend, heare you Sir, speake: 2486
  Thy life's a Myracle. Speake yet againe.   2497
  Enough, enough, and dye. That thing you speake of,   2522
  Had not concluded all. He wakes, speake to him.   2790
  Tell me but truly, but then speake the truth,   2855
  Alb. Ile ouertake you, speake.   2883
  To proue vpon thy heart, where to I speake, | Thou lyest.   3095
  Where they shall rest for euer. Trumpets speake.   3106
  And shall perchance do good, but speake you on,   3164
  Edg. What kinde of helpe? | *Alb*. Speake man.   3171
  Alb. Who dead? Speake man.   3176
  *Speake *Edmund*, where's the King? and where's *Cordelia*?   3193
  Speake what we feele, not what we ought to say: 3299
SPEAKES = 2*1
  Our Sister speakes of. Come, bring away the Stocks.   1219
  Let's see these Pockets; the Letters that he speakes of   2709
  Edg. What's he that speakes for *Edmund* Earle of Glo-|(ster?   3078
SPEAKING = 2*1
  *they'l haue me whipt for speaking true: thou'lt haue me   696

KING LEAR

SPEAKING *cont.*
  She gaue strange Eliads, and most speaking lookes   2412
  Past speaking of in a King. Thou hast a Daughter   2647
SPEAKST = 2
  Me thinkes thy voyce is alter'd, and thou speak'st   2440
  Hast heauy substance, bleed'st not, speak'st, art sound,   2494
SPEAKT = *1
  Reg. And speak't againe my Lord, no more with me.   1553
SPECIAL = *1
  Gent. Though that the Queen on special cause is here   2660
SPECTACLES = 1
  *such neede to hide it selfe. Let's see: come, if it bee no- | thing, I shall
  not neede Spectacles.   369
SPECULATIONS = 1
  Which are to France the Spies and Speculations   1633
SPEECH = 7*2
  A loue that makes breath poore, and speech vnable,   65
  Lear. How, how *Cordelia*? Mend your speech a little,   100
  That can my speech defuse, my good intent   532
  Foole. Sirha, Ile teach thee a speech. | *Lear.* Do.   645
  And found him pight to doe it, with curst speech   1002
  A Mistresses command. Weare this; spare speech,   2289
  Edg. If ere your Grace had speech with man so poore, | Heare me one
  word.   2881
  That if my speech offend a Noble heart,   3081
  Bast. This speech of yours hath mou'd me,   3163
SPEECHES = 2
  And your large speeches, may your deeds approue,   198
  Smoile you my speeches, as I were a Foole?   1155
SPEED = 2*1
  Well, my Legittimate, if this Letter speed,   353
  *forbearance till the speed of his rage goes slower: and as   488
  Gent. Sir, speed you: what's your will?   2651
SPEEDILY = 1*1
  Corn. Poste speedily to my Lord your husband, shew   2060
  So speedily can venge. But (O poore Glouster)   2325
SPEEDY = 3*1
  *if your Dilligence be not speedy, I shall be there afore | you.   878
  This Leter Madam, craues a speedy answer: | 'Tis from your Sister.   2328
  Gent. Neere, and on speedy foot: the maine descry | Stands on the
  hourely thought.   2657
  His speedy taking off. As for the mercie   2912
SPHERICALL = *1
  *Treachers by Sphericall predominance. Drunkards, Ly- | ars,   452
SPIE = 1
  (For now I spie a danger) I entreate you   1544
SPIES = 2
  Which are to France the Spies and Speculations   1633
  As if we were Gods spies: And wee'l weare out   2957
SPIGHT = 1
  Deliuer'd Letters spight of intermission,   1309
SPILL = 1
  Cracke Natures moulds, all germaines spill at once | That makes
  ingratefull Man.   1663
SPIRIT = 3*1
  Foole. Come not in heere Nuncle, here's a spirit, helpe | me, helpe me.   1820
  It is the Cowish terror of his spirit   2280

SPIRIT *cont.*
Let not my worser Spirit tempt me againe | To dye before you please. 2664
Cor. Sir, do you know me? | *Lear.* You are a spirit I know, where did
you dye? 2798
SPIRITE = *2
Foole. A spirite, a spirite, he sayes his name's poore | *Tom.* 1823
SPIRITS = 4
And when he saw my best alarum'd spirits 989
Were very pregnant and potentiall spirits 1013
Would stretch thy Spirits vp into the ayre: 2291
This Sword, this arme, and my best spirits are bent 3094
SPIT = *1
Lear. Rumble thy belly full: spit Fire, spowt Raine: 1669
SPITS = 1
Lear. To haue a thousand with red burning spits | Come hizzing in vpon
'em. 2013
SPLEENE = 1
Create her childe of Spleene, that it may liue 796
SPLIT = 1
Let sorrow split my heart, if euer I | Did hate thee, or thy Father. 3139
SPOAKE = *1
*to be iust? This is the Letter which hee spoake of; 1980
SPOILE = 1
And these same crosses spoile me. Who are you? 3243
SPOKE = 3
By what your selfe too late haue spoke and done, 718
Spoke with how manifold, and strong a Bond 983
Ere you had spoke so farre. He led our Powers, 3003
SPOKEN = 4*1
Haue you not spoken 'gainst the Duke of *Cornewall?* 953
Lear. Is this well spoken? 1532
*receiued a Letter this night, 'tis dangerous to be spoken, 1761
Glou. Me thinkes y'are better spoken. | *Edg.* Come on Sir, 2444
Bast. Th'hast spoken right, 'tis true, 3135
SPORT = 2*1
*there was good sport at his making, and the horson must 26
Do more then this in sport; Father, Father, 968
As Flies to wanton Boyes, are we to th'Gods, | They kill vs for their
sport. 2221
SPOTTED = 1
A most Toad-spotted Traitor. Say thou no, 3093
SPOUSE = *1
*with mans sworne Spouse: set not thy Sweet-heart on | proud array.
Tom's a cold. 1862
SPOUT = 1
You Cataracts, and Hyrricano's spout, 1657
SPOWT = *1
Lear. Rumble thy belly full: spit Fire, spowt Raine: 1669
SPRIGS = 1
Pins, Wodden-prickes, Nayles, Sprigs of Rosemarie: 1267
SPRING = 3
That good effects may spring from words of loue: 199
And from her derogate body, neuer spring 794
Spring with my teares; be aydant, and remediate 2368
SPURNE = 1
By rule of Knight-hood, I disdaine and spurne: 3101

SPY *see also* spie = 1
  that what a man cannot smell out, he may spy into. 897
SQUARE = 1
  Which the most precious square of sense professes, 79
SQUINT = 1
  Gon. Hola, hola, | That eye that told you so, look'd but a squint. 3014
SQUINTS = *1
  *and the Pin, squints the eye, and makes the Hare-lippe; 1897
SQUINY = *1
  *squiny at me? No, doe thy worst blinde Cupid, Ile not 2581
SQUIRE = 1
  No Squire in debt, nor no poore Knight; 1741
SQUIRES = 1
  Heere do you keepe a hundred Knights and Squires, 750
SQUIRE-LIKE = 1
  To knee his Throne, and Squire-like pension beg, 1507
STAGE = 2
  To this great stage of Fooles. This a good blocke: 2625
  Cordelia, and Souldiers, ouer the Stage, and Exeunt. 2919
STAINE = 2
  Staine my mans cheekes. No you vnnaturall Hags, 1578
  If that her breath will mist or staine the stone, | Why then she liues. 3222
STAKE = 2
  Bringing the murderous Coward to the stake: 999
  Glou. I am tyed to'th'Stake, | And I must stand the Course. 2125
STALE = 1
  Then doth within a dull stale tyred bed 347
STAMPE = 1
  Let it stampe wrinkles in her brow of youth, 798
STAND = 14*3
  Stand in the plague of custome, and permit 337
  Now Gods, stand vp for Bastards. 356
  If thou canst serue where thou dost stand condemn'd, 535
  *whipt out, when the Lady Brach may stand by'th'fire | and stinke. 642
  Mumbling of wicked charmes, coniuring the Moone | To stand auspicious Mistris. 973
  If I would stand against thee, would the reposall 1005
  Kent. Strike you slaue: stand rogue, stand you neat | slaue, strike. 1114
  Your horrible pleasure. Heere I stand your Slaue, 1674
  Stand in assured losse. Take vp, take vp, 2054
  Glou. I am tyed to'th'Stake, | And I must stand the Course. 2125
  Reg. Giue me thy Sword. A pezant stand vp thus? | *Killes him.* 2154
  Heere's the place: stand still: how fearefull 2446
  Glou. Set me where you stand. 2460
  Vp, so: How is't? Feele you your Legges? You stand. | *Glou.* Too well, too well. 2508
  How stiffe is my vilde sense | That I stand vp, and haue ingenious feeling 2733
  The which immediacie may well stand vp, 3005
STANDING = *1
  *ditch-Dogge; drinkes the green Mantle of the standing 1912
STANDS = 9*1
  But now her price is fallen: Sir, there she stands, 215
  When it is mingled with regards, that stands 262
  *Crab: thou canst, tell why ones nose stands i'th'middle | on's face? | *Lear.* No. 893
  Then stands on any shoulder that I see | Before me, at this instant. 1168

STANDS *cont.*

Nature in you stands on the very Verge	1427
Stands in some ranke of praise, Ile go with thee,	1556
Stands still in esperance, liues not in feare:	2182
Cor. 'Tis knowne before. Our preparation stands	2375
Gent. Neere, and on speedy foot: the maine descry | Stands on the hourely thought.	2657
Stands on me to defend, not to debate. *Exit.*	2916

STARE = 1

When I do stare, see how the Subiect quakes.	2555

STARRE = *2

*to lay his Goatish disposition on the charge of a Starre,	456
*haue bin that I am, had the maidenlest Starre in the Fir-|mament twinkled on my bastardizing.	460

STARRES = 1*2

*Moone, and Starres, as if we were villaines on necessitie,	450
*the seuen Starres are no mo then seuen, is a pretty reason.	909
Who haue, as who haue not, that their great Starres	1631

STARRE-BLASTING = *1

*blisse thee from Whirle-Windes, Starre-blasting, and ta-|king,	1840

STARTS = *1

Reg. Such vnconstant starts are we like to haue from | him, as this of *Kents* banishment.	325

STARUD = 1

Weele see 'em staru'd first: come. *Exit.*	2968

STATE = 9

Interest of Territory, Cares of State)	55
When Maiesty falls to folly, reserue thy state,	159
From this enormous State, seeking to giue	1246
For the sound man. Death on my state: wherefore	1388
By some discretion, that discernes your state	1429
Intelligent of our State. What hath bin seene,	1634
With others, whom the rigour of our State | Forc'd to cry out.	2867
Shall neuer see his pardon: for my state,	2915
Rule in this Realme, and the gor'd state sustaine.	3295

STAY = 8*1

Lear. Let me not stay a iot for dinner, go get it rea-|dy:	539
Lear. Follow me not, stay here. *Exit.*	1332
But I will tarry, the Foole will stay,	1354
I can be patient, I can stay with *Regan,* | I and my hundred Knights.	1524
Gon. My Lord, entreate him by no meanes to stay.	1602
Reg. Our troopes set forth to morrow, stay with vs: | The wayes are dangerous.	2401
Alb. Stay till I haue read the Letter. | *Edg.* I was forbid it:	2891
Alb. Stay yet, heare reason: *Edmund,* I arrest thee	3027
Cordelia, Cordelia, stay a little. Ha:	3235

STE = 12*1

STEALTH = 1*1

Who in the lustie stealth of Nature, take | More composition, and fierce qualitie,	345
*Hog in sloth, Foxe in stealth, Wolfe in greedinesse, Dog	1873

STEEPE = 1

Glou. Me thinkes the ground is eeuen. | *Edg.* Horrible steepe.	2433

STEEPLES = *1

*Till you haue drench'd our Steeples, drown the Cockes.	1658

STELLED = 1

And quench'd the Stelled fires:	2133

STENCH = *1
  *there is the sulphurous pit; burning, scalding, stench,   2570
STEP = 2
  No vnchaste action or dishonoured step   250
  One step I haue aduanc'd thee, if thou do'st   2971
STEPS = 1
  Kent. That from your first of difference and decay, | Haue follow'd your
  sad steps.   3254
STERNE = 1
  If Wolues had at thy Gate howl'd that sterne time,   2135
STEW = 20*5
STEWARD see also Ste., Stew. = 10
  Enter Gonerill, and Steward.   506
  Enter Steward.   575
  Sir, who am I Sir? | *Enter Steward.* | *Ste*. My Ladies Father.   · 607
  Enter Steward.   856
  Enter Kent, and Steward seuerally.   1075
  Enter Steward.   1468
  Enter Steward.   2072
  Enter Gonerill, Bastard, and Steward.   2267
  Enter Regan, and Steward.   2383
  Enter Steward.   2675
STEWD = 1
  Stew'd in his haste, halfe breathlesse, painting forth   1307
STICKE = 1*1
  *o'th' coxcombs with a sticke, and cryed downe wantons,   1400
  In his Annoynted flesh, sticke boarish phangs.   2130
STIFFE = 1
  How stiffe is my vilde sense | That I stand vp, and haue ingenious
  feeling   2733
STILL = 21*1
  Kent. See better *Lear*, and let me still remaine | The true blanke of
  thine eie.   170
  A still soliciting eye, and such a tongue,   253
  And the remainders that shall still depend,   759
  Let me still take away the harmes I feare,   851
  Not feare still to be taken. I know his heart,   852
  Infirmity doth still neglect all office,   1382
  Storme still. Enter Kent, and a Gentleman, seuerally.   1615
  Storme still. Enter Lear, and Foole.   1655
  The tirrany of the open night's too rough | For Nature to endure.
  Storme still   1779
  *vexes. There could I haue him now, and there, and there | againe, and
  there. *Storme still.*   1842
  *foule Fiend. Still through the Hauthorne blowes the   1878
  Boy *Sesey*: let him trot by. *Storme still.*   1880
  His wits begin t'vnsettle. | *Glou*. Canst thou blame him? *Storm still*   1941
  I will keepe still with my Philosopher.   1959
  His word was still, fie, foh, and fumme,   1967
  Then still contemn'd and flatter'd, to be worst: 2180
  Stands still in esperance, liues not in feare: 2182
  Makes thee the happier: Heauens deale so still: 2251
  Heere's the place: stand still: how fearefull   2446
  How do's the King? | *Gent*. Madam sleepes still.   2761
  Cor. Still, still, farre wide.   2800
STINKE = 1
  *whipt out, when the Lady Brach may stand by'th'fire | and stinke.   642

STINKING = *1
*not a nose among twenty, but can smell him that's stink-|ing; 1343
STIRRE = 1
there's my key: if you do stirre abroad, goe arm'd. 491
STIRRES = 2
Her Fathers heart from her; call *France*, who stirres? 134
If it be you that stirres these Daughters hearts 1574
STIRRILITY = 1
Into her Wombe conuey stirrility, 792
STIRS = 1
Lear. This feather stirs, she liues: if it be so, 3227
STOCKES = 2*1
Foole. And thou hadst beene set i'th' Stockes for that 1337
Lear. Who put my man i'th'Stockes? 1467
How came my man i'th'Stockes? 1490
STOCKING = 1*1
*pound, filthy woosted-stocking knaue, a Lilly-liuered, 1090
Against the Grace, and Person of my Master, | Stocking his Messenger. 1210
STOCKS = 6*1
Corn. Fetch forth the Stockes? 1203
Call not your Stocks for me, I serue the King. 1207
Corn. Fetch forth the Stockes; 1212
Reg. Sir, being his Knaue, I will. *Stocks brought out*. 1217
Our Sister speakes of. Come, bring away the Stocks. 1219
*ouerlustie at legs, then he weares wodden nether-stocks. 1285
Kent. Where learn'd you this Foole? | *Foole*. Not i'th' Stocks Foole. 1359
STOCKT = *2
Lear. Who stockt my Seruant? *Regan*, I haue good hope 1477
*stockt, punish'd, and imprison'd: who hath three Suites | to his backe,
sixe shirts to his body: 1914
STOLNE = 1
And when I haue stolne vpon these Son in Lawes, 2628
STOMACK = 1
From a full flowing stomack. Generall, 3017
STONE = 1
If that her breath will mist or staine the stone, | Why then she liues. 3222
STONES = 2*1
(More harder then the stones whereof 'tis rais'd, 1718
Their precious Stones new lost: became his guide, 3153
Lear. Howle, howle, howle: O you are men of stones, 3217
STONE-CUTTER = *1
Kent. A Taylor Sir, a Stone-cutter, or a Painter, could 1131
STOOD = 4*1
But yet alas, stood I within his Grace, 298
Bast. Here stood he in the dark, his sharpe Sword out, 972
Seeing how lothly opposite I stood 985
Edg. As I stood heere below, me thought his eyes 2514
Should haue stood that night against my fire, 2785
STOP = 3
Stop, stop, no helpe? 969
Or with this paper shall I stop it: hold Sir, 3113
STOPT = 1
Will not be rub'd nor stopt, Ile entreat for thee. 1230
STORD = 1
All the stor'd Vengeances of Heauen, fall 1444
STORM = 1
His wits begin t'vnsettle. | *Glou*. Canst thou blame him? *Storm still* 1941

STORME = 13*1
 And leaue thee in the storme,   1353
 No, Ile not weepe, I haue full cause of weeping. | *Storme and Tempest*.   1583
 Corn. Let vs withdraw, 'twill be a Storme.   1587
 *My *Regan* counsels well: come out oth'storme. *Exeunt*.   1613
 Storme still. Enter Kent, and a Gentleman, seuerally.   1615
 That yet you do not know. Fye on this Storme,   1646
 Storme still. Enter Lear, and Foole.   1655
 The tirrany of the open night's too rough | For Nature to endure.
 Storme still   1779
 Lear. Thou think'st 'tis much that this contentious | (storme   1786
 That bide the pelting of this pittilesse storme,   1810
 *vexes. There could I haue him now, and there, and there | againe, and
 there. *Storme still*.   1842
 Boy *Sesey*: let him trot by. *Storme still*.   1880
 The Sea, with such a storme as his bare head,   2131
 I'th'last nights storme, I such a fellow saw;   2216
STRAIGHT = 3*1
 *so, Ile write straight to my Sister to hold my course; pre-|pare for
 dinner. *Exeunt*.   527
 They summon'd vp their meiney, straight tooke Horse,   1311
 Mine eyes are not o'th'best, Ile tell you straight.   3244
 Kent. No my good Lord, I am the very man. | *Lear*. Ile see that
 straight.   3252
STRAIND = 1
 Which we durst neuer yet; and with strain'd pride,   183
STRAINE = *1
 Alb. Sir, you haue shew'd to day your valiant straine   2983
STRANGE = 5*5
 Fra. This is most strange,   234
 *Gods, Gods! 'Tis strange, that from their cold'st neglect   279
 *Kent banish'd; his offence, honesty. 'Tis strange. *Exit*   446
 Glo. O strange and fastned Villaine, | Would he deny his Letter, said he? 1015
 Cor. Thou art a strange fellow, a Taylor make a man?   1130
 Lea. 'Tis strange that they should so depart from home,   1274
 The Art of our Necessities is strange,   1725
 *my old Master must be relieued. There is strange things | toward
 Edmund, pray you be carefull. *Exit*.   1769
 But that thy strange mutations make vs hate thee,   2191
 She gaue strange Eliads, and most speaking lookes   2412
STRANGENESSE = 2
 (Which I can call but now,) I haue heard strangenesse.   1026
 Edg. This is aboue all strangenesse,   2510
STRANGER = 1
 And as a stranger to my heart and me,   122
STRANGERD = 1
 Dow'rd with our curse, and stranger'd with our oath, | Take her or,
 leaue her.   223
STRATAGEM = 1
 It were a delicate stratagem to shoo | A Troope of Horse with Felt: Ile
 put't in proofe,   2626
STRAW = 3*1
 I am cold my selfe. Where is this straw, my Fellow?   1724
 Kent. What art thou that dost grumble there i'th' | straw? Come forth. 1825
 *ragges, a Pigmies straw do's pierce it. None do's offend,   2610
 In short, and musty straw? Alacke, alacke,   2788

STRAY = 1
I would not from your loue make such a stray,   229
STRENGTH = 5
How in my strength you please: for you *Edmund*,   1054
His nighted life: Moreouer to descry | The strength o'th'Enemy.   2398
Glou. Now let thy friendly hand | Put strength enough too't.   2681
Heere is the guesse of their true strength and Forces,   2898
Maugre thy strength, place, youth, and eminence,   3086
STRENGTHS = 1
Conferring them on yonger strengths, while we   45
STRETCH = 3
That stretch their duties nicely.   1179
Would stretch thy Spirits vp into the ayre: 2291
That would vpon the wracke of this tough world | Stretch him out
longer.   3288
STRIFE = 2
Our daughters seuerall Dowers, that future strife   49
Who were the opposites of this dayes strife: 2985
STRIKE = 8*3
Gon. Did my Father strike my Gentleman for chi- | ding of his Foole? |
Ste. I Madam.   507
Gon. You strike my people, and your disorder'd rable, | make Seruants
of their Betters.   766
Kent. Strike you slaue: stand rogue, stand you neat | slaue, strike.   1114
To strike at me vpon his misconstruction,   1193
Strike in their num'd and mortified Armes.   1266
On her ingratefull top: strike her yong bones   1445
Strike flat the thicke Rotundity o'th'world,   1662
With this vngracious paper strike the sight   2729
Reg. Let the Drum strike, and proue my title thine.   3026
He'le strike and quickly too, he's dead and rotten.   3251
STRIKES = *1
Cor. Keepe peace vpon your liues, he dies that strikes | againe, what is
the matter?   1122
STRIP = *1
*hand: why dost thou lash that Whore? Strip thy owne   2604
STRIUE = 1
Striue to be interest. What can you say, to draw   91
STRIUING = 2
Striuing to better, oft we marre what's well.   870
This hurt you see, striuing to apprehend him.   1049
STROKE = 1
But not without that harmefull stroke, which since | Hath pluckt him
after.   2321
STROKES = 1
Haue humbled to all strokes: that I am wretched   2250
STRONG = 1*1
Spoke with how manifold, and strong a Bond   983
*the strong Lance of Iustice, hurtlesse breakes: Arme it in   2609
STROOKE = 2
Look'd blacke vpon me, strooke me with her Tongue   1442
Gent. None but the Foole, who labours to out-iest | His heart-strooke
iniuries.   1624
STRUCKEN = 1
Ste. Ile not be strucken my Lord.   615
STUBBORNE = 1
You stubborne ancient Knaue, you reuerent Bragart, | Wee'l teach you.   1204

STUDY = 3

Edm. Sir, I shall study deseruing.   34

Gon. Let your study | Be to content your Lord, who hath receiu'd you   302

What is your study? | *Edg.* How to preuent the Fiend, and to kill

Vermine.   1937

STUFFE = *1

Bast. If I finde him comforting the King, it will stuffe   1990

STUMBLED = 1

I stumbled when I saw. Full oft 'tis seene,   2200

STUNG = 1

Each iealous of the other, as the stung   2903

STYLE = *1

Edg. Both style, and gate; Horseway, and foot-path: 2246

SUBDUD = *1

Lear. Death Traitor, nothing could haue subdu'd | (Nature   1851

SUBDUED = 1

For him attempting, who was selfe-subdued,   1198

SUBIECT = 2*1

Lear. If thou be'st as poore for a subiect, as hee's for a   552

When I do stare, see how the Subiect quakes.   2555

I hold you but a subiect of this Warre, | Not as a Brother.   2999

SUBSCRIBE = 1

All Cruels else subscribe: but I shall see   2137

SUBSCRIPTION = 1

You owe me no subscription. Then let fall   1673

SUBSTANCE = 2

If ought within that little seeming substance,   216

Hast heauy substance, bleed'st not, speak'st, art sound,   2494

SUB-CONTRACTED = 1

'Tis she is sub-contracted to this Lord,   3031

SUCCEEDE = *1

Bast. I promise you, the effects he writes of, succeede | vnhappily.   472

SUCCESSE = 1

Not sure, though hoping of this good successe,   3157

SUCH = 35*6

Bur. Pardon me Royall Sir, | Election makes not vp in such conditions.   225

I would not from your loue make such a stray,   229

Must be of such vnnaturall degree,   240

A still soliciting eye, and such a tongue,   253

Haue no such Daughter, nor shall euer see   288

Reg. Such vnconstant starts are we like to haue from | him, as this of   .

Kents banishment.   325

*Father carry authority with such disposition as he beares,   329

*such neede to hide it selfe. Let's see: come, if it bee no-|thing, I shall

not neede Spectacles.   369

Glou. He cannot bee such a Monster. *Edmond* seeke   427

That such a King should play bo-peepe, | And goe the Foole among.   690

To be such men as may besort your Age, | Which know themselues, and

you.   760

And such a Daughter, | Should sure to the Slaughter,   838

And thereto adde such reasons of your owne,   862

Beene well inform'd of them, and with such cautions,   1041

Nature's of such deepe trust, we shall much need: | You we first seize

on.   1057

Kent. That such a slaue as this should weare a Sword,   1145

Who weares no honesty: such smiling rogues as these,   1146

Kent. No contraries hold more antipathy, | Then I, and such a knaue.   1160

SUCH *cont*.
And put vpon him such a deale of Man,   1196
To do vpon respect such violent outrage: 1299
'Tis on such ground, and to such wholesome end,   1423
With such a number? What, must I come to you   1551
I will haue such reuenges on you both,   1579
That all the world shall--- I will do such things,   1580
Loue not such nights as these: The wrathfull Skies   1695
Such sheets of Fire, such bursts of horrid Thunder,   1698
Such groanes of roaring Winde, and Raine, I neuer   1699
No, I will weepe no more; in such a night,   1797
In such a night as this? O *Regan*, *Gonerill*,   1799
From seasons such as these? O I haue tane   1813
To such a lownesse, but his vnkind Daughters.   1852
*man, is no more but such a poore, bare, forked A-|nimall   1887
But Mice, and Rats, and such small Deare,   1917
Reg. So white, and such a Traitor? | *Glou*. Naughty Ladie,   2102
The Sea, with such a storme as his bare head,   2131
The winged Vengeance ouertake such Children.   2138
I'th'last nights storme, I such a fellow saw;   2216
Lear. Vpon such sacrifices my *Cordelia*, | The Gods themselues throw
Incense.   2961
With boote, and such addition as your Honours   3273
SUCKD = *1
*You Fen-suck'd Fogges, drawne by the powrfull Sunne, | To fall, and
blister.   1450
SUDDEN *see* sodaine
SUDDENLY *see* sodainely
SUE = 1
Kent. I must loue you, and sue to know you better.   33
SUFFER = 2
To suffer with the body; Ile forbeare,   1385
Glou. Go in with me; my duty cannot suffer   1926
SUFFERD = *1
*not as it hath power, but as it is suffer'd. Come to me, that of   386
SUFFERING = 1
Who hast not in thy browes an eye-discerning | Thine Honor, from thy
suffering.   2306
SUFFERS = 1
The shame which heere it suffers.   1321
SUGGESTION = 1
To thy suggestion, plot, and damned practise: 1010
SUITE *see* sutors
SUITED = 1*1
*base, proud, shallow, beggerly, three-suited-hundred   1089
Cor. Be better suited,   2753
SUITES = *1
*stockt, punish'd, and imprison'd: who hath three Suites | to his backe,
sixe shirts to his body: 1914
SULPHROUS = 1
You Sulph'rous and Thought-executing Fires,   1659
SULPHUROUS = *1
*there is the sulphurous pit; burning, scalding, stench,   2570
SUMMIT *see* somnet
SUMMOND = 1
They summon'd vp their meiney, straight tooke Horse,   1311

SUMMONERS = 1
These dreadfull Summoners grace. I am a man, | More sinn'd against,
then sinning.   1712
SUMMONS = 1
Your name, your quality, and why you answer | This present Summons?   3071
SUMPTER = 1
Perswade me rather to be slaue and sumpter | To this detested groome.   1509
SUN = 1 *2
*Glou. These late Eclipses in the Sun and Moone por- | tend   433
*behauiour, we make guilty of our disasters, the Sun, the   449
Thou out of Heauens benediction com'st | To the warme Sun.   1238
SUNG = 1
For sodaine ioy did weepe, | And I for sorrow sung,   688
SUNNE = 1 *1
For by the sacred radience of the Sunne,   116
*You Fen-suck'd Fogges, drawne by the powrfull Sunne, | To fall, and
blister.   1450
SUNNES = 1
Glou. Were all thy Letters Sunnes, I could not see.   2584
SUPERFLUOUS = 2
Are in the poorest thing superfluous.   1565
Let the superfluous, and Lust-dieted man,   2252
SUPERFLUX = 1
That thou maist shake the superflux to them,   1816
SUPER-SERUICEABLE = *1
*action-taking, whoreson glasse-gazing super-seruiceable   1091
SUPPER = 1
so, so, wee'l go to Supper i'th'morning.   2042
SUPPLY = *1
*Gaole, from the loathed warmth whereof, deliuer me, and sup- | ply the
place for your Labour.   2720
SUPPORT = 3
And in the most exact regard, support   778
Stew. Wherefore, bold Pezant, | Dar'st thou support a publish'd
Traitor? Hence,   2683
(Alacke too weake the conflict to support)   3160
SUPPOSED = *1
*will maintaine vpon Edmund, supposed Earle of Gloster,   3061
SURE = 9
Cor. Then poore Cordelia, | And yet not so, since I am sure my loue's   82
Sure I shall neuer marry like my Sisters.   110
So many folds of fauour: sure her offence   239
Who I am sure is kinde and comfortable: 825
And such a Daughter, | Should sure to the Slaughter,   838
Edg. I am sure on't, not a word.   958
I am sure of that: and at her late being heere,   2411
Edg. Do you heare ought (Sir) of a Battell toward. | Gent. Most sure,
and vulgar: 2652
Not sure, though hoping of this good successe,   3157
SURFETS = *1
*when we are sicke in fortune, often the surfets of our own   448
SURGE = 1
Almost too small for sight. The murmuring Surge,   2455
SURGEONS = 1
You shall haue ransome. Let me haue Surgeons,   2635
SURRENDER = 1
this last surrender of his will but offend vs.   330

SUSPECTS = 1
That he suspects none: on whose foolish honestie   501
SUSPEND = 1*1
*suspend your indignation against my Brother, til you can   414
Suspend thy purpose, if thou did'st intend | To make this Creature
fruitfull: 790
SUSPITION = *1
*his suspition more fully. I will perseuer in my course of   1991
SUSTAIND = 1
By you to be sustain'd, shall our abode   142
SUSTAINE = 3
If she sustaine him, and his hundred Knights   854
of him, entreat for him, or any way sustaine him.   1757
Rule in this Realme, and the gor'd state sustaine.   3295
SUSTAINING = 1
In our sustaining Corne. A Centery send forth;   2356
SUTE = 1
*Ste. This ancient Ruffian Sir, whose life I haue spar'd | at sute of his
gray-beard.   1135
SUTORS = 1
No Heretiques burn'd, but wenches Sutors;   1739
SUUM = *1
*cold winde: Sayes suum, mun, nonny, Dolphin my Boy,   1879
SWAGGERD see zwaggerd
SWALLOWES = *1
*Cow-dung for Sallets; swallowes the old Rat, and the   1911
SWAY = 3
The name, and all th'addition to a King: the Sway,   144
If you do loue old men; if your sweet sway   1480
I'th'sway of your owne will: is he array'd?   2770
SWAYES = *1
*and fond bondage, in the oppression of aged tyranny, who swayes   385
SWEAR = *1
*Bast. If the matter were good my Lord, I durst swear   398
SWEARE = 3*1
Lear. By Iupiter I sweare no.   1295
Kent. By Iuno, I sweare I.   1296
*keepe thy words Iustice, sweare not, commit not,   1861
I will not sweare these are my hands: let's see,   2807
SWEARST = 1
Kent. Now by Apollo, King | Thou swear'st thy Gods in vaine.   173
SWEET = 5*2
*Foole. Do'st thou know the difference my Boy, be-|tweene a bitter
Foole, and a sweet one.   667
*Lear. O let me not be mad, not mad sweet Heauen: 918
If you do loue old men; if your sweet sway   1480
*them in the sweet face of Heauen. One, that slept in the   1869
Gon. Farewell sweet Lord, and Sister. Exit   2081
clout, i'th'clout: Hewgh. Giue the word. | Edg. Sweet Mariorum.   2539
Reg. Now sweet Lord,   2853
SWEETE = 1
Blesse thy sweete eyes, they bleede.   2244
SWEETEN = *1
*of Ciuet; good Apothecary sweeten my immagination: 2572
SWEETNESSE = 1
That follow'd me so neere, (O our liues sweetnesse,   3147

SWEET-HEART = 1*1
  *with mans sworne Spouse: set not thy Sweet-heart on | proud array.
  Tom's a cold.   1862
  Trey, Blanch, and Sweet-heart: see, they barke at me.   2021
SWELL = 1
  Or swell the curled Waters 'boue the Maine,   1621
SWELS = *1
  *Lear. Oh how this Mother swels vp toward my heart!   1328
SWIFT = *1
  *Postes shall be swift, and intelligent betwixt vs. Fare-|well deere
  Sister, farewell my Lord of Glouster.   2070
SWIMME = *1
  *night to swimme in. Now a little fire in a wilde Field,   1892
SWIMMING = *1
  *Edg. Poore Tom, that eates the swimming Frog, the   1908
SWINE = 1
  To houell thee with Swine and Rogues forlorne,   2787
SWITHOLD = 1
  Swithold footed thrice the old,   1900
SWORD = 11*3
  In cunning, I must draw my Sword vpon you: 960
  *Bast. Here stood he in the dark, his sharpe Sword out,   972
  With his prepared Sword, he charges home   987
  *Kent. That such a slaue as this should weare a Sword,   1145
  *through Sword, and Whirle-Poole, o're Bog, and Quag-|mire,   1834
  Reg. Giue me the Sword. A pezant stand vp thus? | Killes him.   2154
  Oppos'd against the act: bending his Sword   2318
  Breefely thy selfe remember: the Sword is out | That must destroy thee. 2679
  Do's not become a Sword, thy great imployment   2975
  Bast. Himselfe, what saist thou to him? | Edg. Draw thy Sword,   3079
  Despise thy victor-Sword, and fire new Fortune,   3087
  This Sword, this arme, and my best spirits are bent   3094
  This Sword of mine shall giue them instant way,   3105
  Bast. Well thought on, take my Sword,   3208
SWORE = *1
  *her. Swore as many Oathes, as I spake words, & broke   1868
SWORNE = 2*1
  Lear. Nothing, I haue sworne, I am firme.   269
  *with mans sworne Spouse: set not thy Sweet-heart on | proud array.
  Tom's a cold.   1862
  Bast. To both these Sisters haue I sworne my loue: 2902
SYLLABLE see sillable
T = 8
  T'auert your liking a more worthier way,   231
  Then on a wretch whom Nature is asham'd | Almost t'acknowledge
  hers.   232
  Which are t'intrince, t'vnloose: smooth euery passion   1148
  T'obey in all your daughters hard commands: 1927
  His wits begin t'vnsettle. | Glou. Canst thou blame him? Storm still 1941
  To morrow, or at further space, t'appeare   2996
  Into a mad-mans rags, t'assume a semblance   3150
TAD-POLE see tod-pole
TAILE = 1*1
  *taile, and my Natiuity was vnder Vrsa Maior, so   458
  Or Bobtaile tight, or Troudle taile,   2027
TAILOR see taylor

TAILORS *see* taylors
TAINT = 1
    Fall into taint, which to beleeue of her — 242
TAKE = 49*12
    That Lord, whose hand must take my plight, shall carry — 108
    Our potencie made good, take thy reward. — 186
    The Gods to their deere shelter take thee Maid, — 196
    Dow'rd with our curse, and stranger'd with our oath, | Take her or, leaue her. — 223
    And here I take *Cordelia* by the hand, | Dutchesse of *Burgundie*. — 267
    Be it lawfull I take vp what's cast away. — 278
    Who in the lustie stealth of Nature, take | More composition, and fierce qualitie, — 345
    Foole. Sirrah, you were best take my Coxcombe. — 627
    *colde shortly, there take my Coxcombe; why this fellow — 631
    Lear. Take heed Sirrah, the whip. — 640
    By her, that else will take the thing she begges, — 757
    Tarry, take the Foole with thee: — 836
    Let me still take away the harmes I feare, — 851
    Gon. Take you some company, and away to horse, — 860
    My Father hath set guard to take my Brother, — 945
    *the King, and take Vanitie the puppets part, a- |gainst — 1109
    And they will take it so, if not, hee's plaine. — 1175
    The King his Master, needs must take it ill — 1221
    Take vantage heauie eyes, not to behold — 1248
    To take the basest, and most poorest shape — 1258
    To take the indispos'd and sickly fit, — 1387
    Reg. I pray you Sir, take patience, I haue hope — 1416
    Make it your cause: Send downe, and take my part. — 1482
    O *Regan*, will you take her by the hand? — 1484
    Then my out-wall; open this Purse, and take — 1642
    Doth from my sences take all feeling else, — 1793
    Too little care of this: Take Physicke, Pompe, — 1814
    Edgar. Take heed o'th'foule Fiend, obey thy Pa- |rents, — 1860
    And let this Tyrannous night take hold vpon you, — 1929
    Kent. Good my Lord take his offer, | Go into th'house. — 1934
    Let him take the Fellow. — 1961
    Glou. Take him you on. | *Kent*. Sirra, come on: go along with vs. — 1962
    Glou. Heere is better then the open ayre, take it thank- |fully: — 1998
    Edg. My teares begin to take his part so much, | They marre my counterfetting. — 2018
    Glou. Good friend, I prythee take him in thy armes; — 2047
    Both welcome, and protection. Take vp thy Master, — 2051
    Stand in assured losse. Take vp, take vp, — 2054
    *take vppon your Traitorous Father, are not fit for your — 2067
    Corn. My Villaine? | *Seru*. Nay then come on, and take the chance of anger. — 2152
    Thou wilt ore-take vs hence a mile or twaine — 2229
    Glou. Here take this purse, y whom the heau'ns plagues — 2249
    Alb. Where was his Sonne, | When they did take his eyes? — 2335
    Take all my outward worth. — 2360
    Therefore I do aduise you take this note: — 2416
    Edg. I would not take this from report, | It is, and my heart breakes at it. — 2585
    *none, I say none, Ile able 'em; take that of me my Friend, — 2611
    Lear. If thou wilt weepe my Fortunes, take my eyes. — 2618
    Glou. You euer gentle Gods, take my breath from me, — 2663

TAKE *cont.*

Least that th'infection of his fortune take	2685
Stew. Slaue thou hast slaine me: Villain, take my purse;	2699
Lear. You do me wrong to take me out o'th'graue,	2794
Are of the Adder. Which of them shall I take?	2904
If both remaine aliue: To take the Widdow,	2906
Edg. Heere Father, take the shadow of this Tree	2921
Bast. Some Officers take them away: good guard,	2940
And take vpon's the mystery of things,	2956
Bast. Take them away.	2960
Take thou this note, go follow them to prison,	2970
Take thou my Souldiers, prisoners, patrimony,	3018
Bast. Well thought on, take my Sword,	3208

TAKEN *see also* tane = 3

Not feare still to be taken. I know his heart,	852
Cor. If he be taken, he shall neuer more	1052
Glo. The Duke's too blame in this, | 'Twill be ill taken. *Exit.*	1235

TAKING = 4*4

Gon. There is further complement of leaue-taking be-|tweene	327
Lear. Why my Boy? | *Foole.* Why? for taking ones part that's out of fauour,	628
*action-taking, whoreson glasse-gazing super-seruiceable	1091
Do's not attend my taking. Whiles I may scape	1256
You taking Ayres, with Lamenesse. | *Corn.* Fye sir, fie.	1446
*blisse thee from Whirle-Windes, Starre-blasting, and ta-|king,	1840
Well worth a poore mans taking. Fayries, and Gods	2466
His speedy taking off. As for the mercie	2912

TAKT = *1

| *Lear.* To tak't againe perforce; Monster Ingratitude! | 912 |

TALE = 1*1

| *curious tale in telling it, and deliuer a plaine message | 564 |
| *Edg.* By nursing them my Lord. List a breefe tale, | 3144 |

TALES = 2

| Nor tell tales of thee to high-iudging *Ioue*, | 1522 |
| And pray, and sing, and tell old tales, and laugh | 2952 |

TALKD = 1

| My Lord is dead: *Edmond*, and I haue talk'd, | 2417 |

TALKE = 4*2

Gent. I will talke further with you. | *Kent.* No, do not:	1639
*maintaine talke with the Duke, that my charity be not of	1766
Lear. First let me talke with this Philosopher,	1932
Lear. Ile talke a word with this same lerned Theban:	1936
Talke of Court newes, and wee'l talke with them too,	2954

TALL = 1

| Appeare like Mice: and yond tall Anchoring Barke, | 2453 |

TAME = *1

| *Edg.* A most poore man, made tame to Fortunes blows | 2668 |

TAMELY = 1

| To beare it tamely: touch me with Noble anger, | 1576 |

TANE = 2

| From seasons such as these? O I haue tane | 1813 |
| King *Lear* hath lost, he and his Daughter tane, | 2929 |

TARDINESSE = 1

| *Fra.* Is it but this? A tardinesse in nature, | 258 |

TARRY = 3

| tarry, but away, goe too, haue you wisedome, so. | 621 |
| Tarry, take the Foole with thee: | 836 |

TARRY *cont.*
But I will tarry, the Foole will stay,   1354
TART = 1
The Newes is not so tart. Ile read, and answer.   2334
TASK = 1
You are much more at task for want of wisedome,   867
TASTE = 4*1
this but as an essay, or taste of my Vertue.   381
Foole. She will taste as like this as, a Crabbe do's to a   892
And must needs taste his folly.   1591
Ere I taste bread, thou art in nothing lesse   3041
Taste the wages of their vertue, and all Foes   3275
TATTERD = *1
*tatter'd cloathes great Vices do appeare: Robes,   2607
TAUERNE = 1
Makes it more like a Tauerne, or a Brothell,   754
TAUGHT = 1
Rather then die at once) taught me to shift   3149
TAXE = 1
I taxe not you, you Elements with vnkindnesse.   1671
TAYLOR = *3
*you cowardly Rascall, nature disclaimes in thee: a Taylor | made thee.   1128
Cor. Thou art a strange fellow, a Taylor make a man?   1130
Kent. A Taylor Sir, a Stone-cutter, or a Painter, could   1131
TAYLORS = 1
When Nobles are their Taylors Tutors,   1738
TEACH = 3*3
Kent. Come sir, arise, away, Ile teach you differences: 619
Foole. Sirha, Ile teach thee a speech. | *Lear.* Do.   645
Lear. No Lad, teach me.   669
*Pry'thy Nunckle keepe a Schoolemaster that can teach   692
You stubborne ancient Knaue, you reuerent Bragart, | Wee'l teach you.   1204
Foole. Wee'l set thee to schoole to an Ant, to teach   1340
TEARE = 1
Is it not as this mouth should teare this hand   1795
TEARES = 7
With cadent Teares fret Channels in her cheekes,   799
That these hot teares, which breake from me perforce   816
Edg. My teares begin to take his part so much, | They marre my
counterfetting.   2018
Spring with my teares; be aydant, and remediate   2368
My mourning, and importun'd teares hath pittied: 2378
Vpon a wheele of fire, that mine owne teares | Do scal'd, like molten
Lead.   2796
Lear. Be your teares wet?   2827
TEARING = 1
No tearing Lady, I perceiue you know it.   3115
TEEME = 1
A Babe to honor her. If she must teeme,   795
TEETH = *1
Edg. Chill picke your teeth Zir: come, no matter vor | your foynes.   2697
TELL = 25*5
And heere are to be answer'd. Tell me my daughters   53
Ile tell thee thou dost euill.   180
I tell you all her wealth. For you great King,   228
*and tell my Daughter, I would speake with her. Goe you   605
Foole. Prythee tell him, so much the rent of his land   664

TELL *cont*.

Who is it that can tell me who I am? | *Foole*. *Lears* shadow.	743
Alb. What's the matter, Sir? | *Lear*. Ile tell thee:	812
Alb. How farre your eies may pierce I cannot tell;	869
*for though she's as like this, as a Crabbe's like an | Apple, yet I can tell what I can tell.	889
Lear. What can'st tell Boy?	891
*Crab: thou canst, tell why ones nose stands i'th'middle | on's face? | *Lear*. No.	893
Foole. Can'st tell how an Oyster makes his shell? | *Lear*. No.	899
Foole. Nor I neither; but I can tell why a Snaile ha's | a house.	901
Stew. Prythee, if thou lou'st me, tell me. | *Kent*. I loue thee not.	1080
Daughters, as thou canst tell in a yeare.	1327
Fiery? The fiery Duke, tell the hot Duke that---	1380
Goe tell the Duke, and's wife, Il'd speake with them:	1392
Nor tell tales of thee to high-iudging *Ioue*,	1522
And she will tell you who that Fellow is	1645
When Vsurers tell their Gold i'th'Field,	1744
Thou sayest the King growes mad, Ile tell thee Friend	1945
No Father his Sonne deerer: true to tell thee,	1949
Foole. Prythee Nunkle tell me, whether a madman be | a Gentleman, or a Yeoman.	2007
Tell me what more thou know'st. *Exeunt*.	2347
That of thy death, and businesse, I can tell.	2731
Tell me but truly, but then speake the truth,	2855
And pray, and sing, and tell old tales, and laugh	2952
Mine eyes are not o'th'best, Ile tell you straight.	3244
Lear. He's a good fellow, I can tell you that,	3250

TELLING = *1

*curious tale in telling it, and deliuer a plaine message	564

TELLS = *1

Edg. *Fraterretto* cals me, and tells me *Nero* is an Ang-|ler	2004

TEMPER = 1*1

To temper, Clay. Ha? Let it be so.	823
*keepe me in temper, I would not be mad. How now are | the Horses ready?	919

TEMPERANCE = 1

Be by good Madam when we do awake him, | I doubt of his Temperance.	2774

TEMPEST = 4

No, Ile not weepe, I haue full cause of weeping. | *Storme and Tempest*.	1583
Some friendship will it lend you 'gainst the Tempest:	1716
The bodies delicate: the tempest in my mind,	1792
This tempest will not giue me leaue to ponder	1805

TEMPT = 1

Let not my worser Spirit tempt me againe | To dye before you please.	2664

TEN = 2

Gon. Heare me my Lord; | What need you fiue and twenty? Ten? Or fiue?	1559
Ten Masts at each, make not the altitude	2495

TENANT = 2

Oldm. O my good Lord, I haue bene your Tenant,	2193
And your Fathers Tenant, these fourescore yeares.	2194

TEND = 1

To follow in a house, where twice so many | Haue a command to tend you?	1561

TENDED = 1
  That tended vpon my Father?   1034
TENDER = 3
  Nor will you tender lesse?   212
  Which in the tender of a wholesome weale,   722
  Are as the time is; to be tender minded   2974
TENDER-HEFTED = 1
  Thy tender-hefted Nature shall not giue   1455
TENDS = *1
  The deere Father | *Would with his Daughter speake, commands, tends, ser- |(uice,   1377
TENS = 1
  And thou shalt haue more, | Then two tens to a score.   656
TENT = 1
  Alb. She is not well, conuey her to my Tent.   3056
TENTH = 1
  Vpon our kingdome: if on the tenth day following,   190
TERMES = 1*1
  Bast. Parted you in good termes? Found you no dis- |pleasure in him, by word, nor countenance?   478
  All's not offence that indiscretion findes, | And dotage termes so.   1486
TERRIBLE = *1
  Glou. No? what needed then that terrible dispatch of   367
TERRITORY = 1
  Interest of Territory, Cares of State)   55
TERROR = 1
  It is the Cowish terror of his spirit   2280
TERRORS = 1
  The terrors of the earth? you thinke Ile weepe,   1582
TERTIA *l.*505 1751 2348 2937 = 4
TERTIUS *l.*1614 = 1
TESTIMONY = *1
  *deriue from him better testimony of his intent, you shold   415
TH *see also* by'th, i'th, o'th, to'th = 25*3
  The name, and all th'addition to a King: the Sway,   144
  Aloofe from th'intire point, will you haue her?   263
  Goe to th'creating a whole tribe of Fops   348
  As to th'legitimate: fine word: Legitimate.   352
  Th'vntented woundings of a Fathers curse   819
  When I haue shew'd th'vnfitnesse.   855
  Gon. Nay then--- | *Alb.* Well, well, th'euent. *Exeunt*   871
  Bold in the quarrels right, rouz'd to th'encounter,   990
  Which can pursue th'offender; how dost my Lord?   1028
  To haue th'expence and wast of his Reuenues: 1039
  Vnder th'allowance of your great aspect,   1181
  Corn. What was th'offence you gaue him? | *Ste.* I neuer gaue him any: 1190
  Remember to haue heard. Mans Nature cannot carry | Th'affliction, nor the feare.   1700
  Kent. Good my Lord take his offer, | Go into th'house.   1934
  Glou. In fellow there, into th'Houel; keep thee warm.   1955
  Reg. One side will mocke another: Th'other too.   2143
  As Flies to wanton Boyes, are we to th'Gods, | They kill vs for their sport.   2221
  Glou. When shall I come to th'top of that same hill?   2431
  That on th'vnnumbred idle Pebble chafes   2456
  You are now within a foote of th'extreme Verge: 2462
  *who haue the power to seale th'accusers lips. Get thee   2612

TH *cont*.

Least that th'infection of his fortune take	2685
*come not neere th'old man: keepe out che vor'ye, or Ile	2693
Th'vntun'd and iarring senses, O winde vp, | Of this childe-changed Father.	2765
Alb. Let's then determine with th'ancient of warre | On our proceeding.	2873
In a wall'd prison, packs and sects of great ones, | That ebbe and flow by th'Moone.	2958
And from th'extremest vpward of thy head,	3091
By th'law of Warre, thou wast not bound to answer	3109

THAN *see* then

THANKE = 6*1

Lear. I thanke thee fellow. | Thou seru'st me, and Ile loue thee.	617
Lear. Now my friendly knaue I thanke thee, there's | earnest of thy seruice.	622
Glo. For him I thanke your Grace.	1060
Alb. Glouster, I liue | To thanke thee for the loue thou shew'dst the King,	2344
Edg. I thanke you Sir, that's all.	2659
Edg. I thanke you Sir.	2662
Pray you vndo this Button. Thanke you Sir,	3281

THANKES = 2

That he which finds him shall deserue our thankes,	998
Ile leade you to some biding. | *Glou*. Heartie thankes:	2671

THANKFULLY = *1

Glou. Heere is better then the open ayre, take it thank-|fully:	1998

THANKLESSE = 1

To haue a thanklesse Childe. Away, away. *Exit*.	803

THAT *see also* y *l*.*9 *13 42 49 57 65 74 77 88 97 108 124 *140 156 182
197 199 216 *227 235 241 243 246 248 251 252 254 260 262 266 271 273
275 *279 289 305 *323 339 *367 *372 *386 *399 *406 *419 *425 *447
*454 *459 *460 471 *484 501 504 512 522 532 533 *545 *546 *558 560
*565 579 *588 *604 679 690 *692 *703 710 719 723 724 *727 743 752
757 759 769 777 784 796 801 804 807 815 816 822 828 830 *845 858 897
915 931 933 981 998 1000 1019 1020 1034 1036 1042 1045 *1092 *1099
*1122 *1145 1149 1159 1168 1179 *1186 1197 1222 1224 *1237 1241
1255 1259 *1274 1287 1305 *1322 *1323 *1324 *1325 *1337 *1341 *1346
1350 1356 1380 1390 *1401 1411 1419 1429 1431 1435 1437 1469 1471
1486 1498 1505 1529 1535 1540 1571 1574 1580 1607 1622 1631 1641
1645 1646 *1651 1652 1664 1677 *1680 1682 1694 1703 1705 1708 1709
1729 1748 *1754 *1760 *1766 1772 1774 1786 1801 1802 1810 1816
*1825 *1835 *1848 1853 *1865 *1869 *1908 *1909 1924 1943 *1972
*1979 *1982 *1988 *1992 *2010 *2011 2017 2024 *2034 2053 2055 2124
2135 2141 2165 2166 2169 2174 2185 2186 2191 2224 2226 2238 2250
2253 2262 2271 2281 2305 2317 2321 2324 2342 2355 2359 2363 2371
*2377 2411 2424 2425 2431 *2448 2450 2452 2456 2503 2511 *2518 2522
2524 *2533 *2534 2542 *2546 *2552 2556 *2564 2574 *2604 *2605 *2611
2621 2624 2642 2654 *2660 2677 2680 2685 2709 2731 2734 2758 2768
2778 2785 2789 2796 2886 2887 2922 2942 2959 2964 2973 *3012 3015
3020 3046 3047 *3062 3077 *3078 3081 3099 3122 3125 3145 3147 3148
3151 3185 3214 3219 3222 3225 3229 3238 3250 3253 3254 3263 3288
3300 = 235*79

THATS = 9*6

Reg. That's most certaine, and with you: next moneth | (with vs.	313
Edm. That's my feare, I pray you haue a continent	487
Lear. Why my Boy? | *Foole*. Why? for taking ones part that's out of fauour,	628

THATS *cont.*

Weary of all, shall want some. That's a sheal'd Pescod.	711
Fool. She that's a Maid now, & laughs at my departure,	923
That's something yet: *Edgar* I nothing am. *Exit*.	1272
*not a nose among twenty, but can smell him that's stink-|ing;	1343
Or rather a disease that's in my flesh,	1516
Kent. Who's there? | *Foole*. Marry here's Grace, and a Codpiece, that's	
a | Wiseman, and a Foole.	1691
Poore Foole, and Knaue, I haue one part in my heart | That's sorry yet	
for thee.	1727
Which came from one that's of a newtrall heart, | And not from one	
oppos'd.	2116
Edg. I thanke you Sir, that's all.	2659
Ripenesse is all come on. | *Glo*. And that's true too. *Exeunt*.	2935
Reg. That's as we list to grace him.	3001
Mess. Edmund is dead my Lord. | *Alb*. That's but a trifle heere:	3266

THAUE = 1

Lear. Better thou had'st | Not beene borne, then not t'haue pleas'd me	
better.	256

THE *see also* o'the, th', y = 495*233

THEBAN = *1

Lear. Ile talke a word with this same lerned Theban:	1936

THEE *l.*71 85 123 162 180 187 188 *194 196 277 *445 537 *571 *572 617
618 *622 645 *670 *699 737 764 772 813 817 818 820 826 836 *888 *913
928 1005 1006 1014 1023 1044 *1076 1081 1082 *1083 1084 1085 1086
*1099 1100 *1103 1107 *1128 1129 *1228 1230 1279 1288 *1340 *1341
*1346 *1347 1353 1414 1456 1457 1465 1513 1519 1522 1556 1570 1705
1706 1728 1771 1787 1808 1829 *1840 1903 1945 1949 *1955 1987
*1994 2056 2105 2165 2167 2191 2195 2197 2204 2225 2228 2236 2248
2251 2265 2292 2296 2345 2407 2428 2467 2468 2480 2519 2573 *2612
2619 2622 2680 2686 2704 2727 2787 2945 2951 2963 2971 2972 3020
3027 3042 3082 3126 3133 3138 3140 3210 3238 = 106*24

THEEFE = 1*2

Pinnion him like a Theefe, bring him before vs:	2083
*yond Iustice railes vpon yond simple theefe. Hearke in	2596
*the Iustice, which is the theefe: Thou hast seene a Far-|mers	2598

THEEUES = *1

*Fooles by heauenly compulsion, Knaues, Theeues, and	451

THEFT = 1

Yeelds to the Theft. Had he bin where he thought,	2484

THEIR *see also* o'their *l.*52 196 *279 682 683 723 752 767 779 847 1149
1151 1152 1179 1247 1266 1271 1303 1311 1313 *1323 *1324 *1341
*1342 1394 1575 1608 1631 1697 1704 1721 1737 1738 1744 *1754 1854
1928 2222 2342 2713 2714 *2781 2898 2934 2941 2987 3054 3153 3199
3275 3276 = 45*7

THEM *see also* 'em *l.*45 285 324 377 *384 *637 *686 817 1041 1277 1304
1373 *1374 1392 1393 1543 1636 1697 1816 *1869 *2022 *2033 *2037
2320 2376 *2518 2755 2782 2904 2940 2942 2954 2960 2966 2970 2986
*2994 3019 3105 3144 3179 3218 3246 3293 = 35*10

THEMSELUES = 5

To be such men as may besort your Age, | Which know themselues, and	
you.	760
Reg. O Sir, to wilfull men, | The iniuries that they themselues procure,	1606
The knowledge of themselues.	2739
Lear. Vpon such sacrifices my *Cordelia*, | The Gods themselues throw	
Incense.	2961
Your eldest Daughters haue fore-done themselues,	3259

THEN *l.*5 *23 *60 61 63 82 84 88 92 115 211 *227 232 257 270 *321 347
349 *367 *411 426 *544 *599 648 649 650 651 652 653 657 *659 *687
*698 *707 724 755 756 773 802 834 850 868 871 *877 *885 *909 941 968
1037 1082 1161 1168 1178 *1285 *1298 1318 1418 1430 1497 1542 1566
1642 1650 *1666 1673 1713 1718 1736 *1746 1747 *1760 1774 1808
*1881 *1883 *1998 *2033 2148 *2153 2168 2180 2184 2208 2218 2219
2275 2279 2419 2437 2441 2451 2561 2629 2644 *2719 2760 2855 2873
2909 3009 3042 3114 3128 3149 3223 3274 = 80*26
THER *l.*494 *1763 = *2
THERE *l.*26 42 215 219 *327 *577 *631 *878 1043 1202 1213 1277 1306
1491 1616 1628 *1686 1691 1717 *1759 *1769 1794 1822 *1825 *1842
1843 1906 1907 *1955 *2034 2049 2089 2206 *2258 2361 2386 *2545
*2549 *2570 *2589 *2601 *2718 2888 3040 3166 3283 = 28*22
THEREFORE = 5

To match you where I hate, therefore beseech you	230
Better then you your selfe: therefore I pray you,	1430
Glou. I haue no way, and therefore want no eyes:	2199
Therefore I do aduise you take this note:	2416
It was some Fiend: Therefore thou happy Father,	2517

THERES = 5*10

Bast. It was not brought mee, my Lord; there's the	394
*prediction; there's Son against Father, the King fals from	440
*byas of Nature, there's Father against Childe. We haue	441
there's my key: if you do stirre abroad, goe arm'd.	491
*theres a great abatement of kindnesse appeares as well in	589
Lear. Now my friendly knaue I thanke thee, there's | earnest of thy	
seruice.	622
*my selfe, there's mine, beg another of thy | Daughters.	638
*noses, are led by their eyes, but blinde men, and there's	1342
Do sorely ruffle, for many Miles about | There's scarce a Bush.	1604
*doo't. There's my Gauntlet, Ile proue it on a Gyant.	2537
*beneath is all the Fiends. There's hell, there's darke- |nes,	2569
There's money for thee.	2573
Lear. Then there's life in't. Come, and you get it,	2644
Bast. There's my exchange, what in the world hes	3045

THERETO = 1

And thereto adde such reasons of your owne,	862

THEREWITHALL = *1

*therewithall the vnruly way-wardnesse, that infirme and | cholericke	
yeares bring with them.	323

THERFORE = 1*1

That face of hers againe, therfore be gone,	289
*It is thy businesse that I go about: Therfore great France	2377

THERS = *2

*thee ther's no labouring i'th' winter. All that follow their	1341
Lear. Nature's aboue Art, in that respect. Ther's your	2533

THESE *l.*68 *433 *465 470 612 733 816 *875 1146 1176 1201 *1438 1574
1638 1695 1712 *1762 1813 *2035 2104 2140 2194 2324 2628 2709 2754
*2781 2807 2822 2871 2902 2947 3102 3243 = 27*9
THEY = 38*12
THEYL = *1

*they'l haue me whipt for speaking true: thou'lt haue me	696

THHAST = 3

Bast. About it, and write happy, when th'hast done,	2979
If more, the more th'hast wrong'd me.	3129
Bast. Th'hast spoken right, 'tis true,	3135

THICKE = 1
    Strike flat the thicke Rotundity o'th'world,   1662
THINE = 18*6
    We make thee Lady. To thine and *Albanies* issues   71
    Lear. To thee, and thine hereditarie euer,   85
    To wage against thine enemies, nere feare to loose it, | Thy safety being
    motiue.   167
    Kent. See better *Lear*, and let me still remaine | The true blanke of
    thine eie.   170
    Lea. Heare me recreant, on thine allegeance heare me;   181
    Lear. Thou hast her *France*, let her be thine, for we   287
    *both parts, thou boar'st thine Asse on thy backe o're the   676
    *the rod, and put'st downe thine owne breeches, then they   687
    Thee o're to harshnesse: Her eyes are fierce, but thine   1456
    Lear. Prythee go in thy selfe, seeke thine owne ease,   1804
    With thine, and all that offer to defend him,   2053
    Vpon these eyes of thine, Ile set my foote.   2140
    Who hast not in thy browes an eye-discerning | Thine Honor, from thy
    suffering.   2306
    And to reuenge thine eyes. Come hither Friend,   2346
    Do'st thou know me? | *Lear*. I remember thine eyes well enough: dost
    thou   2579
    *goes, with no eyes. Looke with thine eares: See how   2595
    *thine eare: Change places, and handy-dandy, which is   2597
    That eyelesse head of thine, was first fram'd flesh   2677
    And fire vs hence, like Foxes: wipe thine eyes,   2965
    Dispose of them, of me, the walls is thine: 3019
    Alb. The let alone lies not in your good will. | *Bast*. Nor in thine Lord.   3023
    Reg. Let the Drum strike, and proue my title thine.   3026
    Thou worse then any name, reade thine owne euill: 3114
    Gon. Say if I do, the Lawes are mine not thine,   3116
THING = 11*7
    Commit a thing so monstrous, to dismantle   238
    *nor so old to dote on her for any thing. I haue yeares on | my backe
    forty eight.   569
    *my peace. I had rather be any kind o'thing then a foole,   698
    By her, that else will take the thing she begges,   757
    *acquaint my Daughter no further with any thing you   876
    And I haue one thing of a queazie question   946
    Are in the poorest thing superfluous.   1565
    Commend a deere thing to you. There is diuision   1628
    Edgar. Who giues any thing to poore *Tom*? Whom   1832
    *sophisticated. Thou art the thing it selfe; vnaccommo- | dated   1886
    The lowest, and most deiected thing of Fortune,   2181
    Vpon the crowne o'th'Cliffe. What thing was that | Which parted from
    you?   2511
    Enough, enough, and dye. That thing you speake of,   2522
    *no, to euery thing that I said: I, and no too, was no good   2546
    *me, I was euery thing: 'Tis a Lye, I am not Agu-proofe.   2551
    Gent. You shall haue any thing. | *Lear*. No Seconds? All my selfe?   2637
    Is he not here? | *Alb*. Great thing of vs forgot,   3191
    Gentle, and low, an excellent thing in woman.   3237
THINGS = 7*3
    Shall not be a Maid long, vnlesse things be cut shorter. | *Exeunt*.   924
    That all the world shall--- I will do such things,   1580
    That things might change, or cease.   1622
    Kent. Alas Sir are you here? Things that loue night,   1694

THINGS *cont.*

*And can make vilde things precious. Come, your Houel;	1726
*my old Master must be relieued. There is strange things | toward	
Edmund, pray you be carefull. *Exit*.	1769
On things would hurt me more, but Ile goe in,	1806
Some things, I know not what. Ile loue thee much	2407
*things thou dost not. Now, now, now, now. Pull off my | Bootes:	
harder, harder, so.	2614
And take vpon's the mystery of things,	2956

THINKE = 17*4

I thinke our Father will hence to night.	312
Reg. We shall further thinke of it.	331
*it were his: but in respect of that, I would faine thinke it | were not.	399
to no other pretence of danger. | *Glou.* Thinke you so?	421
*backe: wher's my Foole? Ho, I thinke the world's	578
*mistaken, for my duty cannot be silent, when I thinke | your Highnesse	
wrong'd.	594
That Ile resume the shape which thou dost thinke | I haue cast off for	
euer. *Exit*	828
Thou vnpossessing Bastard, dost thou thinke,	1004
Lear. Regan, I thinke you are. I know what reason	1407
I haue to thinke so, if thou should'st not be glad,	1408
Reg. I cannot thinke my Sister in the least	1420
Must be content to thinke you old, and so,	1530
The terrors of the earth? you thinke Ile weepe,	1582
*thus giues way to Loyaltie, something feares mee to | thinke of.	1973
Glou. He that will thinke to liue, till he be old,	2141
Which made me thinke a Man, a Worme. My Sonne	2217
All hearts against vs: *Edmund*, I thinke is gone | In pitty of his misery,	
to dispatch	2396
*Thinke that the cleerest Gods, who make them Honors	2518
My boone I make it, that you know me not, | Till time, and I, thinke	
meet.	2758
For (as I am a man) I thinke this Lady | To be my childe *Cordelia*. |	
Cor. And so I am: I am.	2824
And desperately are dead | *Lear.* I so I thinke.	3260

THINKES = 5

Glou. Me thinkes the ground is eeuen. | *Edg.* Horrible steepe.	2433
Me thinkes thy voyce is alter'd, and thou speak'st	2440
Glou. Me thinkes y'are better spoken. | *Edg.* Come on Sir,	2444
Me thinkes he seemes no bigger then his head.	2451
Me thinkes I should know you, and know this man,	2819

THINKING = *1

Bast. I am thinking Brother of a prediction I read this	469

THINKST = 3

Think'st thou that dutie shall haue dread to speake, | When power to	
flattery bowes?	156
That iustly think'st, and hast most rightly said:	197
Lear. Thou think'st 'tis much that this contentious | (storme	1786

THIRD = 3*2

Remaine this ample third of our faire Kingdome,	86
A third, more opilent then your Sisters? speake.	92
With my two Daughters Dowres, digest the third,	136
*ha's banish'd two on's Daughters, and did the third a	632
*that he is a manifold Traitor, let him appeare by the third	3062

THIRTY = 1

Some fiue or six and thirty of his Knights	2075

THIS *l*.11 *16 *23 *24 *27 48 *68 72 86 111 123 147 161 193 206 234 237 258 284 326 330 353 360 381 *382 *387 *392 393 *404 *420 *424 426 *439 *444 *447 *469 *484 498 601 *631 658 679 712 716 719 739 746 752 784 791 805 821 826 842 865 *889 *892 932 944 950 968 *978 994 1008 1040 1049 1055 *1076 *1135 *1138 *1145 1169 1170 1176 1184 1199 1218 1235 1240 1242 1246 1249 1268 1278 1280 1301 1320 *1326 *1328 1330 1359 1379 1389 1390 1434 1470 1472 1483 1510 1532 *1585 1588 1642 1644 1646 1652 *1666 1679 1703 1717 1724 *1733 1734 *1749 *1753 *1761 1771 1773 1786 1795 1799 1805 1810 1814 1831 *1844 1855 *1858 *1882 *1883 *1895 1929 1932 *1936 1950 1957 *1980 *1982 *1985 *2061 2098 2151 2163 2174 *2176 2211 2223 2231 *2249 2286 2289 2290 2323 2328 2330 2404 2416 2420 2474 2485 *2499 2510 *2536 2577 *2582 2585 *2591 *2594 2625 2639 2729 2764 2766 2777 2782 2808 2819 2821 2824 2866 2869 2884 2921 2970 2972 2973 2985 2999 3029 3031 3058 3069 3072 3090 3094 3105 3108 3113 3118 3125 3151 3157 3163 3168 3173 3185 3186 3194 3224 3227 3247 3269 3271 3281 3282 3288 3295 3298 = 171*50, 1

To this great stage of Fooles. This a good blocke: 2625

THOROUGH = *1

*thou whip'st her. The Vsurer hangs the Cozener. Tho-|rough   2606
THOSE *l*.104 163 221 1310 1529 1540 *1554 1856 2754 2778 = 9*1

THOU *see also* th'hast, thou'dst, thou'lt, thou'rt, y *l*.127 155 156 174 180 182 *194 256 286 287 335 535 536 540 *542 549 *552 553 555 557 562 567 *571 592 *596 618 626 *630 *633 648 649 650 651 652 653 656 *667 *675 *676 *677 *685 *686 *695 *699 *705 *706 *707 *708 771 772 775 780 790 815 827 828 *893 *911 *913 *916 1004 1008 1011 1080 1085 1087 *1096 *1098 *1101 *1102 *1130 *1137 1144 1158 1162 1238 1240 1280 1301 *1326 1327 1329 *1337 *1374 1408 1454 1461 1464 1478 1515 1517 1523 1558 1567 1569 *1661 1704 1706 1707 1786 1816 *1825 *1830 1831 *1845 1864 *1881 *1883 *1886 *1888 *1919 1942 1945 *1994 *2050 2052 2099 2104 2120 2123 2136 *2139 2165 2185 2186 2229 2245 2256 2261 2345 2347 2440 2441 2467 2490 2493 2496 2517 2532 2557 2579 *2580 *2582 *2598 *2601 *2603 *2604 *2605 *2606 *2614 *2618 2620 2621 2647 2678 2684 2689 *2699 2700 2701 2745 2786 2795 2950 2970 2971 2972 2973 3018 3036 3041 3079 3088 3093 3096 3109 3110 3114 3118 3124 3128 3194 3236 3279 = 133*62

THOUDST = 4

question, thoud'st well deseru'd it. | *Kent*. Why Foole?   1338
The lesser is scarce felt. Thou'dst shun a Beare,   1789
Thou'dst meete the Beare i'th' mouth, when the mind's | (free,   1791
Thou'dst shiuer'd like an Egge: but thou do'st breath: 2493

THOUGH = 13*9

*though this Knaue came somthing sawcily to the   24
Kent. Let it fall rather, though the forke inuade   153
That I am glad I haue not, though not to haue it,   254
Bid them farewell *Cordelia*, though vnkinde,   285
*no good to vs: though the wisedome of Nature can   434
your face bids me, though you say nothing.   709
Though I condemne not, yet vnder pardon   866
*for though she's as like this, as a Crabbe's like an | Apple, yet I can tell what I can tell.   889
(As this I would, though thou didst produce   1008
Reg. No maruaile then, though he were ill affected,   1037
*for though it be night, yet the Moone shines, Ile make a   1104
*not haue made him so ill, though they had bin but two | yeares oth'trade.   1132

THOUGH *cont.*

*for my part I will not be, though I should win your | displeasure to
entreat me too't.   1188
Though the Raine it raineth euery day.   1732
Though their Iniunction be to barre my doores,   1928
*Loyalty, though the conflict be sore betweene that, and | my blood.   1992
Though well we may not passe vpon his life   2084
*Downe from the waste they are Centaures, though   2567
*Gent. Though that the Queen on special cause is here   2660
Mine Enemies dogge, though he had bit me,   2784
For him that brought it: wretched though I seeme,   2886
Not sure, though hoping of this good successe,   3157

THOUGHT = 12*1
Kent. | *I thought the King had more affected the   3
I lou'd her most, and thought to set my rest   131
As my great Patron thought on in my praiers.   151
I had thought by making this well knowne vnto you,   716
If they not thought the profits of my death   1012
Of differences, which I best thought it fit   1066
Yeelds to the Theft. Had he bin where he thought,   2484
By this had thought bin past. Aliue, or dead?   2485
Edg. As I stood heere below, me thought his eyes   2514
Gent. Neere, and on speedy foot: the maine descry | Stands on the
hourely thought.   2657
Bast. Sir, I thought it fit, | To send the old and miserable King to some
retention,   2989
Alb. Me thought thy very gate did prophesie   3137
Bast. Well thought on, take my Sword,   3208

THOUGHTS = 3
Edgar. Beare free and patient thoughts.   2525
So should my thoughts be seuer'd from my greefes, | Drum afarre off. 2736
Edg. What in ill thoughts againe?   2932

THOUGHT-EXECUTING = 1
You Sulph'rous and Thought-executing Fires,   1659

THOULT = 3*2
*nay, & thou canst not smile as the wind sits, thou'lt catch   630
*they'l haue me whipt for speaking true: thou'lt haue me   696
I can scarce speake to thee, thou'lt not beleeue   1414
Will not beare question: either say thou'lt do't, | Or thriue by other
meanes.   2976
And thou no breath at all? Thou'lt come no more, | Neuer, neuer,
neuer, neuer, neuer.   3279

THOURT = 1
That hast this Fortune on me? If thou'rt Noble, | I do forgiue thee.   3125

THOUSAND = 2*1
*But this heart shal break into a hundred thousand flawes   1585
Lear. To haue a thousand with red burning spits | Come hizzing in vpon
'em.   2013
Were two full Moones: he had a thousand Noses,   2515

THREATEND = 1
I threaten'd to discouer him; he replied,   1003

THREATNED = *1
*bed, if I die for it, (as no lesse is threatned me) the King   1768

THREAT-ENRAGD = 1
To his great Master, who, threat-enrag'd   2319

THREDDING = *1
*Reg. Thus out of season, thredding darke ey'd night,   1062

THREE = 2*2
    In three our Kingdome: and 'tis our fast intent,   43
    *Wooll; the Cat, no perfume. Ha? Here's three on's are   1885
    *stockt, punish'd, and imprison'd: who hath three Suites | to his backe,
    six shirts to his body: 1914
    Bast. I was contracted to them both, all three | Now marry in an
    instant.   3179
THREE-SUITED-HUNDRED = *1
    *base, proud, shallow, beggerly, three-suited-hundred   1089
THRICE = 1
    Swithold footed thrice the old,   1900
THRILLD = 1
    Mes. A Seruant that he bred, thrill'd with remorse,   2317
THRIUE = 5
    And my inuention thriue, *Edmond* the base | Shall to'th'Legitimate: I
    grow, I prosper: 354
    Do's letcher in my sight. Let Copulation thriue: 2559
    If euer thou wilt thriue, bury my bodie,   2700
    For your good hoast: pray that the right may thriue: 2922
    Will not beare question: either say thou'lt do't, | Or thriue by other
    meanes.   2976
THROATE = 1
    Or whil'st I can vent clamour from my throate,   179
THROND = 1
    Thron'd and set high; Seruants, who seeme no lesse,   1632
THRONE =*1
    To knee his Throne, and Squire-like pension beg,   1507
THRONGS = 1
    Nor Cut-purses come not to throngs;   1743
THROUGH *see also* thorough
THREE *see also* 3.
THROUGH = 1*5
    May carry through it selfe to that full issue   533
    *Edg. Away, the foule Fiend followes me, through the   1827
    *the foule fiend hath led through Fire, and through Flame,   1833
    *through Sword, and Whirle-Poole, o're Bog, and Quag-|mire,   1834
    *foule Fiend. Still through the Hauthorne blowes the   1878
THROW = 2*1
    *Edg. Tom, will throw his head at them: Auaunt you   2022
    Turne out that eyelesse Villaine: throw this Slaue   2174
    Lear. Vpon such sacrifices my *Cordelia*, | The Gods themselues throw
    Incense.   2961
THROWEST = 1
    Set lesse then thou throwest;   653
THROWING = 1
    For with throwing thus my head;   2029
THROWNE = *2
    *Thy dowrelesse Daughter King, throwne to my chance,   281
    *cunning of it. I found it throwne in at the Casement of | my Closset.   395
THRUST = 1
    Reg. Go thrust him out at gates, and let him smell | His way to Douer.
    Exit with Glouster.   2170
THRUSTING = *1
    *influence; and all that we are euill in, by a diuine thru-|sting   454
THUNDER = 4*2
    'Gainst Paricides did all the thunder bend,   982
    *Sindge my white head. And thou all-shaking Thunder,   1661

THUNDER *cont.*	
Nor Raine, Winde, Thunder, Fire are my Daughters;	1670
Such sheets of Fire, such bursts of horrid Thunder,	1698
What is the cause of Thunder?	1933
*winde to make me chatter: when the Thunder would not	2548

THUNDER-BEARER = 1
I do not bid the Thunder-bearer shoote, 1521
THUNDER-BOLTS = 1
Vaunt-curriors of Oake-cleauing Thunder-bolts, 1660
THUS = 16*9
*Kent. Fare thee well King, sith thus thou wilt appeare, 194
Thus Kent, O Princes, bids you all adew, 200
*Glo. Kent banish'd thus? and France in choller parted? 358
*reason it thus, and thus, yet Nature finds it selfe scourg'd 435
*Do's Lear walke thus? Speake thus? Where are his eies? 740
That thou hast power to shake my manhood thus, 815
*Reg. Thus out of season, thredding darke ey'd night, 1062
Ste. Why do'st thou vse me thus? I know thee not. 1085
*Stew. Why, what a monstrous Fellow art thou, thus 1098
That he so slightly valued in his Messenger, | Should haue him thus
restrained. 1222
Should haue thus little mercy on their flesh: 1854
He said it would be thus: poore banish'd man: 1944
*thus giues way to Loyaltie, something feares mee to | thinke of. 1973
For with throwing thus my head; 2029
You should not ruffle thus. What will you do? 2107
Reg. Giue me thy Sword. A pezant stand vp thus? | Killes him. 2154
Edg. Yet better thus, and knowne to be contemn'd, 2179
And when your Mistris heares thus much from you, 2421
Edg. Why I do trifle thus with his dispaire, | Is done to cure it. 2471
Thus might he passe indeed: yet he reuiues. 2487
The safer sense will ne're accommodate | His Master thus. 2528
To see another thus. I know not what to say: 2806
Seest thou this obiect Kent? | Kent. Alacke, why thus? 3194
THWART = 1
And be a thwart disnatur'd torment to her. 797
THY l.111 115 159 160 162 165 168 174 177 178 186 189 191 192 277 *281
335 536 623 *638 654 *675 *676 *677 *678 *686 693 *695 *699 784 785
790 827 *885 *888 *908 914 1007 1010 1097 *1102 1241 1250 1280 1287
*1326 1330 *1344 *1345 1409 1412 1455 1464 1523 1557 *1667 *1669
1790 1804 1815 1822 *1828 *1830 *1839 1849 *1860 *1861 *1862 *1875
*1876 *1877 *1882 *1988 2015 2023 2032 *2047 2051 2128 2129 2135
2154 2159 2166 2187 2191 2196 2203 2236 2244 2264 2291 2306 2307
2308 *2377 2440 2497 2556 *2581 2584 *2603 *2604 2619 2679 2681
2705 2731 2747 2777 2779 2789 *2895 2928 2930 2972 2975 3028 3038
3039 3040 3052 3080 3082 3086 3087 3088 3089 3091 3092 3095 3097
3098 3099 3102 3103 3130 3137 3140 3207 3210 3211 = 114*37
TIDE = *1
*tide by the heads, Dogges and Beares by'th'necke, 1283
TIE see tye
TIED see also tide, tyed = 1
Thy Sisters naught: oh Regan, she hath tied 1412
TIGHT = 1
Or Bobtaile tight, or Troudle taile, 2027
TIKE see tight
TIL = *1
*suspend your indignation against my Brother, til you can 414

TILL = 8*9

*vs, *till our oldnesse cannot rellish them. I begin to finde an idle*	384
this I may speake more. If our Father would sleepe till I wak'd	387
*Hum? Conspiracy? Sleepe till I wake him, you should	390
*forbearance till the speed of his rage goes slower: and as	488
*Kent. I will not sleepe my Lord, till I haue deliuered | your Letter.	
Exit.	880
*Foole. Thou shouldst not haue bin old, till thou hadst | bin wise.	916
As I haue life and Honour, there shall he sit till Noone.	1213
*Reg. Till noone? till night my Lord, and all night too.	1214
Till it crie sleepe to death.	1395
If till the expiration of your Moneth	1495
*Till you haue drench'd our Steeples, drown the Cockes.	1658
Glou. He that will thinke to liue, till he be old,	2141
Glou. I do remember now: henceforth Ile beare | Affliction, till it do cry	
out it selfe	2520
My boone I make it, that you know me not, | Till time, and I, thinke	
meet.	2758
Trouble him no more till further setling.	2839
Alb. Stay till I haue read the Letter. | Edg. I was forbid it:	2891

TIME = 21*6

*Lear. Meane time we shal expresse our darker purpose.	41
The best, the deerest, should in this trice of time	237
*Cor. Time shall vnfold what plighted cunning hides,	306
*Gon. The best and soundest of his time hath bin but	320
*seene the best of our time. Machinations, hollownesse,	442
*some little time hath qualified the heat of his displeasure,	483
beaten for being old before thy time.	914
Cur. You may do then in time,	941
I haue seene better faces in my Time,	1167
Some time I shall sleepe out, the rest Ile whistle:	1232
Of my obscured course. And shall finde time	1245
Some other time for that. Beloued Regan,	1411
Lear. I gaue you all. | Reg. And in good time you gaue it.	1547
Then comes the time, who liues to see't,	1747
*This prophecie Merlin shall make, for I liue before his | (time. | Exit.	1749
If Wolues had at thy Gate howl'd that sterne time,	2135
Thou know'st, the first time that we smell the Ayre	2621
*opportunities to cut him off: if your will want not, time and	2717
Of murtherous Letchers: and in the mature time,	2728
My boone I make it, that you know me not, | Till time, and I, thinke	
meet.	2758
When time shall serue, let but the Herald cry, | And Ile appeare againe.	
Exit.	2893
Alb. We will greet the time. Exit.	2901
Are as the time is; to be tender minded	2974
And more, much more, the time will bring it out.	3123
The time will not allow the complement | Which very manners vrges.	3187
Nay, send in time. | Alb. Run, run, O run.	3204
Edg. The waight of this sad time we must obey,	3298

TIMES = 1*1

*world bitter to the best of our times: keepes our Fortunes from	383
Glou. 'Tis the times plague, | When Madmen leade the blinde:	2234

TINY *see* tyne
TIRED *see* tyred

TIRRANY = 1
  The tirrany of the open night's too rough | For Nature to endure.
  Storme still   1779
TIS *l*.43 *279 *318 *446 *659 742 844 1035 1038 1166 *1228 1243 *1274
  *1298 1423 1457 1538 *1590 1601 *1612 1679 1718 *1761 1786 1787
  *1891 2090 2100 2200 2209 2234 2329 2351 2375 2447 *2551 *2692 2730
  2789 2791 2852 2877 3031 3124 3135 3145 *3174 3232 3239 = 35*14
TITHING *see* tything
TITLE = 2
  Whose age had Charmes in it, whose Title more,   2991
  Reg. Let the Drum strike, and proue my title thine.   3026
TO *see also* t', too, to'th, too't = 365*105
TOAD = *1
  *Toad, the Tod-pole, the wall-Neut, and the water: that   1909
TOAD-SPOTTED = 1
  A most Toad-spotted Traitor. Say thou no,   3093
TOASTED = *1
  *Mouse: peace, peace, this peece of toasted Cheese will 2536
TOD-POLE = *1
  *Toad, the Tod-pole, the wall-Neut, and the water: that   1909
TOE = *1
  *The man y makes his Toe, what he his Hart shold make, 1684
TOGETHER = 3*1
  France and him, pray you let vs sit together, if our   328
  Bast. Spake you with him? | *Edg*. I, two houres together. 476
  Saddle my horses: call my Traine together.   763
  Gone. Combine together 'gainst the Enemie: 2870
TOKEN = 1
  Send thy token of repreeue.   3207
TOLD = 7*3
  *man, if ther be any good meaning toward you: I haue told 494
  But that I told him the reuenging Gods,   981
  I told him of the Army that was Landed: 2271
  He smil'd at it. I told him you were comming,   2272
  And told me I had turn'd the wrong side out: 2276
  *me like a Dogge, and told mee I had the white hayres in 2544
  *out. Go too, they are not men o'their words; they told 2550
  Gon. Hola, hola, | That eye that told you so, look'd but a squint. 3014
  And when 'tis told, O that my heart would burst.   3145
  Told him our pilgrimage. But his flaw'd heart   3159
TOM = 6*7
  *my Cue is villanous Melancholly, with a sighe like *Tom* 464
  Inforce their charitie: poore *Turlygod* poore *Tom*,   1271
  Edg. Fathom, and halfe, Fathom and halfe; poore *Tom*. 1819
  Foole. A spirite, a spirite, he sayes his name's poore | *Tom*. 1823
  Edgar. Who giues any thing to poore *Tom*? Whom   1832
  *do poore *Tom* some charitie, whom the foule Fiend   1841
  Edg. Poore Tom, that eates the swimming Frog, the 1908
  Edg. Tom, will throw his head at them: Auaunt you 2022
  Tom will make him weepe and waile,   2028
  And Market Townes: poore Tom thy horne is dry,   2032
  Old. 'Tis poore mad Tom.   2209
  *poore Tom hath bin scarr'd out of his good wits. Blesse 2247
  Edg. Giue me thy arme; | Poore Tom shall leade thee. *Exeunt*. 2264
TOMBE = 1
  I would diuorce me from thy Mother Tombe,   1409

TOMS = 5*1
   *Blisse thy fiue Wits, *Tom*s a cold. O do, de, do, de, do, de,   1839
   *with mans sworne Spouse: set not thy Sweet-heart on | proud array.
   Tom's a cold.   1862
   Haue bin Toms food, for seuen long yeare: 1918
   Edg. Poore Tom's a cold.   1925
   Noble Philosopher, your company. | *Edg.* Tom's a cold.   1953
   Edg. Poore Tom's a cold. I cannot daub it further.   2241
TONGUE = 4*1
   More ponderous then my tongue.   84
   A still soliciting eye, and such a tongue,   253
   *thou art nothing. Yes forsooth I will hold my tongue, so   708
   Look'd blacke vpon me, strooke me with her Tongue   1442
   And that thy tongue (some say) of breeding breathes,   3099
TONGUES = 2
   When Slanders do not liue in Tongues;   1742
   Had I your tongues and eyes, Il'd vse them so,   3218
TONIGHT *see* night
TOO *see also* t'intrince = 32*4
   Onely she comes too short, that I professe   77
   hath now cast her off, appeares too grossely.   317
   The Contents, as in part I vnderstand them, | Are too blame.   377
   tarry, but away, goe too, haue you wisedome, so.   621
   Foole. Let me hire him too, here's my Coxcombe.   625
   on? You are too much of late i'th'frowne.   704
   By what your selfe too late haue spoke and done,   718
   Lear. Woe, that too late repents: 769
   Alb. Well, you may feare too farre.   849
   Gon. Safer then trust too farre;   850
   Reg. If it be true, all vengeance comes too short   1027
   Glo. I know not Madam, 'tis too bad, too bad.   1035
   Kent. Sir, I am too old to learne: 1206
   You shall doe small respects, show too bold malice   1209
   Reg. Till noone? till night my Lord, and all night too.   1214
   Glo. The Duke's too blame in this, | 'Twill be ill taken. *Exit.*   1235
   Lear. O sides, you are too tough!   1488
   And what they may incense him too, being apt,   1610
   Glo. Go too; say you nothing. There is diuision be-|tweene   1759
   Instantly know, and of that Letter too;   1772
   The tirrany of the open night's too rough | For Nature to endure.
   Storme still   1779
   Too little care of this: Take Physicke, Pompe,   1814
   Reg. One side will mocke another: Th'other too.   2143
   Who is too good to pitty thee.   2167
   Oldm. Madman, and beggar too.   2214
   Almost too small for sight. The murmuring Surge,   2455
   Vp, so: How is't? Feele you your Legges? You stand. | *Glou.* Too well,
   too well.   2508
   *no, to euery thing that I said: I, and no too, was no good   2546
   *out. Go too, they are not men o'their words; they told   2550
   My life will be too short, | And euery measure faile me.   2748
   Ripenesse is all come on. | *Glo.* And that's true too. *Exeunt.*   2935
   Talke of Court newes, and wee'l talke with them too,   2954
   (Alacke too weake the conflict to support)   3160
   He'le strike and quickly too, he's dead and rotten.   3251
TOOKE = 4*1
   They summon'd vp their meiney, straight tooke Horse,   1311

TOOKE *cont*.

Why the hot-bloodied *France*, that dowerlesse tooke — 1505
*they tooke from me the vse of mine owne house, charg'd — 1755
I tooke it for a man: often 'twould say — 2523
All leuied in my name, haue in my name | Tooke their discharge. — 3053

TOOT = 6*1

*so often blush'd to acknowledge him, that now I am | braz'd too't. — 13
*for my part I will not be, though I should win your | displeasure to
entreat me too't. — 1188
For lifting food too't? But I will punish home; — 1796
No, the Wren goes too't, and the small gilded Fly — 2558
Too't Luxury pell-mell, for I lacke Souldiers. — 2562
*the soyled Horse goes too't with a more riotous appe- |tite: — 2566
Glou. Now let thy friendly hand | Put strength enough too't. — 2681

TOOTH = 3

How sharper then a Serpents tooth it is, — 802
Tooth that poysons if it bite: — 2024
Edg. Know my name is lost | By Treasons tooth: bare-gnawne, and
Canker-bit, — 3073

TOOTHD = 1

Sharpe-tooth'd vnkindnesse, like a vulture heere, — 1413

TOP = 2

On her ingratefull top: strike her yong bones — 1445
Glou. When shall I come to th'top of that same hill? — 2431

TOPPLE = 1

Least my braine turne, and the deficient sight | Topple downe headlong. — 2458

TORCH = 1

Enter Gloucester, with a Torch. — 1890

TORCHES = 3

Fly Brother, Torches, Torches, so farewell. | *Exit Edgar*. — 964
Enter Gloster, and Seruants with Torches. — 970

TORMENT = 1

And be a thwart disnatur'd torment to her. — 797

TOSSE = 1

Backe do I tosse these Treasons to thy head, — 3102

TOTH = 6*1

And my inuention thriue, *Edmond* the base | Shall to'th'Legitimate: I
grow, I prosper: — 354
The Child was bound to'th' Father; Sir in fine, — 984
*Fortune that arrant whore, nere turns the key toth' poore. — 1325
Reg. Good Sir, to'th'purpose. *Tucket within*. — 1466
Glou. I am tyed to'th'Stake, | And I must stand the Course. — 2125
I am cut to'th'Braines. — 2636
(Be briefe in it) to'th'Castle, for my Writ — 3202

TOUCH = 2*1

To beare it tamely: touch me with Noble anger, — 1576
Might I but liue to see thee in my touch, — 2204
Lear. No, they cannot touch me for crying. I am the | King himselfe. — 2530

TOUCHES = 1

Touches vs not with pitty: O, is this he? — 3186

TOUGH = 2

Lear. O sides, you are too tough! — 1488
That would vpon the wracke of this tough world | Stretch him out
longer. — 3288

TOWARD = 7*4

*Vnburthen'd crawle toward death. Our son of *Cornwal*, — 46

TOWARD *cont*.
Lear. My Lord of *Burgundie*, | We first addresse toward you, who with
this King 205
*man, if ther be any good meaning toward you: I haue told 494
Cur. Haue you heard of no likely Warres toward, ... 938
Lear. Oh how this Mother swels vp toward my heart! 1328
*my old Master must be relieued. There is strange things | toward
Edmund, pray you be carefull. *Exit*. 1769
But if thy flight lay toward the roaring sea, ... 1790
*And driue toward Douer friend, where thou shalt meete 2050
Are gone with him toward Douer; where they boast | To haue well
armed Friends. 2078
I'th'way toward Douer, do it for ancient loue, ... 2230
Edg. Do you heare ought (Sir) of a Battell toward. | *Gent*. Most sure,
and vulgar: 2652
TOWER = 1
Edg. Childe *Rowland* to the darke Tower came, ... 1966
TOWNES = 1
And Market Townes: poore Tom thy horne is dry, ... 2032
TRADE = 3
*not haue made him so ill, though they had bin but two | yeares
oth'trade. 1132
Bad is the Trade that must play Foole to sorrow, ... 2224
Hangs one that gathers Sampire: dreadfull Trade: 2450
TRAGEDIE = 1
THE TRAGEDIE OF | KING LEAR. 3304
TRAINE = 7
A little to disquantity your Traine, ... 758
Saddle my horses: call my Traine together. 763
My Traine are men of choice, and rarest parts, ... 776
She hath abated me of halfe my Traine; 1441
To grudge my pleasures, to cut off my Traine, ... 1458
Dismissing halfe your traine, come then to me, ... 1497
He is attended with a desperate traine, ... 1609
TRAITOR = 10*4
*incht Bridges, to course his owne shadow for a Traitor. 1838
Lear. Death Traitor, nothing could haue subdu'd | (Nature 1851
*him this Letter, the Army of France is landed: seeke out | the Traitor
Glouster. 2061
Corn. *Edmund* farewell: go seek the Traitor Gloster, ... 2082
Who's there? the Traitor? | *Reg*. Ingratefull Fox, 'tis he. 2089
Reg. Hard, hard: O filthy Traitor. 2096
Reg. So white, and such a Traitor? | *Glou*. Naughty Ladie, ... 2102
If you do chance to heare of that blinde Traitor, ... 2424
To raise my fortunes. Thou old, vnhappy Traitor, ... 2678
Stew. Wherefore, bold Pezant, | Dar'st thou support a publish'd
Traitor? Hence, ... 2683
That names me Traitor, villain-like he lies, ... 3046
that he is a manifold Traitor, let him appeare by the third 3062
Thy valor, and thy heart, thou art a Traitor: 3088
A most Toad-spotted Traitor. Say thou no, ... 3093
TRAITOROUS = *1
*take vppon your Traitorous Father, are not fit for your 2067
TRAITORS = 1*1
Corn. And what confederacie haue you with the Trai-|tors, late footed
in the Kingdome? 2111
Lear. A plague vpon you Murderors, Traitors all, ... 3233

TRANSPORT = 1*1
These dispositions, which of late transport you | From what you rightly
are.   733
*Might not you transport her purposes by word? Belike,   2406
TRAUAILD = 1*1
*Kent. Pray do not Sir, I haue watch'd and trauail'd hard,   1231
They haue trauail'd all the night? meere fetches,   1363
TREACHERIE = *1
*treacherie, and all ruinous disorders follow vs disquietly   443
TREACHEROUS = 1
Reg. Out treacherous Villaine, | Thou call'st on him, that hates thee. It
was he   2164
TREACHERS = *1
*Treachers by Sphericall predominance. Drunkards, Ly-|ars,   452
TREACHERY = 1
His answer was, the worse. Of Glosters Treachery,   2273
TREAD = *1
*my Lord, if you will giue me leaue, I will tread this vn-|boulted   1138
TREASON = 1*2
*in Pallaces, Treason; and the Bond crack'd, 'twixt   438
*of France. O Heauens! that this Treason were not; | or not I the
detector.   1982
On capitall Treason; and in thy arrest,   3028
TREASONS = 4
That made the ouerture of thy Treasons to vs: 2166
Thy heynous, manifest, and many Treasons,   3039
Edg. Know my name is lost | By Treasons tooth: bare-gnawne, and
Canker-bit,   3073
Backe do I tosse these Treasons to thy head,   3102
TREASURY = 1
The Treasury of life, when life it selfe   2483
TREE = 2
And by the happy hollow of a Tree,   1253
Edg. Heere Father, take the shadow of this Tree   2921
TREMBLE = 2
Finde out their enemies now. Tremble thou Wretch,   1704
This iudgement of the Heauens that makes vs tremble.   3185
TRESPASSE = 1
Your Sonne and Daughter found this trespasse worth   1320
TREY = 1
Trey, Blanch, and Sweet-heart: see, they barke at me.   2021
TRIBE = 1
Goe to th'creating a whole tribe of Fops   348
TRICE = 1
The best, the deerest, should in this trice of time   237
TRICKE = *1
*Glou. The tricke of that voyce, I do well remember: 2552
TRICKES = *1
*Reg. Good Sir, no more: these are vnsightly trickes: 1438
TRIFLE = 3
On euery trifle. When he returnes from hunting,   514
Edg. Why I do trifle thus with his dispaire, | Is done to cure it.   2471
Mess. Edmund is dead my Lord. | Alb. That's but a trifle heere: 3266
TRIPT = 2*1
Kent. Nor tript neither, you base Foot-ball plaier.   616
*thou knowest me? Is it two dayes since I tript vp thy   1102
Tript me behind: being downe, insulted, rail'd,   1195

TROOPE = 1*1
  *That troope with Maiesty. Our selfe by Monthly course,   140
  It were a delicate stratagem to shoo | A Troope of Horse with Felt: Ile
  put't in proofe,   2626
TROOPES = 1
  Reg. Our troopes set forth to morrow, stay with vs: | The wayes are
  dangerous.   2401
TROT = 1
  Boy *Sesey*: let him trot by. *Storme still.*   1880
TROTH-PLIGHT = 1
  Bid her a-light, and her troth-plight,   1902
TROTTING = *1
  *Proud of heart, to ride on a Bay trotting Horse, ouer foure   1837
TROUBLE = 3*1
  Degenerate Bastard, Ile not trouble thee;   764
  I will not trouble thee my Child; farewell: 1513
  Kent. Here Sir, but trouble him not, his wits are gon.   2046
  Trouble him no more till further setling.   2839
TROUDLE = 1
  Or Bobtaile tight, or Troudle taile,   2027
TROWEST = 1
  Learne more then thou trowest,   652
TRUE = 11*3
  And prize me at her worth. In my true heart,   75
  Lear. So young, and so vntender? | *Cor.* So young my Lord, and true.   113
  Kent. See better *Lear*, and let me still remaine | The true blanke of
  thine eie.   170
  My minde as generous, and my shape as true   342
  *they'l haue me whipt for speaking true: thou'lt haue me   696
  Reg. If it be true, all vengeance comes too short   1027
  Which scarcely keepes thee warme, but for true need: 1570
  Le. True Boy: Come bring vs to this Houell. *Exit.*   1733
  No Father his Sonne deerer: true to tell thee,   1949
  Corn. True or false, it hath made thee Earle of Glou- | cester: 1987
  Heere is the guesse of their true strength and Forces,   2898
  Ripenesse is all come on. | *Glo.* And that's true too. *Exeunt.*   2935
  Bast. Th'hast spoken right, 'tis true,   3135
  I kill'd the Slaue that was a hanging thee. | *Gent.* 'Tis true (my Lords)
  he did.   3238
TRUELY = 1*1
  *him truely that will put me in trust, to loue him that is   545
  Bast. I shall serue you Sir truely, how euer else.   1059
TRUE-HARTED = 1
  *thee nothing, do it carefully: and the Noble & true-har- | ted   445
TRULY = 2
  Hearke, do you heare the Sea? | *Glou.* No truly.   2435
  Tell me but truly, but then speake the truth,   2855
TRUMPET = 9*2
  If you haue victory, let the Trumpet sound   2885
  Alb. Thou art armed *Gloster*, | Let the Trumpet sound: 3036
  Call by the Trumpet: he that dares approach;   3047
  Come hither Herald, let the Trumpet sound, | And read out this. *A*
  Trumpet sounds.   3057
  sound of the Trumpet: he is bold in his defence. 1 Trumpet. | Her.
  Againe. 2 *Trumpet.*   3063
  Her. Againe. 3 *Trumpet.* | *Trumpet answers within.*   3065

TRUMPET *cont.*
  Alb. Aske him his purposes, why he appeares | Vpon this Call
o'th'Trumpet.   3068
TRUMPETS = 2*1
  *Harke, the Dukes Trumpets, I know not wher he comes;   1017
  Corn. What Trumpet's that?   1469
  Where they shall rest for euer. Trumpets speake.   3106
TRUNKE = 1
  Thy banist trunke be found in our Dominions,   191
TRUNKE-INHERITING = *1
  *finicall Rogue, one Trunke-inheriting slaue, one that   1092
TRUST = 5*2
  *him truely that will put me in trust, to loue him that is   545
  Gon. Safer then trust too farre;   850
  Of any trust, vertue, or worth in thee   1006
  Nature's of such deepe trust, we shall much need: | You we first seize
on.   1057
  Corn. I will lay trust vpon thee: and thou shalt finde | a deere Father
in my loue. *Exeunt.*   1994
  Reg. Sicke, O sicke. | *Gon.* If not, Ile nere trust medicine.   3043
  Trust to thy single vertue, for thy Souldiers   3052
TRUSTIE = 1
  Into my Husbands hands. This trustie Seruant   2286
TRUTH = 6
  Lear. Let it be so, thy truth then be thy dowre: 115
  An honest mind and plaine, he must speake truth,   1174
  Reg. Be simple answer'd, for we know the truth.   2110
  All my reports go with the modest truth, | Nor more, nor clipt, but so.   2751
  Tell me but truly, but then speake the truth,   2855
  On him, on you, who not, I will maintaine | My truth and honor
firmely.   3048
TRUTHS = *1
  Foole. Truth's a dog must to kennell, hee must bee   641
TRY = *1
  *try whither your Costard, or my Ballow be the harder; | chill be plaine
with you.   2694
TUCKET = 2
  To make thee seeke it. *Tucket within.*   1014
  Reg. Good Sir, to'th'purpose. *Tucket within.*   1466
TURKE = *1
  *the Turke. False of heart, light of eare, bloody of hand;   1872
TURLYGOD = 1
  Inforce their charitie: poore *Turlygod* poore *Tom*,   1271
TURND = 1
  And told me I had turn'd the wrong side out: 2276
TURNE = 12*1
  Make with you by due turne, onely we shall retaine   143
  And on the sixt to turne thy hated backe   189
  Turne all her Mothers paines, and benefits   800
  My very Character) I'ld turne it all   1009
  Reuenge, affirme, and turne their Halcion beakes   1151
  Smile once more, turne thy wheele.   1250
  Shall of a Corne cry woe, and turne his sleepe to wake.   1685
  Lear. My wits begin to turne.   1722
  Foole. This cold night will turne vs all to Fooles, and | Madmen.   1858
  Thou should'st haue said, good Porter turne the Key: 2136
  Turne out that eyelesse Villaine: throw this Slaue   2174

TURNE *cont.*
 Least my braine turne, and the deficient sight | Topple downe headlong. 2458
 And turne our imprest Launces in our eies 2993
TURNES = 1
 The knaue turnes Foole that runnes away, 1356
TURNS = *1
 *Fortune that arrant whore, nere turns the key toth' poore. 1325
TUTORS = 1
 When Nobles are their Taylors Tutors, 1738
TWAINE = 4
 Like Rats oft bite the holy cords a twaine, 1147
 Thou wilt ore-take vs hence a mile or twaine 2229
 Who redeemes Nature from the generall curse | Which twaine haue brought her to. 2648
 Is generall woe: Friends of my soule, you twaine, 3294
TWAS = 2*2
 *downe; 'twas her Brother, that in pure kindnesse to his | Horse buttered his Hay. 1401
 Iudicious punishment, 'twas this flesh begot | Those Pelicane Daughters. 1855
 *Mes. I my good Lord: 'twas he inform'd against him 2341
 Is wretchednesse depriu'd that benefit | To end it selfe by death? 'Twas yet some comfort, 2503
TWEENE = 2
 Got 'tweene a sleepe, and wake? Well then, 349
 Then my Daughters got 'tweene the lawfull sheets. 2561
TWELUE = 1
 For that I am some twelue, or fourteene Moonshines 339
TWENTIE = 1
 To bring but fiue and twentie, to no more | Will I giue place or notice. 1545
TWENTY = 4*1
 Then twenty silly-ducking obseruants, 1178
 *not a nose among twenty, but can smell him that's stink-|ing; 1343
 With fiue and twenty? Regan, said you so? 1552
 Thy fifty yet doth double fiue and twenty, 1557
 Gon. Heare me my Lord; | What need you fiue and twenty? Ten? Or fiue? 1559
TWICE = 2
 And thou art twice her Loue. 1558
 To follow in a house, where twice so many | Haue a command to tend you? 1561
TWILL = 2
 Glo. The Duke's too blame in this, | 'Twill be ill taken. Exit. 1235
 Corn. Let vs withdraw, 'twill be a Storme. 1587
TWINKLED = 1
 *haue bin that I am, had the maidenlest Starre in the Fir-|mament twinkled on my bastardizing. 460
TWIXT = 3*1
 *in Pallaces, Treason; and the Bond crack'd, 'twixt 438
 'Twixt the Dukes of Cornwall, and Albany? | Bast. Not a word. 939
 With mutuall cunning) 'twixt Albany, and Cornwall: 1630
 Twixt two extremes of passion, ioy and greefe, | Burst smilingly. 3161
TWO see also 2. = 15*4
 With my two Daughters Dowres, digest the third, 136
 Bast. Spake you with him? | Edg. I, two houres together. 476
 *I will looke further intoo't: but where's my Foole? I | haue not seene him this two daies. 600
 *ha's banish'd two on's Daughters, and did the third a 632

TWO *cont.*
I had two Coxcombes and two Daughters. 635
And thou shalt haue more, | Then two tens to a score. 656
Foole. Nunckle, giue me an egge, and Ile giue thee | two Crownes. 670
Lear. What two Crownes shall they be? 672
*eate vp the meate, the two Crownes of the egge: when 674
*thou knowest me? Is it two dayes since I tript vp thy 1102
*not haue made him so ill, though they had bin but two | yeares
oth'trade. 1132
Should many people, vnder two commands 1537
That will with two pernicious Daughters ioyne 1677
Were two full Moones: he had a thousand Noses, 2515
Repaire those violent harmes, that my two Sisters | Haue in thy
Reuerence made. 2778
We two alone will sing like Birds i'th'Cage: 2949
Twixt two extremes of passion, ioy and greefe, | Burst smilingly. 3161
Kent. If Fortune brag of two, she lou'd and hated, | One of them we
behold. 3245
TWOULD = 1*1
I tooke it for a man: often 'twould say 2523
*'twould not ha' bin zo long as 'tis, by a vortnight. Nay, 2692
TYE = 1
Which tye him to an answer: our wishes on the way 2282
TYED = 1
Glou. I am tyed to'th'Stake, | And I must stand the Course. 2125
TYNE = 1
Foole. He that has and a little-tyne wit, 1729
TYRANNOUS = 1
And let this Tyrannous night take hold vpon you, 1929
TYRANNY *see also* tirrany = *1
*and fond bondage, in the oppression of aged tyranny, who swayes 385
TYRANTS = 1
When misery could beguile the Tyrants rage, | And frustrate his proud
will. 2505
TYRED = 1
Then doth within a dull stale tyred bed 347
TYTHING = *2
*Poole: who is whipt from Tything to Tything, and 1913
VAINE = 3
Kent. Now by *Apollo*, King | Thou swear'st thy Gods in vaine. 173
Gon. Oh vaine Foole. 2311
Alb. He knowes not what he saies, and vaine is it | That we present vs
to him. 3262
VALEWED = 1
Beyond what can be valewed, rich or rare, 62
VALEWES = *1
*not which of the Dukes hee valewes 8
VALIANT = *1
Alb. Sir, you haue shew'd to day your valiant straine 2983
VALIDITIE = 1
No lesse in space, validitie, and pleasure 87
VALOR = 1
Thy valor, and thy heart, thou art a Traitor: 3088
VALOUR = *1
Kent. No Maruell, you haue so bestir'd your valour, 1127
VALUE = 1
You lesse know how to value her desert, | Then she to scant her dutie. 1417

VALUED = 1
That he so slightly valued in his Messenger, | Should haue him thus
restrained.   1222
VANITIE = *1
*the King, and take Vanitie the puppets part, a-|gainst   1109
VANQUISHD = 1
An vnknowne opposite: thou art not vanquish'd, | But cozend, and
beguild.   3110
VANTAGE = 1
Take vantage heauie eyes, not to behold   1248
VARLET = 1*1
*Kent. What a brazen-fac'd Varlet art thou, to deny   1101
Out Varlet, from my sight.   1474
VARRY = 1
With euery gall, and varry of their Masters,   1152
VASSALL = 1
Lear. O Vassall! Miscreant. | Alb. Cor. Deare Sir forbeare.   175
VAULT = 1
That Heauens vault should crack: she's gone for euer.   3219
VAUNT-CURRIORS = 1
Vaunt-curriors of Oake-cleauing Thunder-bolts,   1660
VENGE = 1
So speedily can venge. But (O poore Glouster)   2325
VENGEANCE = 4
Reg. If it be true, all vengeance comes too short   1027
Lear. Vengeance, Plague, Death, Confusion: 1370
The winged Vengeance ouertake such Children.   2138
Corn. If you see vengeance. | Seru. Hold your hand, my Lord: 2144
VENGEANCES = 1
All the stor'd Vengeances of Heauen, fall   1444
VENT = 1
Or whil'st I can vent clamour from my throate,   179
VENTURE = 1
(If you dare venture in your owne behalfe)   2288
VENTURED = 1
Yet haue I ventured to come seeke you out,   1930
VERGE = 2
Nature in you stands on the very Verge   1427
You are now within a foote of th'extreme Verge: 2462
VERITY = 1
Kent. Sir, in good faith, in sincere verity,   1180
VERMINE = *1
What is your study? | *Edg. How to preuent the Fiend, and to kill
Vermine.   1937
VERTUE = 6*1
this but as an essay, or taste of my Vertue.   381
Of any trust, vertue, or worth in thee   1006
Whose vertue and obedience doth this instant   1055
Thou Periur'd, and thou Simular of Vertue   1707
*Forkes presages Snow; that minces Vertue, & do's shake   2564
Trust to thy single vertue, for thy Souldiers   3052
Taste the wages of their vertue, and all Foes   3275
VERTUES = 2
Thee and thy vertues here I seize vpon,   277
Cord. All blest Secrets, | All you vnpublish'd Vertues of the earth 2366
VERTUOUS = 1
A plot vpon her vertuous Husbands life,   2725

VERY = 18*3

I finde she names my very deede of loue:	76
Glou. O Villain, villain: his very opinion in the Let-|ter.	409
any further delay, then this very Euening.	426
Lear. What art thou? | *Kent.* A very honest hearted Fellow, and as poore as | the King.	549
*then as a very pretence and purpose of vnkindnesse;	599
My very Character) I'ld turne it all	1009
Were very pregnant and potentiall spirits	1013
It pleas'd the King his Master very late	1192
Being the very fellow which of late	1316
Nature in you stands on the very Verge	1427
Most Serpent-like, vpon the very Heart.	1443
Gallow the very wanderers of the darke	1696
But lately: very late: I lou'd him (Friend)	1948
Bring me but to the very brimme of it,	2260
I am a very foolish fond old man,	2814
Alb. Our very louing Sister, well be-met:	2865
Alb. Me thought thy very gate did prophesie	3137
That very Dogges disdain'd: and in this habit	3151
The time will not allow the complement | Which very manners vrges.	3187
Kent. No my good Lord, I am the very man. | *Lear.* Ile see that straight.	3252
Edg. Very bootlesse.	3265

VEX = *1

Kent. Vex not his ghost, O let him passe, he hates him,	3287

VEXES = *1

*vexes. There could I haue him now, and there, and there | againe, and there. *Storme still.*	1842

VEXT = 1

As mad as the vext Sea, singing alowd.	2352

VGLY = 1

How vgly did'st thou in *Cordelia* shew?	780

VICES = 2*1

*tatter'd cloathes great Vices do appeare: Robes,	2607
As duteous to the vices of thy Mistris, | As badnesse would desire.	2705
The Gods are iust, and of our pleasant vices | Make instruments to plague vs:	3131

VICIOUS *see also* vitious = 1

It is no vicious blot, murther, or foulenesse,	249

VICTORY = 1

If you haue victory, let the Trumpet sound	2885

VICTOR-SWORD = 1

Despise thy victor-Sword, and fire new Fortune,	3087

VIEW = 1

Bast. The Enemy's in view, draw vp your powers,	2897

VIGILANCE = 1

That guard, and most vnusall vigilance	1255

VILDE = 3*1

*And can make vilde things precious. Come, your Houel;	1726
Glou. Our flesh and blood, my Lord, is growne so | vilde, that it doth hate what gets it.	1923
Corn. Lest it see more, preuent it; Out vilde gelly:	2158
How stiffe is my vilde sense | That I stand vp, and haue ingenious feeling	2733

VILLAGES = 1

Poore pelting Villages, Sheeps-Coates, and Milles,	1269

VILLAIN = *4
   Glou. O Villain, villain: his very opinion in the Let-|ter.   409
   *to our Graues. Find out this Villain, *Edmond*, it shall lose   444
   Stew. Slaue thou hast slaine me: Villain, take my purse;   2699
VILLAINE = 11*4
   *Abhorred Villaine, vnnaturall, detested, brutish   410
   *Villaine; worse then brutish: Go sirrah, seeke him: Ile   411
   apprehend him. Abhominable Villaine, where is he?   412
   *Sonne and Father. This villaine of mine comes vnder the   439
   Edg. Some Villaine hath done me wrong.   486
   Glo. Now *Edmund*, where's the villaine?   971
   Glo. Where is the villaine, *Edmund*?   977
   Glo. O strange and fastned Villaine, | Would he deny his Letter, said he?   1015
   All Ports Ile barre, the villaine shall not scape,   1018
   *villaine into morter, and daube the wall of a   1139
   Corn. To this Chaire binde him, | Villaine, thou shalt finde.   2098
   Corn. My Villaine? | *Seru*. Nay then come on, and take the chance of
   anger.   2152
   Reg. Out treacherous Villaine, | Thou call'st on him, that hates thee. It
   was he   2164
   Turne out that eyelesse Villaine: throw this Slaue   2174
   Edg. I know thee well. A seruiceable Villaine,   2704
VILLAINES = *1
   *Moone, and Starres, as if we were villaines on necessitie,   450
VILLAIN-LIKE = 1
   That names me Traitor, villain-like he lies,   3046
VILLANOUS = *1
   *my Cue is villanous Melancholly, with a sighe like *Tom*   464
VINES = 1
   The Vines of France, and Milke of Burgundie,   90
VIOLENT = 2
   To do vpon respect such violent outrage: 1299
   Repaire those violent harmes, that my two Sisters | Haue in thy
   Reuerence made.   2778
VIOLENTLY = *1
   *run a certaine course: where, if you violently proceed a-|gainst   416
VIRTUE *see* vertue
VIRTUES *see* vertues
VIRTUOUS *see* vertuous
VISAGE = 2
   Shee'l flea thy Woluish visage. Thou shalt finde,   827
   A plague vpon your Epilepticke visage,   1154
VISIT = 1
   Cor. You know not why we came to visit you?   1061
VITIOUS = 1
   The darke and vitious place where thee he got, | Cost him his eyes.   3133
VNABLE = 1
   A loue that makes breath poore, and speech vnable,   65
VNACCOMMODATED = *1
   *sophisticated. Thou art the thing it selfe; vnaccommo-|dated   1886
VNBOULTED = *1
   *my Lord, if you will giue me leaue, I will tread this vn-|boulted   1138
VNBURTHEND = *1
   *Vnburthen'd crawle toward death. Our son of *Cornwal*,   46
VNBUTTON = *1
   *as thou art. Off, off you Lendings: Come, vn-|button heere.   1888

VNCAUGHT = 1
Not in this Land shall he remaine vncaught 994
VNCHASTE = 1
No vnchaste action or dishonoured step 250
VNCONSTANT = *1
*Reg. Such vnconstant starts are we like to haue from | him, as this of
Kents banishment. 325
VNCOUERD = *1
*with thy vncouer'd body, this extremitie of the Skies. Is 1882
VNDER = 5*4
*Sonne and Father. This villaine of mine comes vnder the 439
*My father compounded with my mother vnder the Dra- | gons 457
*taile, and my Natiuity was vnder Vrsa Maior, so 458
Though I condemne not, yet vnder pardon 866
Vnder th'allowance of your great aspect, 1181
Approach thou Beacon to this vnder Globe, 1240
Should many people, vnder two commands 1537
That vnder couert, and conuenient seeming 1709
*that hath laid Kniues vnder his Pillow, and Halters 1835
VNDERSTAND = 2*1
The Contents, as in part I vnderstand them, | Are too blame. 377
To vnderstand my purposes aright: 748
*Lear. Inform'd them? Do'st thou vnderstand me man. | Glo. I my good
Lord. 1374
VNDERSTANDING = 1
Reg. I speake in vnderstanding: Y'are: I know't, 2415
VNDERTAKE = 1
That dares not vndertake: Hee'l not feele wrongs 2281
VNDIVULGED = 1
That hast within thee vndivulged Crimes 1705
VNDO = 1
Pray you vndo this Button. Thanke you Sir, 3281
VNDONE = *1
*Kent. I cannot wish the fault vndone, the issue of it, | being so proper. 20
VNDOO = 1
So distribution should vndoo excesse, 2255
VNFED = 1
How shall your House-lesse heads, and vnfed sides, 1811
VNFEED = *1
*Foole. Then 'tis like the breath of an vnfeed Lawyer, 659
VNFITNESSE = 1
When I haue shew'd th'vnfitnesse. 855
VNFOLD = *1
*Cor. Time shall vnfold what plighted cunning hides, 306
VNFORTUNATE = 1
Glou. A poore vnfortunate Beggar. 2513
VNFRIENDED = 1
Vnfriended, new adopted to our hate, 222
VNGOUERND = 1
Least his vngouern'd rage, dissolue the life | That wants the meanes to
leade it. 2370
VNGRACIOUS = 1
With this vngracious paper strike the sight 2729
VNGRATEFULL see ingratefull
VNHAPPIE = 1
Cor. Vnhappie that I am, I cannot heaue 97

VNHAPPILY = 1
  *_Bast_. I promise you, the effects he writes of, succeede | vnhappily.   472
VNHAPPY = 1
  To raise my fortunes. Thou old, vnhappy Traitor,   2678
VNKIND = 1
  To such a lownesse, but his vnkind Daughters.   1852
VNKINDE = 1
  Bid them farewell _Cordelia_, though vnkinde,   285
VNKINDNESSE = 2*1
  *then as a very pretence and purpose of vnkindnesse;   599
  Sharpe-tooth'd vnkindnesse, like a vulture heere,   1413
  I taxe not you, you Elements with vnkindnesse.   1671
VNKNOWNE = 1
  An vnknowne opposite: thou art not vanquish'd, | But cozend, and beguild.   3110
VNLESSE = 1
  Shall not be a Maid long, vnlesse things be cut shorter. | _Exeunt_.   924
VNLOOSE = 1
  Which are t'intrince, t'vnloose: smooth euery passion   1148
VNMANNERLY = 1
  The region of my heart, be _Kent_ vnmannerly,   154
VNMERCIFULL = 1
  Glou. Vnmercifull Lady, as you are, I'me none.   2097
VNNATURALL = 4*2
  Must be of such vnnaturall degree,   240
  *Abhorred Villaine, vnnaturall, detested, brutish   410
  To his vnnaturall purpose, in fell motion   986
  Staine my mans cheekes. No you vnnaturall Hags,   1578
  *_Glo_. Alacke, alacke _Edmund_, I like not this vnnaturall   1753
  Bast. Most sauage and vnnaturall.   1758
VNNECESSARY = 1*1
  *_Kent_. Thou whoreson Zed, thou vnnecessary letter: 1137
  Age is vnnecessary: on my knees I begge,   1436
VNNUMBRED = 1
  That on th'vnnumbred idle Pebble chafes   2456
VNPOSSESSING = 1
  Thou vnpossessing Bastard, dost thou thinke,   1004
VNPRIZD = 1
  Can buy this vnpriz'd precious Maid of me.   284
VNPROUIDED = 1
  My vnprouided body, latch'd mine arme;   988
VNPUBLISHD = 1
  Cord. All blest Secrets, | All you vnpublish'd Vertues of the earth   2366
VNQUIETLY = 1
  Gen. One minded like the weather, most vnquietly.   1617
VNREMOUEABLE = 1
  How vnremoueable and fixt he is | In his owne course.   1368
VNRULY = *1
  *therewithall the vnruly way-wardnesse, that infirme and | cholericke yeares bring with them.   323
VNSANCTIFIED = 1
  Thee Ile rake vp, the poste vnsanctified   2727
VNSEALE = 1
  Let me vnseale the Letter.   2408
VNSETTLE = 1
  His wits begin t'vnsettle. | _Glou_. Canst thou blame him? _Storm still_   1941

VNSIGHTLY = *1
*Reg. Good Sir, no more: these are vnsightly trickes: 1438
VNSPOKE = 1
Which often leaues the history vnspoke   259
VNSTATE = *1
*after your owne wisedome. I would vnstate my | selfe, to be in a due
resolution.   429
VNSUBSTANTIALL = 1
Thou vnsubstantiall ayre that I embrace: 2185
VNTENDER = 1
Lear. So young, and so vntender? | Cor. So young my Lord, and true.   113
VNTENTED = 1
Th'vntented woundings of a Fathers curse   819
VNTILL = 2*1
*him: and at my entreaty forbeare his presence, vntill   482
Vntill their greater pleasures first be knowne | That are to censure them.   2941
Vntill some halfe houre past when I was arm'd,   3156
VNTIMELY = 1*1
*Vntimely comes this hurt. Giue me your arme. Exeunt.   2176
Vpon the English party. Oh vntimely death, death.   2703
VNTO = 3
I had thought by making this well knowne vnto you,   716
The Wretch that thou hast blowne vnto the worst,   2186
Neuer (O fault) reueal'd my selfe vnto him,   3155
VNTUND = 1
Th'vntun'd and iarring senses, O winde vp, | Of this childe-changed
Father.   2765
VNUSALL = 1
That guard, and most vnusall vigilance   1255
VNWHIPT = 1
Vnwhipt of Iustice. Hide thee, thou Bloudy hand;   1706
VOICE see also voyce = 2
Lear. Passe. | Glou. I know that voice.   2541
What is't thou saist? Her voice was euer soft,   3236
VOICES = 1
Of Bedlam beggers, who with roaring voices,   1265
VOLKE = *1
*volke passe: and 'chud ha' bin zwaggerd out of my life,   2691
VOR = *2
*come not neere th'old man: keepe out che vor'ye, or Ile   2693
*Edg. Chill picke your teeth Zir: come, no matter vor | your foynes.   2697
VORTNIGHT = *1
*'twould not ha' bin zo long as 'tis, by a vortnight. Nay,   2692
VOUCHSAFE = 1
That you'l vouchsafe me Rayment, Bed, and Food.   1437
VOUCHT = 1
That monsters it: Or your fore-voucht affection   241
VOWES = 1*1
That thou hast sought to make vs breake our vowes,   182
*Let our reciprocall vowes be remembred. You haue manie   2716
VOYCE = 1*1
Me thinkes thy voyce is alter'd, and thou speak'st   2440
*Glou. The tricke of that voyce, I do well remember: 2552
VP see also pent-vp = 22*7
Bur. Pardon me Royall Sir, | Election makes not vp in such conditions.   225
Be it lawfull I take vp what's cast away.   278
Now Gods, stand vp for Bastards.   356

VP *cont.*

Glou. Why so earnestly seeke you to put vp y Letter?	363
*eate vp the meate, the two Crownes of the egge: when	674
Drie vp in her the Organs of increase,	793
*thou knowest me? Is it two dayes since I tript vp thy	1102
They summon'd vp their meiney, straight tooke Horse,	1311
Lear. Oh how this Mother swels vp toward my heart!	1328
Must be their Schoole-Masters: shut vp your doores,	1608
Cor. Shut vp your doores my Lord, 'tis a wil'd night,	1612
Ha's practis'd on mans life. Close pent-vp guilts,	1710
Both welcome, and protection. Take vp thy Master,	2051
Stand in assured losse. Take vp, take vp,	2054
In Hell-blacke-night indur'd, would haue buoy'd vp	2132
Reg. Giue me thy Sword. A pezant stand vp thus? | *Killes him*.	2154
Would stretch thy Spirits vp into the ayre:	2291
Edg. You do climbe vp it now. Look how we labor.	2432
Looke vp a height, the shrill-gorg'd Larke so farre	2500
Cannot be seene, or heard: Do but looke vp.	2501
Vp, so: How is't? Feele you your Legges? You stand. | *Glou*. Too well, too well.	2508
*Bring vp the browne Billes. O well flowne Bird: i'th'	2538
Thee Ile rake vp, the poste vnsanctified	2727
How stiffe is my vilde sense | That I stand vp, and haue ingenious feeling	2733
Th'vntun'd and iarring senses, O winde vp, | Of this childe-changed Father.	2765
Bast. The Enemy's in view, draw vp your powers,	2897
The which immediacie may well stand vp,	3005
Kent. Breake heart, I prythee breake. | *Edg*. Looke vp my Lord.	3285

VPBRAIDES = 1

His Knights grow riotous, and himselfe vpbraides vs	513

VPON = 42*4

Vpon the foule disease, reuoke thy guift,	178
Vpon our kingdome: if on the tenth day following,	190
Thee and thy vertues here I seize vpon,	277
Vpon the gad? *Edmond*, how now? What newes?	361
Blastes and Fogges vpon thee:	818
Vpon his partie 'gainst the Duke of *Albany*? | Aduise your selfe.	956
In cunning, I must draw my Sword vpon you:	960
That tended vpon my Father?	1034
Cor. Keepe peace vpon your liues, he dies that strikes | againe, what is the matter?	1122
A plague vpon your Epilepticke visage,	1154
Goose, if I had you vpon *Sarum* Plaine,	1156
To strike at me vpon his misconstruction,	1193
And put vpon him such a deale of Man,	1196
To do vpon respect such violent outrage:	1299
Look'd blacke vpon me, strooke me with her Tongue	1442
Most Serpent-like, vpon the very Heart.	1443
Art not asham'd to looke vpon this Beard?	1483
Kent. Sir, I do know you, | And dare vpon the warrant of my note	1626
And let this Tyrannous night take hold vpon you,	1929
Corn. I will lay trust vpon thee: and thou shalt finde | a deere Father in my loue. *Exeunt*.	1994
Lear. To haue a thousand with red burning spits | Come hizzing in vpon 'em.	2013
I haue ore-heard a plot of death vpon him:	2048

VPON *cont*.

Though well we may not passe vpon his life	2084
Vpon these eyes of thine, Ile set my foote.	2140
Ser. If you did weare a beard vpon your chin,	2150
Vpon the Dunghill: *Regan*, I bleed apace,	2175
May all the building in my fancie plucke | Vpon my hatefull life. Another way	2332
The Fishermen, that walk'd vpon the beach	2452
Vpon the crowne o'th'Cliffe. What thing was that | Which parted from you?	2511
*yond Iustice railes vpon yond simple theefe. Hearke in	2596
And when I haue stolne vpon these Son in Lawes,	2628
Gent. Oh heere he is: lay hand vpon him, Sir.	2631
Vpon the English party. Oh vntimely death, death.	2703
A plot vpon her vertuous Husbands life,	2725
Vpon a wheele of fire, that mine owne teares | Do scal'd, like molten Lead.	2796
Cor. O looke vpon me Sir, | And hold your hand in benediction o're me,	2810
You know the goodnesse I intend vpon you:	2854
Lear. Vpon such sacrifices my *Cordelia*, | The Gods themselues throw Incense.	2961
If none appeare to proue vpon thy person,	3038
Regan. My sicknesse growes vpon me.	3055
will maintaine vpon Edmund, supposed Earle of Gloster,	3061
Alb. Aske him his purposes, why he appeares | Vpon this Call o'th'Trumpet.	3068
To proue vpon thy heart, where to I speake, | Thou lyest.	3095
To lay the blame vpon her owne dispaire, | That she for-did her selfe.	3213
Lear. A plague vpon you Murderors, Traitors all,	3233
That would vpon the wracke of this tough world | Stretch him out longer.	3288

VPONS = 1

And take vpon's the mystery of things,	2956

VPPON = *1

*take vppon your Traitorous Father, are not fit for your	2067

VPRIGHT = 1

For all beneath the Moone would I not leape vpright.	2463

VPWARD = 2*1

*great one that goes vpward, let him draw thee after:	1346
Fourescore and vpward, | Not an houre more, nor lesse:	2815
And from th'extremest vpward of thy head,	3091

VRGD = 1

By dilligent discouerie, but your hast | Is now vrg'd on you.	2899

VRGES = 1

The time will not allow the complement | Which very manners vrges.	3187

VRSA = *1

*taile, and my Natiuity was vnder *Vrsa Maior*, so	458

VS *see also* let's, on's, vpon's *l*.*6 54 56 182 214 282 301 311 314 *328 330 343 *384 *424 *434 *443 512 513 543 1302 1587 *1733 1787 *1858 1963 *2070 2083 2166 2191 2201 2222 2229 2269 2287 2396 2401 2711 2712 2875 2877 2964 2965 2967 3132 3185 3186 3192 3263 3270 = 40*9

VSAGE = 1

Thou might'st deserue, or they impose this vsage, | Comming from vs.	1301

VSD = 1

That going shalbe vs'd with feet.	1748

VSE = 8 *6
*you gaue me nothing for't, can you make no vse of no- | thing Nuncle?   660
*Gon. I would you would make vse of your good wise- | (dome   731
*Fool. Shalt see thy other Daughter will vse thee kind- | ly,   888
Wherein we must haue vse of your aduise.   1064
Your needfull counsaile to our businesses, | Which craues the instant
vse.   1070
Ste. Why do'st thou vse me thus? I know thee not.   1085
Kent. Why Madam, if I were your Fathers dog, | You should not vse
me so.   1215
*they tooke from me the vse of mine owne house, charg'd   1755
*backe, thou hotly lusts to vse her in that kind, for which   2605
The Naturall Foole of Fortune. Vse me well,   2634
*To vse his eyes for Garden water-pots. I wil die brauely,   2640
Her husband being aliue. Now then, wee'l vse   2909
I do require them of you so to vse them,   2986
Had I your tongues and eyes, Il'd vse them so,   3218
VSED = *1
*Foole. I haue vsed it Nunckle, ere since thou mad'st   685
VSURER = *1
*thou whip'st her. The Vsurer hangs the Cozener. Tho- | rough   2606
VSURERS = 1
When Vsurers tell their Gold i'th'Field,   1744
VSURPES = 1
To thee a Womans seruices are due, | My Foole vsurpes my body.   2296
VSURPT = 1
Kent. The wonder is, he hath endur'd so long, | He but vsurpt his life.   3291
VTTERD = 1
What he hath vtter'd I haue writ my Sister: 853
VULGAR = 1
Edg. Do you heare ought (Sir) of a Battell toward. | Gent. Most sure,
and vulgar: 2652
VULTURE = 1
Sharpe-tooth'd vnkindnesse, like a vulture heere,   1413
VURTHER = 1
Edg. Chill not let go Zir, | Without vurther 'casion.   2687
WAGE = 2
To wage against thine enemies, nere feare to loose it, | Thy safety being
motiue.   167
To wage against the enmity oth'ayre,   1502
WAGES = 1
Taste the wages of their vertue, and all Foes   3275
WAGTAILE = 1
Iakes with him. Spare my gray-beard, you wagtaile?   1140
WAIES = 1
*Ile so carbonado your shanks, draw you Rascall, come | your waies.   1111
WAIGHT = 1
Edg. The waight of this sad time we must obey,   3298
WAILE = 1
Tom will make him weepe and waile,   2028
WAIST see waste
WAKD = *2
*this I may speake more. If our Father would sleepe till I wak'd   387
*contriuing of Lust, and wak'd to doe it. Wine lou'd I   1870
WAKE = 3 *1
Got 'tweene a sleepe, and wake? Well then,   349
*Hum? Conspiracy? Sleepe till I wake him, you should   390

KING LEAR

WAKE *cont.*
Shall of a Corne cry woe, and turne his sleepe to wake. 1685
Gent. So please your Maiesty, | That we may wake the King, he hath slept long? 2767
WAKES = 1*1
*Do, de, de, de: sese: Come, march to Wakes and Fayres, 2031
Had not concluded all. He wakes, speake to him. 2790
WAKING = 1
Are Lethargied. Ha! Waking? 'Tis not so? 742
WALKD = 1
The Fishermen, that walk'd vpon the beach 2452
WALKE = 1*1
*Do's *Lear* walke thus? Speake thus? Where are his eies? 740
Cor. Wilt please your Highnesse walke? | *Lear.* You must beare with me: 2840
WALKES = *1
*Curfew, and walkes at first Cocke: Hee giues the Web 1896
WALKING = 1
on's body, cold: Looke, heere comes a walking fire. 1894
WALL = 1*1
*villaine into morter, and daube the wall of a 1139
Then my out-wall; open this Purse, and take 1642
WALLD = 1
In a wall'd prison, packs and sects of great ones, | That ebbe and flow by th'Moone. 2958
WALLS = 1
Dispose of them, of me, the walls is thine: 3019
WALL-NEUT = *1
*Toad, the Tod-pole, the wall-Neut, and the water: that 1909
WANDERERS = 1
Gallow the very wanderers of the darke 1696
WANT = 6*1
If for I want that glib and oylie Art, 246
But euen for want of that, for which I am richer, 252
And well are worth the want that you haue wanted. 305
Weary of all, shall want some. That's a sheal'd Pescod. 711
You are much more at task for want of wisedome, 867
Glou. I haue no way, and therefore want no eyes: 2199
opportunities to cut him off: if your will want not, time and 2717
WANTED = 1
And well are worth the want that you haue wanted. 305
WANTON = 1
As Flies to wanton Boyes, are we to th'Gods, | They kill vs for their sport. 2221
WANTONS = *1
*o'th' coxcombs with a sticke, and cryed downe wantons, 1400
WANTS = 1
Least his vngouern'd rage, dissolue the life | That wants the meanes to leade it. 2370
WARD = *1
*declin'd, the Father should bee as Ward to the Son, and 407
WARDNESSE = *1
*therewithall the vnruly way-wardnesse, that infirme and | cholericke yeares bring with them. 323
WARLIKE = 1
But since thy out-side lookes so faire and Warlike, 3098

311

WARM = *1
*Glou. In fellow there, into th'Houel; keep thee warm.   1955
WARME = 4
Thou out of Heauens benediction com'st | To the warme Sun.   1238
If onely to go warme were gorgeous,   1568
Which scarcely keepes thee warme, but for true need: 1570
*sharpe Hauthorne blow the windes. Humh, goe to thy | bed and warme
thee.   1828
WARMTH = *1
*Gaole, from the loathed warmth whereof, deliuer me, and sup- |ply the
place for your Labour.   2720
WARRANT see also vor = 1
Kent. Sir, I do know you, | And dare vpon the warrant of my note   1626
WARRE = 3
Alb. Let's then determine with th'ancient of warre | On our proceeding.   2873
I hold you but a subiect of this Warre, | Not as a Brother.   2999
By th'law of Warre, thou wast not bound to answer   3109
WARRES = 1
Cur. Haue you heard of no likely Warres toward,   938
WAS see also 'twas = 34*11
WASHD = 1
Cor. The Iewels of our Father, with wash'd eies   293
WAST l.*705 2123 2786 3109 = 3*1, 1
To haue th'expence and wast of his Reuenues: 1039
WASTE see also wast = *1
*Downe from the waste they are Centaures, though   2567
WATCHD = 1*1
*Kent. Pray do not Sir, I haue watch'd and trauail'd hard,   1231
Losses their remedies. All weary and o're-watch'd,   1247
WATCHES = 1
My Father watches: O Sir, fly this place,   950
WATER = 2*3
And let not womens weapons, water drops,   1577
*Foole. O Nunkle, Court holy-water in a dry house, is   1665
*better then this Rain-water out o'doore. Good Nunkle,   1666
When Brewers marre their Malt with water;   1737
*Toad, the Tod-pole, the wall-Neut, and the water: that   1909
WATERS = 2
And cast you with the waters that you loose   822
Or swell the curled Waters 'boue the Maine,   1621
WATER-POTS = *1
*To vse his eyes for Garden water-pots. I wil die brauely,   2640
WATRISH = 1
Not all the Dukes of watrish Burgundy,   283
WAUED = 1
Hornes wealk'd, and waued like the enraged Sea: 2516
WAWLE = 1
We wawle, and cry. I will preach to thee: Marke.   2622
WAXE = 1
Leaue gentle waxe, and manners: blame vs not   2712
WAY = 21*4
T'auert your liking a more worthier way,   231
*Bast. Fled this way Sir, when by no meanes he could.   978
*would'st be a Baud in way of good seruice, and art no- |thing   1093
Resolue me with all modest haste, which way   1300
*Foole. Winters not gon yet, if the wil'd Geese fly that | (way,   1322
Corn. 'Tis best to giue him way, he leads himselfe.   1601

WAY *cont*.

That way, Ile this: He that first lights on him, | Holla the other. *Exeunt*.	1652
of him, entreat for him, or any way sustaine him.	1757
O that way madnesse lies, let me shun that: | No more of that.	1801
Kent. This way, my Lord. | *Lear*. With him;	1957
*thus giues way to Loyaltie, something feares mee to | thinke of.	1973
Kent. All the powre of his wits, haue giuen way to his	2001
Reg. Go thrust him out at gates, and let him smell | His way to Douer.	
Exit with Glouster.	2170
Oldm. You cannot see your way.	2198
Glou. I haue no way, and therefore want no eyes:	2199
I'th'way toward Douer, do it for ancient loue,	2230
Glou. Know'st thou the way to Douer?	2245
Not met vs on the way. Now, where's your Master?	2269
Which tye him to an answer: our wishes on the way	2282
Gon. One way I like this well.	2330
May all the building in my fancie plucke | Vpon my hatefull life.	
Another way	2332
Shew scarse so grosse as Beetles. Halfe way downe	2449
Reg. But haue you neuer found my Brothers way, | To the fore-fended	
place?	2858
As this instructs thee, thou dost make thy way	2972
This Sword of mine shall giue them instant way,	3105

WAYES *see also* waies = 1

Reg. Our troopes set forth to morrow, stay with vs: | The wayes are	
dangerous.	2401

WAY-WARDNESSE = *1

*therewithall the vnruly way-wardnesse, that infirme and | cholericke	
yeares bring with them.	323

WE *see also* wee, wee'l, weele = 54*16

WEAKE = 3

Reg. I pray you Father being weake, seeme so.	1494
A poore, infirme, weake, and dispis'd old man:	1675
(Alacke too weake the conflict to support)	3160

WEAKENS = 1

Either his Notion weakens, his Discernings	741

WEALE = 1

Which in the tender of a wholesome weale,	722

WEALKD = 1

Hornes wealk'd, and waued like the enraged Sea:	2516

WEALTH = 1

I tell you all her wealth. For you great King,	228

WEAPON = 1

Horse to ride, and weapon to weare:	1916

WEAPONS = 2

Glo. Weapons? Armes? what's the matter here?	1121
And let not womens weapons, water drops,	1577

WEARE = 6*3

*needs weare my Coxcombe. How now Nunckle? would	634
And know not how their wits to weare,	682
Kent. That such a slaue as this should weare a Sword,	1145
*Fathers that weare rags, do make their Children blind,	1323
Horse to ride, and weapon to weare:	1916
Ser. If you did weare a beard vpon your chin,	2150
A Mistresses command. Weare this; spare speech,	2289
Glou. O ruin'd peece of Nature, this great world | Shall so weare out to	
naught.	2577

WEARE *cont.*
    As if we were Gods spies: And wee'l weare out   2957
WEARES = 1*2
    Who weares no honesty: such smiling rogues as these,   1146
    Foole. Hah, ha, he weares Cruell Garters Horses are   1282
    *ouerlustie at legs, then he weares wodden nether-stocks.   1285
WEARST = 1
    Why Nature needs not what thou gorgeous wear'st,   1569
WEARY = 4
    Gon. Put on what weary negligence you please,   519
    Weary of all, shall want some. That's a sheal'd Pescod.   711
    Losses their remedies. All weary and o're-watch'd,   1247
    They are sicke, they are weary,   1362
WEATHER = 2
    Kent. Who's there besides foule weather?   1616
    Gen. One minded like the weather, most vnquietly.   1617
WEAUES = 1
    This weaues it selfe perforce into my businesse,   944
WEB = *1
    *Curfew, and walkes at first Cocke: Hee giues the Web   1896
WED = 1
    They loue you all? Happily when I shall wed,   107
WEE *l.**2066 = *1
WEEDES = 2
    Darnell, and all the idle weedes that grow   2355
    These weedes are memories of those worser houres: 2754
WEEDS = 1
    Crown'd with ranke Fenitar, and furrow weeds,   2353
WEEL = 8*1
    Lear. And you lie sirrah, wee'l haue you whipt.   694
    You stubborne ancient Knaue, you reuerent Bragart, | Wee'l teach you.   1204
    Foole. Wee'l set thee to schoole to an Ant, to teach   1340
    Wee'l no more meete, no more see one another.   1514
    so, so, wee'l go to Supper i'th'morning.   2042
    Her husband being aliue. Now then, wee'l vse   2909
    And aske of thee forgiuenesse: So wee'l liue,   2951
    Talke of Court newes, and wee'l talke with them too,   2954
    As if we were Gods spies: And wee'l weare out   2957
WEELE = 1
    Weele see 'em staru'd first: come. *Exit.*   2968
WEEPE = 8*1
    For sodaine ioy did weepe, | And I for sorrow sung,   688
    The terrors of the earth? you thinke Ile weepe,   1582
    No, Ile not weepe, I haue full cause of weepe. | *Storme and Tempest.*   1583
    Or ere Ile weepe; O Foole, I shall go mad. *Exeunt.*   1586
    No, I will weepe no more; in such a night,   1797
    Tom will make him weepe and waile,   2028
    Lear. If thou wilt weepe my Fortunes, take my eyes.   2618
    Yes faith: I pray weepe not,   2828
    Ere they shall make vs weepe?   2967
WEEPING = 1
    No, Ile not weepe, I haue full cause of weeping. | *Storme and Tempest.*   1583
WEIGHD = *1
    *most, for qualities are so weigh'd, that curiosity in nei- | ther, can make
    choise of eithers moity.   9
WEIGHT *see* waight

WEILD = *1
*Gon. Sir, I loue you more then word can weild y matter,   60
WEL = *1
*Lea. Those wicked Creatures yet do look wel fauor'd   1554
WELCOME = 6*1
Glo. I serue you Madam, | Your Graces are right welcome. Exeunt.
Flourish.   1072
Whose welcome I perceiu'd had poison'd mine,   1315
For your fit welcome, giue eare Sir to my Sister,   1528
Both welcome, and protection. Take vp thy Master,   2051
The worst returnes to laughter. Welcome then,   2184
*Gon. Welcome my Lord. I meruell our mild husband   2268
Lear. You are welcome hither. | Kent. Nor no man else: 3256
WELL = 49*11
Be as well neighbour'd, pittied, and releeu'd,   126
*Kent. Fare thee well King, sith thus thou wilt appeare,   194
Your faults as they are named. Loue well our Father: 296
And well are worth the want that you haue wanted.   305
Well may you prosper.   308
When my Dimensions are as well compact,   341
Got 'tweene a sleepe, and wake? Well then,   349
Well, my Legittimate, if this Letter speed,   353
*Bast. I do not well know my L.(ord) If it shall please you to   413
You shall do well, the fault of it Ile answer.   517
Remember what I haue said. | Ste. Well Madam.   523
*Knigh. He saies my Lord, your Daughters is not well.   580
*theres a great abatement of kindnesse appeares as well in   589
*Lear. No more of that, I haue noted it well, goe you   604
I had thought by making this well knowne vnto you,   716
Alb. Well, you may feare too farre.   849
Striuing to better, oft we marre what's well.   870
Gon. Nay then--- | Alb. Well, well, th'euent. Exeunt   871
Fare you well Sir. Exit.   942
Draw, seeme to defend your selfe, | Now quit you well.   961
Beene well inform'd of them, and with such cautions,   1041
Whose disposition all the world well knowes   1229
question, thoud'st well deseru'd it. | Kent. Why Foole?   1338
Glo. Well my good Lord, I haue inform'd them so.   1373
No, but not yet, may be he is not well,   1381
Glo. I would haue all well betwixt you. Exit.   1396
Our yongest borne, I could as well be brought   1506
Lear. Is this well spoken?   1532
Is it not well? What should you need of more?   1534
Reg. This house is little, the old man and's people, | Cannot be well
bestow'd.   1588
*My Regan counsels well: come out oth'storme. Exeunt.   1613
*man no more then this? Consider him well. Thou ow'st   1883
Are gone with him toward Douer; where they boast | To haue well
armed Friends.   2078
Though well we may not passe vpon his life   2084
Conceiue, and fare thee well.   2292
Gon. One way I like this well.   2330
I pray desire her call her wisedome to her. | So fare you well: 2422
Reg. Fare thee well. Exeunt   2428
Well worth a poore mans taking. Fayries, and Gods   2466
Edg. Now fare ye well, good Sir. | Glou. With all my heart.   2469
Now Fellow, fare thee well. | Edg. Gone Sir, farewell: 2480

WELL *cont*.
Vp, so: How is't? Feele you your Legges? You stand. | *Glou*. Too well,
too well.   2508
*Bring vp the browne Billes. O well flowne Bird: i'th'   2538
Glou. The tricke of that voyce, I do well remember: 2552
Do'st thou know me? | *Lear*. I remember thine eyes well enough: dost
thou   2579
I know thee well enough, thy name is Glouster: 2619
The Naturall Foole of Fortune. Vse me well,   2634
Edg. Well pray you Father.   2666
Edg. I know thee well. A seruiceable Villaine,   2704
Of the death-practis'd Duke: for him 'tis well,   2730
Alb. Our very louing Sister, well be-met: 2865
Alb. Why farethee well, I will o're-looke thy paper.   2895
And Fortune led you well: you haue the Captiues   2984
The which immediacie may well stand vp,   3005
Rega. Lady I am not well, else I should answere   3016
Alb. She is not well, conuey her to my Tent.   3056
What safe, and nicely I might well delay,   3100
Bast. Well thought on, take my Sword,   3208
WENCHES = 1
No Heretiques burn'd, but wenches Sutors;   1739
WENT = *1
*young, so out went the Candle, and we were left dark-|ling.   728
WERE *l*.365 *398 *399 400 *450 *588 627 *684 724 *728 *882 1013 1037
   1155 1215 1568 *1893 *1982 2272 2515 *2545 2584 2626 2735 2808 2957
   2985 *3012 = 17*11
WERT *l*.*913 *1881 = *2, *1
Foole. If a mans braines were in's heeles, wert not in | danger of
kybes? | *Lear*. I Boy.   882
WET = 1*1
*Diuinity. When the raine came to wet me once, and the   2547
Lear. Be your teares wet?   2827
WHAT *l*.62 *67 72 91 155 207 247 261 294 *306 311 *316 361 365 *367
   *467 470 *495 519 523 *526 540 *542 549 553 562 *577 *586 672 *695
   *703 718 734 787 810 833 853 858 890 891 897 937 979 1007 *1030 1087
   *1098 *1101 1123 1125 1158 1163 1184 1190 1334 1371 1407 1469 1475
   1531 1533 1534 1551 1560 1563 1569 1581 1610 1634 1643 *1684 1794
   1815 *1825 1864 1906 1907 1920 1924 1933 1937 1950 *1999 *2033 2092
   2107 2109 *2111 2151 2239 2277 2278 2347 2358 2391 2407 2427 2488
   2511 2556 2588 *2594 2633 *2641 2667 2707 2806 2821 2888 2932 3045
   3070 3079 3100 3119 3121 3124 3171 3173 3236 3262 3269
   3299 = 102*23
WHATS = 9*1
Be it lawfull I take vp what's cast away.   278
Lear. What's that? | *Kent*. Authority.   560
Alb. What's the matter, Sir? | *Lear*. Ile tell thee: 812
Striuing to better, oft we marre what's well.   870
Bast. How now, what's the matter? Part.   1118
Glo. Weapons? Armes? what's the matter here?   1121
Lear. What's he, | That hath so much thy place mistooke | To set thee
heere?   1286
Kent. How fares your Grace? | *Lear*. What's he?   1904
Gent. Sir, speed you: what's your will?   2651
Edg. What's he that speakes for *Edmund* Earle of Glo-|(ster?   3078
WHEATE = *1
*Mildewes the white Wheate, and hurts the poore Crea-|ture of earth.   1898

WHEELE = 3*1
Smile once more, turne thy wheele.   1250
*let go thy hold when a great wheele runs downe a   1344
Vpon a wheele of fire, that mine owne teares | Do scal'd, like molten
Lead.   2796
The Wheele is come full circle, I am heere.   3136
WHELKD *see* wealk'd
WHELME = 1
With the hell-hated Lye, ore-whelme thy heart,   3103
WHEN *l.*107 155 157 159 214 262 341 393 *448 474 514 *547 *581 *594
*642 *674 *677 *684 *686 *705 *735 772 826 837 855 *978 989 1001
1194 *1284 1303 *1344 *1347 1352 1384 *1399 1453 1520 1523 1555
*1651 1736 1737 1738 1740 1742 1744 *1754 1775 1791 *1910 2200 2235
2275 2336 2421 2431 2483 2505 *2547 *2548 2555 2624 2628 2774 2893
2950 2979 3145 3156 3220 = 51*21
WHENCE = *1
*I say, retire with me to my lodging, from whence I will   489
WHER *l.*1017 = *1
WHERE *l.*58 230 286 412 *416 *424 535 *740 951 975 977 1078 1330 1359
1561 1595 1724 1788 1809 1931 *1988 2016 2045 *2050 *2068 2078 2120
2159 2212 2335 2395 2460 2484 2799 2803 2804 2823 2997 3095 3106
3133 3142 3249 = 37*6
WHEREFORE = 7
My seruices are bound, wherefore should I   336
Lag of a Brother? Why Bastard? Wherefore base?   340
For the sound man. Death on my state: wherefore   1388
Reg. Wherefore to Douer?   2122
Corn. Wherefore to Douer? Let him answer that.   2124
Reg. Wherefore to Douer? | *Glou*. Because I would not see thy cruell
Nailes   2127
Stew. Wherefore, bold Pezant, | Dar'st thou support a publish'd
Traitor? Hence,   2683
WHEREIN = 2*1
Bast. Bethink your selfe wherein you may haue offen-|ded   481
Wherein we must haue vse of your aduise.   1064
Thy halfe o'th'Kingdome hast thou not forgot, | Wherein I thee
endow'd.   1464
WHEREOF = 4*1
(Whereof I know you are fraught), and put away   732
Alb. Now Gods that we adore, | Whereof comes this?   804
Whereof (perchance) these are but furnishings.   1638
(More harder then the stones whereof 'tis rais'd,   1718
*Gaole, from the loathed warmth whereof, deliuer me, and sup-|ply the
place for your Labour.*   2720
WHERES = 6*5
*ho, dinner, where's my knaue? my Foole? Go you and call   573
*my Foole hither. You you Sirrah, where's my Daughter?   574
asleepe, how now? Where's that Mungrell?   579
*I will looke further intoo't: but where's my Foole? I | haue not seene
him this two daies.   600
Glo. Now *Edmund*, where's the villaine?   971
Kent. I know you: Where's the King?   1618
How now? Where's the King?   2073
Where's my Sonne *Edmund*?   2161
Not met vs on the way. Now, where's your Master?   2269
*Speake *Edmund*, where's the King? and where's *Cordelia*?   3193

WHERESOERE *see* where
WHERETO = 1
    Whereto our health is bound, we are not our selues,   1383
WHEREVPON = *1
    Glou. Sir, this yong Fellowes mother could; where- | vpon   16
WHERS = *1
    *backe: wher's my Foole? Ho, I thinke the world's   578
WHETHER *see also* whither = 4*1
    Or whether gasted by the noyse I made, | Full sodainely he fled.   991
    Corn. Whether is he going?   1599
    Glo. He cals to Horse, but will I know not whether.   1600
    Foole. Prythee Nunkle tell me, whether a madman be | a Gentleman,
    or a Yeoman.   2007
    Or whether since he is aduis'd by ought   2848
WHICH *l*.*8 56 79 137 146 183 185 242 252 259 266 *484 534 559 *565
    *598 720 722 724 733 761 781 816 828 947 998 1026 1028 1066 1071
    1148 1176 *1185 *1187 1300 1310 1316 1321 1350 1499 1517 1570 1633
    1636 *1651 1719 1774 *1980 *1981 2086 2104 2116 2217 2232 2282 2302
    2321 2363 2496 2512 *2597 *2598 *2605 2649 2654 2701 2904 2910 2913
    *2994 3005 3077 3104 3188 3228 = 62*13
WHILE = 3
    Conferring them on yonger strengths, while we   45
    Repose you there, while I to this hard house,   1717
    Let him alone a while.   2802
WHILES = 1
    Do's not attend my taking. Whiles I may scape   1256
WHILST = 1
    Or whil'st I can vent clamour from my throate,   179
WHINING = *1
    *one whom I will beate into clamours whining, if thou   1096
WHIP = 1
    Lear. Take heed Sirrah, the whip.   640
WHIPST = *1
    *thou whip'st her. The Vsurer hangs the Cozener. Tho- | rough   2606
WHIPT = 2*5
    *whipt out, when the Lady Brach may stand by'th'fire | and stinke.   642
    this, let him be whipt that first findes it so.   679
    Lear. And you lie sirrah, wee'l haue you whipt.   694
    *they'l haue me whipt for speaking true: thou'lt haue me   696
    *whipt for lying, and sometimes I am whipt for holding   697
    *Poole: who is whipt from Tything to Tything, and   1913
WHIRLE-POOLE = *1
    *through Sword, and Whirle-Poole, o're Bog, and Quag- | mire,   1834
WHIRLE-WINDES = *1
    *blisse thee from Whirle-Windes, Starre-blasting, and ta- | king,   1840
WHISPERD = *1
    *I meane the whisper'd ones, for they are yet but | ear-kissing
    arguments.   935
WHISTLE = 2
    Some time I shall sleepe out, the rest Ile whistle: 1232
    Gon. I haue beene worth the whistle.   2300
WHITE = 3*5
    *Sindge my white head. And thou all-shaking Thunder,   1661
    So old, and white as this. O, ho! 'tis foule.   1679
    *Mildewes the white Wheate, and hurts the poore Crea- | ture of earth.   1898
    Curres, be thy mouth or blacke or white: 2023
    Reg. So white, and such a Traitor? | *Glou*. Naughty Ladie,   2102

WHITE *cont*.
Lear. Ha! *Gonerill* with a white beard? They flatter'd	2543
*me like a Dogge, and told mee I had the white hayres in	2544
Cor. Had you not bin their Father, these white flakes	2781

WHITHER *see also* whether = *1
*try whither your Costard, or my Ballow be the harder; | chill be plaine with you.	2694

WHO *l*.*23 134 206 303 307 345 *385 393 555 607 743 825 1146 1171 1198 1244 1265 1467 *1477 1479 1623 1624 1631 1632 1645 1747 *1832 *1913 *1914 2077 2167 2189 2207 2306 2319 *2518 2527 *2612 2648 2669 2911 2944 2955 2985 3048 3117 3176 3206 3243 = 45*8

WHOLE = 1
Goe to th'creating a whole tribe of Fops	348

WHOLESOME = 2
Which in the tender of a wholesome weale,	722
'Tis on such ground, and to such wholesome end,	1423

WHOM *l*.119 149 232 235 536 1031 *1096 *1832 *1841 *2249 2867 = 7*4

WHOOP = 1
Whoop Iugge I loue thee.	737

WHORE = 1*2
Leaue thy drinke and thy whore, | And keepe in a dore,	654
*Fortune that arrant whore, nere turns the key toth' poore.	1325
*hand: why dost thou lash that Whore? Strip thy owne	2604

WHORES = 1
And Baudes, and whores, do Churches build,	1745

WHORESON = *3
*action-taking, whoreson glasse-gazing super-seruiceable	1091
*sop oth' Moonshine of you, you whoreson Cullyenly | Barber-monger, draw.	1105
Kent. Thou whoreson Zed, thou vnnecessary letter:	1137

WHORE-MASTER-MAN = *1
*on. An admirable euasion of Whore-master-man,	455

WHORSON *see also* horson = *1
Lear. My Ladies Father? my Lords knaue, you whor-|son dog, you slaue, you curre.	610

WHOS = 8
Kent. Who's there besides foule weather?	1616
Kent. Who's there? | *Foole*. Marry here's Grace, and a Codpiece, that's a | Wiseman, and a Foole.	1691 |
Kent. Giue my thy hand, who's there?	1822
Kent. Who's there? What is't you seeke?	1906
Who's there? the Traitor? | *Reg*. Ingratefull Fox, 'tis he.	2089
Oldm. How now? who's there?	2206
Who looses, and who wins; who's in, who's out;	2955

WHOSE = 17*3
Although our last and least; to whose yong loue,	89
That Lord, whose hand must take my plight, shall carry	108
Nor are those empty hearted, whose low sounds| Reuerbe no hollownesse.	163
Whose nature is so farre from doing harmes,	500
That he suspects none: on whose foolish honestie	501
Whose mind and mine I know in that are one,	522
Whose vertue and obedience doth this instant	1055
Ste. This ancient Ruffian Sir, whose life I haue spar'd | at sute of his gray-beard.	1135
Whose influence like the wreath of radient fire | On flickring *Phoebus* front.	1182

WHOSE *cont*.
   On whose imployment I was sent to you,   1208
   Whose disposition all the world well knowes   1229
   Whose welcome I perceiu'd had poison'd mine,   1315
   Lear. This is a Slaue, whose easie borrowed pride   1472
   Your old kind Father, whose franke heart gaue all,   1800
   Reg. To whose hands | You haue sent the Lunaticke King: Speake.   2113
   Glou. There is a Cliffe, whose high and bending head   2258
   Are many Simples operatiue, whose power | Will close the eye of
   Anguish.   2364
   *Behold yond simpring Dame, whose face betweene her   2563
   Whose age had Charmes in it, whose Title more,   2991
WHY *l*.106 340 343 *363 *581 628 *629 *631 636 662 *673 *893 *896
  *901 903 *904 *908 1061 1082 1085 *1098 1144 1162 1215 1339 1371
  *1485 1505 *1539 1541 1569 2351 2405 2437 2471 *2604 2639 2869
  *2895 3068 3071 3195 3223 3278 = 29*15
WICKED = 2*1
   Mumbling of wicked charmes, coniuring the Moone | To stand
   auspicious Mistris.   973
   Lea. Those wicked Creatures yet do look wel fauor'd   1554
   When others are more wicked, not being the worst   1555
WICKEDNESSE = 1
   Alb. Knowes he the wickednesse?   2340
WIDDOW = 2
   But being widdow, and my Glouster with her,   2331
   If both remaine aliue: To take the Widdow,   2906
WIDE = 1
   Cor. Still, still, farre wide.   2800
WIDE-SKIRTED = 1
   With plenteous Riuers, and wide-skirted Meades   70
WIELD *see* weild
WIFE = 7
   Our deerest *Regan*, wife of *Cornwall?*   73
   I shall not be his wife.   274
   I'ld speake with the Duke of *Cornewall*, and his wife.   1372
   Goe tell the Duke, and's wife, Il'd speake with them: 1392
   Your (*Wife*, so I would say) affectio-|*nate Seruant*. Gonerill.   2722
   I bare it in the interest of my wife,   3030
   Bast. He hath Commission from thy Wife and me, | To hang *Cordelia*
   in the prison, and   3211
WIL *l*.*2640 = *1
WILD = *2
   Foole. Winters not gon yet, if the wil'd Geese fly that | (way, 1322
   Cor. Shut vp your doores my Lord, 'tis a wil'd night,   1612
WILDE = *1
   *night to swimme in. Now a little fire in a wilde Field,   1892
WILFULL = 1
   Reg. O Sir, to wilfull men, | The iniuries that they themselues procure, 1606
WILL *see also* chill, hee'l, he'le, Ile, shee'l, they'l, 'twill, wee'l, weele,
  you'l, you'le *l*.54 96 208 212 221 247 263 312 330 *423 *431 *489 515
  531 *545 *572 *600 *620 665 *708 725 757 *880 *888 *892 *906 932 997
  1020 *1096 *1138 1175 *1188 1217 1230 1257 1352 1354 1453 1484 1489
  1496 1513 1520 1543 1546 1579 1580 1600 1639 1645 1647 1677 1682
  1689 1690 1716 *1763 *1765 1796 1797 1798 1805 *1858 1959 1971
  *1990 *1991 *1994 *1999 2000 *2022 2028 *2037 2055 2105 2107 2141
  2143 2239 2253 2365 2528 *2536 2622 *2641 *2718 2748 2807 2829 2878

WILL *cont*.
2887 *2895 2901 2949 2976 3033 3048 *3061 3123 3187 3222 3270 =
75*30, 8*2

We haue this houre a constant will to publish	48
*blessing against his will, if thou follow him, thou must	633
Is it your will, speake Sir? Prepare my Horses.	770
And am fallen out with my more headier will,	1386
When misery could beguile the Tyrants rage, | And frustrate his proud will.	2505
Gent. Sir, speed you: what's your will?	2651
*opportunities to cut him off: if your will want not, time and	2717
Oh indistinguish'd space of Womans will,	2724
I'th'sway of your owne will: is he array'd?	2770
Alb. The let alone lies not in your good will. | *Bast*. Nor in thine Lord.	3023

WILLES = 1

To quarrell with your great opposelesse willes,	2477

WILT *see also* thou'lt *l*.*194 2229 *2618 2700 = 2*2, 2

Lear. Wilt breake my heart?	1783
Cor. Wilt please your Highnesse walke? | *Lear*. You must beare with me:	2840

WIN = *1

*for my part I will not be, though I should win your | displeasure to entreat me too't.	1188

WIND = *1

*nay, & thou canst not smile as the wind sits, thou'lt catch	630

WINDE = 6*3

*him out: winde me into him, I pray you: frame the Bu- |sinesse	428
Bids the winde blow the Earth into the Sea,	1620
Nor Raine, Winde, Thunder, Fire are my Daughters;	1670
Such groanes of roaring Winde, and Raine, I neuer	1699
With heigh-ho, the Winde and the Raine,	1730
*cold winde: Sayes suum, mun, nonny, Dolphin my Boy,	1879
Alb. Oh *Gonerill*, | You are not worth the dust which the rude winde | Blowes in your face.	2301
*winde to make me chatter: when the Thunder would not	2548
Th'vntun'd and iarring senses, O winde vp, | Of this childe-changed Father.	2765

WINDES = 2*4

The Windes, and persecutions of the skie;	1263
*Glo. Alacke the night comes on, and the high windes	1603
*Lear. Blow windes, & crack your cheeks; Rage, blow	1656
*sharpe Hauthorne blow the windes. Humh, goe to thy | bed and warme thee.	1828
*blisse thee from Whirle-Windes, Starre-blasting, and ta- |king,	1840
To be oppos'd against the iarring windes?	2783

WINDOWD = 1

Your lop'd, and window'd raggednesse defend you	1812

WINE = *1

*contriuing of Lust, and wak'd to doe it. Wine lou'd I	1870

WING = *1

*The Crowes and Choughes, that wing the midway ayre	2448

WINGED = 1

The winged Vengeance ouertake such Children.	2138

WINS = 1

Who looses, and who wins; who's in, who's out;	2955

WINTER = *1

*thee ther's no labouring i'th' winter. All that follow their	1341

WINTERS = *1
   Foole. Winters not gon yet, if the wil'd Geese fly that | (way,   1322
WIPE = 2
   Glou. O let me kisse that hand. | *Lear*. Let me wipe it first,   2574
   And fire vs hence, like Foxes: wipe thine eyes,   2965
WISE = 2*1
   *honest, to conuerse with him that is wise and saies little, to   546
   As you are Old, and Reuerend, should be Wise.   749
   Foole. Thou shouldst not haue bin old, till thou hadst | bin wise.   916
WISEDOME = 6*3
   *after your owne wisedome. I would vnstate my | selfe, to be in a due
   resolution.   429
   *no good to vs: though the wisedome of Nature can   434
   tarry, but away, goe too, haue you wisedome, so.   621
   Gon. I would you would make vse of your good wise- |(dome   731
   You are much more at task for want of wisedome,   867
   To haue his eare abus'd, wisedome bids feare.   1611
   And bring him to our eye. What can mans wisedome   2358
   I pray desire her call her wisedome to her. | So fare you well: 2422
   Bast. In wisedome I should aske thy name,   3097
WISEMAN = 2*1
   *when a wiseman giues thee better counsell giue me mine   1347
   And let the wiseman flie: 1355
   Kent. Who's there? | *Foole*. Marry here's Grace, and a Codpiece, that's
   a | Wiseman, and a Foole.   1691
WISEMEN = 2
   For wisemen are growne foppish,   681
   *in, aske thy Daughters blessing, heere's a night pitties | neither
   Wisemen, nor Fooles.   1667
WISH = 1*1
   Kent. I cannot wish the fault vndone, the issue of it, | being so proper.   20
   Reg. O the blest Gods! | So will you wish on me, when the rash moode
   is on.   1452
WISHES = 1
   Which tye him to an answer: our wishes on the way   2282
WIT = 3*3
   Let me, if not by birth, haue lands by wit,   503
   *durt, thou hadst little wit in thy bald crowne, when thou   677
   *wit o'both sides, and left nothing i'th'middle; heere | comes one o'the
   parings.   700
   Foole. Then I prythee be merry, thy wit shall not go | slip-shod. | *Lear*.
   Ha, ha, ha.   885
   Hauing more man then wit about me, drew;   1318
   Foole. He that has and a little-tyne wit,   1729
WITCH = 1
   And aroynt thee Witch, aroynt thee.   1903
WITH = 146*41
WITHALL = 1
   as I shall find meanes, and acquaint you withall.   432
WITHDRAW = 1
   Corn. Let vs withdraw, 'twill be a Storme.   1587
WITHIN = 15*1
   If ought within that little seeming substance,   216
   But yet alas, stood I within his Grace,   298
   Then doth within a dull stale tyred bed   347
   Hornes within. Enter Lear and Attendants.   538
   Lear. What fiftie of my Followers at a clap? | Within a fortnight?   810

WITHIN *cont*.

To make thee seeke it. *Tucket within*.	1014
Kent. With the Earle Sir, here within.	1331
Reg. Good Sir, to'th'purpose. *Tucket within*.	1466
That hast within thee vndivulged Crimes	1705
Stew. Madam within, but neuer man so chang'd:	2270
You are now within a foote of th'extreme Verge:	2462
The Battaile done, and they within our power,	2914
Alarum within. Enter with Drumme and Colours, Lear,	2918
Glo. Grace go with you Sir. *Exit*. | *Alarum and Retreat within*.	2925
Herald reads. | *If any man of qualitie or degree*, *within the lists of the Ar-|my*,	3059
Her. Againe. 3 *Trumpet*. | *Trumpet answers within*.	3065

WITHOUT = 6*2

Must be a faith that reason without miracle | Should neuer plant in me.	243
Without our Grace, our Loue, our Benizon:	290
*assurance haue your satisfaction, and that without	425
*need to care for her frowning, now thou art an O with-|out	706
daughters, and leaue his hornes without a case.	905
Without the forme of Iustice: yet our power	2085
But not without that harmefull stroke, which since | Hath pluckt him after.	2321
Edg. Chill not let go Zir, | Without vurther 'casion.	2687

WITNESSE = 1

Witnesse the world, that I create thee heere | My Lord, and Master.	3020

WITS = 6*4

And know not how their wits to weare,	682
Lear. My wits begin to turne.	1722
*Blisse thy fiue Wits, *Tom*s a cold. O do, de, do, de, do, de,	1839
His wits begin t'vnsettle. | *Glou*. Canst thou blame him? *Storm still*	1941
The greefe hath craz'd my wits. What a night's this?	1950
Kent. All the powre of his wits, haue giuen way to his	2001
Edg. Blesse thy fiue wits.	2015
Kent. Here Sir, but trouble him not, his wits are gon.	2046
*poore Tom hath bin scarr'd out of his good wits. Blesse	2247
'Tis wonder that thy life and wits, at once	2789

WODDEN = *1

*ouerlustie at legs, then he weares wodden nether-stocks.	1285

WODDEN-PRICKES = 1

Pins, Wodden-prickes, Nayles, Sprigs of Rosemarie:	1267

WOE = 3

Lear. Woe, that too late repents:	769
Shall of a Corne cry woe, and turne his sleepe to wake.	1685
Is generall woe: Friends of my soule, you twaine,	3294

WOES = 1

And woes, by wrong imaginations loose	2738

WOFULL = 1

Alb. If there be more, more wofull, hold it in,	3166

WOLFE = 1*1

To be a Comrade with the Wolfe, and Owle,	1503
*Hog in sloth, Foxe in stealth, Wolfe in greedinesse, Dog	1873

WOLUES = 1

If Wolues had at thy Gate howl'd that sterne time,	2135

WOLUISH = 1

Shee'l flea thy Woluish visage. Thou shalt finde,	827

WOMAN = 2*4
Lear. How old art thou? | **Kent*. Not so young Sir to loue a woman for
singing, 567
*For there was neuer yet faire woman, but shee made | mouthes in a
glasse. 1686
*deerely, Dice deerely; and in Woman, out-Paramour'd 1871
*Nor the rustling of Silkes, betray thy poore heart to wo-|man. 1875
Proper deformitie seemes not in the Fiend | So horrid as in woman. 2309
Gentle, and low, an excellent thing in woman. 3237
WOMANS = 2
To thee a Womans seruices are due, | My Foole vsurpes my body. 2296
Oh indistinguish'd space of Womans will, 2724
WOMBD = *1
*she grew round womb'd, and had indeede (Sir) a 17
WOMBE = 1
Into her Wombe conuey stirrility, 792
WOMEN = *1
*Women all aboue: but to the Girdle do the Gods inhe-|rit, 2568
WOMENS = 1
And let not womens weapons, water drops, 1577
WONDER = 2
'Tis wonder that thy life and wits, at once 2789
Kent. The wonder is, he hath endur'd so long, | He but vsurpt his life. 3291
WONT = *2
*with that Ceremonious affection as you were wont, 588
*Le. When were you wont to be so full of Songs sirrah? 684
WOODEN *see* wodden
WOOLL = *1
*Wooll; the Cat, no perfume. Ha? Here's three on's are 1885
WOOSTED-STOCKING = *1
*pound, filthy woosted-stocking knaue, a Lilly-liuered, 1090
WORD = 10*3
*Gon. Sir, I loue you more then word can weild y matter, 60
As to th'legitimate: fine word: Legitimate. 352
*Bast. Parted you in good termes? Found you no dis-|pleasure in him,
by word, nor countenance? 478
'Twixt the Dukes of *Cornwall*, and *Albany*? | *Bast*. Not a word. 939
Brother, a word, discend; Brother I say, 949
Edg. I am sure on't, not a word. 958
When Priests are more in word, then matter; 1736
*Lear. Ile talke a word with this same lerned Theban: 1936
Lear. Let me aske you one word in priuate. 1939
His word was still, fie, foh, and fumme, 1967
*Might not you transport her purposes by word? Belike, 2406
clout, i'th'clout: Hewgh. Giue the word. | *Edg*. Sweet Mariorum. 2539
*Edg. If ere your Grace had speech with man so poore, | Heare me one
word. 2881
WORDS = 6*3
That good effects may spring from words of loue: 199
Make thy words faith'd? No, what should I denie, 1007
To bandy hasty words, to scant my sizes, 1459
Kent. Few words, but to effect more then all yet; 1650
*keepe thy words Iustice, sweare not, commit not, 1861
*her. Swore as many Oathes, as I spake words, & broke 1868
Glou. No words, no words, hush. 1965
*out. Go too, they are not men o'their words; they told 2550

WORE = *1
*curl'd my haire, wore Gloues in my cap; seru'd the Lust   1866
WORKE = 3*1
Which I must act, Briefenesse, and Fortune worke.   947
(Loyall and naturall Boy) Ile worke the meanes   1022
*a prouoking merit set a-worke by a reprouable badnesse | in himselfe. 1977
Cor. O thou good *Kent*, | How shall I liue and worke | To match thy
goodnesse?   2745
WORKING = 1
Mighty in their working do you that offence,   723
WORLD = 14*5
*world before he was sent for: yet was his Mother fayre,   25
To shield thee from disasters of the world,   188
world bitter to the best of our times: keepes our Fortunes from 383
Bast. This is the excellent foppery of the world, that   447
And thou must make a dullard of the world,   1011
Whose disposition all the world well knowes   1229
That all the world shall--- I will do such things,   1580
Strike flat the thicke Rotundity o'th'world,   1662
But who comes heere? My Father poorely led? | World, World, O
world!   2189
Glou. O you mighty Gods! | This world I do renounce, and in your
sights   2473
Glou. O ruin'd peece of Nature, this great world | Shall so weare out to
naught.   2577
*case, your purse in a light, yet you see how this world | goes. 2591
Lear. What, art mad? A man may see how this world   2594
Your businesse of the world hath so an end,   2889
Witnesse the world, that I create thee heere | My Lord, and Master. 3020
Bast. There's my exchange, what in the world hes   3045
That would vpon the wracke of this tough world | Stretch him out
longer.   3288
WORLDS = *1
*backe: wher's my Foole? Ho, I thinke the world's   578
WORME = 1*1
*the Worme no Silke; the Beast, no Hide; the Sheepe, no   1884
Which made me thinke a Man, a Worme. My Sonne   2217
WORSE = 4*3
*Villaine; worse then brutish: Go sirrah, seeke him: Ile   411
*worse after dinner, I will not part from thee yet. Dinner   572
*They could not, would not do't: 'tis worse then murther,   1298
I am worse then ere I was.   2208
Edg. And worse I may be yet: the worst is not,   2210
His answer was, the worse. Of Glosters Treachery,   2273
Thou worse then any name, reade thine owne euill: 3114
WORSER = 2
Let not my worser Spirit tempt me againe | To dye before you please. 2664
These weedes are memories of those worser houres: 2754
WORSHIPS = 1
The worships of their name. O most small fault,   779
WORSSE = 1*1
Reg. My Sister may recieue it much more worsse,   1225
*the Dukes, and a worsse matter then that: I haue   1760
WORST = 8*1
When others are more wicked, not being the worst   1555
Then still contemn'd and flatter'd, to be worst: 2180
The worst returnes to laughter. Welcome then,   2184

WORST *cont.*
The Wretch that thou hast blowne vnto the worst,	2186
Edg. O Gods! Who is't can say I am at the worst?	2207
Edg. And worse I may be yet: the worst is not,	2210
So long as we can say this is the worst.	2211
*squiny at me? No, doe thy worst blinde Cupid, Ile not	2581
Cor. We are not the first, | Who with best meaning haue incurr'd the worst:	2943

WORTH = 9
And prize me at her worth. In my true heart,	75
And well are worth the want that you haue wanted.	305
Should make thee worth them.	817
Of any trust, vertue, or worth in thee	1006
Your Sonne and Daughter found this trespasse worth	1320
Gon. I haue beene worth the whistle.	2300
Alb. Oh *Gonerill,* | You are not worth the dust which the rude winde | Blowes in your face.	2301
Take all my outward worth.	2360
Well worth a poore mans taking. Fayries, and Gods	2466

WORTHIED = 1
That worthied him, got praises of the King,	1197

WORTHIER = 1
T'auert your liking a more worthier way,	231

WORTHY = 2
My worthy Arch and Patron comes to night,	996
Edg. Worthy Prince I know't.	3141

WOULD *see also* 'chud, I'de, I'ld, 'twould *l.*229 299 *387 *399 *417 *429 485 559 584 585 *605 *634 693 *699 721 *731 840 *919 966 1005 1008 1016 1032 *1083 *1298 *1348 1376 *1378 1396 1409 1421 1471 1806 1944 2128 2132 2192 2291 2426 2463 *2548 2585 2639 2706 2722 2808 2911 3145 3148 3242 3288 = 38*15
WOULDEST *l.*155 = 1
WOULDST *see also* thou'dst *l.*542 553 555 *911 *1093 *1845 = 2*4
WOUNDINGS = 1
Th'vntented woundings of a Fathers curse	819

WRACKE = 1
That would vpon the wracke of this tough world | Stretch him out longer.	3288

WRATH = 3
Come not betweene the Dragon and his wrath,	130
Shall do a curt'sie to our wrath, which men | May blame, but not comptroll.	2086
The food of thy abused Fathers wrath:	2203

WRATHFULL = 1
Loue not such nights as these: The wrathfull Skies	1695

WREATH = 1
Whose influence like the wreath of radient fire | On flickring *Phoebus* front.	1182

WREN = 1
No, the Wren goes too't, and the small gilded Fly	2558

WRENCHT = 1
Which like an Engine, wrencht my frame of Nature	781

WRETCH = 4
Then on a wretch whom Nature is asham'd | Almost t'acknowledge hers.	232
Finde out their enemies now. Tremble thou Wretch,	1704
The Wretch that thou hast blowne vnto the worst,	2186

WRETCH *cont*.
  Gent. A sight most pittifull in the meanest wretch,   2646
WRETCHED = 3
  As full of griefe as age, wretched in both,   1573
  Haue humbled to all strokes: that I am wretched   2250
  For him that brought it: wretched though I seeme,   2886
WRETCHEDNESSE = 1
  Is wretchednesse depriu'd that benefit | To end it selfe by death? 'Twas
  yet some comfort,   2503
WRETCHES = 2
  Poore naked wretches, where so ere you are   1809
  Expose thy selfe to feele what wretches feele,   1815
WRINKLES = 1
  Let it stampe wrinkles in her brow of youth,   798
WRIT = 4*1
  *he hath writ this to feele my affection to your Honor, &   420
  What he hath vtter'd I haue writ my Sister: 853
  What haue you writ that Letter to my Sister? | *Stew*. I Madam.   858
  Our Father he hath writ, so hath our Sister,   1065
  (Be briefe in it) to'th'Castle, for my Writ   3202
WRITE = 2*2
  *hand to write this? A heart and braine to breede it in?   392
  *so, Ile write straight to my Sister to hold my course; pre- | pare for
  dinner. *Exeunt*.   527
  Reg. Why should she write to *Edmund*?   2405
  Bast. About it, and write happy, when th'hast done,   2979
WRITES = *1
  Bast. I promise you, the effects he writes of, succeede | vnhappily.   472
WRONG = 6
  Edg. Some Villaine hath done me wrong.   486
  Lear. I did her wrong.   898
  And told me I had turn'd the wrong side out: 2276
  And woes, by wrong imaginations loose   2738
  Lear. You do me wrong to take me out o'th'graue,   2794
  Haue (as I do remember) done me wrong.   2831
WRONGD = 3
  *mistaken, for my duty cannot be silent, when I thinke | your Highnesse
  wrong'd.   594
  Say you haue wrong'd her.   1432
  If more, the more th'hast wrong'd me.   3129
WRONGS = 3
  Gon. By day and night, he wrongs me, euery howre   510
  That dares not vndertake: Hee'l not feele wrongs   2281
  Gon. Milke-Liuer'd man, | That bear'st a cheeke for blowes, a head for
  wrongs,   2304
WROTE = *1
  Bast. I hope for my Brothers iustification, hee wrote   380
Y = *5
  Gon. Sir, I loue you more then word can weild y matter,   60
  Glou. Why so earnestly seeke you to put vp y Letter?   363
  *The man y makes his Toe, what he his Hart shold make,   1684
  Corn. See't shalt thou neuer. Fellowes hold y Chaire,   2139
  Glou. Here take this purse, y whom the heau'ns plagues   2249
YARD = *1
  *draw mee a Cloathiers yard. Looke, looke, a   2535
YARE = 3
  Reg. I speake in vnderstanding: Y'are: I know't,   2415

YARE *cont.*
    Edg. Y'are much deceiu'd: In nothing am I chang'd | But in my
    Garments.   2442
    Glou. Me thinkes y'are better spoken. | *Edg.* Come on Sir,   2444
YE *l.**490 821 1120 1157 1542 2469 *2693 = 5*2
YEA = 2
    Lear. No. | *Kent.* Yes. | *Lear.* No I say. | *Kent.* I say yea.   1291
    Yea, or so many? Sith that both charge and danger,   1535
YEARE *see also* yeere = 2
    Daughters, as thou canst tell in a yeare.   1327
    Haue bin Toms food, for seuen long yeare: 1918
YEARES = 4*2
    **Glou.* He hath bin out nine yeares, and away he shall | againe. The
    King is comming.   35
    *therewithall the vnruly way-wardnesse, that infirme and | cholericke
    yeares bring with them.   323
    *nor so old to dote on her for any thing. I haue yeares on | my backe
    forty eight.   569
    *not haue made him so ill, though they had bin but two | yeares
    oth'trade.   1132
    And your Fathers Tenant, these fourescore yeares.   2194
    The good yeares shall deuoure them, flesh and fell,   2966
YEELD = 1
    Yeeld, come before my Father, light hoa, here,   963
YEELDE = 1
    Life would not yeelde to age.   2192
YEELDS = 1
    Yeelds to the Theft. Had he bin where he thought,   2484
YEERE = 1*1
    *yeere elder then this; who, yet is no deerer in my ac- | count,   23
    Fooles had nere lesse grace in a yeere,   680
YEOMAN = 1*2
    **Foole.* Prythee Nunkle tell me, whether a madman be | a Gentleman,
    or a Yeoman.   2007
    **Foole.* No, he's a Yeoman, that ha's a Gentleman to   2010
    *his Sonne: for hee's a mad Yeoman that sees his Sonne a | Gentleman
    before him.   2011
YES = 5*3
    *thou art nothing. Yes forsooth I will hold my tongue, so   708
    *At point a hundred Knights: yes, that on euerie dreame,   845
    **Foole.* Yes indeed, thou would'st make a good Foole.   911
    Bast. Yes Madam, he was of that consort.   1036
    Kent. Yes Sir, but anger hath a priuiledge.   1143
    Lear. No. | *Kent.* Yes. | *Lear.* No I say. | *Kent.* I say yea.   1291
    Yes faith: I pray weepe not,   2828
    Alb. Halfe-blooded fellow, yes.   3025
YET = 37*12
    *yeere elder then this; who, yet is no deerer in my ac- | count,   23
    *world before he was sent for: yet was his Mother fayre,   25
    Cor. Then poore *Cordelia*, | And yet not so, since I am sure my loue's   82
    Which we durst neuer yet; and with strain'd pride,   183
    Cor. I yet beseech your Maiesty.   245
    But yet alas, stood I within his Grace,   298
    **Reg.* 'Tis the infirmity of his age, yet he hath euer but | slenderly
    knowne himselfe.   318
    *reason it thus, and thus, yet Nature finds it selfe scourg'd   435
    *worse after dinner, I will not part from thee yet. Dinner   572

ZWAGGERD = *1

*volke passe: and 'chud ha' bin zwaggerd out of my life,   2691
& *l*.*39 *50 *152 *420 *445 *923 *1656 *1868 *2564 = *9, *1

    *nay, & thou canst not smile as the wind sits, thou'lt catch   630
1 *l*.*3063 = *1
2 *l*.3064 = 1
3 *l*.3065 = 1